The Pacific Coast League:
A Statistical History, 1903–1957

The Pacific Coast League: A Statistical History, 1903–1957

by

Dennis Snelling

McFarland & Company, Inc., Publishers
Jefferson, North Carolina, and London

LIBRARY OF CONGRESS CATALOGUING-IN-PUBLICATION DATA

Snelling, Dennis, 1958–
    The Pacific Coast League : a statistical history, 1903–1957 / by
Dennis Snelling.
        p.   cm.

    ISBN-13: 978-0-7864-0045-4
    ISBN-10: 0-7864-0045-5 (softcover : 50# alkaline paper) ∞

    1. Pacific Coast League—History.   2. Pacific Coast League—
Statistics.   3. Baseball teams—United States—Statistics.
I. Title.
GV875.P33S54   2006
796.357'6479—dc20   94-43242
British Library cataloguing data are available

Manufactured in the United States of America

*McFarland & Company, Inc., Publishers
    Box 611, Jefferson, North Carolina 28640
        www.mcfarlandpub.com*

For Andrea

Table of Contents

Acknowledgments

This book would not have been possible without the invaluable help of several individuals. Jim Beggs was most gracious in taking the time to proofread the player sections at a time when he was working on his dissertation. He even consented to review the pitchers, despite his personal distaste for them. Lark Downs gave several formatting suggestions which were helpful in the early stages of the project.

Minor league historian Bob Hoie was extremely helpful in clearing up numerous questions about players, backgrounds of individuals and events in the league, and in providing statistical information. Long-time statistician Bill Weiss provided copies of statistics from his PCL "archives," including pitching statistics from the 1906 and 1918 seasons, "missing" 1920 statistics for the players suspended for gambling activities, and more complete numbers than appear in the guides for players appearing in fewer than 15 games or pitching fewer than 45 innings. He also patiently answered numerous queries on many subjects.

Joe Hoppel of "The Sporting News" provided access to that publication's clip files and transaction cards and helped fill gaps in biographical information.

Baylor Butler, who is very active on SABR's Negro Leagues Committee, helped research and provide statistics for players who played in the league post-1958. Carlos Bauer, who has undertaken research into the early years of the league, reviewed the rough draft of the Team Roster section for the years 1903 through 1918 and helped identify players from that era. The staff at the Research Library at the National Baseball Hall of Fame in Cooperstown was, as always, courteous and prompt in their responses to queries.

Special thanks must go to my wife, Linda, and children, Tyler, Garrett, and Andrea, who put up with too many hours of their husband and father buried in books, papers, and huddled at the computer. Without their help and understanding, this project would have been impossible.

Sources and Methodology

It is important to note at the beginning of this book that minor league records in general, and those of the Pacific Coast League in particular, possess varying degrees of reliability, particularly in the years prior to World War II. Some statistical lines do not round properly, some are incomplete, and some do not make sense.

The Pacific Coast League features its own challenges and obstacles for those who wish to compile its records. There are no official pitching or fielding records for 1906, presumably at least in part due to aftereffects of the San Francisco earthquake. Likewise, there are no official pitching records for 1918 and the fielding records for that year were, according to the *Reach Guide*, "unfortunately . . . lost." Compounding difficulty in accurately representing that season is the identification of several players with San Francisco, when in fact they were members of the Sacramento team.

The league records for the 1920 season add their particular, unique problems. Several star players were suspended by the league in two separate gambling incidents. As part of its response to the scandals, the league expunged the players from all league records for the year, even though one of those deemed guilty missed the batting title by only a fraction of a point.

One other major hurdle in putting together a comprehensive list of league records, especially in the compiling of individual PCL career playing records, involves the information, or lack of same, for players appearing in fewer than 15 games or pitching fewer than 45 innings. The information is very sketchy prior to the 1940s, and in many years is nonexistent. Rudimentary pitching information is often carried only for those pitchers with at least one decision. Hitting lines sometimes carry only a batting average and the number of games played.

All of these problems were addressed, but it is important to know the sources for that information since it does not come from "official" records.

The pitching records for 1906 come from a list compiled by Bob Hoie from the Pacific Coast League boxscores of that season. Defensive positions were determined by the author, also by examining box scores from that year. The same goes for the defensive positions listed here for 1918. The pitching statistics for 1918, also unofficial, were compiled by Bob Hoie with the assistance of L. Robert Davids and Merco Smolich. The 1920 statistics for the suspended players come from the *Los Angeles Times* and were compiled by reporter (and later PCL statistician) Leo Moriarty, except for Tom Seaton's statistics, which were reconstructed by Bob Hoie from box-scores. In addition, runs batted in for 1914 are from a list discovered in the *Los Angeles Times* by Bob Hoie and typed by Ray Nemec. The runs batted in for 1921 and 1924 are not carried in the *Reach Guide*, but are in the *Spalding Guide*. Available records for players appearing in fewer than 15 games or pitching fewer than 45 innings were provided from the files of PCL historian and statistician Bill Weiss.

There were also more subtle, and more common, problems that called for a consistent and logical approach.

The published "official" records were used as the base of information because they are the most complete source, despite their flaws. Therefore, a "benefit of the doubt" was given to the official records, unless they could be shown as obviously wrong. To be changed, the records not only had to be obviously wrong, but the necessary correction had to be easily ascertained, including an explanation of the error. The case of Doc Crandall and his 1919 offensive statistics is an example.

In the *Reach Guide* for that season, Crandall is credited with a .257 batting average, based on 36 hits in 257 at bats. That obviously does not calculate correctly. His other offensive records and those of others in the league were examined to determine, if possible, where the error occurred. The records show that he appeared in 59 games, so 257 at bats appears to be too many, especially when one looks at other pitchers who threw the same number of innings and compares the number of at bats they had. So, knowing that the at bats are wrong, and assuming the batting average is correct, the number of at bats is changed to 140 so the batting average computes. The explanation is one you have probably already guessed when looking at the .257 batting average and the 257 at bats. The batting average was carried over incorrectly into the at bats column.

Because a ready explanation was needed before correcting the records, there are only 14 of these types of corrections made in this book. They are listed at the end of Section X. It is part of the nature of minor league records that further research will probably bring to light more of these corrections.

Another more common problem was one of rounding. All batting averages were recalculated for the years 1903 through 1940, and any years following which had any instances of incorrect rounding come to light. Correcting rounding and other errors in calculations of earned run averages proved a little trickier.

In some of the early official records, fractions of an inning are listed and calculated. Most years, only full innings are shown and there are many apparent rounding errors, up and down, if the full innings are used in the equation. Since is not an uncommon practice to show full innings only, because of space limitations (as is the case with this book), all earned run averages were recalculated for the 1903 through 1950 seasons. Those that were off were then recalculated by adding or subtracting a fraction of an inning. If the new calculated earned run average matched the official record, it was assumed that a fraction existed and the official record was correct. If the use of a fraction did not solve the problem, a full inning was assumed and the official record corrected. The basic idea was not to change the official record unless there was no choice. If the original calculation could be made to work, it was used. A full listing of corrected batting averages and earned run averages is presented in Section X.

In compiling PCL career records, the official statistics still formed the base of information. For some players, other sources were used to save time initially (i.e. SABR's *Minor League Stars, Vol 1, 2 and 3, Sporting News Daguerreotypes*, the *Mutual Baseball Almanac*, etc.), but those records were always double-checked against the *Reach, Spalding* and *Sporting News* guides since the reference books have their own omissions, duplication of error from source materials, and typos. A few, shorter playing records came from going through boxscores.

Biographical information came from a variety of sources: *The Ballplayers*, The *Baseball Encyclopedia*, Dick Beverage's fine team histories of the Los Angeles Angels and Hollywood Stars, contemporary player profiles carried in the *Los Angeles Times, San Francisco Call-Bulletin, San Francisco Examiner*, and *San Francisco Chronicle*, and many other books that paralleled the time period covered here. Additionally, some information was gleaned from interviews with players including Mark Koenig, Gus Zernial, Jimmie Reese, Larry Jansen, George Bamberger, Joe Brovia, Dom Di Maggio, Frank Crosetti, Tony Freitas, Ad Liska, Tommy Byrne, Jim Rivera, Gene Mauch, and several others.

Introduction

This book has grown out of a desire to learn more about the Pacific Coast League, especially from its inception in 1903 to the end of its "golden era" in 1957 when the Brooklyn Dodgers and the New York Giants moved west in a continuance of major league baseball's version of the Oklahoma Land Rush.

Growing up and living in California as I have, coincidentally arriving in the world the same year that the Golden State went "big league," my parent's and grandparent's generations have always spoken of the old PCL as they would an old friend, their nostalgic reminiscences giving way to a feeling of remorse for those not fortunate enough to have witnessed baseball in a setting now long past and never to be revisited. They recall the players, personalities and playing fields of that era with great reverence. Instead of Musial, Mays, Mantle and Feller, their boyhood heroes were named Freitas, Novikoff, Bilko, Liska and Raimondi. Joe DiMaggio is remembered as a San Francisco Seal, Ted Williams as a San Diego Padre and Billy Martin was the second baseman for the Oakland Oaks. To those living west of the Mississippi during that time, the Pacific Coast League *was* the major leagues.

My own familiarity with the league was centered around the Paul Bunyan–like numbers put up by the circuit's offensive stars; players collecting 300 hits, 500 total bases, and driving in 200 runs in a single season, thanks in large part to a schedule that often neared or even topped 200 games.

As a result of these observations, I began work on a book that I hoped would capture the spirit and memories of baseball's greatest minor league, beyond the numbers; an organization that, with better timing, might have become a third major league. While researching the PCL, I began to construct a base of information for each team and many of the league's players for what I originally envisioned to be an appendix for the book. While I had not set out to compile a book of statistics, it soon became apparent that this "appendix" had grown into something that was book-length itself.

What the reader will find within these pages is a team-by-team listing, including statistics for the starters and main reserves for the years 1903 through 1957. Also included are year-by-year playing records for more than 500 of the most important, interesting and talented players to appear in the league during those years. Other sections detail manager listings and yearly records for each franchise, no-hitters and other notable achievements, and the annual league leaders in major statistical categories.

I have made every attempt to provide a lot of statistical information about the league while keeping the format "reader friendly." Many of the names in this book will bring back memories and others will surprise. My hope is that this book will elicit conversation about the league and answer profound questions such as, "Who made up the starting infield of the 1947 Los Angeles Angels?" Books comprised of baseball statistics *can* be fun.

SECTION I

Team Rosters

This section details the starters and reserves for each team in the Pacific Coast League during the years 1903 through 1957. Some statistical information is sketchy at best for the first few years of the league, especially 1906 (the year of the San Francisco earthquake) and 1918; and there are also many errors in the early records. Pitching records are especially sketchy (see the "Sources and Methodology" section at the beginning of this book). The statistics shown here represent the most currently accepted numbers, but later corrections are inevitable.

Teams are arranged by year and order of standing at the conclusion of the regular season (split season results not being recognized). The tables include a listing of starting players at each position and the main reserves. Reserves are listed along with up to three defensive positions, which are shown in order of the number of games played at each position. Those players appearing at more than three positions are listed as "U," which stands for "utility." The players are identified by last name and first initial (space limitations prevent the use of full first names). The first initial represents the name by which the player is now most commonly known, using the *Baseball Encyclopedia* as a common reference. For instance, Alfred Manuel Martin's first initial is shown as "B" instead of "A" since he is better known as "Billy."

The starting outfielders are listed in an order based on the number of official at bats. The number of games played was used to determine the starter at a position, unless there were two players who each had played only the one position. Then the number of at bats was used to determine the starter.

Along the way, many players appeared with more than one team during the course of a season. In each case the player has been listed with the team for which he played the most games. A number in parentheses following the player's last name corresponds to a footnote indicating the other team(s) for which the player appeared.

Pitchers are listed in order based on innings pitched except in seasons where that information is unavailable. In those seasons, the order is based on victories.

Shown below the pitchers are the footnotes corresponding to the players appearing with more than one team, the team's manager(s), team record, and the regular season finish of the team. The managers, like the players, are listed by first initial and last name, the initial representing their most commonly known name.

Generally, all players pitching more than 100 innings or batting more than 200 times are listed. If space allows, players with fewer than the above totals are shown. Offensive statistics for reserves and pitchers are listed below the starters in an order based on the number of at bats. Pitchers are sometimes omitted in favor of reserves with fewer at bats unless the pitcher had strong offensive statistics.

The results of any playoff series that took place are located at the bottom of the page following the last place team for each season. If there was no playoff series in a particular year, that is also indicated.

The statistical categories are self explanatory for both hitting and pitching. Information unavailable is indicated with "--."

1903

LOS ANGELES	AB	HR	RBI	BA	SB	PITCHERS	IP	W–L	BB	SO	ERA
1B P. DILLON	752	––	––	.360	43	D. NEWTON (2)	––	35–12	––	––	––
2B G. WHEELER	760	––	––	.222	35	W. HALL	––	32–18	––	––	––
3B J. SMITH	789	––	––	.294	54	J. CORBETT	––	25–17	––	––	––
SS J. TOMAN	595	––	––	.220	33	D. GRAY	––	25–20	––	––	––
OF D. HOY	806	––	––	.261	46						
OF G. CRAVATH	805	––	––	.272	34						
OF A. ROSS	750	––	––	.292	56						
C H. SPIES	634	––	––	.259	36						
P J. CORBETT	262	––	––	.336	13						
SS T. RAYMOND (1)	232	––	––	.224	9	(1) ALSO WITH SAN FRANCISCO					
C G. HURLBURT	184	––	––	.261	4	(2) ALSO WITH PORTLAND					
P D. NEWTON (2)	177	––	––	.266	5	**MANAGER – J. MORLEY**					
P W. HALL	177	––	––	.147	2	**RECORD W–133 L–78 FINISH–1ST**					

SACRAMENTO	AB	HR	RBI	BA	SB	PITCHERS	IP	W–L	BB	SO	ERA
1B C. TOWNSEND	659	––	––	.296	27	B. THOMAS	––	27–15	––	––	––
2B P. CASEY	818	––	––	.290	65	W. CUTTER (1)	––	19–28	––	––	––
3B T. SHEEHAN	689	––	––	.266	33	B. KEEFE	––	15–14	––	––	––
SS T. EAGAN	818	––	––	.320	56	J. FITZGERALD	––	14–21	––	––	––
OF G. MC LAUGHLIN	791	––	––	.284	75	P. KNELL	––	10–9	––	––	––
OF D. DOYLE	788	––	––	.246	55						
OF G. HILDEBRAND	702	––	––	.296	47						
C C. GRAHAM	583	––	––	.271	25						
1C H. HOGAN	455	––	––	.220	15	(1) ALSO WITH SAN FRANCISCO					
P W. CUTTER (1)	182	––	––	.192	6	**MANAGER – M. FISHER**					
P B. THOMAS	159	––	––	.283	5	**RECORD W–105 L–105 FINISH–2ND**					

SEATTLE	AB	HR	RBI	BA	SB	PITCHERS	IP	W–L	BB	SO	ERA
1B K. BRASHEAR (1)	736	––	––	.296	50	J. HUGHES	––	34–15	––	––	––
2B K. MOHLER	427	––	––	.314	40	F. BARBER	––	14–9	––	––	––
3B H. JANSING	552	––	––	.283	23	J. ST. VRAIN	––	12–10	––	––	––
SS J. DOLAN	321	––	––	.265	12	J. DROHAN	––	7–5	––	––	––
OF Z. ZINZAR (2)	688	––	––	.279	24						
OF C. SMITH	671	––	––	.332	32						
OF H. LUMLEY	465	––	––	.387	28						
C D. BOETTIGER	263	––	––	.224	14						
1B C. ZIEGLER	312	––	––	.208	9						
OF J. HANNIVAN	285	––	––	.214	6	(1) ALSO WITH OAKLAND					
C P. WILSON	252	––	––	.210	7	(2) ALSO WITH PORTLAND					
C B. BYERS	250	––	––	.340	2	**MANAGER – P. WILSON**					
OF J. WARD	221	––	––	.217	6	**RECORD W–98 L–100 FINISH–3RD**					

1903

SAN FRANCISCO	AB	HR	RBI	BA	SB	PITCHERS	IP	W—L	BB	SO	ERA
1B E. PABST	671	—	—	.253	27	J. WHALEN	—	28—21	—	—	—
2B B. DELMAS	708	—	—	.236	24	H. IBURG	—	27—23	—	—	—
3B C. IRWIN	773	—	—	.304	38	H. LINDSEY	—	20—21	—	—	—
SS D. SHAY	721	—	—	.244	83	G. HODSON	—	20—24	—	—	—
OF H. KRUG	832	—	—	.274	34						
OF P. MEANEY	811	—	—	.309	52						
OF H. LYNCH	784	—	—	.224	56						
C T. LEAHY	541	—	—	.259	18						
C D. ZEARFOSS	214	—	—	.224	2	**MANAGER — C. IRWIN**					
C A. KELLY	201	—	—	.194	1	**RECORD W—107 L—110 FINISH—4TH**					

PORTLAND	AB	HR	RBI	BA	SB	PITCHERS	IP	W—L	BB	SO	ERA
1B J. FREEMAN	184	—	—	.304	5	I. BUTLER	—	21—31	—	—	—
2B A. ANDERSON	663	—	—	.279	32	C. SHIELDS	—	19—23	—	—	—
3B I. FRANCIS	401	—	—	.287	7	J. THIELMAN	—	18—7	—	—	—
SS J. RAIDY	382	—	—	.257	22	D. MC FARLAN(2)	—	14—22	—	—	—
OF P. NADEAU	791	—	—	.348	52						
OF D. VAN BUREN	779	—	—	.361	65						
OF H. BLAKE	414	—	—	.254	20						
C D. SHEA	311	—	—	.219	7						
3B J. ANDREWS (1)	395	—	—	.281	24	(1) ALSO WITH SEATTLE					
SS HOLLINGSWORTH	379	—	—	.261	14	(2) ALSO WITH SACRAMENTO					
1C S. VIGNEAUX	247	—	—	.194	14	**MANAGER — S. VIGNEAUX/B. ELY**					
C T. HESS	207	—	—	.266	2	**RECORD W—95 L—108 FINISH—5TH**					

OAKLAND	AB	HR	RBI	BA	SB	PITCHERS	IP	W—L	BB	SO	ERA
1B J. MESSERLY (1)	395	—	—	.248	13	O. GRAHAM	—	27—26	—	—	—
2B C. SCHWARTZ (2)	802	—	—	.278	28	G. COOPER	—	18—30	—	—	—
3B B. DEVEREAUX	587	—	—	.250	40	D. MOSKIMAN	—	12—25	—	—	—
SS B. FRANCKS	188	—	—	.191	11	B. MC KAY	—	6—8	—	—	—
OF W. MURDOCK	853	—	—	.268	53						
OF B. O'HARA (2)	762	—	—	.298	66						
OF A. KRUGER	669	—	—	.239	40						
C L. GORTON	537	—	—	.210	23						
2B M. BAXTER	488	—	—	.221	22	(1) ALSO WITH PORTLAND					
PO D. MOSKIMAN	451	—	—	.313	11	(2) ALSO WITH SEATTLE					
C P. LOHMAN	287	—	—	.261	9	**MANAGER — P. LOHMAN**					
P O. GRAHAM	237	—	—	.329	4	**RECORD W—89 L—126 FINISH—6TH**					

PLAYOFF
NONE

1904

TACOMA	AB	HR	RBI	BA	SB	PITCHERS	IP	W–L	BB	SO	ERA
1B L. NORDYKE	744	3	– –	.304	47	B. KEEFE	– –	34–15	– –	– –	– –
2B P. CASEY	756	1	– –	.279	45	O. OVERALL	– –	32–25	– –	– –	– –
3B T. SHEEHAN	826	1	– –	.292	34	B. THOMAS	– –	27–24	– –	– –	– –
SS T. EAGAN	736	25	– –	.311	29	J. ST. VRAIN	– –	19–14	– –	– –	– –
OF M. LYNCH	807	5	– –	.259	34	J. FITZGERALD	– –	17–13	– –	– –	– –
OF G. MC LAUGHLIN	802	6	– –	.258	35						
OF C. DOYLE	774	0	– –	.234	32						
C C. GRAHAM	488	3	– –	.244	22						
C1O H. HOGAN	420	0	– –	.207	11						
P O. OVERALL	216	1	– –	.181	1						
P B. THOMAS	202	0	– –	.233	1						
OF J. HANNIVAN	170	1	– –	.247	4	MANAGER – M. FISHER					
P B. KEEFE	169	0	– –	.183	2	RECORD W–130 L–94 FINISH–1ST					

LOS ANGELES	AB	HR	RBI	BA	SB	PITCHERS	IP	W–L	BB	SO	ERA
1B H. CHASE	702	2	– –	.279	37	D. NEWTON	– –	39–17	– –	– –	– –
2B T. FLOOD	784	2	– –	.270	52	S. BAUM	– –	24–23	– –	– –	– –
3B J. SMITH	620	0	– –	.279	43	D. GRAY	– –	24–26	– –	– –	– –
SS J. TOMAN	584	0	– –	.223	18	W. HALL	– –	17–21	– –	– –	– –
OF G. CRAVATH	771	13	– –	.268	43	O. JONES	– –	6–3	– –	– –	– –
OF C. BERNARD	755	1	– –	.306	66	D. MASON	– –	3–3	– –	– –	– –
OF A. ROSS	680	2	– –	.250	39						
C H. SPIES	597	1	– –	.219	23						
SS T. RAYMOND (1)	326	0	– –	.206	9						
C B. EAGER	215	0	– –	.232	5	(1) ALSO WITH PORTLAND					
P D. NEWTON	175	0	– –	.194	3	MANAGER – T. FLOOD					
P D. GRAY	161	3	– –	.155	2	RECORD W–119 L–97 FINISH–2ND					

SEATTLE	AB	HR	RBI	BA	SB	PITCHERS	IP	W–L	BB	SO	ERA
1B K. BRASHEAR (1)	516	2	– –	.269	25	S. HALL	– –	28–19	– –	– –	– –
2B K. MOHLER	790	5	– –	.319	38	J. HUGHES	– –	26–19	– –	– –	– –
3B T. DELAHANTY	830	2	– –	.276	36	C. SHIELDS (3)	– –	25–22	– –	– –	– –
SS R. HALL	816	4	– –	.268	24	N. WILLIAMS	– –	19–27	– –	– –	– –
OF G. VAN HALTREN	941	4	– –	.269	38	J. HICKEY	– –	2–5	– –	– –	– –
OF C. SMITH	863	7	– –	.284	40						
OF E. FRISK	808	11	– –	.337	26						
C C. BLANKENSHIP	593	3	– –	.309	49						
						(1) ALSO WITH LOS ANGELES					
C T. LEAHY (2)	487	1	– –	.214	11	(2) ALSO WITH SAN FRANCISCO					
P N. WILLIAMS	233	0	– –	.206	4	(3) ALSO WITH PORTLAND					
1B J. FREEMAN (3)	219	0	– –	.237	8	MANAGER – P. WILSON/R. HALL					
1B M. MURPHY (3)	193	2	– –	.244	6	RECORD W–114 L–106 FINISH–3RD					

1904

OAKLAND		AB	HR	RBI	BA	SB	PITCHERS	IP	W–L	BB	SO	ERA
1B	J. STREIB	765	0	– –	.227	26	J. BUCHANAN	– –	33–20	– –	– –	– –
2B	L. SCHLAFLY	694	1	– –	.277	38	H. SCHMIDT	– –	26–28	– –	– –	– –
3B	B. DEVEREAUX	777	0	– –	.232	49	D. MOSKIMAN	– –	19–15	– –	– –	– –
SS	B. FRANCKS	846	0	– –	.241	40	O. GRAHAM	– –	19–23	– –	– –	– –
OF	B. GANLEY	866	0	– –	.271	72	C. COOPER	– –	3–7	– –	– –	– –
OF	A. KRUGER	820	3	– –	.241	45						
OF	B. DUNLEAVY	651	4	– –	.241	54						
C	J. BYRNES	460	1	– –	.220	10						
PO	D. MOSKIMAN	381	4	– –	.260	9						
P	O. GRAHAM	226	3	– –	.310	5	MANAGER – P. LOHMAN					
P	H. SCHMIDT	209	0	– –	.201	2	RECORD W–116 L–109 FINISH–4TH					

SAN FRANCISCO		AB	HR	RBI	BA	SB	PITCHERS	IP	W–L	BB	SO	ERA
1B	D. VAN BUREN	391	0	– –	.266	27	J. WHALEN	– –	32–23	– –	– –	– –
2B	A. ANDERSON	738	0	– –	.214	20	F. BARBER (1)	– –	26–29	– –	– –	– –
3B	C. IRWIN	782	1	– –	.277	38	B. JONES (3)	– –	24–29	– –	– –	– –
SS	J. GOCHNAUR	285	0	– –	.161	9	G. WHEELER (2)	– –	17–12	– –	– –	– –
OF	I. WALDRON	888	1	– –	.276	48	J. CORBETT	– –	13–9	– –	– –	– –
OF	G. HILDEBRAND	835	4	– –	.284	40	P. KNELL	– –	9–23	– –	– –	– –
OF	P. MEANEY	799	0	– –	.272	37	S. YERKES	– –	7–16	– –	– –	– –
C	P. WILSON (1)	474	0	– –	.259	14						
CO	L. GORTON	355	0	– –	.231	17	(1) ALSO WITH SEATTLE					
2S	J. MILLER	350	0	– –	.211	13	(2) ALSO WITH LOS ANGELES					
P	G. WHEELER (2)	312	0	– –	.272	11	(3) ALSO WITH OAKLAND					
1B	B. MASSEY	240	1	– –	.225	6	MANAGER – C. IRWIN					
1B	C. TOWNSEND	218	0	– –	.234	4	RECORD W–101 L–117 FINISH–5TH					

PORTLAND		AB	HR	RBI	BA	SB	PITCHERS	IP	W–L	BB	SO	ERA
1B	E. BECK	796	4	– –	.271	18	H. IBURG	– –	23–30	– –	– –	– –
2B	H. SPENCER	336	0	– –	.238	19	I. BUTLER	– –	17–31	– –	– –	– –
3B	I. FRANCIS	337	1	– –	.249	6	J. THIELMAN	– –	16–29	– –	– –	– –
SS	L. CASTRO	400	2	– –	.263	18	S. ROACH	– –	14–12	– –	– –	– –
OF	P. NADEAU	774	0	– –	.260	42	A. HASTINGS	– –	4–6	– –	– –	– –
OF	K. DRENNAN	744	0	– –	.245	38	C. STARKELL	– –	3–8	– –	– –	– –
OF	W. MC CREEDIE	516	0	– –	.300	26						
C	F. STEELMAN	471	0	– –	.219	14	(1) ALSO WITH SAN FRANCISCO					
PO	J. THIELMAN	329	2	– –	.252	5	MANAGER – B. ELY/D. DUGDALE/ I. BUTLER					
C	D. SHEA (1)	240	0	– –	.196	5	RECORD W–79 L–136 FINISH–6TH					

PLAYOFF
TACOMA DEFEATED LOS ANGELES 5 GAMES TO 4 WITH 1 TIE

1905

LOS ANGELES	AB	HR	RBI	BA	SB	PITCHERS	IP	W–L	BB	SO	ERA
1B P. DILLON	779	2	– –	.272	53	D. GRAY	– –	30–16	– –	– –	– –
2B T. FLOOD	718	5	– –	.242	61	S. BAUM	– –	24–28	– –	– –	– –
3B J. SMITH	752	3	– –	.247	47	B. TOZER	– –	22–15	– –	– –	– –
SS K. BRASHEAR	650	4	– –	.303	31	W. HALL	– –	19–16	– –	– –	– –
OF C. BERNARD	737	2	– –	.246	55	W. NAGLE	– –	11–0	– –	– –	– –
OF A. ROSS	722	0	– –	.241	46	B. GOODWIN	– –	8–8	– –	– –	– –
OF G. CRAVATH	703	9	– –	.259	44	G. WRIGHT	– –	5–4	– –	– –	– –
C H. SPIES	395	0	– –	.195	15						
C B. EAGER	383	0	– –	.196	7						
SS J. TOMAN	324	0	– –	.167	7	MANAGER – P. DILLON					
P S. BAUM	176	1	– –	.210	3	RECORD W–120 L–94 FINISH–1ST					

SAN FRANCISCO	AB	HR	RDI	BA	SB	PITCHERS	IP	W–L	BB	SO	ERA
1B J. NEALON	726	5	– –	.287	68	J. WHALEN	– –	32–25	– –	– –	– –
2B K. MOHLER	448	1	– –	.243	39	R. HITT	– –	24–14	– –	– –	– –
3B C. IRWIN	705	0	– –	.200	45	C. HENLEY	– –	24–19	– –	– –	– –
SS J. GOCHNAUR	675	0	– –	.159	26	R. MILLER (1)	– –	18–26	– –	– –	– –
OF G. HILDEBRAND	822	2	– –	.264	73	G. WHEELER	– –	13–14	– –	– –	– –
OF I. WALDRON	763	1	– –	.279	43	J. CORBETT	– –	3–3	– –	– –	– –
OF H. SPENCER	681	0	– –	.188	40						
C P. WILSON	499	0	– –	.182	16						
2P G. WHEELER	516	0	– –	.238	29	(1) ALSO WITH SEATTLE					
C D. SHEA	284	1	– –	.176	9	MANAGER – P. WILSON					
P J. WHALEN	189	0	– –	.138	7	RECORD W–125 L–100 FINISH–2ND					

TACOMA–SACRA	AB	HR	RBI	BA	SB	PITCHERS	IP	W–L	BB	SO	ERA
1B L. NORDYKE	838	7	– –	.271	48	B. KEEFE	– –	30–22	– –	– –	– –
2B P. CASEY	596	1	– –	.242	40	F. BROWN	– –	22–21	– –	– –	– –
3B T. SHEEHAN	826	1	– –	.232	46	B. THOMAS	– –	20–16	– –	– –	– –
SS T. EAGAN	774	21	– –	.278	29	J. FITZGERALD	– –	15–22	– –	– –	– –
OF D. DOYLE	896	2	– –	.230	43	E. EMERSON	– –	13–11	– –	– –	– –
OF G. MC LAUGHLIN	772	2	– –	.212	53						
OF M. LYNCH	766	1	– –	.244	35						
C C. GRAHAM	484	0	– –	.202	17						
CO H. HOGAN	410	0	– –	.188	10	MANAGER – M. FISHER					
P B. KEEFE	175	0	– –	.143	3	RECORD W–106 L–107 FINISH–3RD					

1905

OAKLAND

		AB	HR	RBI	BA	SB	PITCHERS	IP	W–L	BB	SO	ERA
1B	D. MOSKIMAN	444	1	– –	.252	10	O. GRAHAM	– –	28–25	– –	– –	– –
2B	W. KELLEY	766	0	– –	.200	31	H. IBURG	– –	22–26	– –	– –	– –
3B	B. DEVEREAUX	721	0	– –	.197	34	H. SCHMIDT	– –	18–17	– –	– –	– –
SS	B. FRANCKS	660	0	– –	.191	32	W. HOGAN	– –	12–17	– –	– –	– –
OF	G. VAN HALTREN	860	2	– –	.256	47	D. MOSKIMAN	– –	9–13	– –	– –	– –
OF	A. KRUGER	824	1	– –	.254	62	M. BLEXRUD	– –	6–12	– –	– –	– –
OF	B. DUNLEAVY	792	6	– –	.264	61	J. SMITH	– –	4–3	– –	– –	– –
C	J. BYRNES	417	0	– –	.194	22						
P	O. GRAHAM	225	0	– –	.196	7						
P	W. HOGAN	193	0	– –	.228	2						

MANAGER–P. LOHMAN/
G. VAN HALTREN

RECORD W–103 L–119 FINISH–4TH

PORTLAND

		AB	HR	RBI	BA	SB	PITCHERS	IP	W–L	BB	SO	ERA
1B	M. MITCHELL	530	4	– –	.251	26	N. GARVIN	– –	26–20	– –	– –	– –
2B	L. SCHLAFLY (1)	660	2	– –	.236	77	B. ESSICK	– –	20–30	– –	– –	– –
3B	J. RUNKLE (2)	424	0	– –	.177	26	B. JONES	– –	17–21	– –	– –	– –
SS	J. ATZ (1)	743	2	– –	.242	46	E. CATES	– –	11–11	– –	– –	– –
OF	HOUSEHOLDER(3)	772	2	– –	.267	43	T. CORBETT	– –	8–10	– –	– –	– –
OF	D. VAN BUREN	727	2	– –	.235	23	E. CALIFF	– –	6–3	– –	– –	– –
OF	W. MC CREEDIE	490	1	– –	.255	16						
C	L. MC LEAN	667	1	– –	.280	8	(1) ALSO WITH LOS ANGELES					
							(2) ALSO WITH SEATTLE					
U	E. CATES	282	0	– –	.188	13	(3) ALSO WITH SAN FRANCISCO					
3B	B. SWEENEY	258	0	– –	.225	2	MANAGER – W. MC CREEDIE					
P	B. ESSICK	185	0	– –	.184	1	RECORD W–94 L–110 FINISH–5TH					

SEATTLE

		AB	HR	RBI	BA	SB	PITCHERS	IP	W–L	BB	SO	ERA
1B	J. STRIEB (1)	635	1	– –	.203	38	N. WILLIAMS (3)	– –	25–23	– –	– –	– –
2B	P. BENNETT	330	1	– –	.306	18	S. HALL	– –	23–27	– –	– –	– –
3B	J. MC HALE (2)	657	2	– –	.240	52	C. SHIELDS	– –	20–24	– –	– –	– –
SS	R. HALL	701	0	– –	.237	17	S. ROACH	– –	16–14	– –	– –	– –
OF	J. KANE	747	1	– –	.253	63	R. VICKERS	– –	12–6	– –	– –	– –
OF	H. WOLTER (3)	731	0	– –	.241	19	FITZPATRICK (4)	– –	2–5	– –	– –	– –
OF	H. HOUTZ	465	0	– –	.249	40	O. JONES	– –	2–5	– –	– –	– –
C	R. FRARY	543	0	– –	.238	21						
C	C. BLANKENSHIP	409	2	– –	.311	47	(1) ALSO WITH OAKLAND					
3B	F. RICHARDS (1)	247	0	– –	.190	14	(2) ALSO WITH PORTLAND					
OF	J. HART	208	1	– –	.298	15	(3) ALSO WITH SAN FRANCISCO					
P	S. HALL	207	0	– –	.193	2	(4) ALSO WITH TACOMA					
OF	D. MILLER	206	1	– –	.204	15						

MANAGER – R. HALL

RECORD W–93 L–111 FINISH–6TH

PLAYOFF
LOS ANGELES DEFEATED TACOMA–SACRAMENTO 5 GAMES TO 1

1906

PORTLAND		AB	HR	RBI	BA	SB	PITCHERS	IP	W–L	BB	SO	ERA
1B	P. LISTER	500	0	––	.218	10	E. CALIFF	––	34–14	––	––	––
2B	B. SWEENEY	526	0	––	.283	39	B. HENDERSON	––	29–10	––	––	––
3B	L. MC LEAN	248	2	––	.355	10	B. ESSICK	––	19–6	––	––	––
SS	J. SMITH	507	0	––	.274	25	F. GUM	––	16–7	––	––	––
OF	J. MC HALE	592	1	––	.311	47	A. SCHIMPFF	––	6–3	––	––	––
OF	M. MITCHELL	578	6	––	.351	33	W. FRENCH	––	3–2	––	––	––
OF	W. MC CREEDIE	486	2	––	.309	20	C. MOORE	––	3–2	––	––	––
C	O. MOORE (1)	455	0	––	.198	8						
C	P. DONAHUE	313	0	––	.233	8	(1) ALSO WITH LOS ANGELES					
P	B. HENDERSON	179	2	––	.268	3	MANAGER – W. MC CREEDIE					
P	A. SCHIMPFF	134	0	––	.305	6	RECORD W–115 L–60 FINISH–1ST					

SEATTLE		AB	HR	RBI	BA	SB	PITCHERS	IP	W–L	BB	SO	ERA
1B	B. CROLL	455	0	––	.248	9	R. VICKERS	––	39–20	––	––	––
2B	J. STRIEB	609	0	––	.220	14	O. JONES	––	31–23	––	––	––
3B	A. MOTT	615	0	––	.184	7	N. GARVIN (2)	––	20–19	––	––	––
SS	R. HALL	224	0	––	.308	1	S. HALL	––	8–13	––	––	––
OF	HOUSEHOLDER(1)	505	1	––	.305	9	WELCH (1)	––	6–15	––	––	––
OF	J. KANE	492	2	––	.341	65						
OF	D. VAN BUREN	461	0	––	.269	20						
C	C. BLANKENSHIP	491	0	––	.253	16						
							(1) ALSO WITH SAN FRANCISCO					
P	R. VICKERS	292	3	––	.240	4	(2) ALSO WITH PORTLAND					
P	O. JONES	272	0	––	.184	7	MANAGER – R. HALL					
C	R. MC KUNE	194	1	––	.278	4	RECORD W–99 L–83 FINISH–2ND					

LOS ANGELES		AB	HR	RBI	BA	SB	PITCHERS	IP	W–L	BB	SO	ERA
1B	P. DILLON	549	1	––	.330	18	F. BERGEMAN	––	25–24	––	––	––
2B	J. TOMAN	574	1	––	.190	8	B. BURNS	––	16–16	––	––	––
3B	MC CLELLAND (1)	422	1	––	.194	6	G. HOPKINS (1)	––	13–23	––	––	––
SS	B. DELMAS (2)	636	4	––	.245	16	W. NAGLE	––	9–16	––	––	––
OF	G. CRAVATH	603	4	––	.284	12	D. GRAY	––	7–2	––	––	––
OF	C. BERNARD	531	0	––	.275	41	B. TOZER	––	7–2	––	––	––
OF	R. ELLIS	469	1	––	.226	8	W. HALL (2)	––	5–14	––	––	––
C	B. EAGER	325	0	––	.157	4						
							(1) ALSO WITH OAKLAND					
C	J. BLISS (3)	333	0	––	.294	15	(2) ALSO WITH FRESNO					
2B	K. BRASHEAR	249	0	––	.369	16	(3) ALSO WITH SAN FRANCISCO					
P	W. NAGLE	206	0	––	.248	9	MANAGER – P. DILLON					
SS	J. ATZ	106	0	––	.272	8	RECORD W–95 L–87 FINISH–3RD					

1906

SAN FRANCISCO		AB	HR	RBI	BA	SB	PITCHERS	IP	W–L	BB	SO	ERA
1B	N. WILLIAMS	472	4	– –	.309	30	R. HITT	– –	32–12	– –	– –	– –
2B	K. MOHLER	555	2	– –	.310	2	R. RANDOLPH (1)	– –	22–14	– –	– –	– –
3B	C. IRWIN	620	0	– –	.231	21	J. MEYERS (3)	– –	11–19	– –	– –	– –
SS	J. GOCHNAUR	524	0	– –	.160	21	F. BROWN	– –	10–9	– –	– –	– –
OF	H. SPENCER	724	2	– –	.225	49	SIMONS	– –	7–4	– –	– –	– –
OF	G. HILDEBRAND	526	0	– –	.260	18	G. WHEELER	– –	6–3	– –	– –	– –
OF	G. WHEELER	467	0	– –	.308	26	N. WILLIAMS	– –	5–4	– –	– –	– –
C	P. WILSON	374	0	– –	.235	5						

(1) ALSO WITH OAKLAND AND LOS ANGELES

OF	F. SEARS	279	0	– –	.211	4
P	R. RANDOLPH (1)	207	0	– –	.169	6
P	R. HITT	146	0	– –	.301	3
C	H. SPIES (2)	138	0	– –	.231	9

(2) ALSO WITH LOS ANGELES

(3) ALSO WITH FRESNO

MANAGER – P. WILSON

RECORD W–91 L–81 FINISH–4TH

OAKLAND		AB	HR	RBI	BA	SB	PITCHERS	IP	W–L	BB	SO	ERA
1B	HEITMULLER (1)	542	2	– –	.306	7	O. GRAHAM	– –	24–24	– –	– –	– –
2B	R. HALEY	365	0	– –	.222	20	E. CATES	– –	24–25	– –	– –	– –
3B	B. DEVEREAUX	587	0	– –	.233	23	B. REIDY	– –	17–28	– –	– –	– –
SS	B. FRANCKS	550	0	– –	.227	23						
OF	G. VAN HALTREN	697	0	– –	.217	36						
OF	A. KRUGER	668	1	– –	.316	33						
OF	G. SMITH	492	0	– –	.236	15						
C	T. HACKETT	474	0	– –	.192	6						

U	E. CATES	251	1	– –	.199	8
P	O. GRAHAM	216	1	– –	.218	5
P	B. REIDY	161	0	– –	.136	6

(1) ALSO WITH SEATTLE

MANAGER – G. VAN HALTREN

RECORD W–77 L–110 FINISH–5TH

FRESNO		AB	HR	RBI	BA	SB	PITCHERS	IP	W–L	BB	SO	ERA
1B	H. HOGAN	472	0	– –	.178	4	J. FITZGERALD	– –	24–25	– –	– –	– –
2B	P. CASEY	645	0	– –	.245	22	H. MC GREGOR	– –	15–22	– –	– –	– –
3B	W. CARTWRIGHT	586	1	– –	.217	9	H. WOLTER	– –	12–21	– –	– –	– –
SS	T. EAGAN	652	2	– –	.261	22	LEMKE	– –	5–13	– –	– –	– –
OF	C. DOYLE	759	1	– –	.192	16	C. STELTZ (1)	– –	3–10	– –	– –	– –
OF	G. MC LAUGHLIN	715	0	– –	.260	29	F. O'BRIEN (2)	– –	3–10	– –	– –	– –
OF	H. WOLTER	549	1	– –	.286	22	HOAG	– –	2–10	– –	– –	– –
C	W. DASHWOOD	539	1	– –	.186	9						

3B	F. ARELLANES	170	0	– –	.165	5

(1) ALSO WITH LOS ANGELES

(2) ALSO WITH SAN FRANCISCO

MANAGER – M. FISHER

RECORD W–64 L–117 FINISH–6TH

PLAYOFFS
NONE

1907

LOS ANGELES	AB	HR	RBI	BA	SB	PITCHERS	IP	W–L	BB	SO	ERA
1B P. DILLON	631	5	––	.304	34	D. GRAY	––	32–14	155	216	––
2B K. BRASHEAR	581	0	––	.270	36	B. BURNS	––	23–16	82	144	––
3B J. SMITH	432	0	––	.243	20	W. NAGLE	––	16–14	50	69	––
SS B. DELMAS	604	2	––	.227	25	F. CARNES (1)	––	16–19	134	124	––
OF W. CARLISLE	648	14	––	.259	39	F. HOSP	––	12–7	96	56	––
OF G. CRAVATH	614	10	––	.303	50	F. BERGMAN	––	6–5	49	27	––
OF R. ELLIS	578	4	––	.239	29						
C H. HOGAN	375	1	––	.168	3						
2O C. BERNARD	539	0	––	.271	35						
CO B. EAGER	282	0	––	.202	6	(1) ALSO WITH OAKLAND					
PO W. NAGLE	213	0	––	.249	8	MANAGER – P. DILLON					
P D. GRAY	161	0	––	.205	4	RECORD W–115 L–74 FINISH–1ST					

SAN FRANCISCO	AB	HR	RBI	BA	SB	PITCHERS	IP	W–L	BB	SO	ERA
1B N. WILLIAMS	682	2	––	.257	27	O. JONES	––	29–21	125	156	––
2B K. MOHLER	385	0	––	.239	25	C. HENLEY	––	24–15	103	197	––
3B C. IRWIN	580	1	––	.240	28	B. JOY	––	18–22	143	170	––
SS G. WHEELER	559	2	––	.227	31	R. WILLIS	––	12–17	96	100	––
OF G. HILDEBRAND	648	1	––	.239	59	H. QUICK	––	11–12	71	56	––
OF H. SPENCER	571	0	––	.163	39	W. ASHLEY	––	6–4	25	25	––
OF SHAUGHNESSY	295	1	––	.237	22						
C G. STREET	523	1	––	.231	8						
2B J. STREIB	275	0	––	.178	7						
SS B. MORIARTY	239	1	––	.301	11						
OF H. MELCHOIR	220	1	––	.305	17						
OF L. PIPER	196	0	––	.281	19						
C C. ESOLA	193	3	––	.228	9						
SS R. ZEIDER	192	0	––	.214	10						
PO C. HENLEY	189	1	––	.238	5						
P O. JONES	158	0	––	.139	5	MANAGER – D. LONG					
PO1 H. QUICK	153	0	––	.183	1	RECORD W–104 L–99 FINISH–2ND					

1907

OAKLAND	AB	HR	RBI	BA	SB	PITCHERS	IP	W–L	BB	SO	ERA
1B G. BIGBEE	696	0	– –	.234	36	E. CATES	– –	26–23	141	226	– –
2B G. HALEY	705	0	– –	.227	36	D. WRIGHT	– –	25–18	134	135	– –
3B B. DEVEREAUX	618	0	– –	.235	28	W. HOGAN	– –	20–14	90	115	– –
SS T. EAGAN	708	10	– –	.335	31	R. RANDOLPH (1)	– –	20–18	108	107	– –
OF H. HEITMULLER	763	4	– –	.262	39	B. REIDY	– –	9–14	32	49	– –
OF G. VAN HALTREN	718	0	– –	.269	47	J. HOPKINS	– –	5–4	32	27	– –
OF J. SMITH	715	1	– –	.269	53						
C J. BLISS	472	1	– –	.225	30						
U W. HOGAN	269	0	– –	.290	13	(1) ALSO WITH LOS ANGELES					
P D. WRIGHT	205	0	– –	.263	6	**MANAGER – G. VAN HALTREN**					
P E. CATES	157	0	– –	.197	5	**RECORD W–97 L–101 FINISH–3RD**					

PORTLAND	AB	HR	RBI	BA	SB	PITCHERS	IP	W–L	BB	SO	ERA
1B C. ATHERTON	220	0	– –	.173	2	E. KINSELLA	– –	20–19	102	167	– –
2B P. CASEY	621	0	– –	.251	20	B. GROOM	– –	20–26	158	191	– –
3B A. MOTT	504	0	– –	.218	20	E. CALIFF	– –	13–22	108	116	– –
SS J. FAY	198	0	– –	.177	10	C. HARTMAN	– –	10–14	100	84	– –
OF W. MC CREEDIE	606	0	– –	.300	31	H. PERNOLL	– –	6–13	73	69	– –
OF J. BASSEY (1)	595	2	– –	.224	36	A. SCHIMPFF	– –	1–9	26	33	– –
OF R. LOVETT	255	0	– –	.263	15						
C P. DONAHUE	570	0	– –	.226	22						
S3 J. SHINN	212	1	– –	.175	8						
1B T. CARSON	212	1	– –	.208	5						
C O. MOORE	204	0	– –	.221	4						
SP A. SCHIMPFF	203	0	– –	.133	6						
P B. GROOM	164	0	– –	.146	2						
OF T. RAFTERY	159	1	– –	.295	16						
1B E. KENNEDY	144	0	– –	.271	12						
SS O. JOHNSON	135	0	– –	.215	2	(1) ALSO WITH OAKLAND					
P E. KINSELLA	133	0	– –	.075	2	**MANAGER – W. MC CREEDIE**					
OF I. BURDETTE	126	1	– –	.246	15	**RECORD W–72 L–114 FINISH–4TH**					

PLAYOFFS
NONE

1908

LOS ANGELES		AB	HR	RBI	BA	SB	PITCHERS	IP	W–L	BB	SO	ERA
1B	P. DILLON	620	7	– –	.271	33	D. GRAY	– –	26–11	– –	– –	– –
2B	C. BERNARD	507	1	– –	.272	29	W. NAGLE	– –	24–10	– –	– –	– –
3B	J. SMITH	612	0	– –	.239	28	F. HOSP	– –	20–15	– –	– –	– –
SS	B. DELMAS	624	2	– –	.248	23	A. BRISWALTER	– –	13–5	– –	– –	– –
OF	R. OAKES	736	0	– –	.288	36	B. KOESTNER	– –	11–23	– –	– –	– –
OF	R. ELLIS	646	5	– –	.269	30	E. THORSEN	– –	5–3	– –	– –	– –
OF	K. BRASHEAR	537	2	– –	.259	25	R. RANDOLPH	– –	5–6	– –	– –	– –
C	T. EASTERLY	376	3	– –	.309	7	G. WHEELER	– –	3–3	– –	– –	– –
U	G. WHEELER	398	1	– –	.211	18						
C	H. HOGAN	275	0	– –	.164	6						
U	W. NAGLE	184	0	– –	.179	5						
PI	F. HOSP	178	0	– –	.174	6						
P	D. GRAY	141	0	– –	.248	1						
2B	I. HOWARD	129	0	– –	.287	8	MANAGER – P. DILLON					
P	B. KOESTNER	112	0	– –	.277	4	RECORD W–110 L–78 FINISH–1ST					

PORTLAND		AB	HR	RBI	BA	SB	PITCHERS	IP	W–L	BB	SO	ERA
1B	B. DANZIG	685	2	– –	.298	27	B. GROOM	– –	29–15	– –	– –	– –
2B	P. CASEY	611	2	– –	.226	20	J. GARRETT	– –	21–16	– –	– –	– –
3B	O. JOHNSON	656	10	– –	.280	38	E. KINSELLA	– –	21–19	– –	– –	– –
SS	P. COONEY	653	1	– –	.187	45	J. GRANEY	– –	12–13	– –	– –	– –
OF	J. BASSEY	609	4	– –	.246	58	E. PINNANCE	– –	4–3	– –	– –	– –
OF	T. RAFTERY	602	2	– –	.276	38	H. PERNOLL	– –	3–2	– –	– –	– –
OF	W. MC CREEDIE	466	0	– –	.245	14	MARSHALL	– –	1–6	– –	– –	– –
C	T. MADDEN	359	0	– –	.273	10	C. ROSE	– –	0–6	– –	– –	– –
O3	B. RYAN	623	0	– –	.249	35						
C	B. WHALING	228	0	– –	.145	2						
P	B. GROOM	162	0	– –	.179	0						
P	E. KINSELLA	132	0	– –	.182	0	MANAGER – W. MC CREEDIE					
PO	J. GRANEY	105	0	– –	.229	1	RECORD W–95 L–90 FINISH–2ND					

1908

SAN FRANCISCO	AB	HR	RBI	BA	SB	PITCHERS	IP	W–L	BB	SO	ERA
1B N. WILLIAMS	741	1	––	.270	41	R. SUTER	––	26–20	––	––	––
2B K. MOHLER	723	1	––	.254	43	C. HENLEY	––	20–18	––	––	––
3B H. MC ARDLE	558	0	––	.197	26	R. WILLIS	––	19–18	––	––	––
SS R. ZEIDER	742	1	––	.245	93	O. JONES	––	11–24	––	––	––
OF H. MELCHOIR	663	6	––	.259	43	F. BROWNING	––	9–2	––	––	––
OF G. HILDEBRAND	621	0	––	.238	37	SKILLMAN	––	6–6	––	––	––
OF F. BECK	347	4	––	.242	14	E. GRIFFIN	––	4–6	––	––	––
C C. BERRY	526	1	––	.243	19	J. BERGER	––	3–4	––	––	––
O3 J. CURTIS	448	1	––	.192	16						
OF L. PIPER	228	1	––	.167	20						
PO C. HENLEY	198	1	––	.182	9						
P R. SUTER	154	1	––	.227	3						
OF P. BODIE	134	3	––	.276	5						
P R. WILLIS	130	0	––	.162	2	**MANAGER – D. LONG**					
P O. JONES	120	0	––	.142	0	**RECORD W–100 L–104 FINISH–3RD**					

OAKLAND	AB	HR	RBI	BA	SB	PITCHERS	IP	W–L	BB	SO	ERA
1B W. HOGAN	546	3	––	.242	30	D. WRIGHT	––	16–15	––	––	––
2B G. HALEY	321	0	––	.240	10	D. HARDY	––	14–23	––	––	––
3B J. ALTMAN	372	0	––	.228	13	T. CHRISTIAN	––	10–10	––	––	––
SS T. EAGAN	687	9	––	.262	17	S. NELSON	––	10–14	––	––	––
OF H. HEITMULLER	791	12	––	.284	39	S. LOUCKS	––	9–15	––	––	––
OF J. COOK	759	1	––	.227	34	J. HOPKINS	––	8–8	––	––	––
OF G. VAN HALTREN	706	2	––	.242	30	H. KILLIAN	––	6–4	––	––	––
C C. LEWIS	254	0	––	.224	3	P. DELLAR	––	6–11	––	––	––
C1 J. SLATTERY	360	0	––	.331	8						
C M. LA LONGE (1)	308	0	––	.244	17						
13S W. MILLER	266	2	––	.195	2						
2B F. TRUESDALE	238	0	––	.252	17						
OF D. LEWIS	186	0	––	.253	4						
P D. HARDY	144	0	––	.188	2	(1) ALSO WITH SAN FRANCISCO					
OF J. SMITH	129	0	––	.163	4	**MANAGER – G. VAN HALTREN**					
P D. WRIGHT	125	0	––	.248	2	**RECORD W–83 L–116 FINISH–4TH**					

PLAYOFFS
NONE

1909

SAN FRANCISCO	AB	HR	RBI	BA	SB	PITCHERS	IP	W–L	BB	SO	ERA
1B T. TENNANT	692	––	––	.230	––	F. BROWNING	––	32–16	––	––	––
2B K. MOHLER	607	––	––	.193	––	C. HENLEY	––	31–10	––	––	––
3B R. ZEIDER	705	––	––	.289	––	R. WILLIS	––	20–9	––	––	––
SS H. MC ARDLE	690	––	––	.197	––	P. EASTLEY	––	19–16	––	––	––
OF H. MELCHOIR	692	––	––	.298	––	E. GRIFFIN	––	12–9	––	––	––
OF P. BODIE	543	––	––	.249	––	J. DURHAM	––	5–4	––	––	––
OF J. LEWIS	303	––	––	.228	––	J. CORBETT	––	4–8	––	––	––
C C. BERRY	577	––	––	.244	––	H. STEWART	––	3–4	––	––	––

	AB	HR	RBI	BA	SB						
C1O N. WILLIAMS	345	––	––	.223	––						
3B H. MUNDORFF	320	––	––	.266	––						
OF J. WILLIAMS	281	––	––	.242	––						
OF G. DAVIS	236	––	––	.263	––	MANAGER – D. LONG					
OF R. MILLER	219	––	––	.347	––	RECORD W–132 L–80 FINISH–1ST					

PORTLAND	AB	HR	RBI	BA	SB	PITCHERS	IP	W–L	BB	SO	ERA
1B G. ORT	682	––	––	.223	––	A. CARSON	––	29–20	––	––	––
2B R. BREEN	459	––	––	.203	––	S. HARKNESS	––	29–21	––	––	––
3B O. JOHNSON	665	––	––	.293	––	J. GARRETT	––	25–19	––	––	––
SS I. OLSON	797	––	––	.215	––	J. GRANEY	––	17–9	––	––	––
OF W. SPEAS	609	––	––	.236	––	H. GUYN	––	6–7	––	––	––
OF W. MC CREEDIE	607	––	––	.272	––	T. SEATON	––	4–3	––	––	––
OF B. RYAN	538	––	––	.232	––						
C G. FISHER	414	––	––	.258	––						

	AB	HR	RBI	BA	SB						
OP J. GRANEY	385	––	––	.252	––						
2B P. COONEY	310	––	––	.210	––						
C C. ARMBRUSTER	202	––	––	.203	––	MANAGER – W. MC CREEDIE					
1B E. KENNEDY	202	––	––	.252	––	RECORD W–112 L–87 FINISH–2ND					

LOS ANGELES	AB	HR	RBI	BA	SB	PITCHERS	IP	W–L	BB	SO	ERA
1B P. DILLON	416	––	––	.243	––	B. TOZER	––	31–12	––	––	––
2B I. HOWARD	596	––	––	.240	––	B. KOESTNER	––	20–16	––	––	––
3B J. SMITH	754	––	––	.223	––	W. NAGLE	––	18–9	––	––	––
SS B. DELMAS	740	––	––	.243	––	F. HOSP	––	15–14	––	––	––
OF J. GODWIN	687	––	––	.224	––	A. BRISWALTER	––	12–13	––	––	––
OF T. DALEY	682	––	––	.264	––	E. THORSEN	––	12–18	––	––	––
OF J. BEALL	626	––	––	.289	––						
C J. ORNDORFF	449	––	––	.171	––						

	AB	HR	RBI	BA	SB						
12 G. WHEELER	428	––	––	.250	––						
OC A. ROSS	404	––	––	.233	––						
P F. HOSP	148	––	––	.203	––	MANAGER – P. DILLON					
C H. SMITH	146	––	––	.171	––	RECORD W–118 L–97 FINISH–3RD					

1909

SACRAMENTO		AB	HR	RBI	BA	SB	PITCHERS		IP	W–L	BB	SO	ERA
1B	C. GANDIL	758	––	––	.282	––	J. WHALEN		––	23–18	––	––	––
2B	F. RAYMER	671	––	––	.240	––	S. BAUM		––	21–20	––	––	––
3B	H. JANSING	331	––	––	.236	––	B. EHMAN		––	19–18	––	––	––
SS	J. SHINN	758	––	––	.239	––	C. BROWN		––	16–23	––	––	––
OF	C. DOYLE	720	––	––	.231	––	J. FITZGERALD		––	14–25	––	––	––
OF	S. FLANNAGAN	617	––	––	.251	––							
OF	J. HOUSE	423	––	––	.258	––							
C	J. BYRNES (1)	421	––	––	.154	––							
C	C. GRAHAM	302	––	––	.228	––	(1) ALSO WITH OAKLAND						
1B	H. MYERS	281	––	––	.292	––	**MANAGER – C. GRAHAM**						
3B	C. DARINGER	233	––	––	.197	––	**RECORD W–97 L–107 FINISH–4TH**						

OAKLAND		AB	HR	RBI	BA	SB	PITCHERS		IP	W–L	BB	SO	ERA
1B	D. CAMERON	669	––	––	.265	––	G. BOICE		––	19–22	––	––	––
2B	G. CUTSHAW	250	––	––	.228	––	J. WIGGS		––	19–23	––	––	––
3B	W. HOGAN	773	––	––	.263	––	T. CHRISTIAN		––	18–17	––	––	––
SS	T. MC KUNE	511	––	––	.200	––	T. TONNESON		––	14–22	––	––	––
OF	D. LEWIS	748	––	––	.279	––	S. NELSON		––	12–25	––	––	––
OF	F. CARROLL	526	––	––	.245	––	L. MAIRE		––	1–7	––	––	––
OF	H. MURPHY	435	––	––	.287	––							
C	C. LEWIS	338	––	––	.198	––							
						––							
C	M. LA LONGE (1)	417	––	––	.213	––							
S2	S. RAGAN	290	––	––	.214	––	(1) ALSO WITH SACRAMENTO						
P2O	T. CHRISTIAN	281	––	––	.210	––	**MANAGER – G. VAN HALTREN/B. REIDY**						
OF	W. KELLY	236	––	––	.203	––	**RECORD W–88 L–125 FINISH–5TH**						

VERNON		AB	HR	RBI	BA	SB	PITCHERS		IP	W–L	BB	SO	ERA
1B	K. BRASHEAR	711	––	––	.246	––	G. SCHAEFER		––	20–16	––	––	––
2B	G. HALEY	515	––	––	.231	––	R. HITT		––	15–29	––	––	––
3B	A. MOTT	470	––	––	.179	––	BRACKENRIDGE		––	14–22	––	––	––
SS	T. EAGAN	647	––	––	.223	––	E. WILLETT (2)		––	13–17	––	––	––
OF	J. STOVALL	765	––	––	.237	––	D. VANCE		––	6–13	––	––	––
OF	F. MARTINKE	735	––	––	.286	––	S. HARKNESS		––	5–14	––	––	––
OF	B. COY	421	––	––	.271	––							
C	H. HOGAN	381	––	––	.184	––							
							(1) ALSO WITH OAKLAND						
O2	C. BERNARD	437	––	––	.261	––	(2) ALSO WITH PORTLAND						
S23	B. MC CAY (1)	350	––	––	.274	––	**MANAGER – H. HOGAN**						
OF	B. CAFFYN	229	––	––	.223	––	**RECORD W–80 L–131 FINISH–6TH**						

PLAYOFFS
NONE

1910

PORTLAND		AB	HR	RBI	BA	SB	PITCHERS	IP	W–L	BB	SO	ERA
1B	W. RAPPS	703	3	––	.236	31	V. GREGG	––	32–18	141	376	––
2B	P. CASEY	569	0	––	.241	10	G. KRAPP	––	29–16	179	256	––
3B	T. SHEEHAN	348	0	––	.201	13	B. STEEN	––	23–17	107	183	––
SS	I. OLSON	798	1	––	.237	39	T. SEATON	––	17–17	102	128	––
OF	B. RYAN	784	13	––	.242	25	R. GARRETT	––	10–15	47	102	––
OF	W. SPEAS	505	1	––	.200	22						
OF	G. ORT	469	0	––	.213	17						
C	G. FISHER	537	5	––	.266	13						
OF	F. MARTINKE (1)	356	2	––	.230	20						
3B	G. HETLING	290	0	––	.234	6						
OF	A. KRUGER	231	0	––	.281	14	(1) ALSO WITH VERNON					
C	T. MURRAY	199	0	––	.161	3	MANAGER – W. MC CREEDIE					
OF	W. MC CREEDIE	166	0	––	.217	0	RECORD W–114 L–87 FINISH–1ST					

OAKLAND		AB	HR	RBI	BA	SB	PITCHERS	IP	W–L	BB	SO	ERA
1B	D. CAMERON	618	4	––	.254	16	J. LIVELY	––	31–15	119	194	––
2B	G. CUTSHAW	820	3	––	.222	45	W. MOSER	––	31–20	107	175	––
3B	H. WOLVERTON	618	2	––	.256	9	S. NELSON	––	18–14	196	136	––
SS	B. WARES	811	1	––	.222	47	T. CHRISTIAN	––	18–15	78	129	––
OF	H. MAGGERT	745	9	––	.254	58	W. HARKINS	––	12–14	47	102	––
OF	P. SWANDER	745	9	––	.230	17						
OF	W. HOGAN	739	2	––	.261	37						
C	C. MITZE	435	2	––	.191	12						
C21	M. SPIESMAN (1)	320	0	––	.144	3						
OF	F. CARROLL	305	1	––	.203	18	(1) ALSO WITH SACRAMENTO					
1O	M. PFYL	181	2	––	.249	5	MANAGER – H. WOLVERTON					
P	W. MOSER	161	0	––	.180	2	RECORD W–112 L–98 FINISH–2ND					

SAN FRANCISCO		AB	HR	RBI	BA	SB	PITCHERS	IP	W–L	BB	SO	ERA
1B	T. TENNANT	856	8	––	.270	32	C. HENLEY	––	34–19	76	224	––
2B	K. MOHLER	670	1	––	.191	26	F. MILLER	––	20–15	82	185	––
3B	O. VITT	720	1	––	.232	41	R. SUTER	––	16–14	82	213	––
SS	H. MC ARDLE	611	0	––	.185	8	R. WILLIS (1)	––	14–17	97	110	––
OF	P. BODIE	768	30	––	.263	29	P. EASTLEY	––	11–17	79	90	––
OF	H. MELCHOIR	681	1	––	.269	30	F. BROWNING	––	9–13	51	79	––
OF	J. LEWIS	459	2	––	.261	19	H. STEWART	––	8–12	71	78	––
C	C. BERRY	492	4	––	.179	12	M. WALKER	––	6–4	26	41	––
							R. AMES	––	4–3	28	21	––
U	H. SHAW	520	2	––	.281	24						
C	N. WILLIAMS	349	2	––	.186	6	(1) ALSO WITH OAKLAND					
OF	T. MADDEN	267	1	––	.266	16	MANAGER – D. LONG					
P	C. HENLEY	172	4	––	.198	0	RECORD W–114 L–106 FINISH–3RD					

1910

VERNON		AB	HR	RBI	BA	SB	PITCHERS		IP	W–L	BB	SO	ERA
1B	K. BRASHEAR	607	5	– –	.232	16	R. HITT		– –	26–18	98	135	– –
2B	R. BRASHEAR	762	18	– –	.236	37	E. WILLETT		– –	20–19	90	117	– –
3B	L. BURRELL	605	1	– –	.240	17	BRACKENRIDGE		– –	20–22	101	95	– –
SS	B. LINDSAY	679	2	– –	.196	20	A. CARSON		– –	19–16	44	128	– –
OF	W. CARLISLE	797	12	– –	.258	34	G. SCHAEFER		– –	11–10	37	53	– –
OF	B. COY	719	5	– –	.229	27	J. RALEIGH		– –	10–9	42	66	– –
OF	J. STOVALL	385	0	– –	.218	25	A. HENSLING		– –	7–8	46	52	– –
C	D. BROWN	424	2	– –	.241	13							
1B	M. FISHER	360	1	– –	.178	11	(1) ALSO WITH LOS ANGELES						
C	H. HOGAN	285	0	– –	.112	4	**MANAGER – H. HOGAN**						
O3S	F. HOSP (1)	184	1	– –	.239	7	**RECORD W–113 L–107 FINISH–4TH**						

LOS ANGELES		AB	HR	RBI	BA	SB	PITCHERS		IP	W–L	BB	SO	ERA
1B	P. DILLON	629	2	– –	.238	27	W. NAGLE		– –	25–15	83	111	– –
2B	I. HOWARD	748	6	– –	.241	77	B. TOZER		– –	18–22	112	109	– –
3B	W. ROTH	431	0	– –	.225	12	E. THORSEN		– –	17–20	137	113	– –
SS	B. DELMAS	663	3	– –	.226	30	E. CRIGER		– –	11–21	95	96	– –
OF	T. DALEY	831	2	– –	.262	51	F. DELHI		– –	9–10	38	87	– –
OF	F. MURPHY	670	1	– –	.228	30	R. CASTLETON		– –	8–15	68	95	– –
OF	C. BERNARD	642	2	– –	.257	38	A. BRISWALTER		– –	6–7	28	21	– –
C	H. SMITH	330	1	– –	.170	11							
OF	A. ROSS (1)	388	0	– –	.229	16							
3B	E. HALLINAN	358	0	– –	.201	14	(1) ALSO WITH VERNON						
C	J. ORNDORFF	250	0	– –	.172	8	**MANAGER – P. DILLON**						
U	G. WHEELER	249	3	– –	.193	11	**RECORD W–101 L–121 FINISH–5TH**						

SACRAMENTO		AB	HR	RBI	BA	SB	PITCHERS		IP	W–L	BB	SO	ERA
1B	B. DANZIG	538	2	– –	.273	16	S. BAUM		– –	17–20	74	111	– –
2B	J. SHINN	693	2	– –	.225	38	J. WHALEN		– –	14–22	85	80	– –
3B	L. BOARDMAN	693	0	– –	.218	6	J. FITZGERALD		– –	13–25	104	135	– –
SS	E. BURNS	424	1	– –	.182	10	B. HUNT		– –	12–18	93	174	– –
OF	J. BRIGGS	731	3	– –	.231	17	C. NOURSE		– –	10–13	85	70	– –
OF	H. PERRY	692	9	– –	.279	33	F. ARELLANES		– –	8–6	31	60	– –
OF	D. VAN BUREN	627	2	– –	.238	20	H. BYRAM		– –	3–7	36	58	– –
C	M. LA LONGE	413	0	– –	.186	2							
OF	A. HEISTER	439	0	– –	.216	13	(1) ALSO WITH OAKLAND						
C	P. THOMAS (1)	243	0	– –	.239	10	**MANAGER – C. GRAHAM**						
2B	F. RAYMER	240	0	– –	.217	7	**RECORD W–83 L–128 FINISH–6TH**						

PLAYOFFS
NONE

1911

PORTLAND		AB	HR	RBI	BA	SB	PITCHERS	IP	W–L	BB	SO	ERA
1B	W. RAPPS	648	––	––	.279	36	B. KOESTNER	405	25–15	127	237	––
2B	B. RODGERS	377	––	––	.265	18	T. SEATON	382	24–16	114	218	––
3B	T. SHEEHAN	673	––	––	.254	22	B. STEEN	367	30–16	117	213	––
SS	R. PECKINPAUGH	702	––	––	.258	35	E. HENDERSON	290	21–12	100	185	––
OF	A. KRUGER	743	––	––	.279	32	S. HARKNESS	127	5–8	34	74	––
OF	B. RYAN	741	––	––	.333	39						
OF	C. CHADBOURNE	689	––	––	.298	53						
C	W. KUHN	346	––	––	.228	15						
C	T. MURRAY	241	––	––	.241	9						
2S	R. MC KUNE	220	––	––	.205	7						
12O	J. BARRY	181	––	––	.193	5						
23	B. LINDSAY	179	––	––	.285	12	MANAGER – W. MC CREEDIE					
P	B. KOESTNER	167	––	––	.215	7	RECORD W–113 L–79 FINISH–1ST					

VERNON		AB	HR	RBI	BA	SB	PITCHERS	IP	W–L	BB	SO	ERA
1B	H. PATTERSON	793	––	––	.285	44	R. CASTLETON	327	22–13	76	146	––
2B	R. BRASHEAR	679	––	––	.297	36	J. RALEIGH	295	20–18	61	113	––
3B	L. BURRELL	707	––	––	.273	25	R. HITT	290	21–15	77	125	––
SS	F. HOSP	521	––	––	.261	14	H. STEWART	273	19–12	67	162	––
OF	W. CARLISLE	805	––	––	.297	55	BRACKENRIDGE	243	16–13	54	68	––
OF	G. STINSON	558	––	––	.317	25	A. CARSON	207	13–7	47	105	––
OF	J. KANE	515	––	––	.254	51	A. GIPE	77	3–3	20	22	––
C	D. BROWN	378	––	––	.246	8						
OS3	C. MC DONNELL	528	––	––	.292	23						
OF	A. ROSS	322	––	––	.273	19	MANAGER – H. HOGAN					
C	H. HOGAN	251	––	––	.191	5	RECORD W–118 L–88 FINISH–2ND					

OAKLAND		AB	HR	RBI	BA	SB	PITCHERS	IP	W–L	BB	SO	ERA
1B	J. TIEDEMANN	429	––	––	.296	14	H. PERNOLL	341	23–16	81	158	––
2B	G. CUTSHAW	782	––	––	.261	90	H. ABLES	324	22–11	88	218	––
3B	H. WOLVERTON	491	––	––	.295	7	T. CHRISTIAN	282	20–12	51	110	––
SS	B. WARES	713	––	––	.240	69	J. FLATER	222	10–16	59	53	––
OF	I. HOFFMAN	769	––	––	.286	45	H. GREGORY	201	16–10	60	64	––
OF	E. ZACHER	646	––	––	.294	22	O. KILROY	196	8–13	68	70	––
OF	B. COY	537	––	––	.255	17	K. KNIGHT (1)	138	6–9	27	46	––
C	C. MITZE	435	––	––	.228	11	J. WIGGS	75	3–5	31	31	––
OF	H. MAGGERT	437	––	––	.314	27						
1B	M. PFYL	389	––	––	.296	19	(1) ALSO WITH SACRAMENTO					
32	G. HETLING	332	––	––	.244	9	MANAGER – H. WOLVERTON					
C	D. PEARCE	274	––	––	.266	5	RECORD W–111 L–99 FINISH–3RD					

1911

SACRAMENTO		AB	HR	RBI	BA	SB	PITCHERS		IP	W−L	BB	SO	ERA
1B	B. DANZIG	761	−−	−−	.292	23	J. FITZGERALD		357	20−17	111	164	−−
2B	P. O'ROURKE	693	−−	−−	.257	24	S. BAUM		320	17−15	49	118	−−
3B	J. SHINN	789	−−	−−	.280	73	H. BYRAM		300	15−17	47	136	−−
SS	D. LERCHEN	619	−−	−−	.210	10	F. THOMPSON		280	12−20	79	100	−−
OF	D. VAN BUREN	695	−−	−−	.262	25	B. HUNT		152	4−13	52	57	−−
OF	A. HEISTER	525	−−	−−	.240	22	C. NOURSE		133	5−5	51	39	−−
OF	C. MAHONEY	523	−−	−−	.247	0	F. ARELLANES		126	7−8	38	38	−−
C	O. THOMAS	571	−−	−−	.277	10							

(1) ALSO WITH SAN FRANCISCO

OF	T. MADDEN (1)	508	−−	−−	.303	36

MANAGER − P. O'ROURKE
RECORD W−95 L−109 FINISH−4TH

SAN FRANCISCO		AB	HR	RBI	BA	SB	PITCHERS		IP	W−L	BB	SO	ERA
1B	T. TENNANT	708	−−	−−	.253	24	F. MILLER		378	20−21	103	238	−−
2B	K. MOHLER	585	−−	−−	.282	25	R. SUTER		365	22−22	105	339	−−
3B	O. VITT	401	−−	−−	.269	44	C. HENLEY		321	17−14	76	158	−−
SS	H. MC ARDLE	681	−−	−−	.267	14	F. BROWNING		239	14−20	50	96	−−
OF	W. POWELL	674	−−	−−	.289	54	W. MEIKLE		216	10−11	47	94	−−
OF	J. LEWIS (1)	464	−−	−−	.254	24	D. MOSKIMAN		134	5−13	32	49	−−
OF	H. SHAW	409	−−	−−	.252	21	S. FANNING		110	5−6	25	63	−−
C	C. BERRY	456	−−	−−	.224	6							

SO2	B. WEAVER	674	−−	−−	.282	30
OF	J. HOLLAND	240	−−	−−	.283	3
C	W. SCHMIDT	230	−−	−−	.265	21
OF	H. MELCHOIR	226	−−	−−	.270	7

(1) ALSO WITH SACRAMENTO

MANAGER − D. LONG
RECORD W−95 L−112 FINISH−5TH

LOS ANGELES		AB	HR	RBI	BA	SB	PITCHERS		IP	W−L	BB	SO	ERA
1B	P. DILLON	580	−−	−−	.253	18	F. DELHI		446	27−23	98	187	−−
2B	C. MOORE	526	−−	−−	.298	54	E. CRIGER		224	8−17	71	88	−−
3B	R. AKIN	464	−−	−−	.244	11	J. AGNEW		220	5−20	64	51	−−
SS	B. DELMAS	570	−−	−−	.254	13	W. LEVERENZ		194	10−12	58	61	−−
OF	T. DALEY	708	−−	−−	.302	71	J. HALLA		152	11−15	34	62	−−
OF	I. HOWARD	646	−−	−−	.251	67	B. TOZER		86	4−5	14	25	−−
OF	T. LOBER	316	−−	−−	.171	4	R. COUCHMAN		73	2−6	28	15	−−
C	H. SMITH	424	−−	−−	.212	8	E. THORSEN		72	2−7	28	18	−−

3S	G. METZGER	735	−−	−−	.253	33
C	P. ABBOTT	307	−−	−−	.215	8
OF	H. HEITMULLER	300	−−	−−	.343	18
OF	C. BERNARD	238	−−	−−	.303	14

MANAGER − P. DILLON
RECORD W−82 L−127 FINISH−6TH

PLAYOFFS
NONE

1912

OAKLAND		AB	HR	RBI	BA	SB	PITCHERS	IP	W–L	BB	SO	ERA
1B	J. TIEDEMANN	432	––	––	.287	8	H. ABLES	363	25–18	134	303	––
2B	B. LEARD	650	––	––	.235	80	B. MALARKEY	290	20–11	43	185	––
3B	G. HETLING	708	––	––	.297	33	H. GREGORY	274	18–14	80	98	––
SS	A. COOK	743	––	––	.241	21	T. CHRISTIAN	258	16–10	51	70	––
OF	E. ZACHER	642	––	––	.277	21	C. PARKIN	182	13–8	56	68	––
OF	B. COY	639	––	––	.297	25	J. KILLILAY	169	15–4	45	106	––
OF	C. PATTERSON	515	––	––	.305	30	H. PERNOLL	118	4–11	19	58	––
C	C. MITZE	434	––	––	.228	8	K. DURBIN	100	4–5	23	32	––
OF	I. HOFFMAN	384	––	––	.255	21						
1B	B. SHARPE	357	––	––	.300	4						
C	D. ROHRER	214	––	––	.234	1	MANAGER – B. SHARPE					
2B	J. FRICK	162	––	––	.235	8	RECORD W–120 L–83 FINISH–1ST					

VERNON		AB	HR	RBI	BA	SB	PITCHERS	IP	W–L	BB	SO	ERA
1B	C. MC DONNELL	302	––	––	.258	6	R. HITT	314	21–12	92	149	––
2B	R. BRASHEAR	692	––	––	.314	27	BRACKENRIDGE	244	16–13	77	87	––
3B	L. BURRELL	546	––	––	.244	15	S. CARSON	238	12–11	61	98	––
SS	L. LITSCHI	589	––	––	.278	18	H. STEWART	237	18–12	68	110	––
OF	W. CARLISLE	749	––	––	.283	76	J. RALEIGH	234	15–12	81	95	
OF	D. BAYLESS	716	––	––	.318	44	R. CASTLETON	222	13–8	83	92	––
OF	J. KANE	616	––	––	.310	66	D. GRAY	147	11–7	51	59	––
C	D. BROWN	333	––	––	.255	9						
S12	F. HOSP	567	––	––	.261	18						
C	S. AGNEW	322	––	––	.283	11						
1B	H. PATTERSON	196	––	––	.204	10	MANAGER – H. HOGAN					
OF	G. STINSON	153	––	––	.183	7	RECORD W–118 L–83 FINISH–2ND					

LOS ANGELES		AB	HR	RBI	BA	SB	PITCHERS	IP	W–L	BB	SO	ERA
1B	P. DILLON	368	––	––	.293	13	C. CHECH	360	25–14	80	118	––
2B	L. HOWARD	742	––	––	.287	68	W. LEVERENZ	334	23–13	111	173	––
3B	G. METZGER	612	––	––	.240	22	B. TOZER	262	16–14	62	84	––
SS	J. BERGER	722	––	––	.278	36	W. SLAGLE	245	16–17	64	68	––
OF	T. DALEY	639	––	––	.332	54	J. HALLA	236	10–12	56	69	––
OF	H. HEITMULLER	556	––	––	.335	27	W. NAGLE	107	8–6	32	26	––
OF	T. LOBER	508	––	––	.244	14						
C	W. BOLES	299	––	––	.231	4						
2B	B. PAGE	321	––	––	.284	27						
1B	C. MOORE	317	––	––	.290	35						
OF	M. DRISCOLL	302	––	––	.235	10						
OF	J. CORE	265	––	––	.283	8	MANAGER – P. DILLON					
C	C. BROOKS	262	––	––	.286	7	RECORD W–110 L–93 FINISH–3RD					

1912

PORTLAND	AB	HR	RBI	BA	SB	PITCHERS	IP	W—L	BB	SO	ERA
1B W. RAPPS	508	—	—	.244	20	B. KOESTNER	345	16—24	113	155	—
2B B. RODGERS	705	—	—	.306	28	A. KLAWITTER	332	23—14	82	145	—
3B B. LINDSAY	318	—	—	.318	7	HIGGINBOTHAM	288	19—12	75	135	—
SS D. BANCROFT	565	—	—	.212	29	S. HARKNESS	227	13—17	87	104	—
OF C. CHADBOURNE	668	—	—	.275	48	D. GREGG	125	5—7	67	79	—
OF A. KRUGER	586	—	—	.299	28	H. SUTOR	119	5—7	69	92	—
OF W. DOANE	505	—	—	.309	47						
C D. HOWLEY	331	—	—	.215	5						
C G. FISHER	314	—	—	.268	12	MANAGER — W. MC CREEDIE					
31O H. BUTCHER	256	—	—	.223	7	RECORD W—85 L—100 FINISH—4TH					

SAN FRANCISCO	AB	HR	RBI	BA	SB	PITCHERS	IP	W—L	BB	SO	ERA
1B B. JACKSON	286	—	—	.266	14	F. MILLER	335	20—22	130	279	—
2B K. MOHLER	381	—	—	.255	12	C. HENLEY	324	14—23	54	161	—
3B J. WUFFLI	453	—	—	.285	18	S. FANNING	245	12—13	52	150	—
SS R. CORHAN	660	—	—	.267	32	J. BAKER	243	12—15	83	149	—
OF H. MUNDORFF	456	—	—	.259	19	B. MC CORRY	234	12—13	92	132	—
OF C. HARTLEY	422	—	—	.306	18	R. TONER	125	5—8	45	47	—
OF J. GEDEON	411	—	—	.263	26	F. DELHI	99	5—8	19	33	—
C W. SCHMIDT	370	—	—	.262	22						
1S2 H. MC ARDLE	434	—	—	.203	6						
1O D. HOWARD	344	—	—	.358	19						
OF B. ZIMMERMAN	255	—	—	.306	11	MANAGER — D. LONG					
C C. BERRY	255	—	—	.145	4	RECORD W—89 L—115 FINISH—5TH					

SACRAMENTO	AB	HR	RBI	BA	SB	PITCHERS	IP	W—L	BB	SO	ERA
1B H. MILLER	592	—	—	.257	25	F. ARELLANES	316	22—16	80	121	—
2B P. O'ROURKE	680	—	—	.287	28	J. WILLIAMS	266	9—16	108	109	—
3B T. SHEEHAN	333	—	—	.261	6	J. GILLIGAN (1)	261	10—20	108	143	—
SS B. ORR	324	—	—	.256	18	S. BAUM (2)	227	14—13	54	73	—
OF J. SHINN	631	—	—	.271	45	J. FITZGERALD	176	6—15	111	84	—
OF J. LEWIS	563	—	—	.288	37	H. SCHWENK	135	5—12	52	43	—
OF C. SWAIN	426	—	—	.286	21	J. MUNSELL	133	8—8	66	68	—
C H. CHEEK	358	—	—	.263	10						
						(1) ALSO WITH PORTLAND					
3S H. IRELAN	398	—	—	.264	15	(2) ALSO WITH VERNON					
O1 D. VAN BUREN	383	—	—	.313	15	MANAGER—P. O'ROURKE/					
3O2 A. HEISTER	371	—	—	.245	16	D. VAN BUREN					
OF T. MADDEN	337	—	—	.264	15	RECORD W—73 L—121 FINISH—6TH					

PLAYOFFS
NONE

1913

PORTLAND	AB	HR	RBI	BA	SB	PITCHERS	IP	W-L	BB	SO	ERA
1B C. DERRICK	551	0	--	.274	34	B. JAMES	328	24-16	113	215	--
2B B. RODGERS	784	5	--	.305	42	HIGGINBOTHAM	302	21-14	73	140	--
3B B. LINDSAY	487	1	--	.300	6	H. KRAUSE	284	17-11	108	175	--
SS A. KORES	586	5	--	.282	22	H. WEST	279	18-11	56	120	--
OF C. CHADBOURNE	789	1	--	.283	39	R. HAGERMAN	233	14-9	108	164	--
OF W. DOANE	582	4	--	.304	37	G. KRAPP	229	12-13	134	139	--
OF T. LOBER (1)	518	1	--	.305	20						
C G. FISHER	390	2	--	.292	23						
1O W. SPEAS	310	0	--	.319	10						
3S K. MC CORMICK	302	1	--	.212	7						
C C. BERRY	277	2	--	.245	9	(1) ALSO WITH LOS ANGELES					
P H. KRAUSE	144	3	--	.278	0	MANAGER - W. MC CREEDIE					
P HIGGINBOTHAM	127	0	--	.299	4	RECORD W-109 L-86 FINISH-1ST					

SACRAMENTO	AB	HR	RBI	BA	SB	PITCHERS	IP	W-L	BB	SO	ERA
1B T. TENNANT	737	1	--	.299	28	S. STROUD	315	25-15	68	202	--
2B D. KENWORTHY	622	8	--	.297	60	A. KLAWITTER	309	18-14	62	158	--
3B E. HALLINAN	699	6	--	.265	18	F. ARELLANES	262	13-17	71	96	--
SS C. YOUNG	575	0	--	.250	25	J. MUNSELL	236	6-14	133	113	--
OF R. MORAN	730	10	--	.274	55	J. LIVELY	235	11-13	51	86	--
OF J. LEWIS	560	12	--	.286	32	J. WILLIAMS	218	17-7	54	92	--
OF J. SHINN	537	3	--	.302	71	E. KINSELLA	111	7-8	36	55	--
C J. BLISS	415	0	--	.205	13						
OF D. VAN BUREN	360	1	--	.283	12						
S2 D. STARK	247	0	--	.219	11	MANAGER - H. WOLVERTON					
C H. CHEEK	158	0	--	.215	2	RECORD W-103 L-94 FINISH-2ND					

VENICE	AB	HR	RBI	BA	SB	PITCHERS	IP	W-L	BB	SO	ERA
1B H. PATTERSON	410	0	--	.244	18	B. KOESTNER	411	24-26	130	205	--
2B R. BRASHEAR	504	1	--	.258	13	S. BAUM	361	23-19	72	140	--
3B L. LITSCHI	651	4	--	.226	22	R. HITT	320	22-15	73	142	--
SS F. HOSP	491	4	--	.255	22	S. HARKNESS	263	16-12	103	127	--
OF D. BAYLESS	709	10	--	.324	28	J. RALEIGH	202	12-10	55	74	--
OF W. CARLISLE	687	7	--	.224	34	E. KLEPFER	111	4-7	27	66	--
OF J. KANE	632	6	--	.280	32						
C R. ELLIOTT	454	2	--	.273	6						
S23 P. O'ROURKE	602	1	--	.244	25						
12 C. MC DONNELL	434	0	--	.247	14						
OF P. MELOAN	393	5	--	.275	24	MANAGER - H. HOGAN					
P B. KOESTNER	143	0	--	.238	4	RECORD W-107 L-102 FINISH-3RD					

1913

SAN FRANCISCO		AB	HR	RBI	BA	SB	PITCHERS	IP	W–L	BB	SO	ERA
1B	H. MC ARDLE	656	0	– –	.212	29	S. FANNING	357	28–15	54	206	– –
2B	R. DOWNS	370	5	– –	.268	14	C. HENLEY	253	15–15	56	106	– –
3B	J. CARTWRIGHT	613	0	– –	.274	22	J. BAKER	182	11–13	76	86	– –
SS	R. CORHAN	645	2	– –	.262	20	F. THOMAS	164	6–10	29	59	– –
OF	J. JOHNSTON	749	2	– –	.304	124	L. LEIFIELD	160	13–8	29	55	– –
OF	H. MUNDORFF	690	5	– –	.270	50	O. OVERALL	147	8–9	31	118	– –
OF	W. HOGAN	478	2	– –	.255	29	P. DOUGLAS	147	6–8	54	87	– –
C	W. SCHMIDT	426	1	– –	.249	33	B. MC CORRY	123	6–9	66	68	– –
2O3	C. CHARLES	276	1	– –	.232	17						
OF	B. ZIMMERMAN	232	0	– –	.289	16	MANAGER – D. LONG					
OF	B. SCHALLER	198	6	– –	.283	25	RECORD W–104 L–103 FINISH–4TH					

LOS ANGELES		AB	HR	RBI	BA	SB	PITCHERS	IP	W–L	BB	SO	ERA
1B	C. MOORE	490	2	– –	.259	44	P. PERRITT	342	20–19	92	124	– –
2B	B. PAGE	716	1	– –	.254	36	J. RYAN	307	17–17	90	125	– –
3B	G. METZGER	382	0	– –	.196	15	C. CHECH	305	18–20	86	84	– –
SS	E. JOHNSON	602	4	– –	.266	33	B. TOZER	254	15–16	88	77	– –
OF	H. MAGGERT	715	13	– –	.316	89	W. SLAGLE	227	12–12	76	49	– –
OF	R. ELLIS	648	8	– –	.275	39	R. CRABBE	204	10–10	76	63	– –
OF	A. KRUGER	540	1	– –	.230	29						
C	W. BOLES	268	0	– –	.231	4						
U	I. HOWARD	770	9	– –	.265	71						
S32	P. GOODWIN	290	1	– –	.276	5	MANAGER – P. DILLON					
C	C. ARBOGAST	205	2	– –	.195	2	RECORD W–100 L–108 FINISH–5TH					

OAKLAND		AB	HR	RBI	BA	SB	PITCHERS	IP	W–L	BB	SO	ERA
1B	J. NESS	503	5	– –	.264	19	B. MALARKEY	373	25–16	51	175	– –
2B	B. LEARD	729	2	– –	.224	70	J. KILLILAY	299	12–23	97	105	– –
3B	G. HETLING	581	0	– –	.265	17	H. PERNOLL (1)	246	15–14	68	98	– –
SS	A. COOK	693	0	– –	.258	38	H. ABLES	229	9–15	73	130	– –
OF	B. COY	716	18	– –	.278	19	H. GREGORY (2)	187	5–16	75	50	– –
OF	E. ZACHER	665	8	– –	.284	18	T. PRUIETT	175	9–9	63	84	– –
OF	G. SCHIRM	338	1	– –	.237	23	T. CHRISTIAN	140	9–7	41	59	– –
C	D. ROHRER	309	0	– –	.178	4	B. O'BRIEN	111	5–5	43	56	– –
1O	R. GARDNER	404	3	– –	.285	13	(1) ALSO WITH SAN FRANCISCO					
32S	A. GUEST	327	0	– –	.226	13	(2) ALSO WITH LOS ANGELES					
OF	T. KAYLOR	303	3	– –	.284	14	MANAGER – C. MITZE/A. DEVLIN					
OF	C. CLEMENS	215	1	– –	.209	9	RECORD W–90 L–120 FINISH–6TH					

PLAYOFFS
NONE

1914

PORTLAND		AB	HR	RBI	BA	SB	PITCHERS	IP	W-L	BB	SO	ERA
1B	F. DERRICK	520	4	45	.298	35	HIGGINBOTHAM	418	31-20	102	155	2.28
2B	B. RODGERS	773	2	66	.292	71	H. KRAUSE	356	22-18	114	155	2.22
3B	A. KORES	692	5	94	.296	30	E. RIEGER	195	12-11	36	50	2.72
SS	D. BANCROFT	668	2	58	.277	29	H. WEST	185	11-10	47	57	2.82
OF	W. DOANE	639	3	75	.293	34	E. MARTINONI	176	11-2	58	69	2.20
OF	T. LOBER	582	9	59	.246	13	B. EVANS	158	11-10	53	76	2.62
OF	B. RYAN	530	3	64	.293	19	J. LUSH	107	7-4	28	47	1.43
C	G. FISHER	440	1	58	.355	11	P. EASTLEY	61	4-2	14	17	2.80
O1	W. SPEAS	416	1	48	.276	17						
3S	B. DAVIS	366	0	41	.246	13						
P	HIGGINBOTHAM	174	0	8	.218	3	MANAGER - W. MC CREEDIE					
C	E. YANTZ	164	0	20	.207	3	RECORD W-113 L-84 FINISH-1ST					

LOS ANGELES		AB	HR	RBI	BA	SB	PITCHERS	IP	W-L	BB	SO	ERA
1B	B. ABSTEIN	760	1	101	.308	37	T. HUGHES	348	24-16	115	191	1.91
2B	B. PAGE	486	1	52	.237	33	J. RYAN	342	24-11	87	102	1.84
3B	G. METZGER	656	0	61	.239	22	C. CHECH	297	20-16	82	72	2.88
SS	E. JOHNSON	581	4	67	.289	37	P. PERRITT	295	17-14	65	86	2.26
OF	H. WOLTER	802	8	76	.020	44	3. LOVE	288	10-9	81	95	1.56
OF	R. ELLIS	756	6	120	.310	44	H. EHMKE	232	12-11	91	89	2.79
OF	H. MAGGERT	754	3	82	.288	51	P. MUSSER	166	8-12	80	72	3.46
C	W. BOLES	318	1	24	.242	13						
2S	C. MOORE	393	0	32	.239	33						
C	C. BROOKS	283	1	31	.244	10	MANAGER - P. DILLON					
C1	D. MEEK	172	2	20	.308	5	RECORD W-116 L-94 FINISH-2ND					
OF	G. HARPER	132	0	21	.288	4						

SAN FRANCISCO		AB	HR	RBI	BA	SB	PITCHERS	IP	W-L	BB	SO	ERA
1B	C. CHARLES	461	1	33	.243	17	S. FANNING	369	24-18	76	168	2.27
2B	R. DOWNS	755	3	96	.277	24	H. PERNOLL	358	22-22	77	101	2.09
3B	P. O'LEARY	660	0	41	.248	14	L. LEIFIELD	357	21-19	105	137	2.22
SS	R. CORHAN	634	3	73	.293	33	P. STANDRIDGE	326	18-19	77	112	2.13
OF	B. SCHALLER	762	8	78	.278	49	S. BAUM	303	21-12	74	120	2.02
OF	M. FITZGERALD	601	5	46	.308	44	J. WILLIAMS	64	3-6	15	21	3.10
OF	H. MUNDORFF	516	3	61	.252	27	W. BARHAM	47	3-0	23	13	2.87
C	W. SCHMIDT	442	0	46	.262	51						
OF	J. TOBIN	430	5	29	.240	13						
13O	J. CARTWRIGHT	281	1	25	.221	12						
1B	D. HOWARD	227	1	41	.352	6						
C	N. CLARKE	176	1	18	.222	5	MANAGER - D. LONG					
P	H. PERNOLL	131	0	11	.221	0	RECORD W-115 L-96 FINISH-3RD					

1914

VENICE		AB	HR	RBI	BA	SB	PITCHERS		IP	W–L	BB	SO	ERA
1B	B. BORTON	636	2	72	.307	23	E. KLEPFER		378	23–15	92	212	2.19
2B	B. LEARD	758	4	60	.268	49	R. HITT		364	25–18	116	152	2.05
3B	L. LITSCHI	645	2	64	.279	19	C. HENLEY		269	17–13	59	109	2.78
SS	H. MC ARDLE	598	2	64	.236	13	D. WHITE		259	17–13	56	99	2.43
OF	W. CARLISLE	785	5	41	.262	28	F. DECANNIERE		152	10–7	46	78	2.07
OF	D. BAYLESS	662	8	103	.296	22	B. KOESTNER		126	3–9	57	33	3.99
OF	J. KANE	448	3	53	.288	26	S. HARKNESS		101	6–3	44	26	4.90
C	R. ELLIOTT	453	3	54	.309	6	P. SMITH		48	1–1	26	14	6.41
							J. MC GINNITY		37	1–4	5	7	3.65
OF	P. MELOAN	405	6	47	.304	25							
S32	F. HOSP	342	1	35	.208	9							
OF	J. WILHOIT	192	2	15	.349	8	MANAGER – H. HOGAN						
13	C. MC DONNELL	182	0	26	.209	10	RECORD W–113 L–98 FINISH–4TH						

SACRA–MISSION		AB	HR	RBI	BA	SB	PITCHERS		IP	W–L	BB	SO	ERA
1B	T. TENNANT	773	3	73	.276	14	S. STROUD		331	20–18	62	130	2.01
2B	R. YOUNG	720	0	48	.275	50	L. WILLIAMS		276	13–20	64	167	2.05
3B	E. HALLINAN	544	0	37	.246	21	F. ARELLANES		265	10–18	59	80	2.96
SS	B. ORR	498	1	38	.305	13	B. MALARKEY (1)		260	11–17	53	76	2.77
OF	B. COY (1)	687	3	71	.279	24	H. GREGORY		249	13–14	80	67	2.74
OF	J. SHINN	576	1	45	.264	28	R. KREMER		137	2–8	42	34	5.20
OF	R. MORAN	561	3	50	.260	37							
C	T. HANNAH	374	0	44	.273	7							
							(1) ALSO WITH OAKLAND						
OF	D. VAN BUREN	473	1	37	.245	13	MANAGER – H. WOLVERTON						
C	D. ROHRER	291	1	20	.234	6	RECORD W–90 L–121 FINISH–5TH						

OAKLAND		AB	HR	RBI	BA	SB	PITCHERS		IP	W–L	BB	SO	ERA
1B	R. GARDNER	510	1	44	.306	17	A. KLAWITTER		403	20–26	109	182	2.73
2B	J. NESS	681	1	69	.292	25	B. PROUGH		328	14–23	75	175	2.86
3B	G. HETLING	559	0	61	.261	17	R. GEYER		289	9–18	56	88	2.59
SS	W. MENGES	263	0	18	.228	14	J. KILLILAY		277	12–18	82	96	2.86
OF	R. MIDDLETON	767	1	39	.288	40	H. ABLES		223	13–17	82	95	2.02
OF	F. QUINLAN	701	2	47	.290	43	T. PRUIETT		155	9–13	52	92	3.25
OF	E. ZACHER	695	3	78	.276	33	T. CHRISTIAN		101	3–3	21	24	3.48
C	C. MITZE	338	0	33	.231	9	J. BROMLEY		47	1–4	11	17	2.13
S23	A. GUEST	552	0	49	.230	10							
C	W. ALEXANDER	323	2	32	.282	9							
OF	T. KAYLOR	297	1	25	.273	10	MANAGER – A. DEVLIN/T. CHRISTIAN						
2S	R. MURPHY	172	1	10	.297	13	RECORD W–79 L–133 FINISH–6TH						

PLAYOFFS
NONE

1915

SAN FRANCISCO	AB	HR	RBI	BA	SB	PITCHERS	IP	W−L	BB	SO	ERA
1B H. HEILMANN	371	12	−−	.364	26	S. BAUM	382	30−15	65	153	2.45
2B R. DOWNS	642	9	−−	.282	19	S. FANNING	364	25−15	62	202	2.65
3B B. JONES	674	9	−−	.277	30	C. SMITH	221	17−8	63	66	3.09
SS R. CORHAN	604	4	−−	.276	34	J. KILLILAY (1)	193	8−10	66	53	3.31
OF B. SCHALLER	770	20	−−	.301	62	C. BROWN	177	11−8	35	91	2.75
OF P. BODIE	720	19	−−	.325	37	B. REISIGL	147	4−10	63	51	3.80
OF M. FITZGERALD	697	9	−−	.321	55	B. STEEN	122	10−5	20	64	1.55
C W. SCHMIDT	416	2	−−	.245	25	J. COUCH	98	6−5	46	34	2.47
			−−			P. CAVET	94	5−6	35	28	4.29
O1 P. MELOAN	417	11	−−	.285	27						
23S B. LEARD	324	1	−−	.213	17	(1) ALSO WITH SALT LAKE CITY					
C B. BLOCK	164	0	−−	.226	10	**MANAGER − H. WOLVERTON**					
C L. SEPULVEDA	160	0	−−	.237	5	**RECORD W−118 L−89 FINISH−1ST**					

SALT LAKE CITY	AB	HR	RBI	BA	SB	PITCHERS	IP	W−L	BB	SO	ERA
1B T. TENNANT	479	0	−−	.250	9	L. WILLIAMS	419	33−12	115	294	2.84
2B J. GEDEON	739	19	−−	.317	25	P. FITTERY	312	22−17	111	177	3.03
3B E. HALLINAN	421	3	−−	.216	4	B. HALL	311	19−14	132	119	3.50
SS B. ORR	776	3	−−	.280	26	J. WILLIAMS (1)	207	7−12	57	66	4.05
OF J. SHINN	756	6	−−	.312	47	H. GREGORY	204	10−11	81	85	4.27
OF B. RYAN	754	12	−−	.340	21	L. LA ROY	143	6−9	50	55	3.97
OF E. ZACHER	526	6	−−	.283	12	H. WEST (2)	102	5−6	39	27	4.31
C T. HANNAH	436	3	−−	.271	6						
13 B. BRIEF	328	8	−−	.363	16	(1) ALSO WITH LOS ANGELES					
OF F. QUINLAN	288	0	−−	.306	13	(2) ALSO WITH VERNON AND LOS ANGELES					
3B J. BARBEAU	287	1	−−	.279	5	**MANAGER − C. BLANKENSHIP**					
C B. LYNN	161	2	−−	.311	7	**RECORD W−108 L−89 FINISH−2ND**					

LOS ANGELES	AB	HR	RBI	BA	SB	PITCHERS	IP	W−L	BB	SO	ERA
1B P. KOERNER (1)	529	8	−−	.318	18	J. RYAN	373	26−21	98	154	2.72
2B F. MC MULLIN	681	1	−−	.279	31	S. LOVE	359	23−15	138	173	1.95
3B G. METZGER	397	1	−−	.171	8	T. HUGHES	279	19−16	100	127	3.03
SS Z. TERRY	548	1	−−	.264	13	L. SCOGGINS	244	12−9	102	116	3.10
OF H. MAGGERT	736	12	−−	.307	55	C. CHECH (2)	228	12−14	46	60	3.28
OF R. ELLIS	705	5	−−	.271	34	P. PERRITT	185	9−12	34	49	3.06
OF H. WOLTER	518	5	−−	.359	29	BRANDT	76	3−4	40	29	3.33
C W. BOLES	425	0	−−	.289	17						
U A. BEAUMILLER	381	2	−−	.228	31						
C C. BROOKS	232	0	−−	.267	7	(1) ALSO WITH OAKLAND					
3B J. BUTLER	209	1	−−	.230	5	(2) ALSO WITH VERNON					
OF G. HARPER	192	2	−−	.286	7	**MANAGER − P. DILLON**					
P J. RYAN	182	2	−−	.297	2	**RECORD W−110 L−98 FINISH−3RD**					

1915

VERNON		AB	HR	RBI	BA	SB	PITCHERS	IP	W–L	BB	SO	ERA
1B	GLEISCHMANN	455	4	– –	.246	15	B. PIERCY	292	15–15	90	104	2.19
2B	B. PURTELL	685	2	– –	.255	15	C. HENLEY	276	15–21	50	96	2.78
3B	D. RADER	404	0	– –	.257	6	R. HITT	258	15–11	56	88	2.51
SS	J. BERGER	737	5	– –	.251	23	F. DECANNIERE	226	13–10	69	96	2.19
OF	J. WILHOIT	682	3	– –	.323	27	R. MITCHELL	178	7–9	36	69	3.28
OF	D. BAYLESS	594	1	– –	.268	15	A. FROMME	154	11–9	42	45	2.28
OF	W. CARLISLE (1)	577	8	– –	.241	16	C. JOHNSON	139	8–6	52	52	1.95
C	T. SPENCER	354	5	– –	.257	3						
1O2	S. RISBERG	602	10	– –	.274	28	(1) ALSO WITH PORTLAND					
OF	J. KANE	428	1	– –	.290	10	MANAGER – H. HOGAN/D. BAYLESS/					
C	C. MITZE	346	2	– –	.231	6	D. WHITE					
3B	G. HETLING	274	0	– –	.223	2	RECORD W–102 L–104 FINISH–4TH					

OAKLAND		AB	HR	RBI	BA	SB	PITCHERS	IP	W–L	BB	SO	ERA
1B	J. NESS	700	16	– –	.339	16	A. KLAWITTER	394	26–18	111	157	2.97
2B	MARCAN	428	1	– –	.222	8	B. PROUGH	357	15–25	72	194	3.08
3B	L. LITSCHI	553	6	– –	.253	13	T. PRUIETT	286	16–20	118	130	2.95
SS	A. GUEST	311	1	– –	.232	6	B. BURNS (1)	274	14–15	48	73	2.79
OF	J. JOHNSTON	788	11	– –	.348	82	H. ABLES (2)	229	8–16	78	99	3.46
OF	R. MIDDLETON	750	3	– –	.288	29	S. BEER	158	9–5	33	74	2.73
OF	R. GARDNER	510	3	– –	.324	19	R. BOYD	134	6–5	45	50	2.62
C	R. ELLIOTT	415	1	– –	.301	4						
							(1) ALSO WITH LOS ANGELES					
C	W. KUHN	365	0	– –	.236	10	(2) ALSO WITH SAN FRANCISCO					
OF	H. MUNDORFF	293	0	– –	.222	7	MANAGER – T. CHRISTIAN/R. ELLIOTT					
SS	F. HOSP	189	0	– –	.233	1	RECORD W–93 L–113 FINISH–5TH					

PORTLAND		AB	HR	RBI	BA	SB	PITCHERS	IP	W–L	BB	SO	ERA
1B	F. DERRICK	691	4	– –	.250	29	HIGGINBOTHAM	330	14–17	92	105	3.11
2B	B. STUMPF	748	5	– –	.295	26	S. COVELESKI	293	17–17	82	171	2.67
3B	R. BATES	669	11	– –	.294	23	H. KRAUSE	267	11–15	76	111	3.34
SS	B. DAVIS	444	2	– –	.245	13	J. LUSH	266	12–18	90	145	2.67
OF	W. SPEAS	632	3	– –	.288	32	R. EVANS	242	9–22	83	90	3.20
OF	T. LOBER	612	4	– –	.275	16	G. KAHLER	212	9–17	77	71	3.10
OF	W. DOANE (1)	500	5	– –	.278	14						
C	G. FISHER	475	2	– –	.318	14						
OF	D. HILLYARD	336	6	– –	.268	14	(1) ALSO WITH VERNON					
C	F. CARISCH	313	0	– –	.268	11	MANAGER – W. MC CREEDIE					
SS	C. WARD	186	0	– –	.269	3	RECORD W–78 L–116 FINISH–6TH					

PLAYOFFS
NONE

1916

LOS ANGELES		AB	HR	RBI	BA	SB	PITCHERS	IP	W−L	BB	SO	ERA
1B	P. KOERNER	720	3	−−	.276	21	J. RYAN	350	29−10	92	134	2.19
2B	P. MC LARRY	553	5	−−	.293	22	Z. ZABEL	272	17−13	119	84	2.38
3B	J. GALLOWAY	544	9	−−	.244	7	P. STANDRIDGE	267	20−10	91	90	2.53
SS	B. DAVIS (1)	618	3	−−	.265	14	D. CRANDALL (1)	234	11−17	80	70	2.96
OF	R. ELLIS	755	2	−−	.254	32	O. HORSTMANN	232	11−14	104	109	2.56
OF	H. MAGGERT	672	6	−−	.274	42	B. HOGG	232	16−9	96	74	2.64
OF	H. WOLTER	615	6	−−	.296	40	L. SCOGGINS	144	11−8	50	61	3.70
C	J. BASSLER	349	0	−−	.304	18	S. HALL	128	6−6	44	39	3.37
SS	J. BUTLER (1)	380	1	−−	.184	11						
C	W. BOLES	307	2	−−	.287	6	(1) ALSO WITH OAKLAND					
O3	J. KANE (2)	232	0	−−	.220	14	(2) ALSO WITH SALT LAKE CITY					
3B	J. SCHULTZ	221	0	−−	.281	7	MANAGER − F. CHANCE					
PO	D. CRANDALL (1)	148	0	−−	.257	1	RECORD W−119 L−79 FINISH−1ST					

VERNON		AB	HR	RBI	BA	SB	PITCHERS	IP	W−L	BB	SO	ERA
1B	G. GLEISCHMANN	756	5	−−	.245	33	A. FROMME	319	23−14	89	91	1.92
2B	S. RISBERG	691	6	−−	.263	25	J. QUINN	289	16−13	85	149	2.93
3B	R. BATES	789	5	−−	.285	29	F. DECANNIERE	258	16−13	111	85	2.20
SS	P. MC GAFFIGAN	548	2	−−	.248	33	E. JOHNSON	229	15−10	108	75	3.03
OF	W. MATTICK	699	0	−−	.255	16	C. JOHNSON	200	8−14	73	75	3.87
OF	T. DALEY	650	3	−−	.255	45	R. MITCHELL	197	14−8	74	85	2.33
OF	W. DOANE	501	0	−−	.271	26	O. HESS	191	13−11	86	63	2.69
C	B. WHALING	215	1	−−	.200	2	F. ARELLANES	135	8−6	39	52	2.46
OF	A. GRIGGS	386	7	−−	.275	9						
C	T. SPENCER	211	1	−−	.261	2						
S2	D. RADER	202	0	−−	.188	8						
C	C. MITZE	166	1	−−	.241	7	MANAGER − H. PATTERSON					
SO2	W. CALLAHAN	158	0	−−	.259	5	RECORD W−115 L−91 FINISH−2ND					

SALT LAKE CITY		AB	HR	RBI	BA	SB	PITCHERS	IP	W−L	BB	SO	ERA
1B	B. BRIEF	723	33	−−	.314	23	P. FITTERY	448	29−19	158	203	2.97
2B	G. GISLASON	190	1	−−	.195	4	B. PIERCY	292	20−15	132	108	3.26
3B	M. RATH	657	0	−−	.300	32	B. HALL	256	14−19	115	114	4.04
SS	B. ORR	683	5	−−	.249	16	T. HUGHES	209	9−11	93	98	3.87
OF	F. QUINLAN	771	2	−−	.313	26	C. HOFF	86	8−2	41	26	3.75
OF	B. RYAN	701	8	−−	.310	18	P. PERRITT	83	4−3	18	20	4.12
OF	J. SHINN	447	0	−−	.280	25	D. RUETHER	80	4−5	41	43	2.49
C	T. HANNAH	469	9	−−	.260	9						
							(1) ALSO WITH LOS ANGELES					
23S	F. MURPHY (1)	371	0	−−	.240	13	MANAGER − C. BLANKENSHIP/					
OF	D. BAYLESS	267	2	−−	.292	13	B. BERNHARD/B. O'CONNOR					
2S	T. DOWNEY	197	0	−−	.213	2	RECORD W−99 L−96 FINISH−3RD					

1916

SAN FRANCISCO	AB	HR	RBI	BA	SB	PITCHERS	IP	W–L	BB	SO	ERA
1B C. AUTRY	558	1	– –	.258	8	S. BAUM	330	20–19	90	110	2.81
2B R. DOWNS	734	4	– –	.287	14	J. COUCH	319	18–15	115	70	2.68
3B B. JONES	703	6	– –	.273	41	B. STEEN	276	19–19	78	82	2.96
SS J. COFFEY	457	0	– –	.223	21	R. OLDHAM	262	10–13	117	141	2.89
OF P. BODIE	769	20	– –	.303	16	C. BROWN	216	13–14	73	113	3.16
OF B. SCHALLER	737	21	– –	.269	35	E. ERICKSON	192	12–9	112	158	2.35
OF M. FITZGERALD	421	3	– –	.316	24	P. PERRITT	83	4–3	18	20	4.10
C L. SEPULVEDA	332	0	– –	.205	7	S. FANNING	80	2–5	32	36	3.60
C C. BROOKS (1)	305	0	– –	.252	9	(1) ALSO WITH LOS ANGELES					
OF J. DALTON	247	0	– –	.255	4	MANAGER – H. WOLVERTON					
PO C. BROWN	200	0	– –	.265	2	RECORD W–104 L–102 FINISH–4TH					

PORTLAND	AB	HR	RBI	BA	SB	PITCHERS	IP	W–L	BB	SO	ERA
1B L. GUISTO	426	14	– –	.286	13	A. SOTHORON	397	30–17	158	202	2.65
2B B. RODGERS	500	0	– –	.258	12	W. NOYES	341	21–19	121	144	3.14
3B J. EVANS	346	1	– –	.263	14	B. HOUCK	316	17–19	130	126	3.36
SS C. WARD	528	0	– –	.235	13	H. KELLY	220	8–13	85	70	2.78
OF D. WILIE	663	5	– –	.293	36	R. HAGERMAN	136	6–11	93	51	4.30
OF B. SOUTHWORTH	627	12	– –	.300	32	HIGGINBOTHAM(2)	109	4–9	29	21	4.29
OF A. NIXON	486	1	– –	.263	17						
C J. ROCHE	408	0	– –	.299	14						
23 B. VAUGHN	572	0	– –	.264	23						
O1 W. SPEAS (1)	366	0	– –	.251	13	(1) ALSO WITH SAN FRANCISCO					
C G. FISHER	288	0	– –	.288	7	(2) ALSO WITH OAKLAND					
3S1 B. STUMPF	259	0	– –	.266	7	MANAGER – W. MC CREEDIE					
OF K. WILLIAMS	183	4	– –	.284	14	RECORD W–93 L–98 FINISH–5TH					

OAKLAND	AB	HR	RBI	BA	SB	PITCHERS	IP	W–L	BB	SO	ERA
1B J. BARRY	727	3	– –	.281	14	B. PROUGH	389	18–23	57	142	2.68
2B D. KENWORTHY	735	1	– –	.314	44	R. BOYD	300	8–23	108	71	3.12
3B J. BARBEAU	455	0	– –	.240	11	S. BEER	277	12–23	103	91	3.09
SS J. BERGER	565	0	– –	.241	10	S. MARTIN	275	16–18	94	90	2.81
OF R. MIDDLETON	713	2	– –	.273	34	A. KLAWITTER (1)	210	6–19	111	53	4.08
OF B. LANE	691	4	– –	.276	56	B. BURNS	209	10–14	43	50	2.42
OF R. GARDNER	442	0	– –	.290	6						
C R. ELLIOTT	339	1	– –	.274	6						
						(1) ALSO WITH SALT LAKE CITY					
C J. VANN (1)	227	0	– –	.308	4	MANAGER – R. ELLIOTT/D. HOWARD					
3B R. MURPHY	186	1	– –	.269	19	RECORD W–72 L–136 FINISH–6TH					

PLAYOFFS
NONE

1917

SAN FRANCISCO	AB	HR	RBI	BA	SB	PITCHERS	IP	W–L	BB	SO	ERA
1B P. KOERNER	741	8	– –	.275	25	E. ERICKSON	444	31–15	153	307	1.93
2B R. DOWNS	610	1	– –	.239	28	C. JOHNSON (1)	399	25–23	130	147	2.44
3B C. PICK	795	0	– –	.302	66	S. BAUM	352	24–17	85	91	2.50
SS R. CORHAN	680	2	– –	.253	42	R. OLDHAM	344	18–19	144	172	2.88
OF M. FITZGERALD	704	2	– –	.324	51	C. SMITH	293	17–15	132	60	2.33
OF B. SCHALLER	657	4	– –	.314	51	B. STEEN	97	8–7	30	33	2.51
OF G. MAISEL	616	0	– –	.308	48						
C D. BAKER	349	1	– –	.266	12						
OF J. CALVO	498	1	– –	.263	36						
C R. MC KEE	209	1	– –	.268	6	(1) ALSO WITH VERNON					
P E. ERICKSON	150	0	– –	.140	0	**MANAGER – H. WOLVERTON/R. DOWNS**					
P C. JOHNSON (1)	136	0	– –	.115	1	**RECORD W–119 L–93 FINISH–1ST**					

LOS ANGELES	AB	HR	RBI	BA	SB	PITCHERS	IP	W–L	BB	SO	ERA
1B J. FOURNIER	512	7	– –	.305	38	D. CRANDALL	364	26–15	83	91	2.77
2B D. KENWORTHY	510	1	– –	.302	29	B. HOGG	335	27–13	88	129	2.23
3B B. DAVIS	511	1	– –	.213	5	S. HALL	313	14–19	104	73	3.04
SS Z. TERRY	509	0	– –	.251	26	C. BROWN	309	18–13	65	93	2.80
OF I. MEUSEL	811	7	– –	.311	69	P. STANDRIDGE	196	10–13	69	33	3.90
OF R. ELLIS (1)	616	4	– –	.273	24	J. RYAN	187	12–11	87	96	2.70
OF H. MAGGERT	597	0	– –	.256	32	T. SEATON	129	8–8	71	62	2.93
C W. BOLES	428	0	– –	.266	19						
U R. KILLEFER	594	0	– –	.295	42						
C J. BASSLER	264	0	– –	.284	5						
3B J. SCHULTZ	161	0	– –	.261	6						
P D. CRANDALL	136	0	– –	.206	0	(1) ALSO WITH SAN FRANCISCO					
3B F. GROEHLING	112	0	– –	.196	1	**MANAGER – F. CHANCE**					
2B E. GARDNER	100	0	– –	.300	2	**RECORD W–116 L–94 FINISH–2ND**					

SALT LAKE CITY	AB	HR	RBI	BA	SB	PITCHERS	IP	W–L	BB	SO	ERA
1B E. SHEELY	749	19	– –	.303	14	R. EVANS	369	22–19	109	100	3.39
2B G. GISLASON	456	0	– –	.235	12	J. DUBUC	352	22–16	146	98	3.13
3B M. RATH	721	0	– –	.341	40	W. LEVERENZ	349	22–18	147	126	2.73
SS B. ORR	753	0	– –	.255	26	T. HUGHES	191	9–14	76	65	4.71
OF J. TOBIN	800	2	– –	.331	41	C. HOFF	189	8–9	96	70	4.91
OF B. RYAN	730	9	– –	.319	28	A. SCHINKLE	183	11–9	60	36	3.15
OF F. QUINLAN	673	0	– –	.254	27	A. KIRMEYER	139	5–10	61	52	5.17
C T. HANNAH	569	3	– –	.292	9						
2O3 K. CRANDALL	469	7	– –	.292	17						
P J. DUBUC	147	1	– –	.279	0	**MANAGER – B. BERNHARD**					
P W. LEVERENZ	139	0	– –	.194	17	**RECORD W–102 L–97 FINISH–3RD**					

1917

PORTLAND		AB	HR	RBI	BA	SB	PITCHERS	IP	W–L	BB	SO	ERA
1B	B. BORTON	332	4	– –	.286	11	K. PENNER	375	21–18	120	100	3.33
2B	B. RODGERS	594	0	– –	.263	16	B. HOUCK	366	23–15	106	140	2.21
3B	P. SIGLIN	741	0	– –	.231	26	L. BRENTON	335	16–22	137	117	3.12
SS	C. HOLLOCHER	813	1	– –	.276	33	B. FINCHER	261	10–19	67	53	3.10
OF	J. FARMER	744	8	– –	.286	47	H. GARDNER	124	7–6	33	24	2.10
OF	K. WILLIAMS	737	24	– –	.313	61	B. JAMES	119	7–9	51	25	3.94
OF	D. WILIE	724	4	– –	.296	46	A. HELFRICH	79	5–4	39	17	3.21
C	G. FISHER	402	4	– –	.226	7						
				– –								
C	E. BALDWIN	242	0	– –	.219	3	**MANAGER – W. MC CREEDIE**					
3B	B. PINELLI	211	0	– –	.199	8	**RECORD W–98 L–102 FINISH–4TH**					

OAKLAND		AB	HR	RBI	BA	SB	PITCHERS	IP	W–L	BB	SO	ERA
1B	R. GARDNER	342	0	– –	.260	15	H. KRAUSE	429	28–26	142	131	2.98
2B	E. MENSOR	590	1	– –	.225	27	B. PROUGH	374	22–22	54	108	2.36
3B	R. MURPHY	752	1	– –	.303	52	T. GOODBRED	328	17–19	91	95	3.16
SS	T. SHEEHAN	350	0	– –	.217	19	R. KREMER	224	9–15	76	55	3.29
OF	R. MIDDLETON	696	0	– –	.263	26	S. MARTIN	144	12–5	46	43	2.06
OF	H. MILLER	696	3	– –	.296	7	S. BEER	132	6–8	41	31	3.01
OF	CHADBOURNE (1)	590	0	– –	.266	32	P. ARLETT	115	4–7	39	42	3.22
C	C. MITZE	387	0	– –	.222	7	B. BURNS	88	4–5	15	19	4.48
OF	B. LANE	564	4	– –	.230	57	(1) ALSO WITH VERNON					
SS	B. STUMPF (2)	431	1	– –	.262	24	(2) ALSO WITH PORTLAND					
C	D. MURRAY	320	0	– –	.234	5	**MANAGER – D. HOWARD**					
OF	W. LEE	317	0	– –	.293	30	**RECORD W–103 L–108 FINISH–5TH**					

VERNON		AB	HR	RBI	BA	SB	PITCHERS	IP	W–L	BB	SO	ERA
1B	A. GRIGGS (1)	684	10	– –	.311	31	J. QUINN	409	24–20	84	160	2.35
2B	B. VAUGHN (2)	611	1	– –	.273	50	R. MITCHELL	366	13–26	113	114	2.92
3B	J. GALLOWAY	781	5	– –	.246	17	A. FROMME	350	21–19	84	89	2.57
SS	W. CALLAHAN	529	0	– –	.233	21	E. HOVLIK	178	6–15	92	63	4.24
OF	T. DALEY	680	0	– –	.276	34	D. MARION	161	5–14	58	40	4.42
OF	F. SNODGRASS	642	0	– –	.277	34	DECANNIERE (3)	155	4–12	72	50	3.19
OF	W. DOANE	641	0	– –	.268	43						
C	M. SIMON	304	0	– –	.224	3						
							(1) ALSO WITH PORTLAND					
1B	GLEISCHMANN (2)	366	0	– –	.216	15	(2) ALSO WITH LOS ANGELES					
2S	H. HUNTER (3)	326	0	– –	.248	16	(3) ALSO WITH SAN FRANCISCO					
C	H. MOORE	219	2	– –	.196	5	**MANAGER – G. STOVALL**					
1B	G. STOVALL	218	0	– –	.261	5	**RECORD W–84 L–128 FINISH–6TH**					

PLAYOFFS
NONE

1918

VERNON		AB	HR	RBI	BA	SB	PITCHERS	IP	W–L	BB	SO	ERA
1B	B. BORTON	275	2	– –	.265	8	J. QUINN	213	13–9	20	99	1.48
2B	F. HOSP	347	0	– –	.239	3	W. DELL	208	14–7	74	78	1.69
3B	T. WESTERZIL	316	1	– –	.272	.7	A. FROMME	169	8–7	30	55	2.34
SS	J. MITCHELL	382	0	– –	.251	27	C. CHECH	141	9–7	18	24	2.11
OF	C. CHADBOURNE	400	1	– –	.288	26	R. MITCHELL	123	7–7	33	37	1.83
OF	P. DALEY	369	1	– –	.295	9	E. RIEGER	93	7–6	27	19	3.28
OF	S. ALCOCK	236	0	– –	.237	7						
C	A. DE VORMER	278	0	– –	.302	13						
INF	J. MATHES	210	1	– –	.219	14						
OF	T. LONG	133	1	– –	.248	8						
C	H. MOORE	119	0	– –	.210	1	MANAGER – B. ESSICK					
P	J. QUINN	75	0	– –	.147	0	RECORD W–58 L–44 FINISH–1ST					

LOS ANGELES		AB	HR	RBI	BA	SB	PITCHERS	IP	W–L	BB	SO	ERA
1B	J. FOURNIER	400	4	– –	.325	37	D. CRANDALL	222	16–9	35	69	2.06
2B	J. PEPE	316	5	– –	.237	7	P. FITTERY	210	11–13	86	85	2.66
3B	R. KILLEFER	387	0	– –	.295	29	B. PERTICA	180	12–7	65	80	2.25
SS	Z. TERRY	342	0	– –	.263	17	C. BROWN	173	12–7	30	65	1.56
OF	R. ELLIS	366	1	– –	.279	16	R. VALENCIA	88	1–6	30	31	2.25
OF	S. CRAWFORD	356	1	– –	.292	8	P. STANDRIDGE	80	5–5	25	12	2.94
OF	C. COOPER	248	1	– –	.270	16						
C	W. BOLES	266	0	– –	.256	4						
SS	K. BUTLER	128	0	– –	.258	4						
C	P. LAPAN	123	0	– –	.252	2	MANAGER – R. KILLEFER					
P	D. CRANDALL	105	5	– –	.314	0	RECORD W–57 L–47 FINISH–2ND					

SAN FRANCISCO		AB	HR	RBI	BA	SB	PITCHERS	IP	W–L	BB	SO	ERA
1B	P. KOERNER	386	1	– –	.275	14	L. O'DOUL	185	12–8	67	62	2.63
2B	R. DOWNS (1)	329	2	– –	.289	10	T. SEATON	167	11–8	48	75	2.53
3B	C. PICK	382	0	– –	.333	55	E. KANTLEHNER	160	10–11	49	32	2.30
SS	R. CORHAN	303	1	– –	.238	15	S. BAUM	156	8–7	42	30	2.02
OF	H. HUNTER	400	1	– –	.293	24	C. SMITH	105	6–7	53	25	3.61
OF	J. HUMMEL	338	0	– –	.296	3	C. JOHNSON	76	2–6	27	15	3.19
OF	H. MAGGERT	304	1	– –	.247	19	D. CRESPI	59	2–4	21	12	1.98
C	R. MC KEE	204	0	– –	.270	12						
							(1) ALSO WITH LOS ANGELES					
C	C. BROOKS	164	0	– –	.256	4	MANAGER – C. GRAHAM					
P	L. O'DOUL	120	1	– –	.200	2	RECORD W–51 L–51 FINISH–3RD					

1918

SACRAMENTO	AB	HR	RBI	BA	SB	PITCHERS	IP	W–L	BB	SO	ERA
1B A. GRIGGS	344	12	– –	.378	22	H. GARDNER	195	12–8	34	78	2.22
2B B. RODGERS	366	1	– –	.243	18	L. BRENTON	188	6–15	56	66	2.63
3B B. PINELLI	348	0	– –	.267	.15	J. BROMLEY	177	12–10	63	62	3.15
SS T. DOWNEY	199	1	– –	.271	4	H. WEST	141	9–6	34	78	3.06
OF B. ELDRED	398	4	– –	.264	22	A. LEAKE	139	7–8	27	43	2.08
OF D. WILIE	366	5	– –	.279	25						
OF H. WOLTER	294	2	– –	.221	12						
C T. EASTERLY	282	1	– –	.259	6						
C G. FISHER	125	1	– –	.312	4						
U R. ELLIOTT	102	1	– –	.216	0	MANAGER – B. RODGERS					
OF E. FORSYTH	82	0	– –	.220	1	RECORD W–48 L–48 FINISH–4TH					

SALT LAKE CITY	AB	HR	RBI	BA	SB	PITCHERS	IP	W–L	BB	SO	ERA
1B E. SHEELY	330	12	– –	.300	9	W. LEVERENZ	192	16–5	74	74	2.25
2B P. SIGLIN	290	0	– –	.283	19	T. MC CABE	168	11–10	63	38	3.76
3B H. SAND	241	0	– –	.232	10	J. DUBUC	158	9–9	78	44	3.60
SS B. ORR	359	0	– –	.262	17	K. PENNER	118	7–5	50	40	3.52
OF J. FARMER	350	4	– –	.269	21	E. EVANS	71	3–8	31	15	5.96
OF L. CHAPPELL	289	5	– –	.325	18	A. CONKWRIGHT	56	1–2	39	10	5.43
OF W. MILLER	217	0	– –	.230	7	E. WILLETT	47	2–4	11	14	4.79
C M. KONNICK	246	1	– –	.236	6						
23 K. CRANDALL	239	0	– –	.272	4						
OF B. RYAN	197	5	– –	.305	3	MANAGER – W. MC CREEDIE					
C J. DUNN	92	0	– –	.196	0	RECORD W–48 L–49 FINISH–5TH					

OAKLAND	AB	HR	RBI	BA	SB	PITCHERS	IP	W–L	BB	SO	ERA
1B R. GARDNER	355	0	– –	.265	6	B. PROUGH	226	13–12	33	68	1.95
2B H. CHRISTENSEN	293	0	– –	.201	6	S. MARTIN	192	8–16	69	63	2.82
3B P. ARLETT	226	0	– –	.265	5	H. KRAUSE	170	10–11	53	66	2.60
SS B. WARES	254	0	– –	.185	5	R. KREMER	158	5–14	35	69	3.31
OF H. MILLER	414	6	– –	.316	18	B. ARLETT	153	4–9	43	34	2.70
OF R. MIDDLETON	377	3	– –	.302	15						
OF R. CROLL	350	0	– –	.186	10						
C C. MITZE	199	0	– –	.196	4						
3O N. HAWKS	222	1	– –	.248	11						
P H. KRAUSE	151	4	– –	.252	0						
C D. MURRAY	148	0	– –	.277	2	MANAGER – D. HOWARD					
U LEIFER	110	1	– –	.236	5	RECORD W–40 L–63 FINISH–6TH					

PLAYOFF
LOS ANGELES DEFEATED VERNON 5 GAMES TO 2

1919

VERNON	AB	HR	RBI	BA	SB	PITCHERS	IP	W–L	BB	SO	ERA
1B B. BORTON	587	14	– –	.303	16	W. DELL	351	25–16	99	162	2.38
2B B. FISHER	563	2	– –	.290	17	B. HOUCK	278	19–16	74	108	3.88
3B B. MEUSEL	655	14	– –	.337	31	A. FROMME	250	20–7	56	83	2.23
SS J. MITCHELL	720	0	– –	.283	41	R. DAWSON	231	16–11	61	102	2.96
OF C. CHADBOURNE	721	2	– –	.294	21	H. FINNERNAN	195	14–4	54	54	2.49
OF S. EDINGTON	593	2	– –	.302	11	W. MITCHELL	155	9–5	45	73	2.61
OF H. HIGH	445	0	– –	.317	15	S. ROSS	84	4–1	37	23	2.45
C A. DE VORMER	328	2	– –	.213	5						
3B Z. BECK	312	0	– –	.212	12	(1) ALSO WITH SAN FRANCISCO					
C C. BROOKS (1)	286	1	– –	.311	10	**MANAGER – B. ESSICK**					
P W. DELL	128	1	– –	.227	2	**RECORD W–111 L–70 FINISH–1ST**					

LOS ANGELES	AB	HR	RBI	BA	SB	PITCHERS	IP	W–L	BB	SO	ERA
1B J. FOURNIER	638	11	– –	.328	44	D. CRANDALL	355	28–10	43	99	2.41
2B KENWORTHY (1)	520	3	– –	.227	10	C. BROWN	314	25–8	44	78	2.03
3B B. NIEHOFF (1)	426	5	– –	.223	10	B. PERTICA	306	17–20	108	123	3.23
SS B. FABRIQUE (2)	630	0	– –	.235	19	P. FITTERY	301	18–20	121	102	3.02
OF R. KILLEFER	691	5	– –	.320	43	V. ALDRIDGE	221	15–10	56	87	2.89
OF S. CRAWFORD	664	14	– –	.360	14	W. SCHULTZ	107	5–4	39	32	4.37
OF R. ELLIS	616	3	– –	.258	5						
C W. BOLES	273	2	– –	.223	1						
3O1 R. BATES	301	2	– –	.279	11						
2B F. HOSP (3)	298	1	– –	.255	2	(1) ALSO WITH SEATTLE & SALT LAKE CITY					
C J. BASSLER	259	1	– –	.274	3	(2) ALSO WITH SEATTLE					
P D. CRANDALL	140	0	– –	.257	0	(3) ALSO WITH SEATTLE & VERNON					
SS P. DRISCOLL	121	1	– –	.264	1	**MANAGER – R. KILLEFER**					
P P. FITTERY	108	0	– –	.259	1	**RECORD W–108 L–72 FINISH–2ND**					
3S F. HANEY	103	0	– –	.252	7						

SALT LAKE CITY	AB	HR	RBI	BA	SB	PITCHERS	IP	W–L	BB	SO	ERA
1B E. SHEELY	646	28	– –	.305	15	A. GOULD	325	15–16	125	96	3.52
2B M. KRUG	658	10	– –	.310	24	C. MARKLE	320	18–15	123	162	3.80
3B E. MULLIGAN	465	5	– –	.269	18	S. BAUM (2)	219	11–16	41	69	3.45
SS E. JOHNSON (1)	581	3	– –	.324	54	J. DALE	217	13–13	85	85	4.48
OF H. MAGGERT	671	5	– –	.274	36	W. LEVERENZ	216	13–11	96	94	3.74
OF E. MULVEY	630	2	– –	.259	18	S. STROUD	215	14–11	37	75	3.85
OF B. RUMLER	591	17	– –	.362	15	A. MAIN	86	3–5	29	36	3.87
C T. SPENCER	326	4	– –	.322	4						
						(1) ALSO WITH VERNON					
C C. BYLER	286	0	– –	.203	2	(2) ALSO WITH SAN FRANCISCO					
3O R. SMITH	253	4	– –	.241	6	**MANAGER – E. HERR**					
P J. DALE	126	2	– –	.325	0	**RECORD W–88 L–83 FINISH–3RD**					

1919

SACRAMENTO		AB	HR	RBI	BA	SB	PITCHERS	IP	W–L	BB	SO	ERA
1B	A. GRIGGS	545	9	– –	.288	7	B. PIERCY	369	26–18	148	163	2.27
2B	P. MC GAFFIGAN	459	0	– –	.246	42	W. MAILS (3)	301	19–17	99	134	3.14
3B	B. PINELLI	548	1	– –	.252	51	D. VANCE	294	10–18	81	86	2.82
SS	B. ORR	554	0	– –	.204	12	B. PROUGH	185	12–13	22	69	2.53
OF	R. MIDDLETON	644	5	– –	.292	29	E. LARKIN	130	6–8	42	32	2.91
OF	B. ELDRED	617	4	– –	.311	41						
OF	H. WOLTER	578	10	– –	.329	22						
C	L. COOK (1)	303	1	– –	.155	2						
S32	B. STUMPF (2)	529	0	– –	.225	15	(1) ALSO WITH VERNON AND SEATTLE					
C	G. FISHER	193	2	– –	.249	2	(2) ALSO WITH OAKLAND					
2B	B. RODGERS	184	0	– –	.196	0	(3) ALSO WITH SEATTLE					
P	B. PIERCY	136	0	– –	.199	2	MANAGER – B. RODGERS					
C	H. CADY	122	0	– –	.246	4	RECORD W–85 L–83 FINISH–4TH					

OAKLAND		AB	HR	RBI	BA	SB	PITCHERS	IP	W–L	BB	SO	ERA
1B	L. GUISTO	262	0	– –	.252	6	B. ARLETT	348	22–17	112	79	3.00
2B	B. WARES (1)	411	1	– –	.226	10	C. FALKENBERG	314	15–18	75	115	2.89
3B	P. ARLETT	314	0	– –	.217	5	C. HOLLING	300	14–20	103	106	2.94
SS	S. BOHNE	520	1	– –	.287	47	R. KREMER	298	15–23	88	94	3.83
OF	B. LANE	647	3	– –	.255	59	D. GEARIN	170	12–7	40	36	3.46
OF	C. COOPER (2)	555	3	– –	.315	27	H. WEAVER	84	0–7	51	21	6.08
OF	D. WILIE	522	2	– –	.326	34	H. KRAUSE	51	3–3	15	16	1.75
C	C. MITZE	330	0	– –	.248	9						
C	R. ELLIOTT	304	1	– –	.293	4	(1) ALSO WITH SEATTLE					
2B	R. GROVER	295	0	– –	.227	10	(2) ALSO WITH LOS ANGELES					
OF	H. MILLER	217	5	– –	.346	9	MANAGER – D. HOWARD					
P	B. ARLETT	140	1	– –	.286	2	RECORD W–86 L–96 FINISH–5TH					

SAN FRANCISCO		AB	HR	RBI	BA	SB	PITCHERS	IP	W–L	BB	SO	ERA
1B	P. KOERNER	613	9	– –	.313	27	T. SEATON	354	25–16	115	107	2.84
2B	K. CRANDALL (1)	520	4	– –	.263	17	C. SMITH	305	17–19	145	82	3.57
3B	W. KAMM	485	3	– –	.235	13	J. COUCH	267	12–19	117	62	3.27
SS	J. CAVENEY	654	8	– –	.272	20	J. SCOTT	237	13–11	71	76	2.43
OF	M. SCHICK (1)	689	6	– –	.276	38	J. BROMLEY (2)	194	7–13	87	69	4.45
OF	M. FITZGERALD	629	2	– –	.334	45	D. CRESPI (3)	86	3–5	31	5	4.50
OF	H. HUNTER	434	1	– –	.263	11						
C	R. MC KEE	265	1	– –	.260	5						
							(1) ALSO WITH LOS ANGELES					
S23	R. CORHAN	437	1	– –	.259	24	(2) ALSO WITH SACRAMENTO					
OF	J. CONNOLLY	261	0	– –	.253	9	(3) ALSO WITH SALT LAKE CITY					
C	E. BALDWIN	240	2	– –	.217	2	MANAGER – C. GRAHAM					
U	C. ZAMLOCH	172	1	– –	.285	8	RECORD W–84 L–94 FINISH–6TH					

1919

PORTLAND		AB	HR	RBI	BA	SB	PITCHERS	IP	W−L	BB	SO	ERA
1B	L. BLUE	679	9	−−	.281	44	R. OLDHAM	370	21−23	116	144	2.82
2B	P. SIGLIN	602	3	−−	.279	32	K. PENNER	337	15−20	89	111	3.61
3B	T. WESTERZIL (1)	553	0	−−	.271	13	S. SUTHERLAND	235	14−14	75	55	3.45
SS	D. RADER	417	1	−−	.249	13	D. JONES	194	9−10	65	59	3.06
OF	G. MAISEL	381	0	−−	.262	17	C. SCHROEDER	89	4−6	31	38	2.62
OF	D. COX	374	2	−−	.273	12	O. HARSTAD	88	6−5	35	24	3.99
OF	J. FARMER	366	6	−−	.276	20						
C	D. BAKER	377	0	−−	.265	4						
OF	W. SPEAS	355	3	−−	.265	9						
C1	A. KOEHLER	299	1	−−	.247	1						
OF	J. WALKER	280	3	−−	.300	8	(1) ALSO WITH VERNON					
OF	B. SCHALLER (2)	269	6	−−	.275	4	(2) ALSO WITH SEATTLE AND SAN FRANCISCO					
PO	R. OLDHAM	196	2	−−	.230	4	MANAGER − W. MC CREEDIE					
S2	W. KINGDON	149	0	−−	.174	3	RECORD W−78 L−96 FINISH−7TH					

SEATTLE		AB	HR	RBI	BA	SB	PITCHERS	IP	W−L	BB	SO	ERA
1B	GLEISCHMANN	279	5	−−	.244	3	E. REIGER (5)	256	14−16	48	53	2.67
2B	J. KNIGHT	523	2	−−	.300	8	L. BIGBEE	218	11	19	140	09	4.58
3B	R. MURPHY	656	1	−−	.270	32	C. THOMAS	210	10−16	47	59	2.95
SS	R. FRENCH	299	0	−−	.221	6	L. BRENTON	203	13−11	63	82	3.81
OF	P. COMPTON	629	10	−−	.294	31	E. SCHORR (4)	174	6−12	74	63	3.78
OF	J. WALSH	586	1	−−	.265	24	H. GARDNER	168	10−12	44	56	3.32
OF	B. CUNNINGHAM	515	1	−−	.274	15	M. REGAN	83	3−5	31	21	5.20
C	P. LAPAN (1)	411	3	−−	.238	14						
1B	J. ROCHE (2)	280	0	−−	.239	1	(1) ALSO WITH LOS ANGELES					
OF	G. HARPER (3)	264	2	−−	.269	12	(2) ALSO WITH OAKLAND					
3S2	F. MURPHY	263	0	−−	.221	2	(3) ALSO WITH SAN FRANCISCO					
3B	H. SAND (4)	178	0	−−	.236	7	(4) ALSO WITH SALT LAKE CITY					
C	E. SWEENEY	154	0	−−	.279	3	(5) ALSO WITH VERNON					
PO	L. BIGBEE	139	3	−−	.244	4	MANAGER − W. CLYMER/C. MULLEN					
1B	C. MULLEN	136	1	−−	.272	7	RECORD W−62 L−108 FINISH−8TH					

PLAYOFFS
NONE

1920

VERNON		AB	HR	RBI	BA	SB	PITCHERS		IP	W–L	BB	SO	ERA
1B	B. BORTON	439	11	– –	.321	10	W. DELL		370	27–15	126	123	2.99
2B	B. FISHER	787	2	– –	.310	20	W. MITCHELL		348	25–13	86	161	2.38
3B	R. SMITH	616	1	– –	.292	10	SHELLENBACK		299	18–12	79	104	2.71
SS	J. MITCHELL	790	1	– –	.270	29	B. HOUCK		244	10–17	59	102	2.62
OF	C. CHADBOURNE	775	3	– –	.286	16	B. PIERCY		232	13–10	112	94	2.44
OF	H. HIGH	664	4	– –	.288	13	W. SMALLWOOD		165	10–10	43	56	3.94
OF	T. LONG	392	0	– –	.273	7	A. FROMME		108	6–8	22	19	2.67
C	A. DE VORMER	550	3	– –	.242	9							
O1	S. EDINGTON	394	3	– –	.272	7							
3O2	H. MORSE	196	0	– –	.230	5							
1B	A. MUELLER	161	0	– –	.248	1							
CO	S. ALCOCK	149	0	– –	.282	2	MANAGER – B. ESSICK						
P	W. DELL	135	0	– –	.222	0	RECORD W–110 L–88 FINISH–1ST						

SEATTLE		AB	HR	RBI	BA	SB	PITCHERS		IP	W–L	BB	SO	ERA
1B	R. MURPHY	674	10	– –	.307	63	B. GEARY		353	22–14	71	122	2.65
2B	D. KENWORTHY	616	5	– –	.313	12	H. GARDNER		279	20–15	54	115	2.52
3B	S. BOHNE	684	6	– –	.333	42	A. DEMAREE		251	16–13	64	63	2.61
SS	B. STUMPF	532	3	– –	.256	4	S. SEIBOLD		228	13–14	78	53	3.48
OF	R. MIDDLETON	718	2	– –	.287	27	L. BRENTON (1)		225	10–14	82	61	2.43
OF	B. ELDRED	682	3	– –	.339	35	E. SCHORR		223	13–11	70	66	2.83
OF	B. CUNNINGHAM	521	3	– –	.288	9							
C	E. BALDWIN	325	0	– –	.240	5							
C	J. ADAMS	297	0	– –	.215	3							
1B	C. ZAMLOCK	272	2	– –	.320	7	(1) ALSO WITH SAN FRANCISCO						
C	F. TOBIN	180	0	– –	.233	3	MANAGER – B. WARES						
SS	H. HARTFORD	135	0	– –	.178	0	RECORD W–102 L–91 FINISH–2ND						

LOS ANGELES		AB	HR	RBI	BA	SB	PITCHERS		IP	W–L	BB	SO	ERA
1B	A. GRIGGS	373	2	– –	.306	1	L. THOMAS		304	21–19	78	72	3.02
2B	K. CRANDALL	572	2	– –	.250	12	V. ALDRIDGE		297	18–15	80	123	2.88
3B	B. NIEHOFF	548	3	– –	.250	12	B. PERTICA		296	15–13	84	117	2.82
SS	I. MC AULEY	640	3	– –	.255	15	P. KEATING		292	18–14	97	90	3.05
OF	R. KILLEFER	730	0	– –	.286	56	D. CRANDALL		278	15–13	51	90	2.92
OF	S. CRAWFORD	719	12	– –	.332	3	C. BROWN		228	7–14	52	51	3.35
OF	R. ELLIS	619	3	– –	.249	4	T. HUGHES		94	7–4	42	47	3.63
C	J. BASSLER	454	1	– –	.319	10							
123	R. ZEIDER	484	0	– –	.258	14							
OF	J. STATZ	386	0	– –	.236	11							
C	P. LAPAN	279	0	– –	.219	4	MANAGER – R. KILLEFER						
3O	T. MC DONALD	177	1	– –	.226	6	RECORD W–102 L–95 FINISH–3RD						

1920

SAN FRANCISCO	AB	HR	RBI	BA	SB	PITCHERS	IP	W−L	BB	SO	ERA
1B P. KOERNER	281	3	– –	.263	10	J. SCOTT	354	23−14	82	122	2.29
2B D. WALSH	422	2	– –	.280	10	S. LEWIS	350	22−21	103	146	2.96
3B W. KAMM	596	7	– –	.237	24	J. COUCH	328	22−17	90	88	2.72
SS J. CAVENEY	723	1	– –	.279	27	S. LOVE	290	12−19	112	149	2.67
OF M. SCHICK	810	6	– –	.301	32	H. MC QUAID	199	8−7	47	48	2.44
OF J. CONNOLLY	647	3	– –	.283	16	G. JORDAN	126	5−13	43	39	5.08
OF M. FITZGERALD	619	2	– –	.336	33						
C S. AGNEW	495	8	– –	.271	11						
OF H. WOLTER	503	4	– –	.266	14						
23S R. CORHAN	353	1	– –	.280	18						
O1 J. O'CONNELL	305	0	– –	.262	5						
C A. YELLE	252	0	– –	.242	2	MANAGER − C. GRAHAM					
1B Z. HASBROOK	251	0	– –	.299	18	RECORD W−103 L−96 FINISH−4TH					

SALT LAKE CITY	AB	HR	RBI	BA	SB	PITCHERS	IP	W−L	BB	SO	ERA
1B E. SHEELY	700	33	– –	.371	14	S. STROUD	323	26−13	112	149	3.20
2B M. KRUG	653	9	– –	.289	15	W. LEVERENZ	277	18−13	110	111	3.73
3B E. MULLIGAN	662	6	– –	.299	50	J. BROMLEY	245	14−14	110	63	4.04
SS E. JOHNSON	647	2	– –	.338	46	S. THURSTON	220	9−13	50	76	4.38
OF B. RUMLER	531	24	– –	.352	31	N. CULLOP	196	11−12	47	50	3.62
OF H. MAGGERT	469	4	– –	.371	29	S. BAUM	149	7−10	32	48	5.07
OF W. HOOD	398	1	– –	.307	16	A. GOULD	140	6−8	46	44	4.30
C C. BYLER	440	0	– –	.243	8	E. RIEGER	88	4−6	18	20	5.32
32O H. SAND	052	1	– –	.216	11						
C J. JENKINS	289	6	– –	.260	3	MANAGER − E. JOHNSON					
O2 F. HOSP	206	1	– –	.272	6	RECORD W−95 L−92 FINISH−5TH					

OAKLAND	AB	HR	RBI	BA	SB	PITCHERS	IP	W−L	BB	SO	ERA
1B L. GUISTO	355	3	– –	.287	8	B. ARLETT	427	29−17	134	105	2.89
2B P. ARLETT	355	0	– –	.217	5	C. HOLLING	367	22−20	99	113	3.29
3B J. KNIGHT	693	6	– –	.283	9	R. KREMER	321	13−22	66	90	3.02
SS R. BRUBAKER	435	0	– –	.228	10	H. KRAUSE	213	11−16	41	51	4.13
OF H. MILLER	806	17	– –	.347	22	E. ALTEN	168	11−8	38	33	2.41
OF D. WILIE	695	1	– –	.294	25	J. BOEHLING	84	4−4	47	36	2.90
OF C. COOPER	629	0	– –	.296	37	G. WINN	70	2−6	16	21	2.69
C C. MITZE	406	0	– –	.246	5						
O2 B. LANE	589	3	– –	.272	29						
3S H. GINGLIARDI	204	4	– –	.240	1						
P B. ARLETT	177	5	– –	.254	2						
C C. DORMAN	166	0	– –	.193	2	MANAGER − D. HOWARD					
S3 B. HAMILTON	154	0	– –	.260	2	RECORD W−95 L−103 FINISH−6TH					

1920

SACRAMENTO	AB	HR	RBI	BA	SB	PITCHERS	IP	W–L	BB	SO	ERA
1B F. MOLLWITZ	576	2	––	.281	33	K. PENNER	379	19–23	90	122	3.47
2B P. MC GAFFIGAN	585	1	––	.258	55	B. PROUGH	348	20–20	40	105	3.21
3B L. SHEEHAN	480	1	––	.225	15	P. FITTERY	331	19–21	110	153	3.07
SS B. ORR	673	5	––	.264	9	W. MAILS	292	18–17	187	105	3.23
OF P. COMPTON	742	14	––	.307	31	E. KUNZ	171	3–11	59	44	4.78
OF M. KOPP	740	9	––	.261	50	D. NIEHAUS	95	6–6	25	29	2.36
OF B. RYAN	393	7	––	.298	7	D. JONES	92	5–5	36	16	3.70
C H. CADY	294	3	––	.262	5	T. FAETH	84	3–5	24	25	3.84
CO3 B. SCHANG	413	3	––	.220	13						
32S R. GROVER	353	1	––	.190	6						
C L. COOK	288	1	––	.215	3	MANAGER – B. RODGERS					
P K. PENNER	169	0	––	.237	0	RECORD W–89 L–109 FINISH–7TH					

PORTLAND	AB	HR	RBI	BA	SB	PITCHERS	IP	W–L	BB	SO	ERA
1B L. BLUE	626	4	––	.291	37	S. SUTHERLAND	352	21–17	102	84	2.68
2B P. SIGLIN	675	3	––	.230	7	S. ROSS (1)	301	12–20	98	70	2.78
3B T. WESTERZIL	666	1	––	.285	17	H. POLSON	255	11–19	107	96	3.21
SS W. KINGDON	388	0	––	.196	5	R. KALLIO	211	9–10	62	66	3.37
OF B. SCHALLER	689	13	––	.290	24	BROOKS	134	6–10	27	32	3.03
OF D. COX	646	0	––	.299	18	J. GLASIER	124	9–6	41	47	3.40
OF G. MAISEL	629	2	––	.323	30	F. JUNEY	101	4–7	36	40	3.54
C A. KOEHLER	414	1	––	.234	7	C. SCHROEDER	75	4–2	37	34	4.08
U K. SPRANGER	458	0	––	.221	8	(1) ALSO WITH VERNON					
C D. BAKER	193	0	––	.280	5	MANAGER – W. MC CREEDIE					
P S. SUTHERLAND	165	0	––	.297	1	RECORD W–81 L–103 FINISH–8TH					

PLAYOFFS
NONE

1921

LOS ANGELES	AB	HR	RBI	BA	SB	PITCHERS	IP	W–L	BB	SO	ERA
1B A. GRIGGS	678	10	119	.294	6	D. CRANDALL	328	24–13	53	106	3.13
2B B. NIEHOFF	646	11	87	.293	20	V. ALDRIDGE	283	20–10	62	116	2.16
3B H. LINDEMORE	457	1	51	.269	4	T. HUGHES	241	14–14	89	130	2.84
SS I. MC AULEY	665	0	53	.299	21	A. REINHART	233	15–5	64	84	3.05
OF D. CARROLL	686	3	93	.292	45	G. LYONS	232	14–14	124	91	3.92
OF S. CRAWFORD	626	9	103	.318	10	L. THOMAS	225	12–17	46	44	3.52
OF J. STATZ	584	2	34	.310	52	N. DUMOVICH	148	8–7	56	48	2.61
C E. BALDWIN	339	1	30	.242	2						
O1 R. KILLEFER	349	1	28	.272	11						
C O. STANAGE	323	0	17	.279	2						
2O B. MC CABE	254	1	19	.315	6	MANAGER – R. KILLEFER					
P D. CRANDALL	117	2	12	.265	0	RECORD W–108 L–80 FINISH–13T					

SACRAMENTO	AB	HR	RBI	BA	SB	PITCHERS	IP	W–L	BB	SO	ERA
1B F. MOLLWITZ	615	3	57	.299	47	P. FITTERY	361	25–14	82	164	2.89
2B P. MC GAFFIGAN	708	5	55	.220	55	B. PROUGH	320	20–12	61	118	3.01
3B C. PICK	717	13	96	.328	43	T. FAETH (1)	286	18–17	100	93	4.25
SS B. ORR	686	3	76	.286	2	K. PENNER	201	17–14	71	115	3.65
OF M. KOPP	663	12	59	.281	45	D. NIEHAUS	237	14–16	106	87	4.41
OF B. RYAN	621	9	90	.320	7	E. KUNZ	228	14–12	103	99	3.79
OF P. COMPTON	616	18	95	.278	24	E. SHEA	156	12–9	55	50	4.33
C R. ELLIOTT	355	4	39	.296	5						
O12 L. SHEEHAN	339	5	55	.277	10	(1) ALSO WITH VERNON					
C L. COOK	285	3	29	.207	4	MANAGER – B. RODGERS					
3C B. SCHANG	101	1	10	.297	3	RECORD W–105 L–80 FINISH–2ND					

SAN FRANCISCO	AB	HR	RBI	BA	SB	PITCHERS	IP	W–L	BB	SO	ERA
1B J. O'CONNELL	600	17	101	.337	23	J. COUCH	345	25–15	68	90	3.08
2B M. RATH	436	1	11	.264	11	L. O'DOUL	312	25–9	92	97	2.39
3B W. KAMM	598	13	105	.288	21	J. SCOTT	296	18–15	68	64	3.65
SS J. CAVENEY	689	11	76	.325	29	S. LEWIS	235	15–15	86	80	3.60
OF M. SCHICK	692	8	55	.296	24	R. CRUMPLER	234	13–16	105	100	3.04
OF J. KELLY	619	4	83	.284	23	H. MC QUAID	122	6–8	33	34	3.69
OF M. FITZGERALD	521	3	64	.307	33						
C A. YELLE	352	0	30	.293	3						
O21 B. ELLISON	634	18	102	.311	10						
C S. AGNEW	352	11	54	.295	9						
U D. WALSH	265	1	25	.260	4						
P L. O'DOUL	136	5	23	.338	2						
P J. COUCH	125	1	9	.192	1	MANAGER – C. GRAHAM					
P J. SCOTT	120	1	19	.242	0	RECORD W–106 L–82 FINISH–3RD					

1921

SEATTLE		AB	HR	RBI	BA	SB	PITCHERS	IP	W–L	BB	SO	ERA
1B	R. MURPHY	599	15	92	.316	20	E. JACOBS	292	19–14	87	124	3.67
2B	D. KENWORTHY	654	5	101	.343	21	H. GARDNER	291	18–12	75	115	2.94
3B	T. WESTERZIL	402	0	34	.289	14	A. DEMAREE	247	16–9	59	69	4.19
SS	B. STUMPF	565	8	93	.301	10	R. FRANCIS	228	12–11	72	69	3.63
OF	B. LANE	639	7	54	.296	47	E. SCHORR	183	15–7	60	42	3.93
OF	B. ELDRED	590	6	84	.319	17	J. DAILEY	141	9–13	51	51	4.91
OF	R. MIDDLETON	384	2	26	.276	7	B. GEARY	136	7–6	54	33	3.97
C	E. SPENCER	251	5	33	.323	0	L. BRENTON	105	5–6	36	33	3.69
1B	R. BATES	340	5	53	.338	6						
OF	B. CUNNINGHAM	337	4	51	.341	7						
3S	P. PATTERSON	299	3	30	.227	4						
C	F. TOBIN	238	3	27	.252	1	**MANAGER – B. WARES/D. KENWORTHY**					
C	J. ADAMS	196	2	17	.230	2	**RECORD W–103 L–82 FINISH–4TH**					

OAKLAND		AB	HR	RBI	BA	SB	PITCHERS	IP	W–L	BB	SO	ERA
1B	L. GUISTO	560	8	82	.320	7	E. ALTEN	319	19–21	97	101	3.98
2B	J. KNIGHT	667	15	129	.342	10	B. ARLETT	319	19–18	115	101	4.37
3B	B. PINELLI	720	2	57	.339	47	H. KRAUSE	294	24–13	59	111	2.91
SS	R. BRUBAKER	522	4	52	.299	14	R. KREMER	294	16–14	66	123	3.61
OF	H. MILLER	726	11	137	.347	14	G. WINN	226	14–7	72	56	4.74
OF	D. WILIE	700	0	73	.310	23	S. SEIBOLD	87	3–8	44	42	7.34
OF	C. COOPER	670	4	53	.328	49						
C	A. KOEHLER	440	5	57	.293	1						
2S	A. WHITE	296	2	25	.236	4						
C	C. MITZE	174	0	11	.207	2	**MANAGER – D. HOWARD**					
OF	T. CATHER	157	0	18	.217	2	**RECORD W–101 L–85 FINISH–5TH**					

VERNON		AB	HR	RBI	BA	SB	PITCHERS	IP	W–L	BB	SO	ERA
1B	H. HYATT	514	17	81	.323	4	W. DELL	336	28–14	112	134	2.95
2B	L. ZEIDER (1)	402	0	35	.216	9	SHELLENBACK	268	18–10	64	84	3.19
3B	R. SMITH	610	10	89	.320	11	W. MITCHELL	249	12–15	66	122	4.05
SS	R. FRENCH	616	2	69	.269	6	B. MC GRAW	233	10–13	79	83	3.94
OF	C. CHADBOURNE	713	0	51	.288	24	S. LOVE	182	5–14	72	88	4.55
OF	H. HIGH	465	6	54	.284	9						
OF	S. EDINGTON	464	3	54	.300	4						
C	T. HANNAH	452	5	49	.305	4						
OF	P. SCHNEIDER	458	14	69	.325	5						
2B	C. GORMAN	346	0	30	.246	5						
1B	D. LOCKER	285	0	18	.228	2	(1) ALSO WITH LOS ANGELES					
C	D. MURPHY	250	0	30	.260	5	**MANAGER – B. ESSICK**					
U	S. ALCOCK	250	0	19	.280	3	**RECORD W–96 L–90 FINISH–6TH**					

1921

SALT LAKE CITY	AB	HR	RBI	BA	SB	PITCHERS	IP	W–L	BB	SO	ERA
1B T. JOURDAN	430	5	61	.309	5	R. KALLIO (1)	277	9–21	82	107	4.48
2B P. SIGLIN	784	22	87	.344	11	J. BROMLEY	274	13–17	105	120	4.99
3B D. BROWN	648	15	98	.309	20	A. GOULD	248	18–20	88	83	4.94
SS H. SAND	738	17	91	.320	23	W. LEVERENZ	246	11–19	113	119	5.45
OF P. STRAND	589	9	95	.314	15	E. RIEGER	234	13–12	46	58	5.19
OF J. WILHOIT	478	3	60	.339	5	S. THURSTON	158	7–13	40	64	5.58
OF D. LEWIS	424	14	84	.403	3						
C B. LYNN	267	4	31	.247	1						
OF G. CRAVATH	341	18	64	.326	3						
C1 C. BYLER	341	1	39	.261	5	(1) ALSO WITH PORTLAND					
31S F. GAY	297	0	25	.306	10	MANAGER – G. CRAVATH					
C J. JENKINS	184	11	37	.337	2	RECORD W–73 L–110 FINISH–7TH					

PORTLAND	AB	HR	RBI	BA	SB	PITCHERS	IP	W–L	BB	SO	ERA
1B J. POOLE	731	20	107	.330	20	H. PILLETTE	326	13–30	104	141	4.20
2B M. KRUG	679	7	54	.274	12	S. ROSS	310	13–25	138	100	4.65
3B S. HALE	530	9	78	.342	14	S. JOHNSON	304	18–20	97	119	3.82
SS G. GRANTHAM	269	1	30	.305	7	H. POLSON (1)	198	3–18	114	88	6.45
OF M. WOLFER	731	2	63	.274	25	R. COLEMAN	156	4–12	51	43	4.50
OF D. COX	702	5	95	.301	17	G. ELLISON	118	3–7	37	42	5.57
OF W. GENIN	541	3	17	.259	7	B. PLUMMER	89	1–11	44	22	5.76
C G. FISHER	365	4	50	.288	1						
O3 H. GINGLIARDI (1)	452	7	33	.268	5						
C D. BAKER	294	0	25	.276	2	(1) ALSO WITH SALT LAKE CITY					
SS C. YOUNG	267	0	12	.169	3	MANAGER – W. MC CREEDIE					
3B K. BUTLER	187	0	10	.241	7	RECORD W–51 L–134 FINISH–8TH					

PLAYOFFS
NONE

1922

SAN FRANCISCO		AB	HR	RBI	BA	SB	PITCHERS	IP	W–L	BB	SO	ERA
1B	B. ELLISON	718	16	114	.308	20	O. MITCHELL	289	24–7	67	117	2.90
2B	P. KILDUFF	616	6	75	.287	21	J. SCOTT	276	25–9	52	75	2.22
3B	W. KAMM	650	20	124	.342	35	B. GEARY	264	20–9	48	79	2.52
SS	H. RHYNE	699	0	93	.285	19	E. ALTEN	233	13–10	50	67	3.55
OF	J. O'CONNELL	671	13	92	.335	39	F. COUMBE	180	10–7	58	68	3.40
OF	J. KELLY	573	5	68	.333	32	D. MC WEENY	175	15–7	59	130	2.78
OF	G. VALLA	547	1	48	.333	12						
C	S. AGNEW	389	11	61	.337	8						
OP	C. SEE	352	1	40	.307	10						
C	A. YELLE	331	0	24	.254	2						
23	D. WALSH	212	1	25	.269	4	MANAGER – D. MILLER					
U	R. MILLER	153	1	10	.268	6	RECORD W–127 L–72 FINISH–1ST					

VERNON		AB	HR	RBI	BA	SB	PITCHERS	IP	W–L	BB	SO	ERA
1B	H. HYATT	548	15	84	.318	9	W. DELL	369	23–17	104	143	3.17
2B	C. SAWYER	467	5	66	.293	21	J. MAY	362	35–9	100	238	1.84
3B	R. SMITH	719	8	101	.349	7	J. DOYLE	313	20–15	89	91	3.13
SS	R. FRENCH	741	4	83	.279	27	B. JAMES	297	21–12	137	134	3.27
OF	C. CHADBOURNE	830	3	62	.296	22	R. GILDER	191	9–11	37	53	2.87
OF	H. HIGH	614	2	56	.296	2	J. JOLLEY	99	3–3	35	35	3.64
OF	P. BODIE	502	6	87	.293	7						
C	T. HANNAH	399	4	53	.278	5						
OF	N. HAWKS	319	3	51	.279	6						
C	D. MURPHY	314	5	39	.290	3						
23	R. ZEIDER	287	0	22	.233	13						
OF	P. SCHNEIDER	234	15	51	.346	1						
1B	D. LOCKER	202	0	21	.287	4	MANAGER – B. ESSICK					
P	W. DELL	145	0	12	.179	0	RECORD W–123 L–76 FINISH–2ND					

LOS ANGELES		AB	HR	RBI	BA	SB	PITCHERS	IP	W–L	BB	SO	ERA
1B	A. GRIGGS	639	20	129	.338	10	G. LYONS	333	17–17	111	120	2.70
2B	H. LINDEMORE	672	1	71	.271	18	N. DUMOVICH	294	20–11	79	82	2.36
3B	C. DEAL	667	6	87	.331	7	D. CRANDALL	269	17–19	34	95	3.65
SS	I. MC AULEY	639	0	34	.213	14	L. THOMAS	263	18–11	75	51	2.98
OF	B. MC CABE	722	0	84	.291	39	T. HUGHES	231	17–9	88	95	3.08
OF	D. CARROLL	710	3	63	.297	35	B. WALLACE	159	7–10	41	38	4.02
OF	B. TWOMBLY	671	2	79	.300	24	E. PONDER	122	10–2	24	46	2.14
C	T. DALY	412	0	45	.294	0						
C	E. BALDWIN	323	1	35	.266	4						
OF	E. SPENCER	158	0	2	.203	1	MANAGER – R. KILLEFER					
OF	R. KILLEFER	139	0	10	.295	6	RECORD W–111 L–88 FINISH–3RD					

1922

SALT LAKE CITY	AB	HR	RBI	BA	SB	PITCHERS	IP	W-L	BB	SO	ERA
1B P. STRAND	752	28	138	.384	10	A. GOULD	278	16-14	98	91	5.28
2B P. SIGLIN	789	16	106	.316	11	R. KALLIO	264	17-12	92	118	3.48
3B O. VITT	642	4	52	.315	8	S. THURSTON	255	15-16	44	69	4.31
SS H. SAND	748	21	95	.267	13	E. MYERS	244	13-17	65	79	4.24
OF M. SCHICK	770	18	89	.270	25	G. BLAEHOLDER	200	10-10	74	86	4.99
OF J. WILHOIT	624	6	81	.317	10	E. RIEGER	145	2-8	34	32	6.39
OF D. LEWIS	566	20	108	.362	5	H. BETTS	126	7-10	45	40	5.21
C J. JENKINS	351	8	40	.299	1	S. LEWIS	83	4-7	29	31	4.34
C C. BYLER	247	2	33	.251	4						
C E. ANFINSON	189	4	27	.259	3	MANAGER - D. LEWIS					
1B G. GLEISCHMANN	146	0	17	.226	3	RECORD W-95 L-106 FINISH-4TH					

SEATTLE	AB	HR	RBI	BA	SB	PITCHERS	IP	W-L	BB	SO	ERA
1B B. STUMPF	548	2	61	.274	8	V. GREGG	327	19-20	74	150	3.36
2B S. ADAMS	429	1	33	.256	4	E. JACOBS	306	23-17	65	95	3.50
3B T. WESTERZIL	518	0	53	.290	10	H. GARDNER	287	17-15	73	128	3.26
SS S. CRANE	482	1	50	.266	11	G. BURGER	249	12-15	79	78	3.22
OF D. ELDRED	734	9	131	.354	23	E. SCHORR	100	8-12	50	33	5.51
OF B. LANE	716	10	66	.285	60	F. MACK	102	2-8	44	43	4.68
OF E. BARNEY	391	8	55	.286	14						
C F. TOBIN	424	5	43	.248	2						
O1 W. HOOD	507	11	71	.316	12						
U B. ORR (1)	421	2	57	.299	10	(1) ALSO WITH SACRAMENTO					
32 M. CUETO	317	1	33	.268	11	MANAGER - W. MC CREEDIE/J. ADAMS					
C J. ADAMS	213	2	24	.249	1	RECORD W-90 L-107 FINISH-5TH					

OAKLAND	AB	HR	RBI	BA	SB	PITCHERS	IP	W-L	BB	SO	ERA
1B G. LAFAYETTE	661	3	86	.310	12	B. ARLETT	374	25-19	112	128	2.77
2B T. CATHER	663	3	92	.288	20	R. KREMER	356	20-18	74	154	2.78
3B B. MARRIOTT	434	2	49	.286	9	H. KRAUSE	344	21-19	65	134	3.19
SS R. BRUBAKER	740	1	73	.258	21	L. BRENTON	262	5-24	100	77	4.23
OF E. BROWN	682	6	70	.268	37	G. JONES	187	7-10	73	41	4.48
OF D. WILIE	672	5	67	.307	14	H. ELLER	108	6-10	44	33	4.67
OF C. COOPER	580	3	60	.298	48						
C A. KOEHLER	478	3	40	.243	2						
OF F. SCHULTE (1)	362	4	34	.229	2	(1) ALSO WITH SEATTLE					
2S1 J. KNIGHT	262	1	30	.267	5	(2) ALSO WITH SALT LAKE CITY					
32S D. KERNS (2)	216	0	16	.278	2	(3) ALSO WITH PORTLAND					
P B. ARLETT	174	4	21	.241	0	MANAGER - D. HOWARD					
C C. MITZE (3)	170	0	6	.224	0	RECORD W-88 L-112 FINISH-6TH					

1922

PORTLAND		AB	HR	RBI	BA	SB	PITCHERS		IP	W—L	BB	SO	ERA
1B	J. POOLE	752	22	109	.299	13	J. MIDDLETON		277	15—16	103	72	4.03
2B	F. BRAZILL	456	13	51	.318	9	W. LEVERENZ		266	15—18	86	103	3.18
3B	S. HALE	525	10	93	.358	18	R. CRUMPLER		222	13—17	117	104	4.38
SS	E. MC CANN	582	2	41	.280	13	S. SUTHERLAND		213	13—10	61	61	2.07
OF	C. HIGH	649	24	107	.316	12	R. WALBERG		209	9—13	79	84	4.48
OF	M. WOLFER	638	1	45	.251	10	H. BIEMILLER		138	6—10	91	64	5.87
OF	T. GRESSETT	556	6	54	.308	11	R. YARRISON		82	6—4	26	20	1.87
C	R. ELLIOTT	284	1	29	.278	3							
OF	D. COX	552	6	67	.295	10							
32S	J. SARGENT	425	4	41	.256	6							
C	A. KING	198	8	32	.258	0	MANAGER—D. KENWORTHY/T. TURNER/						
C	O. FUHRMAN	181	0	11	.199	1	A. DEMAREE/J. MIDDLETON						
OF	J. THORPE	120	1	14	.308	5	RECORD W—87 L—112 FINISH—7TH						

SACRAMENTO		AB	HR	RBI	BA	SB	PITCHERS		IP	W—L	BB	SO	ERA
1B	F. MOLLWITZ	665	0	74	.310	37	P. FITTERY		334	16—26	107	152	3.31
2B	P. MC GAFFIGAN	493	0	30	.223	19	E. KUNZ		304	15—18	118	126	4.12
3B	B. SCHANG	438	2	30	.272	24	B. PROUGH		243	11—14	42	77	3.44
SS	W. PEARCE	554	3	39	.238	23	K. PENNER		232	11—17	49	90	3.30
OF	B. RYAN	623	4	82	.305	16	E. SHEA		229	11—17	72	72	4.36
OF	P. COMPTON (1)	432	8	43	.306	12	C. CANFIELD		168	4—13	92	65	5.14
OF	M. KOPP	349	1	25	.287	23							
C	O. STANAGE	307	1	31	.267	4							
O21	L. SHEEHAN	627	8	85	.273	12							
13O	R. MURPHY (2)	480	6	65	.277	23							
O3	E. MC NEELY	315	0	15	.213	10							
OF	A. SCHINKEL	279	6	30	.294	5	(1) ALSO WITH SAN FRANCISCO						
C	L. COOK	237	0	17	.203	4	(2) ALSO WITH SEATTLE						
32	C. PICK	221	0	13	.281	18	MANAGER — C. PICK						
OF	FITZGERALD (1)	211	1	15	.265	7	RECORD W—76 L—124 FINISH—8TH						

PLAYOFFS
NONE

1923

SAN FRANCISCO		AB	HR	RBI	BA	SB	PITCHERS	IP	W–L	BB	SO	ERA
1B	B. ELLISON	757	23	129	.358	12	R. SHEA	291	21–10	69	83	3.62
2B	P. KILDUFF	622	10	122	.328	16	B. GEARY	262	21–11	50	59	3.61
3B	E. MULLIGAN	620	9	77	.329	30	S. HODGE	256	18–15	81	78	3.48
SS	H. RHYNE	611	5	77	.296	21	D. MC WEENY	253	20–12	73	160	3.91
OF	G. VALLA	829	1	65	.334	30	H. COURTNEY	251	19–6	113	97	2.80
OF	P. COMPTON	527	7	68	.324	7	O. MITCHELL	204	10–9	71	81	3.40
OF	T. HENDRYX	475	6	89	.339	13	J. SCOTT	173	11–9	51	58	4.06
C	S. AGNEW	369	13	66	.312	2						
OF	J. KELLY	443	5	41	.348	15						
C	A. YELLE	356	2	38	.281	4						
O1	P. WANER	325	3	39	.369	4	(1) ALSO WITH VERNON					
S23	FLASKAMPER (1)	270	0	28	.267	5	MANAGER – D. MILLER/B. ELLISON					
U	D. WALSH	268	4	31	.343	2	RECORD W–124 L–77 FINISH–1ST					

SACRAMENTO		AB	HR	RBI	BA	SB	PITCHERS	IP	W–L	BB	SO	ERA
1B	F. MOLLWITZ	665	4	70	.313	36	YELLOWHORSE	311	22–13	79	99	3.68
2B	P. SIGLIN	707	10	96	.303	19	B. HUGHES	292	14–13	80	112	3.91
3B	E. HEMMINGWAY	727	0	50	.293	39	B. PROUGH	285	20–11	38	81	3.60
SS	G. MC GINNIS	578	3	57	.253	7	H. THOMPSON	242	18–12	42	51	0.70
OF	M. KOPP	829	5	62	.337	80	K. PENNER	234	12–17	59	103	4.27
OF	E. BROWN	591	14	82	.276	6	P. FITTERY	225	15–14	71	83	3.84
OF	C. COCHRAN	552	10	88	.303	20	C. CANFIELD	112	4–3	54	56	5.46
C	A. KOEHLER	506	10	95	.356	12	E. SHEA	102	6–4	40	32	4.59
3O	C. ROHWER	353	0	56	.295	15						
C	B. SCHANG	267	2	47	.348	24						
OF	E. MC NEELY	213	1	27	.333	20	MANAGER – C. PICK					
OF	B. RYAN	203	0	30	.256	4	RECORD W–112 L–87 FINISH–2ND					

PORTLAND		AB	HR	RBI	BA	SB	PITCHERS	IP	W–L	BB	SO	ERA
1B	J. POOLE	756	27	136	.339	17	C. ECKERT	286	19–11	64	80	3.90
2B	E. MC CANN	399	3	36	.303	10	S. SUTHERLAND	279	16–17	55	76	3.39
3B	F. BRAZILL	659	19	91	.316	12	W. LEVERENZ	245	17–11	62	98	3.49
SS	B. JONES	642	3	70	.302	22	J. MIDDLETON	230	12–10	54	74	3.52
OF	M. WOLFER	560	6	34	.298	13	CRUMPLER (2)	211	12–14	94	97	5.67
OF	C. HIGH	558	20	94	.339	8	R. YARRISON	207	16–8	47	47	3.00
OF	A. KING	480	18	76	.288	11	C. SCHROEDER	185	13–10	84	92	4.14
C	C. BYLER (1)	353	2	54	.249	7	T. PILLETTE (2)	162	9–10	70	51	4.56
OF	D. COX	414	9	65	.321	7	(1) ALSO WITH LOS ANGELES					
OF	T. GRESSETT	373	4	46	.300	8	(2) ALSO WITH SALT LAKE CITY					
2S	B. STUMPF	343	4	26	.271	9	MANAGER – J. MIDDLETON					
C	J. ONSLOW	252	0	25	.266	0	RECORD W–107 L–89 FINISH–THIRD					

1923

SEATTLE		AB	HR	RBI	BA	SB	PITCHERS		IP	W–L	BB	SO	ERA
1B	D. JOHNSTON	584	3	73	.308	21	E. JACOBS		312	24–10	91	143	3.14
2B	W. MEARKLE	367	0	24	.297	8	H. GARDNER		305	22–12	59	98	3.10
3B	H. BALDWIN	476	3	56	.282	17	V. GREGG		281	17–15	71	173	2.75
SS	B. ORR	598	1	61	.263	6	S. BLAKE		256	13–20	115	125	4.71
OF	B. ELDRED	742	7	116	.353	23	G. BURGER		146	7–8	44	32	3.45
OF	B. LANE	695	4	62	.311	44	C. WILLIAMS		107	5–9	29	24	5.30
OF	R. ROHWER	655	37	135	.325	12							
C	Y. YARYAN	339	15	54	.280	1							
S23	S. CRANE	561	0	65	.253	12	(1) ALSO WITH SAN FRANCISCO						
1O	J. WELSH	374	6	37	.283	6	MANAGER – H. WOLVERTON/						
C	F. TOBIN	299	3	38	.261	1	R. KILLEFER						
C	P. RITCHIE (1)	149	0	12	.322	6	RECORD W–99 L–97 FINISH–4TH						

SALT LAKE CITY		AB	HR	RBI	BA	SB	PITCHERS		IP	W–L	BB	SO	ERA
1B	R. LESLIE	765	15	140	.340	9	J. SINGLETON		271	15–15	125	112	6.28
2B	L. SHEEHAN	804	36	130	.338	14	A. GOULD		268	16–21	92	94	5.98
3B	O. VITT	811	19	112	.337	18	R. MC CABE		261	14–16	44	112	4.97
SS	W. PEARCE	322	2	31	.233	7	R. KALLIO		234	14–9	96	106	4.73
OF	P. STRAND	825	43	187	.394	22	F. COUMBE		230	13–12	78	45	5.99
OF	J. WILHOIT	662	8	86	.360	9	E. MYERS		219	11–16	50	63	6.04
OF	J. FREDERICK	585	16	82	.328	4							
C	J. PETERS	517	11	74	.338	8							
O1	D. LEWIS	478	28	115	.358	4							
C	J. JENKINS	303	9	51	.350	5							
SS	D. KERNS	176	0	10	.239	0							
P1	F. COUMBE	155	3	23	.290	1	MANAGER – D. LEWIS						
SS	T. LAZZERI	130	7	21	.354	4	RECORD W–94 L–105 FINISH–5TH						

LOS ANGELES		AB	HR	RBI	BA	SB	PITCHERS		IP	W–L	BB	SO	ERA
1B	A. GRIGGS	495	21	88	.329	1	G. LYONS		269	18–16	71	72	3.41
2B	H. LINDEMORE	407	1	35	.290	7	P. JONES		267	16–17	111	100	3.88
3B	C. DEAL (1)	349	4	53	.315	8	D. CRANDALL		258	17–12	28	84	3.10
SS	I. MC AULEY	668	1	47	.238	9	L. THOMAS		247	9–15	66	44	3.94
OF	B. TWOMBLY	781	5	74	.332	33	T. HUGHES		235	14–16	93	88	4.29
OF	W. HOOD	745	21	128	.340	19	B. WALLACE		205	9–18	89	22	5.71
OF	B. MC CABE	674	6	82	.286	17	E. PONDER		172	7–9	50	54	3.61
C	T. DALY (2)	395	0	31	.266	3							
23	M. KRUG	545	4	49	.299	12	(1) ALSO WITH VERNON						
1B	W. GOLVIN	327	2	45	.248	6	(2) ALSO WITH PORTLAND						
C	E. BALDWIN	307	2	33	.293	4	MANAGER – M. KRUG						
OF	D. CARROLL	190	1	17	.316	4	RECORD W–93 L–109 FINISH–6TH						

1923

OAKLAND	AB	HR	RBI	BA	SB	PITCHERS	IP	W−L	BB	SO	ERA
1B G. LAFAYETTE	627	12	103	.317	9	R. KREMER	357	25−16	77	127	3.08
2B M. MASSEY	398	1	22	.279	9	W. MAILS	356	23−18	125	206	2.96
3B A. MADERAS	604	4	63	.267	19	H. KRAUSE	328	19−20	60	113	3.10
SS R. BRUBAKER	584	0	49	.301	9	I. COLWELL	259	7−20	77	86	4.38
OF T. CATHER	782	10	109	.344	20	G. MURCHIO	231	9−17	83	34	4.83
OF C. COOPER	718	0	53	.319	37	B. ARLETT	125	4−9	47	34	5.76
OF B. ARLETT	445	19	101	.330	9	O. ELEY	82	2−4	32	26	3.73
C D. BAKER	409	2	55	.279	4						
12 J. KNIGHT	378	6	58	.336	4						
C A. READ	234	1	27	.303	5						
OF O. JOHNSON	207	1	20	.295	2						
OF D. WILLE	199	0	13	.201	4						
C P. THOMAS	158	0	18	.323	1						
SS R. SMITH	156	1	9	.199	0						
2B P. MC GAFFIGAN	144	0	8	.222	8	MANAGER − I. HOWARD					
1B L. GUISTO	116	1	21	.293	3	RECORD W−91 L−111 FINISH−7TH					

VERNON	AB	HR	RBI	BA	SB	PITCHERS	IP	W−L	BB	SO	ERA
1B R. MURPHY	694	8	76	.324	14	J. MAY	320	19−22	89	149	3.43
2B D. RADER	464	1	44	.265	4	SHELLENBACK	286	19−19	53	98	4.37
3B J. WARNER	510	1	43	.278	2	W. DELL (2)	236	12−11	72	88	4.04
SS G. SLADE	177	0	12	.209	1	E. ALTEN (3)	203	10−11	47	58	4.52
OF C. CHADBOURNE	756	1	50	.317	7	R. GILDER	167	7−12	41	48	4.63
OF P. SCHNEIDER	598	19	110	.360	3	R. FOSTER	106	3−9	29	11	4.08
OF P. BODIE	485	8	105	.295	1	E. RIEGER	96	3−7	16	18	4.78
C T. HANNAH	370	6	55	.346	1	C. CRUZ	79	1−8	27	22	5.47
						C. CARSON	71	3−4	28	16	3.93
3B R. SMITH (1)	548	7	60	.327	7						
OF H. HIGH	427	4	48	.340	5						
C D. MURPHY	316	4	43	.282	2	(1) ALSO WITH LOS ANGELES					
O1 H. HYATT	198	7	37	.303	1	(2) ALSO WITH SEATTLE					
2B C. GORMAN	189	0	12	.238	2	(3) ALSO WITH SAN FRANCISCO					
2B C. SAWYER	158	2	19	.278	1	MANAGER − B. ESSICK					
23 BOTT	158	0	8	.228	2	RECORD W−77 L−122 FINISH−8TH					

PLAYOFFS
NONE

1924

SEATTLE	AB	HR	RBI	BA	SB	PITCHERS	IP	W–L	BB	SO	ERA
1B E. BOWMAN	528	10	81	.301	6	V. GREGG	326	25–11	75	175	2.90
2B C. BRADY	763	4	83	.261	14	G. STUELAND	261	18–13	138	110	4.55
3B H. BALDWIN	758	6	140	.299	27	S. SUTHERLAND	218	9–13	72	65	4.66
SS S. CRANE	573	1	58	.269	18	P. JONES	218	13–11	112	161	4.37
OF B. ELDRED	684	7	131	.351	21	J. BAGBY	202	16–10	41	40	4.76
OF R. ROHWER	644	33	155	.325	11	W. DELL	183	9–14	86	74	5.56
OF B. LANE	598	1	45	.336	45	C. WILLIAMS	152	9–10	53	32	3.85
C E. BALDWIN	504	10	76	.282	3	B. PLUMMER	130	6–6	68	34	4.91
O1 J. WELSH	599	16	90	.342	17						
C F. TOBIN	215	0	14	.260	1	(1) ALSO WITH SACRAMENTO					
SS F. EMMER	205	4	24	.293	1	MANAGER – R. KILLEFER					
OF B. BECKER (1)	203	6	39	.310	6	RECORD W–109 L–91 FINISH–1ST					

LOS ANGELES	AB	HR	RBI	BA	SB	PITCHERS	IP	W–L	BB	SO	ERA
1B W. GOLVIN	328	2	29	.216	7	C. ROOT	322	21–16	102	199	3.69
2B M. KRUG	456	2	65	.265	8	G. PAYNE	315	21–13	42	86	2.83
3B R. JACOBS	517	9	76	.277	2	E. MYERS	260	15–17	61	49	4.61
SS C. BECK	482	6	53	.268	4	D. CRANDALL	256	19–11	32	72	2.71
OF W. HOOD	757	22	184	.338	0	T. HUGHES	208	12–14	99	73	4.67
OF C. DURST	705	17	130	.342	16	N. DUMOVICH	158	9–12	75	34	6.15
OF B. WHALEY	704	2	82	.328	12	C. RAMSEY	143	7–3	51	51	2.89
C J. JENKINS (1)	333	9	66	.288	2						
S2 I. MC AULEY	514	3	48	.276	6						
OF B. TWOMBLY	471	2	46	.312	14						
1B R. GRIMES	247	4	46	.320	0						
C E. SPENCER	217	3	27	.281	3	(1) ALSO WITH SALT LAKE CITY					
O1 W. CRUISE	151	5	23	.318	1	MANAGER – M. KRUG					
C C. BYLER	137	0	13	.241	0	RECORD W–107 L–92 FINISH–2ND					

SAN FRANCISCO	AB	HR	RBI	BA	SB	PITCHERS	IP	W–L	BB	SO	ERA
1B B. ELLISON	805	33	188	.381	10	O. MITCHELL	330	28–15	102	97	4.06
2B P. KILDUFF	695	13	108	.294	5	B. GEARY	297	19–15	78	83	5.24
3B E. MULLIGAN	820	13	114	.306	28	R. SHEA	252	14–14	106	68	5.43
SS H. RHYNE	751	2	80	.298	26	M. GRIFFIN	251	16–14	69	54	3.20
OF G. VALLA	730	6	78	.367	28	G. WILLIAMS	243	14–12	129	130	3.63
OF J. KELLY	638	8	65	.301	21						
OF P. WANER	587	8	97	.356	12						
C A. YELLE	347	1	36	.248	0						
OF T. HENDRYX	373	9	69	.319	2						
C S. AGNEW	223	8	38	.314	2	MANAGER – B. ELLISON					
O2 D. WALSH	191	5	28	.288	0	RECORD W–108 L–93 FINISH–3RD					

1924

OAKLAND	AB	HR	RBI	BA	SB	PITCHERS	IP	W-L	BB	SO	ERA
1B L. GUISTO	513	11	81	.294	4	G. BOEHLER	396	26-21	172	216	4.00
2B S. ADAMS	806	4	90	.273	13	W. MAILS	382	24-22	140	190	3.73
3B A. MADERAS	392	5	34	.235	11	E. KUNZ	364	23-18	140	143	3.76
SS R. BRUBAKER	601	4	59	.313	13	R. FOSTER	256	12-18	92	78	3.59
OF B. ARLETT	698	33	145	.328	24	H. KRAUSE	242	16-16	51	122	4.09
OF G. LAFAYETTE	676	9	83	.325	19						
OF T. CATHER	637	5	97	.300	8						
C D. BAKER	342	2	49	.301	6						
C A. READ	367	0	33	.267	2						
OF E. GOEBEL	296	2	24	.236	4	MANAGER - I. HOWARD					
3B B. MC CARREN	253	4	26	.241	2	RECORD W-103 L-99 FINISH-4TH					

SALT LAKE CITY	AB	HR	RBI	BA	SB	PITCHERS	IP	W-L	BB	SO	ERA
1B R. LESLIE	755	18	147	.339	11	J. SINGLETON	322	21-15	132	130	4.61
2B H. LINDEMORE	764	15	114	.339	6	R. MC CABE	260	18-15	87	95	5.64
3B O. VITT	435	15	90	.333	4	R. KALLIO	244	18-14	93	102	3.87
SS P. PITTENGER	555	6	70	.319	29	E. PONDER	208	10-14	74	78	5.45
OF J. FREDERICK	790	28	132	.353	8	P. MULCAHY	187	8-12	101	84	6.50
OF L. SHEEHAN	622	22	118	.346	3	H. O'NEILL	153	10-8	68	64	5.65
OF D. LEWIS	528	28	154	.392	7	L. O'DOUL	128	7-9	56	39	6.54
C J. PETERS	447	11	96	.336	2						
OP L. O'DOUL	416	11	101	.392	11						
C3 L. COOK	345	3	57	.301	4						
OP1 F. COUMBE	380	12	64	.297	3						
S3 T. LAZZERI	293	16	61	.283	8	MANAGER - D. LEWIS					
S3 W. PEARCE	225	0	24	.240	7	RECORD W-101 L-100 FINISH-5TH					

VERNON	AB	HR	RBI	BA	SB	PITCHERS	IP	W-L	BB	SO	ERA
1B J. MC DOWELL	650	26	132	.289	5	K. PENNER	346	24-13	84	130	4.00
2B W. GRIFFIN	645	7	84	.268	3	C. CHRISTIAN	315	16-22	95	115	3.94
3B C. DEAL	553	12	99	.324	4	SHELLENBACK	212	14-7	38	55	3.65
SS J. WARNER	604	3	76	.303	8	L. THOMAS	181	10-11	52	37	4.17
OF J. BLAKESLEY	692	11	101	.315	9	E. BRYAN	173	13-5	42	34	3.27
OF C. CHADBOURNE	642	3	52	.255	8	W. LUDOLPH	138	7-10	36	45	4.63
OF M. MENOSKY	542	15	84	.328	9	L. CADORE	92	6-6	29	32	6.16
C D. MURPHY	428	5	60	.301	3						
C T. HANNAH	349	4	70	.318	2						
S2 G. SLADE	280	0	29	.232	1						
32 W. KIMMICK	254	1	22	.315	0						
O12 R. MURPHY	253	3	43	.316	5	MANAGER - B. ESSICK					
OF P. SCHNEIDER	235	16	52	.328	0	RECORD W-97 L-104 FINISH-6TH					

1924

PORTLAND		AB	HR	RBI	BA	SB	PITCHERS	IP	W–L	BB	SO	ERA
1B	J. POOLE	722	38	159	.353	8	J. WINTERS	285	16–20	101	93	4.11
2B	E. MC CANN	671	11	73	.320	17	C. ECKERT	264	13–21	82	77	4.91
3B	F. BRAZILL	638	36	148	.351	8	M. RACHAC	234	13–14	90	71	4.31
SS	S. BENTON	486	1	33	.265	11	W. LEVERENZ	218	14–14	75	84	4.38
OF	D. COX	696	25	141	.356	5	C. SCHROEDER	180	11–12	79	49	5.00
OF	C. HIGH	612	20	139	.322	4	H. BEDIENT	178	6–12	42	55	5.66
OF	M. WOLFER	597	4	62	.327	11	D. KEEFE	109	5–3	35	48	6.77
C	T. DALY	349	2	52	.272	1						
S31	D. DISTEL	539	5	68	.286	7	MANAGER – D. KENWORTHY/					
C	M. COCHRANE	300	7	56	.333	1	FRANK BRAZILL					
OF	J. MILLER	289	3	39	.291	2	RECORD W–88 L–110 FINISH–7TH					

SACRAMENTO		AB	HR	RBI	BA	SB	PITCHERS	IP	W–L	BB	SO	ERA
1B	F. MOLLWITZ	549	6	51	.266	10	B. HUGHES	355	20–19	120	145	4.28
2B	P. SIGLIN	728	7	95	.288	16	S. HALL	305	16–21	96	51	4.22
3B	C. ROHWER	409	7	47	.284	0	C. CANFIELD	266	16–16	147	144	4.33
SS	G. MC GINNIS	327	1	35	.226	3	B. PROUGH	242	10–17	50	75	4.95
OF	M. KOPP	742	5	71	.298	44	H. THOMPSON	212	13–15	46	54	4.59
OF	C. COCHRAN	473	5	58	.283	6	L. VINCI	124	6–8	61	39	4.50
OF	E. MC NEELY	460	8	41	.333	14						
C	A. KOEHLER	396	9	78	.341	2						
S32	E. HEMINGWAY	584	1	63	.284	26						
O1	R. SMITH	364	4	57	.277	6						
C	B. SCHANG	255	3	41	.302	7						
C3	M. SHEA	216	4	28	.338	3	MANAGER – C. PICK/B. RYAN					
OF	W. MATTHEWS	182	0	12	.264	7	RECORD W–88 L–112 FINISH–8TH					

PLAYOFFS
NONE

1925

SAN FRANCISCO	AB	HR	RBI	BA	SB	PITCHERS	IP	W−L	BB	SO	ERA
1B B. ELLISON	708	22	160	.325	8	B. GEARY	287	20−12	49	80	4.01
2B P. KILDUFF	670	20	126	.306	11	O. MITCHELL	277	20−8	69	106	4.29
3B E. MULLIGAN	751	10	77	.286	12	D. MC WEENY	263	20−5	78	175	2.70
SS H. RHYNE	724	3	97	.315	17	G. WILLIAMS	249	21−10	140	133	3.79
OF G. VALLA	769	6	72	.333	13	M. GRIFFIN	209	16−4	76	49	4.26
OF T. BROWER	705	36	163	.362	17	J. PFEFFER	193	15−15	57	62	5.27
OF P. WANER	699	11	130	.401	8	J. CROCKETT	189	12−11	87	82	4.38
C S. AGNEW	384	20	85	.326	0	D. MOUDY	82	3−5	37	48	4.83
OF T. HENDRYX	330	4	41	.303	6						
C A. YELLE	266	1	21	.267	1						
OF S. JOLLEY	132	12	43	.447	1						
P O. MITCHELL	120	1	7	.008	0	MANAGER − B. ELLISON					
C P. RITCHIE	111	1	26	.315	0	RECORD W−128 L−71 FINISH−1ST					

SALT LAKE CITY	AB	HR	RBI	BA	SB	PITCHERS	IP	W−L	BB	SO	ERA
1B F. COUMBE	540	21	99	.331	8	J. SINGLETON	303	17−19	119	122	4.60
2B J. KERR	552	7	78	.330	26	R. MC CABE	266	17−15	56	86	4.64
3B O. VITT	579	6	73	.345	8	B. PIERCY	255	21−11	118	102	4.44
SS T. LAZZERI	710	60	222	.355	39	E. PONDER	244	17−9	215	95	5.09
OF L. O'DOUL	825	24	191	.375	12	P. MULCAHY	244	14−10	117	97	4.24
OF L. SHEEHAN	734	33	170	.342	17	H. HULVEY	142	11−2	43	51	5.07
OF J. FREDERICK	640	10	79	.309	3	R. KALLIO	109	8−5	34	46	3.63
C J. PETERS	449	14	79	.312	1	S. STROUD	81	5−5	26	34	4.66
23 H. LINDEMORE	566	6	70	.332	5						
1B R. LESLIE	308	4	65	.305	7						
OF J. CONNOLLY	268	9	39	.317	3						
C L. COOK	258	1	29	.244	2	MANAGER − O. VITT					
P H. HULVEY	112	0	12	.330	0	RECORD W−116 L−84 FINISH−2ND					

SEATTLE	AB	HR	RBI	BA	SB	PITCHERS	IP	W−L	BB	SO	ERA
1B B. HERMAN	651	15	131	.316	22	J. MILJUS	295	20−15	99	115	3.14
2B C. BRADY	730	2	66	.266	17	B. HASTY (1)	271	14−18	102	119	4.45
3B F. BRAZILL	708	29	155	.395	12	D. STRYKER	234	16−10	62	67	3.65
SS F. EMMER	523	7	85	.329	21	N. DUMOVICH	169	12−8	71	67	5.38
OF B. ELDRED	739	7	142	.327	21	F. FUSSELL	146	8−7	74	75	4.87
OF B. LANE	656	1	32	.280	34	B. PLUMMER	142	9−7	78	48	4.82
OF B. MC CABE	622	11	105	.280	18	R. LUCAS	121	9−5	33	47	2.82
C E. BALDWIN	405	6	54	.269	4						
O3 H. BALDWIN	430	0	55	.267	13	(1) ALSO WITH PORTLAND					
C T. DALY	281	0	24	.228	2	MANAGER − R. KILLEFER					
P J. MILJUS	112	1	7	.205	0	RECORD W−103 L−91 FINISH−3RD					

1925

LOS ANGELES	AB	HR	RBI	BA	SB	PITCHERS	IP	W−L	BB	SO	ERA
1B R. GRIMES	623	6	104	.294	7	C. ROOT	324	25−13	91	211	2.86
2B C. BECK	539	13	75	.310	18	G. PAYNE	319	18−19	42	88	3.94
3B M. KRUG	490	6	59	.294	12	W. GLAZNER	259	14−18	84	120	4.31
SS R. JACOBS	668	17	104	.272	7	D. CRANDALL	239	20−7	40	89	3.46
OF W. HOOD	758	27	157	.327	31	R. WRIGHT	229	10−16	93	85	4.29
OF B. TWOMBLY	656	1	75	.329	27	E. JACOBS	121	9−5	24	50	2.75
OF J. STATZ	545	2	45	.264	17	C. RAMSEY (1)	104	6−7	46	26	3.55
C G. SANBERG	471	2	55	.231	6	T. HUGHES	89	5−4	38	36	3.94
O3 B. WHALEY	404	0	56	.257	4	(1) ALSO WITH SEATTLE					
SS I. MC AULEY	331	1	22	.205	2	MANAGER − M. KRUG					
C R. ENNIS	181	0	18	.238	2	RECORD W−105 L−93 FINISH−4TH					

PORTLAND	AB	HR	RBI	BA	SB	PITCHERS	IP	W−L	BB	SO	ERA
1B G. LAFAYETTE (1)	717	22	95	.287	11	HOLLINGSWORTH	281	15−15	162	167	3.87
2B E. MC CANN	689	4	88	.309	30	R. MEEKER	266	13−13	83	112	3.65
3B H. RICONDA	513	7	78	.320	16	D. BURNS	256	13−18	112	106	4.88
SS B. HUNNEFIELD	732	13	76	.291	42	M. RACHAC	236	16−12	78	85	4.00
OF R. ROWHER	677	40	153	.334	12	C. ECKERT (3)	229	9−14	59	47	5.03
OF C. HIGH	608	20	107	.337	9	R. YARRISON	215	11−12	89	79	4.73
OF D. LEWIS	442	15	71	.294	5	W. LEVERENZ	193	11−11	77	61	3.73
C F. TOBIN (2)	384	7	46	.273	1						
						(1) ALSO WITH OAKLAND					
3O C. DEAL	427	6	58	.279	11	(2) ALSO WITH SEATTLE					
C T. HANNAH (3)	350	3	45	.283	5	(3) ALSO WITH VERNON					
OF L. LAMB	249	1	19	.233	2	MANAGER − D. LEWIS/T. HANNAH					
SS B. JONES	200	1	30	.305	4	RECORD W−92 L−104 FINISH−5TH					

OAKLAND	AB	HR	RBI	BA	SB	PITCHERS	IP	W−L	BB	SO	ERA
1B J. FENTON	345	0	27	.229	0	G. BOEHLER	417	23−25	209	278	4.10
2B R. BRUBAKER	536	3	66	.306	4	A. DELANEY	293	17−16	69	142	3.74
3B G. MAKIN	709	4	56	.257	8	E. KUNZ	271	13−18	139	85	4.94
SS J. FLOWERS	470	19	78	.304	18	H. KRAUSE	223	11−15	52	96	4.88
OF B. ARLETT	710	25	146	.344	26	H. PRUETT	209	10−15	111	95	3.49
OF H. MILLER	574	16	99	.321	8	R. FOSTER	171	9−15	80	53	4.94
OF C. COOPER	391	2	32	.261	10						
C A. READ	255	0	22	.251	3						
2S J. REESE	463	0	37	.248	13						
1B L. GUISTO	335	5	50	.337	6						
OF J. BRATCHER	286	0	17	.297	6						
SS L. LARY	241	0	21	.257	6						
OF U. PICKERING	193	7	22	.264	5	MANAGER − I. HOWARD					
C D. BAKER	167	0	18	.246	0	RECORD W−88 L−112 FINISH−6TH					

1925

SACRAMENTO	AB	HR	RBI	BA	SB	PITCHERS	IP	W–L	BB	SO	ERA
1B J. DAVIS	690	13	119	.330	10	B. HUGHES	326	19–16	100	131	3.78
2B P. SIGLIN	679	5	81	.256	8	S. MARTIN	283	13–19	114	149	2.89
3B J. MC LAUGHLIN	476	2	58	.292	16	SHELLENBACK	264	14–17	61	91	3.27
SS R. FRENCH	680	0	47	.271	32	L. VINCI	219	10–19	117	86	4.85
OF M. KOPP	805	8	76	.282	27	E. SHEA	199	10–12	70	83	4.74
OF C. HOFFMAN	454	3	46	.300	7	R. KEATING	199	8–20	95	71	5.02
OF B. CUNNINGHAM	438	0	52	.283	8	C. CANFIELD	170	5–11	111	83	5.29
C M. SHEA	451	8	64	.319	5						
O1 H. BROWN	394	3	37	.223	9						
3O J. WATSON	375	7	47	.296	9	(1) ALSO WITH OAKLAND					
O32 T. CATHER (1)	257	2	32	.257	2	**MANAGER – B. RYAN**					
C A. KOEHLER	256	4	39	.262	1	**RECORD W–82 L–119 FINISH–7TH**					

VERNON	AB	HR	RBI	BA	SB	PITCHERS	IP	W–L	BB	SO	ERA
1B J. MC DOWELL	697	21	94	.261	7	C. BARFOOT	354	26–15	83	76	3.20
2B W. GRIFFIN	525	8	73	.305	6	H. PILLETTE	285	11–26	71	78	3.66
3B J. WARNER	638	0	64	.296	2	W. LUDOLPH	266	13–12	89	60	3.65
SS E. HEMINGWAY	550	2	38	.282	10	E. BRYAN	251	9–18	59	72	4.91
OF M. WOLFER	692	2	79	.277	11	S. JOHNSON	168	3–17	53	95	4.66
OF J. BLAKESLEY	420	13	62	.286	8	K. PENNER	74	2–6	20	24	5.47
OF S. HORAN (1)	276	4	49	.254	3	R. OLDHAM	73	4–7	28	25	4.19
C R. WHITNEY	355	0	35	.248	3	J. CHRISTIAN	71	3–5	34	24	5.96
2S M. FINN	311	0	25	.232	6						
OF E. SWANSON	266	1	31	.293	15						
OF T. OLIVER	255	0	26	.255	4						
SS G. SLADE	188	0	19	.250	0						
C3 B. SCHANG	163	0	13	.274	2						
OF B. BECKER	157	2	27	.268	3	(1) ALSO WITH LOS ANGELES					
P C. BARFOOT	143	6	16	.203	0	**MANAGER – B. ESSICK/R. ELLIS**					
OF B. GILLESPIE	136	0	6	.287	5	**RECORD W–80 L–120 FINISH–8TH**					

PLAYOFFS
NONE

1926

LOS ANGELES		AB	HR	RBI	BA	SB	PITCHERS	IP	W–L	BB	SO	ERA
1B	R. JACOBS	580	21	102	.255	13	E. HAMILTON	279	24–8	68	138	2.48
2B	E. HEMINGWAY	628	0	64	.279	20	E. JACOBS	278	20–12	69	103	2.20
3B	F. BRAZILL	551	19	111	.336	19	D. CRANDALL	245	20–8	48	86	2.20
SS	J. MITCHELL	651	0	83	.264	30	R. WRIGHT	222	19–7	47	59	3.08
OF	J. STATZ	823	4	59	.354	19	W. GLAZNER	209	11–15	68	68	3.88
OF	A. JAHN	623	8	118	.337	7	R. YARRISON	176	13–8	52	58	4.09
OF	A. WEIS	543	7	80	.317	3	P. DAY	160	6–11	26	57	3.65
C	T. HANNAH	389	4	55	.237	3						
O1	W. HOOD	502	13	82	.301	9						
2B	G. STALEY	242	0	16	.244	2						
C	G. SANBERG	234	2	18	.226	2	MANAGER – M. KRUG					
3B	M. KRUG	131	2	29	.389	2	RECORD W–121 L–81 FINISH–1ST					

OAKLAND		AB	HR	RBI	BA	SB	PITCHERS	IP	W–L	BB	SO	ERA
1B	L. GUISTO	385	4	55	.273	3	A. DELANEY	290	21–13	66	110	3.04
2B	J. REESE	709	4	48	.267	11	H. PRUETT	277	22–13	98	135	2.47
3B	J. CAVENEY (1)	654	7	81	.309	10	H. KRAUSE	263	19–12	46	114	2.87
SS	L. LARY	566	7	44	.253	6	E. KUNZ (2)	166	7–11	65	45	3.58
OF	B. ARLETT	667	35	140	.382	26	L. DICKERMAN	161	12–5	67	82	2.96
OF	T. GOVERNOR	552	1	56	.274	17	J. OESCHGER(3)	146	5–14	46	44	4.19
OF	J. BRATCHER	435	4	45	.324	9	A. GOULD	143	8–8	55	29	2.96
C	A. BOOL	344	5	34	.265	2						
							(1) ALSO WITH SEATTLE					
3O	R. BRUBAKER	401	0	46	.254	1	(2) ALSO WITH SAN FRANCISCO					
OF	R. SHINNERS	369	7	45	.276	3	(3) ALSO WITH MISSION					
C	D. BAKER	322	0	40	.280	5	MANAGER – I. HOWARD					
1B	J. FENTON	294	3	44	.293	4	RECORD W–111 L–92 FINISH–2ND					

MISSION		AB	HR	RBI	BA	SB	PITCHERS	IP	W–L	BB	SO	ERA
1B	J. MC DOWELL	545	17	80	.250	4	B. COLE	325	29–12	93	102	2.63
2B	M. FINN	528	2	49	.261	15	H. PILLETTE	322	21–16	76	99	3.10
3B	B. JONES	621	2	105	.308	11	W. LUDOLPH	253	15–13	88	85	3.81
SS	G. SLADE	562	2	70	.288	5	C. BARFOOT	235	13–14	46	49	4.56
OF	E. SWANSON	763	2	55	.316	43	J. CHRISTIAN	230	11–14	85	61	4.07
OF	I. BOONE	626	32	137	.380	16	E. BRYAN	194	7–10	46	41	3.39
OF	R. GILLESPIE	497	6	64	.308	9	C. ECKERT	116	7–7	29	18	3.72
C	D. MURPHY	334	2	38	.269	1						
21O	W. GRIFFIN	409	5	56	.296	4						
S23	W. RODDA	288	1	31	.271	7	MANAGER–W. MCCREEDIE/W. SCHMIDT/					
OF	T. VACHE	285	4	37	.302	7	B. LEARD					
C	R. WALTERS	253	0	15	.182	0	RECORD W–106 L–94 FINISH–3RD					

1926

PORTLAND	AB	HR	RBI	BA	SB	PITCHERS	IP	W–L	BB	SO	ERA
1B G. LAFAYETTE	282	7	38	.280	1	L. MANGUM	328	19–20	88	106	3.84
2B E. JOHNSON	443	9	28	.282	11	B. HUGHES (1)	317	17–21	76	114	3.35
3B D. PROTHRO	474	14	67	.327	11	G. PAYNE	276	13–19	51	87	4.57
SS R. SMITH	667	3	66	.264	11	R. MEEKER	239	15–14	68	83	3.77
OF E. SMITH	669	46	133	.336	20	F. ORTMAN	194	11–12	90	86	3.90
OF B. BAGWELL	450	19	96	.391	6	BAUMGARTNER	183	14–10	28	46	3.20
OF P. STRAND	386	11	52	.326	3	R. LINGREL	171	13–6	42	40	3.74
C C. BERRY	292	5	33	.236	1	M. RACHAC (1)	142	6–7	55	30	4.12
						D. LEVERETTE	98	3–5	34	38	6.52
32 L. METZ	524	0	17	.288	6						
OF R. ELSH	342	1	16	.240	13						
12O R. WASHBURN	305	7	52	.282	1						
C F. TOBIN	252	3	30	.246	1	(1) ALSO WITH SACRAMENTO					
1B A. MC CURDY	228	2	38	.316	4	MANAGER – E. JOHNSON					
C L. WENDELL	207	3	27	.237	1	RECORD W–100 L–101 FINISH–4TH					

SACRAMENTO	AB	HR	RBI	BA	SB	PITCHERS	IP	W–L	BB	SO	ERA
1B J. DAVIS	585	12	93	.308	6	R. KALLIO	326	18–16	85	123	3.23
2B J. MONROE	779	13	97	.295	26	L. VINCI	298	15–21	128	137	3.47
3B J. MCLAUGHLIN	578	2	71	.272	13	R. KEATING	240	14–14	61	122	3.63
SS R. FRENCH	625	1	42	.293	29	S. MARTIN	235	14–12	80	69	3.18
OF R. ROHWER (1)	565	22	107	.262	14	E. SHEA	228	15–11	58	76	3.79
OF F. OSBORN	549	3	65	.264	9						
OF C. HOFFMAN	541	6	68	.250	6						
C A. KOEHLER	578	10	98	.301	7						
OF M. KOPP	486	1	47	.292	7	(1) ALSO WITH PORTLAND					
OF B. CUNNINGHAM	410	0	52	.300	4	MANAGER – B. RYAN					
13 J. KNIGHT	324	5	50	.281	3	RECORD W–99 L–102 FINISH–5TH					

HOLLYWOOD	AB	HR	RBI	BA	SB	PITCHERS	IP	W–L	BB	SO	ERA
1B R. LESLIE	399	6	50	.258	2	R. MC CABE	239	15–19	45	62	3.28
2B J. KERR	705	16	75	.272	31	J. SINGLETON	235	10–13	90	99	3.18
3B O. VITT	341	1	25	.252	11	SHELLENBACK	230	16–12	49	93	2.97
SS D. LEE	558	0	42	.228	8	C. FULLERTON	230	10–17	89	67	4.34
OF J. FREDERICK	667	8	63	.277	3	P. MULCAHY	192	7–12	92	79	3.38
OF L. O'DOUL	659	20	116	.338	10	H. O'NEILL	166	9–9	55	59	3.20
OF F. ZOELLER	585	7	56	.268	11	H. HULVEY	150	13–10	36	54	3.90
C J. PETERS	403	3	53	.290	3	G. HOLLERSON	133	9–7	39	29	3.52
3S C. GOOCH	404	0	36	.262	5						
O1 L. SHEEHAN	395	5	46	.306	4						
1B F. COUMBE	323	7	28	.250	3	MANAGER – O. VITT					
C L. COOK	226	0	18	.208	2	RECORD W–94 L–107 FINISH–6TH					

1926

SEATTLE		AB	HR	RBI	BA	SB	PITCHERS		IP	W–L	BB	SO	ERA
1B	H. SCHWABB	476	8	57	.273	8	J. ELLIOTT		367	26–20	121	203	2.55
2B	C. BRADY	609	0	42	.258	11	B. HASTY		286	16–20	92	99	3.97
3B	H. BALDWIN	508	2	53	.246	12	J. MILJUS		233	14–13	80	89	4.48
SS	J. SHERLOCK	540	4	99	.306	4	H. BRETT		226	9–18	103	97	3.54
OF	M. CALLAGHAN	733	4	75	.330	26	S. MARTIN		137	7–7	53	39	4.60
OF	B. LANE	600	3	61	.272	37	C. BEST		124	7–9	53	45	4.93
OF	F. HUFFT	550	16	94	.311	8	W. PETERS		100	2–7	37	22	3.51
C	E. BALDWIN	395	2	48	.278	1	C. RAMSEY		87	4–3	31	20	3.62
OF	B. ELDRED	312	2	59	.340	3							
S32	F. ELLSWORTH	253	3	24	.253	6							
C	J. JENKINS	247	4	45	.283	1							
1B	A. GRIGGS	234	5	36	.346	0	MANAGER – R. KILLEFER						
3B	D. JESSEE	147	1	9	.292	2	RECORD W–89 L–111 FINISH–7TH						

SAN FRANCISCO		AB	HR	RBI	BA	SB	PITCHERS		IP	W–L	BB	SO	ERA
1B	B. ELLISON	321	3	48	.302	1	D. MOUDY		278	15–22	146	144	4.05
2B	P. KILDUFF	346	8	56	.288	1	O. MITCHELL		269	18–12	64	122	3.61
3B	E. MULLIGAN	715	3	52	.263	8	B. GEARY		259	14–15	40	46	4.24
SS	L. BAKER	299	1	28	.258	1	G. WILLIAMS		252	10–19	138	168	4.29
OF	G. VALLA (1)	702	1	23	.268	14	M. GRIFFIN		215	7–17	85	43	4.56
OF	E. AVERILL	679	23	119	.348	9	W. MAILS		176	9–13	54	54	4.19
OF	S. JOLLEY	575	25	132	.346	3	D. KERR		99	3–8	32	18	4.27
C	S. AGNEW	362	12	36	.251	4							
2S	G. SUHR	611	14	71	.282	6							
O1	T. BROWER	591	16	99	.330	5							
1B	D. CAMILLI	298	7	41	.312	3	(1) ALSO WITH OAKLAND						
C	A. YELLE	216	0	13	.241	0	(2) ALSO WITH OAKLAND AND HOLLYWOOD						
SS	L. TAYLOR	166	1	16	.253	0	MANAGER – R. WILLIAMS						
OF	J. CONNALLY (2)	154	2	24	.241	3	RECORD W–84 L–116 FINISH–8TH						

PLAYOFFS
NONE

1927

OAKLAND	AB	HR	RBI	BA	SB	PITCHERS	IP	W–L	BB	SO	ERA
1B J. FENTON	648	12	110	.278	5	G. BOEHLER	296	22–12	75	160	3.10
2B J. REESE	722	2	83	.295	18	A. DELANEY	239	14–10	71	89	3.05
3B J. CAVENEY	588	5	71	.279	2	W. COOPER	231	15–12	51	65	3.35
SS L. LARY	765	12	102	.293	12	B. HASTY	198	12–11	66	71	4.14
OF B. ARLETT	658	30	123	.351	20	H. KRAUSE	172	15–6	28	51	3.56
OF J. BRATCHER	602	12	101	.321	11	A. GOULD	167	17–5	53	76	3.61
OF T. GOVERNOR	517	3	48	.325	7	L. DICKERMAN	166	9–10	91	74	3.90
C A. READ	312	1	24	.253	1	H. SPARKS	107	6–4	38	24	4.04
						H. CRAGHEAD	100	4–4	41	49	3.42
OF R. SHINNERS	313	6	44	.297	4						
C A. BOOL	257	3	34	.280	1	MANAGER – I. HOWARD					
O3 R. BRUBAKER	155	3	33	.323	0	RECORD W–120 L–75 FINISH–1ST					

SAN FRANCISCO	AB	HR	RBI	BA	SB	PITCHERS	IP	W–L	BB	SO	ERA
1B P. BODIE	336	12	80	.324	5	E. KUNZ	305	18–19	110	70	4.30
2B G. SUHR	679	27	118	.293	6	H. MAY	298	20–16	93	134	3.74
3B E. MULLIGAN	665	6	65	.274	23	O. MITCHELL	269	17–13	76	101	4.68
SS C. DITTMAR	570	4	71	.268	5	D. MOUDY	244	19–11	116	90	3.46
OF E. AVERILL	754	20	116	.324	10	W. MAILS	217	11–11	75	102	4.39
OF L. O'DOUL	736	33	158	.378	40	B. GEARY	129	7–7	35	18	4.19
OF S. JOLLEY	625	33	163	.397	3	H. TURPIN	97	6–4	26	21	4.45
C S. AGNEW (1)	224	6	36	.290	2	H. BRETT	87	4–6	38	28	4.45
OF R. JOHNSON	327	4	24	.306	6						
1B D. CAMILLI	254	2	31	.244	3						
C T. REGO	196	1	14	.250	1						
C F. MC CREA	192	2	22	.245	1	(1) ALSO WITH HOLLYWOOD					
C A. VARGAS	181	1	15	.210	0	MANAGER – R. WILLIAMS					
1B S. MISHKIN	169	2	19	.260	0	RECORD W–106 L–90 FINISH–2ND					

SEATTLE	AB	HR	RBI	BA	SB	PITCHERS	IP	W–L	BB	SO	ERA
1B J. HUDGENS	481	25	95	.299	4	J. EDWARDS	281	20–17	75	87	3.36
2B C. BRADY	599	0	51	.247	5	E. BRANDT	261	19–11	107	144	3.96
3B W. KIMMICK	451	5	77	.359	12	J. KNIGHT	205	12–12	48	68	4.17
SS F. ELLSWORTH	567	3	65	.282	16	K. GRAHAM	200	13–10	78	76	3.64
OF M. CALLAGHAN	651	3	86	.350	19	J. MILJUS	179	13–5	56	53	2.36
OF E. PURDY	603	8	76	.367	22	S. MARTIN	122	7–8	37	19	3.76
OF F. HUFFT	496	19	138	.355	10	S. SUTHERLAND	90	4–7	36	16	4.40
C W. SCHMIDT	314	0	34	.271	3						
1S2 J. SHERLOCK	388	5	48	.265	2						
OF B. ELDRED	369	2	48	.325	10						
3B P. BALLENGER	241	1	24	.332	1	MANAGER – R. KILLEFER					
C J. JENKINS	198	3	22	.323	0	RECORD W–98 L–92 FINISH–3RD					

1927

SACRAMENTO		AB	HR	RBI	BA	SB	PITCHERS	IP	W–L	BB	SO	ERA
1B	F. MC GEE	360	1	32	.225	20	R. KEATING	293	20–15	84	91	3.31
2B	J. MONROE	592	4	70	.296	12	J. SINGLETON	290	16–13	74	94	3.25
3B	J. MC LAUGHLIN	582	9	71	.304	14	M. RACHAC	259	15–14	87	50	3.99
SS	R. FRENCH	636	5	87	.259	14	R. KALLIO	239	12–16	85	69	4.18
OF	M. KOPP	608	5	64	.273	14	L. VINCI	232	11–19	119	105	4.76
OF	F. OSBORN	474	5	80	.323	5	E. SHEA	220	13–8	70	68	4.09
OF	C. COOPER	450	0	34	.293	16	D. KEEFE	149	13–7	44	35	4.65
C	A. KOEHLER	383	12	57	.290	5						
OF	R. ROHWER	422	14	95	.334	11						
OF	C. HOFFMAN	362	5	54	.348	3						
C	H. SEVEREID	356	5	72	.326	1						
1B	J. KNIGHT	270	10	46	.311	5	MANAGER – B. RYAN					
23	L. BACKER	254	2	30	.303	1	RECORD W–100 L–95 FINISH–4TH					

PORTLAND		AB	HR	RBI	BA	SB	PITCHERS	IP	W–L	BB	SO	ERA
1B	D. BRANOM	377	13	81	.374	5	B. HUGHES	262	15–15	85	86	4.26
2B	F. SIGAFOOS	559	10	76	.335	11	J. COUCH	232	18–15	62	41	4.03
3B	D. PROTHRO	616	10	100	.330	13	E. PONDER	223	10–15	55	80	3.79
SS	B. CISSELL	696	5	64	.323	18	E. TOMLIN	220	16–9	88	57	4.33
OF	E. SMITH	653	40	141	.368	11	L. FRENCH	181	11–12	98	71	4.77
OF	P. STRAND	622	18	105	.355	11	W. KINNEY	172	9–9	72	36	4.50
OF	C. BIGBEE (1)	255	0	22	.294	10	C. YERKES	157	7–10	41	58	3.61
C	A. YELLE	289	0	30	.260	2						
1B	A. MC CURDY	382	10	63	.280	4						
23O	E. JOHNSON	318	2	23	.299	5	(1) ALSO WITH SEATTLE					
23	L. METZ (2)	297	1	19	.246	1	(2) ALSO WITH OAKLAND					
OF	B. BAGWELL	216	9	46	.292	2	MANAGER – E. JOHNSON					
PO	E. TOMLIN	181	3	20	.304	0	RECORD W–95 L–95 FINISH–5TH					

HOLLYWOOD		AB	HR	RBI	BA	SB	PITCHERS	IP	W–L	BB	SO	ERA
1B	M. HEATH	330	9	51	.282	7	SHELLENBACK	265	19–12	68	106	3.05
2B	J. KERR	660	18	91	.276	41	C. FULLERTON	263	13–19	90	84	3.93
3B	C. GOOCH	437	1	40	.252	8	H. HULVEY	224	17–14	49	74	2.97
SS	D. LEE	689	2	39	.242	7	P. MULCAHY	208	6–13	90	69	4.24
OF	J. FREDERICK	623	9	93	.305	9	R. MC CABE	196	11–16	35	53	3.63
OF	B. TWOMBLY	521	0	54	.309	16	W. MURPHY	191	14–8	57	37	3.39
OF	P. MC NULTY	362	0	43	.312	12	A. JACOBS	136	3–9	49	23	4.96
C	D. MURPHY	351	7	53	.293	1	A. TREACHOUT	103	6–6	46	22	3.84
OF	L. SHEEHAN	361	6	44	.288	7						
1B	J. MC DOWELL	240	5	30	.242	3	MANAGER – O. VITT					
OF	J. SWEENEY	231	6	24	.251	5	RECORD W–92 L–104 FINISH–6TH					

1927

MISSION		AB	HR	RBI	BA	SB	PITCHERS	IP	W–L	BB	SO	ERA
1B	O. MC DANIEL	654	19	121	.321	2	C. BARFOOT	308	15–18	54	55	3.56
2B	M. FINN	461	1	53	.321	8	H. PILLETTE	297	13–20	63	74	4.69
3B	B. JONES	383	3	44	.261	7	W. LUDOLPH	238	9–20	72	74	5.03
SS	G. SLADE	625	7	72	.298	5	L. WEINERT	232	17–12	91	107	3.14
OF	E. ROSE	677	15	102	.334	5	C. ECKERT	165	8–10	36	44	5.02
OF	E. SWANSON	642	3	55	.294	32	E. BRYAN	164	8–7	49	45	5.15
OF	R. GILLESPIE	277	5	32	.249	1	J. CHRISTIAN	112	4–13	66	27	6.99
C	R. WHITNEY	406	0	36	.236	1						
3S2	W. RODDA	546	1	48	.284	12						
O12	W. GRIFFIN	269	8	51	.301	0						
OF	R. WADE	256	5	31	.297	2						
OF	H. HOOPER	218	1	19	.284	4	MANAGER – B. LEARD/H.HOOPER					
2B	S. PARKER	166	0	16	.217	4	RECORD W–56 L–110 FINISH–7TH					

LOS ANGELES		AB	HR	RBI	BA	SB	PITCHERS	IP	W–L	BB	SO	ERA
1B	W. HOOD	600	17	116	.298	7	E. WEATHERSBY	293	16–18	107	101	4.45
2B	G. STALEY	563	1	64	.318	6	B PIERCY	267	12–20	105	72	4.88
3B	F. BRAZILL	545	21	76	.327	11	W. PETERS (1)	251	16–15	76	80	4.69
SS	J. MITCHELL	381	0	34	.215	9	W. WRIGHT	227	13–11	73	55	4.56
OF	A. JAHN	682	17	146	.343	9	B. CUNNINGHAM	175	9–10	111	65	4.57
OF	D. COX	618	13	90	.345	7	E. HAMILTON	145	7–16	50	49	5.09
OF	A. WEIS	527	13	77	.317	4						
C	G. SANBERG	344	2	60	.273	2						
12S	R. JACOBS	359	13	64	.323	9						
231	E. HEMINGWAY	322	1	36	.295	6						
C	T. HANNAH	317	7	37	.265	2	(1) ALSO WITH SEATTLE					
3B	M. KRUG	173	0	19	.266	3	MANAGER – M. KRUG					
SS	O. KAHN	167	2	17	.192	1	RECORD W–80 L–116 FINISH–8TH					

PLAYOFFS
NONE

1928

SAN FRANCISCO

SAN FRANCISCO		AB	HR	RBI	BA	SB	PITCHERS	IP	W–L	BB	SO	ERA
1B	S. THURSTON	420	24	98	.348	5	D. RUETHER	303	29–7	57	110	3.03
2B	G. SUHR	741	22	133	.314	5	E. JACOBS	277	22–8	64	159	2.56
3B	B. PINELLI	422	2	31	.310	3	W. MAILS	277	20–12	101	152	3.96
SS	H. RHYNE	692	6	106	.312	17	D. MOUDY	213	10–10	88	93	4.09
OF	S. JOLLEY	765	45	188	.404	9	H. MAY	205	11–13	55	90	4.74
OF	E. AVERILL	763	36	173	.354	13	O. MITCHELL	200	13–11	70	66	3.87
OF	R. JOHNSON	650	22	76	.360	29	S. THURSTON	137	9–7	22	37	4.59
C	J. SPRINZ	505	4	49	.236	10						
3B	F. CROSETTI	326	4	22	.248	4	**MANAGER – R. WILLIAMS**					
1B	S. MISHKIN	248	2	28	.274	0	**RECORD W–120 L–71 FINISH–1ST**					

HOLLYWOOD

HOLLYWOOD		AB	HR	RBI	BA	SB	PITCHERS	IP	W–L	BB	SO	ERA
1B	M. HEATH	662	19	109	.307	10	SHELLENBACK	272	23–11	66	125	3.34
2B	J. KERR	775	16	82	.301	30	J. COUCH (1)	236	9–17	46	51	4.88
3B	J. WERA	294	3	45	.303	6	G. RHODES	229	17–10	95	129	3.26
SS	D. LEE	802	5	77	.273	7	H. HULVEY	226	14–9	54	85	4.42
OF	B. TWOMBLY	697	0	75	.314	12	R. MC CABE	224	16–10	45	59	3.93
OF	E. SMITH (1)	657	26	126	.320	10	W. KINNEY	210	17–8	92	81	4.67
OF	C. CARLYLE	440	14	72	.289	8	K. BONNELLY (3)	127	7–6	34	27	4.60
C	J. BASSLER	373	2	33	.300	3	P. MULCAHY	104	4–6	48	42	4.67
							W. MURPHY	95	5–6	44	23	4.83
OF	W. REHG	261	3	47	.307	4						
C	S. AGNEW	252	4	38	.321	2	(1) ALSO WITH PORTLAND					
OF	B. ROTH	226	1	37	.283	1	(2) ALSO WITH SAN FRANCISCO					
3B	L. OSTERBERG	221	8	35	.294	2	(3) ALSO WITH SACRAMENTO					
OF	T. BOROJA	169	1	13	.308	3	**MANAGER – O. VITT**					
OF	F. WELCH (2)	161	4	23	.292	0	**RECORD W–112 L–79 FINISH–2ND (T)**					

SACRAMENTO

SACRAMENTO		AB	HR	RBI	BA	SB	PITCHERS	IP	W–L	BB	SO	ERA
1B	E. SHEELY	630	21	128	.381	3	L. VINCI	330	23–11	129	141	3.57
2B	J. MONROE	731	10	84	.321	14	R. KEATING	309	27–10	60	116	3.14
3B	J. MC LAUGHLIN	542	10	81	.310	4	A. GOULD (1)	209	13–8	61	58	3.01
SS	R. FRENCH	814	9	77	.287	9	R. KALLIO	179	12–11	58	65	4.32
OF	D. HOFFMAN	740	11	96	.335	15	E. SHEA (1)	148	7–12	50	45	5.04
OF	F. OSBORN	624	12	97	.316	16	M. RACHAC	134	9–8	32	32	4.03
OF	R. ROHWER	478	10	84	.289	13	E. KUNZ	132	4–8	51	36	5.18
C	H. SEVEREID	385	10	59	.301	0	D. CRANDALL	81	6–4	19	22	3.89
C	A. KOEHLER	370	8	60	.305	1						
23	L. BACKER	225	1	27	.267	3						
OF	M. KOPP	202	2	16	.282	3	(1) ALSO WITH OAKLAND					
OF	W. BURKE	176	2	23	.324	1	**MANAGER – B. RYAN**					
O1	L. SHEEHAN	176	3	31	.261	2	**RECORD W–112 L–79 FINISH–2ND (T)**					

1928

MISSION		AB	HR	RBI	BA	SB	PITCHERS	IP	W–L	BB	SO	ERA
1B	O. MC DANIEL	562	25	102	.327	6	H. PILLETTE	301	16–18	59	71	3.11
2B	M. FINN	662	1	69	.284	14	C. HOLLING	255	17–14	66	65	3.63
3B	W. RODDA	584	3	65	.264	7	B. HUGHES	220	11–12	87	112	3.92
SS	G. SLADE	667	6	90	.306	13	E. NEVERS	206	14–11	69	54	4.37
OF	E. SWANSON	740	4	58	.346	49	M. NELSON	186	9–7	67	71	4.30
OF	I. BOONE (1)	594	9	104	.354	8	H. KRAUSE (4)	180	15–10	36	56	4.35
OF	F. HUFFT (2)	561	30	143	.371	7						
C	E. BALDWIN	365	3	47	.277	0	(1) ALSO WITH PORTLAND					
							(2) ALSO WITH SEATTLE					
OF	P. BODIE (3)	333	10	62	.348	2	(3) ALSO WITH SAN FRANCISCO					
C	R. WHITNEY (1)	319	1	44	.266	1	(4) ALSO WITH OAKLAND					
OF	W. GRIFFIN	201	1	34	.343	3	**MANAGER – R. KILLEFER**					
1B	H. GREEN	153	4	20	.196	2	**RECORD W–99 L–92 FINISH–4TH**					

OAKLAND		AB	HR	RBI	BA	SB	PITCHERS	IP	W–L	BB	SO	ERA
1B	J. FENTON	645	9	71	.299	4	H. CRAGHEAD	282	18–13	104	147	3.41
2B	J. REESE	478	1	35	.247	5	G. BOEHLER	257	17–14	124	140	4.09
3B	J. CAVENEY (1)	457	6	47	.263	1	P. DAGLIA	252	18–11	90	110	3.75
SS	L. LARY	614	7	94	.314	19	W. COOPER	212	10–16	45	45	3.48
OF	B. ARLETT	561	25	113	.365	10	M. DUMOVICH	180	9–11	86	67	3.05
OF	T. GOVERNOR	522	0	38	.274	9	B. WETZEL (2)	146	5–6	72	36	5.11
OF	I. MEUSEL	374	11	65	.267	4	B. HASTY	123	6–7	37	34	3.58
C	A. READ	325	2	25	.225	3	L. MC EVOY	78	3–5	32	23	3.35
23S	M. DEAN	389	1	43	.278	3						
OF	J. BROOKS	367	5	58	.305	11						
C	E. LOMBARDI	318	8	47	.377	1	(1) ALSO WITH SAN FRANCISCO					
O2	R. BRUBAKER	255	1	40	.290	2	(2) ALSO WITH PORTLAND AND HOLLYWOOD					
3B	J. VERGEZ	241	3	32	.245	3	**MANAGER – I. HOWARD**					
OF	F. FRAZIER	230	0	14	.257	6	**RECORD W–91 L–100 FINISH–5TH**					

LOS ANGELES		AB	HR	RBI	BA	SB	PITCHERS	IP	W–L	BB	SO	ERA
1B	C. TOLSON	501	28	108	.351	1	C. BARFOOT	311	20–19	59	57	3.84
2B	G. STALEY	608	2	51	.301	12	B. CUNNINGHAM	277	17–13	105	89	4.22
3B	B. JONES	594	1	55	.296	3	W. PETERS	246	14–11	71	75	3.99
SS	C. DITTMAR	626	2	63	.254	15	N. PLITT	236	12–19	90	60	5.11
OF	SCHULMERICH	717	19	96	.317	9	E. WEATHERSBY	212	12–18	88	58	5.01
OF	W. HOOD	599	20	106	.290	9	R. OSBORN	120	5–9	73	58	5.70
OF	W. BERGER	535	20	94	.327	5	R. WRIGHT	104	5–8	41	16	4.33
C	T. HANNAH	262	3	27	.271	0	G. GABLER	80	1–4	24	19	4.84
321	H. BURKETT	357	2	30	.261	2						
C	G. SANBERG	221	2	29	.231	4	**MANAGER – M. KRUG**					
OF	W. JENSEN	150	1	16	.240	3	**RECORD W–87 L–104 FINISH–6TH**					

1928

PORTLAND		AB	HR	RBI	BA	SB	PITCHERS	IP	W–L	BB	SO	ERA
1B	J. KEESEY	678	9	104	.336	18	J. KNIGHT (3)	331	17–17	69	105	3.35
2B	F. SIGAFOOS	695	8	76	.296	32	FULLERTON (4)	271	15–20	95	96	3.45
3B	F. BRAZILL (1)	303	8	50	.330	3	L. FRENCH	251	11–17	128	105	4.05
SS	Y. WUESTLING	365	2	32	.269	4	B. COLE (3)	246	10–20	58	73	5.16
OF	E. ROSE (1)	457	4	40	.278	7	E. PONDER	226	11–13	59	94	4.10
OF	B. LEBOURVEAU	357	7	37	.353	12	C. YERKES	202	11–12	70	115	3.74
OF	C. BATES	318	6	38	.280	10	F. ORTMAN	166	8–15	68	49	5.15
C	T. REGO	262	0	31	.294	0						
							(1) ALSO WITH MISSION					
23	E. JOHNSON	378	0	30	.310	12	(2) ALSO WITH LOS ANGELES					
OP1	E. TOMLIN	324	3	43	.327	4	(3) ALSO WITH SEATTLE					
OF	C. BIGBEE (2)	301	0	17	.229	6	(4) ALSO WITH HOLLYWOOD					
3S	F. KNOTHE	264	1	28	.258	9	**MANAGER – E. JOHNSON/B. RODGERS**					
3S2	I. DAVIS (3)	259	0	16	.220	3	**RECORD W–79 L–112 FINISH–7TH**					

SEATTLE		AB	HR	RBI	BA	SB	PITCHERS	IP	W–L	BB	SO	ERA
1B	W. OLNEY	289	1	43	.304	0	H. COLLARD	232	5–23	62	57	4.22
2B	J. SHERLOCK	660	10	88	.289	13	E. BRYAN (2)	191	8–11	51	48	4.71
3B	F. MULLER	468	8	37	.231	5	A. TREACHOUT	189	8–13	65	66	4.66
SS	F. ELLSWORTH	595	2	51	.272	6	K. GRAHAM	187	10–17	71	57	4.33
OF	A. RUBLE	648	10	71	.326	17	T. WILSON	161	7–11	30	35	5.53
OF	M. WOLFER	359	0	22	.267	5	C. NANCE (2)	139	9–1	25	19	3.36
OF	B. NEIS	350	4	29	.286	3	C. SULLIVAN	122	5–8	44	43	5.09
C	E. AINSMITH (1)	327	3	42	.242	3	S. MARTIN (2)	92	4–6	35	34	5.58
3O	D. BARBEE (1)	483	16	89	.327	8						
23S	J. MITCHELL (2)	326	2	27	.316	9						
23S	J. CHAMBERLAIN	203	3	29	.256	0	(1) ALSO WITH PORTLAND					
C	C. BORREANI	179	0	8	.240	1	(2) ALSO WITH MISSION					
OF	T. SULLIVAN	172	3	31	.221	5	**MANAGER – J. MIDDLETON**					
C	W. SCHMIDT	168	0	15	.298	3	**RECORD W–64 L–127 FINISH–8TH**					

PLAYOFF
SAN FRANCISCO DEFEATED SACRAMENTO 4 GAMES TO 2

1929

MISSION

		AB	HR	RBI	BA	SB	PITCHERS	IP	W–L	BB	SO	ERA
1B	J. SHERLOCK	782	14	156	.336	25	B. COLE	279	24–12	90	103	3.45
2B	M. FINN	704	5	64	.347	17	H. PILLETTE	273	23–13	52	82	3.59
3B	E. MULLIGAN	734	3	56	.279	42	M. NELSON	249	17–10	106	115	4.80
SS	G. SLADE	734	16	115	.302	19	D. RUETHER	208	14–9	64	76	4.71
OF	I. BOONE	794	55	218	.407	9	H. MC QUAID	170	12–4	52	64	4.29
OF	F. HUFFT	754	39	187	.379	7	H. KRAUSE	167	7–9	35	55	5.34
OF	C. CHRISTENSEN	505	0	47	.319	19	B. HUBBELL	154	11–7	48	45	3.79
C	F. HOFMANN	390	11	72	.300	3	E. NEVERS	148	7–8	60	44	4.56
O1	P. SCOTT	260	12	55	.335	5	**MANAGER – R. KILLEFER**					
C	E. BALDWIN	259	3	25	.247	1	**RECORD W–123 L–78 FINISH–1ST**					

SAN FRANCISCO

		AB	HR	RBI	BA	SB	PITCHERS	IP	W–L	BB	SO	ERA
1B	G. SUHR	785	51	177	.381	19	E. JACOBS	290	21–11	63	130	3.47
2B	J. CAVENEY	530	9	87	.334	6	S. THURSTON	282	22–11	45	78	4.40
3B	B. PINELLI	679	5	65	.311	12	L. GOMEZ	267	18–11	108	159	3.43
SS	F. CROSETTI	784	12	81	.314	5	W. MAILS	250	15–16	103	119	4.86
OF	S. JOLLEY	812	35	159	.387	6	C. DAVIS	240	17–13	61	79	3.97
OF	A. WINGO	597	24	124	.060	2	J. WALTERS (1)	160	12–5	61	55	3.77
OF	E. COLEMAN	405	16	72	.343	2	V. GLYNN	123	1–8	48	46	5.12
C	R. REED	351	0	37	.259	3	J. COUCH	113	9–8	28	30	5.42
23S	L. BAKER	486	9	56	.282	2						
O3P	J. WALTERS (1)	438	13	79	.304	10	(1) ALSO WITH PORTLAND					
OF	J. DONOVAN	318	15	61	.302	3	(2) ALSO WITH OAKLAND					
OF	S. SCHINO (2)	314	8	31	.274	8	**MANAGER – R. WILLIAMS**					
PO	S. THURSTON	182	8	37	.302	0	**RECORD W–114 L–87 FINISH–2ND**					

HOLLYWOOD

		AB	HR	RBI	BA	SB	PITCHERS	IP	W–L	BB	SO	ERA
1B	M. HEATH	680	38	156	.349	20	SHELLENBACK	335	26–12	68	163	3.97
2B	M. MALONEY	292	1	34	.236	0	B. WETZEL	269	18–15	92	113	4.04
3B	R. ROLLINGS	738	6	86	.324	14	G. HOLLERSON	247	13–13	51	67	4.40
SS	D. LEE	848	4	71	.262	9	H. HULVEY	240	14–11	53	81	6.07
OF	C. CARLYLE	666	20	136	.347	21	W. KINNEY	203	12–12	104	81	4.25
OF	L. FUNK	547	13	125	.384	16	A. JOHNS	201	17–10	38	88	3.89
OF	B. RUMLER	503	26	120	.386	6	MARTICORENA	145	9–9	79	87	5.77
C	H. SEVEREID (1)	474	24	124	.359	3						
2S3	C. FALK	451	5	57	.273	5						
23S	H. BURKETT (2)	430	5	53	.242	5						
C	J. BASSLER	299	0	37	.251	1	(1) ALSO WITH SACRAMENTO					
OF	W. ALBERT	203	2	30	.286	4	(2) ALSO WITH LOS ANGELES					
OF	W. REHG	200	2	38	.305	8	**MANAGER – O. VITT**					
O1	H. GREEN	190	9	45	.279	3	**RECORD W–113 L–89 FINISH–3RD**					

1929

OAKLAND		AB	HR	RBI	BA	SB	PITCHERS	IP	W−L	BB	SO	ERA
1B	J. FENTON	487	3	60	.322	5	L. MC EVOY	329	22−12	134	138	3.83
2B	J. REESE	766	1	56	.337	24	H. CRAGHEAD	298	21−12	128	190	4.04
3B	J. VERGEZ	711	46	165	.323	11	P. DAGLIA	281	17−17	113	101	3.97
SS	M. DEAN	522	1	45	.215	3	J. EDWARDS (1)	277	18−15	89	113	4.74
OF	B. ARLETT	722	39	189	.374	22	N. DUMOVICH	217	15−17	82	68	4.81
OF	R. CARLYLE	604	22	108	.348	2	R. HURST	134	8−7	43	50	2.88
OF	F. FRAZIER	494	1	27	.263	11	C. JEFFCOAT	119	4−6	51	40	3.40
C	E. LOMBARDI	516	24	109	.366	3	C. KASICH	116	7−4	70	45	5.51
OF	T. GOVERNOR	358	1	25	.274	4	(1) ALSO WITH SEATTLE					
U	R. BRUBAKER	261	2	31	.268	2	MANAGER − I. HOWARD					
C	A. READ	215	1	28	.293	3	RECORD W−111 L−91 FINISH−4TH					

LOS ANGELES		AB	HR	RBI	BA	SB	PITCHERS	IP	W−L	BB	SO	ERA
1B	C. TOLSON	487	28	122	.359	1	A. WALSH	294	21−14	123	104	4.83
2B	R. JACOBS	591	20	118	.332	11	C. BARFOOT	236	18−12	58	64	4.53
3B	B. JONES	441	2	58	.281	15	V. ROBERTS	225	10−14	81	81	5.32
SS	C. DITTMAR	505	5	43	.303	14	N. PLITT	200	10−11	62	63	4.63
OF	J. STATZ	799	3	75	.308	37	E. BAECHT (1)	183	14−7	60	109	3.44
OF	W. BERGER	744	40	166	.335	19	C. HOLLING	163	8−13	44	51	6.07
OF	E. WEBB	658	37	164	.357	14	W. PETERS	156	7−8	57	52	5.07
C	G. SANBERG	377	7	55	.289	3	H. CHESLEY	98	4−5	75	47	6.52
3S2	F. HANEY	586	1	51	.292	56	(1) ALSO WITH PORTLAND					
OF	SCHULMERICH	360	19	77	.328	6	MANAGER − M. KRUG/J. LELIVELT					
C	D. WARREN	202	6	31	.272	0	RECORD W−104 L−98 FINISH−5TH					

PORTLAND		AB	HR	RBI	BA	SB	PITCHERS	IP	W−L	BB	SO	ERA
1B	J. KEESEY	705	12	124	.349	17	R. MAHAFFEY	370	21−25	113	165	4.01
2B	M. HILLIS	441	4	57	.283	4	J. KNIGHT (1)	313	15−21	79	87	4.94
3B	G. STALEY	280	0	24	.271	3	C. FULLERTON	270	19−18	92	102	4.50
SS	B. CHATHAM	263	6	23	.312	14	J. CASCARELLA	238	13−15	90	90	4.81
OF	C. BATES	661	11	82	.300	23	F. ORTMAN	181	8−15	55	62	5.07
OF	A. JAHN (1)	619	3	92	.304	5	CHESTERFIELD (2)	163	5−7	67	86	4.25
OF	D. HARRIS	309	15	70	.366	19						
C	L. WOODALL	347	1	34	.282	0						
OF	C. FREY	285	0	19	.284	10						
OF	B. JOHNSON	264	5	27	.254	6						
3B	F. SIGAFOOS	204	2	28	.270	5						
S2	J. CRONIN	199	0	9	.256	10	(1) ALSO WITH SAN FRANCISCO					
SS	J. HASSLER	194	4	19	.242	1	(2) ALSO WITH HOLLYWOOD					
C	T. REGO	194	0	14	.263	1	MANAGER − B. RODGERS					
23	R. ODELL	187	1	18	.282	1	RECORD W−90 L−112 FINISH−6TH					

1929

SACRAMENTO		AB	HR	RBI	BA	SB	PITCHERS	IP	W-L	BB	SO	ERA
1B	D. CAMILLI	446	12	74	.296	3	E. BRYAN	328	20-12	80	79	4.41
2B	J. MONROE	589	6	58	.336	13	L. VINCI	242	13-20	96	99	5.35
3B	J. MC LAUGHLIN	474	3	65	.316	6	A. GOULD	223	10-18	82	71	5.12
SS	R. FRENCH	619	1	53	.296	8	D. CRANDALL (1)	202	11-13	58	50	4.18
OF	F. OSBORN	528	5	82	.324	11	R. KEATING	192	12-11	82	72	4.50
OF	R. ROHWER	495	11	70	.257	8	J. CANO	153	5-9	64	47	5.82
OF	M. HOAG	414	6	54	.280	5	G. JONES (2)	152	8-10	67	53	5.21
C	A. KOEHLER	457	13	74	.344	2	M. RACHAC	123	4-7	27	25	7.24
							L. GILLICK	86	3-5	37	26	6.28
S32	L. BACKER	634	8	88	.334	4	T. FREITAS	59	2-4	20	27	6.41
OF	W. BURKE	321	0	27	.283	3						
1B	H. STOEVEN	255	3	35	.286	2						
OF	J. HARRIS	190	6	42	.342	0	(1) ALSO WITH LOS ANGELES					
231	T. KRASNOVICH	160	1	24	.264	2	(2) ALSO WITH SAN FRANCISCO AND HOLLYWOOD					
P	E. BRYAN	157	2	16	261	0	MANAGER - B. RYAN					
OF	I. MEUSEL	153	2	21	.327	2	RECORD W-85 L-117 FINISH-7TH					

SEATTLE		AB	HR	RBI	BA	SB	PITCHERS	IP	W-L	BB	SO	ERA
1B	H. TAYLOR	456	5	47	.272	10	R. KALLIO	278	15-19	91	85	4.04
2B	E. JOHNSON	266	5	30	.335	17	F. PIPGRAS	248	9-21	129	96	5.08
3B	F. KNOTHE (1)	630	10	70	.287	37	E. FISCH	219	5-22	69	80	3.90
SS	F. ELLSWORTH	465	1	37	.232	7	F. LAMANSKI	159	6-8	48	60	5.09
OF	C. WADE	645	22	133	.321	7	K. GRAHAM	152	6-11	59	45	4.26
OF	D. BARBEE	613	22	118	.316	4	G. SMITH	129	4-12	48	50	4.81
OF	O. ECKHARDT	571	7	70	.354	16	H. COLLARD	128	5-9	40	33	4.85
C	C. BORREANI	322	2	34	.276	1	A. HOUSE	122	3-15	70	63	5.75
2S3	F. MULLER	436	10	37	.255	1						
O1	L. ALMADA	417	4	44	.305	6						
C	B. STEINECKE	240	5	32	.317	3	(1) ALSO WITH PORTLAND					
OF	B. ALLINGTON	202	1	12	.312	11	MANAGER - E. JOHNSON					
C	F. COX	181	0	26	260	0	RECORD W-67 L-135 FINISH-8TH					

PLAYOFF
HOLLYWOOD DEFEATED MISSION 4 GAMES TO 2

1930

HOLLYWOOD	AB	HR	RBI	BA	SB	PITCHERS	IP	W–L	BB	SO	ERA
1B M. HEATH	546	37	136	.324	19	J. TURNER	258	21–9	58	92	3.80
2B O. BRANNAN	742	18	130	.307	6	SHELLENBACK	252	19–7	59	111	4.64
3B M. GAZELLA	650	11	94	.303	9	G. HOLLERSON	203	13–10	60	70	6.03
SS D. LEE	717	3	57	.275	27	B. WETZEL	200	13–11	89	87	5.58
OF C. CARLYLE	616	12	97	.326	14	A. JOHNS	195	12–11	68	96	4.38
OF D. BARBEE (1)	588	41	155	.325	5	E. YDE	179	13–10	69	118	5.33
OF J. HILL	480	18	71	.356	10	V. PAGE	172	8–12	56	39	3.87
C H. SEVEREID	376	13	93	.367	6	H. HULVEY	171	11–10	34	69	4.89
						G. RHODES	117	9–2	59	76	5.23
O1 H. GREEN	431	14	80	.329	4						
C J. BASSLER	348	0	71	.365	5	(1) ALSO WITH SEATTLE					
OF B. RUMLER	346	14	82	.353	8	MANAGER – O. VITT					
3S2 L. CATINA	184	0	10	.212	1	RECORD W–119 L–81 FINISH–1ST					

LOS ANGELES	AB	HR	RBI	BA	SB	PITCHERS	IP	W–L	BB	SO	ERA
1B R. JACOBS	710	20	130	.304	11	E. BAECHT	364	26–12	125	179	3.24
2B F. SIGAFOOS	702	19	103	.305	25	A. DELANEY	278	13–19	74	100	3.91
3B F. HANEY	673	7	80	.312	52	W. BALLOU	238	16–7	95	129	3.78
SS C. DITTMAR	622	14	125	.310	13	C. YERKES (1)	194	12–13	67	90	4.59
OF SCHULMERICH	692	28	130	.380	12	C. BARFOOT	186	12–10	42	32	5.03
OF J. STATZ	558	5	84	.360	37	B. HORNE	175	13–7	107	98	4.47
OF G. HARPER	546	8	97	.308	9	W. PETERS	172	12–12	69	47	5.07
C T. HANNAH	329	4	48	.267	1	A. WALSH	85	6–5	49	34	6.99
OF J. MOORE	546	26	101	.342	15						
C D. WARREN	205	6	30	.224	2	(1) ALSO WITH PORTLAND					
23 A. PARKER	204	0	26	.289	4	MANAGER – J. LELIVELT					
C B. SKIFF	149	0	13	.215	1	RECORD W–113 L–84 FINISH–2ND					

SACRAMENTO	AB	HR	RBI	BA	SB	PITCHERS	IP	W–L	BB	SO	ERA
1B D. CAMILLI	619	17	118	.275	8	F. THOMAS	298	18–20	131	228	3.95
2B M. HILLIS (1)	569	5	70	.297	5	T. FREITAS	275	19–6	74	121	3.24
3B L. BACKER	709	12	114	.330	7	R. KEATING (1)	251	14–15	87	89	4.41
SS R. FRENCH	848	3	72	.264	28	E. BRYAN	250	18–12	67	84	4.21
OF M. HOAG	725	17	121	.337	19	T. FLYNN	247	15–14	113	104	3.93
OF F. OSBORN	603	8	87	.325	7	L. VINCI	219	7–18	76	79	4.93
OF R. ROHWER	392	13	83	.298	6	A. GOULD (2)	127	5–9	56	44	4.74
C A. KOEHLER	369	3	47	.279	4						
3B J. MC LAUGHLIN	385	1	36	.304	7						
2B A. WARD	344	7	35	.247	6	(1) ALSO WITH PORTLAND					
C K. WIRTZ	305	2	41	.249	0	(2) ALSO WITH SAN FRANCISCO					
OF B. ELDRED	203	6	42	.369	3	MANAGER – B. RYAN					
OF H. STEINBACHER	153	0	26	.314	5	RECORD W–102 L–96 FINISH–3RD					

1930

SAN FRANCISCO	AB	HR	RBI	BA	SB	PITCHERS	IP	W−L	BB	SO	ERA
1B E. SHEELY	718	29	180	.403	6	J. ZINN	316	26−12	80	132	4.07
2B J. CAVENEY	575	8	84	.336	4	C. DAVIS	305	17−18	80	103	4.87
3B B. PINELLI	579	3	55	.313	16	E. JACOBS	275	17−13	81	120	3.89
SS F. CROSETTI	782	27	113	.334	21	A. MC DOUGALL	227	9−17	117	124	5.55
OF J. DONOVAN	652	13	96	.336	15	H. TURPIN	205	10−11	41	65	3.86
OF A. WINGO	537	21	117	.348	6	J. MILJUS	157	8−8	67	68	4.24
OF E. COLEMAN	396	12	68	.301	3	C. PERRY	124	7−7	74	54	6.02
C A. GASTON	398	11	67	.286	0						
23 L. BAKER	619	9	86	.291	6						
OF P. OANA	298	11	53	.326	7						
C A. PENEBSKY	285	2	41	.298	1						
OF E. SULIK	215	3	21	.279	2	MANAGER − R. WILLIAMS					
P J. ZINN	103	5	36	.326	0	RECORD W−101 L−98 FINISH−4TH					

OAKLAND	AB	HR	RBI	BA	SB	PITCHERS	IP	W−L	BB	SO	ERA
1B J. FENTON	595	7	100	.308	6	H. CRAGHEAD	343	21−22	125	199	3.64
2B M. DEAN	475	2	39	.286	5	P. DAGLIA	294	18−16	149	125	4.10
3B J. VERGEZ	687	29	125	.307	16	R. HURST	229	14−12	71	92	4.52
SS B. DE VIVEIROS	498	3	46	.253	4	J. EDWARDS	215	12−16	92	86	3.81
OF F. UHALT	749	0	49	.311	18	B. HUBBELL (1)	178	8−15	58	68	5.51
OF B. ARLETT	618	31	143	.361	8	B. HENDERSON	131	8−7	91	78	4.32
OF L. MARTIN	454	3	49	.295	9	N. DUMOVICH	114	3−7	58	30	6.39
C E. LOMBARDI	473	22	105	.370	1						
OF P. GRIFFIN	425	4	66	.294	7						
23O R. BRUBAKER	305	0	47	.344	7	(1) ALSO WITH SEATTLE AND SACRAMENTO					
2B J. MELLANA	290	9	34	.321	13	MANAGER − C. ZAMLOCH					
C A. READ	245	1	24	.290	2	RECORD W−97 L−103 FINISH−5TH					

SEATTLE	AB	HR	RBI	BA	SB	PITCHERS	IP	W−L	BB	SO	ERA
1B H. TAYLOR	681	2	64	.298	21	R. KALLIO	267	18−16	92	140	3.67
2B F. MULLER	467	13	59	.274	6	P. ZAHNISER	264	18−14	90	89	4.06
3B F. KNOTHE	717	11	70	.304	34	D. RUETHER	254	17−15	78	61	3.43
SS F. ELLSWORTH	456	3	38	.292	11	A. HOUSE	222	7−18	114	71	4.82
OF D. HOLLAND	792	20	141	.332	16	F. LAMANSKI	188	7−14	81	100	5.74
OF L. ALMADA	676	19	113	.296	10	E. KUNZ	174	8−8	93	64	5.17
OF B. LAWRENCE	408	3	45	.275	12	E. HANSEN	165	10−7	52	51	4.58
C C. BORREANI	381	1	44	.273	7						
S21 M. OWEN	443	3	55	.300	16						
2B E. JOHNSON	260	2	31	.300	6						
C F. COX	239	0	31	.351	3	MANAGER − E. JOHNSON					
OF C. LEE	233	1	31	.296	4	RECORD W−92 L−107 FINISH−6TH					

1930

MISSION		AB	HR	RBI	BA	SB	PITCHERS	IP	W–L	BB	SO	ERA
1B	G. BURNS	767	22	131	.349	27	B. COLE	267	16–13	70	100	4.61
2B	J. MONROE	689	28	106	.350	7	H. PILLETTE	261	18–14	58	66	4.34
3B	E. MULLIGAN	828	5	56	.300	27	D. LIEBER	240	13–18	85	85	5.17
SS	W. RODDA	524	7	81	.274	9	T. PILLETTE	213	14–9	111	90	5.40
OF	F. HUFFT	721	37	178	.356	8	H. MC QUAID (1)	201	10–13	52	66	4.83
OF	E. KELLY	459	2	34	.275	10	J. KNOTT	183	7–11	67	57	5.45
OF	I. BOONE	310	22	96	.448	5	G. CASTER	128	8–10	78	47	5.48
C	F. HOFMANN	369	9	49	.268	1	M. NELSON	92	4–6	41	26	6.85
C	B. BRENZEL	270	4	34	.307	0						
OF	H. ROSENBERG	239	11	53	.368	3						
2S	A. WRIGHT	174	0	8	.196	0						
OF	D. HAFEY	173	3	18	.208	0						
OF	F. BERGER	148	2	24	.297	5						
P	B. COLE	135	0	10	.289	1						
OF	E. BIGELOW	121	1	11	.298	4	(1) ALSO WITH OAKLAND					
OF	C. CHRISTENSEN	105	0	11	.267	1	**MANAGER – R. KILLEFER**					
SS	J. COSCARART	100	3	13	.240	1	**RECORD W–91 L–110 FINISH–7TH**					

PORTLAND		AB	HR	RBI	BA	SB	PITCHERS	IP	W–L	BB	SO	ERA
1B	O. ORWOLL	611	11	80	.301	15	F. ORTMAN	294	15–18	105	95	4.10
2B	B. RHIEL	423	7	79	.348	4	J. WALTERS	240	17–15	89	90	4.31
3B	G. ROBERTSON	592	0	53	.292	4	W. MAILS	234	11–16	112	144	4.38
SS	J. CRONIN	453	0	42	.265	7	C. FULLERTON	221	11–18	107	102	5.90
OF	W. FRENCH	644	0	49	.309	9	CHESTERFIELD(1)	184	6–12	78	97	4.20
OF	K. WILLIAMS	546	14	110	.350	23	C. MAYS	144	5–9	36	43	4.75
OF	H. SUMMA	376	4	47	.316	10	J. CASCARELLA	109	5–5	59	49	6.61
C	J. PALMISANO	357	1	61	.308	3	H. MC DONALD	90	4–4	52	60	5.20
OS1	B. JOHNSON	501	21	93	.265	5						
C	L. WOODALL	336	1	44	.345	4						
OF	D. CRAMER	300	5	46	.347	6						
P3O	J. WALTERS	240	6	40	.296	2	(1) ALSO WITH SACRAMENTO					
SS	B. CHATHAM	184	0	13	.283	7	**MANAGER – L. WOODALL**					
3B	S. HALE	140	1	18	.293	4	**RECORD W–81 L–117 FINISH–8TH**					

PLAYOFF
HOLLYWOOD DEFEATED LOS ANGELES 4 GAMES TO 1

1931

SAN FRANCISCO	AB	HR	RBI	BA	SB	PITCHERS	IP	W–L	BB	SO	ERA
1B J. KEESEY	665	10	113	.358	14	S. GIBSON	337	28–12	59	204	2.48
2B A. GARIBALDI	478	4	77	.314	12	C. DAVIS	236	14–14	56	106	4.19
3B J. WERA	651	1	103	.306	4	E. JACOBS	217	12–11	51	78	3.98
SS F. CROSETTI	734	5	143	.343	23	A. MC DOUGALL	201	14–7	96	109	3.27
OF P. OANA	742	23	161	.345	12	C. WILLOUGHBY	159	10–11	46	64	3.56
OF F. FRAZIER	588	7	84	.327	23	J. ZINN	146	9–7	31	49	3.32
OF E. SULIK	462	2	52	.329	18	B. HENDERSON	113	8–3	58	85	3.34
C M. MEALEY	269	0	19	.242	1	K. DOUGLASS	109	6–3	27	42	2.64
O1 J. DONOVAN	419	3	32	.301	12						
23 J. CAVENEY	407	3	55	.334	3						
OF M. HUNT	228	5	43	.302	1	MANAGER – R. WILLIAMS					
C E. BALDWIN	187	0	20	.246	0	RECORD W–107 L–80 FINISH–1ST					

HOLLYWOOD	AB	HR	RBI	BA	SB	PITCHERS	IP	W–L	BB	SO	ERA
1B J. SHERLOCK	614	10	99	.279	9	SHELLENBACK	306	27–7	61	127	2.85
2B O. BRANNAN	555	7	85	.283	2	J. TURNER	292	17–14	80	106	4.28
3B M. GAZELLA	653	8	77	.314	11	E. YDE	210	15–16	88	118	4.32
SS D. LEE	651	3	55	.275	14	V. PAGE	201	17–8	44	69	4.34
OF D. BARBEE	650	47	166	.332	4	E. BRAY	166	6–11	52	63	5.42
OF J. HILL	600	19	97	.318	18	D. WETZEL	164	11–9	60	56	4.50
OF C. CARLYLE	490	10	89	.320	3	A. JOHNS	89	4–5	30	46	5.16
C J. BASSLER	316	0	43	.354	0						
OF M. CALLAHAN	372	1	54	.304	3						
C H. SEVEREID	308	17	65	.347	1						
1B H. GREEN	176	2	16	.239	1						
2S3 L. CATINA	167	1	24	.242	2	MANAGER – O. VITT					
OF A. MC NEELEY	154	0	17	.299	2	RECORD W–104 L–83 FINISH–2ND					

PORTLAND	AB	HR	RBI	BA	SB	PITCHERS	IP	W–L	BB	SO	ERA
1B J. FENTON	676	8	116	.293	6	J. BOWMAN	246	18–11	62	126	3.80
2B J. MONROE (1)	607	7	64	.362	15	O. ORWOLL	237	13–16	94	113	4.06
3B S. HALE	555	2	80	.323	7	W. MAILS	212	13–13	140	124	5.01
SS Y. WUESTLING	645	3	78	.256	5	J. WALTERS	190	15–11	62	45	5.25
OF E. COLEMAN	768	37	183	.358	4	J. KILLEEN (2)	158	11–4	74	77	4.10
OF B. RHIEL	674	7	112	.346	7	B. POSEDEL	131	7–6	59	39	5.22
OF F. BERGER	494	9	76	.275	6	A. HOUSE (3)	129	7–4	61	62	4.60
C L. WOODALL	376	0	35	.266	0						
						(1) ALSO WITH MISSION					
O21 B. JOHNSON	504	22	94	.337	12	(2) ALSO WITH HOLLYWOOD					
C J. FITZPATRICK	347	0	46	.271	0	(3) ALSO WITH OAKLAND					
23 ROBERTSON (1)	219	0	16	.201	2	MANAGER – S. ABBOTT					
S23 G. WISE	163	0	17	.233	0	RECORD W–100 L–87 FINISH–3RD					

1931

LOS ANGELES	AB	HR	RBI	BA	SB	PITCHERS	IP	W–L	BB	SO	ERA
1B R. JACOBS	386	18	73	.298	5	W. BALLOU	286	24–13	89	160	3.71
2B L. BAKER	556	8	71	.273	7	J. PETTY	267	15–16	64	120	4.51
3B D. FARRELL	727	11	127	.327	8	L. HERRMANN	251	20–11	88	152	4.08
SS C. DITTMAR	470	8	95	.285	11	M. MOSS	243	15–14	96	118	4.59
OF H. SUMMA	754	4	89	.341	25	L. NELSON	163	5–9	69	61	5.85
OF J. STATZ	748	6	107	.332	45	A. SHEALY	109	4–8	68	48	6.61
OF V. BARTON	334	17	67	.302	4	C. YERKES	87	2–4	42	27	5.90
C G. CAMPBELL	261	10	56	.307	4						
3B F. HANEY	335	3	37	.301	24						
OF J. MOORE	317	6	69	.366	8						
C J. SCHULTE	240	5	33	.283	4	(1) ALSO WITH OAKLAND					
OF G. HARPER (1)	220	3	33	.268	2	**MANAGER – J. LELIVELT**					
C T. HANNAH	204	0	28	.265	0	**RECORD W–98 L–89 FINISH–4TH**					

OAKLAND	AB	HR	RBI	BA	SB	PITCHERS	IP	W–L	BB	SO	ERA
1B L. ANTON	570	3	56	.312	15	P. DAGLIA	279	13–20	115	132	4.64
2B R. BRUBAKER	441	1	57	.349	3	M. PEARSON	234	17–16	123	158	4.46
3B B. PINELLI (1)	553	0	63	.268	11	H. CRAGHEAD	229	13–15	100	156	4.17
SS E. MOORE	495	6	83	.315	15	F. ORTMAN	186	7–12	57	50	5.32
OF F. UHALT	691	1	62	.291	21	W. LUDOLPH	184	10–12	50	72	4.94
OF F. HUFFT (2)	645	14	92	.343	10	F. THOMAS	163	12–10	59	123	3.86
OF G. BLACKERBY	435	9	61	.292	7	R. HURST	96	1–7	42	36	4.69
C A. READ	335	0	23	.209	1						
C H. MC MULLEN	220	3	31	.341	2						
S2 M. DEAN	219	0	12	.196	2	(1) ALSO WITH SAN FRANCISCO					
OF M. POWERS	207	0	19	.300	7	(2) ALSO WITH MISSION					
O3 A. REESE	188	4	28	.271	3	**MANAGER – C. ZAMLOCH**					
2S C. LIND	150	0	10	.180	6	**RECORD W–86 L–101 FINISH–5TH (T)**					

SACRAMENTO	AB	HR	RBI	BA	SB	PITCHERS	IP	W–L	BB	SO	ERA
1B D. CAMILLI	714	16	100	.294	7	T. FREITAS	297	19–13	102	156	3.09
2B J. MC LAUGHLIN	403	1	28	.278	9	E. BRYAN	280	14–18	60	71	4.31
3B S. HACK	660	2	37	.352	20	T. FLYNN	233	16–18	92	86	4.55
SS R. FRENCH	644	1	67	.244	15	B. HUBBELL	216	13–14	50	55	4.37
OF F. DEMAREE	674	16	104	.312	13	L. GILLICK	187	8–11	69	62	3.46
OF H. STEINBACHER	503	4	66	.294	8	L. VINCI	172	3–11	62	62	5.18
OF R. ROHWER	356	10	47	.247	5	CHESTERFIELD(1)	139	7–12	72	58	6.34
C K. WIRTZ	390	5	53	.303	2						
OF F. OSBORN	259	1	44	.251	2	(1) ALSO WITH SEATTLE					
OF F. BORDAGARAY	252	5	32	.373	4	**MANAGER – B. RYAN**					
2B H. WHITE	200	0	28	.285	7	**RECORD W–86 L–101 FINISH–5TH (T)**					

1931

MISSION

		AB	HR	RBI	BA	SB	PITCHERS	IP	W–L	BB	SO	ERA
1B	G. BURNS (1)	696	18	129	.325	33	H. PILLETTE	273	16–11	44	68	3.52
2B	S. CLARKE	609	10	85	.258	17	A. COLE	273	15–17	70	110	3.82
3B	E. MULLIGAN	390	0	27	.279	12	G. CASTER	236	13–17	79	83	5.07
SS	J. COSCARART	457	0	48	.271	12	D. LIEBER	213	11–16	51	63	4.86
OF	O. ECKHARDT	745	7	117	.369	9	P. ZAHNISER (4)	196	8–16	89	58	5.09
OF	J. WELSH	628	8	89	.315	19	E. WALSH	190	14–12	68	62	4.40
OF	E. KELLY	344	2	31	.291	6	C. BRIGGS	150	5–9	64	64	5.88
C	B. BRENZEL	377	1	60	.284	2	T. PILLETTE	130	3–8	63	39	6.02
OF	P. SCOTT	256	2	34	.324	7						
SS	B. DE VIVEIROS	256	4	21	.262	5						
1B	B. DAHLGREN	234	1	23	.244	3	(1) ALSO WITH LOS ANGELES					
1B	N. HAWKS (2)	208	1	14	.296	5	(2) ALSO WITH SAN FRANCISCO					
C	F. HOFMANN	201	1	34	.299	4	(3) ALSO WITH SACRAMENTO					
OF	D. HAFEY	198	6	32	.293	0	(4) ALSO WITH SEATTLE					
C	P. RICCI (3)	162	0	17	.315	1	MANAGER – G. BURNS/ J. DEVINE					
2B	A. WRIGHT	149	0	14	.309	1	RECORD W–84 L–103 FINISH–7TH					

SEATTLE

		AB	HR	RBI	BA	SB	PITCHERS	IP	W–L	BB	SO	ERA
1B	H. TAYLOR	716	8	72	.310	30	P. PAGE	233	15–15	94	57	5.06
2B	F. MULLER	687	15	105	.281	8	R. KEATING (1)	210	8–15	03	72	4.45
3B	F. KNOTHE	675	8	109	.317	44	H. TURPIN (2)	197	9–14	50	64	5.07
SS	F. ELLSWORTH	514	3	45	.253	12	R. KALLIO (1)	194	12–13	81	78	5.71
OF	D. HOLLAND	681	19	131	.308	17	D. RUETHER (1)	160	9–13	40	43	5.00
OF	B. LAWRENCE	618	2	99	.324	14	K. BONNELLY	155	9–9	77	42	4.58
OF	L. ALMADA	584	4	75	.289	14	MC QUILLAN (1)	152	8–7	64	58	4.97
C	F. COX	426	3	60	.357	8	J. MILJUS	107	7–6	40	28	4.71
2B	S. STEWART	297	0	23	.306	20	(1) ALSO WITH PORTLAND					
OF	I. FLAGSTEAD (1)	229	1	28	.231	3	(2) ALSO WITH SAN FRANCISCO					
C	A. GASTON	196	0	35	.367	1	MANAGER – E. JOHNSON					
C	J. BOTTARINI	135	1	16	.222	0	RECORD W–83 L–104 FINISH–8TH					

PLAYOFF
SAN FRANCISCO DEFEATED HOLLYWOOD 4 GAMES TO 0

1932

PORTLAND		AB	HR	RBI	BA	SB	PITCHERS	IP	W–L	BB	SO	ERA
1B	J. KEESEY (1)	674	5	122	.309	6	B. SHORES	260	19–11	95	164	3.84
2B	J. MONROE	415	5	59	.328	11	P. ZAHNISER	229	14–10	65	65	3.98
3B	P. HIGGINS	721	33	132	.326	21	H. MC DONALD	192	13–10	59	90	3.38
SS	M. CHOSEN	351	0	22	.219	1	L. KOUPAL	183	16–6	68	67	3.25
OF	L. FINNEY	764	5	98	.351	15	J. PETERSON	180	14–9	52	68	3.90
OF	F. BERGER	574	18	105	.305	9	A. JACOBS	153	11–7	47	63	5.47
OF	B. JOHNSON	545	29	111	.330	9	J. PRUDHOMME	139	7–5	60	33	4.61
C	J. FITZPATRICK	408	0	54	.306	4	J. BOWMAN	133	10–7	47	66	4.19
							B. DIETRICH	112	5–7	51	58	3.86
2S	B. REEVES	360	1	39	.253	7						
OF	F. OSBORN (2)	311	1	32	.296	1	(1) ALSO WITH SAN FRANCISCO					
C	J. PALMISANO	289	0	28	.253	3	(2) ALSO WITH SACRAMENTO					
1B	R. JACOBS	149	5	34	.289	2	**MANAGER – S. ABBOTT**					
OF	J. MOORE	146	4	17	.336	2	**RECORD W–111 L–78 FINISH–1ST**					

HOLLYWOOD		AB	HR	RBI	BA	SB	PITCHERS	IP	W–L	BB	SO	ERA
1B	J. SHERLOCK	674	11	114	.292	25	SHELLENBACK	322	26–10	48	119	3.13
2B	O. BRANNAN	697	17	111	.311	9	V. PAGE	258	13–19	81	87	4.23
3B	M. GAZELLA	474	5	42	.232	12	M. THOMAS	229	14–18	77	88	3.66
SS	D. LEE	611	1	44	.265	10	E. YDE	226	17–9	102	112	3.94
OF	C. CARLYLE	673	16	106	.346	16	J. TURNER	194	11–10	55	52	4.59
OF	A. MC NEELEY	553	11	82	.284	9	T. SHEEHAN	181	13–6	50	87	3.03
OF	M. CALLAGHAN	511	0	42	.311	14	F. ORTMAN	82	5–4	29	26	4.06
C	J. BASSLER	443	1	66	.357	3						
3S	A. STRANGE	354	2	40	.277	4						
OF	B. MEUSEL	228	4	26	.329	4						
C	T. MAYER	175	4	32	.246	3						
OF	G. QUELLICH	175	5	30	.269	1	**MANAGER – O. VITT**					
P	SHELLENBACK	135	8	29	.296	0	**RECORD W–106 L–83 FINISH–2ND**					

SACRAMENTO		AB	HR	RBI	BA	SB	PITCHERS	IP	W–L	BB	SO	ERA
1B	D. CAMILLI	727	17	107	.308	18	E. BRYAN	271	19–13	55	59	3.79
2B	A. KAMPOURIS	549	11	88	.281	10	T. FLYNN	239	13–17	92	92	4.22
3B	L. BACKER	563	2	56	.313	8	J. DE SHONG	228	19–6	82	111	3.16
SS	R. FRENCH	661	0	71	.257	30	L. VINCI	214	13–13	80	71	4.12
OF	F. BORDAGARAY	692	5	77	.322	20	L. GILLICK	178	10–10	60	45	4.70
OF	H. STEINBACHER	578	5	82	.322	9	B. TINCUP	168	9–12	62	66	4.35
OF	F. DEMAREE	437	12	84	.364	6	M. SALVO	127	7–4	38	28	4.54
C	L. WOODALL	390	2	54	.321	2	T. FREITAS	65	6–4	28	35	3.60
O3	E. MC NEELY	377	1	28	.281	6						
C	K. WIRTZ	288	1	34	.260	3	**MANAGER – B. RYAN/E. MC NEELY**					
OF	C. LAHMAN	259	6	43	.293	1	**RECORD W–101 L–88 FINISH–3RD**					

1932

SAN FRANCISCO	AB	HR	RBI	BA	SB	PITCHERS	IP	W–L	BB	SO	ERA
1B J. DONOVAN	760	18	68	.293	18	C. DAVIS	326	22–16	57	122	2.24
2B A. GARIBALDI	740	5	81	.307	49	B. HENDERSON	276	17–12	95	172	3.10
3B J. WERA	692	0	106	.308	13	J. ZINN	258	18–15	53	95	4.47
SS A. GALAN	712	6	75	.291	14	A. MC DOUGALL	247	17–15	98	128	4.09
OF E. SULIK	662	14	101	.313	17	L. STINE	167	7–13	74	86	5.17
OF M. HUNT	529	14	84	.316	2	K. DOUGLASS	159	11–9	37	47	4.70
OF P. OANA	440	2	52	.239	5						
C C. WALLGREN	247	1	22	.247	0						
C A. PENEBSKY (1)	212	1	26	.250	2						
OF V. DI MAGGIO	200	6	31	.270	2						
C B. BRENZEL	173	0	20	.295	3	(1) ALSO WITH OAKLAND					
P J. ZINN	145	2	23	.269	2	MANAGER – J. CAVENEY					
P C. DAVIS	134	1	14	.269	0	RECORD W–96 L–90 FINISH–4TH					

LOS ANGELES	AB	HR	RBI	BA	SB	PITCHERS	IP	W–L	BB	SO	ERA
1B E. SHEELY	417	11	102	.319	6	W. BALLOU	305	18–21	87	157	4.36
2B L. BAKER	527	1	59	.202	4	F. BAECHT	258	12–14	117	133	4.58
3B F. HANEY	617	6	62	.300	29	H. STITZEL	256	13–17	86	81	4.72
SS C. DITTMAR	583	4	78	.298	9	L. HERRMANN	211	21–7	46	117	3.71
OF J. STATZ	737	6	93	.347	21	C. MONCRIEF	160	6–12	91	71	4.83
OF M. KREEVICH	561	15	70	.294	13	M. MOSS	148	11–8	76	66	4.68
OF H. SUMMA	543	0	64	.297	7	L. SWEETLAND	102	6–8	35	35	6.26
C G. CAMPBELL	498	9	93	.319	11						
OF T. STAINBACK	433	10	91	.356	17						
1B J. OGLESBY	263	5	61	.323	5						
C B. CRONIN	199	0	24	.216	1	MANAGER – J. LELIVELT					
3B G. LILLARD	141	5	28	.312	2	RECORD W–96 L–93 FINISH–5TH					

SEATTLE	AB	HR	RBI	BA	SB	PITCHERS	IP	W–L	BB	SO	ERA
1B G. BURNS	687	11	140	.354	22	P. PAGE	314	18–20	115	67	3.98
2B F. MULLER	682	38	121	.282	15	H. HAID	291	18–15	105	119	4.21
3B E. MULLIGAN (1)	548	3	42	.296	15	L. NELSON	295	22–17	104	133	4.37
SS F. ELLSWORTH	693	4	46	.255	25	R. KALLIO	285	11–20	105	121	3.79
OF J. WELSH (2)	627	7	75	.309	11	J. WALTERS	265	16–16	130	77	5.00
OF D. HOLLAND	519	15	76	.335	15						
OF L. ALMADA	438	6	45	.311	20						
C F. COX	478	3	56	.291	2						
OF P. SCOTT	367	10	71	.302	12	(1) ALSO WITH MISSION AND PORTLAND					
OF H. MAGGERT	219	10	57	.256	2	(2) ALSO WITH MISSION					
C J. BOTTARINI	198	3	28	.278	0	MANAGER – E. JOHNSON/G. BURNS					
P J. WALTERS	163	4	26	.294	2	RECORD W–90 L–95 FINISH–6TH					

1932

OAKLAND		AB	HR	RBI	BA	SB	PITCHERS	IP	W–L	BB	SO	ERA
1B	L. ANTON	562	13	88	.315	22	E. WALSH	288	19–15	85	147	3.16
2B	R. BRUBAKER	407	1	33	.270	3	W. LUDOLPH	271	16–14	62	99	2.76
3B	B. PINELLI	554	0	57	.307	16	F. THOMAS	255	12–19	93	196	3.25
SS	G. MULLEAVY	504	1	58	.321	22	R. JOINER	204	10–13	54	83	4.60
OF	F. UHALT	655	0	58	.296	15	A. WALSH (2)	146	6–15	57	56	6.10
OF	G. BLACKERBY	629	4	94	.302	11	C. FIEBER	142	8–11	83	44	5.77
OF	E. MAILHO	456	2	42	.316	16	P. DAGLIA	102	8–4	35	41	3.45
C	A. GASTON	200	1	18	.260	2	B. PHEBUS	101	2–9	50	56	5.17
OF	F. HUFFT	449	11	70	.283	5						
2S	DE VIVEIROS (1)	342	5	41	.225	2	(1) ALSO WITH SACRAMENTO AND LOS ANGELES					
3OS	H. GLAISTER	277	2	33	.256	4	(2) ALSO WITH MISSION AND LOS ANGELES					
2B	L. KINTANA	209	0	27	.249	6	**MANAGER – C. ZAMLOCH**					
C	B. RAIMONDI	121	0	6	.281	0	**RECORD W–80 L–107 FINISH–7TH**					

MISSION		AB	HR	RBI	BA	SB	PITCHERS	IP	W–L	BB	SO	ERA
1B	B. DAHLGREN	722	11	101	.287	8	B. COLE	236	12–16	51	79	3.52
2B	A. WRIGHT	533	2	68	.287	4	T. PILLETTE	228	13–14	64	53	3.83
3B	J. COSCARART	391	1	34	.271	3	H. PILLETTE	209	11–12	40	52	4.31
SS	B. SANKEY (1)	555	0	42	.250	1	D. LIEBER	241	13–18	46	60	4.03
OF	L. ALMADA (2)	557	3	89	.320	30	C. BRIGGS	131	4–11	53	53	4.76
OF	O. ECKHARDT	539	5	82	.371	15	D. RUETHER	103	3–9	30	29	4.21
OF	D. HAFEY	457	10	67	.293	15	W. OSBORNE	100	2–6	35	29	5.31
C	F. HOFMANN	287	2	33	.251	1	G. BOWLER	92	4–3	34	37	4.31
23S	V. SHERLOCK	377	1	35	.263	7						
S3	M. KOENIG	322	0	23	.335	4						
C	P. RICCI (3)	297	0	21	.222	0	(1) ALSO WITH PORTLAND					
OF	F. FRAZIER (3)	254	2	42	.319	12	(2) ALSO WITH SEATTLE					
3B	D. GYSELMAN	226	1	34	.319	0	(3) ALSO WITH SAN FRANCISCO					
OF	P. KELMAN	132	0	7	.242	4	**MANAGER – J. DEVINE/F. HOFMANN**					
OF	H. ANDERSON	124	0	13	.306	5	**RECORD W–71 L–117 FINISH–8TH**					

PLAYOFFS
NONE

1933

LOS ANGELES	AB	HR	RBI	BA	SB	PITCHERS	IP	W–L	BB	SO	ERA
1B J. OGLESBY	723	20	137	.313	14	B. NEWSOM	320	30–11	124	212	3.17
2B J. REESE	393	5	38	.331	3	F. THOMAS	300	20–14	104	159	3.75
3B G. LILLARD	645	43	149	.307	2	D. WARD	285	25–9	114	172	3.25
SS C. DITTMAR	478	5	49	.264	2	W. BALLOU	217	12–19	69	122	3.69
OF T. STAINBACK	789	19	148	.335	19	L. HERRMANN	188	16–9	54	98	4.59
OF J. STATZ	767	10	73	.325	17	H. STITZEL	105	4–3	45	26	4.80
OF M. GUDAT	741	10	113	.333	25	E. NELSON	96	3–6	55	45	4.86
C H. MC MULLEN	400	11	59	.268	3						
S3 O. MOHLER (1)	484	8	68	.287	15						
C B. CRONIN	254	2	31	.303	1	(1) ALSO WITH MISSION					
2B M. GAZELLA	235	7	47	.264	4	MANAGER – J. LELIVELT					
P B. NEWSOM	123	0	15	.285	0	RECORD W–114 L–73 FINISH–1ST					

PORTLAND	AB	HR	RBI	BA	SB	PITCHERS	IP	W–L	BB	SO	ERA
1B E. SHEELY	454	13	100	.359	0	J. BOWMAN	283	23–11	65	155	4.17
2B J. MONROE	576	7	62	.323	20	S. GIBSON	234	15–14	60	132	4.00
3B E. MULLIGAN	694	2	56	.294	43	W. RADONITZ	220	13–15	64	60	4.30
SS B. SANKEY	587	2	47	.261	5	R. KALLIO	211	17–7	58	97	3.42
OF P. OANA	686	29	163	.332	11	L. KOUPAL	210	16–9	82	68	4.25
OF G. BLACKERBY	614	4	92	.340	11	A. JACOBS	185	17–7	65	68	4.61
OF F. BERGER	595	14	93	.313	5	H. TURPIN	104	6–9	23	35	2.93
C J. PALMISANO	437	2	41	.295	4	T. FREITAS	75	4–7	15	48	3.98
1B J. KEESEY	334	4	56	.299	1						
S23 B. REEVES	209	1	24	.239	4	MANAGER – S. ABBOTT					
OF B. LOANE	156	10	40	.288	4	RECORD W–105 L–77 FINISH–2ND					

HOLLYWOOD	AB	HR	RBI	BA	SB	PITCHERS	IP	W–L	BB	SO	ERA
1B R. JACOBS	564	36	125	.284	9	SHELLENBACK	314	21–12	74	124	4.53
2B O. BRANNAN	717	14	108	.303	11	A. CAMPBELL	311	22–15	124	137	4.08
3B F. HANEY	719	2	65	.317	63	V. PAGE	293	20–15	82	93	4.54
SS A. STRANGE	490	6	81	.324	10	T. SHEEHAN	271	21–13	88	95	4.25
OF C. DURST	730	14	80	.318	23	B. WETZEL	177	14–10	59	59	4.92
OF C. CARLYLE	584	9	94	.320	14						
OF D. TAITT	378	15	67	.336	3						
C J. BASSLER	330	0	50	.336	1						
OF V. DI MAGGIO (1)	339	11	65	.333	7						
S3 J. BERKOWITZ	266	0	26	.305	4						
C L. SUMMERS	162	1	15	.235	2						
OF L. MARTIN	144	3	24	.299	2	(1) ALSO WITH SAN FRANCISCO					
C F. TOBIN	138	3	11	.254	1	MANAGER – O. VITT					
P F. SHELLENBACK	140	8	30	.243	0	RECORD W–107 L–80 FINISH–3RD					

1933

SACRAMENTO		AB	HR	RBI	BA	SB	PITCHERS		IP	W–L	BB	SO	ERA
1B	D. CAMILLI	622	20	116	.293	10	E. BRYAN		318	21–17	54	78	5.15
2B	A. KAMPOURIS	724	13	123	.304	47	L. VINCI		262	18–12	103	80	3.64
3B	L. BACKER	633	3	72	.333	5	T. FLYNN		227	16–11	101	99	4.56
SS	R. FRENCH	624	4	75	.269	23	L. GILLICK		195	11–12	65	68	5.02
OF	H. STEINBACHER	628	5	112	.307	4	B. HORNE (1)		142	9–7	50	86	3.48
OF	F. BORDAGARAY	416	7	65	.351	10	M. SALVO		114	5–11	18	49	3.86
OF	C. LAHMAN	462	3	66	.262	6	W. HARTWIG		108	5–7	44	37	4.83
C	L. WOODALL	346	2	31	.312	3	J. NOONAN		100	4–4	47	30	6.22
							H. SANDERS		83	6–7	39	24	5.00
O3	T. BOROJA	487	14	58	.298	10							
C	K. WIRTZ	295	3	36	.261	0	(1) ALSO WITH OAKLAND						
OF	E. MC NEELY	279	5	20	.308	15	**MANAGER – E. MC NEELY**						
P	E. BRYAN	162	0	25	.290	0	**RECORD W–96 L–85 FINISH–4TH**						

OAKLAND		AB	HR	RBI	BA	SB	PITCHERS		IP	W–L	BB	SO	ERA
1B	L. ANTON	623	5	104	.305	37	R. JOINER		283	22–14	54	123	4.14
2B	C. LAVAGETTO	509	7	100	.312	18	W. LUDOLPH		262	19–9	59	74	3.09
3B	J. WERA	582	1	74	.259	7	G. GABLER		235	9–15	73	82	4.64
SS	B. DE VIVEIROS	307	2	32	.244	0	L. MC EVOY		227	13–15	87	62	5.95
OF	E. MAILHO	690	4	58	.303	52	E. WALSH		193	13–8	78	61	4.76
OF	F. UHALT	632	4	89	.350	62	M. SALINSEN		182	9–12	56	35	4.90
OF	H. POOL	630	5	126	.348	21	C. FIEBER		113	5–9	101	66	5.40
C	A. VELTMAN	500	12	86	.332	10							
2S1	L. KINTANA	487	5	59	.255	6							
C	B. RAIMONDI	270	0	34	.289	3	(1) ALSO WITH LOS ANGELES						
SS	M. CHOSEN (1)	209	2	22	.258	1	**MANAGER – R. BRUBAKER**						
OF	P. SCOTT	162	0	26	.327	5	**RECORD W–93 L–92 FINISH–5TH**						

SAN FRANCISCO		AB	HR	RBI	BA	SB	PITCHERS		IP	W–L	BB	SO	ERA
1B	J. FENTON	619	4	75	.315	3	J. ZINN		317	20–19	69	99	4.12
2B	A. GARIBALDI	729	7	102	.309	26	C. DAVIS		283	20–16	56	86	3.97
3B	L. OSTENBERG	470	23	113	.328	3	L. STINE		244	12–14	122	134	4.72
SS	A. GALAN	745	9	102	.356	41	B. HENDERSON		189	7–16	104	83	5.33
OF	J. DI MAGGIO	762	28	169	.340	10	E. STUTZ		157	6–9	71	51	5.57
OF	E. SULIK	488	2	59	.293	13	K. DOUGLASS		143	7–9	47	65	4.72
OF	L. FUNK	426	3	48	.298	13	B. CUNNINGHAM		115	5–10	42	38	5.48
C	J. BOTTARINI	396	13	69	.301	1	A. MC DOUGALL		81	3–7	37	37	5.22
OF	J. DONOVAN	287	4	38	.307	2							
C	E. MC ISSAC	263	0	28	.240	0							
P	J. ZINN	178	4	22	.275	0	(1) ALSO WITH MISSION						
OF	M. HUNT (1)	168	6	42	.304	3	**MANAGER – J. CAVENEY**						
P	C. DAVIS	154	4	18	.305	1	**RECORD W–81 L–106 FINISH–6TH**						

1933

MISSION		AB	HR	RBI	BA	SB	PITCHERS	IP	W−L	BB	SO	ERA
1B	B. DAHLGREN	733	6	110	.315	4	L. JOHNSON	281	16−20	111	126	4.39
2B	V. SHERLOCK	543	1	56	.276	8	J. BABICH	274	20−15	99	133	3.62
3B	B. WALTERS	362	16	92	.376	7	D. LIEBER	253	15−16	61	80	5.05
SS	C. SEVER (1)	680	1	45	.269	4	T. PILLETTE	206	10−17	69	51	5.76
OF	O. ECKHARDT	760	12	143	.414	15	B. COLE	203	8−17	59	44	6.02
OF	L. ALMADA	625	6	72	.357	11	B. PHEBUS	166	7−12	80	72	5.43
OF	D. HAFEY	490	16	94	.292	12	W. OSBORNE	146	2−7	55	57	5.25
C	J. FITZPATRICK	477	2	71	.306	4						
OF	A. MOORE (2)	452	2	65	.296	4						
23S	A. WRIGHT	325	0	33	.249	2	(1) ALSO WITH SAN FRANCISCO					
3B	B. FRIBERG	254	2	30	.272	1	(2) ALSO WITH PORTLAND					
P	B. COLE	138	0	12	.295	0	**MANAGER − F. HOFMANN**					
C	M. DUGGAN	137	0	15	.263	0	**RECORD W−79 L−108 FINISH−7TH**					

SEATTLE		AB	HR	RBI	BA	SB	PITCHERS	IP	W−L	BB	SO	ERA
1B	G. BURNS	640	27	128	.337	11	P. PAGE	286	10−24	103	82	5.72
2B	F. MULLER	294	20	66	.327	5	G. GASIER	264	12−19	126	114	5.80
3B	J. COSCARART	602	14	81	.306	4	H. PILLETTE (1)	254	13−14	57	73	4.68
SS	F. ELLSWORTH	585	5	52	.244	12	H. ULRICH	173	5−15	54	40	5.57
OF	J. WELSH	696	8	79	.290	10	E. SEWELL	151	6−17	72	54	5.89
OF	L. ALMADA	632	5	44	.323	28	H. HAID	150	6−8	44	51	3.35
OF	N. BONGIOVANNI	300	0	28	.263	4	J. WALTERS	114	4−8	51	25	5.77
C	A. BRADBURY	399	12	68	.283	0						
SS	A. MC LARNEY	317	2	28	.268	2						
OF	H. SUMMA	288	2	33	.354	6						
C	F. COX	278	0	30	.263	2						
23	D. JOHNSON	269	1	16	.234	8	(1) ALSO WITH MISSION					
OP	J. WALTERS	268	17	52	.284	2	**MANAGER − G. BURNS**					
PO	E. SEWELL	149	3	14	.255	2	**RECORD W−65 L−119 FINISH−8TH**					

PLAYOFFS
NONE

1934

LOS ANGELES		AB	HR	RBI	BA	SB	PITCHERS	IP	W–L	BB	SO	ERA
1B	J. OGLESBY	725	15	139	.312	11	F. THOMAS	295	28–4	118	204	2.59
2B	J. REESE	733	3	85	.311	14	L. GARLAND	249	21–9	80	91	2.67
3B	G. LILLARD	592	27	119	.289	10	M. MEOLA	248	20–5	90	93	2.90
SS	C. DITTMAR	517	3	73	.294	7	J. CAMPBELL	243	19–15	80	80	2.63
OF	J. STATZ	760	6	66	.324	61	R. HENSHAW	196	16–4	90	120	2.75
OF	M. GUDAT	758	4	125	.319	43	E. NELSON	171	14–5	57	72	2.53
OF	F. DEMAREE	702	45	173	.383	41	D. WARD	137	13–4	53	54	2.63
C	G. CAMPBELL	459	17	97	.305	14						
C	W. GOBEL	148	2	29	.297	0						
SS	B. MATTICK	137	0	10	.277	2						
32S	M. GAZELLA	116	1	13	.190	0	MANAGER – J. LELIVELT					
P	F. THOMAS	113	1	18	.257	0	RECORD W–137 L–50 FINISH–1ST					

MISSION		AB	HR	RBI	BA	SB	PITCHERS	IP	W–L	BB	SO	ERA
1B	B. DAHLGREN	735	20	136	.302	11	D. LIEBER	284	19–13	83	77	2.50
2B	A. WRIGHT	674	0	83	.286	5	W. OSBORNE	266	16–19	87	107	3.65
3B	J. STRONER	602	5	101	.282	5	C. MITCHELL	253	19–12	70	63	3.67
SS	C. BECK	626	2	66	.208	2	S. THURSTON	233	15–10	65	66	3.20
OF	L. ALMADA	797	2	65	.332	23	L. JOHNSON	148	7–10	55	45	4.82
OF	O. ECKHARDT	707	6	106	.378	7	J. BABICH	120	10–3	43	46	2.03
OF	D. HAFEY	612	16	88	.322	10	B. HORNE (1)	114	7–7	38	52	4.33
C	J. FITZPATRICK	521	0	65	.278	4	P. DAGLIA	111	4–7	33	34	4.31
OF	A. MOORE	191	0	22	.199	2						
C	M. DUGGAN	137	0	15	.226	1	(1) ALSO WITH SACRAMENTO					
P	S. THURSTON	119	2	14	.252	0	MANAGER – G. STREET					
3S	H. SAND	111	0	8	.243	1	RECORD W–101 L–85 FINISH–2ND					

HOLLYWOOD		AB	HR	RBI	BA	SB	PITCHERS	IP	W–L	BB	SO	ERA
1B	R. JACOBS	597	24	112	.288	9	J. SULLIVAN	288	25–11	132	163	2.88
2B	J. BERKOWITZ	373	3	23	.279	4	T. SHEEHAN	237	16–14	77	102	3.69
3B	F. HANEY	702	1	76	.306	71	J. DENSMORE	230	14–11	92	123	4.84
SS	J. LEVEY	718	7	63	.256	39	SHELLENBACK	229	14–12	50	80	4.17
OF	S. JOLLEY	631	23	133	.360	7	A. CAMPBELL	191	12–13	74	76	4.81
OF	V. DI MAGGIO	587	17	91	.288	7	W. HEBERT	170	11–11	49	53	4.23
OF	C. CARLYLE	459	4	58	.272	9						
C	HERSHBERGER	332	3	46	.307	7						
O1	C. DURST	438	4	61	.299	3						
C	J. BASSLER	308	0	55	.351	2						
2B	B. DOERR	201	0	11	.259	1						
OF	F. BELL	145	8	30	.283	2	MANAGER – O. VITT					
P	J. SULLIVAN	114	0	9	.228	0	RECORD W–97 L–88 FINISH–3RD					

1934

SAN FRANCISCO	AB	HR	RBI	BA	SB	PITCHERS	IP	W–L	BB	SO	ERA
1B J. FENTON	498	6	70	.293	6	L. HERRMANN	325	27–13	78	151	3.10
2B A. GARIBALDI	725	1	86	.286	28	J. ZINN	320	14–17	64	71	3.48
3B S. BARATH	172	3	18	.256	3	S. GIBSON	313	21–17	74	171	2.96
SS H. RHYNE	675	0	65	.258	15	W. BALLOU	210	13–12	64	117	3.39
OF L. FUNK	619	0	47	.288	12	K. SHEEHAN	187	5–10	75	101	3.46
OF J. MARTY	513	2	55	.275	19	W. MAILS	167	4–13	62	74	4.14
OF E. SULIK	427	1	31	.246	14	E. STUTZ	138	8–10	53	35	2.94
C L. WOODALL	402	0	39	.251	1						
23 L. BACKER	407	2	53	.263	3						
OF J. DI MAGGIO	375	12	69	.341	8						
OF J. THOMAS	195	1	18	.215	5						
31S F. GIRA	191	0	15	.230	1						
C V. MONZO	169	0	24	.278	0	MANAGER – J. CAVENEY					
P J. ZINN	135	1	22	.296	0	RECORD W–93 L–95 FINISH–4TH					

OAKLAND	AB	HR	RBI	BA	SB	PITCHERS	IP	W–L	BB	SO	ERA
1B L. ANTON	653	19	100	.312	31	K. DOUGLASS(3)	240	14–10	74	89	3.48
2B L. KINTANA	594	0	82	.285	9	H. HAID	237	13–18	77	82	4.11
3B E. MULLIGAN	722	0	44	.269	45	L. MC EVOY	235	12–15	95	64	3.87
SS B. DE VIVEIROS	436	2	47	.253	3	W. LUDOLPH	231	16–12	53	58	3.97
OF S. KEYES	680	19	99	.310	18	T. CONLAN	220	16–13	81	54	3.57
OF E. KELLY	532	0	51	.299	10	J. REGO	177	6–9	99	104	4.52
OF F. UHALT	304	0	28	.299	23	E. WALSH	158	7–11	70	46	5.22
C B. RAIMONDI	529	1	70	.284	10						
						(1) ALSO WITH SACRAMENTO					
SS R. FRENCH (1)	241	0	19	.228	9	(2) ALSO WITH SEATTLE					
OF J. WELSH (2)	206	1	12	.194	2	(3) ALSO WITH MISSION					
OF H. POOL	170	0	25	.329	4	MANAGER – R. BRUBAKER					
OF A. RUBLE	126	0	13	.254	1	RECORD W–90 L–98 FINISH–5TH					

SEATTLE	AB	HR	RBI	BA	SB	PITCHERS	IP	W–L	BB	SO	ERA
1B E. SHEELY (1)	640	7	101	.313	5	H. CRAGHEAD	280	16–21	110	145	4.34
2B A. HARRINGTON	575	3	54	.299	7	H. PILLETTE	260	17–11	45	87	2.60
3B J. COSCARART	700	6	63	.294	19	W. RADONITS	233	13–15	76	80	4.40
SS F. ELLSWORTH	472	4	36	.265	7	G. CASTER (1)	233	13–15	95	104	3.40
OF F. BERGER	659	19	112	.323	10	H. ULRICH (1)	189	6–15	57	49	5.57
OF M. HUNT	644	30	128	.346	8	C. YERKES	132	10–12	57	47	5.24
OF B. LAWRENCE (1)	591	3	84	.298	11						
C J. BOTTARINI	425	8	52	.299	0						
SS C. SMITH	266	4	30	.226	3	(1) ALSO WITH PORTLAND					
C A. BRADBURY	163	5	30	.282	1	MANAGER – G. BURNS/D. RUETHER					
21 H. MICHAEL	147	3	15	.218	1	RECORD W–81 L–102 FINISH–6TH					

1934

SACRAMENTO		AB	HR	RBI	BA	SB	PITCHERS	IP	W–L	BB	SO	ERA
1B	L. POWERS	751	0	77	.286	20	M. SALVO	271	15–18	82	112	3.32
2B	A. KAMPOURIS	422	19	64	.277	21	T. FLYNN	258	16–16	83	91	3.72
3B	L. OSTENBERG	614	23	104	.277	1	O. NITCHOLAS	223	11–13	50	68	4.44
SS	T. KRASOVICH	344	3	29	.235	7	P. GREGORY	221	15–16	72	70	4.11
OF	H. STEINBACHER	755	2	97	.313	15	L. KOUPAL	212	11–15	66	79	3.94
OF	J. DONOVAN	670	8	65	.278	17	L. VINCI (1)	194	6–10	81	58	3.15
OF	F. BORDAGARAY	483	6	46	.321	23	W. HARTWIG	179	3–15	68	60	4.32
C	K. WIRTZ	276	2	32	.236	0	G. GABLER (2)	136	3–9	44	28	3.58
O23	T. BOROJA	447	9	53	.251	8						
C	B. SALKELD	204	1	18	.255	1						
C	T. MAYER	191	4	26	.314	1	(1) ALSO WITH SEATTLE					
SS	H. WARREN	156	0	17	.224	1	(2) ALSO WITH OAKLAND					
OF	C. LAHMAN (1)	156	2	11	.244	1	**MANAGER – E. MC NEELY**					
SS	H. COSBEY	136	0	11	.228	2	**RECORD W–79 L–109 FINISH–7TH**					

PORTLAND		AB	HR	RBI	BA	SB	PITCHERS	IP	W–L	BB	SO	ERA
1B	G. BURNS (1)	394	2	54	.292	3	H. TURPIN	320	15–22	58	89	4.05
2B	S. COSCARART	595	3	60	.311	7	E. BRYAN	309	11–24	81	77	3.53
3B	G. ENGLISH	634	9	73	.279	11	R. KALLIO (1)	207	13–18	93	74	4.22
SS	C. WILBURN	741	2	50	.283	6	E. BRAME (3)	180	10–16	44	36	5.30
OF	G. BLACKERBY	623	8	83	.270	6	J. WILSON	158	9–9	96	71	4.26
OF	BONGIOVANNI (1)	543	2	57	.346	8						
OF	M. CLABAUGH	443	16	73	.305	17						
C	F. COX	442	3	54	.317	2						
1B	R. GARRETSON	256	2	22	.227	1	(1) ALSO WITH SEATTLE					
C	H. DOERR (1)	199	1	14	.256	2	(2) ALSO WITH LOS ANGELES					
2B	P. COSCARART	198	1	20	.253	2	(3) ALSO WITH MISSION					
OF	B. LOANE (2)	183	1	10	.213	8	**MANAGER – W. MC CREEDIE/T. TURNER/**					
2B	J. MC LEOD	152	1	8	.211	1	**G. BURNS/G. BLACKERBY**					
P	E. BRYAN	134	1	12	.254	0	**RECORD W–66 L–117 FINISH–8TH**					

PLAYOFFS
NONE

1935

SAN FRANCISCO	AB	HR	RBI	BA	SB	PITCHERS	IP	W−L	BB	SO	ERA
1B L. POWERS	704	4	79	.308	30	S. GIBSON	252	22−4	48	121	3.46
2B A. GARIBALDI	731	7	89	.298	26	J. DENSMORE	247	14−14	105	120	3.94
3B L. BACKER	525	0	78	.310	6	W. BALLOU	220	18−8	69	94	3.28
SS H. RHYNE	523	1	81	.294	12	R. JOINER (2)	200	14−5	33	84	3.74
OF J. DI MAGGIO	679	34	154	.398	24	K. SHEEHAN	173	7−8	97	87	3.49
OF J. MARTY	609	6	98	.287	25	E. STUTZ	163	11−13	50	62	4.81
OF T. NORBERT	524	11	103	.302	30	J. ZINN (1)	134	7−7	29	42	4.43
C L. WOODALL	257	0	43	.354	1	H. STITZEL (3)	132	7−14	52	56	4.49
						F. NEWKIRK	112	8−5	54	43	5.24
3O S. BARATH	218	1	39	.330	6						
C V. MONZO	208	2	33	.322	1	(1) ALSO WITH SACRAMENTO					
C J. BECKER	207	0	42	.372	2	(2) ALSO WITH LOS ANGELES					
OF L. O'DOUL	134	2	25	.269	3	(3) ALSO WITH MISSION					
SS F. GIRA	110	0	3	.309	3	MANAGER − L. O'DOUL					
P J. ZINN (1)	101	1	11	.238	0	RECORD W−103 L−70 FINISH−1ST					

LOS ANGELES	AB	HR	RBI	BA	SB	PITCHERS	IP	W−L	BB	SO	ERA
1B J. OGLESBY	678	24	132	.350	18	M. MEOLA	258	19−8	74	103	3.00
2B J. REESE	578	1	66	.297	9	L. GARLAND	238	19−11	98	93	3.48
3B G. LILLARD	642	56	147	.361	8	J. CAMPBELL	191	13−10	81	70	4.15
SS S. MESNER	634	13	99	.331	6	N. KIMBALL	169	8−10	94	101	5.80
OF M. GUDAT	735	2	65	.309	52	G. GABLER	151	14−8	37	37	4.04
OF J. STATZ	716	2	65	.330	53	R. BUXTON	134	7−7	47	64	3.90
OF C. CARLYLE	653	11	100	.297	13	E. NELSON	121	11−5	37	68	3.13
C W. GOBEL	287	4	36	.258	2	H. HARRIS	100	3−7	34	30	4.95
						K. FRAZIER	71	1−7	44	19	6.08
S2 C. DITTMAR	215	0	36	.260	2						
C G. GIBSON	180	2	21	.194	0	MANAGER − J. LELIVELT					
SS B. MATTICK	131	0	18	.267	2	RECORD W−98 L−76 FINISH−2ND					

OAKLAND	AB	HR	RBI	BA	SB	PITCHERS	IP	W−L	BB	SO	ERA
1B L. ANTON	585	13	76	.306	23	W. LUDOLPH	283	20−13	40	74	3.09
2B F. MULLER	556	13	109	.266	9	K. DOUGLASS	245	16−12	57	75	4.15
3B F. HAWKINS	578	3	55	.292	7	H. MC DONALD	216	14−11	49	95	3.25
SS K. MOLESWORTH	597	0	97	.313	8	T. CONLAN	211	11−12	88	54	5.08
OF E. MAILHO	652	2	88	.353	36	J. TOBIN	152	11−8	59	68	4.14
OF F. UHALT	581	4	52	.324	33	H. HAID	117	5−6	18	45	3.69
OF S. KEYES	468	17	84	.293	3	G. DARROW	95	4−10	36	31	5.21
C B. RAIMONDI	355	0	38	.256	3	J. REGO	75	6−4	38	43	4.46
U B. DE VIVEIROS	320	3	24	.253	3						
C N. KIES	213	1	27	.244	0	(1) ALSO WITH MISSION					
OF F. BELL	156	2	26	.314	3	MANAGER − O. VITT					
OF WORTHINGTON (1)	154	2	19	.247	1	RECORD W−91 L−83 FINISH−3RD					

1935

PORTLAND		AB	HR	RBI	BA	SB	PITCHERS		IP	W−L	BB	SO	ERA
1B	H. DAVIS	566	2	64	.314	7	H. CARSON		272	18−14	61	58	3.71
2B	B. CISSELL	646	8	84	.316	14	J. WADE		263	17−15	166	153	3.98
3B	G. ENGLISH	675	8	118	.327	9	H. ULRICH		216	13−12	64	62	5.13
SS	C. WILBURN	710	5	60	.317	28	S. CHANDLER (3)	179		7−9	51	82	4.27
OF	N. BONGIOVANNI	722	5	63	.338	18	B. POSEDEL		161	12−7	31	93	3.69
OF	M. CLABAUGH	565	16	116	.342	21	W. RADONITS (1)	126		7−6	29	49	4.93
OF	G. HOLT	305	8	55	.298	3							
C	B. CRONIN	456	0	52	.246	5	(1) ALSO WITH MISSION AND SEATTLE						
							(2) ALSO WITH LOS ANGELES						
O3	H. RICE (1)	537	2	70	.305	8	(3) ALSO WITH OAKLAND						
OF	G. BLACKERBY	217	1	34	.286	4	MANAGER − B. RYAN/B. CISSELL						
C	H. DOERR (2)	140	0	18	.214	1	RECORD W−87 L−86 FINISH−4TH						

MISSION		AB	HR	RBI	BA	SB	PITCHERS		IP	W−L	BB	SO	ERA
1B	R. MORT	572	6	90	.267	7	W. BECK		354	23−18	143	202	4.07
2B	A. WRIGHT	698	1	84	.288	9	W. OSBORNE		253	18−11	75	101	3.56
3B	E. JOOST	533	1	83	.287	8	O. NITCHOLAS		243	12−17	85	91	5.07
SS	C. BECK	604	5	96	.276	4	S. THURSTON		201	15−10	49	46	4.80
OF	L. ALMADA	741	3	65	.301	14	C. MITCHELL		152	6−11	31	32	5.09
OF	O. ECKHARDT	710	2	114	.399	8	L. JOHNSON		149	7−9	71	62	6.28
OF	F. BERGER	633	23	137	.310	5							
C	C. OUTEN	428	7	62	.367	1							
3B	E. MULLIGAN (1)	245	0	21	.257	11							
1P	S. THURSTON	223	2	35	.220	1	(1) ALSO WITH HOLLYWOOD						
C	M. FRANKOVICH	212	2	26	.283	0	MANAGER − G. STREET						
P	W. BECK	141	0	11	.191	1	RECORD W−87 L−87 FINISH−5TH						

SEATTLE		AB	HR	RBI	BA	SB	PITCHERS		IP	W−L	BB	SO	ERA
1B	H. MICHAEL	430	11	73	.319	4	D. BARRETT		305	22−13	119	191	3.51
2B	A. HARRINGTON	399	3	43	.282	5	H. CRAGHEAD		276	18−16	101	120	4.07
3B	D. GYSELMAN	611	9	100	.303	18	E. BRYAN (1)		259	15−19	62	54	4.27
SS	C. SMITH	571	13	56	.266	10	H. PILLETTE (2)		201	14−15	40	63	4.66
OF	M. HUNT	639	25	112	.330	12	P. DAGLIA		181	13−8	42	92	3.93
OF	B. LAWRENCE	608	7	86	.319	23	C. PICKREL		176	6−16	75	67	5.16
OF	J. DONOVAN	530	18	80	.298	22	R. LUCAS (3)		123	6−11	54	26	5.40
C	J. BOTTARINI	312	12	50	.276	2	L. VINCI		95	1−5	54	44	7.86
							M. THOMAS		72	4−6	25	38	5.62
2S	E. TAYLOR	322	4	24	.280	5							
C	H. SPINDEL	228	4	31	.276	6	(1) ALSO WITH PORTLAND						
1B	G. GRANTHAM	168	1	13	.286	1	(2) ALSO WITH HOLLYWOOD						
OF	H. BONETTI	134	0	7	.254	5	(3) ALSO WITH MISSION						
P	E. BRYAN (1)	125	0	24	.296	1	MANAGER − D. RUETHER						
P	D. BARRETT	117	1	19	.282	1	RECORD W−80 L−93 FINISH−6TH						

1935

SACRAMENTO		AB	HR	RBI	BA	SB	PITCHERS	IP	W−L	BB	SO	ERA
1B	J. FREDERICK	628	3	93	.363	6	A. HERRING	267	19−14	78	134	4.41
2B	D. JOHNSON	630	7	81	.271	21	M. SALVO	248	11−17	83	121	3.33
3B	T. BOROJA	457	4	64	.276	4	T. FLYNN	248	11−15	93	106	3.70
SS	R. OLSEN	566	1	39	.265	10	L. KOUPAL	239	12−19	45	103	3.95
OF	H. STEINBACHER	661	4	85	.309	10	P. GREGORY	236	11−16	51	83	4.27
OF	H. ROSENBERG	567	10	80	.354	15	W. HARTWIG	179	6−14	48	67	4.12
OF	M. WEST	319	5	54	.266	0						
C	B. SALKELD	322	2	37	.261	5						
S3	F. ELLSWORTH	298	2	25	.245	2						
C	R. BERRES	285	1	35	.225	2						
2B	G. CHAPMAN	177	3	26	.311	4						
1B	R. DE FORREST	167	0	10	.198	0	MANAGER − K. WIRTZ/E. MC NEELY					
1B	J. MC CARTHY	165	0	13	.218	0	RECORD W−75 L−100 FINISH−7TH					

HOLLYWOOD		AB	HR	RBI	BA	SB	PITCHERS	IP	W−L	BB	SO	ERA
1B	R. JACOBS	402	13	69	.296	11	E. WELLS	264	9−20	55	80	4.33
2B	B. DOERR	647	4	74	.317	5	A. CAMPBELL	241	12−17	99	105	4.51
3B	J. LEVEY	532	2	47	.278	7	W. HEBERT	219	10−17	50	79	4.94
SS	G. MYATT	530	1	33	.311	22	SHELLENBACK	200	14−9	33	82	3.42
OF	V. DI MAGGIO	659	24	112	.278	15	B. HORNE (1)	174	13−7	50	73	3.99
OF	C. DURST	639	6	72	.324	9	J. HILE	148	1−7	52	51	5.24
OF	S. JOLLEY	599	29	128	.372	0						
C	G. DESAUTELS	426	6	55	.265	8						
S3	J. BERKOWITZ	222	0	21	.275	4						
1B	G. MC DONALD	212	0	23	.255	1						
C	J. KERR	193	4	31	.269	0	(1) ALSO WITH MISSION					
OF	V. WIRTHMAN	131	1	9	.260	1	MANAGER − F. SHELLENBACK					
P	E. WELLS	121	0	10	.240	0	RECORD W−73 L−99 FINISH−8TH					

PLAYOFF
SAN FRANCISCO DEFEATED LOS ANGELES 4 GAMES TO 2

1936

PORTLAND	AB	HR	RBI	BA	SB	PITCHERS	IP	W–L	BB	SO	ERA
1B J. FREDERICK	644	9	103	.352	4	G. CASTER	339	25–13	102	234	2.79
2B P. COSCARART	602	3	58	.233	7	B. POSEDEL	265	20–10	87	175	2.82
3B F. BEDORE	629	4	100	.337	3	A. LISKA	223	15–12	68	97	2.91
SS D. LEE	613	0	49	.250	9	H. CARSON	210	12–13	59	45	4.37
OF N. BONGIOVANNI	610	2	46	.264	16	D. FRENCH	128	4–7	60	104	3.66
OF M. CLABAUGH	559	20	112	.317	6	T. FLYNN	115	8–8	46	39	5.24
OF S. COSCARART	278	2	54	.259	5	W. RADONITS	100	7–6	14	52	4.14
C E. BRUCKER	469	9	82	.339	3	S. LARKIN	96	4–7	56	48	5.34
1B B. SWEENEY	314	3	37	.309	1						
O3 G. HOLT	283	6	40	.272	0						
OS R. HOWELL	212	0	20	.278	3	MANAGER – M. BISHOP/B. SWEENEY					
C B. CRONIN	167	0	20	.228	0	RECORD W–96 L–79 FINISH–1ST					

OAKLAND	AB	HR	RBI	BA	SB	PITCHERS	IP	W–L	BB	SO	ERA
1B L. ANTON	555	7	70	.317	37	J. LA ROCCA	258	17–13	104	154	3.03
2B D. LODIGIANI	554	4	60	.280	10	W. LUDOLPH	250	21–6	45	80	2.70
3B J. HITCHCOCK	667	3	74	.271	20	K. DOUGLASS	244	15–16	69	101	3.21
SS J. GORDON	533	6	56	.300	9	J. TOBIN	230	16–8	65	110	4.38
OF J. GLYNN	714	3	95	.297	15	F. OLDS	191	11–16	58	56	4.29
OF E. BOLYARD	608	3	73	.306	12	H. HAID	134	6–6	42	59	2.42
OF F. BELL	479	9	80	.313	7	T. CONLAN	100	5–9	36	31	4.86
C C. HARTJE	276	2	30	.322	6	H. MC DONALD	70	3–3	29	19	3.98
C HERSHBERGER	259	1	40	.263	5						
S23 B. DE VIVEIROS	241	0	21	.241	5						
OF H. POOL	221	0	43	.394	1						
OF F. UHALT	157	1	20	.299	7	MANAGER – B. MEYER					
P1 J. TOBIN	153	0	18	.261	2	RECORD W–95 L–81 FINISH–2ND (T)					

SAN DIEGO	AB	HR	RBI	BA	SB	PITCHERS	IP	W–L	BB	SO	ERA
1B G. MC DONALD	334	0	52	.317	3	M. SALVO	239	15–12	74	145	3.31
2B B. DOERR	695	2	77	.342	30	W. HEBERT	229	18–12	51	87	3.03
3B E. HOLMAN	627	6	108	.314	17	E. WELLS (1)	196	9–13	60	62	4.32
SS G. MYATT	652	1	50	.276	33	H. PILLETTE	191	11–8	37	63	3.16
OF V. DI MAGGIO	641	19	102	.293	22	D. WARD (2)	184	15–7	100	83	3.42
OF C. DURST	621	1	81	.306	14	B. HORNE	164	7–14	78	76	4.39
OF V. WIRTHMAN	428	1	49	.287	6	A. CAMPBELL	129	6–9	73	45	4.95
C G. DESAUTELS	480	3	69	.319	4	SHELLENBACK	102	6–7	13	38	3.53
1B R. JACOBS	332	5	46	.280	8	(1) ALSO WITH SEATTLE					
OF I. SHIVER	191	7	41	.309	2	(2) ALSO WITH SACRAMENTO					
C J. KERR	124	1	17	.258	2	MANAGER – F. SHELLENBACK					
OF T. WILLIAMS	107	0	11	.271	2	RECORD W–95 L–81 FINISH–2ND (T)					

1936

SEATTLE		AB	HR	RBI	BA	SB	PITCHERS	IP	W–L	BB	SO	ERA
1B	J. SHEVLIN	356	1	35	.289	3	D. BARRETT	284	22–13	109	187	3.36
2B	F. MULLER	561	30	105	.305	11	L. KOUPAL	281	23–11	68	121	2.69
3B	D. GYSELMAN	655	10	77	.282	15	P. GREGORY	241	15–14	79	96	3.88
SS	C. SMITH	272	2	20	.243	7	CRAGHEAD (2)	235	16–12	83	109	3.60
OF	M. HUNT	670	30	135	.316	6	D. OSBORN	190	11–9	67	56	3.36
OF	B. LAWRENCE	633	4	81	.300	18	R. LUCAS	161	7–12	63	75	4.42
OF	J. DONOVAN	625	23	81	.306	13	MC DOUGALL (1)	106	5–5	34	50	4.67
C	H. SPINDEL	370	5	43	.300	5						
S1	G. WRIGHT	369	9	57	.274	5						
12O	H. MICHAEL	300	2	32	.250	1	(1) ALSO WITH PORTLAND					
C	J. BASSLER	260	0	38	.354	2	(2) ALSO WITH SAN DIEGO					
S2	E. TAYLOR (1)	225	0	14	.209	2	**MANAGER – D. RUETHER**					
OF	H. BONETTI	181	2	19	.249	2	**RECORD W–93 L–92 FINISH–4TH**					

LOS ANGELES		AB	HR	RBI	BA	SB	PITCHERS	IP	W–L	BB	SO	ERA
1B	D. HURST	558	19	113	.303	2	J. SALVESON	251	21–7	70	127	2.76
2B	J. REESE	515	0	54	.270	7	F. THOMAS	206	15–10	75	134	3.10
3B	S. MESNER	703	17	132	.326	3	D. LIEBER	183	12–12	50	55	4.77
SS	C. DITTMAR	427	1	44	.286	5	R. PRIM	161	13–8	48	69	4.47
OF	C. CARLYLE	654	3	82	.339	15	B. JOYCE	149	5–13	64	37	4.77
OF	J. STATZ	631	3	62	.322	43	J. BERRY	125	7–7	28	70	3.74
OF	SCHULMERICH	462	14	85	.301	2	G. GABLER	115	7–6	45	39	4.69
C	J. BOTTARINI	393	12	51	.295	2	H. CASEY	106	5–8	36	66	4.92
OF	M. GUDAT	346	1	46	.324	13						
SS	B. MATTICK	241	1	30	.278	3						
12	R. RUSSELL	201	5	33	.249	3	**MANAGER – J. LELIVELT**					
C	R. STEINER	129	0	7	.202	0	**RECORD W–88 L–88 FINISH–5TH (T)**					

MISSION		AB	HR	RBI	BA	SB	PITCHERS	IP	W–L	BB	SO	ERA
1B	R. MORT	656	1	70	.326	3	B. BECK	304	18–21	119	135	3.73
2B	A. WRIGHT	331	0	34	.233	3	O. NITCHOLAS	248	16–14	36	65	3.63
3B	E. JOOST	668	6	72	.286	36	S. THURSTON	197	13–10	55	68	4.52
SS	C. BECK	390	0	36	.205	6	F. LAMANSKE	187	9–8	77	63	4.66
OF	L. ALMADA	700	1	53	.286	25	W. OSBORNE	172	12–9	75	88	3.98
OF	H. ROSENBERG	668	3	99	.334	11	L. STEWART	166	11–13	45	54	4.66
OF	M. WEST	579	1	91	.307	5	L. JOHNSON	138	7–9	48	52	4.37
C	C. OUTEN	344	2	59	.334	1	H. STITZEL	83	2–3	38	34	4.55
2S3	E. LEISHMAN (1)	360	1	32	.258	16						
C	J. SPRINZ	309	2	47	.285	5	(1) ALSO WITH OAKLAND					
OF	J. STONEHAM	199	0	37	.332	5	**MANAGER – W. KAMM**					
32	D. JOHNSON	156	0	21	.314	3	**RECORD W–88 L–88 FINISH–5TH (T)**					

1936

SAN FRANCISCO		AB	HR	RBI	BA	SB	PITCHERS		IP	W–L	BB	SO	ERA
1B	H. BOSS	641	1	75	.303	2	S. GIBSON		298	18–15	70	172	2.81
2B	B. HOLDER	581	1	50	.289	17	K. SHEEHAN		280	15–20	103	127	4.31
3B	S. BARATH	523	6	69	.256	8	E. STUTZ		243	17–18	74	90	4.44
SS	H. RHYNE	518	1	53	.255	11	W. BALLOU		220	11–16	63	132	4.79
OF	J. MARTY	599	17	92	.359	33	R. COLE		168	11–5	63	54	4.55
OF	T. NORBERT	597	21	126	.313	16	P. DAGLIA		145	6–11	46	43	4.97
OF	T. BOROJA	510	4	62	.265	7	J. CAMPBELL (1)		119	4–10	47	35	6.73
C	V. MONZO	284	1	39	.335	4							
S2	F. GIRA	360	0	28	.222	5							
OF	J. GRAVES	208	1	24	.260	1	(1) ALSO WITH LOS ANGELES AND SEATTLE						
C	B. SALKELD	204	0	15	.221	2	**MANAGER – L. O'DOUL**						
C	L. WOODALL	163	0	18	.276	1	**RECORD W–83 L–93 FINISH–7TH**						

SACRAMENTO		AB	HR	RBI	BA	SB	PITCHERS		IP	W–L	BB	SO	ERA
1B	J. GRILK	592	10	76	.258	6	J. CHAMBERS		280	17–19	86	127	4.37
2B	K. PETERS	340	0	30	.206	6	C. PIPPEN		215	16–9	51	65	3.56
3B	J. VERGEZ	354	7	42	.274	8	N. ANDREWS		197	11–14	60	85	4.34
SS	F. MOREHOUSE	539	10	43	.267	8	D. NEWSOME		171	7–16	56	63	3.53
OF	L. VEZELICH	656	7	104	.296	16	W. SEINSOTH		114	3–8	74	59	5.84
OF	B. ADAMS	542	16	71	.256	9	J. LYONS		96	1–11	20	25	4.22
OF	WORTHINGTON	392	2	39	.306	1	R. ROSS		94	2–12	66	49	8.23
C	L. HEAD	295	0	35	.271	4	J. WAHONICK		84	2–7	58	39	5.04
							M. BELCHER		81	2–5	27	24	4.11
U	J. DOBBINS	404	1	34	.265	15							
OF	F. DOLJACK	266	3	36	.312	3							
23	A. GARIBALDI	258	2	19	.326	11							
OF	H. EPPS	167	0	18	.287	7	**MANAGER – B. KILLEFER**						
C	S. NARRON	167	2	14	.222	2	**RECORD W–65 L–111 FINISH–8TH**						

PLAYOFFS
OAKLAND DEFEATED SAN DIEGO 4 GAMES TO 1
PORTLAND DEFEATED SEATTLE 4 GAMES TO 0

FINAL
PORTLAND DEFEATED OAKLAND 4 GAMES TO 1

1937

SACRAMENTO	AB	HR	RBI	BA	SB	PITCHERS	IP	W-L	BB	SO	ERA
1B M. PRATHER	347	6	69	.256	2	T. FREITAS	290	23-12	36	108	2.86
2B D. WILLIAMS	494	9	62	.298	8	B. KLINGER	279	19-13	81	108	3.77
3B A. GARIBALDI	568	18	106	.327	23	C. PIPPEN	238	15-14	59	75	4.20
SS J. ORENGO	580	11	70	.257	10	W. SCHMIDT	229	15-11	49	103	3.89
OF L. VEZELICH	704	7	87	.317	31	T. SEATS	186	11-10	53	76	3.87
OF B. ADAMS	592	19	82	.299	19	D. NEWSOME	182	12-10	53	62	3.76
OF N. CULLOP	532	19	127	.310	4	G. MURRAY	78	6-3	37	23	6.00
C H. FRANKS	313	3	39	.265	4						
S3O J. VERGEZ	461	13	66	.282	15						
C W. COOPER	241	3	29	.266	3						
1B W. PROUT	198	1	22	.232	1	MANAGER - B. KILLEFER					
SS F. MOREHOUSE	116	0	11	.224	4	RECORD W-102 L-76 FINISH-1ST					

SAN FRANCISCO	AB	HR	RBI	BA	SB	PITCHERS	IP	W-L	BB	SO	ERA
1B H. BOSS	716	5	130	.304	8	S. GIBSON	260	19-8	55	146	2.83
2B A. WRIGHT	606	0	75	.277	10	E. STUTZ	241	15-9	75	89	4.66
3B F. HAWKINS	479	12	95	.324	5	G. LILLARD	214	14-10	116	145	4.41
SS H. RHYNE	416	0	46	.255	3	B. SHORES	193	14-8	86	98	2.47
OF T. NORBERT	497	16	91	.304	7	W. BALLOU	153	13-12	55	86	3.70
OF D. DI MAGGIO	496	5	46	.306	15	R. COLE	143	6-9	58	52	4.40
OF B. HOLDER	486	2	65	.319	10	K. SHEEHAN	142	11-12	73	90	4.94
C L. WOODALL	305	0	44	.292	1	W. FLOWERS (1)	88	3-11	50	25	6.13
OF E. LONGACRE	372	1	40	.277	10						
S3 T. JENNINGS	367	2	39	.289	9						
C V. MONZO	291	2	21	.234	7	(1) ALSO WITH LOS ANGELES					
OF J. GILL	238	2	35	.273	1	MANAGER - L. O'DOUL					
P3 G. LILLARD	175	4	38	.326	2	RECORD W-98 L-80 FINISH-2ND					

SAN DIEGO	AB	HR	RBI	BA	SB	PITCHERS	IP	W-L	BB	SO	ERA
1B G. MC DONALD	632	4	102	.312	5	J. CHAPLIN	318	23-15	114	151	2.72
2B J. REESE	506	2	78	.314	4	D. WARD	284	18-18	116	92	4.44
3B E. HOLMAN	305	1	28	.223	2	M. SALVO	278	19-13	107	196	3.08
SS G. MYATT	565	6	51	.281	33	H. CRAGHEAD	245	16-13	74	119	3.27
OF H. PATCHETT	689	8	66	.306	21	W. HEBERT	244	17-14	42	90	3.02
OF R. THOMPSON	647	16	92	.326	13	H. PILLETTE	126	4-5	29	38	3.78
OF C. DURST	458	2	57	.293	4						
C G. DETORE	434	3	72	.334	16						
OF T. WILLIAMS	454	23	98	.291	1						
323 J. BERKOWITZ	422	0	35	.254	3						
C B. STARR	278	0	34	.219	0	MANAGER - F. SHELLENBACK					
P J. CHAPLIN	124	2	18	.242	0	RECORD W-97 L-81 FINISH-3RD					

1937

PORTLAND		AB	HR	RBI	BA	SB	PITCHERS	IP	W–L	BB	SO	ERA
1B	B. SWEENEY	463	1	71	.313	4	A. LISKA	319	24–18	74	135	3.07
2B	P. COSCARART	434	2	41	.253	8	B. POSEDEL	300	21–12	87	172	3.09
3B	F. BEDORE	533	1	67	.263	2	W. RADONITS	250	19–14	70	114	3.74
SS	D. LEE	631	0	49	.235	2	H. CARSON	178	11–11	63	54	4.90
OF	N. BONGIOVANNI	734	11	78	.322	6	J. HARE	100	4–6	27	41	4.23
OF	J. FREDERICK	667	12	107	.301	0						
OF	M. CLABAUGH	571	17	114	.326	11						
C	B. CRONIN	367	1	47	.270	0						
2O3	S. COSCARART	374	5	42	.262	7	MANAGER – B. SWEENEY					
CO	M. TRESH	355	3	38	.270	3	RECORD W–90 L–86 FINISH–4TH					

LOS ANGELES		AB	HR	RBI	BA	SB	PITCHERS	IP	W–L	BB	SO	ERA
1B	R. RUSSELL	407	13	69	.278	6	F. THOMAS	294	23–11	112	181	3.21
2B	C. DITTMAR	228	0	37	.276	1	R. PRIM	293	21–13	59	176	3.72
3B	S. MESNER	505	10	91	.329	4	J. BERRY	266	13–13	48	91	2.77
SS	B. MATTICK	612	2	66	.279	10	R. EVANS	203	11–14	47	88	3.99
OF	M. GUDAT	621	6	73	.332	7	D. LIEBER	165	8–10	38	42	4.36
OF	J. STATZ	558	2	57	.290	18	E. OVERMAN	93	5–6	49	32	5.32
OF	C. CARLYLE	488	7	63	.297	15	J. SALVESON	73	5–5	10	24	3.08
C	B. COLLINS	560	13	93	.279	8						
1B	D. HURST	284	10	50	.271	2						
23	K. RICHARDSON	258	7	19	.221	5						
OF	R. HARGRAVE	242	3	30	.293	0						
2O3	G. HOLT	229	6	36	.227	1						
32	B. MC WILLIAMS	204	9	31	.314	3	MANAGER – T. HANNAH					
OF	R. HOWELL	154	5	26	.260	0	RECORD W–90 L–88 FINISH–5TH					

SEATTLE		AB	HR	RBI	BA	SB	PITCHERS	IP	W–L	BB	SO	ERA
1B	H. MICHAEL	616	14	89	.292	3	P. GREGORY	276	20–15	88	80	3.88
2B	F. MULLER	559	26	111	.288	6	D. BARRETT	275	20–18	118	186	3.89
3B	D. GYSELMAN	666	11	53	.297	8	C. PICKREL	266	16–17	99	128	4.26
SS	A. STRANGE	642	6	56	.280	7	B. THOMAS (1)	242	11–17	40	85	3.83
OF	M. HUNT	647	39	131	.312	2	H. TURPIN	157	9–11	50	64	4.59
OF	H. POOL	458	6	65	.334	2	D. OSBORN	121	2–10	41	41	5.13
OF	B. LAWRENCE	439	0	54	.251	5						
C	E. FERNANDES	387	9	57	.305	1						
OF	J. DONOVAN	274	7	24	.226	2						
OF	L. MC CORMACK	267	5	27	.288	2						
C	H. SPINDEL	182	1	7	.214	4	(1) ALSO WITH PORTLAND					
S2	E. TAYLOR	126	2	15	.262	0	MANAGER – J. BASSLER					
C	J. BASSLER	99	0	10	.313	1	RECORD W–81 L–96 FINISH–6TH					

1937

OAKLAND	AB	HR	RBI	BA	SB	PITCHERS	IP	W–L	BB	SO	ERA
1B R. GIBSON	413	8	59	.289	6	E. BONHAM	278	17–16	89	188	3.66
2B D. LODIGIANI	538	18	84	.327	12	F. OLDS	258	15–16	74	58	4.15
3B P. MAY	424	3	61	.304	9	K. DOUGLASS	219	8–23	74	76	3.99
SS J. HITCHCOCK	620	3	37	.268	10	J. LA ROCCA	166	13–6	71	101	3.20
OF W. JUDNICH	651	11	81	.317	21	R. MILLER	122	6–10	67	41	5.53
OF E. KOY	522	16	77	.310	15	A. PIECHOTA	112	9–4	32	54	3.21
OF A. BROWNE	495	3	48	.301	2	W. LUDOLPH	99	7–4	24	35	2.45
C B. BAKER	319	2	41	.292	4	M. BREUER	85	0–12	23	28	4.02
						H. HAID	81	2–4	36	40	7.11
2OS E. LEISHMAN	308	2	26	.221	8						
C B. RAIMONDI	303	1	34	.248	2						
SS B. BLAIR	206	1	19	.296	4						
1O F. BELL	194	3	29	.289	3						
OF E. SAWYER	162	2	31	.284	1	MANAGER – B. MEYER					
OF E. BOLYARD	101	3	9	.297	1	RECORD W–79 L–98 FINISH–7TH					

MISSION	AB	HR	RBI	BA	SB	PITCHERS	IP	W–L	BB	SO	ERA
1B R. MORT	553	0	63	.304	11	B. BECK	226	11	22	90	108	4.42
2B D. JOHNSON	410	1	31	.251	9	S. BOLEN	224	11–13	76	81	3.46
3B S. BARATH	576	4	53	.253	9	O. NITCHOLAS	207	11–17	40	53	4.43
SS J. VITTER (1)	457	3	39	.284	15	L. TOST	204	9–8	82	102	3.52
OF H. ROSENBERG	612	10	76	.330	7	L. HERRMANN	194	11–18	83	71	5.75
OF M. WEST	555	16	95	.330	10	F. LAMANSKE (1)	176	9–13	68	75	4.65
OF F. DOLJACK	531	10	89	.301	8	J. BABICH	157	12–8	95	95	4.64
C J. SPRINZ	307	0	36	.257	5	W. OSBORNE	120	3–9	74	33	5.25
S2 G. SLADE	574	2	58	.280	4						
OF L. ALMADA	484	2	42	.252	9	(1) ALSO WITH SAN FRANCISCO					
C C. OUTEN	282	3	44	.316	1	MANAGER – W. KAMM					
2B M. KOENIG	90	0	19	.289	1	RECORD W–73 L–105 FINISH–8TH					

PLAYOFFS
SAN DIEGO DEFEATED SACRAMENTO 4 GAMES TO 0
PORTLAND DEFEATED SAN FRANCISCO 4 GAMES TO 0

FINAL
SAN DIEGO DEFEATED PORTLAND 4 GAMES TO 0

1938

LOS ANGELES	AB	HR	RBI	BA	SB	PITCHERS	IP	W–L	BB	SO	ERA
1B R. RUSSELL	679	21	114	.318	7	R. PRIM	230	17–10	42	126	3.29
2B E. MAYO	416	9	59	.332	9	J. SALVESON	205	11–10	44	91	4.13
3B C. ENGLISH	709	19	143	.303	3	G. LILLARD	203	16–10	83	144	3.50
SS E. CIHOCKI	646	11	86	.248	7	F. THOMAS	200	18–8	68	123	3.29
OF J. STATZ	630	2	44	.317	12	J. BERRY	187	16–11	51	90	3.42
OF J. ROTHROCK	516	6	84	.287	5	D. LIEBER	167	10–6	32	57	3.18
OF J. MOORE	492	21	86	.305	2	G. BUSH	108	8–5	16	44	3.92
C B. COLLINS	475	11	57	.253	8						
OF P. CARPENTER	259	4	35	.324	2						
2B G. SANFORD	196	2	16	.235	1	MANAGER – T. HANNAH					
C H. SUEME	142	0	14	.176	0	RECORD W–105 L–73 FINISH–1ST					

SEATTLE	AB	HR	RBI	BA	SB	PITCHERS	IP	W–L	BB	SO	ERA
1B L. GABRIELSON	636	5	96	.310	7	D. BARRETT	328	18–17	132	188	3.24
2B F. MULLER	627	20	110	.297	4	F. HUTCHINSON	290	25–7	99	145	2.48
3B D. GYSELMAN	701	12	86	.305	12	P. GREGORY	260	21–15	74	128	3.67
SS A. STRANGE	546	6	63	.245	5	H. TURPIN	217	17–14	53	81	2.90
OF B. LAWRENCE	564	4	87	.277	5	C. PICKREL	157	8–8	65	69	4.47
OF M. HUNT	539	13	77	.291	1						
OF E. VANNI	436	0	38	.301	8						
C H. SPINDEL	400	8	54	.310	2						
C E. FERNANDES	245	4	34	.282	0						
OF L. MC CORMACK	215	1	24	.288	1						
OF A. MARCHAND	180	1	14	.244	1						
P D. BARRETT	118	0	16	.220	0	MANAGER – J. LELIVELT					
P F. HUTCHINSON	115	2	23	.313	1	RECORD W–100 L–75 FINISH–2ND					

SACRAMENTO	AB	HR	RBI	BA	SB	PITCHERS	IP	W–L	BB	SO	ERA
1B L. BARTON	580	17	74	.264	7	T. FREITAS	290	24–11	46	159	2.67
2B D. WILLIAMS	675	15	88	.281	13	W. SCHMIDT	280	16–19	74	111	3.66
3B J. VERGEZ	583	16	80	.249	19	B. WALKER	226	17–12	59	99	2.95
SS J. ORENGO	622	18	83	.277	11	C. PIPPEN	223	17–8	40	68	3.15
OF M. MARSHALL	656	11	57	.267	16	D. NEWSOME	180	11–11	64	70	3.50
OF N. CULLOP	485	20	66	.256	7	L. SHERRILL	159	5–10	55	75	3.79
OF W. JAMES	334	2	40	.254	4						
C H. FRANKS	470	9	67	.274	2						
OF B. ADAMS	270	9	36	.293	24						
C F. GRUBE	181	0	18	.221	0						
OF D. HAFEY	172	3	11	.215	2	MANAGER – B. KILLEFER					
OF R. DIEFFENBACH	106	1	10	.198	0	RECORD W–95 L–82 FINISH–3RD					

1938

SAN FRANCISCO	AB	HR	RBI	BA	SB	PITCHERS	IP	W–L	BB	SO	ERA
1B H. BOSS	647	5	96	.306	5	S. GIBSON	284	23–12	59	151	2.66
2B A. WRIGHT	644	0	53	.267	4	B. SHORES	230	17–14	113	78	3.87
3B F. HAWKINS	664	14	110	.309	3	L. KOUPAL	210	9–16	76	73	5.01
SS T. JENNINGS	488	5	65	.283	7	E. STUTZ	196	10–11	50	51	4.50
OF T. NORBERT	677	30	163	.284	7	K. FRAZIER	182	7–14	97	62	4.95
OF D. DI MAGGIO	659	5	60	.307	16	A. WILKIE	110	1–8	57	48	3.93
OF B. HOLDER	585	2	95	.330	11	W. BALLOU	86	10–2	36	43	2.41
C J. SPRINZ	402	0	42	.299	6						
SS B. LILLARD	278	1	20	.335	8						
C L. WOODALL	194	1	17	.294	0						
PO K. FRAZIER	149	4	23	.262	0	**MANAGER – L. O'DOUL**					
P S. GIBSON	118	0	19	.314	1	**RECORD W–93 L–85 FINISH–4TH**					

SAN DIEGO	AB	HR	RBI	BA	SB	PITCHERS	IP	W–L	BB	SO	ERA
1B G. MC DONALD	549	0	61	.268	7	J. CHAPLIN	285	20–16	85	137	3.57
2B J. REESE	349	0	28	.232	2	H. CRAGHEAD	271	18–18	79	138	2.86
3B J. BERKOWITZ	443	1	52	.298	8	W. HEBERT	243	12–16	58	102	3.11
SS J. GRIFFITHS	613	0	69	.282	6	M. SALVO	238	22–9	82	191	2.60
OF H. PATCHETT	668	3	57	.302	10	D. WARD	174	9–12	65	55	5.02
OF S. HARRIS	545	7	92	.301	4	B. HUMPHREY	166	9–12	35	50	2.33
OF DALLESSANDRO	541	22	91	.309	8	H. PILLETTE	78	2–2	18	29	2.65
C S. HOGAN	331	1	42	.257	1						
23 A. NIEMIEC	461	2	66	.304	4						
C3 G. DETORE	296	3	40	.260	8						
OF B. STEWART	230	0	15	.270	0						
OF J. WILLIAMS	116	1	9	.207	0	**MANAGER – F. SHELLENBACK**					
P J. CHAPLIN	116	1	16	.241	0	**RECORD W–92 L–85 FINISH–5TH**					

PORTLAND	AB	HR	RBI	BA	SB	PITCHERS	IP	W–L	BB	SO	ERA
1B B. SWEENEY	531	5	54	.273	1	B. THOMAS	292	18–19	48	117	3.51
2B J. MORRISSEY	620	2	61	.247	3	W. HILCHER	285	21–19	91	143	3.25
3B I. JEFFRIES	687	5	78	.284	6	A. LISKA	278	16–18	75	126	3.69
SS D. MARSHALL	334	0	24	.269	1	G. DARROW	212	8–15	79	92	4.67
OF J. FREDERICK	617	5	102	.319	3	W. RADONITS	184	7–12	49	62	3.91
OF S. COSCARART	588	4	48	.260	4						
OF H. ROSENBERG	575	4	82	.320	12						
C G. DICKEY	355	8	48	.251	0						
OF E. WILSON	301	0	21	.272	4						
C B. CRONIN	239	1	23	.230	0	**MANAGER – B. SWEENEY**					
SS D. LEE	227	0	14	.247	2	**RECORD W–79 L–96 FINISH–6TH**					

1938

HOLLYWOOD		AB	HR	RBI	BA	SB	PITCHERS	IP	W–L	BB	SO	ERA
1B	R. MORT	605	1	73	.266	5	J. BABICH	275	19–17	119	180	3.27
2B	D. JOHNSON	389	2	28	.221	9	W. OSBORNE	246	12–18	116	77	5.01
3B	J. COSCARART	564	6	69	.271	3	L. TOST	220	11–16	91	103	3.48
SS	T. CAREY	629	3	65	.297	4	O. NITCHOLAS	217	14–13	46	59	4.15
OF	F. UHALT	635	5	65	.332	32	S. BOLEN	208	12–17	89	63	4.67
OF	C. DURST (1)	474	4	46	.308	3	HERRMANN (3)	141	10–6	52	66	3.96
OF	S. JOLLEY (2)	414	6	54	.350	2	B. BECK (4)	108	7–10	40	42	6.67
C	B. BRENZEL	410	0	52	.251	0						
OF	G. PUCCINELLI	298	22	59	.305	2						
2S	J. HOOVER	288	3	26	.257	6						
OF	W. NORMAN	242	12	47	.293	2						
OF	V. METTLER	241	0	18	.249	4	(1) ALSO WITH SAN DIEGO					
OF	F. BELL	187	5	30	.305	3	(2) ALSO WITH OAKLAND					
31	B. MC WILLIAMS	130	0	10	.192	1	(3) ALSO WITH SAN FRANCISCO					
C	J. ANUNZIO	109	1	11	.239	0	(4) ALSO WITH SEATTLE					
P	J. BABICH	107	0	14	.234	1	**MANAGER – R. KILLEFER**					
C	C. OUTEN	103	0	13	.320	0	**RECORD W–79 L–99 FINISH–7TH**					

OAKLAND		AB	HR	RBI	BA	SB	PITCHERS	IP	W–L	BB	SO	ERA
1B	R. GIBSON	517	5	49	.228	4	B. JOYCE	287	18–18	100	66	3.01
2B	H. LUBY	580	4	70	.295	20	D. VAN FLEET(2)	234	12–16	80	104	4.58
3B	J. WARNER	450	1	26	.216	2	J. BITTNER	215	10–17	93	114	3.60
SS	E. MONTAGUE	495	4	40	.226	7	K. SHEEHAN	212	4–27	120	87	4.88
OF	J. ABREU	569	11	77	.299	9	K. DOUGLASS (3)	182	8–14	54	100	3.76
OF	J. HILL	539	9	46	.249	25	J. LINDELL	166	9–8	77	68	3.42
OF	E. BOLYARD	342	4	40	.278	2	F. OLDS	137	3–10	51	20	4.86
C	B. RAIMONDI	441	0	47	.270	4	E. PYLE	121	6–6	56	46	4.24
							W. MOORE	59	2–1	24	18	5.03
C1	W. CONROY	340	4	46	.247	6						
OF	M. GUDAT (1)	216	2	32	.296	6	(1) ALSO WITH HOLLYWOOD					
PO	J. LINDELL	144	4	27	.368	2	(2) ALSO WITH LOS ANGELES					
P	B. JOYCE	108	0	10	.195	0	(3) ALSO WITH PORTLAND					
OF	J. DONOVAN	104	0	10	.250	6	**MANAGER – D. ZWILLING**					
3B	B. RIGNEY	83	0	4	.265	0	**RECORD W–65 L–113 FINISH–8TH**					

PLAYOFFS
SACRAMENTO DEFEATED LOS ANGELES 4 GAMES TO 1
SAN FRANCISCO DEFEATED SEATTLE 4 GAMES TO 1

FINAL
SACRAMENTO DEFEATED SAN FRANCISCO 4 GAMES TO 1

1939

SEATTLE		AB	HR	RBI	BA	SB	PITCHERS	IP	W–L	BB	SO	ERA
1B	G. ARCHIE	654	7	88	.330	27	D. BARRETT	308	22–15	113	144	3.22
2B	J. MORRISSEY	365	4	53	.296	2	H. TURPIN	270	23–10	46	100	2.50
3B	D. GYSELMAN	476	2	68	.296	11	P. GREGORY	245	18–11	79	86	4.08
SS	A. STRANGE	666	8	90	.335	18	B. WALKER	241	16–18	76	82	3.32
OF	J. WHITE	648	1	54	.287	47	L. WEBBER	201	17–7	56	78	2.78
OF	B. LAWRENCE	566	3	92	.295	8						
OF	E. VANNI	458	2	51	.325	20						
C	G. CAMPBELL	438	1	69	.313	7						
OF	M. HUNT	371	15	76	.259	3						
23	J. COSCARART	310	0	32	.300	2						
C	B. HANCKEN	186	1	14	.237	1	MANAGER – J. LELIVELT					
P	D. BARRETT	142	0	20	.223	0	RECORD W–101 L–73 FINISH–1ST					

SAN FRANCISCO		AB	HR	RBI	BA	SB	PITCHERS	IP	W–L	BB	SO	ERA
1B	K. FRAZIER	366	3	52	.257	3	S. GIBSON	265	22–9	51	136	2.24
2B	A. WRIGHT	593	0	71	.285	7	E. STUTZ	237	13–16	56	65	3.34
0B	J. WARNER	399	0	59	.306	6	B. SHORES	225	13–12	89	89	3.40
SS	H. STOREY	459	9	85	.351	5	L. POWELL	184	12–11	92	125	2.79
OF	D. DI MAGGIO	664	14	82	.360	39	L. KOUPAL	161	9–12	45	61	3.86
OF	B. HOLDER	636	5	87	.314	14	O. JORGENS	157	13–5	76	59	3.90
OF	T. NORBERT	564	25	104	.305	9	W. BALLOU	99	8–7	48	37	2.82
C	J. SPRINZ	276	0	26	.312	2						
S3	T. JENNINGS	378	4	44	.262	4						
1B	H. BOSS	216	0	42	.296	5						
C	L. WOODALL	213	0	26	.239	0	MANAGER – L. O'DOUL					
3B	E. RAIMONDI	188	0	12	.271	0	RECORD W–97 L–78 FINISH–2ND					

LOS ANGELES		AB	HR	RBI	BA	SB	PITCHERS	IP	W–L	BB	SO	ERA
1B	R. COLLINS	586	26	128	.334	5	R. PRIM	280	20–17	43	107	3.57
2B	L. STRINGER	548	16	85	.272	6	F. THOMAS	246	17–13	91	139	2.75
3B	C. ENGLISH	660	13	89	.279	2	J. BONETTI	238	20–5	24	69	3.25
SS	E. CIHOCKI	564	3	78	.280	0	L. STINE	208	13–15	70	101	5.02
OF	J. STATZ	557	4	62	.311	9	J. FLORES	173	9–9	59	100	3.54
OF	J. MOORE	491	17	99	.301	2	J. BERRY	122	8–7	48	62	4.43
OF	J. ROTHROCK	370	5	44	.292	2	D. VAN FLEET(1)	117	6–6	26	52	4.08
C	B. COLLINS	482	8	52	.306	20						
32S	E. MAYO	464	6	61	.263	3						
OF	P. CARPENTER	340	2	30	.229	4						
C	H. SUEME	148	1	19	.230	0	(1) ALSO WITH SEATTLE					
OF	L. NOVIKOFF	135	8	37	.452	2	MANAGER – T. HANNAH					
P	R. PRIM	110	0	16	.255	1	RECORD W–97 L–79 FINISH–3RD					

1939

SACRAMENTO		AB	HR	RBI	BA	SB	PITCHERS	IP	W–L	BB	SO	ERA
1B	L. BARTON	593	11	87	.297	8	T. FREITAS	332	21–18	37	172	2.87
2B	D. WILLIAMS	538	8	68	.266	5	T. SEATS	292	21–14	63	130	3.02
3B	A. GARIBALDI	637	16	85	.292	25	W. SCHMIDT	244	15–13	52	89	3.14
SS	J. ORENGO	463	17	61	.272	13	A. SHERER	182	6–12	59	48	3.76
OF	M. MARSHALL	715	18	61	.297	8	I. SMITH	122	12–4	33	57	2.29
OF	C. WIECZOREK	437	12	67	.291	13	HERRMANN (1)	114	2–7	43	43	4.66
OF	L. VEZELICH	227	2	31	.291	5	J. HUBBELL	85	7–7	40	49	4.10
C	B. OGRODOWSKI	341	1	43	.217	2	L. SHERRILL	79	3–5	32	32	4.34
							L. GUAY	76	3–2	42	24	4.28
C	J. GRILK	273	3	33	.238	1						
OF	A. CASTANO	203	0	8	.281	3	(1) ALSO WITH OAKLAND					
OF	L. SCOFFIC	192	2	14	.245	3	MANAGER – B. BORGMANN					
2B	B. BORGMANN	186	0	15	.231	4	RECORD W–88 L–88 FINISH–4TH					

SAN DIEGO		AB	HR	RBI	BA	SB	PITCHERS	IP	W–L	BB	SO	ERA
1B	G. MC DONALD	490	1	50	.229	4	W. HEBERT	299	20–10	64	104	3.13
2B	A. NIEMIEC	531	0	63	.279	3	B. HUMPHREY	208	9–15	55	54	4.07
3B	M. HASLIN	537	11	79	.345	8	H. CRAGHEAD	203	11–16	56	94	4.75
SS	J. GRIFFITHS	384	0	25	.227	4	P. TOBIN	186	7–15	119	124	3.92
OF	H. PATCHETT	610	0	32	.290	6	A. OLSEN	164	7–12	94	76	4.72
OF	DALLESSANDRO	541	18	98	.368	12	J. GONZALES	138	11–7	46	42	3.52
OF	J. WILLIAMS	289	2	30	.280	5	H. PILLETTE	89	8–6	21	22	2.32
C	G. DETORE	411	4	72	.355	12						
U	J. BERKOWITZ	402	0	43	.261	2						
OF	C. CARLYLE	258	2	31	.271	1						
C	B. STARR	248	1	21	.226	2	MANAGER – C. DURST					
O3	B. STEWART	186	4	17	.306	1	RECORD W–83 L–93 FINISH–5TH					

HOLLYWOOD		AB	HR	RBI	BA	SB	PITCHERS	IP	W–L	BB	SO	ERA
1B	B. HERMAN	350	13	71	.317	2	W. OSBORNE	277	16–17	77	77	4.61
2B	B. CISSELL	696	3	83	.269	4	J. BITTNER	237	13–14	96	100	4.14
3B	B. KAHLE	405	6	43	.247	3	R. ARDIZOIA	235	14–9	118	135	3.99
SS	J. HOOVER	457	6	72	.298	16	L. FLEMING	234	12–16	105	133	4.00
OF	F. UHALT	585	2	54	.284	16	B. MUNCRIEF	169	11–11	40	93	4.32
OF	G. PUCCINELLI	413	16	70	.298	1	L. TOST	121	5–10	41	54	4.98
OF	S. HARRIS	383	6	58	.339	1	C. MONCRIEF	83	7–7	40	21	4.10
C	B. BRENZEL	275	1	33	.262	0						
1B	L. GABRIELSON	315	1	34	.276	2						
SS	MOREHOUSE (1)	312	3	25	.266	2						
OF	W. NORMAN	231	10	45	.260	4	(1) ALSO WITH SACRAMENTO					
OF	J. TYACK	214	4	40	.290	5	MANAGER – R. KILLEFER					
C	C. DAPPER	209	1	32	.316	1	RECORD W–82 L–94 FINISH–6TH					

1939

OAKLAND		AB	HR	RBI	BA	SB	PITCHERS	IP	W−L	BB	SO	ERA
1B	R. GIBSON (1)	362	2	48	.251	2	J. SALVESON	233	12−15	42	75	3.82
2B	H. LUBY	681	3	56	.283	20	B. CANTWELL	227	13−15	53	57	3.33
3B	J. ABREU	493	4	44	.288	9	J. FALLON	219	13−13	88	82	4.61
SS	W. LYMAN	511	0	28	.250	6	H. BITHORN	210	13−14	100	129	3.64
OF	M. GUDAT	516	1	71	.324	10	R. BUXTON	200	13−10	72	95	2.88
OF	S. JOLLEY	499	9	76	.309	4	J. GAY	154	9−14	78	79	4.56
OF	A. BROWNE	454	0	48	.262	8						
C	B. RAIMONDI	316	1	27	.304	3						
S31	J. VERGEZ	449	12	65	.287	8						
OF	M. CHRISTOFF	315	7	42	.244	5						
C	B. CONROY	286	3	43	.266	6						
1B	E. LEVY	191	4	26	.215	6	(1) ALSO WITH SAN FRANCISCO					
OF	J. HILL	166	3	21	.193	4	MANAGER − J. VERGEZ					
3B	P. AMBROSE	122	0	11	.205	1	RECORD W−78 L−98 FINISH−7TH					

PORTLAND		AB	HR	RBI	BA	SB	PITCHERS	IP	W−L	BB	SO	ERA
1B	B. SWEENEY	527	6	60	.338	0	B. THOMAS	303	20−17	64	151	4.81
2B	I. JEFFRIES	645	5	69	.316	2	A. LISKA	285	20−16	54	137	3.35
OB	F. HAWKINS	491	15	91	.320	0	D. NEWSOME (1)	178	6−14	61	60	5.26
SS	C. WILBURN	479	1	56	.271	3	W. HILCHER	160	6−15	58	36	5.04
OF	E. WILSON	681	8	74	.283	17	C. PICKREL (2)	133	7−10	55	36	4.74
OF	H. ROSENBERG	646	8	95	.331	5	W. RADONITS	132	4−9	31	55	5.87
OF	J. FREDERICK	479	4	85	.326	1	R. BIRKHOFER	103	2−8	24	50	6.29
C	V. MONZO	290	1	40	.307	0	G. GABLER	97	5−6	21	32	4.73
S32	D. MARSHALL	352	0	34	.241	1	(1) ALSO WITH SAN DIEGO					
OF	E. COLEMAN	320	16	77	.344	0	(2) ALSO WITH SEATTLE					
C	E. FERNANDES	283	2	49	.329	0	MANAGER − B. SWEENEY					
P	B. THOMAS	113	0	12	.212	0	RECORD W−75 L−98 FINISH−8TH					

PLAYOFFS
SACRAMENTO DEFEATED SAN FRANCISCO 4 GAMES TO 1
LOS ANGELES DEFEATED SEATTLE 4 GAMES TO 2

FINAL
SACRAMENTO DEFEATED LOS ANGELES 4 GAMES TO 2

1940

SEATTLE		AB	HR	RBI	BA	SB	PITCHERS	IP	W–L	BB	SO	ERA
1B	G. ARCHIE	670	8	95	.324	26	H. TURPIN	297	23–11	65	96	2.73
2B	A. NIEMIEC	588	1	70	.274	6	D. BARRETT	258	24–5	121	164	2.48
3B	D. GYSELMAN	608	2	73	.289	12	B. WALKER	202	12–14	72	51	4.19
SS	B. SCHUSTER	645	2	74	.291	26	P. GREGORY	199	12–10	71	92	3.66
OF	J. WHITE	600	8	53	.295	35	L. WEBBER	177	13–10	56	63	3.25
OF	E. VANNI	538	0	74	.333	24	A. WILKIE	144	13–5	55	45	2.69
OF	B. LAWRENCE	477	1	56	.273	3	I. SCRIBNER	123	10–5	36	51	3.37
C	G. CAMPBELL	372	1	45	.280	2						
OF	S. HARRIS	277	2	34	.271	2						
C	E. KEARSE	252	3	47	.302	0	MANAGER – J. LELIVELT					
OF	F. KELLEHER	203	7	40	.281	0	RECORD W–112 L–66 FINISH–1ST					

LOS ANGELES		AB	HR	RBI	BA	SB	PITCHERS	IP	W–L	BB	SO	ERA
1B	R. COLLINS	630	18	111	.327	6	L. STINE	257	18–10	71	94	2.83
2B	L. STRINGER	638	14	89	.263	11	R. PRIM	240	18–11	47	110	2.59
3B	E. MAYO	643	11	85	.320	17	J. BONETTI	193	14–10	43	54	4.28
SS	E. CIHOCKI	499	5	56	.257	5	B. WEILAND	164	12–7	77	87	3.78
OF	L. NOVIKOFF	714	41	171	.363	3	F. THOMAS	161	6–11	64	77	4.97
OF	J. STATZ	453	1	48	.289	11	J. BERRY	143	9–5	41	69	2.39
OF	J. MOORE	380	9	69	.311	2	J. FALLON	141	13–9	55	51	4.72
C	C. HERNANDEZ	308	6	36	.269	1	J. FLORES	132	7–5	67	99	4.43
OF	P. CARPENTER	338	4	38	.216	2						
C	B. HOLM	281	1	31	.231	2						
OF	J. ROTHROCK (1)	253	1	37	.245	2	(1) ALSO WITH HOLLYWOOD					
S3	P. LOWREY	216	1	12	.250	12	MANAGER – J. STATZ					
OF	W. CARROLL	126	0	9	.302	1	RECORD W–102 L–75 FINISH–2ND					

OAKLAND		AB	HR	RBI	BA	SB	PITCHERS	IP	W–L	BB	SO	ERA
1B	C. DUNN	670	27	102	.233	4	J. SALVESON	286	19–13	43	71	2.30
2B	H. LUBY	689	4	57	.257	21	S. CORBETT	277	17–18	72	88	2.79
3B	J. VERGEZ	259	4	31	.270	5	R. BUXTON	252	17–13	90	149	3.07
SS	W. LYMAN	606	0	40	.216	10	C. PIPPEN	172	10–13	48	63	3.55
OF	M. GUDAT	626	1	67	.313	13	B. CANTWELL	151	13–5	32	35	2.56
OF	M. CHRISTOFF	561	16	98	.321	11	G. DARROW	135	8–8	47	44	3.06
OF	L. CHRISTOPHER	561	8	72	.276	11	J. MULLIGAN	115	7–8	43	31	4.07
C	B. RAIMONDI	358	0	43	.237	4	V. JOHNSON	76	0–2	48	24	5.92
3O	G. CHAPMAN	291	1	36	.275	4						
C	B. CONROY	243	7	30	.230	5						
3B	E. RAIMONDI	215	0	24	.274	0						
3B	P. AMBROSE	146	0	10	.199	2	MANAGER – J. VERGEZ					
P	J. SALVESON	116	1	20	.328	0	RECORD W–94 L–84 FINISH–3RD					

1940

SAN DIEGO		AB	HR	RBI	BA	SB	PITCHERS	IP	W–L	BB	SO	ERA
1B	G. MC DONALD	537	2	63	.289	3	D. NEWSOME	315	23–11	74	128	2.63
2B	S. SPERRY	551	0	76	.303	8	W. HEBERT	280	15–18	100	106	3.92
3B	M. HASLIN	616	9	103	.321	16	B. HUMPHREY	216	13–14	55	48	3.71
SS	S. MESNER	680	0	97	.341	6	H. CRAGHEAD	175	8–14	74	66	4.88
OF	B. STEWART	723	6	71	.320	10	A. OLSEN	118	7–7	39	47	4.11
OF	H. PATCHETT	686	0	51	.284	9	J. MORRIS	100	4–1	50	34	4.14
OF	J. JENSEN	481	1	64	.304	4	H. PILLETTE	89	7–2	18	31	2.82
C	B. SALKELD	431	20	81	.288	0						
C	G. DETORE	265	2	35	.321	3	**MANAGER – C. DURST**					
P	W. HEBERT	116	0	16	.259	0	**RECORD W–92 L–85 FINISH–4TH**					

SACRAMENTO		AB	HR	RBI	BA	SB	PITCHERS	IP	W–L	BB	SO	ERA
1B	L. BARTON	345	7	41	.235	4	T. FREITAS	332	20–19	48	146	2.71
2B	D. WILLIAMS	545	7	92	.305	1	O. JUDD	295	22–13	115	148	2.90
3B	A. GARIBALDI (1)	582	5	70	.251	6	W. SCHMIDT	256	15–14	56	139	3.03
SS	B. BLATTNER	442	4	54	.278	9	N. KLEINKE	240	15–12	52	99	2.40
OF	L. KING	668	1	46	.289	12	R. MUNGER	190	9–14	99	96	3.17
OF	C. WIECZOREK	508	21	84	.315	5	F. GABLER	88	3–5	23	25	5.60
OF	M. ALMADA	306	2	24	.232	9						
C	B. OGRODOWSKI	311	1	39	.257	1						
3S2	G. HANDLEY	377	1	50	.273	12						
C1	J. GRILK	331	6	48	.299	0						
SS	E. LAKE	237	15	35	.295	13						
1B	J. BOLLING	223	2	25	.229	4						
OF	R. LANG	165	2	24	.268	0	(1) ALSO WITH SAN DIEGO					
OF	M. MARSHALL	153	0	9	.261	0	**MANAGER – B. BORGMANN**					
P	O. JUDD	133	1	17	.256	0	**RECORD W–90 L–88 FINISH–5TH**					

HOLLYWOOD		AB	HR	RBI	BA	SB	PITCHERS	IP	W–L	BB	SO	ERA
1B	B. SWEENEY	313	4	50	.268	8	R. ARDIZOIA	264	14–20	105	145	4.09
2B	B. CISSELL	629	4	76	.289	7	W. OSBORNE	262	18–17	86	67	4.06
3B	B. KAHLE	641	2	83	.312	5	L. FLEMING	231	17–12	82	143	2.77
SS	J. HOOVER	583	3	49	.250	14	H. BITHORN	181	10–17	100	125	4.37
OF	F. UHALT	651	1	52	.269	23	F. GAY	171	6–6	85	70	4.69
OF	B. HERMAN	469	9	80	.307	0	J. BITTNER	158	10–9	62	61	3.42
OF	R. THOMPSON	447	5	53	.210	4	L. TOST	135	4–6	50	72	4.07
C	B. BRENZEL	255	3	35	.294	1						
1B	B. GRAY	230	4	27	.226	2						
C	C. DAPPER	209	2	17	.249	2						
OF	G. MANDISH	202	2	16	.272	0	**MANAGER – B. SWEENEY**					
C	V. MONZO	181	1	20	.238	3	**RECORD W–84 L–94 FINISH–6TH**					

1940

SAN FRANCISCO	AB	HR	RBI	BA	SB	PITCHERS	IP	W-L	BB	SO	ERA
1B F. FAIN	446	7	50	.238	3	S. GIBSON	263	14-14	57	126	2.84
2B A. WRIGHT	558	0	68	.258	3	E. STUTZ	252	19-14	78	65	3.54
3B T. JENNINGS	680	13	89	.319	12	F. DASSO	212	10-15	121	126	3.31
SS N. FERNANDEZ	369	0	37	.304	5	A. EPPERLY	204	11-16	83	50	3.92
OF J. BARRETT	629	12	79	.267	40	L. POWELL	141	12-7	71	72	3.57
OF T. NORBERT	594	20	94	.320	5	L. GUAY	138	1-10	72	63	4.11
OF B. HOLDER	521	1	60	.274	6	R. JENSEN	86	2-3	77	50	5.13
C J. SPRINZ	378	0	51	.249	2	W. BALLOU	67	6-7	25	36	3.63
1B J. BURNS	241	0	30	.270	2						
SS H. STOREY	232	1	36	.323	5						
C E. BOTELHO	131	0	14	.206	3						
32 J. WARNER	130	0	16	.262	1	MANAGER - L. O'DOUL					
OF D. WHITE	115	1	10	.322	0	RECORD W-81 L-97 FINISH-7TH					

PORTLAND	AB	HR	RBI	BA	SB	PITCHERS	IP	W-L	BB	SO	ERA
1B J. FREDERICK	415	2	43	.306	5	B. THOMAS (1)	294	16-20	70	96	3.91
2B D. MARSHALL	421	0	23	.247	3	W. HILCHER	246	12-21	75	101	4.47
3B F. HAWKINS	403	6	65	.288	2	R. HARRELL	203	6-23	98	130	3.77
SS L. BROWN	571	0	49	.200	9	A. LISKA	190	9-12	41	99	3.36
OF H. ROSENBERG	659	4	70	.314	10	B. SPEECE	173	7-9	43	62	3.95
OF H. REICH	592	11	54	.230	7	J. ORRELL	165	7-14	97	89	5.67
OF J. GILL	530	16	87	.323	6	J. GONZALES	126	2-12	42	41	4.57
C E. ADAMS	178	0	21	.213	0	L. FALLIN	87	1-7	38	28	5.79
23 A. SCHWAB	301	0	24	.199	0						
OF E. COLEMAN	268	9	47	.317	0						
2B F. MULLER	244	3	31	.234	0						
OF R. BERGSTROM	187	2	19	.289	0						
C E. FERNANDES	153	2	22	.333	2	(1) ALSO WITH SAN DIEGO					
C J. ANNUNZIO	153	0	6	.235	0	MANAGER - J. FREDERICK					
C J. SCHULTZ	120	1	23	.325	0	RECORD W-56 L-122 FINISH-8TH					

PLAYOFFS
SEATTLE DEFEATED OAKLAND 4 GAMES TO 1
LOS ANGELES DEFEATED SAN DIEGO 4 GAMES TO 3

FINAL
SEATTLE DEFEATED LOS ANGELES 4 GAMES TO 1

1941

SEATTLE		AB	HR	RBI	BA	SB	PITCHERS	IP	W–L	BB	SO	ERA
1B	L. SCARSELLA	637	10	110	.322	14	D. BARRETT	291	20–12	109	163	2.75
2B	A. NIEMIEC	536	3	66	.297	3	H. TURPIN	269	20–6	35	68	2.51
3B	D. GYSELMAN	560	3	55	.255	15	P. GREGORY	197	11–14	50	56	3.65
SS	N. STICKLE	403	0	44	.280	10	I. SCRIBNER	155	11–9	55	56	3.72
OF	J. WHITE	547	2	49	.291	28	S. JOHNSON	151	13–7	13	59	2.80
OF	W. MATHESON	535	12	84	.290	17	E. COLE	123	11–6	43	40	3.00
OF	S. HARRIS	414	4	53	.302	6	D. SORIANO	109	6–5	46	47	3.80
C	G. CAMPBELL (1)	395	0	42	.268	3	L. BROWN	105	5–7	31	46	4.20
							L. WEBBER	104	7–3	24	32	2.16
C	C. FALLON	303	0	29	.274	4						
OF	L. KING (2)	255	0	26	.220	2						
OF	B. LAWRENCE	241	1	29	.278	4	(1) ALSO WITH LOS ANGELES					
OF	E. AVERILL	223	1	17	.247	2	(2) ALSO WITH SACRAMENTO					
23S	L. BERGER	130	1	17	.246	2	MANAGER – B. SKIFF					
P	H. TURPIN	106	1	14	.226	1	RECORD W–104 L–70 FINISH–1ST					

SACRAMENTO		AB	HR	RBI	BA	SB	PITCHERS	IP	W–L	BB	SO	ERA
1B	M. STURDY	627	10	81	.308	20	T. FREITAS	300	21–15	38	112	2.70
2B	B. BLATTNER	620	17	100	.294	23	R. MUNGER	261	17–16	87	159	3.07
3B	D. GUTTERIDGE	680	13	88	.309	46	W. SCHMIDT	224	13–9	52	90	2.03
SS	S. SCALZI	355	1	47	.256	4	HOLLINGSWORTH	213	21–9	58	92	3.17
OF	B. ENDICOTT	591	5	38	.298	13	N. KLEINKE	158	12–8	32	56	3.19
OF	B. ADAMS	571	17	92	.285	23	G. TURBEVILLE	116	8–4	84	79	4.42
OF	P. MARTIN	245	2	35	.322	10	W. CAPLINGER	100	3–5	40	71	3.78
C	C. WIECZOREK	504	16	96	.286	2						
S3	G. HANDLEY	326	1	43	.313	13						
C	C. KLUTTZ	232	1	22	.336	3	MANAGER – P. MARTIN					
OF	L. BLAKELY	223	1	26	.300	2	RECORD W–102 L–75 FINISH–2ND					

SAN DIEGO		AB	HR	RBI	BA	SB	PITCHERS	IP	W–L	BB	SO	ERA
1B	G. MC DONALD	611	1	58	.283	4	Y. TERRY	315	26–8	74	172	2.31
2B	S. SPERRY	523	2	60	.268	6	W. HEBERT	279	22–10	58	102	3.00
3B	M. HASLIN	458	5	75	.301	10	B. THOMAS	272	15–17	61	78	3.31
SS	E. PELLAGRINI	659	8	70	.273	13	A. OLSEN	247	14–16	90	107	3.72
OF	M. MAZZERA	626	16	104	.268	6	W. RICH	139	9–9	60	66	3.50
OF	H. PATCHETT	622	0	60	.296	25	HUMPHREY (1)	128	5–12	41	35	5.06
OF	J. JENSEN	509	7	55	.305	3	R. DILBECK	95	6–4	32	43	2.65
C	B. SALKELD	324	7	51	.225	1						
C1	G. DETORE	378	5	61	.320	9						
3O2	A. GARIBALDI	329	5	49	.286	5	(1) ALSO WITH LOS ANGELES					
P	W. HEBERT	113	0	9	.292	0	MANAGER – C. DURST					
C	D. BALLINGER	102	0	9	.294	0	RECORD W–101 L–76 FINISH–3RD					

1941

HOLLYWOOD		AB	HR	RBI	BA	SB	PITCHERS	IP	W–L	BB	SO	ERA
1B	B. GRAY	325	3	45	.283	1	L. TOST	243	13–10	71	112	3.85
2B	H. SCHULTE	676	0	62	.280	4	F. DASSO	230	15–15	116	147	3.91
3B	B. KAHLE	693	5	95	.319	9	H. BITHORN	228	17–15	99	111	3.59
SS	J. HOOVER	531	8	62	.235	11	J. BITTNER	215	12–14	82	80	4.19
OF	J. DICKSHOT	608	10	86	.298	6	W. OSBORNE	207	12–12	65	67	4.22
OF	F. UHALT	534	2	44	.288	18	F. GAY	144	11–7	64	73	3.31
OF	J. BARRETT	517	4	66	.313	24	R. JOINER	126	2–12	35	44	4.79
C	C. DAPPER	433	8	63	.277	9						
OF	H. ROSENBERG	420	1	55	.286	9						
1B	B. HERMAN	272	11	63	.346	2						
C	B. BRENZEL	228	4	22	.268	1	MANAGER – B. SWEENEY					
1B	B. SWEENEY	121	1	16	.273	4	RECORD W–85 L–91 FINISH–4TH					

SAN FRANCISCO		AB	HR	RBI	BA	SB	PITCHERS	IP	W–L	BB	SO	ERA
1B	F. FAIN	649	5	66	.310	8	T. SEATS	261	14–18	58	114	3.03
2B	T. LAZZERI	315	3	39	.248	5	L. JANSEN	238	16–10	75	70	2.80
3B	T. JENNINGS	273	5	43	.326	5	E. STUTZ	233	14–16	70	50	3.21
SS	N. FERNANDEZ	706	19	129	.327	14	S. GIBSON	163	13–7	41	72	3.31
OF	B. HOLDER	624	2	53	.280	11	A. EPPERLY	146	5–7	46	44	4.25
OF	D. WHITE	612	4	53	.302	10	B. JOYCE	135	6–12	43	31	4.80
OF	W. CARROLL (1)	405	1	54	.269	8						
C	B. OGRODOWSKI	399	0	46	.276	0						
23	D. TROWER	394	3	36	.246	5						
OF	J. POWELL	241	0	40	.278	9						
3B	E. GOORABIAN	221	2	25	.249	1	(1) ALSO WITH LOS ANGELES					
OF	J. BROVIA	195	0	27	.318	0	MANAGER – L. O'DOUL					
C	J. SPRINZ	131	0	15	.168	1	RECORD W–81 L–95 FINISH–5TH (T)					

OAKLAND		AB	HR	RBI	BA	SB	PITCHERS	IP	W–L	BB	SO	ERA
1B	C. DUNN	392	9	50	.245	1	J. SALVESON	288	15–20	63	100	3.75
2B	H. LUBY	677	5	73	.301	17	C. PIPPEN	263	17–16	69	104	3.56
3B	M. DUEZABOU	624	4	55	.296	20	S. CORBETT	249	15–15	97	70	4.15
SS	B. RIGNEY	605	3	61	.208	8	R. BUXTON	243	14–18	103	97	3.52
OF	M. GUDAT	640	2	65	.291	9	G. DARROW	176	9–12	65	54	3.32
OF	F. TAUBY	432	4	61	.299	7	T. ANANICS	125	4–8	72	50	3.60
OF	E. DEVAURS	411	0	28	.258	8	J. MULLIGAN	100	3–4	58	31	5.40
C	B. RAIMONDI	307	1	37	.283	6						
OF	M. CHRISTOFF	348	5	41	.221	7						
OF	G. CHAPMAN	298	3	34	.272	4						
C	B. CONROY	297	6	36	.290	4	MANAGER – J. VERGEZ					
13	J. VERGEZ	134	1	19	.284	0	RECORD W–81 L–95 FINISH–5TH (T)					

1941

LOS ANGELES	AB	HR	RBI	BA	SB	PITCHERS	IP	W–L	BB	SO	ERA
1B P. WEINTRAUB	417	18	75	.302	2	R. PRIM	255	16–15	38	119	2.86
2B J. STAMPER	286	0	25	.238	0	J. FLORES	223	12–15	89	139	3.23
3B E. MAYO	412	13	72	.286	8	L. STINE	168	9–14	64	39	5.41
SS B. SCHUSTER (1)	492	2	53	.276	25	F. THOMAS	154	10–13	65	72	4.09
OF P. LOWREY	653	6	69	.311	26	J. BERRY	125	6–10	51	48	5.26
OF J. MOORE	474	18	100	.331	2	J. BONETTI	111	7–3	20	37	3.24
OF H. STOREY	465	2	50	.280	5	G. COFFMAN	80	1–3	47	19	5.74
C B. COLLINS (1)	375	3	58	.296	12	F. TATARO	77	3–3	59	42	6.19
						J. DOBERNIC	72	3–7	45	53	3.25
23S R. WARSTLER	276	0	25	.254	0						
SS L. MERULLO	275	1	17	.218	12						
C B. HOLM	198	5	17	.197	3						
OF R. SAMHAMMER	154	0	3	.214	3						
P1 L. STINE	148	1	13	.297	1	(1) ALSO WITH SEATTLE					
OF J. STATZ	142	0	21	.268	1	MANAGER – J. STATZ					
OF W. BERGER	141	8	18	.241	0	RECORD W–72 L–98 FINISH–7TH					

PORTLAND	AB	HR	RBI	BA	SB	PITCHERS	IP	W–L	BB	SO	ERA
1B H. REICH	556	11	66	.306	8	A. LISKA	301	18–18	87	154	3.71
2B A. WRIGHT	523	0	56	.224	1	W. HILCHER	253	15–17	85	87	3.66
3B M. OWEN	501	1	70	.299	3	R. HARRELL (1)	226	9–17	94	74	4.78
SS L. BROWN	642	0	51	.245	7	E. REID	184	13–10	73	66	3.96
OF R. THOMPSON	594	11	46	.285	5	B. SPEECE	148	9–12	30	42	3.53
OF T. NORBERT	503	20	73	.278	1	J. GONZALES	134	4–12	33	36	4.70
OF J. GILL	421	12	56	.283	0	J. ORRELL	124	5–9	64	65	3.48
C F. HAWKINS	290	3	46	.283	4	J. CALLAHAN	80	1–4	53	34	4.28
O1 D. ESCOBAR	440	6	61	.282	4						
C J. SCHULTZ	284	0	24	.275	1	(1) ALSO WITH SAN FRANCISCO					
C J. ANNUNZIO	135	0	18	.207	1	MANAGER – O. VITT					
23 J. COSCARART	111	0	7	.180	0	RECORD W–71 L–97 FINISH–8TH					

PLAYOFFS
SEATTLE DEFEATED HOLLYWOOD 4 GAMES TO 3
SACRAMENTO DEFEATED SAN DIEGO 4 GAMES TO 0

FINAL
SEATTLE DEFEATED SACRAMENTO 4 GAMES TO 3

1942

SACRAMENTO		AB	HR	RBI	BA	SB	PITCHERS	IP	W–L	BB	SO	ERA
1B	M. STURDY	587	1	57	.300	6	T. FREITAS	295	24–13	36	98	2.93
2B	G. HANDLEY	312	0	34	.256	3	B. DONNELLY	270	21–10	128	165	2.84
3B	S. MESNER	680	1	74	.301	3	K. WICKER	250	16–12	63	83	3.24
SS	E. LAKE	633	19	69	.278	23	C. BEERS	210	16–12	56	72	3.81
OF	B. ADAMS	647	27	107	.309	9	H. LYONS	164	10–10	68	76	3.62
OF	D. GARMS	606	7	96	.314	15	W. SCHMIDT	140	10–8	27	36	3.09
OF	A. THOMPSON	553	1	54	.316	20						
C	R. MUELLER	565	16	102	.297	3						
O1	P. MARTIN	223	0	24	.247	6						
2B	C. MARSHALL	188	1	19	.229	1						
OF	W. SHEWEY	154	0	14	.299	6	MANAGER – P. MARTIN					
3B	G. LILLARD	97	3	20	.340	2	RECORD W–105 L–73 FINISH–1ST					

LOS ANGELES		AB	HR	RBI	BA	SB	PITCHERS	IP	W–L	BB	SO	ERA
1B	E. WAITKUS	699	9	81	.336	7	R. PRIM	277	21–10	39	121	2.47
2B	R. HUGHES	630	1	61	.298	21	RAFFENSBERGER	242	17–18	51	138	3.46
3B	E. MAYO	635	12	110	.307	10	R. LYNN	211	11–12	67	108	3.11
SS	B. SCHUSTER	640	6	78	.298	26	P. GEHRMAN	196	11–6	60	81	2.57
OF	B. OLSEN	645	15	87	.302	33	J. FLORES	185	14–5	63	100	2.63
OF	J. MOORE	487	7	85	.347	3	G. MALLORY	154	10–8	48	47	3.21
OF	P. LOWREY	393	5	39	.257	10	J. DOBERNIC	98	5–5	51	64	4.96
C	A. TODD	375	5	44	.256	4						
OF	F. BELL (1)	427	5	43	.246	6	(1) ALSO WITH HOLLYWOOD & OAKLAND					
OF	J. STATZ	263	2	22	.228	2	MANAGER – J. STATZ					
C	G. CAMPBELL	249	1	19	.201	1	RECORD W–104 L–74 FINISH–2ND					

SEATTLE		AB	HR	RBI	BA	SB	PITCHERS	IP	W–L	BB	SO	ERA
1B	E. TORGESON	523	4	52	.312	32	D. BARRETT	330	27–13	101	178	1.72
2B	A. NIEMIEC	612	1	67	.266	5	H. TURPIN	321	23–9	44	67	2.07
3B	D. GYSELMAN	647	2	64	.280	6	C. FISCHER	190	10–15	63	81	2.60
SS	N. STICKLE	669	1	37	.260	17	L. GUAY	138	9–5	53	40	3.39
OF	W. MATHESON	627	5	87	.313	13	M. BUDNICK	123	7–6	62	49	2.78
OF	J. WHITE	590	2	69	.297	27	D. SORIANO	116	5–7	73	60	3.18
OF	L. KING	470	0	43	.281	11	A. LIBKE	109	6–10	55	34	4.21
C	R. COLLINS	332	3	42	.259	11	E. CARNETT	84	4–6	37	26	3.54
OF	S. HARRIS	261	2	26	.276	0						
C	W. BEARD	172	0	10	.233	2						
OF	B. LAWRENCE	142	0	13	.310	0	MANAGER – B. SKIFF					
C	E. KEARSE	123	0	18	.260	1	RECORD W–96 L–82 FINISH–3RD					

1942

SAN DIEGO	AB	HR	RBI	BA	SB	PITCHERS	IP	W-L	BB	SO	ERA
1B G. MC DONALD	272	0	19	.268	0	W. HEBERT	319	22-15	78	125	2.37
2B M. SKELLEY	489	2	49	.252	4	A. OLSEN	293	18-16	93	94	2.76
3B J. HILL	544	2	62	.283	2	F. DASSO	284	15-18	127	155	2.88
SS J. CALVEY	545	4	66	.281	14	N. BROWN	197	13-12	80	76	3.58
OF H. PATCHETT	663	0	43	.288	8	POFFENBERGER	168	9-10	80	40	3.86
OF J. JENSEN	578	11	64	.275	11	B. THOMAS (1)	163	9-13	35	57	2.65
OF M. MAZZERA	575	14	90	.308	3	R. DILBECK	123	11-6	23	48	3.29
C B. SALKELD	354	7	60	.285	3						
C1 G. DETORE	303	2	38	.251	3						
32O A. GARIBALDI	298	0	25	.225	3	(1) ALSO WITH HOLLYWOOD					
1B F. STINSON	259	1	18	.263	0	**MANAGER - C. DURST**					
OF J. WHIPPLE	259	3	20	.251	1	**RECORD W-91 L-87 FINISH-4TH**					

SAN FRANCISCO	AB	HR	RBI	BA	SB	PITCHERS	IP	W-L	BB	SO	ERA
1B F. FAIN	519	4	53	.216	3	T. SEATS	250	10-18	56	89	3.67
2B O. BEJMA	344	1	32	.273	1	S. GIBSON	249	20-12	41	87	2.78
3B T. JENNINGS	376	3	60	.293	1	B. JOYCE	234	22-10	41	59	3.19
SS D. TROWER	607	1	35	.252	15	E. STUTZ	170	8-10	40	42	4.17
OF R. HODGIN	675	4	112	.320	6	L. JANSEN	173	11-14	39	46	4.31
OF B. HOLDER	652	6	51	.298	4	R. HARRELL	137	4-8	50	39	3.74
OF K. LEWIS	628	20	115	.312	7	A. EPPERLY	130	7-10	42	38	4.22
C J. SPRINZ	302	0	33	.242	1	A. LIEN	120	6-8	25	49	2.77
32 R. PERRY	536	12	75	.256	4						
C B. OGRODOWSKI	297	1	23	.300	0	(1) ALSO WITH PORTLAND					
1B C. HENSON	130	0	16	.177	0	**MANAGER - L. O'DOUL**					
1B F. HAWKINS (1)	124	2	11	.258	0	**RECORD W-88 L-90 FINISH-5TH**					

OAKLAND	AB	HR	RBI	BA	SB	PITCHERS	IP	W-L	BB	SO	ERA
1B L. SCARSELLA (1)	640	7	97	.267	5	J. SALVESON	310	24-12	60	93	2.58
2B H. LUBY	667	3	75	.310	10	C. PIPPEN	211	11-17	66	51	4.18
3B J. VERGEZ	335	3	31	.263	5	R. BUXTON	204	13-16	65	74	3.39
SS B. RIGNEY	638	1	57	.288	13	I. CHELINI	188	9-13	44	38	2.58
OF E. MAILHO	599	1	42	.294	15	S. CORBETT	181	8-11	54	49	4.47
OF W. WESTLAKE	593	7	74	.268	10	V. DI BIASI	181	10-13	73	74	3.43
OF M. GUDAT	369	0	41	.271	4	J. YELOVIC	112	4-7	56	68	3.05
C B. RAIMONDI	415	0	33	.246	6						
C J. GLENN	232	1	22	.246	3						
O3 F. TAUBY	194	1	30	.294	1						
OF M. DUEZABOU	173	1	17	.301	4	(1) ALSO WITH SEATTLE					
P J. SALVESON	155	1	16	.219	1	**MANAGER - J. VERGEZ**					
OF M. CHRISTOFF	107	1	8	.177	4	**RECORD W-85 L-92 FINISH-6TH**					

1942

HOLLYWOOD	AB	HR	RBI	BA	SB	PITCHERS	IP	W–L	BB	SO	ERA
1B W. GARBE	355	2	36	.265	3	R. JOINER	234	12–18	38	80	3.85
2B H. SCHULTE (1)	547	1	45	.260	5	F. GAY	229	8–19	82	76	3.69
3B B. KAHLE	634	0	62	.263	2	M. PEREZ	227	14–15	87	95	3.33
SS J. HOOVER	590	11	62	.327	14	C. ROOT	215	11–14	39	103	3.18
OF F. UHALT	669	1	40	.275	14	W. OSBORNE (2)	175	10–14	64	46	5.40
OF J. DICKSHOT	623	11	87	.303	14	J. BITTNER	174	13–8	59	70	2.48
OF F. KALIN	450	13	79	.304	1	B. BEVENS (3)	126	4–11	84	65	4.44
C B. ATWOOD	300	4	26	.253	0						
2S3 D. YOUNG	425	2	37	.249	3	(1) ALSO WITH OAKLAND					
C B. BRENZEL	287	1	20	.226	0	(2) ALSO WITH PORTLAND					
1B C. SYLVESTER	250	0	27	.232	0	(3) ALSO WITH SEATTLE					
OF B. CARNEY (2)	183	0	12	.279	1	**MANAGER – O. VITT**					
1B B. HERMAN	149	5	42	.322	0	**RECORD W–75 L–103 FINISH–7TH**					

PORTLAND	AB	HR	RBI	BA	SB	PITCHERS	IP	W–L	BB	SO	ERA
1B L. BARTON	564	10	74	.305	12	A. LISKA	322	15–21	73	164	3.64
2B A. WRIGHT	395	0	18	.228	1	J. ORRELL	280	11–22	94	131	4.00
3B M. OWEN	535	3	66	.303	5	S. COHEN	224	10–14	56	48	3.90
SS L. BROWN	492	0	31	.220	5	W. HILCHER (1)	220	7–16	63	59	3.60
OF R. THOMPSON	650	11	49	.308	6	W. SCHUBEL	141	8–8	51	43	4.98
OF T. NORBERT	481	28	99	.378	4	B. SPEECE	124	9–6	36	48	3.92
OF J. GILL	387	11	57	.302	7						
C J. LEOVICH	337	1	31	.190	0						
23S H. MARTINEZ	284	3	26	.243	8						
OF L. STINE	281	2	40	.278	2						
OF D. AMARAL	250	2	27	.308	3	(1) ALSO WITH HOLLYWOOD					
3O B. BERGSTROM	160	0	14	.238	1	**MANAGER – F. BRAZILL**					
C T. MAYER	127	0	9	.213	0	**RECORD W–67 L–110 FINISH–8TH**					

PLAYOFFS
SEATTLE DEFEATED SACRAMENTO 4 GAMES TO 1
LOS ANGELES DEFEATED SAN DIEGO 4 GAMES TO 3

FINAL
SEATTLE DEFEATED LOS ANGELES 4 GAMES TO 2

1943

LOS ANGELES	AB	HR	RBI	BA	SB	PITCHERS	IP	W–L	BB	SO	ERA
1B W. QUINN	572	11	80	.236	10	R. LYNN	248	21–8	64	110	2.47
2B R. HUGHES	461	0	41	.323	18	RAFFENSBERGER	244	19–11	53	134	2.14
3B C. ENGLISH	591	16	98	.323	2	P. GEHRMAN	226	20–7	49	80	2.43
SS B. SCHUSTER	618	5	67	.275	16	J. PHIPPS	202	17–5	69	80	3.03
OF A. PAFKO	604	18	118	.356	13	G. MALLORY	192	11–8	47	81	3.08
OF J. OSTROWSKI	472	21	82	.282	7	O. BAKER	111	10–3	18	34	2.84
OF C. GARRIOTT	286	10	47	.255	11	D. OSBORN	102	10–1	29	30	2.65
C B. HOLM	271	2	28	.292	4						
OF J. MOORE	217	1	31	.290	1						
2B E. MALLORY	159	3	18	.346	5	MANAGER – B. SWEENEY					
OF R. RUSSELL	153	7	26	.320	1	RECORD W–110 L–45 FINISH–1ST					

SAN FRANCISCO	AB	HR	RBI	BA	SB	PITCHERS	IP	W–L	BB	SO	ERA
1B G. SUHR	527	1	65	.247	1	B. JOYCE	259	20–12	37	75	2.43
2B D. YOUNG	549	4	56	.246	0	R. HARRELL	241	17–16	74	106	3.17
3B C. PETERSEN	516	0	49	.286	5	T. SEATS	229	14–11	41	75	2.48
SS D. TROWER	263	2	18	.221	5	A. LIEN	222	13–12	39	76	2.55
OF H. STEINBACHER	569	2	105	.318	0	A. EPPERLY	166	16–5	45	60	3.47
OF F. UHALT	512	1	47	.313	17	S. GIBSON	125	6–5	27	34	2.45
OF G. METKOVICH	268	3	38	.325	4						
C J. SPRINZ	298	0	22	.211	3						
S2 J. ADAIR (1)	301	0	36	.239	2						
C B. OGRODOWSKI	248	0	22	.262	0						
3O W. ENOS	223	6	38	.305	2	(1) ALSO WITH HOLLYWOOD					
OF L. HOOPER	188	1	16	.240	0	MANAGER – L. O'DOUL					
3B E. PAUL	173	0	11	.249	2	RECORD W–89 L–66 FINISH–2ND					

SEATTLE	AB	HR	RBI	BA	SB	PITCHERS	IP	W–L	BB	SO	ERA
1B L. GABRIELSON	421	0	54	.306	22	J. DEMORAN	256	16–15	73	66	2.57
2B M. MULLEN	426	0	31	.272	17	P. JONAS	193	12–14	78	78	2.98
3B D. GYSELMAN	518	0	49	.297	14	B. SPEECE	175	13–9	41	54	2.83
SS J. DOBBINS (1)	412	0	54	.316	9	G. ELLIOTT	136	6–7	41	36	3.84
OF W. MATHESON	548	6	67	.265	16	H. TURPIN	106	7–6	17	25	2.89
OF E. CARNETT	403	2	28	.300	21	S. JOHNSON	104	8–7	7	38	2.51
OF L. KING	263	0	14	.255	6	C. FISCHER	103	10–3	36	36	2.71
C H. SUEME	398	2	49	.281	3	E. CARNETT	63	4–4	22	18	3.14
OF B. LAWRENCE	256	0	17	.242	1						
OF W. KATS	227	0	22	.233	9						
12S J. JEWELL	197	1	12	.228	3	(1) ALSO WITH HOLLYWOOD					
OF L. CHRISTOPHER	137	4	15	.277	6	MANAGER – B. SKIFF					
2S3 S. GRAY	130	0	12	.246	3	RECORD W–85 L–70 FINISH–3RD					

1943

PORTLAND		AB	HR	RBI	BA	SB	PITCHERS		IP	W–L	BB	SO	ERA
1B	L. BARTON	499	11	72	.285	3	A. LISKA		254	17–11	31	122	1.98
2B	B. FLOYD	440	0	32	.264	5	J. WILSON		183	8–10	52	76	2.75
3B	M. OWEN	260	0	32	.308	1	J. ORRELL		170	8–11	61	90	2.33
SS	J. O'NEIL	453	0	49	.254	3	S. COHEN		154	10–8	31	40	3.16
OF	R. THOMPSON	524	2	35	.280	2	E. COOK		148	5–12	51	42	3.83
OF	T. GULLIC	513	17	82	.269	5	M. PIERETTI		135	8–11	50	55	3.07
OF	J. GILL	393	2	60	.323	2	W. OSBORNE		127	9–5	39	35	2.48
C	E. ADAMS	299	3	34	.247	0	W. HERRING		121	8–5	41	44	2.90
23	P. ROGERS	551	3	52	.247	5	**MANAGER – M. SHEA**						
OF	S. HARRIS	366	6	44	.276	1	**RECORD W–79 L–76 FINISH–4TH**						

HOLLYWOOD		AB	HR	RBI	BA	SB	PITCHERS		IP	W–L	BB	SO	ERA
1B	C. MORAN	592	4	64	.284	10	B. THOMAS		249	11–21	66	78	3.90
2B	KNICKERBOCKER	236	0	26	.284	1	R. JOINER		174	11–11	56	50	5.28
3B	H. CLEMENTS	612	0	51	.306	12	R. SMITH		168	12–9	62	68	3.91
SS	T. DAVIS	362	2	37	.221	3	C. ROOT		166	15–5	28	70	3.09
OF	J. DICKSHOT	583	13	99	.352	9	C. BLANTON		150	9–9	43	70	2.70
OF	B. HOLDER	543	6	62	.273	12	E. ERAUTT		115	5–9	40	33	3.29
OF	R. YOUNKER	414	13	67	.280	0	P. MC LAUGHLIN		113	4–5	49	23	4.22
C	B. BRENZEL	271	2	26	.247	0	ESCALANTE (1)		106	5–8	44	29	3.57
2O	K. RICHARDSON	310	6	43	.258	4							
2B	A. LILLY	189	0	10	.206	4	(1) ALSO WITH PORTLAND						
C	J. HILL	157	1	9	.229	2	**MANAGER – C. ROOT**						
OF	B. HERMAN	147	4	22	.354	1	**RECORD W–73 L–82 FINISH–5TH (T)**						

OAKLAND		AB	HR	RBI	BA	SB	PITCHERS		IP	W–L	BB	SO	ERA
1B	L. SCARSELLA	589	3	85	.326	12	C. PIPPEN		270	20–15	69	56	3.03
2B	H. LUBY	587	3	69	.313	16	J. LOTZ		216	11–16	73	42	3.75
3B	ROSENLUND (1)	374	0	34	.243	1	R. BUXTON		183	11–11	51	92	2.75
SS	J. CAULFIELD	537	0	42	.246	4	V. DI BIASI		154	7–11	73	70	4.15
OF	E. MAILHO	598	2	46	.314	13	I. CHELINI		147	12–7	30	26	3.67
OF	F. BELL	529	3	72	.263	10	N. KLEINKE		106	1–10	45	34	4.41
OF	J. DEVINCENZI	426	5	54	.225	5	E. JONES		91	5–6	47	39	2.17
C	B. RAIMONDI	430	1	41	.277	7	F. STROMME		73	2–2	37	31	4.44
3B	J. VERGEZ	244	0	16	.189	5	(1) ALSO WITH SAN FRANCISCO						
OF	J. GONZALES	202	0	21	.183	3	**MANAGER – J. VERGEZ**						
C	W. LEONARD	119	0	8	.168	0	**RECORD W–73 L–82 FINISH–5TH (T)**						

1943

SAN DIEGO	AB	HR	RBI	BA	SB	PITCHERS	IP	W—L	BB	SO	ERA
1B G. MC DONALD	391	0	50	.330	5	C. SCHANZ	276	17—18	130	137	3.23
2B E. WHEELER	493	3	32	.304	14	C. JOHNSON	242	14—16	97	106	3.27
3B W. LOWE	499	2	55	.265	1	J. BRILLHEART	213	9—14	99	53	3.51
SS J. CALVEY	534	0	54	.272	19	F. DASSO	177	12—8	93	154	2.75
OF H. PATCHETT	522	1	49	.284	25	R. CECIL	137	8—10	51	81	2.89
OF M. GUDAT (1)	407	0	26	.256	8	R. DILBECK	118	7—9	24	37	3.51
OF M. ABBOTT	247	1	27	.243	3						
C B. SALKELD	309	2	47	.275	3						
OF J. WHIPPLE	225	1	25	.218	2						
C G. DETORE	187	1	29	.321	1						
32 A. CAILTEAUX	185	0	13	.227	2						
OF J. JENSEN	153	3	21	.255	1						
2B G. MORGAN	152	0	16	.270	2	(1) ALSO WITH HOLLYWOOD					
C D. BALLINGER	135	2	16	.281	3	MANAGER — C. DURST/G. DETORE					
3B L. ESTES	115	0	11	.209	0	RECORD W—70 L—85 FINISH—7TH					

SACRAMENTO	AB	HR	RBI	BA	SB	PITCHERS	IP	W—L	BB	SO	ERA
1B J. ANGLE	512	3	48	.225	14	B. BYERLY	246	9—21	91	98	2.49
2B N. JONES	477	4	37	.304	9	C. DREISEWERD	236	9—20	37	65	3.89
3B F. HENSLEY	434	1	44	.274	0	J. PINTAR	221	5—27	57	63	4.69
SS O. BURNETT	552	6	43	.275	32	A. BRAZLE	160	11—8	60	69	1.69
OF E. KAVANAUGH	485	1	40	.266	16	J. ROY	73	1—8	44	29	4.81
OF B. RAMSEY	379	0	21	.235	28	B. FITZKE	70	0—8	26	9	5.53
OF M. VIAS	346	0	24	.243	6	S. LE GAULT	69	3—6	29	20	2.22
C E. MALONE	359	1	28	.262	5	H. POLLY	58	1—7	22	21	4.50
CO1 E. PETERSEN	278	5	34	.270	3						
3B G. JUMONVILLE	241	3	27	.207	3						
OF J. MOLINA	211	1	12	.223	1	MANAGER — K. PENNER					
1B C. SUYTAR	168	0	10	.220	0	RECORD W—41 L—114 FINISH—8TH					

PLAYOFFS
SAN FRANCISCO DEFEATED PORTLAND 4 GAMES TO 2
SEATTLE DEFEATED LOS ANGELES 4 GAMES TO 0

FINAL
SAN FRANCISCO DEFEATED SEATTLE 4 GAMES TO 2

1944

LOS ANGELES	AB	HR	RBI	BA	SB	PITCHERS	IP	W–L	BB	SO	ERA
1B R. OTERO	421	0	54	.306	6	R. PRIM	286	22–10	40	139	1.70
2B R. RUSSELL	585	17	89	.315	4	G. COMELLAS	276	18–14	94	128	2.61
3B C. ENGLISH (1)	447	2	59	.293	7	D. OSBORN	216	15–13	44	47	3.25
SS G. MILLER	519	0	47	.233	3	R. ADAMS	186	10–7	56	87	3.58
OF C. GARRIOTT	619	13	70	.286	24	D. CONGER	169	13–7	35	65	2.88
OF E. SAUER	392	5	52	.293	19	C. HORTON	91	9–4	31	26	2.87
OF T. NORBERT	363	10	57	.289	1	G. MALLORY	73	6–3	17	46	2.59
C E. FERNANDES	400	5	57	.280	2						
O3 J. OSTROWSKI	475	10	67	.282	7						
C B. SARNI	229	5	24	.227	0	(1) ALSO WITH OAKLAND					
2B G. OGOREK	188	0	14	.245	4	MANAGER – B. SWEENEY					
SS R. SMALLEY	160	1	11	.188	1	RECORD W–99 L–70 FINISH–1ST					

PORTLAND	AB	HR	RBI	BA	SB	PITCHERS	IP	W–L	BB	SO	ERA
1B L. BARTON	462	4	53	.253	6	M. PIERETTI	322	26–13	125	139	2.46
2B M. NUNES	302	1	21	.219	2	R. HELSER	280	20–16	120	156	2.41
3B M. OWEN	449	1	63	.290	9	A. LISKA	236	18–9	40	124	2.48
SS J. O'NEIL	631	0	43	.236	8	S. COHEN	150	10–13	56	44	3.54
OF F. SHONE	509	0	48	.275	17	C. FEDERMEYER	144	6–6	109	59	4.19
OF J. GILL	425	3	49	.287	6	D. PULFORD	121	3–10	43	48	3.72
OF S. HARRIS	373	5	45	.273	1						
C E. ADAMS	310	0	37	.297	1						
O13 T. GULLIC	358	8	54	.260	3						
23O C. PETERSEN	355	0	28	.273	6	MANAGER – M. OWEN					
OF N. DE WEESE	332	2	33	.253	2	RECORD W–87 L–82 FINISH–2ND					

SAN FRANCISCO	AB	HR	RBI	BA	SB	PITCHERS	IP	W–L	BB	SO	ERA
1B G. SUHR	588	0	75	.279	6	B. JOYCE	324	21–20	73	105	2.80
2B D. YOUNG	541	0	53	.231	4	T. SEATS	320	25–13	51	129	2.36
3B J. TRUTTA	241	0	28	.261	4	R. HARRELL	300	20–18	91	168	2.61
SS J. FUTERNICK	398	0	28	.291	15	B. WERLE	289	14–19	84	129	4.05
OF F. UHALT	612	0	52	.276	37	S. GIBSON	114	4–8	26	27	3.95
OF H. STEINBACHER	492	1	86	.248	10						
OF B. GUINTINI	408	2	59	.245	10						
C J. SPRINZ	272	0	28	.276	3						
S3 J. CAVALLI	387	2	44	.214	3						
C B. OGRODOWSKI	266	0	29	.271	1						
OF B. ENOS	241	1	31	.282	2						
OF L. HOOPER	159	0	13	.289	11						
OF N. SHERIDAN	150	4	21	.293	6	MANAGER – L. O'DOUL					
OF D. RESTELLI	137	1	19	.343	6	RECORD W–86 L–83 FINISH–3RD (T)					

1944

OAKLAND		AB	HR	RBI	BA	SB	PITCHERS	IP	W–L	BB	SO	ERA
1B	D. CAMILLI	357	14	60	.289	12	J. LOTZ	254	18–13	78	68	3.22
2B	A. WRIGHT	256	0	26	.215	4	M. SALVO	210	18–7	38	58	1.86
3B	C. ROSENLUND	592	1	59	.252	8	F. STROMME	182	11–11	78	55	2.57
SS	J. CAULFIELD	605	2	45	.258	8	C. PIPPEN	176	8–11	31	77	3.17
OF	L. SCARSELLA	596	6	96	.329	9	N. KLEINKE (1)	138	5–10	57	45	3.91
OF	J. KREEVICH	501	2	50	.267	20	J. SULLIVAN (2)	134	3–14	58	41	4.23
OF	E. MAILHO	465	0	27	.277	16	D. HAYES	110	7–6	38	56	2.62
C	B. RAIMONDI	452	0	45	.290	10						

(1) ALSO WITH SAN DIEGO

OF	F. HAWKINS	334	3	45	.311	11	(2) ALSO WITH PORTLAND
2S	J. HERRERA	220	0	27	.250	7	**MANAGER – D. CAMILLI**
23	L. STORTI	135	0	12	.193	1	**RECORD W–86 L–83 FINISH–3RD (T)**

SEATTLE		AB	HR	RBI	BA	SB	PITCHERS	IP	W–L	BB	SO	ERA
1B	A. LIBKE	397	5	51	.307	13	J. DEMORAN	264	18–16	79	64	2.42
2B	J. DOBBINS	445	1	49	.222	6	C. FISCHER	234	16–13	47	144	1.86
3B	D. GYSELMAN	607	0	49	.305	23	H. TURPIN	229	13–15	33	52	3.10
SS	W. LYMAN	375	0	31	.224	14	B. SPEECE	180	10–13	30	67	2.80
OF	W. MATHESON	567	2	52	.275	21	F. TINCUP	164	8–10	72	78	2.80
OF	L. CHRISTOPHER	398	6	35	.284	13	J. BABICH	134	8–8	66	38	3.16
OF	R. JOHNSON	369	2	35	.260	12	G. ELLIOTT	131	6–6	42	58	3.43
C	H. SUEME	314	1	29	.226	8						

OF	P. CARPENTER	333	3	39	.225	7	
2S	R. GORBOULD	327	0	23	.248	12	
C	H. SPINDEL	211	0	32	.355	2	
OF	C. CREEDEN	207	2	24	.280	15	**MANAGER – B. SKIFF**
OF	W. KATS	155	1	10	.200	10	**RECORD W–84 L–85 FINISH–5TH**

HOLLYWOOD		AB	HR	RBI	BA	SB	PITCHERS	IP	W–L	BB	SO	ERA
1B	C. MORAN	521	2	65	.315	8	R. SMITH	213	16–12	79	64	3.63
2B	K. RICHARDSON	536	7	62	.252	7	R. MISHASEK	209	16–10	74	73	3.79
3B	B. FAUSETT	381	0	35	.312	11	E. ESCALANTE	200	10–14	96	89	4.10
SS	T. DAVIS	604	4	77	.248	1	J. INTLEKOFER	145	11–6	45	46	2.92
OF	B. HOLDER	583	6	54	.280	21	C. HUFFORD	137	7–6	70	32	3.61
OF	F. KELLEHER	487	29	121	.329	0	J. SHARP	134	6–10	103	60	4.90
OF	D. JONES	367	0	20	.281	13	A. WELDON	125	6–8	53	47	3.89
C	J. HILL	375	2	35	.253	5	C. ROOT	87	3–5	28	58	3.20

23	R. OLSEN	302	5	35	.232	2	
CO	R. YOUNKER	299	3	27	.237	0	
OF	O. MEYERS (1)	284	0	23	.243	3	(1) ALSO WITH SACRAMENTO
O1	L. POWERS	239	3	32	.280	2	**MANAGER – C. ROOT**
3B	H. CLEMENTS	148	1	15	.243	0	**RECORD W–83 L–86 FINISH–6TH**

1944

SACRAMENTO		AB	HR	RBI	BA	SB	PITCHERS	IP	W-L	BB	SO	ERA
1B	C. SUYTAR	466	2	45	.219	1	G. FLETCHER	268	12-19	94	126	2.82
2B	G. HANDLEY	499	0	44	.259	15	C. DREISEWERD	252	20-9	21	137	1.61
3B	M. SERAFINI	308	6	29	.237	0	S. LE GAULT	218	9-16	65	86	3.84
SS	R. WATSON	369	0	23	.217	5	G. BABBITT	203	8-15	73	42	3.24
OF	B. RAMSEY	687	2	70	.278	45	E. PORTER	190	10-13	62	68	3.65
OF	A. MC ELREATH	425	2	42	.289	15	D. POWERS	136	7-9	56	37	2.98
OF	F. ROGERS	328	0	20	.244	2	B. BEASLEY	105	5-6	32	21	3.00
C	J. STEINER	314	0	34	.312	4						
U	J. ANGLE	351	1	25	.279	15						
C	L. MARCUCCI	156	1	17	.269	1						
C	J. ROSSI	154	1	17	.214	3						
3B	P. BOWA	145	0	8	.221	7						
O3	W. COX	140	0	17	.257	1	**MANAGER - E. SHEELY**					
OF	E. WEIGANDT	112	0	5	.232	1	**RECORD W-76 L-93 FINISH-7TH**					

SAN DIEGO		AB	HR	RBI	BA	SB	PITCHERS	IP	W-L	BB	SO	ERA
1B	G. MC DONALD	313	0	34	.310	5	F. DASSO	298	20-19	131	253	2.81
2B	V. REYNOLDS	371	0	39	.267	6	R. CECIL	246	19-11	103	186	2.16
3B	E. WHEELER	655	2	56	.267	43	J. BRILLHEART	190	8-14	65	43	3.08
SS	J. CALVEY	514	1	44	.249	25	C. JOHNSON	186	12-11	94	138	3.53
OF	H. PATCHETT	426	1	56	.275	19	J. VALENZUELA	137	3-10	98	58	4.66
OF	M. GUDAT	369	0	31	.282	8	J. WOOD	79	5-4	37	35	2.50
OF	M. STEINER (1)	345	1	36	.267	13						
C	B. SALKELD	340	3	49	.241	4						
C	D. BALLINGER	278	0	26	.241	2						
O1	L. VEZELICH	265	1	31	.275	5						
2S3	G. MORGAN	224	0	15	.232	6						
OF	M. ABBOTT	197	5	25	.254	1						
OF	J. WHIPPLE	152	0	12	.243	6						
1B	W. LOWE	148	0	27	.277	2						
OF	R. THOMPSON	127	0	8	.213	0	(1) ALSO WITH OAKLAND					
OF	J. LAZOR	124	1	7	.306	3	**MANAGER - G. DETORE**					
2B	A. CAILTEAUX	119	0	7	.176	0	**RECORD W-75 L-94 FINISH-8TH**					

PLAYOFFS
SAN FRANCISCO DEFEATED OAKLAND 4 GAMES TO 1
LOS ANGELES DEFEATED PORTLAND 4 GAMES TO 2

FINAL
SAN FRANCISCO DEFEATED LOS ANGELES 4 GAMES TO 3

1945

PORTLAND		AB	HR	RBI	BA	SB	PITCHERS		IP	W–L	BB	SO	ERA
1B	L. BARTON	509	6	76	.318	8	D. PULFORD		274	20–11	84	152	2.37
2B	C. ENGLISH	449	4	52	.283	2	A. LISKA		273	20–12	59	127	2.34
3B	M. OWEN	566	1	83	.311	10	R. HELSER		270	20–14	99	136	3.37
SS	J. O'NEIL	585	0	88	.315	10	S. COHEN		199	14–8	56	67	3.26
OF	F. SHONE	642	5	63	.304	39	W. MOSSOR		157	13–7	71	138	2.92
OF	T. GULLIC	517	9	81	.259	10	J. MOOTY		156	11–5	63	72	3.12
OF	F. DEMAREE	514	3	78	.304	5	J. TISING		145	11–10	38	52	2.92
C	E. ADAMS	344	2	39	.235	3							
2O3	C. PETERSEN	325	0	43	.258	5	(1) ALSO WITH SAN FRANCISCO						
2B	M. NUNES	311	0	38	.273	5	(2) ALSO WITH LOS ANGELES						
OF	N. RHABE (2)	228	0	19	.285	2	**MANAGER – M. OWEN**						
C	F. SOUZA	138	0	7	.203	0	**RECORD W–112 L–68 FINISH–1ST**						

SEATTLE		AB	HR	RBI	BA	SB	PITCHERS		IP	W–L	BB	SO	ERA
1B	G. MC DONALD	552	1	69	.332	26	J. DEMORAN		262	20–10	72	77	2.85
2B	R. GORBOULD	594	1	54	.283	37	C. FISCHER		253	17–14	60	108	2.63
3B	C. ALENO	536	9	84	.289	8	H. TURPIN		229	18–8	26	29	2.40
SS	W. LYMAN	385	0	38	.286	18	G. ELLIOTT		196	14–12	67	80	0.01
OF	T. NORBERT	527	23	109	.258	6	C. JOHNSON		178	14–12	82	117	3.44
OF	J. WHIPPLE	229	1	22	.262	15	A. PALICA		164	10–9	82	55	4.39
OF	W. KATS	221	0	21	.290	6							
C	H. SUEME	340	0	00	.268	7							
S23	J. DOBBINS	477	1	63	.323	12							
C	B. FINLEY	261	4	48	.307	3							
O1	J. GILL (1)	241	2	32	.266	5	(1) ALSO WITH PORTLAND						
OF	R. JOHNSON	214	1	29	.271	11	**MANAGER – B. SKIFF**						
O1	W. MATHESON	152	0	17	.289	0	**RECORD W–105 L–78 FINISH–2ND**						

SACRAMENTO		AB	HR	RBI	BA	SB	PITCHERS		IP	W–L	BB	SO	ERA
1B	E. ZIPAY	427	0	83	.311	6	G. FLETCHER		335	24–14	92	144	2.33
2B	G. HANDLEY	700	1	66	.307	56	J. WOOD		205	9–14	89	64	5.22
3B	L. MARCUCCI	523	7	93	.287	7	J. MC CARTHY		159	10–10	51	50	4.13
SS	J. CALVEY	553	6	80	.271	13	G. BABBITT		140	6–13	53	37	3.99
OF	J. WHITE	688	1	87	.355	40	S. LE GAULT (2)		136	5–8	49	32	3.84
OF	G. MANDISH	471	4	92	.333	9	E. PORTER (2)		134	6–7	48	34	5.10
OF	A. MC ELREATH	406	0	69	.291	14	B. BEASLEY		132	12–4	30	22	3.14
C	N. SCHLEUTER	427	2	44	.246	4	D. POWERS		108	5–6	35	22	4.67
U	J. LANDRUM	618	2	99	.298	11	(1) ALSO WITH PORTLAND						
1CO	R. YOUNKER (1)	366	5	53	.251	4	(2) ALSO WITH HOLLYWOOD						
OF	T. GREENHALGH	224	0	26	.295	5	**MANAGER – E. SHEELY**						
3B	J. GRANT	126	1	22	.310	0	**RECORD W–95 L–85 FINISH–3RD**						

1945

SAN FRANCISCO	AB	HR	RBI	BA	SB	PITCHERS	IP	W–L	BB	SO	ERA
1B G. SUHR	399	0	56	.311	3	B. JOYCE	344	31–11	55	100	2.17
2B D. YOUNG	456	0	47	.272	3	F. SEWARD	257	18–13	106	113	3.85
3B R. PERRY	469	5	67	.271	8	R. BARTHELSON	233	12–14	97	50	4.29
SS R. NICELY	484	1	44	.250	7	E. ORELLA	187	11–11	72	46	3.37
OF N. SHERIDAN	527	3	68	.290	30	K. BRONDELL	110	4–10	55	33	4.25
OF F. UHALT	508	0	41	.301	26	F. EHRMAN	96	8–4	44	27	2.62
OF E. MAILHO	484	1	69	.306	9	A. BUZOLICH	96	4–10	60	11	4.97
C J. SPRINZ	307	0	33	.303	5						
OF B. GUINTINI	304	2	35	.283	4						
1B B. SANDERS	287	1	60	.310	4						
OF B. ENOS	286	5	57	.346	2	**MANAGER – L. O'DOUL**					
C B. OGRODOWSKI	282	0	28	.248	0	**RECORD W–96 L–87 FINISH–4TH**					

OAKLAND	AB	HR	RBI	BA	SB	PITCHERS	IP	W–L	BB	SO	ERA
1B V. PICETTI	546	1	86	.282	13	G. MANN	222	15–9	95	131	2.88
2B G. STEWART	608	1	86	.331	5	L. GILMORE	220	14–13	90	91	4.46
3B C. ROSENLUND	470	0	35	.253	10	F. STROMME	218	16–13	94	93	3.92
SS J. CAULFIELD	676	3	72	.296	10	M. CHETKOVICH	168	10–11	72	65	3.32
OF H. PATCHETT (1)	580	0	47	.307	19	D. HAYES	130	9–9	52	45	4.57
OF L. SCARSELLA	508	10	77	.325	11	J. BABICH	129	4–9	62	36	4.39
OF T. HAFEY	429	9	67	.242	7	J. LOTZ	125	5–9	48	38	6.12
C B. RAIMONDI	341	2	40	.267	3	I. CHELINI	101	5–10	24	28	3.74
OF F. HAWKINS	399	5	66	.341	6						
OF N. DE WEESE	361	4	56	.321	4						
3B J. DIFANI	187	0	19	.294	8	(1) ALSO WITH SEATTLE					
OF C. METRO	186	2	19	.242	3	**MANAGER – D. CAMILLI/B. RAIMONDI**					
C S. FENECH	165	0	18	.267	0	**RECORD W–90 L–93 FINISH–5TH**					

SAN DIEGO	AB	HR	RBI	BA	SB	PITCHERS	IP	W–L	BB	SO	ERA
1B W. PROUT (1)	356	0	59	.292	0	V. EAVES	312	21–15	127	187	3.00
2B B. BOKEN	233	8	57	.330	2	C. DUMLER	282	21–16	104	143	2.42
3B D. GYSELMAN	576	2	74	.321	27	J. BRILLHEART	236	15–13	101	87	4.50
SS F. GIRA	225	0	16	.204	0	B. FERGUSON	211	5–21	114	108	3.54
OF T. CRISCOLA	689	1	58	.311	40	G. KNOWLES (1)	153	8–7	83	43	4.29
OF L. VEZELICH	628	6	110	.307	9	V. TRAHD	121	5–10	75	41	5.21
OF R. THOMPSON	344	1	26	.346	8						
C D. BALLINGER	562	2	82	.299	9						
O2 J. KREEVICH	294	1	25	.252	10						
S23 J. DUNPHY	283	0	12	.216	7	(1) ALSO WITH SACRAMENTO					
OF M. ABBOTT	268	5	42	.280	2	**MANAGER – P. MARTIN**					
1B M. GUDAT	238	0	25	.265	3	**RECORD W–82 L–101 FINISH–6TH**					

1945

LOS ANGELES	AB	HR	RBI	BA	SB	PITCHERS	IP	W–L	BB	SO	ERA
1B M. HICKS	606	10	87	.299	2	R. ADAMS	298	21–15	90	160	2.72
2B R. VIERS	606	2	53	.244	4	D. OSBORN	269	18–13	38	41	2.68
3B P. ELKO	630	4	59	.284	5	C. CUELLAR	225	13–17	83	121	4.40
SS C. BREWSTER	261	1	28	.284	8	G. COMELLAS	156	6–16	55	79	4.44
OF R. RUSSELL	538	14	89	.342	2	K. HICKS	134	6–10	109	40	5.24
OF J. TYACK	518	8	69	.326	19	P. LAMMERS	119	4–11	83	38	5.45
OF L. NOVIKOFF	390	9	52	.310	5	G. WOODEND	90	3–11	57	28	7.50
C M. KREITNER	328	0	36	.277	0	W. MERKLE	88	2–4	39	25	5.62
1B R. OTERO	302	0	23	.344	2						
OF L. PATON	247	0	18	.247	8						
C L. GREENE	223	6	32	.247	0						
S3 G. MILLER	158	0	18	.203	1						
OF D. DOUGLAS	142	1	9	.303	1	MANAGER – B. SWEENEY					
2B R. PETERSON	124	0	8	.226	1	RECORD W–76 L–107 FINISH–7TH					

HOLLYWOOD	AB	HR	RBI	BA	SB	PITCHERS	IP	W–L	BB	SO	ERA
1B C. MORAN	625	6	101	.302	14	N. KIMBALL	301	19–21	57	71	3.44
2B K. RICHARDSON	469	14	85	.301	11	H. SMITH	281	15–20	110	97	4.29
3B B. FAUSETT	644	2	60	.315	21	R. MISHASEK	252	16–16	86	84	5.14
SS H. WILLINGHAM	359	10	63	.256	1	J. MARSHALL (4)	148	5–12	103	63	5.41
OF B. CANTRELL	502	3	69	.281	1	R. WILLIAMS	131	7–10	100	35	5.36
OF L. POWERS	397	4	56	.287	3	J. INTELKOFER	100	1–8	41	35	5.94
OF M. STEINER	339	3	27	.221	19						
C J. HILL	465	1	47	.284	5						
U V. REYNOLDS (1)	473	0	42	.233	7	(1) ALSO WITH SAN DIEGO					
S2 J. CAVALLI (2)	356	1	47	.258	3	(2) ALSO WITH SAN FRANCISCO					
OF S. HARRIS (3)	316	3	46	.250	4	(3) ALSO WITH PORTLAND					
OF B. HOLDER	312	5	41	.256	13	(4) ALSO WITH OAKLAND					
OF B. STEWART	251	0	34	.323	9	MANAGER – B. FAUSETT					
2B M. CHOZEN	140	0	15	.200	1	RECORD W–73 L–110 FINISH–8TH					

PLAYOFFS
SEATTLE DEFEATED PORTLAND 4 GAMES TO 3
SAN FRANCISCO DEFEATED SACRAMENTO 4 GAMES TO 3

FINAL
SAN FRANCISCO DEFEATED SEATTLE 4 GAMES TO 2

1946

SAN FRANCISCO	AB	HR	RBI	BA	SB	PITCHERS	IP	W−L	BB	SO	ERA
1B F. FAIN	615	11	112	.301	24	L. JANSEN	321	30−6	69	171	1.57
2B H. LUBY	678	2	60	.294	22	C. MELTON	248	17−12	72	99	2.83
3B T. JENNINGS	495	3	53	.303	11	F. SEWARD	219	15−13	79	72	3.12
SS R. NICELY	446	1	46	.220	5	B. WERLE	175	12−8	59	72	2.26
OF D. WHITE	553	4	90	.288	4	R. HARRELL	167	13−6	62	70	2.91
OF F. UHALT	520	1	24	.263	24	A. LIEN	143	8−9	52	67	2.90
OF N. SHERIDAN	357	5	55	.269	9	F. ROSSO	141	11−9	67	60	2.68
C B. OGRODOWSKI	312	0	34	.244	1						
OF S. TAORMINA	357	4	69	.255	5						
SS R. HOOVER	215	1	27	.200	3	MANAGER − L. O'DOUL					
3B D. TROWER	193	0	11	.207	9	RECORD W−115 L−68 FINISH−1ST					

OAKLAND	AB	HR	RBI	BA	SB	PITCHERS	IP	W−L	BB	SO	ERA
1B L. SCARSELLA	428	22	91	.332	4	R. ARDIZOIA	207	15−7	76	105	2.83
2B O. BURNETT	563	1	42	.238	14	C. PIPPEN	184	14−11	56	58	2.84
3B B. HART	458	6	70	.227	2	F. SPEER	184	11−8	56	72	2.93
SS R. HAMRICK	346	1	35	.266	6	S. SHEA	174	15−5	60	124	1.66
OF B. HOLDER	477	13	59	.283	14	G. BEARDEN	167	15−4	75	81	3.13
OF H. MARTIN	447	10	46	.255	6	B. STEPHENS	159	10−9	65	91	3.40
OF W. WESTLAKE	429	7	57	.315	5	T. HAFEY	137	6−8	38	62	2.63
C B. RAIMONDI	347	0	32	.300	6	R. BUXTON	119	10−5	32	68	2.57
						C. GASSAWAY	89	7−5	39	52	3.13
OF M. MARSHALL	345	9	56	.278	8						
2O T. SABOL	301	0	23	.246	11						
C E. KEARSE	209	1	30	.273	0						
1B V. BUCCOLA	196	4	22	.265	3	MANAGER − C. STENGEL					
3B C. BIGGS	159	0	12	.245	5	RECORD W−111 L−72 FINISH−2ND					

HOLLYWOOD	AB	HR	RBI	BA	SB	PITCHERS	IP	W−L	BB	SO	ERA
1B T. LUPIEN	633	9	77	.295	43	E. ERAUTT	290	20−14	77	234	2.76
2B G. STEWART (1)	591	4	68	.271	8	A. CUCCURULLO	180	7−11	79	102	2.70
3B B. FAUSETT	252	0	22	.258	12	M. PEREZ	199	7−13	88	79	2.94
SS A. ANDERSON	550	0	31	.264	15	X. RESCIGNO	155	11−9	52	76	3.19
OF C. RIKARD	456	8	68	.325	6	F. DASSO	146	12−5	71	88	3.27
OF F. KALIN	389	11	60	.311	3	A. WILKIE	142	9−7	41	46	2.85
OF T. O'BRIEN	348	17	73	.276	4	R. SMITH	112	7−6	45	49	2.49
C A. UNSER	475	13	68	.259	3	J. BITTNER	97	4−7	31	34	3.34
S3 J. CAVALLI	331	1	24	.211	7						
O1 C. MORAN	305	1	33	.285	6						
OF F. KELLEHER	297	18	54	.286	3	(1) ALSO WITH OAKLAND					
OF B. STEWART	246	2	32	.285	8	MANAGER − B. FAUSETT/J. DYKES					
3B K. RICHARDSON	236	5	37	.246	5	RECORD W−95 L−88 FINISH−3RD					

1946

LOS ANGELES	AB	HR	RBI	BA	SB	PITCHERS	IP	W–L	BB	SO	ERA
1B R. OTERO	399	1	46	.273	2	R. LYNN	271	17–16	123	165	2.79
2B A. GLOSSOP	284	5	26	.250	0	C. CHAMBERS	268	18–15	93	215	3.02
3B G. ARCHIE	457	4	62	.258	5	Y. TERRY	192	12–15	47	84	2.86
SS B. SCHUSTER	626	4	69	.286	26	D. OSBORN	189	10–14	31	39	3.38
OF E. SAUER	685	20	82	.273	45	A. DOBERNIC	134	4–5	86	93	3.22
OF L. CHRISTOPHER	569	26	96	.304	1	D. CONGER	116	7–8	38	59	3.88
OF L. TREADWAY	496	0	27	.286	17	R. ADAMS	104	9–4	25	61	2.68
C D. WILLIAMS	260	1	21	.200	1	L. FLEMING	88	9–5	33	57	3.17
2B E. MALLORY	279	1	11	.219	6						
OF B. OLSEN	208	3	23	.255	6	MANAGER – B. SWEENEY					
OF J. TYACK	168	0	16	.244	3	RECORD W–94 L–89 FINISH–4TH					

SACRAMENTO	AB	HR	RBI	BA	SB	PITCHERS	IP	W–L	BB	SO	ERA
1B E. ZIPAY	444	1	33	.291	8	T. FREITAS	296	16–20	50	126	2.34
2B A. KAMPOURIS	515	11	56	.231	17	A. SMITH	261	18–11	56	116	2.52
3B S. MESNER	698	4	85	.292	5	G. STALEY	236	13–12	79	89	2.94
SS J. CALVEY	507	0	37	.205	12	G. FLETCHER	225	19–12	74	92	3.36
OF J. MARTY	518	14	74	.307	10	B. MANN (2)	207	11–10	74	110	2.61
OF J. WHITE (1)	510	1	40	.312	14	B. BEASLEY	71	6–3	19	16	2.92
OF G. LILLARD	441	22	59	.268	9						
C L. MARCUCCI	330	1	43	.236	1						
1B G. CORBETT	319	4	30	.263	2	(1) ALSO WITH SEATTLE					
C B. CONROY	264	7	27	.212	0	(2) ALSO WITH OAKLAND					
OF A. THOMPSON	209	3	21	.278	4	MANAGER – E. SHEELY					
OF J. LANDRUM	168	2	23	.238	3	RECORD W–94 L–92 FINISH–5TH					

SAN DIEGO	AB	HR	RBI	BA	SB	PITCHERS	IP	W–L	BB	SO	ERA
1B MC DONALD (1)	506	1	56	.277	7	A. OLSEN	288	17–15	68	104	2.91
2B P. COSCARART	251	4	24	.215	2	T. SEATS	236	11–18	52	96	3.13
3B D. GYSELMAN	619	0	58	.281	16	V. KENNEDY	225	18–13	103	95	2.92
SS J. LOHRKE	350	8	48	.303	3	E. VITALICH	213	11–16	82	78	3.42
OF T. CRISCOLA	603	2	56	.274	13	C. DUMLER	114	1–11	43	48	4.18
OF J. JENSEN	496	4	53	.300	8	E. CHAPPLE	108	2–6	74	50	4.33
OF D. GARMS	466	1	44	.270	16	M. SALVO	92	3–6	20	20	3.33
C L. RICE	286	0	26	.245	11						
1S2 J. ANGLE	368	2	24	.250	5						
S2 S. BREARD	318	1	32	.217	2						
OF B. GUINTINI (2)	257	4	24	.257	3	(1) ALSO WITH SEATTLE					
2B A. LANIFERO	224	0	19	.214	2	(2) ALSO WITH HOLLYWOOD					
OF E. BOEHM	206	4	17	.204	1	MANAGER – P. MARTIN/J. BRILLHEART					
C J. MC DONNELL	189	0	13	.238	1	RECORD W–78 L–108 FINISH–6TH					

1946

PORTLAND	AB	HR	RBI	BA	SB	PITCHERS	IP	W–L	BB	SO	ERA
1B H. REICH	629	9	75	.302	5	R. HELSER	293	20–16	118	175	3.04
2B J. BUCHER	215	0	10	.242	1	J. SALVESON	261	15–14	41	119	2.48
3B H. STOREY (1)	556	17	89	.326	3	D. BARRETT	251	9–21	89	143	3.73
SS L. BROWN	383	0	28	.185	1	J. MOOTY	230	11–19	108	93	3.37
OF D. ESCOBAR	433	10	56	.291	9	A. LISKA	195	7–16	43	87	3.09
OF M. SMITH	397	2	29	.249	3	D. PULFORD (2)	139	5–12	56	56	3.88
OF F. SHONE	325	1	25	.268	6						
C B. HOLM	238	1	16	.176	3						
3O2 G. CRAWFORD	398	7	35	.259	5						
2S3 E. WHEELER	298	2	15	.248	9						
OF MATHESON (2)	288	2	32	.288	3						
C D. BALLINGER (3)	276	1	32	.275	0	(1) ALSO WITH LOS ANGELES					
1B G. VICO	168	5	27	.286	1	(2) ALSO WITH SEATTLE					
C T. TURNER	159	0	18	.239	1	(3) ALSO WITH SAN DIEGO					
OF N. HARRIS	158	4	16	.228	0	**MANAGER – M. OWEN**					
C F. SOUZA	131	0	10	.244	2	**RECORD W–74 L–109 FINISH–7TH (T)**					

SEATTLE	AB	HR	RBI	BA	SB	PITCHERS	IP	W–L	BB	SO	ERA
1B E. TORGESON	354	5	53	.285	20	L. TOST	240	16–13	68	158	2.70
2B J. DOBBINS (1)	348	2	36	.224	4	G. ELLIOTT	235	12–13	71	142	3.26
3B B. KAHLE	554	1	72	.287	5	J. DEMORAN	166	5–12	45	68	3.63
SS T. YORK	546	2	51	.251	11	D. SORIANO	166	9–12	62	70	3.58
OF B. RAMSEY (2)	747	3	57	.293	43	J. TOBIN (3)	157	10–10	43	42	4.01
OF E. VANNI	402	0	21	.296	12	C. FISCHER (1)	122	6–11	47	51	4.72
OF L. NOVIKOFF	312	2	34	.301	4	I. PEARSON	110	6–10	41	42	4.75
C H. SUEME	262	1	24	.240	0						
O32 C. METRO (3)	330	4	25	.206	3						
OF K. LEWIS (4)	244	5	25	.221	1						
OF H. PATCHETT	238	0	14	.244	6						
SS N. STICKLE	232	0	19	.246	5						
12 J. BUZAS	189	0	26	.291	12	(1) ALSO WITH PORTLAND					
O1 E. CARNETT	181	1	13	.204	1	(2) ALSO WITH SACRAMENTO					
3S C. ALENO	176	4	28	.233	1	(3) ALSO WITH OAKLAND					
2B R. GORBOULD	167	0	10	.228	6	(4) ALSO WITH SAN FRANCISCO					
C W. BEARD	152	0	9	.217	1	**MANAGER – B. SKIFF/J. WHITE**					
OF C. MAPES	145	4	19	.241	5	**RECORD W–74 L–109 FINISH–7TH (T)**					

PLAYOFFS
SAN FRANCISCO DEFEATED HOLLYWOOD 4 GAMES TO 0
OAKLAND DEFEATED LOS ANGELES 4 GAMES TO 3

FINAL
SAN FRANCISCO DEFEATED OAKLAND 4 GAMES TO 2

1947

LOS ANGELES	AB	HR	RBI	BA	SB	PITCHERS	IP	W−L	BB	SO	ERA
1B L. BARTON (1)	550	18	83	.269	4	C. CHAMBERS	273	24−9	99	175	3.13
2B L. STRINGER	547	13	72	.293	4	R. LYNN	273	16−16	110	145	3.36
3B J. OSTROWSKI	654	24	110	.292	3	R. ADAMS	236	14−12	57	134	3.51
SS B. SCHUSTER	687	6	70	.262	17	R. BAUERS	147	10−8	63	84	3.92
OF C. GARRIOTT	639	22	77	.283	25	J. DOBERNIC	141	8−4	72	111	3.57
OF E. SAUER	568	17	86	.280	17	O. BAKER	132	6−4	41	65	3.14
OF C. MADDERN	458	15	83	.332	1	B. FLEMING	131	11−6	65	42	4.19
C E. MALONE	447	10	72	.260	2	D. MC CALL	119	5−12	77	109	3.86
OF T. STAINBACK	290	2	34	.279	0	(1) ALSO WITH OAKLAND					
23S A. GLOSSOP	239	8	41	.264	1	MANAGER − B. KELLY					
OF L. CHRISTOPHER	206	5	23	.228	2	RECORD W−106 L−81 FINISH−1ST					

SAN FRANCISCO	AB	HR	RBI	BA	SB	PITCHERS	IP	W−L	BB	SO	ERA
1B W. MATHESON	412	4	69	.250	1	J. BREWER	287	16−14	81	122	2.79
2B H. LUBY	711	9	70	.266	12	C. MELTON	261	17−11	56	123	2.72
3B R. ORTEIG	462	6	64	.299	1	B. JOYCE	261	15−15	52	55	3.62
SS R. NICELY	637	8	73	.253	7	B. CHESNES	233	22−8	83	114	2.32
OF D. WHITE	730	7	76	.292	8	B. WERLE	205	12−12	42	80	3.29
OF N. SHERIDAN	618	16	95	.286	9	A. LIEN	190	11−12	51	76	3.60
OF J. BROVIA	359	10	63	.309	1						
C J. GLADD	250	5	33	.252	1						
OF D. RESTELLI	356	10	55	.292	6						
1B B. SANDERS	243	2	37	.263	2						
C W. LEONARD	241	0	22	.241	1	MANAGER − L. O'DOUL					
OF F. UHALT	239	1	16	.280	11	RECORD W−105 L−82 FINISH−2ND					

PORTLAND	AB	HR	RBI	BA	SB	PITCHERS	IP	W−L	BB	SO	ERA
1B G. VICO	462	9	64	.307	7	J. SALVESON	287	17−14	52	96	3.64
2B M. MULLEN	223	0	19	.323	8	R. HELSER	199	10−11	86	139	4.48
3B H. STOREY	681	14	119	.305	9	V. DI BIASI	196	13−10	83	130	2.98
SS L. RATTO	507	0	34	.268	9	A. LISKA	148	10−10	35	70	3.41
OF D. ESCOBAR	459	10	69	.237	6	J. MOOTY	127	12−12	61	64	4.96
OF J. LAZOR	451	7	55	.304	9	J. BIANCO	105	8−7	65	46	4.03
OF M. SMITH	437	5	53	.311	9	T. BRIDGES	104	7−3	31	73	1.64
C C. SILVERA	356	1	39	.247	0	A. SIERRA	92	3−4	52	45	4.40
						V. RASCHI	85	8−2	42	68	2.75
O1 H. REICH	533	18	98	.281	13	J. ROBINSON	81	3−6	41	26	5.89
OF R. WENNER	314	12	41	.242	1						
S1 J. DOBBINS	237	1	22	215	5						
C E. MURATORE	234	2	14	.205	0						
2B E. BASINSKI	209	2	30	.278	5	MANAGER − J. TURNER					
2B W. RADULOVICH	208	4	27	.264	1	RECORD W−97 L−89 FINISH−3RD					

1947

OAKLAND		AB	HR	RBI	BA	SB	PITCHERS	IP	W–L	BB	SO	ERA
1B	L. SCARSELLA	341	13	56	.255	1	G. BEARDEN	198	16–7	82	80	2.86
2B	D. LODIGIANI	498	11	92	.311	7	F. SPEER	189	16–14	74	83	4.38
3B	G. LILLARD	291	7	46	.258	1	D. HAYES	183	12–10	84	96	3.93
SS	R. HAMRICK	473	0	52	.266	5	C. GASSAWAY	183	12–11	61	89	4.23
OF	B. HOLDER	599	16	78	.311	9	A. WILKIE	135	7–7	43	49	4.67
OF	V. DI MAGGIO	473	22	81	.241	7	R. BUXTON	125	8–8	42	52	3.89
OF	H. MARTIN	294	4	48	.361	3	D. SORIANO	114	7–7	54	59	4.82
C	B. RAIMONDI	418	0	47	.297	10	W. HAFEY	107	7–5	49	40	3.28
							T. HAFEY	98	7–6	44	50	6.15
1O	M. VAN ROBAYS	380	8	77	.295	4	H. MULCAHY	89	1–6	40	20	6.67
OF	M. DUEZABOU	238	5	24	.315	8						
2S	O. BURNETT	224	3	26	.295	5						
23S	G. CRAWFORD	215	6	30	.298	4	MANAGER – C. STENGEL					
OF	C. WORKMAN	213	12	40	.268	1	RECORD W–96 L–90 FINISH–4TH					

SEATTLE		AB	HR	RBI	BA	SB	PITCHERS	IP	W–L	BB	SO	ERA
1B	M. ROCCO	504	18	99	.300	9	D. BARRETT	286	14–17	110	130	3.18
2B	T. YORK	506	7	41	.283	5	M. DUBIEL	260	15–17	79	139	3.88
3B	H. LAYNE	499	1	64	.367	6	R. CECIL (1)	205	13–11	79	102	3.91
SS	J. O'NEIL	628	0	66	.272	6	C. RIPPLE (1)	190	8–14	96	96	5.12
OF	B. RAMSEY (1)	650	8	58	.272	26	H. BESSE	167	11–8	77	95	3.23
OF	L. NOVIKOFF	647	21	114	.325	1	S. JAKUCKI (1)	166	11–12	60	86	3.58
OF	J. WHITE	382	3	47	.312	8	B. POSEDEL	121	12–8	40	34	4.26
C	R. HEMSLEY	240	3	31	.263	1						
OF	B. JOHNSON	342	7	50	.295	6	(1) ALSO WITH SACRAMENTO					
32S	G. SCHAREIN	228	0	31	.263	1	MANAGER – J. WHITE					
C	H. SUEME	223	0	21	.238	1	RECORD W–91 L–95 FINISH–5TH					

HOLLYWOOD		AB	HR	RBI	BA	SB	PITCHERS	IP	W–L	BB	SO	ERA
1B	T. LUPIEN	696	21	110	.341	40	J. KRAKAUSKAS	244	11–17	87	117	4.35
2B	F. VAUGHN	380	12	56	.300	0	R. ARDIZOIA	212	11–10	88	102	3.48
3B	D. ROSS	476	11	67	.307	1	F. DASSO (1)	194	9–18	108	117	4.69
SS	C. COX	570	3	54	.293	6	P. WOODS	179	13–10	82	79	4.47
OF	J. DELSING	572	5	53	.316	3	X. RESCIGNO	150	11–9	39	60	4.38
OF	A. LIBKE	506	10	81	.310	2	R. SMITH (1)	144	9–7	37	67	5.37
OF	F. KELLEHER	427	21	93	.314	5	E. ALBOSTA	140	11–6	59	82	3.47
C	C. CAMERON	265	3	38	.272	1	C. HUFFORD	122	7–6	47	33	5.16
							A. YAYLIAN	111	5–7	56	56	4.05
S3	T. DAVIS	380	6	44	.234	3						
OF	G. ZERNIAL	372	12	77	.344	4						
OF	A. SKURSKI	335	4	32	.260	15	(1) ALSO WITH SACRAMENTO					
23	G. STEWART	267	1	35	.273	0	MANAGER – J. DYKES					
C	A. UNSER	230	2	29	.265	2	RECORD W–88 L–98 FINISH–6TH					

1947

SACRAMENTO		AB	HR	RBI	BA	SB	PITCHERS	IP	W–L	BB	SO	ERA
1B	E. ZIPAY	320	2	39	.278	2	G. FLETCHER (1)	284	18–13	87	121	3.61
2B	A. KAMPOURIS	368	10	49	.288	5	T. FREITAS	215	13–17	46	104	3.85
3B	S. MESNER	636	2	71	.255	0	G. MANN (1)	189	11–10	64	83	5.10
SS	L. WELLS	652	2	58	.278	12	H. ORPHAN (2)	151	8–10	86	72	4.71
OF	J. MARTY	568	13	100	.327	8	K. HOLCOMBE	122	8–9	64	56	3.84
OF	J. RUCKER (1)	540	7	52	.276	25	B. SOMENZI	100	4–5	43	32	4.59
OF	A. THOMPSON	474	5	71	.283	11						
C	E. FITZGERALD	411	5	49	.363	26						
OF	J. RIZZO	353	19	74	.297	3						
1B	R. RUSSELL	237	8	33	.329	2						
2S	T. NELSON	216	2	25	.273	2						
OF	J. WARNER	180	4	26	.211	7	(1) ALSO WITH SEATTLE					
1B	M. SCHEMER	158	0	15	.297	1	(2) ALSO WITH HOLLYWOOD					
SS	J. CAULFIELD	138	0	16	.239	1	MANAGER – D. BARTELL					
C1	D. MOORE	133	0	13	.301	1	RECORD W–83 L–103 FINISH–7TH					

SAN DIEGO		AB	HR	RBI	BA	SB	PITCHERS	IP	W–L	BB	SO	ERA
1B	V. SHUPE	669	9	97	.262	4	T. SEATS	306	17–17	39	130	3.65
2B	P. COSCARART	545	6	55	.255	21	A. TREICHEL	249	14–15	151	147	4.12
3B	D. GYSELMAN (1)	446	1	36	.253	11	M. SALVO	200	14–13	44	77	3.83
SS	R. TRAN	531	0	44	.213	3	V. KENNEDY	195	9–15	82	102	4.11
OF	D. CLAY	668	10	62	.313	40	B. KERRIGAN	185	9–12	64	61	4.67
OF	M. WEST	562	43	124	.306	6	E. VITALICH	181	7–15	67	60	3.78
OF	J. BARRETT	524	9	70	.277	25	A. OLSEN	162	6–13	41	48	4.72
C	F. KERR	433	11	60	.300	4						
OF	J. JENSEN	462	5	59	.307	7						
2B	L. LEE	343	1	13	.245	1	(1) ALSO WITH SEATTLE					
C	L. RICE	237	1	18	.236	5	MANAGER – J. COLLINS					
O2	R. HAMILTON	186	0	13	.226	3	RECORD W–79 L–107 FINISH–8TH					

PLAYOFFS
LOS ANGELES DEFEATED SAN FRANCISCO 5–0 IN PLAYOFF TO DECIDE PENNANT

LOS ANGELES DEFEATED PORTLAND 4 GAMES TO 1
OAKLAND DEFEATED SAN FRANCISCO 4 GAMES TO 1

FINAL
LOS ANGELES DEFEATED OAKLAND 4 GAMES TO 1

1948

OAKLAND		AB	HR	RBI	BA	SB	PITCHERS		IP	W–L	BB	SO	ERA
1B	N. ETTEN	578	43	155	.313	3	C. GASSAWAY		198	15–8	59	68	3.09
2B	B. MARTIN	401	3	42	.277	7	E. JONES		196	13–6	110	82	2.98
3B	D. LODIGIANI	581	7	72	.303	7	A. WILKIE		185	11–6	70	56	3.79
SS	M. COMBS	580	10	69	.271	11	W. HAFEY		183	13–10	102	75	4.47
OF	G. METKOVICH	500	23	88	.336	9	D. HAYES (1)		173	6–17	75	84	4.32
OF	B. HOLDER	482	10	57	.297	11	L. WEBBER		131	8–5	55	68	5.50
OF	M. DUEZABOU	389	7	52	.303	21	F. SPEER		108	12–3	42	55	5.17
C	B. RAIMONDI	302	0	31	.285	14	R. BUXTON		96	13–3	29	52	3.19
OF	L. CHRISTOPHER	352	14	61	.318	3							
O1	L. SCARSELLA	329	14	72	.271	5	(1) ALSO WITH SACRAMENTO						
3B	C. LAVAGETTO	286	3	38	.304	1	MANAGER – C. STENGEL						
S2	R. HAMRICK	243	1	26	.259	2	RECORD W–114 L–74 FINISH–1ST						

SAN FRANCISCO		AB	HR	RBI	BA	SB	PITCHERS		IP	W–L	BB	SO	ERA
1B	M. ROCCO	670	27	149	.300	10	B. WERLE		250	17–7	61	136	2.74
2B	H. LUBY	646	12	77	.286	19	J. BREWER		242	15–11	61	96	4.28
3B	S. SHOFNER	333	2	41	.264	4	C. DEMPSEY		219	16–11	61	171	2.10
SS	R. NICELY	613	4	85	.235	4	C. MELTON		215	16–10	48	98	3.14
OF	G. WOODLING	524	22	107	.385	6	A. LIEN		184	15–8	31	81	3.38
OF	D. RESTELLI	505	10	80	.289	6	M. PEREZ		161	11–8	64	58	3.47
OF	J. BROVIA	444	9	89	.322	0	K. GABLES		96	6–7	37	61	4.97
C	D. HOWELL	336	4	38	.292	3	T. FINE		95	5–6	55	43	5.59
							D. SORIANO		84	6–2	49	38	3.96
O31	J. TOBIN	582	5	45	.301	37							
C	W. LEONARD	266	0	31	.256	1							
3B	R. ORTEIG	262	7	51	.271	0	MANAGER – L. O'DOUL						
OF	B. GUINTINI	200	7	25	.220	3	RECORD W–112 L–76 FINISH–2ND						

LOS ANGELES		AB	HR	RBI	BA	SB	PITCHERS		IP	W–L	BB	SO	ERA
1B	J. SANFORD	361	6	44	.247	0	R. LYNN		244	19–10	114	131	3.73
2B	O. BURNETT	314	3	40	.271	4	R. ADAMS		226	14–11	61	102	3.54
3B	J. OSTROWSKI	397	15	56	.295	4	D. ADKINS		212	17–10	71	149	2.25
SS	B. SCHUSTER	617	11	60	.264	8	L. ANTHONY		197	16–11	45	99	3.93
OF	C. GARRIOTT	581	19	65	.232	24	T. HAFEY (1)		154	7–11	56	71	4.62
OF	E. SAUER	571	16	121	.305	20	D. CARLSEN		116	7–6	44	67	5.20
OF	DALLESSANDRO	514	21	87	.307	1	H. KLEINE		110	6–5	70	68	4.01
C	E. MALONE	385	9	48	.268	0	LANFRANCONI		101	5–5	38	31	6.06
							R. BAUERS		95	3–9	49	43	4.93
32	A. GLOSSOP	474	17	75	.283	2							
OF	C. ABERSON	389	34	103	.329	1							
1B	E. LUKON	296	11	46	.257	2	(1) ALSO WITH OAKLAND						
2B	D. JOHNSON	285	5	28	.288	1	MANAGER – B. KELLY						
C	R. NOVOTNEY	256	4	26	.270	0	RECORD W–102 L–86 FINISH–3RD						

1948

SEATTLE	AB	HR	RBI	BA	SB	PITCHERS	IP	W–L	BB	SO	ERA
1B C. MORAN	177	2	25	.305	1	G. FLETCHER	249	16–15	82	114	3.69
2B T. YORK	547	8	60	.256	3	D. BARRETT	246	15–13	78	96	3.33
3B H. LAYNE	664	6	80	.342	5	H. BESSE	232	16–12	92	117	4.38
SS J. O'NEIL	417	0	40	.242	5	J. GORSICA	225	13–14	50	95	3.56
OF B. RAMSEY	662	9	70	.285	26	H. KARPEL	212	11–14	60	92	4.03
OF E. RAPP	564	17	96	.298	10	B. HALL	134	7–11	56	96	3.96
OF N. SHERIDAN	532	17	82	.312	5	C. SCHANZ	106	7–6	42	58	2.29
C M. GRASSO	380	5	27	.261	1	S. PEEK	85	3–5	42	32	4.66
S2 S. NEWSOME	449	0	26	.249	4						
O12 L. MOHR	261	0	15	.280	8						
C R. HEMSLEY	205	0	18	.268	2						
OF L. NOVIKOFF	168	3	30	.327	1	MANAGER – J. WHITE					
OF J. WHITE	167	0	21	.269	5	RECORD W–93 L–95 FINISH–4TH					

PORTLAND	AB	HR	RBI	BA	SB	PITCHERS	IP	W–L	BB	SO	ERA
1B F. MOLE	632	22	83	.283	12	V. DI BIASI	250	17–12	131	128	4.18
2B E. BASINSKI	632	4	50	.277	8	R. HELSER	195	12–11	78	132	4.80
3B H. STOREY	627	10	91	.305	3	T. BRIDGES	195	15–11	75	123	2.86
SS F. ZAK	439	0	27	.248	11	D. PILLETTE	189	14–11	115	83	4.00
OF H. REICH	677	19	100	.323	7	J. MOOTY	168	7–15	70	77	4.39
OF J. RUCKER	607	8	76	.311	16	B. FLEMING (1)	119	7–2	59	44	4.54
OF J. LAZOR	309	5	47	.265	3	A. LISKA	107	5–10	33	47	5.38
C C. SILVERA	501	5	85	.301	5	J. TOTE	102	8–5	64	48	4.23
OF M. SMITH	297	2	37	.286	3	(1) ALSO WITH LOS ANGELES					
OF R. WENNER	269	17	44	.271	2	MANAGER – J. TURNER					
23 M. MULLEN	240	1	21	.300	2	RECORD W–89 L–99 FINISH–5TH					

HOLLYWOOD	AB	HR	RBI	BA	SB	PITCHERS	IP	W–L	BB	SO	ERA
1B R. RUSSELL (1)	484	13	57	.293	2	P. WOODS	279	15–20	167	161	4.52
2B L. STRINGER	651	7	99	.333	10	R. ARDIZOIA	228	13–11	103	109	4.10
3B D. ROSS	416	4	65	.313	3	P. GEBRIAN	197	11–12	83	95	3.84
SS T. DAVIS	381	12	55	.252	5	E. SMITH (1)	194	13–14	72	101	3.90
OF G. ZERNIAL	737	40	156	.322	3	V. KENNEDY	183	9–12	94	97	3.93
OF J. DELSING	463	6	56	.333	4	J. KRAKAUSKAS	157	5–7	73	98	4.18
OF F. KELLEHER	439	25	107	.333	3	E. ALBOSTA	117	4–9	59	58	5.85
C J. GLADD	358	7	35	.246	1	B. BUTLAND	111	7–8	40	49	5.59
						MALTZBERGER	93	7–8	24	32	3.00
3S2 G. HANDLEY	442	2	50	.321	11						
OF A. SKURSKI	360	3	36	.258	11	(1) ALSO WITH SACRAMENTO					
C L. KAHN	277	2	37	.296	6	MANAGER – J. DYKES/L. STRINGER/					
O1 A. LIBKE	238	2	33	.231	0	M. HAAS					
SS C. COX	170	1	16	.224	0	RECORD W–84 L–104 FINISH–6TH					

1948

SAN DIEGO	AB	HR	RBI	BA	SB	PITCHERS	IP	W–L	BB	SO	ERA
1B V. SHUPE	469	6	60	.245	3	T. SEATS	258	12–14	39	114	4.15
2B S. MESNER (1)	586	8	76	.297	3	J. FLORES	225	11–19	81	111	4.36
3B L. HANDLEY	703	5	65	.300	24	X. RESCIGNO	221	18–14	70	87	4.64
SS L. WELLS (1)	474	3	61	.268	3	A. JURISICH	189	11–12	73	124	5.62
OF D. CLAY	756	15	77	.291	22	A. OLSEN	159	10–14	52	76	4.81
OF J. BARRETT	513	14	90	.339	18	B. KERRIGAN	131	3–6	58	31	4.74
OF J. GRAHAM	473	48	136	.298	6	P. WALDEN	113	3–4	48	31	5.65
C L. RICE	305	0	34	.279	1	M. BUDNICK	104	4–8	46	53	4.67
						G. THOMPSON	72	8–3	40	31	2.00
2S P. COSCARART	309	3	25	.207	6						
OF B. ADAMS	273	8	34	.253	2						
OF J. JENSEN	251	6	34	.279	5	(1) ALSO WITH SACRAMENTO					
C J. RITCHEY	217	4	44	.323	2	MANAGER – R. COLLINS/J. BRILLHEART					
C H. CAMELLI	202	4	22	.267	0	RECORD W–83 L–105 FINISH–7TH					

SACRAMENTO	AB	HR	RBI	BA	SB	PITCHERS	IP	W–L	BB	SO	ERA
1B B. DAHLGREN	379	8	41	.298	0	J. SALVESON (4)	245	13–18	55	95	4.74
2B A. KAMPOURIS	354	10	42	.271	2	L. TOST (4)	226	12–15	68	107	3.70
3B J. TABOR (1)	502	17	58	.275	3	R. CECIL	210	13–18	43	32	4.93
SS L. RATTO (2)	506	0	33	.227	12	T. FREITAS	192	12–11	32	59	3.09
OF A. WHITE (3)	693	7	63	.306	20	M. GRISSOM	190	11–7	83	95	4.03
OF J. MARTY	556	24	95	.320	2	K. HOLCOMBE	150	9–10	65	58	5.04
OF J. GRACE	505	17	77	.301	4	S. NAGY	149	5–10	74	56	3.56
C D. MOORE	327	4	43	.309	4	M. SALVO (5)	121	5–7	46	59	4.39
2S1 W. WIETELMANN	481	8	43	.233	2						
32 T. JENNINGS	315	6	38	.286	8	(1) ALSO WITH LOS ANGELES					
C E. LOMBARDI (4)	284	11	55	.264	1	(2) ALSO WITH PORTLAND					
OF F. HAWKINS	201	3	35	.289	0	(3) ALSO WITH HOLLYWOOD					
OF J. WARNER	186	4	16	.204	0	(4) ALSO WITH OAKLAND					
OF J. COOKSON	175	1	14	.257	1	(5) ALSO WITH SAN DIEGO					
C V. CASTINO	170	1	17	.229	0	MANAGER – J. ORENGO					
C N. PESUT	127	1	12	.173	0	RECORD W–75 L–113 FINISH–8TH					

PLAYOFFS
OAKLAND DEFEATED LOS ANGELES 4 GAMES TO 2
SEATTLE DEFEATED SAN FRANCISCO 4 GAMES TO 1

FINAL
OAKLAND DEFEATED SEATTLE 4 GAMES TO 1

1949

HOLLYWOOD	AB	HR	RBI	BA	SB	PITCHERS	IP	W–L	BB	SO	ERA
1B C. STEVENS	679	10	82	.297	12	P. WOODS	275	23–12	100	128	4.12
2B G. HANDLEY	520	1	45	.294	13	W. RAMSDELL	267	18–12	85	152	2.60
3B J. BAXES	641	24	108	.287	10	MALTZBERGER	232	18–10	49	79	3.34
SS J. O'NEIL	458	0	41	.218	1	G. MOULDER	193	14–9	86	80	4.38
OF I. NOREN	678	29	130	.330	10	A. SCHALLOCK	167	12–9	63	121	4.20
OF F. KELLEHER	609	29	90	.253	4	J. SALVESON	148	11–7	35	59	2.98
OF H. GORMAN	507	10	110	.310	10						
C M. SANDLOCK	379	1	54	.243	0						
C A. UNSER	269	5	45	.271	2						
SS G. GENOVESE	251	1	25	.259	1						
2B G. FALLON	184	1	17	.217	2	MANAGER – F. HANEY					
OF A. SKURSKI	176	4	25	.273	6	RECORD W–109 L–78 FINISH–1ST					

OAKLAND	AB	HR	RBI	BA	SB	PITCHERS	IP	W–L	BB	SO	ERA
1B D. KRYHOSKI	253	5	50	.328	4	C. GASSAWAY	217	15–9	79	97	3.94
2B B. MARTIN	623	12	92	.286	11	F. NELSON	208	14–11	78	74	3.25
3B C. LAVAGETTO	459	6	58	.290	2	M. CANDINI	176	15–9	67	88	4.04
SS A. WILSON (1)	607	0	37	.348	47	F. JONES	162	10–10	78	52	4.33
OF J. JENSEN	467	9	77	.261	5	L. TOST	157	14–7	48	78	4.01
OF M. DUEZABOU	441	6	65	.308	15	D. THOMPSON	111	11–8	46	37	3.16
OF L. CHRISTOPHER	395	21	69	.276	4						
C D. PADGETT	424	12	79	.292	3						
OF E. RAPP	340	15	86	.344	6						
OF G. METKOVICH	285	14	50	.337	9	(1) ALSO WITH SAN DIEGO					
C F. KERR (2)	284	6	37	.257	0	(2) ALSO WITH SACRAMENTO					
OF M. VAN ROBAYS	238	3	42	.298	1	MANAGER – C. DRESSEN					
1B L. SCARSELLA	226	12	44	.261	1	RECORD W–104 L–83 FINISH–2ND					

SACRAMENTO	AB	HR	RBI	BA	SB	PITCHERS	IP	W–L	BB	SO	ERA
1B W. DROPO	481	17	85	.287	6	B. GILLESPIE	254	17–13	118	130	3.05
2B P. COSCARART(1)	481	5	65	.272	6	K. HOLCOMBE	249	19–10	108	128	2.85
3B J. TABOR	598	21	113	.318	2	F. DASSO	214	17–10	93	108	3.74
SS L. RATTO	493	0	33	.258	18	O. GROVE	177	9–7	85	78	3.40
OF A. WHITE	749	5	95	.326	23	C. JOHNSON	171	8–14	79	98	3.95
OF R. HODGIN	512	10	85	.311	1						
OF J. MARTY	477	16	112	.327	3						
C B. RAIMONDI (2)	429	0	33	.266	4						
O1 J. GRACE	383	8	70	.282	7	(1) ALSO WITH SAN DIEGO					
S32 F. MARSH	280	3	22	.211	8	(2) ALSO WITH OAKLAND					
OF B. WILSON	267	11	44	.247	5	MANAGER – D. BAKER					
C V. PLUMBO	175	2	15	.223	2	RECORD W–102 L–85 FINISH–3RD					

1949

SAN DIEGO		AB	HR	RBI	BA	SB	PITCHERS	IP	W–L	BB	SO	ERA
1B	M. WEST	619	48	166	.291	4	J. FLORES	279	21–10	74	139	3.03
2B	B. WILSON	683	1	67	.268	15	L. LINDE	226	14–15	100	105	4.42
3B	H. STOREY (1)	491	17	97	.301	3	A. JURISICH	191	13–11	59	104	4.85
SS	S. MESNER	343	0	40	.297	1	X. RESCIGNO	178	10–15	59	74	5.61
OF	D. CLAY	605	11	43	.294	9	R. ADAMS (3)	161	8–7	58	73	3.86
OF	M. MINOSO	532	22	75	.297	13	D. BARRETT (4)	135	12–6	68	62	3.73
OF	B. ADAMS	514	21	69	.272	4						
C	D. MOORE (2)	383	11	54	.311	5	(1) ALSO WITH PORTLAND					
							(2) ALSO WITH SACRAMENTO					
S2	WIETELMANN (2)	496	4	37	.240	4	(3) ALSO WITH LOS ANGELES					
C	J. RITCHEY	327	3	35	.257	12	(4) ALSO WITH SEATTLE					
31	A. ROSEN	273	14	51	.319	5	MANAGER – B. HARRIS					
1B	L. EASTER	268	25	92	.363	1	RECORD W–96 L–92 FINISH–4TH					

SEATTLE		AB	HR	RBI	BA	SB	PITCHERS	IP	W–L	BB	SO	ERA
1B	H. BECKER	524	16	101	.313	2	C. SCHANZ	321	22–17	106	158	3.25
2B	T. YORK	414	4	47	.297	1	G. FLETCHER	318	23–12	113	162	3.28
3B	H. LAYNE	439	2	36	.289	2	H. BESSE	196	8–19	85	83	3.90
SS	J. ALBRIGHT	496	6	47	.258	5	H. KARPEL	176	14–6	65	76	4.40
OF	B. RAMSEY	533	4	52	.274	16	R. ARDIZOIA	154	8–9	58	74	4.20
OF	T. NEILL	520	10	67	.285	2	D. GALEHOUSE	143	10–12	31	74	4.09
OF	A. LYONS	495	23	67	.273	13						
C	M. GRASSO	299	7	31	.251	1						
OF	N. SHERIDAN	486	14	67	.259	10						
2O	L. MOHR	395	0	30	.306	4						
1O	F. COLMAN	306	13	67	.320	1						
C	S. WHITE	173	2	20	.301	2	MANAGER – J. WHITE/B. LAWRENCE					
C	J. WARREN	167	3	33	.306	2	RECORD W–95 L–93 FINISH–5TH					

PORTLAND		AB	HR	RBI	BA	SB	PITCHERS	IP	W–L	BB	SO	ERA
1B	V. SHUPE (1)	627	8	81	.276	7	H. SALTZMAN	276	23–13	111	120	3.26
2B	E. BASINSKI	592	12	79	.267	4	R. HELSER	223	16–10	77	125	2.94
3B	L. THOMAS	709	18	95	.293	15	V. DI BIASI	201	9–16	98	102	4.07
SS	F. AUSTIN	429	4	34	.242	2	R. LYNN (2)	194	10–18	95	85	4.64
OF	J. RUCKER	687	17	95	.295	13	T. BRIDGES	184	11–11	75	110	3.82
OF	L. MARQUEZ	511	4	46	.294	32	B. FLEMING	142	6–8	61	56	3.99
OF	J. BROVIA	364	11	51	.313	2	A. LISKA	140	4–11	42	44	3.86
C	J. GLADD	366	9	57	.268	3	G. DIEHL	110	4–7	43	39	4.58
OF	R. WENNER	295	8	48	.231	2	(1) ALSO WITH SAN DIEGO					
32S	M. MULLEN	208	1	12	.226	1	(2) ALSO WITH LOS ANGELES					
C	J. BURGHER	145	3	17	.255	1	MANAGER – B. SWEENEY					
SS	F. ZAK (1)	140	0	12	.221	1	RECORD W–85 L–102 FINISH–6TH					

1949

SAN FRANCISCO		AB	HR	RBI	BA	SB	PITCHERS	IP	W-L	BB	SO	ERA
1B	M. ROCCO	557	25	114	.276	9	A. LIEN	264	17-18	70	99	4.26
2B	D. LODIGIANI (1)	662	10	65	.269	11	C. DEMPSEY	262	17-14	113	164	4.23
3B	S. SHOFNER	520	15	89	.271	7	S. NAGY	244	15-14	117	123	2.65
SS	R. NICELY	530	0	35	.194	2	E. SINGLETON	188	8-14	76	123	4.02
OF	J. TOBIN	512	0	34	.252	20	M. PEREZ	160	9-8	68	61	4.84
OF	R. CHESO	395	6	46	.248	1	J. BREWER	139	5-11	51	63	5.12
OF	W. JUDNICH	379	18	63	.269	0	H. FELDMAN	119	6-9	42	38	4.31
C	R. JARVIS	307	5	42	.277	2	C. MELTON	115	5-6	46	57	3.83
OF	A. VAUGHAN	281	2	26	.288	6						
C	R. PARTEE	278	1	30	.281	3						
OF	D. RESTELLI	268	10	65	.351	7						
OF	B. HOLDER	237	5	36	.312	0						
OF	C. RICKARD	176	1	15	.273	0	(1) ALSO WITH OAKLAND					
2B	J. MORAN (2)	172	?	16	.273	5	(2) ALSO WITH SACRAMENTO					
S2	D. LAJESKIE	130	1	11	.192	0	MANAGER - L. O'DOUL					
1B	J. WESTLAKE	121	1	10	.215	0	RECORD W-84 L-103 FINISH-7TH					

LOS ANGELES		AB	HR	RBI	BA	SB	PITCHERS	IP	W-L	BB	SO	ERA
1B	C. MORAN	419	8	43	.243	2	B. KELLY	205	9-16	127	77	4.57
2B	W. TERWILLIGER	432	8	46	.275	13	D. WATKINS	204	8-11	99	90	4.81
3B	J. OSTROWSKI	478	32	90	.314	1	O. ANTHONY	182	7-19	50	80	5.09
SS	B. SCHUSTER (1)	616	8	68	.256	19	C. MC LISH	150	8-11	107	68	5.76
OF	C. MAURO	500	12	63	.292	10	D. CARLSEN	135	9-8	74	65	4.73
OF	C. MADDERN	495	14	83	.307	1	K. GABLES (5)	130	6-6	54	56	5.26
OF	C. GARRIOTT	494	10	47	.255	11	A. IHDE	118	7-6	102	45	5.34
C	E. MALONE	293	6	46	.341	0	B. MC DANIELS	113	8-9	59	60	4.22
							B. STEPHENS	102	3-11	51	45	6.00
SS	B. STURGEON (2)	526	0	41	.272	1						
1B	GOLDSBERRY (3)	316	6	32	.247	5						
OF	C. ABERSON	313	17	49	.230	1						
32	A. GLOSSOP	254	5	37	.213	1	(1) ALSO WITH SACRAMENTO					
C	N. BURBINK	239	4	28	.272	0	(2) ALSO WITH SEATTLE					
3B	L. HANDLEY (4)	202	1	24	.282	0	(3) ALSO WITH OAKLAND					
2B	F. GUSTINE	170	4	22	.294	3	(4) ALSO WITH SAN DIEGO					
3B	B. RHAWN	150	1	10	.267	2	(5) ALSO WITH SAN FRANCISCO					
C	R. NOVOTNEY	138	1	7	.210	0	MANAGER - B. KELLY					
OF	DALLESSANDRO	117	8	28	.291	1	RECORD W-74 L-113 FINISH-8TH					

PLAYOFFS
HOLLYWOOD DEFEATED SACRAMENTO 4 GAMES TO 1
SAN DIEGO DEFEATED OAKLAND 4 GAMES TO 3

FINAL
HOLLYWOOD DEFEATED SAN DIEGO 4 GAMES TO 2

1950

OAKLAND	AB	HR	RBI	BA	SB	PITCHERS	IP	W–L	BB	SO	ERA
1B R. ZIMMERMAN	496	20	114	.266	5	A. GETTEL	241	23–7	89	128	3.62
2B B. HOFMAN	558	15	83	.296	2	G. BAMBERGER	236	17–13	112	133	4.23
3B C. LAVAGETTO	490	8	66	.286	3	C. SHOUN	233	16–10	74	84	4.56
SS A. WILSON	848	1	48	.311	31	E. HARRIST	229	18–8	99	148	3.69
OF G. METKOVICH	739	24	141	.315	23	H. BEHRMAN	218	17–8	138	158	4.25
OF E. RAPP	639	24	145	.347	7	E. GROTH	161	7–11	83	49	5.09
OF L. CHRISTOPHER	327	14	74	.303	0	C. GASSAWAY	103	7–7	38	42	5.07
C R. NOBLE	345	15	76	.316	4	L. TOST	94	6–5	40	47	4.98
						F. NELSON	93	2–5	55	44	5.32
13O A. GALAN	447	13	72	.282	10						
OF D. WAKEFIELD	246	7	38	.293	2						
C D. PADGETT	221	10	55	.348	0	MANAGER – C. DRESSEN					
32 B. HERMAN	202	4	29	.307	2	RECORD W–118 L–82 FINISH–1ST					

SAN DIEGO	AB	HR	RBI	BA	SB	PITCHERS	IP	W–L	BB	SO	ERA
1B J. GRAHAM	663	33	136	.293	8	G. ZUVERINK	279	20–14	116	116	3.71
2B R. WILSON	710	2	55	.256	21	A. OLSEN	272	20–15	56	96	3.71
3B M. MINOSO	599	20	115	.339	30	C. EMBREE	255	18–12	99	113	3.32
SS W. WIETELMANN	418	2	35	.261	1	R. WELMAKER	213	16–10	107	143	4.27
OF H. SIMPSON	697	33	156	.323	2	H. SALTZMAN	179	11–10	79	62	4.93
OF M. NIELSEN	429	8	41	.298	6	J. KRAUS (1)	141	6–8	55	78	4.72
OF B. ADAMS	340	15	62	.318	0	R. SAVAGE	122	6–8	59	68	4.65
C D. MOORE	370	1	35	.281	6	D. BARRETT (2)	111	9–5	58	34	5.76
						A. JURISICH	97	8–2	39	60	2.69
O1 M. WEST	520	30	109	.285	1						
U A. SMITH	326	10	50	.248	11	(1) ALSO WITH LOS ANGELES					
3B H. STOREY	297	6	54	.266	0	(2) ALSO WITH HOLLYWOOD					
1B H. CONYERS	220	1	24	.223	2	MANAGER – D. BAKER					
SS M. COMBS	173	3	23	.283	0	RECORD W–114 L–86 FINISH–2ND					

HOLLYWOOD	AB	HR	RBI	BA	SB	PITCHERS	IP	W–L	BB	SO	ERA
1B C. STEVENS	605	12	82	.288	2	B. WADE	248	14–13	83	156	3.67
2B G. HANDLEY	548	1	42	.290	13	O. ANTHONY	198	13–9	58	82	3.95
3B J. BAXES	408	31	76	.243	5	P. WOODS	184	10–11	81	91	3.72
SS B. HICKS	507	7	48	.239	4	MALTZBERGER	172	13–13	33	73	3.61
OF F. KELLEHER	589	40	135	.270	3	J. SALVESON	165	15–4	37	62	2.84
OF E. SAUER	566	9	65	.260	26	K. LEHMAN	158	10–11	69	92	3.47
OF H. GORMAN	534	13	96	.305	0	G. MOULDER	142	7–8	55	57	4.50
C M. SANDLOCK	411	2	32	.297	3	P. MONDORFF	130	7–7	60	61	3.81
						G. SHALLOCK	128	5–7	60	83	4.09
32S M. FRANKLIN	507	8	59	.260	2						
SS J. O'NEIL	236	0	18	.263	3						
OF C. CONATSER	212	7	27	.231	3	MANAGER – F. HANEY					
C C. DAPPER	192	3	23	.245	2	RECORD W–104 L–96 FINISH–3RD					

1950

PORTLAND	AB	HR	RBI	BA	SB	PITCHERS	IP	W−L	BB	SO	ERA
1B M. ROCCO	623	26	108	.258	3	R. DRILLING	253	14−17	71	94	3.59
2B E. BASINSKI	722	15	75	.240	1	R. LYNN	239	14−10	92	117	3.54
3B L. THOMAS	285	4	38	.274	1	J. CREEL	185	12−11	83	96	4.23
SS F. AUSTIN	523	3	55	.277	3	R. ADAMS	181	9−10	76	92	4.62
OF L. MARQUEZ	775	9	86	.311	38	V. DI BIASI	179	12−12	88	111	4.37
OF J. BROVIA	649	39	114	.280	1	L. LINDE	168	5−13	83	75	4.66
OF J. RUCKER	532	6	67	.288	7	R. HELSER	144	12−8	47	71	3.19
C J. GLADD	415	16	55	.267	0						
3O H. LAYNE (1)	250	1	22	.216	1	(1) ALSO WITH SEATTLE					
C J. RITCHEY	241	2	34	.270	1	MANAGER − B. SWEENEY					
S3 J. POLICH	218	1	17	.239	0	RECORD W−101 L−99 FINISH−4TH					

SAN FRANCISCO	AB	HR	RBI	BA	SB	PITCHERS	IP	W−L	BB	SO	ERA
1B L. FLEMING	637	25	138	.292	2	C. JOHNSON	310	22−13	132	164	3.51
2B J. MORAN	567	4	81	.277	2	A. LIEN	276	20−13	86	106	4.11
3B D. LODIGIANI	536	6	68	.300	1	C. MELTON	240	11−18	96	120	5.10
SS J. CONWAY	332	1	35	.238	0	H. FELDMAN	230	11−16	95	78	4.38
OF J. GRACE	520	13	91	.335	4	C. DEMPSEY	194	9−9	78	100	4.36
OF B. HOLDER	511	11	77	.295	2	M. PEREZ	162	9−8	58	57	3.33
OF D. WHITE	503	1	44	.300	1	E. SINGLETON	119	5−10	61	79	4.24
C R. ORTEIG	390	6	49	.300	1	R. BUXTON	77	6−3	37	33	5.03
OF J. TOBIN	379	1	42	.243	12						
3B D. LANG	337	5	53	.264	1						
OF N. SHERIDAN	319	12	54	.288	3						
OF D. RESTELLI	290	17	62	.341	1						
SS R. NICELY	283	2	20	.194	1	MANAGER − L. O'DOUL					
C R. PARTEE	220	1	32	.232	0	RECORD W−100 L−100 FINISH−5TH					

SEATTLE	AB	HR	RBI	BA	SB	PITCHERS	IP	W−L	BB	SO	ERA
1B G. VICO	469	16	83	.286	5	J. WILSON	293	24−11	76	228	2.95
2B T. DAVIS	344	13	51	.262	4	H. BROWN	222	13−13	78	87	4.66
3B L. FREY	375	2	29	.267	10	G. FLETCHER	217	11−12	83	88	4.35
SS J. ALBRIGHT	499	8	60	.269	10	V. KINDSFATHER	193	12−9	76	66	3.73
OF W. JUDNICH	505	19	84	.285	3	A. GERHAUSER	164	10−10	42	65	4.39
OF A. LYONS	475	22	83	.274	18	J. DAVIS	164	9−10	68	73	4.77
OF M. RACKLEY	340	5	26	.294	12	D. GALEHOUSE	109	6−7	40	49	4.38
C B. SALKELD	249	10	39	.205	1	C. SCHANZ	103	4−11	45	43	6.29
O1 F. COLMAN	477	18	97	.319	3						
3S2 B. SCHUSTER	405	6	40	.254	10						
OF B. RAMSEY	224	0	17	.219	20	MANAGER − P. RICHARDS					
2S3 T. YORK	215	3	18	.219	3	RECORD W−96 L−104 FINISH−6TH					

1950

LOS ANGELES	AB	HR	RBI	BA	SB	PITCHERS	IP	W–L	BB	SO	ERA
1B E. FLETCHER	506	9	72	.289	0	C. MC LISH	260	20–11	104	129	3.60
2B J. LUCADELLO (1)	459	2	43	.237	1	B. MUNCRIEF	244	15–17	61	138	3.84
3B L. BRINKOPF	311	4	40	.267	2	R. HAMNER	225	13–16	86	81	3.80
SS G. BAKER	375	2	16	.280	12	H. BESSE	195	11–14	95	95	5.12
OF F. BAUMHOLTZ	670	15	89	.379	27	F. MARINO	149	9–9	50	64	5.13
OF C. MADDERN	573	14	102	.283	0	G. MALLORY	145	4–12	54	63	4.78
OF L. LAYTON	503	27	96	.296	3	J. ADKINS	96	2–6	56	67	6.56
C R. NOVOTNEY	393	8	46	.254	0						
OF C. GARRIOTT	451	10	53	.268	4						
O1 S. SPENCE	438	22	66	.228	1						
S2 R. STURGEON	342	0	17	.202	0						
32 A. GLOSSOP	341	5	47	.217	0						
2S L. KLEIN	331	14	76	.332	3	(1) ALSO WITH SACRAMENTO					
C R. CASH	197	7	30	.239	0	**MANAGER – B. KELLY**					
SS F. WHITMAN	159	0	8	.277	0	**RECORD W–86 L–114 FINISH–7TH**					

SACRAMENTO	AB	HR	RBI	BA	SB	PITCHERS	IP	W–L	BB	SO	ERA
1B S. SOUCHOCK	625	30	99	.291	12	B. EVANS	317	15–22	131	95	3.44
2B D. JOHNSON	229	1	22	.218	4	O. GROVE	309	17–20	131	124	3.32
3B J. TABOR	631	21	94	.266	3	M. SURKONT	255	18–13	86	159	2.96
SS L. RATTO	629	1	38	.256	17	B. GILLESPIE	210	12–12	96	102	3.30
OF A. WHITE	653	1	75	.323	5	H. GUMBERT	138	7–12	34	38	5.35
OF R. HODGIN	552	7	66	.268	9	F. DASSO	100	4–9	65	48	5.49
OF J. BUSBY	416	3	31	.310	17	G. LIERMAN	99	3–4	46	50	5.51
C J. STEINER	399	2	38	.268	0	J. DOBERNIC (2)	94	1–7	34	28	4.88
1O H. REICH	410	10	65	.273	6						
OF J. MARTY	388	9	69	.309	1						
C B. RAIMONDI	277	0	16	.242	4	(1) ALSO WITH SAN DIEGO					
OF T. DEL GUERCIO	226	2	32	.252	4	(2) ALSO WITH LOS ANGELES					
2S J. BERARDINO (1)	197	3	15	.228	4	**MANAGER – R. KRESS/J. MARTY**					
2S R. MYERS	144	1	19	.222	1	**RECORD W–81 L–119 FINISH–8TH**					

PLAYOFFS
NONE

1951

SEATTLE		AB	HR	RBI	BA	SB	PITCHERS	IP	W–L	BB	SO	ERA
1B	G. GOLDSBERRY	405	12	41	.240	6	M. GRISSOM	252	20–11	100	146	3.04
2B	G. HAMNER	526	1	47	.260	5	H. BROWN	168	16–6	36	70	3.05
3B	R. KRSNICH	538	4	53	.251	4	J. DAVIS	162	11–6	46	74	2.44
SS	A. GARBOWSKI	437	3	37	.222	4	B. HALL	133	7–8	51	80	3.72
OF	J. RIVERA	657	20	112	.352	33	C. SCHANZ	121	9–5	50	49	3.87
OF	W. JUDNICH	517	21	102	.329	4	S. NAGY	104	5–5	52	74	4.50
OF	A. LYONS	447	20	94	.286	2	E. JOHNSON	97	8–3	30	40	3.43
C	J. MONTALVO	230	5	49	.287	3	P. CALVERT	95	6–5	28	32	3.51
							A. LYONS	81	8–4	31	40	2.78
103	G. VICO	344	10	62	.247	0						
C	B. SHEELY	191	5	36	.340	0						
23	J. ALBRIGHT	186	2	17	.242	1						
2B	E. VERBAN	145	0	4	.255	0	MANAGER – R. HORNSBY					
C	J. ERAUTT	135	1	18	.304	0	RECORD W–99 L–68 FINISH–1ST					

HOLLYWOOD		AB	HR	RBI	BA	SB	PITCHERS	IP	W–L	BB	SO	ERA
1B	C. STEVENS	489	10	67	.292	1	J. SALVESON	219	15–10	55	74	3.16
2B	G. HANDLEY	524	0	39	.271	5	B. WADE	200	16–6	76	134	2.61
3B	L. STRINGER	525	11	64	.284	5	J. LINDELL	190	12–9	112	89	3.03
SS	G. GENOVESE	384	0	19	.211	0	P. WOODS	162	12–9	54	97	4.06
OF	G. SCHMEES	485	26	100	.328	14	V. LOMBARDI	162	10–11	66	82	3.94
OF	F. KELLEHER	470	28	94	.253	2	G. SHALLOCK	127	11–5	42	96	3.40
OF	D. RESTELLI	270	10	46	.281	0	MALTZBERGER	101	7–8	35	47	3.83
C	M. SANDLOCK	311	3	38	.248	0						
3B	M. FRANKLIN	311	13	49	.257	1						
OF	H. GORMAN	262	8	53	.275	7						
OF	C. CONATSER	247	9	42	.231	0						
SS	J. O'NEIL	218	0	16	.271	0						
PO1	J. LINDELL	178	9	31	.292	0	MANAGER – F. HANEY					
C	C. DAPPER	151	3	22	.219	1	RECORD W–93 L–74 FINISH–2ND					

LOS ANGELES		AB	HR	RBI	BA	SB	PITCHERS	IP	W–L	BB	SO	ERA
1B	C. CONNORS	390	22	77	.321	8	B. SPICER	248	17–13	98	84	3.70
2B	J. HOLLIS	561	3	54	.283	2	F. BACZEWSKI	232	12–10	121	129	4.03
3B	L. BRINKOPF	530	25	93	.279	5	W. HACKER	193	8–15	54	100	3.87
SS	G. BAKER	666	11	62	.278	10	D. LADE	148	8–6	63	56	3.89
OF	D. TALBOT	598	9	51	.249	6	B. MOISAN	142	10–8	75	48	4.12
OF	L. LAYTON	498	23	100	.305	1	R. HAMNER	105	4–6	42	46	4.37
OF	M. WEST	472	35	110	.282	2	H. BESSE	98	8–5	53	54	3.67
C	L. PEDEN	402	11	54	.249	1	E. CHANDLER	90	5–7	49	30	5.50
OF	T. NEILL	293	7	50	.273	0	MANAGER – S. HACK					
1B	D. FONDY	274	11	45	.376	7	RECORD W–86 L–81 FINISH–3RD					

1951

PORTLAND		AB	HR	RBI	BA	SB	PITCHERS	IP	W−L	BB	SO	ERA
1B	J. LAFATA (1)	442	10	63	.217	4	M. PIERETTI	256	18−13	75	86	3.30
2B	E. BASINSKI	687	16	73	.266	3	L. LINDE	212	12−12	68	75	4.29
3B	L. THOMAS	638	27	106	.310	1	R. LYNN	192	13−12	87	68	3.75
SS	F. AUSTIN	597	4	70	.293	1	R. HELSER	161	8−16	73	68	4.64
OF	J. BROVIA	574	32	133	.303	2	R. ADAMS	153	11−9	53	80	4.06
OF	E. BARR	574	12	55	.260	12	L. WARD	121	7−7	60	62	4.54
OF	B. HOLDER	377	6	54	.305	0	J. CREEL	120	9−9	60	43	4.28
C	J. ROSSI	369	10	57	.304	0						
							(1) ALSO WITH OAKLAND					
OF	D. WHITE (2)	242	5	26	.264	0	(2) ALSO WITH SAN DIEGO					
OF	G. GLADSTONE	161	1	14	.230	2	MANAGER − B. SWEENEY					
C	L. MARCUCCI	121	2	12	.231	1	RECORD W−83 L−85 FINISH−4TH					

OAKLAND		AB	HR	RBI	BA	SB	PITCHERS	IP	W−L	BB	SO	ERA
1B	J. MARSHALL	209	9	30	.225	1	W. AYERS	222	20−13	88	91	3.85
2B	P. PAVLICK	569	4	29	.271	19	E. HARRIST	207	16−16	99	130	3.78
3B	B. HAAS	332	10	59	.331	3	W. BAILEY	147	9−8	60	61	4.35
SS	B. JENNINGS (1)	350	9	37	.249	1	J. RAGNI	138	9−7	70	64	4.17
OF	L. CHRISTOPHER	375	11	83	.309	0	L. HITTLE	137	3−3	45	64	3.74
OF	E. RAPP	357	10	74	.322	5	A. GETTEL	72	4−6	26	42	5.25
OF	A. GALAN	323	13	64	.307	4	F. HARDY	68	3−5	28	29	5.56
C	D. PADGETT	241	6	25	.303	1	J. VANDERMEER	63	2−6	35	37	5.14
							D. DAHLE	63	1−4	29	26	3.43
SS	A. WILSON	349	0	22	.255	6						
123	J. MORAN (2)	294	3	33	.286	1	(1) ALSO WITH SAN DIEGO					
O1	L. DAVIS	289	4	35	.266	5	(2) ALSO WITH SAN FRANCISCO					
OP	J. RAGNI	275	2	38	.298	0	(3) ALSO WITH HOLLYWOOD					
3B	S. JORGENSEN	260	5	27	.308	4	MANAGER − M. OTT					
C	E. MALONE (3)	251	6	43	.267	0	RECORD W−80 L−88 FINISH−5TH					

SAN DIEGO		AB	HR	RBI	BA	SB	PITCHERS	IP	W−L	BB	SO	ERA
1B	J. GRAHAM (1)	536	30	105	.271	0	S. JONES	267	16−13	175	246	2.76
2B	R. WILSON	628	0	48	.268	20	R. KERRIGAN	182	14−8	51	52	3.12
3B	H. STOREY	352	14	54	.253	0	C. SIPPLE	201	11−14	88	75	4.25
SS	W. WIETELMANN	390	8	44	.262	3	G. FLETCHER (1)	170	9−12	62	91	3.44
OF	C. MADDERN	373	14	76	.311	1	C. EMBREE	176	11−15	65	70	4.70
OF	S. LOCKLIN	277	5	21	.267	3	A. OLSEN	138	7−10	33	47	4.70
OF	J. TOBIN	246	0	18	.252	8						
C	H. NARAGON	278	2	22	.252	0						
31	J. TABOR (2)	366	7	57	.301	1	(1) ALSO WITH SAN FRANCISCO					
O1	J. ROWELL	271	8	39	.266	0	(2) ALSO WITH SACRAMENTO					
C	F. KERR	261	6	51	.261	2	MANAGER − D. BAKER					
SS	H. MALMBERG	259	0	27	.247	3	RECORD W−79 L−88 FINISH−6TH					

1951

SACRAMENTO	AB	HR	RBI	BA	SB	PITCHERS	IP	W—L	BB	SO	ERA
1B B. BOYD	555	5	64	.342	41	G. ELLIOTT	244	15—14	69	101	3.10
2B J. GORDON	485	43	136	.299	2	K. GABLES	237	11—13	75	101	3.53
3B K. KELTNER	325	6	41	.249	1	W. CLOUGH	191	11—11	62	58	3.82
SS L. RATTO	423	1	30	.210	3	B. GILLESPIE	172	9—11	75	101	4.24
OF A. WHITE	573	0	30	.265	7	O. GROVE	159	8—9	82	76	4.42
OF R. HODGIN	462	5	58	.294	7	A. BENTON (1)	130	5—7	43	43	4.02
OF G. SCALA	418	2	33	.270	8	F. NELSON (2)	119	4—6	58	44	3.63
C V. SMITH	216	1	18	.269	1						
O1 H. REICH	388	9	49	.247	3						
OF J. MARTY	370	12	81	.286	2	(1) ALSO WITH SAN DIEGO					
3S2 L. RIGHETTI	352	3	27	.202	0	(2) ALSO WITH OAKLAND					
C S. HAIRSTON	190	0	18	.253	3	MANAGER — J. GORDON					
C A. LAKEMAN	163	2	19	.227	0	RECORD W—75 L—92 FINISH—7TH					

SAN FRANCISCO	AB	HR	RBI	BA	SB	PITCHERS	IP	W—L	BB	SO	ERA
1B J. DOUGLAS	179	0	17	.246	0	L. BURDETTE	210	14—12	78	118	3.21
2B E. LAKE	579	27	58	.261	7	C. JOHNSON (3)	181	7—18	98	91	5.67
3B D. LODIGIANI	387	5	45	.302	6	A. LIEN	179	13—10	39	65	3.87
SS J. BRIDEWESER	575	3	44	.283	7	L. DICKEY	147	8—10	85	51	4.90
OF W. MC CAWLEY	578	16	73	.287	3	M. PEREZ	137	5—5	58	50	4.80
OF E. SAUER (1)	459	1	61	.264	10	C. DEMPSEY	92	7—7	53	51	3.91
OF B. THURMAN	379	13	63	.274	11	E. SINGLETON	77	5—3	15	44	3.04
C R. ORTEIG	417	16	71	.285	0						
O1 J. GRACE	450	2	56	.302	1	(1) ALSO WITH HOLLYWOOD & SAN DIEGO					
OF B. ADAMS (2)	232	8	42	.250	0	(2) ALSO WITH SAN DIEGO					
C A. TORNAY	208	0	23	.240	1	(3) ALSO WITH OAKLAND					
2B B. SERRELL	169	0	15	.243	3	MANAGER — L. O'DOUL					
1B D. LONG	128	1	23	.266	0	RECORD W—74 L—93 FINISH—8TH					

PLAYOFFS
SEATTLE DEFEATED LOS ANGELES 2 GAMES TO 1
HOLLYWOOD DEFEATED PORTLAND 2 GAMES TO 0

FINAL
SEATTLE DEFEATED HOLLYWOOD 3 GAMES TO 2

1952

HOLLYWOOD		AB	HR	RBI	BA	SB	PITCHERS	IP	W–L	BB	SO	ERA
1B	C. STEVENS	490	2	57	.278	1	J. LINDELL	282	24–9	108	190	2.52
2B	M. BASGALL	578	8	63	.279	6	M. QUEEN	205	14–9	84	131	2.41
3B	G. HANDLEY	456	0	46	.274	10	P. PETTIT	197	15–8	99	74	3.70
SS	D. COLE	602	8	73	.286	2	J. WALSH	172	10–9	78	93	3.19
OF	C. BERNIER	652	9	79	.301	65	P. WOODS	160	11–9	75	79	3.88
OF	T. SAFFELL	495	4	57	.273	16	R. LYNN (1)	121	9–6	56	30	4.24
OF	T. BEARD	390	11	53	.269	24	L. SHEPARD	107	6–4	56	32	3.11
C	M. SANDLOCK	374	0	31	.286	1						
31	J. PHILLIPS	353	9	53	.300	1	(1) ALSO WITH PORTLAND					
OF	F. KELLEHER	222	11	33	.239	5	MANAGER – F. HANEY					
PO	J. LINDELL	174	8	25	.213	1	RECORD W–109 L–71 FINISH–1ST					

OAKLAND		AB	HR	RBI	BA	SB	PITCHERS	IP	W–L	BB	SO	ERA
1B	T. GILBERT	625	31	118	.259	2	A. GETTEL	284	17–14	91	132	3.30
2B	H. SCHENZ	627	2	51	.278	18	B. AYERS	204	13–12	73	78	3.66
3B	S. JORGENSEN	529	10	60	.244	5	L. HITTLE	187	11–10	37	64	2.98
SS	J. BERO	313	7	27	.173	1	G. BAMBERGER	150	14–6	36	67	2.88
OF	S. CHAPMAN	617	16	98	.263	2	M. CANDINI	133	9–6	49	69	2.57
OF	W. MILNE	574	5	57	.286	6	J. VAN CUYK	118	9–3	63	63	2.67
OF	J. OSTROWSKI (1)	415	22	69	.253	1	H. GREGG	108	11–3	48	65	4.25
C	R. NOBLE	366	12	60	.298	2	R. BOWMAN	96	7–5	31	65	3.28
							B. EVANS	95	5–4	34	51	4.26
3O2	L. DAVIS	399	8	44	.306	1	J. MAHRT	86	6–7	46	37	3.98
OF	J. RAGNI	258	2	25	.267	3						
C	L. NEAL	182	0	12	.258	1	(1) ALSO WITH SACRAMENTO					
OF	L. CHRISTOPHER	151	5	26	.258	0	MANAGER – M. OTT					
SS	E. LAKE	138	4	24	.210	2	RECORD W–104 L–76 FINISH–2ND					

SEATTLE		AB	HR	RBI	BA	SB	PITCHERS	IP	W–L	BB	SO	ERA
1B	B. BOYD	641	3	75	.320	33	V. KINDSFATHER	278	21–11	78	148	2.40
2B	N. FERNANDEZ	595	9	68	.269	2	A. WIDMAR	246	20–12	67	106	2.30
3B	R. KRSNICH	437	1	58	.295	2	S. NAGY	231	16–16	71	115	3.04
SS	A. WILSON	683	1	59	.316	25	A. DEL DUCA	208	9–11	63	93	3.68
OF	W. JUDNICH	668	15	105	.287	4	B. HALL (1)	203	14–11	88	119	3.28
OF	C. MADDERN	545	8	77	.294	1	J. DAVIS	132	7–10	50	56	3.61
OF	A. LYONS	428	11	50	.245	2	C. SCHANZ	124	5–7	43	52	3.41
C	R. WILSON	562	7	75	.297	3						
3B	L. THOMAS	186	3	26	.280	1						
1B	G. VICO	171	5	21	.205	0						
2B	P. PAVLICK	162	1	7	.265	3	(1) ALSO WITH SACRAMENTO					
OF	B. CHORLTON	156	1	7	.218	1	MANAGER – B. SWEENEY					
OF	E. HUTSON	139	6	14	.245	0	RECORD W–96 L–84 FINISH–3RD					

1952

PORTLAND	AB	HR	RBI	BA	SB	PITCHERS	IP	W–L	BB	SO	ERA
1B H. REICH (1)	326	4	28	.221	3	M. PIERETTI	276	16–18	82	77	3.42
2B E. BASINSKI	552	10	58	.246	4	R. ADAMS	269	15–16	67	162	2.17
3B D. EGGERT	635	19	82	.252	11	F. SANFORD	230	17–9	83	107	3.44
SS F. AUSTIN	702	4	38	.265	17	L. LINDE	200	11–15	60	119	3.11
OF J. BROVIA	551	21	85	.290	0	R. LINT (2)	167	13–5	58	68	3.61
OF J. RUSSELL	440	7	43	.252	13	L. WARD	156	12–13	56	65	3.06
OF E. BARR	310	3	20	.232	8	WELMAKER (2)	116	4–8	41	72	3.34
C J. GLADD	315	6	41	.194	0						
OF C. CONATSER	272	8	38	.268	1						
1B H. ARFT	268	3	45	.291	5	(1) ALSO WITH SACRAMENTO					
C A. ROBINSON	248	7	29	.173	0	(2) ALSO WITH HOLLYWOOD					
OF E. TIPTON	236	2	23	.263	6	**MANAGER – C. HOPPER**					
23O J. MAGUIRE	186	0	7	.258	4	**RECORD W–92 L–88 FINISH–4TH**					

SAN DIEGO	AB	HR	RBI	BA	SB	PITCHERS	IP	W–L	BB	SO	ERA
1B J. GRAHAM	552	22	88	.274	8	M. LUNA	260	15–16	96	138	2.94
2B M. FRANKLIN	458	6	45	.227	5	G. FLETCHER	232	14–16	87	108	3.76
3B L. STRINGER (1)	538	17	85	.275	3	J. SALVESON	168	10–10	34	57	3.80
SS A. RICHTER	516	1	61	.248	6	B. FLOWERS	167	11–10	62	114	3.18
OF J. TOBIN	599	3	33	.287	20	T. SMITH	147	9–10	60	75	3.24
OF H. FABER	438	5	35	.231	11	A. OLSEN	147	6–13	28	87	3.87
OF H. GORMAN	352	8	39	.261	0	B. HENRY	123	7–9	55	85	3.59
C L. SUMMERS	340	7	57	.241	2	B. MALLOY	94	4–2	39	27	3.26
32 L. KLEIN	418	4	44	.280	5						
1B T. ALSTON	258	2	26	.244	0						
OF D. CLAY	239	0	27	.280	3	(1) ALSO WITH HOLLYWOOD					
C F. KERR	174	3	19	.213	2	**MANAGER – L. O'DOUL**					
OF J. DAVIS	167	6	36	.263	1	**RECORD W–88 L–92 FINISH–5TH**					

LOS ANGELES	AB	HR	RBI	BA	SB	PITCHERS	IP	W–L	BB	SO	ERA
1B C. CONNORS	406	6	51	.259	0	B. MOISAN	238	16–12	101	118	3.82
2B J. HOLLIS	609	3	56	.250	4	E. CHANDLER	236	16–14	60	82	3.51
3B L. BRINKOPF	450	27	67	.238	4	C. MC LISH	212	10–15	60	84	3.78
SS G. BAKER	696	15	73	.260	11	D. LADE	171	8–12	71	53	3.95
OF D. TALBOT	623	6	50	.279	8	B. SPICER	114	6–7	42	57	3.95
OF B. USHER	461	10	47	.293	10	J. HATTEN	104	8–8	35	91	2.25
OF L. LAYTON	400	5	44	.240	5	B. ZICK	104	4–2	57	53	4.41
C L. PEDEN	527	18	71	.279	0	W. RAMSDELL	89	5–6	38	42	3.64
O1 M. WEST	497	35	91	.262	2						
OF R. NORTHEY	235	11	38	.255	1	**MANAGER – S. HACK**					
3B T. DAVIS	184	2	20	.228	1	**RECORD W–87 L–93 FINISH–6TH**					

1952

SAN FRANCISCO	AB	HR	RBI	BA	SB	PITCHERS	IP	W–L	BB	SO	ERA
1B J. GRACE	568	4	62	.299	0	E. SINGLETON	276	17–15	76	170	2.67
2B J. MORAN	687	0	32	.258	7	G. BOEMLER	227	14–16	99	109	3.21
3B R. CHESO	400	3	57	.278	1	A. LIEN	207	9–16	57	60	4.30
SS L. RATTO	538	0	30	.223	7	B. BRADFORD	206	15–11	75	96	3.58
OF W. MC CAWLEY	511	4	78	.256	6	W. CLOUGH (1)	158	6–6	38	33	3.76
OF B. THURMAN	393	9	52	.280	9	B. BEVENS	155	6–12	79	64	4.47
OF F. KALIN	333	12	64	.294	0	B. MUNCRIEF	147	6–13	55	69	2.69
C R. ORTEIG	432	3	53	.266	3	B. REEDER	91	2–9	51	34	5.93
OF G. KLINGLER	255	0	15	.259	5						
OF W. HAFEY	198	5	20	.252	0	(1) ALSO WITH SACRAMENTO					
1B W. ANDRING	187	2	11	.257	2	**MANAGER – T. HEATH**					
OF S. TAORMINA	161	4	22	.286	1	**RECORD W–78 L–102 FINISH–7TH**					

SACRAMENTO	AB	HR	RBI	BA	SB	PITCHERS	IP	W–L	BB	SO	ERA
1B B. GLYNN	409	12	55	.303	1	G. ELLIOTT	254	12–18	41	117	3.19
2B J. GORDON	370	16	46	.246	5	J. FLORES	240	10–20	60	123	2.78
3B B. DILLINGER	585	0	51	.287	12	C. JOHNSON	206	10–17	90	99	4.06
SS R. MYERS	633	7	39	.250	13	K. GABLES	205	9–11	76	92	2.55
OF L. ATTYD (1)	426	2	22	.235	4	O. GROVE	146	6–12	89	65	4.19
OF D. RESTELLI	249	7	31	.357	4	B. BARKELEW	116	4–4	51	50	3.65
OF J. MARTY	228	3	25	.237	1	F. NELSON	115	6–7	31	24	3.83
C J. MC KEEGAN	301	5	23	.166	0						
32S E. BOCKMAN (2)	442	5	44	.258	1						
OF MC CORMICK (2)	315	2	26	.251	1						
C V. SMITH	283	0	22	.226	0						
1B B. TAYLOR	222	0	23	.252	0						
OF J. STEINAGEL	184	2	8	.185	1						
OF A. ANICICH	178	1	8	.185	0	(1) ALSO WITH OAKLAND					
OF E. ROBERTS	161	0	6	.255	2	(2) ALSO WITH PORTLAND					
2B R. STURGEON	155	1	16	.239	1	**MANAGER – J. GORDON**					
OF A. WHITE	125	0	7	.200	0	**RECORD W–66 L–114 FINISH–8TH**					

PLAYOFFS
NONE

1953

HOLLYWOOD	AB	HR	RBI	BA	SB	PITCHERS	IP	W−L	BB	SO	ERA
1B D. LONG	599	35	116	.272	5	G. O'DONNELL	281	20−12	86	67	3.61
2B M. BASGALL	578	10	77	.249	2	J. WALSH	190	16−9	75	81	3.13
3B G. HANDLEY	428	1	35	.259	11	R. MUNGER	166	12−10	58	61	3.37
SS J. PHILLIPS	515	16	77	.270	0	L. HITTLE (1)	156	8−11	35	52	4.15
OF T. SAFFELL	630	13	61	.273	29	H. FISHER	155	10−10	71	72	3.65
OF L. WALLS	593	10	83	.268	14	M. QUEEN	144	8−7	79	97	3.69
OF T. BEARD	402	17	60	.286	21	R. LYNN	143	10−4	63	42	3.72
C E. MALONE	303	9	39	.261	1	B. MACDONALD	84	5−2	40	29	3.42
C B. BRAGAN	303	4	28	.251	5						
1B C. STEVENS	274	5	35	.230	0						
OF F. KELLEHER	249	15	65	.329	1	(1) ALSO WITH OAKLAND					
S3 D. DAHLKE	198	1	10	.237	1	MANAGER − B. BRAGAN					
3O B. BUNDY	102	2	15	.324	1	RECORD W−106 L−74 FINISH−1ST					

SEATTLE	AB	HR	RBI	BA	SB	PITCHERS	IP	W−L	BB	SO	ERA
1B G. GOLDSBERRY	549	6	53	.244	1	A. WIDMAR	272	20−14	108	83	3.70
2B A. WILSON	638	2	76	.332	9	B. EVANS	259	16−13	105	134	3.23
3B L. THOMAS	668	13	100	.297	4	V. KINDSFATHER	248	16−16	87	87	3.01
SS M. COMBS	563	8	58	.265	0	J. DAVIS	217	13−8	64	68	3.02
OF J. TOBIN	709	3	58	.296	10	S. NAGY	186	13−8	88	80	4.16
OF W. JUDNICH	583	16	101	.298	0	T. LOVRICH	153	8−4	63	46	3.95
OF C. MADDERN	411	14	65	.294	1	A. DEL DUCA	145	10−16	66	53	4.72
C R. ORTEIG	489	28	99	.276	2						
O1 G. SCHMEES	412	7	56	.279	5						
C C. CHRISTIE	145	1	17	.283	0	MANAGER − B. SWEENEY					
SS A. GARBOWSKI	130	1	6	.231	0	RECORD W−98 L−82 FINISH−2ND					

LOS ANGELES	AB	HR	RBI	BA	SB	PITCHERS	IP	W−L	BB	SO	ERA
1B F. RICHARDS	740	26	92	.296	4	C. MC LISH	235	16−11	60	114	3.71
2B F. DI PRIMA	497	9	60	.268	2	J. HATTEN	224	17−11	81	152	3.34
3B B. HARDIN	425	0	28	.261	0	B. MOISAN	223	10−11	69	93	3.03
SS G. BAKER	595	20	99	.284	20	B. SPICER	196	12−10	47	76	3.90
OF D. TALBOT	762	14	70	.287	10	E. CHANDLER	179	7−12	42	59	4.48
OF B. USHER	672	15	90	.304	7	W. PADGET	178	11−7	58	60	4.30
OF D. SMITH	338	12	42	.225	2	R. GUMPERT	100	7−9	28	52	3.07
C L. PEDEN	340	11	55	.268	0	A. IHDE	91	4−4	41	35	4.34
OF D. UPRIGHT	245	12	42	.306	3						
C A. EVANS	235	2	26	.285	1						
3B T. DAVIS	204	14	27	.294	1						
P B. MOISAN	141	4	23	.284	0	MANAGER − S. HACK					
C E. TAPPE	114	0	16	.281	1	RECORD W−93 L−87 FINISH−3RD					

1953

PORTLAND	AB	HR	RBI	BA	SB	PITCHERS	IP	W–L	BB	SO	ERA
1B H. ARFT	490	21	64	.227	2	R. LINT	249	22–10	67	100	3.10
2B E. BASINSKI	529	6	61	.240	2	G. ELLIOTT	227	12–14	45	112	3.02
3B D. EGGERT	434	14	56	.235	2	J. HEARD	226	16–12	92	85	3.19
SS F. AUSTIN	739	7	62	.280	14	L. LINDE	203	13–10	64	66	3.36
OF F. ROBBE	472	7	52	.316	1	R. ADAMS	177	9–10	63	82	4.38
OF J. RUSSELL	470	6	37	.262	8	L. WARD	141	5–11	55	64	3.90
OF H. REICH	399	12	53	.296	1	F. SANFORD	135	7–11	59	53	3.93
C J. GLADD	347	3	49	.282	2	R. WAIBEL	123	6–8	24	36	3.95
						WELMAKER (1)	90	4–2	32	49	4.10
C A. ROBINSON	274	13	39	.248	0						
32 C. GRANT	259	13	29	.216	0						
31 D. KOLLOWAY	259	3	33	.251	0						
OF D. RESTELLI	256	12	41	.340	7	(1) ALSO WITH HOLLYWOOD					
OF G. GLADSTONE	244	5	33	.246	0	MANAGER – C. HOPPER					
OF B. MARQUIS	210	6	24	.271	4	RECORD W–92 L–88 FINISH–4TH					

SAN FRANCISCO	AB	HR	RBI	BA	SB	PITCHERS	IP	W–L	BB	SO	ERA
1B G. VICO	582	11	93	.261	2	E. SINGLETON	253	15–17	74	126	3.23
2B J. MORAN	582	3	44	.266	6	B. BRADFORD	191	10–8	74	69	3.35
3B R. CHESO	529	11	80	.297	1	B. MUNCRIEF	169	10–12	39	83	2.67
SS L. RIGHETTI	532	3	61	.258	0	G. BOEMLER	164	8–17	90	97	4.60
OF A. LYONS	510	22	77	.269	2	T. SHANDOR	154	9–9	61	44	4.16
OF S. TAORMINA	448	8	62	.297	3	A. LIEN	153	12–8	37	43	4.07
OF J. ZUVELA	385	16	50	.273	1	J. MC CALL	151	12–7	55	91	3.05
C A. TORNAY	396	2	34	.230	3	W. CLOUGH	135	3–6	49	36	3.79
32O L. STRINGER (1)	396	2	30	.258	3						
OF F. KALIN	355	16	55	.293	1	(1) ALSO WITH SAN DIEGO					
OF W. MC CAWLEY	350	3	45	.251	0	MANAGER – T. HEATH					
C W. TISIERA	168	1	16	.214	1	RECORD W–91 L–89 FINISH–5TH					

SAN DIEGO	AB	HR	RBI	BA	SB	PITCHERS	IP	W–L	BB	SO	ERA
1B T. ALSTON	697	23	101	.297	8	M. LUNA	263	17–12	98	90	2.67
2B A. FEDEROFF	531	0	30	.277	9	B. KERRIGAN	259	16–16	79	103	3.19
3B J. MERSON	327	4	44	.229	1	C. FANNIN	214	14–12	70	137	3.24
SS B. PETERSON	666	5	60	.279	7	W. THOMASON	194	11–10	101	104	3.99
OF R. FABER	634	19	92	.254	8	T. SMITH	185	13–16	84	80	4.52
OF E. RAPP	630	24	108	.311	11	L. DICKEY	132	7–9	41	50	3.01
OF W. POCEKAY	401	14	58	.279	0	R. MALLOY	105	4–3	41	31	4.47
C W. MATHIS	407	6	47	.224	2						
						(1) ALSO WITH LOS ANGELES					
23 F. MURRAY	275	1	19	.218	7	(2) ALSO WITH SAN FRANCISCO					
3O M. FRANKLIN (1)	274	2	27	.259	0	MANAGER – L. O'DOUL					
OF J. GRACE (2)	221	1	20	.231	2	RECORD W–88 L–92 FINISH–6TH					

1953

OAKLAND		AB	HR	RBI	BA	SB	PITCHERS	IP	W-L	BB	SO	ERA
1B	J. MARSHALL	556	24	99	.273	6	A. GETTEL	309	24-14	75	141	3.20
2B	L. DAVIS	670	13	97	.296	1	G. BAMBERGER	245	15-16	100	111	5.00
3B	S. JORGENSEN	610	13	70	.279	4	B. WATERS (3)	177	5-12	54	42	4.01
SS	J. BERO	297	9	32	.209	0	J. ATKINS	170	9-15	62	58	4.24
OF	P. MILNE	650	4	66	.323	10	J. FLORES (2)	153	8-9	34	47	3.94
OF	S. CHAPMAN	617	22	93	.263	2	C. DEMPSEY	106	4-10	61	62	5.18
OF	B. HOWERTON	500	32	106	.256	2	D. FERRARESE	86	4-4	84	56	6.25
C	L. NEAL	603	9	69	.239	2	R. MURPHY	82	4-5	45	33	4.15
SS	J. O'NEIL (1)	301	0	27	.249	2						
S2	E. LAKE	262	2	15	.225	0	(1) ALSO WITH HOLLYWOOD & SAN FRANCISCO					
23	DANDRIDGE (2)	254	0	13	.268	1	(2) ALSO WITH SACRAMENTO					
2B	H. SCHENZ (2)	177	0	18	.288	0	(3) ALSO WITH HOLLYWOOD					
OC	A. CUITTI	130	1	14	.292	1	MANAGER - A. GALAN					
P	A. GETTEL	120	1	0	.240	0	RECORD W-77 L-103 FINISH-7TH					

SACRAMENTO		AB	HR	RBI	BA	SB	PITCHERS	IP	W-L	BB	SO	ERA
1B	N. JONES	641	13	102	.287	2	M. PIERETTI	249	12-17	87	91	4.16
2B	P. PAVLICK	384	0	21	.250	6	K. GABLES	230	9-17	82	100	3.01
3B	E. BOCKMAN	590	11	64	.259	2	C. SCHANZ	199	8-12	70	73	3.84
SS	R. MYERS	496	3	42	.268	5	C. JOHNSON	195	12-14	55	81	3.59
OF	B. DILLINGER	645	0	51	.366	10	H. BESSE	143	6-10	55	52	3.41
OF	N. SHERIDAN (1)	591	13	83	.293	12	K. KIMBALL	121	4-11	46	39	3.71
OF	J. BROVIA	525	20	97	.314	1	R. OSENBAUGH	98	4-7	64	58	4.15
C	J. RITCHEY	454	5	55	.291	10	A. YAYLIAN	84	6-2	36	35	3.96
U	L. ATTYD	419	1	20	.215	10	(1) ALSO WITH OAKLAND					
C	J. MONTALVO	145	2	10	.193	0	MANAGER - G. DESAUTELS					
OF	J. METKOVICH	140	3	17	.214	4	RECORD W-75 L-105 FINISH-8TH					

PLAYOFFS
NONE

1954

SAN DIEGO		AB	HR	RBI	BA	SB	PITCHERS		IP	W–L	BB	SO	ERA
1B	D. SISLER	591	19	90	.318	2	E. ERAUTT		274	16–12	85	115	3.12
2B	A. FEDEROFF	630	0	29	.278	15	B. KERRIGAN		240	17–11	60	104	2.77
3B	M. SMITH	388	9	51	294	14	L. DICKEY		218	14–11	68	86	2.69
SS	B. PETERSON	591	10	61	.289	10	B. WIGHT		210	17–5	72	87	1.93
OF	H. ELLIOTT	640	15	110	.350	8	W. THOMASON		138	10–9	92	65	4.37
OF	E. RAPP	566	24	111	.337	2	C. FANNIN		131	8–5	60	99	2.54
OF	R. FABER	243	6	28	.210	6	T. SMITH		83	3–2	32	36	4.03
C	M. SANDLOCK	229	0	22	.183	0	C. CHAMBERS		75	6–4	45	27	5.30
OP	A. LYONS (1)	264	10	42	.265	3							
3S	J. MERSON	207	2	20	.227	0							
3B	B. ELLIOTT	203	12	39	.256	1	(1) ALSO WITH SAN FRANCISCO						
C	W. POCEKAY	199	1	20	.281	2	**MANAGER – L. O'DOUL**						
1B	L. EASTER	198	13	42	.278	1	**RECORD W–102 L–67 FINISH–1ST**						

HOLLYWOOD		AB	HR	RBI	BA	SB	PITCHERS		IP	W–L	BB	SO	ERA
1B	D. LONG	410	23	68	.280	3	R. BOWMAN		258	22–13	99	165	2.51
2B	M. BASGALL	457	4	59	.252	9	R. MUNGER		218	17–8	63	96	2.32
3B	J. PHILLIPS	577	17	88	.300	3	L. DONOSO		205	19–8	51	141	2.37
SS	D. SMITH	517	0	51	.294	23	M. QUEEN		200	16–8	73	112	3.19
OF	L. WALLS	601	16	93	.290	18	J. WALSH		168	10–7	65	53	3.21
OF	T. SAFFELL	567	8	58	.279	48	E. WOLFE		92	7–4	27	33	2.65
OF	C. BERNIER	431	6	41	.313	38							
C	B. BRAGAN	182	2	19	.258	6							
32S	J. LOHRKE	418	8	52	.263	3							
OF	F. KELLEHER	191	10	38	.246	2	**MANAGER – B. BRAGAN**						
C	E. MALONE	158	1	22	.241	0	**RECORD W–101 L–68 FINISH–2ND**						

OAKLAND		AB	HR	RBI	BA	SB	PITCHERS		IP	W–L	BB	SO	ERA
1B	J. MARSHALL	603	31	123	.285	15	A. GETTEL		284	17–15	79	140	3.07
2B	R. SAMFORD	419	2	48	.253	7	D. FERRARESE		250	18–15	174	184	3.74
3B	S. JORGENSEN	591	14	62	.283	7	G. BAMBERGER		179	11–8	81	61	3.53
SS	R. ROSE	623	0	35	.271	15	H. NICHOLAS		132	4–6	66	66	4.92
OF	S. CHAPMAN	473	11	63	.290	7	J. ATKINS		130	5–7	65	53	5.12
OF	P. MILNE	397	3	43	.270	2	C. VAN CUYK		120	5–6	47	59	3.96
OF	G. HERMANSKI	322	11	48	.270	3	A. SCHALLOCK		99	12–4	39	67	4.10
C	L. NEAL	344	5	44	.271	2							
O2	L. DAVIS	365	9	59	.288	3							
OF	A. CUITTI	282	5	35	.284	1							
3B	B. WILSON	220	4	33	.282	3							
C	L. LANDINI	212	0	13	.250	0	**MANAGER – C. DRESSEN**						
OF	B. HOWERTON	178	3	18	.258	1	**RECORD W–85 L–82 FINISH–3RD**						

1954

SAN FRANCISCO		AB	HR	RBI	BA	SB	PITCHERS	IP	W–L	BB	SO	ERA
1B	J. WESTLAKE	459	5	70	.285	4	T. PONCE	237	14–16	61	69	3.41
2B	J. MORAN	633	0	34	.291	5	E. SINGLETON	213	13–13	65	102	3.00
3B	R. CHESO	395	4	41	.251	6	K. HOLCOMBE	205	10–10	85	75	3.07
SS	L. RIGHETTI	455	2	34	.255	6	E. CHANDLER (2)	179	12–11	56	50	3.32
OF	T. BEARD (1)	563	11	62	.300	30	F. HILLER	166	11–8	33	58	2.92
OF	S. TAORMINA	342	5	56	.272	1	A. ZABALA	112	11–8	43	43	3.22
OF	B. DI PIETRO	331	7	49	.269	2	B. MUNCRIEF	107	3–7	36	59	2.95
C	A. TORNAY	264	1	30	.258	0	B. BRADFORD	104	6–2	36	55	3.39
3S	M. BAXES	452	2	54	.248	9	(1) ALSO WITH HOLLYWOOD					
OF	D. MELTON	329	9	54	.301	5	(2) ALSO WITH LOS ANGELES					
C	W. TISIERA	185	1	18	.259	0	MANAGER – T. HEATH					
1B	C. STEVENS (1)	132	2	23	.242	2	RECORD W–84 L–84 FINISH–4TH					

SEATTLE		AB	HR	RBI	BA	SB	PITCHERS	IP	W–L	BB	SO	ERA
1B	A. WILSON	660	0	50	.336	20	T. BYRNE	260	20–10	118	199	3.15
2B	J. BUKOWATZ	329	1	24	.240	2	B. HALL (2)	242	12–17	101	138	3.53
3B	L. THOMAS	505	4	64	.255	3	G. BEARDEN	202	11–13	97	82	4.05
SS	D. MALLOTT	175	0	11	.223	0	A. WIDMAR	178	8–13	60	63	4.75
OF	J. TOBIN	528	0	26	.248	8	S. NAGY	132	7–11	55	53	3.76
OF	C. MADDERN	456	12	72	.270	2	B. EVANS	114	5–7	52	58	4.66
OF	A. ZARILLA	347	3	32	.216	2	L. MYERS	114	4–7	51	45	4.83
C	R. ORTEIG	354	14	65	.254	0	J. KINDSFATHER	107	4–6	64	30	4.21
O1	G. SCHMEES	360	15	69	.297	9						
21	J. PRIDDY	275	0	24	.247	1	(1) ALSO WITH PORTLAND					
P1	T. BYRNE	176	7	39	.295	1	(2) ALSO WITH HOLLYWOOD					
C	L. JENNEY	134	1	12	.231	0	MANAGER – J. PRIDDY					
1O	H. REICH (1)	131	2	19	.260	0	RECORD W–77 L–85 FINISH–5TH					

LOS ANGELES		AB	HR	RBI	BA	SB	PITCHERS	IP	W–L	BB	SO	ERA
1B	F. RICHARDS	497	24	61	.227	2	C. MC LISH	245	13–15	74	120	3.53
2B	G. MAUCH	565	11	58	.287	12	J. HATTEN	232	13–17	94	138	3.53
3B	B. EDWARDS	393	9	64	.298	0	R. SPICER	231	13–16	54	122	3.07
SS	B. HARDIN	434	2	21	.242	5	J. PYECHA	147	7–7	61	63	3.24
OF	B. USHER	574	13	73	.254	16	B. CHURCH	134	11–9	67	91	3.89
OF	T. BROWN	502	14	61	.263	3	B. MOISAN	101	1–7	60	41	4.09
OF	D. UPRIGHT	235	10	28	.234	2						
C	A. EVANS	269	5	29	.268	1						
C	J. PRAMESA	231	11	37	.294	1						
OF	D. ROBERTSON	219	7	28	.237	4						
SS	H. NASTERNAK	211	3	16	.237	1	MANAGER – B. SWEENEY					
O1	M. WEST	169	12	37	.260	1	RECORD W–73 L–92 FINISH–6TH					

1954

SACRAMENTO		AB	HR	RBI	BA	SB	PITCHERS	IP	W–L	BB	SO	ERA
1B	N. JONES	596	12	82	.304	3	M. PIERETTI	277	16–16	84	122	3.48
2B	H. SCHENZ	646	11	61	.279	9	C. JOHNSON	201	8–15	82	80	3.94
3B	FERNANDEZ (1)	444	12	62	.255	3	A. CICOTTE	186	6–15	113	105	4.75
SS	R. MYERS	261	6	36	.303	2	B. DALEY	180	13–8	55	117	2.80
OF	B. DILLINGER	588	0	38	.301	5	E. PATRICK	156	4–9	72	55	4.67
OF	J. BROVIA	504	13	91	.302	0	C. SCHANZ	132	4–6	50	48	3.95
OF	L. ATTYD	401	1	33	.262	6	K. GABLES	106	3–7	38	42	5.28
C	J. RITCHEY	283	0	23	.272	5	M. CANDINI	72	11–4	30	42	2.25
S3	M. COMBS (1)	404	4	43	.245	2						
O3S	T. GLAVIANO	329	6	34	.213	9	(1) ALSO WITH SEATTLE					
OF	HUMPHREY (2)	216	2	19	.250	5	(2) ALSO WITH HOLLYWOOD					
C	B. SHEELY	171	1	22	.228	0	**MANAGER – G. DESAUTELS/T. FREITAS**					
SS	J. STREETER	131	0	9	.260	1	**RECORD W–73 L–94 FINISH–7TH**					

PORTLAND		AB	HR	RBI	BA	SB	PITCHERS	IP	W–L	BB	SO	ERA
1B	H. ARFT	380	5	29	.261	4	R. WAIBEL	193	11–10	47	51	2.89
2B	E. BASINSKI	551	14	54	.258	4	B. ALEXANDER	190	10–12	102	134	3.22
3B	R. KRSNICH	511	9	77	.252	2	G. ELLIOTT	181	12–15	38	93	3.29
SS	F. AUSTIN	661	4	53	.269	3	R. FIEDLER	173	11–12	72	49	3.96
OF	W. JUDNICH	547	18	81	.272	1	G. BOEMLER	166	7–12	109	77	4.22
OF	G. GLADSTONE	392	10	54	.219	3	R. ADAMS	129	7–11	48	62	5.11
OF	F. ROBBE	378	17	58	.275	0	J. FLORES (1)	91	3–8	27	34	3.67
C	J. ROSSI	282	2	16	.230	5	O. ANTHONY	88	2–4	29	28	2.76
							J. HEARD	87	3–3	26	47	3.43
O3	D. EGGERT	382	13	46	.259	1						
1O	D. RESTELLI	357	12	44	.261	9	(1) ALSO WITH OAKLAND					
C	J. GLADD	252	1	17	.198	1	**MANAGER – C. HOPPER**					
							RECORD W–71 L–94 FINISH–8TH					

PLAYOFFS

SAN DIEGO DEFEATED HOLLYWOOD 7–2 IN PLAYOFF TO DECIDE PENNANT

OAKLAND DEFEATED SAN DIEGO 2 GAMES TO 0
SANFRANCISCO DEFEATED HOLLYWOOD 2 GAMES TO 0

FINAL
OAKLAND DEFEATED SAN FRANCISCO 3 GAMES TO 0

1955

SEATTLE		AB	HR	RBI	BA	SB	PITCHERS	IP	W–L	BB	SO	ERA
1B	B. GLYNN	466	13	56	.270	7	E. SINGLETON	249	19–12	45	150	2.20
2B	M. BASGALL	420	8	42	.245	5	H. JUDSON	186	10–9	68	93	2.90
3B	G. VERBLE	436	2	51	.257	3	V. LOMBARDI	182	8–11	52	81	3.61
SS	L. RIGHETTI (1)	405	3	38	.264	1	L. KRETLOW	150	14–3	74	110	2.47
OF	C. MAURO	569	3	56	.293	7	L. JANSEN	137	7–7	26	66	3.34
OF	B. BALCENA	536	7	60	.291	9	J. OLDHAM	122	9–6	82	53	3.84
OF	A. SCHULT	516	10	79	.287	5	BLACKWELL (1)	112	5–5	47	31	4.09
C	J. GINSBERG	475	7	66	.293	6	B. KENNEDY	94	8–6	18	77	1.92
13	H. ZERNIA	248	2	26	.254	0	(1) ALSO WITH SAN FRANCISCO					
OF	G. SCHMEES	188	3	13	.261	3	**MANAGER – F. HUTCHINSON**					
3B	V. STEPHENS	160	7	36	.338	0	**RECORD W–95 L–77 FINISH–1ST**					

SAN DIEGO		AB	HR	RBI	BA	SB	PITCHERS	IP	W–L	BB	SO	ERA
1B	J. BECQUER	392	7	54	.291	2	E. ERAUTT	241	18–10	64	94	2.78
2B	A. FEDEROFF	587	0	25	.274	6	C. MC LISH (2)	233	17–12	69	116	3.09
3B	M. SMITH	414	9	65	.338	10	J. CARMICHAEL	224	13–10	72	77	3.46
SS	B. PETERSON	576	2	38	.306	4	B. KERRIGAN	159	7–9	47	79	3.62
OF	E. RAPP	582	30	133	.302	1	L. DICKEY	145	7–11	41	30	4.21
OF	R. FABER	422	4	30	.213	4	T. HERRERA	122	5–8	39	39	3.60
OF	F. KAZAK	421	12	67	.302	2	W. THOMASON	109	5–5	43	58	3.48
C	E. BAILEY	344	16	60	.282	0	C. BISHOP	107	7–8	42	38	3.87
							A. LYONS (3)	74	10–5	30	36	5.81
1O	D. SISLER	427	11	52	.255	0						
2S3	J. MERSON	298	6	31	.282	2	(1) ALSO WITH SAN FRANCISCO & PORTLAND					
OF	C. MADDERN (1)	223	4	39	.269	0	(2) ALSO WITH LOS ANGELES					
C	D. AYLWARD	216	0	17	.227	1	(3) ALSO WITH HOLLYWOOD					
3O	R. JABLONSKI	213	13	40	.282	0	**MANAGER – B. ELLIOTT**					
PO	A. LYONS (3)	102	1	5	.108	0	**RECORD W–92 L–80 FINISH–2ND**					

HOLLYWOOD		AB	HR	RBI	BA	SB	PITCHERS	IP	W–L	BB	SO	ERA
1B	R. STEVENS	316	9	44	.241	2	B. GARBER	292	20–16	93	199	2.84
2B	C. ROBERTS	452	8	49	.321	17	R. MUNGER	272	23–8	57	133	1.85
3B	J. LOHRKE	338	3	36	.251	3	J. TRIMBLE	135	11–4	56	91	3.27
SS	D. SMITH	493	0	34	.282	24	R. BOWMAN	131	5–10	46	80	3.70
OF	C. BERNIER	580	12	73	.279	29	G. O'DONNELL	129	9–7	40	33	3.41
OF	L. WALLS	568	24	99	.283	10	B. WADE	123	7–8	44	72	3.30
OF	B. DEL GRECO	481	13	73	.287	21	C. NARANJO	104	4–10	39	37	4.40
C	B. HALL	339	1	47	.257	2						
OF	B. PRESCOTT	381	9	57	.276	8						
3O1	G. FREESE	235	10	40	.302	0						
C	B. BRAGAN	201	2	21	.254	2	**MANAGER – B. BRAGAN**					
1B	G. VICO	166	8	30	.283	1	**RECORD W–91 L–81 FINISH–3RD (T)**					

1955

LOS ANGELES	AB	HR	RBI	BA	SB	PITCHERS	IP	W–L	BB	SO	ERA
1B S. BILKO	622	37	124	.328	4	G. ELSTON	224	17–6	77	146	3.06
2B G. MAUCH	584	8	49	.296	22	J. BROSNAN	223	17–10	66	133	2.38
3B J. CLARKSON	316	13	46	.294	1	J. HATTEN	188	11–9	65	116	3.73
SS E. WINCENIAK	415	12	51	.248	5	G. PIKTUZIS	183	7–13	94	152	4.04
OF H. RICE	493	25	78	.262	6	B. CHURCH	143	11–7	41	67	3.66
OF B. USHER (1)	395	10	46	.225	8	T. LOWN	114	12–5	49	96	2.13
OF G. WADE	378	8	27	.310	23	B. ZICK	106	2–7	49	42	5.01
C J. FANNING	234	4	27	.226	2						
						(1) ALSO WITH SAN DIEGO					
3O L. DAVIS (2)	369	6	41	.244	1	(2) ALSO WITH OAKLAND					
OF R. COATS	337	2	33	.276	12	MANAGER – B. SWEENEY/J. WARNER/					
S32 B. HARDIN	299	0	24	.261	1	B. SCHEFFING					
OF D. TALBOT	200	3	14	.225	4	RECORD W–91 L–81 FINISH–3RD (T)					

PORTLAND	AB	HR	RBI	BA	SB	PITCHERS	IP	W–L	BB	SO	ERA
1B E. MICKELSON	604	12	87	.308	1	B. WERLE	221	17–8	30	76	3.54
2B A. WILSON	616	2	23	.307	12	R. ADAMS	220	12–12	33	108	2.05
3B D. EGGERT	463	22	68	.266	4	R. LINT	211	9–11	68	74	3.76
SS F. AUSTIN	604	3	46	.233	1	B. HALL	174	7–15	53	76	4.13
OF D. WHITMAN	477	9	50	.304	4	B. ALEXANDER	162	10–10	66	92	2.66
OF C. POWIS	411	9	35	.268	6	R. WAIBEL	128	9–7	31	52	3.72
OF L. MARQUEZ	381	8	57	.312	5	G. ELLIOTT	123	7–6	19	57	3.28
C J. ROBERTSON	319	5	28	.229	0	M. BURTSCHY	83	6–8	30	53	3.02
						C. SCHEIB	73	7–4	20	40	3.45
32 E. BASINSKI	280	5	32	.271	1						
OF J. TAYLOR	271	10	55	.295	2	(1) ALSO WITH OAKLAND					
OF W. WESTLAKE (1)	236	5	32	.258	2	MANAGER – C. HOPPER					
C S. CALDERONE	192	2	18	.240	0	RECORD W–86 L–86 FINISH–5TH					

SAN FRANCISCO	AB	HR	RBI	BA	SB	PITCHERS	IP	W–L	BB	SO	ERA
1B C. STEVENS	252	5	29	.234	2	G. BEARDEN	248	18–12	66	84	3.52
2B J. MORAN	533	2	34	.268	1	D. FRACCHIA	225	14–12	87	82	3.28
3B B. SERENA (1)	412	18	71	.270	0	T. PONCE	184	10–12	48	61	4.26
SS M. BAXES	504	5	64	.323	4	J. WALSH	166	8–10	71	60	4.45
OF D. MELTON	616	19	116	.299	5	B. BRADFORD	149	12–5	42	63	3.13
OF T. BEARD	522	8	34	.245	13	B. GREENWOOD	147	5–15	72	89	4.83
OF W. JUDNICH (2)	451	9	60	.279	2	S. NAGY	140	6–12	47	67	4.04
C J. RITCHEY	375	6	41	.285	10	M. FISHER	83	1–6	35	44	3.36
3O J. KIRRENE (1)	334	3	43	.257	1						
OF S. TAORMINA	333	10	45	.261	1	(1) ALSO WITH OAKLAND					
23S R. CHESO	307	4	35	.228	1	(2) ALSO WITH PORTLAND					
1B B. DI PIETRO	221	6	39	.371	2	MANAGER – T. HEATH					
1B W. BELARDI	193	13	43	.269	1	RECORD W–80 L–92 FINISH–6TH					

1955

OAKLAND	AB	HR	RBI	BA	SB	PITCHERS	IP	W−L	BB	SO	ERA
1B J. MARSHALL	593	30	86	.239	7	A. GETTEL	218	12−13	85	101	4.09
2B B. CONSOLO	590	14	68	.276	10	K. DREWS	197	9−13	62	109	4.71
3B S. JORGENSEN	516	15	54	.244	6	G. BAMBERGER	180	12−14	61	70	4.15
SS R. ROSE	585	2	48	.244	8	C. VAN CUYK	151	8−8	38	79	3.58
OF G. METKOVICH	532	17	79	.335	10	F. BESANA	146	6−10	100	103	3.75
OF J. BROVIA	372	19	73	.325	0	H. BROWN	92	9−2	12	37	2.95
OF A. VAN ALSTYNE	363	2	12	.240	8	D. FERRARESE	81	3−7	42	49	3.76
C L. NEAL	483	2	44	.217	1						
OF A. CUITTI	281	6	39	.274	0	(1) ALSO WITH SEATTLE					
OF D. MOITOZA	143	0	8	.238	4	**MANAGER − L. O'DOUL**					
C B. SWIFT (1)	141	1	12	.248	0	**RECORD W−77 L−95 FINISH−7TH**					

SACRAMENTO	AB	HR	RBI	BA	SB	PITCHERS	IP	W−L	BB	SO	ERA
1B N. JONES	666	7	91	.309	3	M. PIERETTI	293	19−15	73	110	3.01
2B J. STREETER	486	4	33	.245	5	B. DALEY	259	18−16	87	118	3.44
3B H. BRIGHT	459	12	73	.305	0	J. BRIGGS	251	15−15	118	118	3.44
OO R. MYERS	544	8	44	.256	1	C. JOHNSON	176	10−9	64	49	3.98
OF A. HEIST	470	7	33	.262	8	R. JONES	147	3−13	45	62	3.99
OF R. CRAWFORD	388	13	54	.289	2	E. HARRIST	114	5−7	41	74	3.31
OF P. MILNE	245	2	33	.237	0	E. CEREGHINO	79	2−5	49	36	5.81
C D. BAICH	335	6	43	.290	0	M. CANDINI	71	2−9	24	34	3.41
OS T. GLAVIANO	324	6	32	.228	7						
OF J. TOBIN	222	0	12	.270	3						
OF E. MIERKOWICZ	217	3	20	.272	2						
C B. SHEELY	212	3	16	.217	0						
3B L. THOMAS	116	2	11	.198	0	**MANAGER − T. FREITAS**					
OF B. DILLINGER	114	0	2	.281	1	**RECORD W−76 L−96 FINISH−8TH**					

PLAYOFF
HOLLYWOOD DEFEATED LOS ANGELES 3 GAMES TO 2 FOR THIRD PLACE

1956

LOS ANGELES		AB	HR	RBI	BA	SB	PITCHERS	IP	W−L	BB	SO	ERA
1B	S. BILKO	597	55	164	.360	4	D. HILLMAN	210	21−7	60	130	3.38
2B	G. MAUCH	566	20	84	.348	2	D. DROTT	197	13−10	108	184	4.39
3B	G. FREESE	474	22	113	.291	5	E. FODGE	192	19−7	82	122	4.31
SS	C. WISE	705	7	60	.287	7	B. THORPE	156	7−7	60	77	4.86
OF	J. BOLGER	592	28	147	.326	3	M. PIERETTI	156	7−9	53	68	4.90
OF	B. SPEAKE	580	25	111	.300	14	B. ANDERSON	105	12−4	52	61	2.65
OF	G. WADE	383	20	67	.292	16	R. ADAMS (1)	100	6−4	21	36	4.49
C	E. TAPPE	303	3	36	.267	0	H. PERKOWSKI	90	4−6	41	52	4.78
C	J. HANNAH	239	1	33	.272	0						
OF	R. COATS	237	0	29	.316	3	(1) ALSO WITH PORTLAND					
32	L. DAVIS	152	6	24	.316	1	MANAGER − B. SCHEFFING					
OF	E. HAAS	149	4	19	.275	1	RECORD W−107 L−61 FINISH−1ST					

SEATTLE		AB	HR	RBI	BA	SB	PITCHERS	IP	W−L	BB	SO	ERA
1B	B. GLYNN	551	17	74	.265	2	E. SINGLETON	226	18−8	58	110	2.55
2B	A. WILSON (1)	273	0	25	.293	6	B. PODBELIAN	199	13−11	50	96	3.31
3B	M. SMITH	516	9	58	.273	15	D. FRACCHIA	188	10−14	70	70	4.44
SS	L. RIGHETTI	578	0	49	.280	1	H. JUDSON	175	10−13	69	109	4.63
OF	B. BALCENA	560	14	62	.295	5	A. SCHALLOCK	163	11−9	52	98	3.42
OF	A. SCHULT	552	15	75	.306	2	L. JANSEN	98	11−2	20	59	2.58
OF	J. TAYLOR	484	24	89	.260	5						
C	R. ORTEIG	385	9	53	.278	2						
OF	C. MAURO	275	9	39	.295	1						
C	D. AYLWARD (2)	206	1	27	.262	0	(1) ALSO WITH PORTLAND					
31	V. STEPHENS	188	6	27	.266	0	(2) ALSO WITH SAN DIEGO					
23	J. LOHRKE	158	0	13	.272	0	MANAGER − L. SEWELL/B. BRENNER					
2B	S. DIXON	117	2	6	.231	2	RECORD W−91 L−77 FINISH−2ND					

PORTLAND		AB	HR	RBI	BA	SB	PITCHERS	IP	W−L	BB	SO	ERA
1B	E. MICKELSON	583	21	101	.309	5	R. VALDES	254	22−11	69	148	3.43
2B	D. YOUNG	491	5	33	.253	6	B. WERLE	247	16−15	40	82	4.41
3B	J. BAXES	333	16	57	.240	1	B. ALEXANDER	222	12−11	93	102	3.86
SS	J. LITTRELL	528	22	80	.307	4	B. DARNELL	215	16−12	57	111	3.94
OF	L. MARQUEZ	602	25	110	.344	18	J. MARTIN	137	7−2	55	50	3.16
OF	R. BORKOWSKI	570	16	96	.289	1	R. LINT	112	4−9	46	40	4.34
OF	T. SAFFELL	538	4	41	.290	9						
C	S. CALDERONE	433	17	66	.289	1						
2S3	E. BASINSKI	309	5	25	.259	2						
OF	L. MERRIMAN	269	2	18	.242	2						
OF	F. CARSWELL	229	13	54	.310	0	MANAGER − T. HOLMES/B. SWEENEY					
C	R. BOTTLER	172	3	20	.227	0	RECORD W−86 L−82 FINISH−3RD					

1956

HOLLYWOOD		AB	HR	RBI	BA	SB	PITCHERS		IP	W–L	BB	SO	ERA
1B	R. STEVENS	427	27	72	.262	3	B. WADE		184	13–18	56	106	4.05
2B	S. JACOBS	302	0	24	.341	4	R. SAWYER		146	6–4	65	64	3.38
3B	G. ALLIE	219	4	21	.292	1	B. GARBER		129	11–6	51	75	3.76
SS	D. SMITH	505	2	48	.269	16	J. TRIMBLE		124	4–11	52	82	4.49
OF	C. BERNIER	626	3	57	.283	48	C. NARANJO		118	8–6	39	90	3.05
OF	R. MEJIAS	594	15	71	.274	32	B. PURKEY		118	6–8	23	60	3.36
OF	J. DUHEM	449	13	68	.256	5	L. ARROYO		115	7–5	45	76	2.81
C	B. HALL	253	3	24	.198	0	C. RAYDON		100	5–5	51	59	4.23
							G. O'DONNELL		94	10–5	21	33	3.15
3S2	J. BAUMER	288	6	34	.264	1	F. GREEN		82	5–4	37	53	4.72
O1	P. PETTIT	284	10	45	.236	1							
2B	B. MAZEROSKI	284	9	36	.306	4	**MANAGER – C. HOPPER**						
3B	G. FREESE	223	11	36	.274	6	**RECORD W–85 L–83 FINISH–4TH**						

SACRAMENTO		AB	HR	RBI	BA	SB	PITCHERS		IP	W–L	BB	SO	ERA
1B	N. JONES	487	14	72	.296	1	G. BEARDEN		207	15–14	56	54	3.48
2B	H. BRIGHT	479	12	61	.284	1	E. HARRIST		205	16–10	58	97	3.52
3B	G. RISLEY	610	8	54	.289	2	J. STANKA		173	5–14	84	108	4.31
SS	J. KOPPE	352	5	00	.270	0	R. OGENDAUGH		166	11	12	72 84	4.23
OF	A. HEIST	547	12	71	.287	12	C. BOYER		164	10–9	77	64	3.95
OF	R. CRAWFORD	362	8	42	.243	2	R. WATKINS		129	6–11	50	49	4.60
OF	W. WESTLAKE	293	12	50	.273	1	R. JONES		103	7–1	48	61	3.66
C	D. BAICH	267	8	27	.270	1	G. ELLIOTT		95	5–3	18	39	3.40
							M. CANDINI		66	3–4	25	39	2.04
O1	J. TOBIN	304	0	14	.283	5							
O2	T. AGOSTA	238	1	22	.239	7							
SS	F. MANTILLA	206	4	24	.272	2	**MANAGER – T. HEATH**						
2B	J. STREETER	201	2	11	.229	1	**RECORD W–84 L–84 FINISH–5TH**						

SAN FRANCISCO		AB	HR	RBI	BA	SB	PITCHERS		IP	W–L	BB	SO	ERA
1B	B. DI PIETRO	365	11	60	.268	2	R. KEMMERER		233	12–14	93	137	3.48
2B	K. ASPROMONTE	549	3	42	.281	4	J. CASALE		228	19–11	81	143	4.10
3B	F. MALZONE	324	6	42	.296	1	R. SMITH		174	9–10	94	107	4.44
SS	J. MAHONEY	499	3	37	.228	7	B. SMITH		156	8–11	53	91	4.38
OF	T. UMPHLETT	467	5	61	.285	5	B. HENRY		105	5–6	34	50	4.73
OF	G. WINDHORN	446	8	45	.307	13	M. SURKONT		102	4–6	29	57	2.38
OF	S. TAORMINA	305	13	56	.298	1	E. GRBA		93	7–4	49	37	4.82
C	H. SULLIVAN	476	11	77	.296	3							
32S	J. TANNER	306	8	37	.281	11							
OF	M. KEOUGH	295	9	38	.315	9							
OF	D. LENHARDT	294	16	49	.299	1							
1B	L. DI PIPPO	264	10	45	.250	1	**MANAGER – E. JOOST/J. GORDON**						
C	E. SADOWSKI	213	7	24	.235	2	**RECORD W–77 L–88 FINISH–6TH**						

1956

SAN DIEGO	AB	HR	RBI	BA	SB	PITCHERS	IP	W−L	BB	SO	ERA
1B D. SISLER	504	11	82	.329	0	R. MESA	241	13−12	137	141	3.85
2B A. FEDEROFF	617	0	47	.290	9	J. CARMICHAEL	233	10−16	52	122	3.82
3B E. KAZAK	505	18	83	.305	4	E. ERAUTT	189	9−19	60	91	4.71
SS C. MOORE	462	5	46	.258	6	A. ATKINS (1)	161	12−6	87	121	4.46
OF B. USHER	595	12	74	.350	5	D. HOSKINS	158	7−11	63	87	4.60
OF H. ELLIOTT	474	9	52	.291	5	V. LOMBARDI (1)	157	9−10	50	81	3.61
OF E. RAPP	414	9	65	.300	3						
C J. ASTROTH	284	6	45	.246	0						
OF F. ROBINSON	406	11	39	.271	4						
2S3 J. MERSON	332	2	29	.253	0	(1) ALSO WITH SEATTLE					
C E. ST. CLAIRE	217	7	25	.263	0	MANAGER − B. ELLIOTT					
OF R. COLAVITO	133	12	32	.368	0	RECORD W−72 L−96 FINISH−7TH					

VANCOUVER	AB	HR	RBI	BA	SB	PITCHERS	IP	W−L	BB	SO	ERA
1B R. JACKSON	303	9	49	.301	2	R. DUREN	205	11−11	87	183	4.13
2B S. JORGENSEN	516	8	42	.273	10	G. BAMBERGER	186	9−14	45	69	4.07
3B K. SEGRIST	318	9	62	.333	0	C. BEAMON	165	13−6	65	84	3.54
SS F. MARSH	370	3	27	.241	7	BACZEWSKI (1)	115	4−6	36	48	5.26
OF J. PISONI	584	20	86	.265	6	F. BESANA	101	1−13	65	43	6.62
OF G. METKOVICH	489	6	43	.294	9	W. FISCHER	97	6−8	26	40	4.66
OF A. DAGRES	431	8	49	.232	14	C. DRUMMOND	96	6−4	64	61	4.11
C L. NEAL	296	5	38	.274	2	R. HARRISON	88	6−6	53	64	3.08
						J. MC DONALD	83	4−5	25	37	2.81
1O J. WESTLAKE	362	10	59	.246	6						
3S F. AUSTIN	281	0	27	.285	0						
C J. ROMANO	241	8	41	.241	2						
SS P. QUINTANA	201	2	15	.214	7	(1) ALSO WITH SEATTLE					
O2 G. JACOBS	187	4	28	.219	1	MANAGER − L. O'DOUL					
23 D. LEPPERT	117	2	12	.256	2	RECORD W−67 L−98 FINISH−8TH					

PLAYOFFS
NONE

1957

SAN FRANCISCO		AB	HR	RBI	BA	SB	PITCHERS	IP	W–L	BB	SO	ERA
1B	F. KELLERT	587	22	107	.308	5	R. SMITH	191	13–10	74	120	3.35
2B	K. ASPROMONTE	512	7	73	.334	1	H. DORISH	190	9–12	59	70	3.32
3B	G. HATTON	379	3	63	.317	0	T. HURD	174	8–6	62	82	3.36
SS	H. MALMBERG	534	4	54	.277	1	J. SPRING	169	11–9	53	72	3.19
OF	A. PEARSON	592	5	50	.297	9	L. KIELY	146	21–6	24	38	2.22
OF	M. KEOUGH	513	13	53	.214	9	W. PROUT	124	6–6	75	87	4.20
OF	W. RENNA	484	29	105	.281	1	W. ABERNATHIE	115	13–2	52	39	4.23
C	E. SADOWSKI	314	7	38	.245	3	B. THIEL	110	5–4	23	40	2.79
OF	T. UMPHLETT	305	4	35	.233	2						
3S	J. PHILLIPS	288	9	38	.274	0						
C	H. SULLIVAN	225	6	33	.293	1						
OF	S. TAORMINA	142	3	37	.296	1	MANAGER – J. GORDON					
C	A. TORNAY	133	0	0	.241	0	RECORD W–101 L–67 FINISH–1ST					

VANCOUVER		AB	HR	RBI	BA	SB	PITCHERS	IP	W–L	BB	SO	ERA
1B	J. MARSHALL	661	30	102	.284	17	E. PALICA	225	15–12	52	95	2.80
2B	S. JORGENSEN	422	16	55	.291	1	G. BAMBERGER	200	14–12	46	73	4.01
3B	K. SEGRIST	520	15	70	.265	1	C. BEAMON	178	12–10	88	99	3.80
SS	B. PETERSON	617	9	55	.298	11	M. MARTIN	176	14–4	30	87	1.90
OF	L. GREEN	505	5	57	.311	11	M. HELD	166	10–7	36	74	2.71
OF	J. FRAZIER	471	15	72	.257	2	D. FERRARESE	140	11–5	43	138	2.86
OF	C. POWIS	247	3	28	.227	2	A. HOUTTEMAN	91	5–6	27	50	3.97
C	C. WHITE	318	1	48	.277	1	E. ERAUTT (1)	83	5–5	20	39	2.39
							S. CONSUEGRA	77	7–1	10	29	1.99
2SO	O. FRIEND	449	21	73	.243	0						
C	T. ATWELL	220	2	27	.245	1	(1) ALSO WITH SAN DIEGO					
OF	C. DIERING	177	2	21	.271	2	MANAGER – C. METRO					
OF	R. CRAWFORD	111	4	13	.234	0	RECORD W–97 L–70 FINISH–2ND					

HOLLYWOOD		AB	HR	RBI	BA	SB	PITCHERS	IP	W–L	BB	SO	ERA
1B	T. BARTIROME	253	0	22	.316	2	B. DANIELS	229	17–8	121	116	2.95
2B	S. JACOBS	526	0	34	.295	5	G. WITT	185	18–7	58	114	2.24
3B	J. BAUMER	486	14	76	.300	1	C. RAYDON	169	10–10	57	137	3.30
SS	L. RODRIGUEZ	536	5	63	.287	0	B. WADE	164	9–10	54	99	3.30
OF	W. CAUSION	552	13	80	.301	1	B. GARBER	154	10–8	40	88	3.56
OF	P. PETTIT	542	20	102	.284	2	C. CHURN	136	9–7	43	64	2.78
OF	C. BERNIER	445	3	49	.290	12	H. PEPPER	136	5–9	50	53	4.50
C	B. HALL	453	6	62	.276	0	F. WATERS	122	5–7	56	63	3.55
							D. ROWE	109	8–6	60	71	4.69
OF	J. DUHEM	393	6	43	.265	5						
S3	D. SMITH	351	1	32	.299	5						
1B	R. STEVENS	240	11	32	.225	1	MANAGER – C. KING					
C	P. NATON	151	5	28	.232	1	RECORD W–94 L–74 FINISH–3RD					

1957

SAN DIEGO		AB	HR	RBI	BA	SB	PITCHERS		IP	W–L	BB	SO	ERA
1B	P. WARD	327	22	70	.330	2	M. GRANT		218	18–7	102	178	2.32
2B	B. MORAN	513	4	45	.211	3	R. MESA		171	10–11	96	130	4.06
3B	R. REGALADO	480	8	50	.306	2	R. BRODOWSKI		169	13–6	59	107	2.93
SS	B. HARRELL	467	6	42	.276	5	E. GASQUE		136	9–7	80	107	4.71
OF	F. ROBINSON	498	11	41	.279	27	H. AGUIRRE		132	6–13	69	100	3.75
OF	D. POPE	460	18	83	.313	8	V. LOMBARDI		106	6–6	20	61	3.32
OF	B. LENNON	325	12	53	.308	1	D. NICHOLS (3)		106	8–5	34	51	4.08
C	A. JONES	340	8	40	.244	1							

(1) ALSO WITH SEATTLE

CO	E. AVERILL	381	19	67	.273	3
2B	A. FEDEROFF (1)	359	0	21	.226	0
3O	E. KAZAK	339	4	50	.289	4
1O	B. DI PIETRO (2)	208	5	21	.274	1

(2) ALSO WITH SAN FRANCISCO
(3) ALSO WITH PORTLAND

MANAGER – B. ELLIOTT/G. METKOVICH

RECORD W–89 L–79 FINISH–4TH

SEATTLE		AB	HR	RBI	BA	SB	PITCHERS		IP	W–L	BB	SO	ERA
1B	B. GLYNN (1)	468	8	41	.256	3	C. RABE		238	16–10	101	143	3.37
2B	E. BASINSKI (1)	436	10	42	.271	3	D. PILLETTE (2)		205	16–8	65	75	3.16
3B	H. BEVAN	560	23	90	.271	1	L. JANSEN		180	10–12	25	82	3.16
SS	M. WILLS	491	0	33	.267	21	M. FRICANO		163	10–11	60	74	3.58
OF	J. DYCK	546	12	70	.310	1	G. HAYDEN		153	4–6	80	91	4.24
OF	B. BALCENA	500	6	49	.286	8	R. MUNGER		138	6–10	48	55	3.65
OF	J. TAYLOR	394	22	72	.305	3	B. PODBELIAN		117	8–4	23	40	2.91
C	R. ORTEIG	343	3	47	.262	2							

(1) ALSO WITH SAN DIEGO

OF	J. DELIS	383	2	40	.285	6
C	D. AYLWARD	243	1	26	.243	1
SS	L. LUTTRELL	181	4	22	.204	2

(2) ALSO WITH SAN FRANCISCO

MANAGER – L. O'DOUL

RECORD W–87 L–80 FINISH–5TH

LOS ANGELES		AB	HR	RBI	BA	SB	PITCHERS		IP	W–L	BB	SO	ERA
1B	S. BILKO	536	56	140	.300	8	J. JANCSE		180	9–12	82	61	3.74
2B	S. ANDERSON	619	2	35	.260	8	R. MAURIELLO		156	11–5	82	110	4.21
3B	R. HARTSFIELD	459	7	63	.281	4	W. BIRRER (1)		135	6–8	43	68	4.87
SS	W. LAMMERS	395	5	36	.248	4	T. LASORDA		132	7–10	59	72	3.90
OF	T. SAFFELL	443	6	30	.262	7	G. MICKENS		119	8–8	37	60	4.40
OF	B. HAMRICK	357	19	56	.291	11	W. GEORGE		116	4–1	30	54	2.25
OF	G. WADE	329	7	33	.237	14	B. DARNELL		116	4–11	46	57	5.14
C	E. TAPPE	214	0	12	.182	2	V. VALETINETTI		111	9–5	40	68	3.96
							C. GROB		87	6–3	15	29	2.18

3B	J. BAXES	297	16	48	.259	2
OF	J. FRIDLEY	275	13	43	.273	0
OF	R. JENKINS	261	13	54	.310	2
SS	R. DOLAN	200	3	24	.260	5
C	H. OLSON	149	5	18	.181	2
C	E. BATTEY	143	9	20	.252	0

(1) ALSO WITH VANCOUVER

MANAGER – C. BRYANT

RECORD W–80 L–88 FINISH–6TH

1957

SACRAMENTO	AB	HR	RBI	BA	SB	PITCHERS	IP	W-L	BB	SO	ERA
1B J. WESTLAKE	477	5	44	.285	1	M. BRIDGES	207	12-16	96	104	4.53
2B A. WILSON	315	0	17	.263	3	J. STANKA	203	10-14	88	133	3.51
3B H. BRIGHT	502	6	51	.263	3	R. WATKINS	177	8-10	75	70	3.25
SS L. RIGHETTI (1)	594	2	32	.242	1	R. OSENBAUGH	159	9-14	62	61	4.36
OF J. GREENGRASS	527	20	76	.283	2	E. HARRIST	158	5-13	57	69	3.52
OF A. HEIST	557	8	62	.257	6	M. COEN	152	2-11	70	82	4.44
OF E. WHITE	203	1	15	.266	1	R. BOWMAN	119	6-11	55	58	4.32
C C. BARRAGAN	316	5	19	.193	1	M. CANDINI	100	9-6	30	47	1.98
1B N. JONES	283	7	35	.293	4						
3S K. HERON	271	3	33	.218	2						
2B T. AGOSTA	188	4	8	.287	2	(1) ALSO WITH SEATTLE					
3B L. OLSEN	185	3	18	.254	2	(2) ALSO WITH VANCOUVER					
C L. NEAL (2)	187	2	25	.273	0	MANAGER — T. HEATH					
C J. MANGAN	119	0	12	.252	0	RECORD W-63 L-105 FINISH-7TH					

PORTLAND	AB	HR	RBI	BA	SB	PITCHERS	IP	W-L	BB	SO	ERA
1B E. MICKELSON	219	2	28	.338	1	B. THORPE	209	7-15	87	152	4.05
2B C. WISE	297	0	27	.246	2	R. ALEXANDER	204	14-13	91	126	3.49
3B B. DE MARS	356	3	34	.242	4	B. WERLE (2)	174	9-8	17	58	3.88
SS E. WINCENIAK	464	5	51	.250	10	CARMICHAEL (2)	164	8-18	55	91	5.20
OF S. DRAKE	624	4	41	.290	36	R. FIEDLER	150	4-13	46	76	4.97
OF L. MARQUEZ	610	31	85	.277	13	R. MARLOWE (3)	114	1-8	41	53	5.15
OF BORKOWSKI (1)	504	12	58	.304	3	R. BAUER	102	4-4	38	39	4.15
C D. BAICH	192	2	8	.208	1						
3B G. FREESE	253	11	39	.261	1						
231 B. ADAMS	247	2	21	.279	1						
OF F. CARSWELL	217	9	49	.263	1						
OF E. RAPP (2)	205	3	19	.278	1	(1) ALSO WITH LOS ANGELES					
C S. CALDERONE	173	2	12	.191	0	(2) ALSO WITH SAN DIEGO					
C R. BOTTLER	146	3	5	.212	0	(3) ALSO WITH VANCOUVER					
1B R. BOWEN	129	2	14	.202	0	MANAGER — B. SWEENEY/F. CARSWELL					
OF J. LITTRELL	108	5	17	.259	0	B. POSEDEL					
OF F. ERNAGA	107	3	10	.252	1	RECORD W-60 L-108 FINISH-8TH					

PLAYOFFS
NONE

SECTION II

Player Register — Hitters

Included in this section are the year-by-year Pacific Coast League statistics for more than 330 of the most important, interesting, and talented players to have appeared in the league during the years 1903 through 1957. While the inclusion of specific players in this section is subjective, there were general criteria used in making selections.

Players who appeared in 10 or more major league seasons and or 10 or more Pacific Coast League seasons were given priority. Allowances have been made for players not reaching those benchmarks but who still had significant major league or PCL careers. For instance, a player who was the Cubs' starting third baseman for eight years is not left out in favor of a utility player who played ten seasons but had only cameo appearances in four of those years.

Other allowances have been made for careers shortened by injury, military service, racial barriers, untimely death, or, admittedly, the author's own prejudices.

Among those players included in the last category are Bill Allington, the most successful manager in the history of the All-American Girls Professional Baseball League; legendary USC baseball coach Rod Dedeaux; actors Chuck Connors and Johnny Berardino; major league baseball's only in-season suicide, Willard Hershberger; multi-sport athlete Jim Thorpe; and songwriter Harry Ruby. Those included because of long major league service as managers include Sparky Anderson, Gene Mauch, Bill Rigney, and John McNamara.

Each player's listing in the register includes their year-by-year PCL playing record, biographical information showing full name, birth and death dates, and a few lines indicating PCL and or major league career highlights or other interesting information. For those players whose Pacific Coast League careers began prior to 1957 and extended beyond the years covered in this book, their full PCL record is shown.

The statistical categories are self-explanatory. They include the year and team for which the player appeared (a listing of team abbreviations appears below), games played (G), at bats (AB), runs (R), hits (H), doubles (2B), triples (3B), home runs (HR), runs batted in (RBI), batting average (BA), slugging average (SA), total bases (TB), and stolen bases (SB). Information unavailable is noted with "--."

In calculating the Pacific Coast League career totals for each player, the categories that include any unavailable information are not totaled unless the number of games involved is insignificant (one percent or less) in comparison with the player's total number of games played. The lifetime batting averages and slugging averages are computed only on seasons that have complete information, provided that information is available for at least 75 percent of the player's career. For some players, career totals will not foot to the averages displayed because of this approach.

Teams in the league are given two types of abbreviations due to space limitations. One is the regular abbreviation, the other is an alternate abbreviation used if the player appeared with more than one team during the season. The following is the abbreviation table:

Team	Abbreviation	Alternate
Dallas–Ft. Worth	DFW	D
Fresno	Fre	F
Hawaii	Haw	Hw
Hollywood	Hol	H
Indianapolis	Ind	I
Los Angeles	LA	LA
Mission	Miss	M
Oakland	Oak	O
Oklahoma City	OkC	OC
Phoenix	Phx	Phx
Portland	Port	P
Sacramento	Sac	Sac
Salt Lake City	SLC	SL
San Diego	SD	SD
San Francisco	SF	SF
Seattle	Sea	Sea
Spokane	Spo	Sp
Tacoma	Tac	Tac
Tucson	Tuc	Tuc
Vancouver	Van	Van
Venice	Ven	Ven
Vernon	Ver	Ver

BUSTER ADAMS   Elvin Clark Adams. Born 6/24/1915, Trinidad, CO. Died 9/1/1990, Rancho Mirage, CA. Outfielder had 109 RBI for the Phillies and Cardinals in 1945. In the final week of the 1942 PCL season, he and Ray Mueller twice hit key back—to—back homers in a dramatic pennant race.

	G	AB	R	H	2B	3B	HR	RBI	BA	SA	TB	SB
1936 Sac	152	542	76	139	29	9	16	71	.256	.432	234	9
1937 Sac	149	592	100	177	49	8	19	82	.299	.505	299	19
1938 Sac	67	270	41	79	11	6	9	36	.293	.478	129	24
1939 Sac	46	164	32	46	7	7	3	14	.280	.463	76	7
1941 Sac	159	571	97	163	40	10	17	92	.285	.480	274	23
1942 Sac	178	647	99	200	43	8	27	107	.309	.526	340	9
1948 SD	102	273	31	69	13	1	8	34	.253	.396	108	2
1949 SD	144	514	78	140	23	5	21	69	.272	.459	236	4
1950 SD	123	340	53	108	26	3	15	62	.318	.544	185	0
1951 SD—SF	103	232	31	58	11	0	8	42	.250	.401	93	0
	1223	4145	638	1179	252	57	143	609	.284	.476	1974	97

SAM AGNEW   Samuel Lester Agnew. Born 4/12/1887, Farmington, MO. Died 7/19/1951, Sonoma, CA. Caught in AL from 1913 through 1919 with St. Louis, Boston and Washington. Always positive, a popular teammate.

	G	AB	R	H	2B	3B	HR	RBI	BA	SA	TB	SB
1912 Ver	105	322	34	91	20	1	5	— —	.283	.398	128	11
1920 SF	144	495	50	134	30	4	8	— —	.271	.396	196	11
1921 SF	116	352	49	104	20	3	11	54	.295	.460	103	9
1922 SF	118	389	67	131	27	4	11	61	.337	.512	199	8
1923 SF	110	369	54	115	21	3	13	66	.312	.491	181	2
1924 SF	79	223	33	70	12	4	8	38	.314	.511	114	2
1925 SF	122	384	46	125	20	1	20	85	.326	.539	207	0
1926 SF	136	362	36	91	17	1	12	36	.251	.403	146	4
1927 SF—H	84	224	17	65	16	2	6	36	.290	.460	103	2
1928 Hol	88	252	39	81	19	1	4	38	.321	.452	114	2
	1102	3372	425	1007	202	24	98	— —	.299	.460	1551	51

EDDIE AINSMITH   Edward Wilbur Ainsmith. Born 2/4/1890, Cambridge, MA. Died 9/6/1981, Ft. Lauderdale, FL. Major league catcher for fifteen years. Served as a test case for the "Work or Fight" rule of World War One.

	G	AB	R	H	2B	3B	HR	RBI	BA	SA	TB	SB
1928 P—Sea	111	327	27	79	14	4	3	42	.242	.336	110	3

BILL ALLINGTON   William Baird Allington. Born 10/26/1903, St. Clair, MI. Died 8/17/1966, Tucson, AZ. While his sarcastic manner often wore thin, as pilot of the Rockford Peaches he was most successful manager in the history of the All—American Girls Professional Baseball League.

	G	AB	R	H	2B	3B	HR	RBI	BA	SA	TB	SB
1929 Sea	76	202	26	63	6	1	1	12	.312	.366	74	11

SPARKY ANDERSON   George Lee Anderson. Born 2/22/1934, Bridgewater, SD. Batboy for the Hollywood Stars in 1949, went on to become the only manager to win World Series titles for teams in both the NL and AL.

SPARKY ANDERSON (cont.)

	G	AB	R	H	2B	3B	HR	RBI	BA	SA	TB	SB
1957 LA	168	619	74	161	15	0	2	35	.260	.294	182	8

BUZZ ARLETT   Russell Loris Arlett. Born 1/3/1899, Elmhurst, CA. Died 5/16/1964, Minneapolis, MN. Pacific Coast League career leader in home runs and runs batted in. Began career as a pitcher. Won 20 games three times in the PCL, including a league–leading 29 in 1920. A switch–hitter with 432 career home runs in the minors, twice hit four homers in a game.

	G	AB	R	H	2B	3B	HR	RBI	BA	SA	TB	SB
1918 Oak	26	71	9	15	4	0	1	8	.211	.310	22	1
1919 Oak	56	140	14	40	7	2	1	19	.286	.386	54	2
1920 Oak	64	177	26	45	5	4	5	26	.254	.412	73	2
1921 Oak	64	128	12	28	5	1	3	14	.219	.344	44	1
1922 Oak	74	174	23	42	9	4	4	21	.241	.408	71	0
1923 Oak	149	445	76	147	31	5	19	101	.330	.551	245	9
1924 Oak	193	698	122	229	57	19	33	145	.328	.606	423	24
1925 Oak	190	710	121	244	49	13	25	146	.344	.555	394	26
1926 Oak	194	667	140	255	52	16	35	140	.382	.666	444	26
1927 Oak	187	658	122	231	54	7	30	123	.351	.591	389	20
1928 Oak	160	561	111	205	47	3	25	113	.365	.594	333	10
1929 Oak	200	722	146	270	70	8	39	189	.374	.655	473	22
1930 Oak	176	618	132	223	57	7	31	143	.361	.626	387	8
	1735	5769	1054	1974	447	89	251	1188	.342	.581	3352	151

JOE ASTROTH   Joseph Henry Astroth. Born 9/1/1922, East Alton, IL. Once drove in six runs in one inning in majors. Ten year big league career as a catcher for the Athletics in both Philadelphia and Kansas City. Favorite of Bobby Shantz among A's catchers during the pitcher's 1952 MVP season.

	G	AB	R	H	2B	3B	HR	RBI	BA	SA	TB	SB
1956 SD	96	284	29	70	14	1	6	45	.246	.366	104	2

EARL AVERILL   Howard Earl Averill. Born 5/21/1902, Snohomish, WA. Died 8/16/1983, Everett, WA. A .318 hitter during thirteen year big league career. Joined Lefty O'Doul and Smead Jolley to form one of PCL's great outfields on the SF Seals in 1927. Elected to the Hall of Fame in 1975.

	G	AB	R	H	2B	3B	HR	RBI	BA	SA	TB	SB
1926 SF	188	679	131	236	49	6	23	119	.348	.539	366	9
1927 SF	183	754	134	244	47	6	20	116	.324	.481	363	10
1928 SF	189	763	178	270	53	11	36	173	.354	.594	453	13
1941 Sea	78	223	24	55	9	0	1	17	.247	.300	67	2
	638	2419	467	805	158	23	80	425	.333	.516	1249	34

ED BAILEY   Lonas Edgar Bailey. Born 4/15/1931, Strawberry Plains,TN. Five–time NL All–Star catcher, hit twenty or more home runs three times. Hit eight pinch–hit home runs during his career, two of which were grand slams. He and brother Jim, a pitcher, were teammates on the 1959 Reds.

	G	AB	R	H	2B	3B	HR	RBI	BA	SA	TB	SB
1955 SD	108	344	52	97	16	0	16	60	.282	.468	161	0

DEL BAKER   Delmar David Baker. Born 5/3/1892, Sherwood, OR. Died 9/11/1973, San Antonio, TX. Managed the Detroit Tigers to the American League pennant in 1940. One of baseball's greatest sign—stealers, Hank Greenberg reportedly had Baker signal pitches to him during his at bats.

	G	AB	R	H	2B	3B	HR	RBI	BA	SA	TB	SB
1917 SF	121	349	42	93	14	1	1	— —	.266	.321	112	12
1919 Port	115	377	33	100	21	0	0	— —	.265	.321	121	4
1920 Port	71	193	20	54	7	2	0	— —	.280	.337	65	5
1921 Port	102	294	22	81	14	0	0	25	.276	.323	95	2
1923 Oak	123	409	42	114	23	3	2	55	.279	.364	149	4
1924 Oak	131	342	53	103	16	0	2	49	.301	.365	125	6
1925 Oak	68	167	18	41	9	0	0	18	.246	.299	50	0
1926 Oak	114	322	39	90	11	2	0	40	.280	.326	105	5
1927 Oak	39	85	12	21	3	1	0	9	.247	.306	26	1
1928 Oak	4	7	0	2	— —	— —	— —	— —	.286	— —	— — — —	
	888	2545	281	699	118	9	5	— —	.275	.334	850	39

DAVE BANCROFT   David James Bancroft. Born 4/20/1891, Sioux City, IA. Died 10/9/1972, Superior, WI. One of the majors best shortstops, played the cut—off position for McGraw's Giants and threw out three Yankees at home plate in the 1922 World Series. Elected to the Hall of Fame in 1971.

	G	AB	R	H	2B	3B	HR	RBI	BA	SA	TB	SB
1912 Port	166	565	68	120	29	8	0	— —	.212	.292	165	29
1914 Port	177	668	99	185	35	14	2	58	.277	.380	254	29
	343	1233	167	305	64	22	2	— —	.247	.340	419	58

DAVE BARBEE   David Monroe Barbee. Born 5/7/1905, Greensboro, NC. Died 7/1/1968, Albemarle, NC. Outfielder played briefly in majors with the Pirates and A's. Led Pacific Coast League in home runs in 1930 and 1931.

	G	AB	R	H	2B	3B	HR	RBI	BA	SA	TB	SB
1928 P—Sea	144	483	78	158	32	11	16	89	.327	.538	260	8
1929 Sea	180	613	110	194	42	10	22	118	.316	.525	322	4
1930 Sea—H	149	588	132	191	30	3	41	155	.325	.595	350	5
1931 Hol	168	650	131	216	42	2	47	166	.332	.620	403	4
	641	2334	451	759	146	26	126	528	.325	.572	1335	21

LARRY BARTON   Lawrence Barton. Born 11/21/1912, Pueblo, CO. Died 3/6/1992, Eufaula, OK. First baseman played pro ball twenty—four years; had over 3,000 career hits, but never played in majors. Scouted for Reds.

	G	AB	R	H	2B	3B	HR	RBI	BA	SA	TB	SB
1938 Sac	164	580	74	153	40	4	17	74	.264	.434	252	7
1939 Sac	173	593	80	176	40	1	11	87	.297	.423	251	8
1940 Sac	100	345	38	81	19	1	7	41	.235	.357	123	4
1942 Port	155	564	82	172	33	6	10	74	.305	.438	247	12
1943 Port	145	499	74	142	28	4	11	72	.285	.423	211	3
1944 Port	128	462	71	117	28	4	4	53	.253	.357	165	6
1945 Port	144	509	89	162	32	4	6	76	.318	.432	220	8
1946 Port	44	126	12	28	7	0	0	4	.222	.278	35	0
1947 O—LA	169	550	72	148	27	3	18	83	.269	.427	235	4

LARRY BARTON (cont.)

	G	AB	R	H	2B	3B	HR	RBI	BA	SA	TB	SB
1948 LA	17	53	2	7	2	0	1	8	.132	.226	12	0
	1239	4281	594	1186	256	27	85	572	.277	.409	1751	52

EDDIE BASINSKI   Edwin Frank Basinski. Born 11/4/1922, Buffalo, NY. Star second baseman at University of Buffalo. Also an accomplished violinist.

	G	AB	R	H	2B	3B	HR	RBI	BA	SA	TB	SB
1947 Port	59	209	22	58	9	2	2	30	.278	.368	77	5
1948 Port	175	632	83	175	24	3	4	50	.277	.343	217	8
1949 Port	164	592	74	158	32	7	12	79	.267	.405	240	4
1950 Port	202	722	80	173	39	1	15	75	.240	.359	259	1
1951 Port	169	687	109	183	32	6	16	73	.266	.400	275	3
1952 Port	166	552	60	136	25	1	10	58	.246	.350	193	4
1953 Port	156	529	49	127	18	1	6	61	.240	.312	165	2
1954 Port	157	551	73	142	34	2	14	54	.258	.403	222	4
1955 Port	98	280	31	76	16	0	5	32	.271	.382	107	1
1956 Port	114	309	32	80	11	3	5	25	.259	.362	112	2
1957 P–Sea	136	436	53	118	22	1	10	42	.271	.394	172	3
1958 Sea	107	349	42	105	28	1	8	47	.301	.456	159	1
1959 Van	43	94	12	13	2	0	2	8	.138	.223	21	0
	1746	5942	720	1544	292	28	109	634	.260	.373	2219	38

JOHNNY BASSLER   John Landis Bassler. Born 6/3/1895, Lancaster, PA. Died 6/29/1979, Santa Monica, CA. As catcher for the Detroit Tigers from 1921–1927, he finished in the top seven in AL MVP voting three times.

	G	AB	R	H	2B	3B	HR	RBI	BA	SA	TB	SB
1915 LA	48	108	13	30	5	0	0	– –	.278	.324	35	5
1916 LA	124	349	42	106	16	3	0	– –	.304	.367	128	18
1917 LA	94	264	32	75	6	4	0	– –	.284	.337	89	5
1919 LA	78	259	31	71	10	2	1	– –	.274	.340	88	3
1920 LA	147	454	69	145	26	8	1	– –	.319	.419	190	10
1928 Hol	127	373	44	112	12	2	2	33	.300	.359	134	3
1929 Hol	107	299	39	75	15	1	0	37	.251	.308	92	1
1930 Hol	123	348	49	127	18	1	0	71	.365	.422	147	5
1931 Hol	103	316	48	112	15	0	0	43	.354	.402	127	0
1932 Hol	156	443	52	158	23	1	1	66	.357	.420	186	3
1933 Hol	122	330	47	111	18	2	0	50	.336	.403	133	1
1934 Hol	123	308	30	108	16	1	0	55	.351	.409	126	2
1935 Hol	6	5	0	0	0	0	0	0	.000	.000	0	0
1936 Sea	111	260	25	92	16	2	0	38	.354	.431	112	2
1937 Sea	56	99	11	31	2	0	0	10	.313	.333	33	1
	1525	4215	532	1353	198	27	5	– –	.321	.384	1620	59

EARL BATTEY   Earl Jesse Battey. Born 1/5/1935, Los Angeles, CA. A star basketball player in high school, he turned down an offer from the Harlem Globetrotters. Four–time AL All–Star catcher with three Gold Gloves.

	G	AB	R	H	2B	3B	HR	RBI	BA	SA	TB	SB
1957 LA	42	143	28	36	8	1	9	20	.252	.510	73	0

FRANKIE BAUMHOLTZ   Frank Conrad Baumholtz. Born 10/7/1918, Midvale, OH. Played two seasons of pro basketball after starring at Ohio University. Led PCL in hitting and doubles in only season there. Second to Stan Musial for the 1952 National League batting title.

	G	AB	R	H	2B	3B	HR	RBI	BA	SA	TB	SB
1950 LA	172	670	126	254	53	10	15	89	.379	.555	372	27

GUS BELL   David Russell Bell. Born 11/15/1928, Louisville, KY. Was sent to the PCL after landing in Branch Rickey's doghouse for wanting to take his family along on road trips. Traded to Cincinnati, he drove in 100 runs four times with the Reds. Son Buddy played eighteen years in the majors.

	G	AB	R	H	2B	3B	HR	RBI	BA	SA	TB	SB
1952 Hol	17	64	12	19	3	1	2	13	.297	.469	30	1

JOHNNY BERARDINO   John Berardino. Born 5/1/1917, Los Angeles, CA. Eleven year major leaguer valued for ability to play all infield positions. A former child actor, went on to star on television in "General Hospital".

	G	AB	R	H	2B	3B	HR	RBI	BA	SA	TB	SB
1950 SD–Sac	57	197	18	45	8	0	3	15	.228	.315	62	4

WALLY BERGER   Walter Antone Berger. Born 10/10/1905, Chicago, IL. Died 11/30/1988, Redondo Beach, CA. Still shares, with Frank Robinson, the NL record for home runs by a rookie. Four–time All–Star, he led the National League in runs batted in and home runs in 1935.

	G	AB	R	H	2B	3B	HR	RBI	BA	SA	TB	SB
1927 LA	14	63	12	23	5	0	3	15	.365	.587	37	0
1928 LA	138	535	94	175	34	7	20	94	.327	.529	283	5
1929 LA	199	744	170	249	41	5	40	166	.335	.565	420	19
1941 LA	59	141	19	34	7	0	8	18	.241	.461	65	0
	410	1483	295	481	87	12	71	293	.324	.543	805	24

CARLOS BERNIER   Carlos Rodriguez Bernier. Born 1/28/1929, Juana Diaz, PR. Died 4/6/1989, Juana Diaz, PR. Nicknamed "The Comet", both fast and exciting to watch, he was one of the most popular players in the PCL. Won six minor league stolen base titles, including three in the PCL. Had a notoriously quick temper; once suspended for hitting an umpire.

	G	AB	R	H	2B	3B	HR	RBI	BA	SA	TB	SB
1952 Hol	171	652	105	196	24	9	9	79	.301	.406	265	65
1954 Hol	119	431	85	135	24	6	6	41	.313	.439	189	38
1955 Hol	168	580	93	162	24	8	12	73	.279	.410	238	29
1956 Hol	159	626	91	177	22	15	3	57	.283	.380	238	48
1957 Hol	126	445	62	129	17	5	3	49	.290	.371	165	12
1958 SLC	151	546	121	181	27	11	15	86	.332	.504	275	34
1959 SLC	152	513	73	144	19	10	9	81	.281	.409	210	21
1961 Haw	127	433	89	152	18	6	20	87	.351	.559	242	22
1962 Haw	121	380	81	119	20	2	17	72	.313	.511	194	7
1963 Haw	153	544	113	163	16	4	26	98	.300	.487	265	10
1964 Haw	124	432	92	127	14	5	27	68	.294	.537	232	22
	1571	5582	1005	1685	225	81	147	791	.302	.450	2513	308

RAY BERRES   Raymond Frederick Berres. Born 8/21/1908, Kenosha, WI. An excellent defensive catcher, played eleven seasons in the majors with four teams. Later a long–time coach with the Chicago White Sox.

	G	AB	R	H	2B	3B	HR	RBI	BA	SA	TB	SB
1935 Sac	93	285	20	64	13	2	1	35	.225	.295	84	2

CHARLIE BERRY   Charles Francis Berry. Born 10/18/1902, Phillipsburg, NJ. Died 9/6/1972, Evanston, IL. Played eleven years in majors as a catcher. The son of a major leaguer, he was a football star in college and the NFL. Later, he was both an AL umpire and a head linesman for NFL, officiating the famous 1958 "Sudden Death" title game in the latter role.

	G	AB	R	H	2B	3B	HR	RBI	BA	SA	TB	SB
1926 Port	99	292	24	69	14	2	5	33	.236	.349	102	1

CARSON BIGBEE   Carson Lee Bigbee. Born 3/31/1895, Waterloo, OR. Died 10/17/1964, Portland, OR. Played eleven seasons for Pirates; came to PCL after his release following the 1926 season in a contract dispute.

	G	AB	R	H	2B	3B	HR	RBI	BA	SA	TB	SB
1927 Sea–P	98	255	41	75	17	1	0	22	.294	.369	94	10
1928 P–LA	110	301	33	69	15	1	0	17	.229	.286	86	6
	208	556	74	144	32	2	0	39	.259	.324	180	16

STEVE BILKO   Stephen Thomas Bilko. Born 11/13/1928, Nanticoke, PA. Died 3/7/1978, Wilkes–Barre, PA. A three–time PCL MVP; won league's Triple Crown in 1956. Won three straight PCL home run championships. Later returned to LA's Wrigley Field with the AL expansion Angels.

	G	AB	R	H	2B	3B	HR	RBI	BA	SA	TB	SB
1955 LA	168	622	105	204	35	3	37	124	.328	.572	356	4
1956 LA	162	597	163	215	18	6	55	164	.360	.687	410	4
1957 LA	158	536	111	161	22	1	56	140	.300	.659	353	8
1959 Spo	135	478	76	146	24	1	26	92	.305	.523	250	2
	623	2233	455	726	99	11	174	520	.325	.613	1369	18

BUDDY BLATTNER   Robert Garnett Blattner. Born 2/8/1920, St. Louis, MO. A table tennis champion as a youngster, went on to a long career in the broadcast booth with several major league teams after playing days.

	G	AB	R	H	2B	3B	HR	RBI	BA	SA	TB	SB
1940 Sac	135	442	55	123	15	8	4	54	.278	.376	166	9
1941 Sac	176	620	96	182	33	6	17	100	.294	.448	278	23
	311	1062	151	305	48	14	21	154	.287	.418	444	32

LU BLUE   Luzerne Atwell Blue. Born 3/5/1897, Washington, D.C. Died 7/28/1958, Alexandria, VA. First baseman joined Detroit in 1921, playing regularly there through 1927. Scored one hundred or more runs six times in majors. Noted for his being buried at Arlington National Cemetery.

	G	AB	R	H	2B	3B	HR	RBI	BA	SA	TB	SB
1919 Port	174	679	91	191	35	7	9	– –	.281	.393	267	44
1920 Port	165	626	94	182	22	11	4	– –	.291	.380	238	37
	339	1305	185	373	57	18	13	– –	.286	.387	505	81

PING BODIE   Frank Stephan Bodie. Born 10/8/1887, San Francisco, CA. Died 12/17/1961, San Francisco, CA. He received his nickname from the sound made when his bat made contact with the ball. A roommate of the Babe's with the Yankees; was the first to hit thirty home runs in the PCL.

	G	AB	R	H	2B	3B	HR	RBI	BA	SA	TB	SB
1908 SF	36	134	19	37	6	1	3	— —	.276	.403	54	5
1909 SF	157	543	62	135	— —	— —	— —	— —	.249	— —	— —	— —
1910 SF	212	768	102	202	34	5	30	— —	.263	.438	336	29
1915 SF	192	720	117	234	52	3	19	— —	.325	.485	349	37
1916 SF	206	769	104	233	48	5	20	— —	.303	.456	351	16
1922 Ver	145	502	69	147	33	5	6	87	.293	.414	208	7
1923 Ver	136	485	70	143	31	10	8	105	.295	.449	218	1
1927 SF	109	336	55	109	16	1	12	80	.324	.485	163	5
1928 SF—M	117	333	58	116	22	1	10	62	.348	.511	170	2
	1310	4590	656	1356	— —	— —	— —	— —	.295	.457	— —	— —

IKE BOONE   Isaac Morgan Boone. Born 2/17/1897, Samantha, AL. Died 8/1/1958, Northport, AL. Winner of the PCL Triple Crown in 1929, set the all—time organized baseball record for total bases that year. Compiled a career .319 batting average in the majors and .370 lifetime in the minors.

	G	AB	R	H	2B	3B	HR	RBI	BA	SA	TB	SB
1926 Miss	172	626	140	238	55	3	32	137	.380	.631	395	16
1928 P—M	166	594	92	210	46	1	9	104	.354	.480	285	8
1929 Miss	198	704	195	323	49	8	55	210	.407	.096	553	9
1930 Miss	83	310	76	139	22	3	22	96	.448	.752	233	5
	619	2324	503	910	172	15	118	555	.392	.631	1466	38

RAY BOONE   Raymond Otis Boone. Born 7/27/1923, San Diego, CA. Led AL in RBI in 1955, two years after setting AL record with four grand slams in one season. Both his son and grandson played in the major leagues.

	G	AB	R	H	2B	3B	HR	RBI	BA	SA	TB	SB
1948 Hol	23	96	14	24	3	2	1	11	.250	.354	34	1

FRENCHY BORDAGARAY   Stanley George Bordagaray. Born 1/3/1910, Coalinga, CA. Eleven year big league utility man, earned reputation as a colorful character while playing for the Brooklyn Dodgers in the 1930's.

	G	AB	R	H	2B	3B	HR	RBI	BA	SA	TB	SB
1931 Sac	70	252	35	94	19	4	5	32	.373	.540	136	4
1932 Sac	173	692	131	223	33	10	5	77	.322	.421	291	20
1933 Sac	117	416	67	146	26	3	7	65	.351	.478	199	10
1934 Sac	117	483	84	155	34	1	6	46	.321	.433	209	23
	477	1843	317	618	112	18	23	220	.335	.453	835	57

BABE BORTON   William Baker Borton. Born 8/14/1888, Marion, IL. Died 7/29/1954, Berkeley, CA. Played first base four seasons in majors. Was a central figure in the gambling scandal that rocked the PCL in 1920. He was effectively suspended for life as a result of his involvement.

	G	AB	R	H	2B	3B	HR	RBI	BA	SA	TB	SB
1914 Ven	181	636	72	195	21	10	2	72	.307	.381	242	23

BABE BORTON (cont.)

	G	AB	R	H	2B	3B	HR	RBI	BA	SA	TB	SB
1917 Port	95	332	46	95	26	4	4	– –	.286	.425	141	11
1918 Ver	84	275	32	73	13	3	2	– –	.265	.356	98	8
1919 Ver	166	587	91	178	15	10	14	– –	.303	.434	255	16
1920 Ver	123	439	76	141	26	7	11	– –	.321	.487	214	10
	649	2269	317	682	101	34	33	– –	.301	.419	950	68

BOB BOYD   Robert Richard Boyd. Born 10/1/1926, Potts Camp, MS. Line–drive hitting first baseman, became the Baltimore Orioles' first .300 hitter. Led PCL in batting average in 1952 and in stolen bases in 1951.

	G	AB	R	H	2B	3B	HR	RBI	BA	SA	TB	SB
1951 Sac	145	555	82	190	32	11	5	64	.342	.467	259	41
1952 Sea	161	641	100	205	29	18	3	75	.320	.435	279	33
1963 OkC	67	233	19	56	12	1	2	23	.251	.326	76	0
1964 OkC	9	8	1	0	0	0	0	0	.000	.000	0	0
	382	1437	202	451	73	30	10	162	.314	.427	614	74

BOBBY BRAGAN   Robert Randall Bragan. Born 10/30/1917, Birmingham, AL. Among the PCL's most colorful and successful player–managers, he managed seven years in the majors. Last big league at bat was a pinch–hit triple in the 1947 World Series.

	G	AB	R	H	2B	3B	HR	RBI	BA	SA	TB	SB
1953 Hol	98	303	29	76	12	0	4	28	.251	.330	100	5
1954 Hol	76	182	16	47	5	0	2	19	.258	.319	58	6
1955 Hol	72	201	13	51	5	0	2	21	.254	.308	62	2
1959 Spo	3	6	0	1	0	0	0	0	.167	.167	1	0
	249	692	58	175	22	0	8	68	.253	.319	221	13

KITTY BRASHEAR   Robert Norman Brashear. Born 8/27/1877, Mansfield, OH. Died 12/22/1934, Los Angeles, CA. Joined PCL after one season as a regular with St. Louis in the National League. Won batting title in 1905.

	G	AB	R	H	2B	3B	HR	RBI	BA	SA	TB	SB
1903 O–Sea	193	736	106	218	37	9	1	– –	.296	.375	276	50
1904 Sea–LA	142	516	80	139	34	4	2	– –	.269	.362	187	25
1905 LA	189	650	84	197	35	7	4	– –	.303	.397	258	31
1906 LA	65	249	48	92	10	4	0	– –	.369	.442	110	16
1907 LA	159	581	65	157	30	3	0	– –	.270	.332	193	36
1908 LA	156	537	57	139	20	1	2	– –	.259	.311	167	25
1909 Ver	201	711	82	175	37	1	2	– –	.246	.309	220	27
1910 Ver	185	607	46	141	32	0	5	– –	.232	.310	188	16
1912 Ver	30	85	5	18	2	0	0	– –	.212	.235	20	2
	1320	4672	573	1276	237	29	16	– –	.273	.347	343	228

FRANK BRAZILL   Frank Leo Brazill. Born 8/11/1899, Spangler, PA. Died 11/3/1976, Oakland, CA. Infielder hit over .300 thirteen consecutive years in the minors, compiling a .331 lifetime batting average.

	G	AB	R	H	2B	3B	HR	RBI	BA	SA	TB	SB
1922 Port	131	456	75	145	26	7	13	51	.318	.491	224	9

FRANK BRAZILL (cont.)

	G	AB	R	H	2B	3B	HR	RBI	BA	SA	TB	SB
1923 Port	176	659	111	208	35	12	19	91	.316	.492	324	12
1924 Port	180	638	157	224	55	12	36	148	.351	.644	411	8
1925 Sea	185	708	174	280	67	11	29	155	.395	.644	456	12
1926 LA	170	551	123	185	30	4	19	111	.336	.508	280	19
1927 LA	148	545	128	178	34	3	21	76	.327	.516	281	11
1928 M−P	91	303	55	100	20	3	8	50	.330	.495	150	3
	1081	3860	823	1320	267	52	145	682	.342	.551	2126	74

BUNNY BRIEF   Anthony Vincent Brief. Born 7/3/1892, Remus, MI. Died 2/10/1963, Milwaukee, WI. One of the great early minor league sluggers, won eight minor league home run titles, including one in the PCL in 1916.

	G	AB	R	H	2B	3B	HR	RBI	BA	SA	TB	SB
1915 SLC	82	328	63	119	23	3	8	− −	.363	.524	172	16
1916 SLC	195	723	149	227	38	5	33	133	.314	.517	374	23
	277	1051	212	346	61	8	41	− −	.329	.520	546	39

JOE BROVIA   Joseph John Brovia. Born 2/18/1922, Davenport, CA. Died 8/15/1994, Santa Cruz, CA. One of the PCL's great competitors, hit a 560 foot homer vs. Seattle in 1947. Led the league in walks in 1952 and 1953. A great fastball hitter, fanned only 78 times in the two seasons combined.

	G	AB	R	H	2B	3B	HR	RBI	BA	SA	TB	SB
1941 SF	92	195	20	62	6	3	0	27	.318	.379	74	0
1942 SF	24	36	4	6	2	0	0	4	.167	.222	8	0
1946 SF	9	9	0	1	0	0	0	1	.111	.111	1	0
1947 SF	114	359	45	111	29	4	10	63	.309	.496	178	1
1948 SF	127	444	53	143	28	4	9	89	.322	.464	206	0
1949 Port	117	364	59	114	21	2	11	51	.313	.473	172	2
1950 Port	193	649	88	182	28	0	39	114	.280	.504	327	1
1951 Port	161	574	76	174	25	2	32	133	.303	.521	299	2
1952 Port	170	551	78	160	25	1	21	85	.290	.454	250	0
1953 Sac	165	525	76	165	36	1	20	97	.314	.501	263	1
1954 Sac	149	504	59	152	32	0	13	91	.302	.442	223	0
1955 Oak	114	372	59	121	19	4	19	73	.325	.551	205	0
	1435	4582	617	1391	251	21	174	828	.304	.481	2206	7

SMOKEY BURGESS   Forrest Harrill Burgess. Born 2/6/1927, Caroleen, NC. Died 9/15/1991, Asheville, NC. A six−time All−Star catcher in the big leagues, he ended his career as one of baseball's greatest pinch−hitters.

	G	AB	R	H	2B	3B	HR	RBI	BA	SA	TB	SB
1946 LA	1	2	0	1	0	0	0	0	.500	.500	1	0
1949 LA	19	43	5	12	1	0	2	12	.279	.442	19	0
	20	45	5	13	1	0	2	12	.289	.444	20	0

GEORGE BURNS   George Henry Burns. Born 1/31/1893, Niles, OH. Died 1/7/1978, Kirkland, WA. Winner of MVP Award in the American League in 1926, spent sixteen years in the majors with a .307 lifetime average. Had the game−winning hit in Game Seven of the 1920 World Series.

GEORGE BURNS (cont.)

	G	AB	R	H	2B	3B	HR	RBI	BA	SA	TB	SB
1930 Miss	200	767	106	268	58	4	22	131	.349	.522	400	27
1931 M–LA	178	696	131	226	52	4	18	129	.325	.489	340	33
1932 Sea	172	687	125	243	53	7	11	140	.354	.499	343	22
1933 Sea	169	643	116	217	32	5	27	128	.337	.529	340	11
1934 Sea–P	118	394	45	115	10	1	2	54	.292	.338	133	3
	837	3187	523	1069	205	21	80	582	.335	.488	1556	96

JIM BUSBY

James Franklin Busby. Born 1/8/1927, Kenedy, TX. A former quarterback at TCU on its Cotton Bowl squad, was one of baseball's top centerfielders during the 1950's. An American League All–Star in 1951.

	G	AB	R	H	2B	3B	HR	RBI	BA	SA	TB	SB
1950 Sac	111	416	76	129	23	8	3	31	.310	.425	177	17

JOE BUSH

Leslie Ambrose Bush. Born 11/27/1892, Brainerd, MN. Died 11/1/1974, Ft. Lauderdale, FL. Won 194 games as a major league pitcher, including twenty–six for the 1922 New York Yankees. Finished up career in the Pacific Coast League as an outfielder.

	G	AB	R	H	2B	3B	HR	RBI	BA	SA	TB	SB
1929 Port	27	95	10	26	6	1	3	19	.274	.453	43	0

DOLF CAMILLI

Adolf Louis Camilli. Born 4/23/1907, San Francisco, CA. Two–time All–Star and captain of the Dodgers, was former boxer whose brother died in a bout with Heavyweight Champion Max Baer. He led the National League in home runs and RBI, winning the MVP Award in 1941.

	G	AB	R	H	2B	3B	HR	RBI	BA	SA	TB	SB
1926 SF	81	298	37	93	25	2	7	41	.312	.480	143	3
1927 SF	81	254	22	62	18	0	2	31	.244	.339	86	3
1929 Sac	117	446	72	132	25	6	12	74	.296	.460	205	3
1930 Sac	166	619	94	170	44	4	17	118	.275	.441	273	8
1931 Sac	185	714	120	210	42	9	16	100	.294	.445	318	7
1932 Sac	187	727	141	224	56	9	17	107	.308	.480	349	18
1933 Sac	159	622	133	182	52	9	20	116	.293	.502	312	10
1944 Sac	113	357	78	103	16	4	14	60	.289	.473	169	12
1945 Sac	11	17	––	6	––	––	––	––	.353	.353	6	0
	1100	4054	697	1182	278	43	105	647	.292	.459	1861	64

WALTER CARLISLE

Walter G. Carlisle. Born 7/6/1883, Yeadon, England. Died 5/27/1945, Hollywood, CA. Turned in the only unassisted triple play by an outfielder in history of organized baseball July 9, 1911.

	G	AB	R	H	2B	3B	HR	RBI	BA	SA	TB	SB
1906 LA	35	117	10	32	8	2	1	––	.274	.402	47	2
1907 LA	179	648	113	168	21	8	14	––	.259	.381	247	39
1910 Ver	224	797	134	206	49	10	12	––	.258	.390	311	34
1911 Ver	206	805	181	239	36	17	17	––	.297	.447	360	55
1912 Ver	200	749	177	212	32	14	14	––	.283	.419	314	76
1913 Ven	187	687	123	154	21	13	7	––	.224	.323	222	34
1914 Ven	204	785	122	206	35	16	5	41	.262	.367	288	28

WALTER CARLISLE (cont.)

	G	AB	R	H	2B	3B	HR	RBI	BA	SA	TB	SB
1915 Ver–P	153	577	72	139	25	14	8	– –	.241	.374	216	16
	1388	5165	932	1356	227	94	78	– –	.263	.388	2005	284

CLEO CARLYLE

Hiram Cleo Carlyle. Born 9/7/1902, Fairburn, GA. Died 11/12/1967 Los Angeles, CA. Consistently productive centerfielder for the Hollywood Stars, played one season with the Boston Red Sox. Had more than 2,500 hits in the minors during his long career. His brother Roy hit a homer in 1929 vs. Mission measured at 618 feet, longest in PCL history.

	G	AB	R	H	2B	3B	HR	RBI	BA	SA	TB	SB
1928 Hol	126	440	77	127	16	4	14	72	.289	.439	193	8
1929 Hol	195	666	146	231	42	12	20	136	.347	.536	357	21
1930 Hol	172	616	142	201	41	4	12	97	.326	.464	286	14
1931 Hol	135	490	89	157	25	4	10	89	.320	.449	220	3
1932 Hol	181	673	123	233	54	9	16	106	.346	.525	353	16
1933 Hol	158	584	105	187	40	7	9	94	.320	.459	268	14
1934 Hol	122	459	71	125	22	0	4	58	.272	.346	159	9
1935 LA	173	653	104	104	25	2	11	100	.297	.392	256	18
1936 LA	167	654	118	222	29	7	3	82	.339	.419	274	15
1937 LA	139	488	74	145	24	4	7	63	.297	.406	198	15
1939 SD	77	258	30	70	12	3	2	31	.271	.364	94	1
	1645	5981	1079	1892	330	56	108	928	.316	.444	2658	129

JAKE CAVENEY

James Christopher Caveney. Born 12/10/1894, San Francisco, CA. Died 7/6/1949, San Francisco, CA. Joe Di Maggio's first professional manager, he moved the eighteen year old from shortstop to the outfield. Was the Cincinnati Reds' regular shortstop for four seasons, beginning in 1922 and holding the job through the 1925 season.

	G	AB	R	H	2B	3B	HR	RBI	BA	SA	TB	SB
1919 SF	170	654	87	178	29	5	8	– –	.272	.369	241	20
1920 SF	191	723	82	202	41	8	1	– –	.279	.362	262	27
1921 SF	173	689	118	224	58	5	11	76	.325	.472	325	29
1926 Sea–O	177	654	73	202	29	5	7	81	.309	.401	262	10
1927 Oak	169	588	69	164	33	7	5	71	.279	.384	226	2
1928 O–SF	125	457	51	120	22	3	6	47	.263	.363	166	1
1929 SF	148	530	67	177	30	3	9	87	.334	.453	240	6
1930 SF	169	575	87	193	39	1	8	84	.336	.449	258	4
1931 SF	115	407	48	136	26	6	3	55	.334	.450	183	3
1932 SF	43	76	8	22	5	0	0	10	.289	.355	27	1
1933 SF	29	60	4	20	3	1	0	8	.333	.417	25	0
1934 SF	21	19	0	5	0	1	0	1	.263	.368	7	0
	1530	5432	694	1643	315	45	58	– –	.302	.409	2222	103

CHESTER CHADBOURNE

Chester James Chadbourne. Born 10/26/1884, Parkman, ME. Died 6/23/1943, Los Angeles, CA. An excellent fly chaser. Collected more than 3,200 hits during his minor league career.

	G	AB	R	H	2B	3B	HR	RBI	BA	SA	TB	SB
1911 Port	196	689	82	205	22	4	0	– –	.298	.341	235	53

CHESTER CHADBOURNE (cont.)

	G	AB	R	H	2B	3B	HR	RBI	BA	SA	TB	SB
1912 Port	176	668	90	184	22	7	1	— —	.275	.334	223	48
1913 Port	191	789	96	223	31	8	1	— —	.283	.346	273	39
1917 O–Ver	154	590	75	157	10	1	0	— —	.266	.286	169	32
1918 Ver	104	400	49	115	17	6	1	— —	.288	.368	147	26
1919 Ver	182	721	122	212	33	9	2	— —	.294	.373	269	21
1920 Ver	195	775	107	222	43	10	3	— —	.286	.379	294	16
1921 Ver	178	713	105	205	42	10	0	51	.288	.374	267	24
1922 Ver	200	830	144	246	48	7	3	62	.296	.382	317	22
1923 Ver	188	756	135	240	38	8	1	50	.317	.393	297	7
1924 Ver	166	642	89	164	28	4	3	52	.255	.326	209	8
	1930	7573	1094	2173	334	74	15	— —	.287	.357	2700	296

FRANK CHANCE

Frank Leroy Chance. Born 9/9/1877, Fresno, CA. Died 9/15/1924, Los Angeles, CA. Hall of Fame first baseman for the Cubs, he later was part–owner of Los Angeles Angels in the Pacific Coast League. Part of most famous, if not most prolific, double play combo in history.

	G	AB	R	H	2B	3B	HR	RBI	BA	SA	TB	SB
1904 LA	— —	73	15	20	4	1	0	— —	.274	.356	26	11
1916 LA	11	7	0	2	1	0	0	— —	.286	.429	3	0
	— —	80	15	22	5	1	0	— —	.275	.363	29	11

SAM CHAPMAN

Samuel Blake Chapman. Born 4/11/1916, Tiburon, CA. Star football player at University of California. Was starter in outfield with Philadelphia A's for ten seasons. An American League All–Star in 1946.

	G	AB	R	H	2B	3B	HR	RBI	BA	SA	TB	SB
1952 Oak	173	617	94	162	28	7	16	98	.263	.408	252	2
1953 Oak	174	617	77	162	31	6	22	93	.263	.439	271	2
1954 Oak	129	473	62	137	34	3	11	63	.290	.444	210	7
	476	1707	233	461	93	16	49	254	.270	.429	733	11

HAL CHASE

Harold Homer Chase. Born 2/13/1883, Los Gatos, CA. Died 5/18/1947, Colusa, CA. Won a Federal League home run title in 1915 and NL batting title in 1916. Was considered the best first baseman of his era, but remembered today for his central role in fixing games. He was finally blacklisted for his part in "Black Sox" and other gambling scandals.

	G	AB	R	H	2B	3B	HR	RBI	BA	SA	TB	SB
1904 LA	— —	702	78	196	32	6	2	— —	.279	.350	246	37

BILLY CISSELL

Chalmer William Cissell. Born 1/3/1904, Perryville, MO. Died 3/15/1949, Chicago, IL. Purchased from Portland by the White Sox for a reported $127,000. Went through hard times after retirement, dying penniless in Chicago while working as Comiskey Park maintenance man.

	G	AB	R	H	2B	3B	HR	RBI	BA	SA	TB	SB
1926 Port	22	85	10	22	5	0	0	12	.259	.318	27	1
1927 Port	183	696	112	225	32	6	5	64	.323	.408	284	18
1935 Port	165	646	106	204	43	4	8	84	.316	.432	279	14
1939 Hol	167	696	92	187	38	8	3	83	.269	.359	250	4

BILLY CISSELL (cont.)

	G	AB	R	H	2B	3B	HR	RBI	BA	SA	TB	SB
1940 Hol	162	629	89	182	32	3	4	76	.289	.369	232	7
1941 H—SF	40	77	7	19	1	0	0	8	.247	.260	20	0
	739	2829	416	839	151	21	20	327	.297	.386	1092	44

MOOSE CLABAUGH   John William Clabaugh. Born 11/13/1901, Albany, MO. Died 7/11/1984, Tucson, AZ. Won five minor league batting titles to finish career with .339 average. His 62 homers in the East Texas League in 1926 set a new pro record. Had only fourteen at bats in the majors.

	G	AB	R	H	2B	3B	HR	RBI	BA	SA	TB	SB
1934 Port	130	443	79	135	24	5	16	73	.305	.490	217	17
1935 Port	158	565	112	193	56	7	16	116	.342	.550	311	21
1936 Port	170	559	108	177	29	4	20	112	.317	.490	274	6
1937 Port	171	571	96	186	39	15	17	114	.326	.536	306	11
1940 Port	14	34	6	4	1	0	1	5	.118	.235	8	1
	643	2172	401	695	149	31	70	420	.320	.514	1116	56

MICKEY COCHRANE   Gordon Stanley Cochrane. Born 4/6/1903, Bridgewater, MA. Died 6/28/1962, Lake Forest, IL. Hall of Fame catcher; was unable to make Boston University baseball team until his junior year.

	G	AB	R	H	2B	3B	HR	RBI	BA	SA	TB	SB
1924 Port	99	300	43	100	8	5	7	56	.333	.463	139	1

ROCKY COLAVITO   Rocco Domenico Colavito. Born 8/10/1933, New York, NY. Slugging outfielder, hit 374 home runs in major leagues. Three times he hit more than 40 home runs in a season. Six—time AL All—Star.

	G	AB	R	H	2B	3B	HR	RBI	BA	SA	TB	SB
1956 SD	35	133	31	49	10	1	12	32	.368	.729	97	0

ED COLEMAN   Parke Edward Coleman. Born 12/1/1901, Canby, OR. Died 8/5/1964, Oregon City, OR. Led PCL in games played, at—bats, hits, runs, doubles, and runs batted in 1931. Acquired by A's in 1932, hit .342 in twenty—six games before a broken ankle ended his rookie season.

	G	AB	R	H	2B	3B	HR	RBI	BA	SA	TB	SB
1929 SF	121	405	73	139	24	2	16	72	.343	.531	215	2
1930 SF	125	396	55	119	18	2	12	68	.301	.447	177	3
1931 Port	187	768	134	275	53	14	37	183	.358	.608	467	4
1939 Port	105	320	56	110	17	1	16	77	.344	.553	177	0
1940 Port	73	268	38	85	10	0	9	47	.317	.455	122	0
	611	2157	356	728	122	19	90	447	.338	.537	1158	9

RIPPER COLLINS   James Anthony Collins. Born 3/30/1904, Altoona, PA. Died 4/16/1970, New Haven, NY. Three—time All—Star, was main slugger of the "Gas House Gang". Led NL in 1934 in homers and RBI as their first baseman; led in same categories in PCL in 1939. Only 5—9 and 160 lbs.

	G	AB	R	H	2B	3B	HR	RBI	BA	SA	TB	SB
1939 LA	172	586	113	196	40	9	26	128	.334	.567	332	5
1940 LA	174	630	93	206	42	5	18	111	.327	.495	312	6

RIPPER COLLINS (cont.)

	G	AB	R	H	2B	3B	HR	RBI	BA	SA	TB	SB
1947 SD	9	13	0	2	0	0	0	1	.154	.154	2	0
	355	1229	206	404	82	14	44	240	.329	.526	646	11

CHUCK CONNORS   Kevin Joseph Aloysius Connors. Born 4/10/1921, Brooklyn, NY. Died 11/10/1992, Los Angeles, CA. Two–sport athlete, he also played pro basketball with the Boston Celtics. Well–known actor.

	G	AB	R	H	2B	3B	HR	RBI	BA	SA	TB	SB
1951 LA	98	390	75	125	28	2	22	77	.321	.572	223	8
1952 LA	113	406	50	105	27	2	6	51	.259	.379	154	4
	211	796	125	230	55	4	28	128	.289	.474	377	12

BILLY CONSOLO   William Angelo Consolo. Born 8/18/1934, Cleveland, OH. Given a $60,000 bonus to join Cincinnati Reds directly out of high school. Was a utility infielder in the major leagues for ten seasons.

	G	AB	R	H	2B	3B	HR	RBI	BA	SA	TB	SB
1955 Oak	159	590	93	163	33	8	14	68	.276	.431	254	10
1961 Van	99	389	63	110	10	7	4	40	.283	.375	146	11
	258	979	156	273	43	15	18	108	.279	.409	400	21

WALKER COOPER   William Walker Cooper. Born 1/8/1915, Atherton, MO. Named catcher on the NL All–Star team eight times in a row. Once purchased by Giants for $175,000, played in majors for eighteen years.

	G	AB	R	H	2B	3B	HR	RBI	BA	SA	TB	SB
1937 Sac	83	241	28	64	12	3	3	29	.266	.378	91	3

DOC CRAMER   Roger Maxwell Cramer. Born 7/22/1906, Beach Haven, NJ. Died 9/9/1990, Manahawkin, NJ. One of the best centerfielders of his era, he twice had six hits in a game and retired with 2,705 hits in the majors.

	G	AB	R	H	2B	3B	HR	RBI	BA	SA	TB	SB
1930 Port	74	300	53	104	24	3	5	46	.347	.497	149	6
1950 Sea	2	2	0	0	0	0	0	0	.000	.000	0	0
	76	302	53	104	24	3	5	46	.344	.493	149	6

SAMMY CRANE   Samuel Byren Crane. Born 9/13/1894, Harrisburg, PA. Died 11/12/1955, Philadelphia, PA. Shortstop was great fielder, but weak hitter. In headlines after killing girlfriend and another man in a bar fight.

	G	AB	R	H	2B	3B	HR	RBI	BA	SA	TB	SB
1922 Sea	131	482	52	128	21	5	1	50	.266	.336	162	11
1923 Sea	155	561	67	142	24	6	0	65	.253	.317	178	12
1924 Sea	160	573	71	154	22	3	1	58	.269	.323	185	18
1925 Sea	14	––	––	––	––	––	––	––	.176	––	–– ––	
	460	1616	190	424	67	14	2	173	.262	.325	525	41

GAVVY CRAVATH   Clifford Carlton Cravath. Born 3/23/1881, Escondido, CA. Died 5/23/1963, Laguna Beach, CA. Won six NL home run titles over seven seasons; was top slugger of "dead ball" era. After drawing a short straw he spent the last 36 years of his life as a Justice of the Peace.

GAVVY CRAVATH (cont.)

	G	AB	R	H	2B	3B	HR	RBI	BA	SA	TB	SB
1903 LA	208	805	109	219	––	––	––	––	.272	––	––	34
1904 LA	––	771	107	207	39	4	13	––	.268	.380	293	43
1905 LA	204	703	––	182	33	9	9	––	.259	.370	260	44
1906 LA	181	603	90	171	33	12	4	––	.284	.398	240	12
1907 LA	182	614	106	186	45	5	10	––	.303	.441	271	50
1921 SLC	112	341	62	111	22	0	18	64	.326	.548	187	3
	––	3837	––	1076	––	––	––	––	.280	.413	––	186

SAM CRAWFORD

Samuel Earl Crawford. Born 4/18/1880, Wahoo, NE. Died 6/15/1968, Hollywood, CA. The all–time major league career leader in triples with 312, also led AL in home runs twice and RBI three times. Ty Cobb successfully pushed his old teammate's election to Hall of Fame in spite of their differences. Crawford umpired in PCL after his playing days.

	G	AB	R	H	2B	3B	HR	RBI	BA	SA	TB	SB
1918 LA	96	356	38	104	14	7	1	––	.292	.379	135	8
1919 LA	173	664	103	239	41	18	14	––	.360	.539	358	14
1920 LA	187	719	99	239	46	21	12	––	.332	.505	363	3
1921 LA	175	626	92	199	44	10	9	103	.318	.463	290	10
	631	2365	332	781	145	56	36	––	.330	.485	1146	35

FRANK CROSETTI

Frank Peter Joseph Crosetti. Born 10/4/1910, San Francisco, CA. Participated in twenty four World Series with Yankees as a player and/or coach. A smart player, master of the "hidden ball" trick.

	G	AB	R	H	2B	3B	HR	RBI	BA	SA	TB	SB
1928 SF	96	326	79	81	18	1	4	22	.248	.347	113	4
1929 SF	184	784	151	246	54	5	12	81	.314	.441	346	5
1930 SF	189	782	171	261	66	8	27	113	.334	.542	424	21
1931 SF	183	734	141	252	48	13	5	143	.343	.465	341	23
	652	2626	542	840	186	27	48	359	.320	.466	1224	53

NICK CULLOP

Heinrich Nicholas Cullop. Born 10/16/1900, Weldon Spring, MO. Died 12/8/1978, Westerville, OH. Pitcher–turned–home run hitter, holds the all–time career record for RBI. Named the Minor League Manager of the Year twice. Played five years in majors with five teams.

	G	AB	R	H	2B	3B	HR	RBI	BA	SA	TB	SB
1937 Sac	151	532	83	165	45	4	19	127	.310	.517	275	4
1938 Sac	138	485	72	124	19	1	20	66	.256	.423	205	7
	289	1017	155	289	64	5	39	193	.284	.472	480	11

GEORGE CUTSHAW

George William Cutshaw. Born 7/27/1887, Wilmington, DE. Died 8/22/1973, San Diego, CA. One of the best fielding second basemen of his era, led the PCL in stolen bases in 1911.

	G	AB	R	H	2B	3B	HR	RBI	BA	SA	TB	SB
1909 Oak	66	250	18	57	––	––	––	––	.228	––	––	––
1910 Oak	223	820	81	182	22	2	3	––	.222	.265	217	45
1911 Oak	206	782	85	204	––	––	––	––	.261	––	––	90
1924 Sea	43	53	7	13	1	1	0	6	.245	.302	16	0

GEORGE CUTSHAW (cont.)

	G	AB	R	H	2B	3B	HR	RBI	BA	SA	TB	SB
1925 Sea	42	70	9	26	6	1	0	9	.371	.486	34	0
1926 Sea	5	––	––	––	––	––	––	––	.000	.000	0	––
	585	1975	200	482	––	––	––	––	.244	––	––	––

BABE DAHLGREN

Ellsworth Tenney Dahlgren. Born 6/15/1912, San Francisco, CA. Played first base for the Yankees on May 2, 1939, in place of Lou Gehrig. Played for eight teams in his twelve major league seasons.

	G	AB	R	H	2B	3B	HR	RBI	BA	SA	TB	SB
1931 Miss	58	234	25	57	11	2	1	23	.244	.321	75	3
1932 Miss	188	722	69	207	40	4	11	101	.287	.399	288	8
1933 Miss	189	733	98	231	28	9	6	110	.315	.402	295	4
1934 Miss	186	735	106	222	34	10	20	136	.302	.457	336	11
1948 Sac	115	379	39	113	21	0	8	41	.298	.417	158	0
	736	2803	337	830	134	25	46	411	.296	.411	1152	26

TOM DALEY

Thomas Francis Daley. Born 11/13/1884, Du Bois, PA. Died 12/2/1934, Los Angeles, CA. Lost PCL batting race in 1912 to a teammate who had died of typhoid two weeks before. Once set fire in the outfield of SF's Ewing Field to protest playing a game there in cold weather.

	G	AB	R	H	2B	3B	HR	RBI	BA	SA	TB	SB
1909 LA	198	682	111	180	––	––	––	––	.264	––	––	––
1910 LA	224	831	104	218	29	2	2	––	.262	.309	257	51
1911 LA	194	708	104	214	––	––	––	––	.302	––	––	71
1912 LA	174	639	90	212	––	––	––	––	.332	––	––	54
1916 Ver	194	650	89	166	17	4	3	––	.255	.308	200	45
1917 Ver	190	680	87	188	27	4	0	––	.276	.328	223	34
1918 Ver	104	369	49	109	15	8	1	––	.295	.388	143	9
	1278	4559	634	1287	––	––	––	––	.282	––	––	––

DOM DALLESSANDRO

Nicholas Dominic Dallessandro. Born 10/3/1913, Reading, PA. Died 4/29/1988, Indianapolis, IN. Outfielder for eight seasons in majors. Beat out Dom Di Maggio for 1939 batting title.

	G	AB	R	H	2B	3B	HR	RBI	BA	SA	TB	SB
1938 SD	155	541	108	167	29	8	22	91	.309	.514	278	8
1939 SD	157	541	101	199	50	9	18	98	.368	.593	321	12
1948 LA	159	514	101	158	27	6	21	87	.307	.506	260	1
1949 LA	39	117	21	34	6	0	8	28	.291	.547	64	1
	510	1713	331	558	112	23	69	304	.326	.539	923	22

CLAY DALRYMPLE

Clayton Errol Dalrymple. Born 12/3/1936, Chico, CA. Great defensive catcher with strong arm, set an NL mark with ninety–nine errorless games in a row. Twelve years in majors with Phils and Orioles.

	G	AB	R	H	2B	3B	HR	RBI	BA	SA	TB	SB
1956 Sac	15	7	0	2	0	0	0	0	.286	.286	2	0
1958 Sac	106	272	19	52	14	0	5	21	.191	.298	81	0
1959 Sac	127	374	37	86	16	0	12	48	.230	.369	138	0
	248	653	56	140	30	0	17	69	.214	.338	221	0

RAY DANDRIDGE   Raymond Dandridge. Born 8/31/1913, Richmond, VA. Died 2/12/1994, Palm Bay, FL. Hall of Fame Negro League third baseman noted for bow—legs and great glove. Named the American Association's MVP in 1950; followed Willie Mays in the Minneapolis batting order in '51.

	G	AB	R	H	2B	3B	HR	RBI	BA	SA	TB	SB
1953 Sac—O	87	254	32	68	10	1	0	13	.268	.315	80	1

CHARLIE DEAL   Charles Albert Deal. Born 10/30/1891, Wilkinsburg, PA. Died 9/16/1979, Covina, CA. Ten year big league third baseman, acquired by Los Angeles from the Chicago Cubs in exchange for Jigger Statz.

	G	AB	R	H	2B	3B	HR	RBI	BA	SA	TB	SB
1922 LA	168	667	95	221	52	4	6	87	.331	.448	299	7
1923 LA—Ver	94	349	50	110	23	2	4	53	.315	.427	149	8
1924 Ver	140	553	87	179	37	7	12	99	.324	.481	266	4
1925 Port	134	427	50	119	16	0	6	58	.279	.358	153	11
	536	1996	282	629	128	13	28	297	.315	.434	867	30

ROD DEDEAUX   Raoul Dedeaux. Born 2/17/1915, New Orleans, LA. Legendary head baseball coach at the University of Southern California.

	G	AB	R	H	2B	3B	HR	RBI	BA	SA	TB	SB
1939 SD—H	30	79	9	13	1	0	0	5	.165	.177	14	1

JIM DELSING   James Henry Delsing. Born 11/13/1925, Rudolph, WI. Best remembered as the pinch—runner for Eddie Gaedel, spent a decade in the major leagues and made All—Star teams in three minor leagues.

	G	AB	R	H	2B	3B	HR	RBI	BA	SA	TB	SB
1947 Hol	153	572	92	181	24	12	5	53	.316	.427	244	3
1948 Hol	122	463	82	154	30	5	6	56	.333	.458	212	4
	275	1035	174	335	54	17	11	109	.324	.441	456	7

FRANK DEMAREE   Joseph Franklin Demaree. Born 6/10/1910, Winters, CA. Died 8/30/1958, Los Angeles, CA. One of only three players to blast thirty home runs and steal thirty bases in the same season, (Lefty O'Doul and Tony Lazzeri being the others), and the only "40—40" man ever in the league. Won PCL triple crown and Most Valuable Player award in 1934.

	G	AB	R	H	2B	3B	HR	RBI	BA	SA	TB	SB
1930 Sac	41	127	24	29	6	3	1	18	.228	.346	44	0
1931 Sac	180	674	89	210	41	10	16	104	.312	.473	319	13
1932 Sac	109	437	71	159	20	6	12	84	.364	.519	227	6
1934 LA	186	702	190	269	51	4	45	173	.383	.660	463	41
1944 Port	35	104	12	27	7	0	0	12	.260	.327	34	2
1945 Port	136	514	87	156	36	3	3	78	.304	.403	207	5
	687	2558	473	850	161	26	77	469	.332	.506	1294	67

GENE DESAUTELS   Eugene Abraham Desautels. Born 6/13/1907, Worcester, MA. Thirteen years in majors as a catcher for Tigers, Red Sox, Indians, and Athletics. A product of Holy Cross, managed in the PCL.

	G	AB	R	H	2B	3B	HR	RBI	BA	SA	TB	SB
1935 Hol	129	426	48	113	26	3	6	55	.265	.383	163	8

GENE DESAUTELS (cont.)

	G	AB	R	H	2B	3B	HR	RBI	BA	SA	TB	SB
1936 SD	148	480	68	153	18	5	3	69	.319	.396	190	4
	277	906	116	266	44	8	9	124	.294	.390	353	12

BOB DILLINGER   Robert Bernard Dillinger. Born 9/17/1918, Glendale, CA
Third baseman led the AL in stolen bases three times. Retired from majors following 1951 season and joined PCL, winning the batting title in 1953.

	G	AB	R	H	2B	3B	HR	RBI	BA	SA	TB	SB
1952 Sac	153	585	67	168	29	8	0	51	.287	.364	213	12
1953 Sac	171	645	104	236	34	7	0	51	.366	.440	284	10
1954 Sac	155	588	76	177	21	3	0	38	.301	.347	204	5
1955 Sac	34	114	11	32	3	0	0	2	.281	.307	35	1
	513	1932	258	613	87	18	0	142	.317	.381	736	28

POP DILLON   Frank Edward Dillon. Born 10/17/1873, Normal, IL. Died
9/12/1931, Pasadena, CA. Captain of Brooklyn in NL in 1904, left team to become player–manager for Los Angeles in PCL. Cousin of Clark Griffith.

	G	AB	R	H	2B	3B	HR	RBI	BA	SA	TB	SB
1903 LA	190	752	115	271	45	12	4	– –	.360	.468	352	43
1905 LA	216	779	101	212	35	6	2	– –	.272	.340	265	53
1906 LA	165	549	61	181	21	10	1	– –	.330	.410	225	18
1907 LA	181	631	88	192	33	5	5	– –	.304	.396	250	34
1908 LA	168	620	77	168	24	7	7	– –	.271	.366	227	33
1909 LA	119	416	44	101	14	5	1	– –	.243	.308	128	12
1910 LA	189	629	63	150	20	4	2	– –	.238	.293	184	27
1911 LA	172	580	63	147	13	8	3	– –	.253	.319	185	18
1912 LA	121	368	52	108	18	0	1	– –	.293	.351	129	13
1913 LA	22	55	4	20	1	0	0	– –	.364	.382	21	1
1914 LA	3	2	0	1	0	1	0	– –	.500	1.500	3	0
1915 LA	18	37	4	7	0	1	0	– –	.189	.243	9	0
	1564	5418	672	1558	224	59	26	– –	.288	.365	1978	252

DOM DI MAGGIO   Dominic Paul Di Maggio. Born 2/12/1917, San Francisco,
CA. Great outfielder and seven–time AL All–Star, he seven times scored more than one hundred runs in a season. A 34–game hit streak in 1949.

	G	AB	R	H	2B	3B	HR	RBI	BA	SA	TB	SB
1937 SF	140	496	109	152	33	7	5	46	.306	.431	214	15
1938 SF	163	659	120	202	42	9	5	60	.307	.420	277	16
1939 SF	170	664	165	239	48	18	14	82	.360	.550	365	39
	473	1819	394	593	123	34	24	188	.326	.471	856	70

JOE DI MAGGIO   Joseph Paul Di Maggio. Born 11/25/1914, Martinez,
CA. Had a PCL record 61–game hitting streak as an eighteen year old in 1933. Lost the PCL batting title by one point in 1935 in comeback from a serious knee injury the year before. Elected to the Hall of Fame in 1955.

	G	AB	R	H	2B	3B	HR	RBI	BA	SA	TB	SB
1932 SF	3	9	2	2	1	1	0	2	.222	.556	5	0
1933 SF	187	762	129	259	45	13	28	169	.340	.543	414	10

JOE DI MAGGIO (cont.)

	G	AB	R	H	2B	3B	HR	RBI	BA	SA	TB	SB
1934 SF	101	375	58	128	18	6	12	69	.341	.517	194	8
1935 SF	172	679	173	270	48	18	34	154	.398	.672	456	24
	463	1825	362	659	112	38	74	394	.361	.586	1069	42

VINCE DI MAGGIO
Vincent Paul Di Maggio. Born 9/6/1912, Martinez, CA. Died 10/3/1986, North Hollywood, CA. A two–time NL All–Star, had strongest arm of the Di Maggio brothers. He hit four grand slams in 1945.

	G	AB	R	H	2B	3B	HR	RBI	BA	SA	TB	SB
1932 SF	59	200	35	54	13	2	6	31	.270	.445	89	2
1933 SF–H	96	339	54	113	24	4	11	65	.333	.525	178	7
1934 Hol	166	587	89	169	25	3	17	91	.288	.428	251	7
1935 Hol	174	659	107	183	36	4	24	112	.278	.454	299	15
1936 SD	176	641	109	188	43	14	19	102	.293	.493	316	22
1946 SF	43	129	19	34	10	2	1	21	.264	.395	51	3
1947 Oak	140	473	80	114	20	4	22	81	.241	.440	208	7
	854	3028	493	855	171	33	100	503	.282	.460	1392	63

CARL DITTMAR
Carl Henry Dittmar. Born 3/21/1901, Baltimore, MD. With Jimmie Reese, formed double–play combination for PCL's greatest team, the 1934 LA Angels. Buried in the Cubs system, never played in majors.

	G	AB	R	H	2B	3B	HR	RBI	BA	SA	TB	SB
1927 SF	164	570	86	153	32	3	4	71	.268	.356	203	5
1928 LA	180	626	71	159	22	6	2	63	.254	.318	199	15
1929 LA	154	505	83	153	30	4	5	43	.303	.408	206	14
1930 LA	166	622	94	193	39	5	14	125	.310	.457	284	13
1931 LA	139	470	78	134	25	5	8	95	.285	.411	193	11
1932 LA	174	583	86	174	40	3	4	78	.298	.398	232	9
1933 LA	149	478	61	126	19	2	5	49	.264	.343	164	2
1934 LA	151	517	75	152	33	2	3	73	.294	.383	198	7
1935 LA	78	215	21	56	6	1	0	36	.260	.298	64	2
1936 LA	125	427	47	122	16	2	1	44	.286	.340	145	5
1937 LA	72	228	20	63	8	1	0	37	.276	.320	73	1
1938 LA	11	19	1	4	2	0	0	2	.211	.316	6	0
	1563	5260	723	1489	272	34	46	716	.283	.374	1967	84

BOBBY DOERR
Robert Pershing Doerr. Born 4/7/1918, Los Angeles, CA. Starter at second base for Hollywood while still in high school, had Hall of Fame career with Boston Red Sox that included nine All–Star selections.

	G	AB	R	H	2B	3B	HR	RBI	BA	SA	TB	SB
1934 Hol	67	201	12	52	6	0	0	11	.259	.289	58	1
1935 Hol	172	647	87	205	22	8	4	74	.317	.394	255	5
1936 SD	175	695	100	238	37	12	2	77	.342	.439	305	30
	414	1543	199	495	65	20	6	162	.321	.401	618	36

WALT DROPO
Walter Dropo. Born 1/30/1923, Moosup, CT. All–Star and the American League Rookie of the Year in 1950. First baseman led AL in RBI that same year. Shares major league record of twelve straight hits.

WALT DROPO (cont.)

	G	AB	R	H	2B	3B	HR	RBI	BA	SA	TB	SB
1949 Sac	132	481	60	138	30	3	17	85	.287	.468	225	6
1951 SD	33	126	17	36	4	0	5	13	.286	.437	55	0
	165	607	77	174	34	3	22	98	.287	.461	280	6

TRUCK EAGAN   Charles Eugene Eagan. Born 8/10/1877, Oakland, CA. Died 3/19/1949, San Francisco, CA. The PCL's first real slugger, leading the league in home runs three times. Led PCL in batting average in 1907. He was known to knock down balls with his bare hand at shortstop.

	G	AB	R	H	2B	3B	HR	RBI	BA	SA	TB	SB
1903 Sac	206	818	137	262	56	24	13	– –	.320	.495	405	56
1904 Tac	191	736	121	229	52	7	25	– –	.311	.503	370	29
1905 Tac	210	774	104	215	49	3	21	– –	.278	.430	333	29
1906 Fre	167	652	70	170	18	12	2	– –	.261	.334	218	22
1907 Oak	194	708	96	237	45	2	10	– –	.335	.446	316	31
1908 Oak	184	687	81	180	28	2	9	– –	.262	.348	239	17
1909 Ver	188	647	65	144	27	2	9	– –	.223	.312	202	14
	1340	5022	674	1437	275	52	89	– –	.286	.415	2083	198

LUKE EASTER   Luscious Luke Easter. Born 8/4/1914, St. Louis, MO. Died 3/29/1979, Euclid, OH. Negro League star was an instant fan favorite and a leading drawing card soon after his PCL debut. Averaged nearly an RBI per game in the PCL. Later had three solid seasons for Cleveland.

	G	AB	R	H	2B	3B	HR	RBI	BA	SA	TB	SB
1949 SD	80	273	56	99	23	0	25	92	.363	.722	197	1
1954 SD	56	198	43	55	8	1	13	42	.278	.525	104	1
	136	471	99	154	31	1	38	134	.327	.639	301	2

OX ECKHARDT   Oscar George Eckhardt. Born 12/23/1901, Yorktown, TX. Died 4/22/1951, Yorktown, TX. Won PCL record four batting titles and had a lifetime minor league batting average of .367. A lack of power combined with weak glove work limited major league career to only fifty–two at bats.

	G	AB	R	H	2B	3B	HR	RBI	BA	SA	TB	SB
1929 Sea	161	571	84	202	35	17	7	70	.354	.511	292	16
1931 Miss	185	745	129	275	52	10	7	117	.369	.494	368	9
1932 Miss	134	539	80	200	33	13	5	82	.371	.508	274	15
1933 Miss	189	760	145	315	56	16	12	143	.414	.578	439	15
1934 Miss	184	707	126	267	36	11	6	106	.378	.485	343	7
1935 Miss	172	710	149	283	40	11	2	114	.399	.494	351	8
	1025	4032	713	1542	252	78	39	632	.382	.513	2067	70

BRICK ELDRED   Ross C. Eldred. Born 7/26/1893, Sacramento, CA. Led the PCL in doubles in 1918 and 1920. Outfielder had nearly 600 doubles in minor league career. Lifetime average of .327; never played in majors.

	G	AB	R	H	2B	3B	HR	RBI	BA	SA	TB	SB
1916 SLC	19	32	3	7	2	0	0	– –	.219	.281	9	0
1918 SF	97	398	54	105	26	5	4	– –	.264	.384	153	22
1919 Sac	166	617	111	192	34	13	4	– –	.311	.428	264	41

BRICK ELDRED (cont.)

	G	AB	R	H	2B	3B	HR	RBI	BA	SA	TB	SB
1920 Sea	188	682	111	231	59	17	3	— —	.339	.488	333	35
1921 Sea	154	590	109	188	60	3	6	84	.319	.461	272	17
1922 Sea	187	734	102	260	55	10	9	131	.354	.493	362	23
1923 Sea	193	742	129	262	71	11	7	116	.353	.507	376	23
1924 Sea	177	684	129	240	71	5	7	131	.351	.500	342	21
1925 Sea	191	739	120	242	66	6	7	142	.327	.461	341	21
1926 Sea	125	312	49	106	30	2	2	59	.340	.468	146	3
1927 Sea	122	369	53	120	31	1	2	48	.325	.431	159	10
1928 Sea	11	19	2	6	1	0	0	2	.316	.368	7	0
1930 Sac	79	203	31	75	10	1	6	42	.369	.517	105	3
	1709	6121	1003	2034	516	74	57	— —	.332	.469	2869	219

BOB ELLIOTT

Robert Irving Elliott. Born 11/26/1916, San Francisco, CA. Died 5/4/1966, San Diego, CA. Converted from outfield to third base, was NL MVP in 1947. Drove in 100 or more runs six times in majors. Homered twice in playoff vs. Hollywood to clinch 1954 PCL pennant for San Diego.

	G	AB	R	H	2B	3B	HR	RBI	BA	SA	TB	SB
1954 SD	81	203	28	52	6	1	12	39	.256	.473	96	1

RUBE ELLIS

George William Ellis. Born 11/17/1885, Downey, CA. Died 3/13/1938, Rivera, CA. Starting outfielder in NL for St. Louis 1909—1912.

	G	AB	R	H	2B	3B	HR	RBI	BA	SA	TB	SB
1905 LA	5	18	— —	6	3	0	0	— —	.333	.500	9	1
1906 LA	143	469	34	106	15	3	1	— —	.226	.277	130	8
1907 LA	171	578	59	138	15	7	4	— —	.239	.310	179	29
1908 LA	184	646	91	174	19	13	5	— —	.269	.362	234	30
1913 LA	183	648	94	178	25	7	8	— —	.275	.372	241	39
1914 LA	208	756	97	234	34	15	6	120	.310	.418	316	44
1915 LA	200	705	97	191	25	8	5	— —	.271	.350	247	34
1916 LA	197	755	108	192	28	10	2	— —	.254	.326	246	32
1917 SF—LA	179	616	59	168	27	7	4	— —	.273	.359	221	24
1918 LA	104	366	49	102	21	4	1	— —	.279	.366	134	16
1919 LA	176	616	71	159	21	4	3	— —	.258	.320	197	5
1920 LA	176	619	47	154	20	1	3	— —	.249	.299	185	4
1921 LA	48	89	16	21	3	0	0	6	.236	.270	24	0
1925 Ver	1	— —	— —	— —	— —	— —	— —	— —	.000	— —	— —	— —
	1975	6881	822	1823	256	79	42	— —	.265	.343	2363	266

BABE ELLISON

Herbert Spencer Ellison. Born 11/15/1895, Rutland, AR. Died 8/11/1955, San Francisco, CA. Became the player—manager for SF in 1923 when Dots Miller contracted a fatal illness. Twice led PCL in RBI. Went 25 for 37 with ten home runs vs. Salt Lake City, May 20—25, 1924.

	G	AB	R	H	2B	3B	HR	RBI	BA	SA	TB	SB
1921 SF	171	634	124	197	46	4	18	102	.311	.481	305	10
1922 SF	187	718	116	220	30	10	16	141	.306	.443	318	20
1923 SF	192	757	145	271	67	10	23	139	.358	.564	427	12
1924 SF	201	805	142	307	68	11	33	188	.381	.616	496	10

BABE ELLISON (cont.)

	G	AB	R	H	2B	3B	HR	RBI	BA	SA	TB	SB
1925 SF	174	708	122	230	38	7	22	160	.325	.492	348	8
1926 SF	105	321	36	97	28	0	3	48	.302	.417	134	1
1927 SF	12	28	5	7	1	1	1	5	.250	.464	13	0
	1042	3971	690	1329	278	43	116	783	.335	.514	2041	61

NICK ETTEN

Nicholas Raymond Thomas Etten. Born 9/19/1913, Spring Grove, IL. Died 10/18/1990 Hinsdale, IL. A war–time big league star, led the American League in home runs in 1944 and RBI in 1945 with Yankees.

	G	AB	R	H	2B	3B	HR	RBI	BA	SA	TB	SB
1947 Oak	46	140	27	42	13	1	4	30	.300	.493	69	3
1948 Oak	164	578	115	181	27	1	43	155	.313	.587	339	3
	210	718	142	223	40	2	47	185	.311	.568	408	6

FERRIS FAIN

Ferris Roy Fain. Born 3/29/1922, San Antonio, TX. Five time All–Star first baseman; streak ended by serious knee injury in 1954. AL batting champ in 1951 and 1952, was one of the game's best fielders.

	G	AB	R	H	2B	3B	HR	RBI	BA	SA	TB	SB
1939 SF	12	33	4	7	2	0	1	8	.212	.364	12	0
1940 SF	146	446	64	106	21	7	7	50	.238	.363	162	3
1941 SF	174	649	122	201	27	8	5	66	.310	.399	259	8
1942 SF	162	519	57	112	17	4	4	53	.216	.287	149	3
1946 SF	180	615	117	185	35	6	11	112	.301	.431	265	24
1956 Sac	70	147	18	37	6	0	0	16	.252	.293	43	0
	744	2409	382	648	108	25	28	305	.269	.369	890	38

LOU FINNEY

Louis Klopsche Finney. Born 8/13/1910, Buffalo, AL. Died 4/22/1966, Lafayette, AL. A fifteen year big league outfielder, replaced Al Simmons in Athletics lineup in 1933. American League All–Star in 1940.

	G	AB	R	H	2B	3B	HR	RBI	BA	SA	TB	SB
1932 Port	185	764	125	268	50	7	5	98	.351	.454	347	15

GUS FISHER

Augustus Harris Fisher. Born 10/21/1885, Pottsborough, TX. Died 4/9/1970, Portland, OR. Catcher had PCL's top batting average in 1914 but did not qualify for title. Played in AL for NY and Cleveland.

	G	AB	R	H	2B	3B	HR	RBI	BA	SA	TB	SB
1909 Port	123	414	43	107	––	––	––	––	.258	––	––	––
1910 Port	163	537	66	143	31	8	5	––	.266	.382	205	13
1912 Port	96	314	32	84	––	––	––	––	.268	––	––	12
1913 Port	139	390	49	114	19	3	2	––	.292	.372	145	23
1914 Port	139	440	64	156	25	8	1	58	.355	.455	200	11
1915 Port	148	475	38	151	30	3	2	––	.318	.406	193	14
1916 Port	98	288	31	83	17	0	0	––	.288	.347	100	7
1917 Port	123	402	35	91	11	0	4	––	.226	.284	114	7
1918 Sac	36	125	15	39	7	0	1	––	.312	.392	49	2
1919 Sac	61	193	23	48	6	1	2	––	.249	.321	62	2
1921 Port	124	365	28	105	15	1	4	50	.288	.367	134	1
	1250	3943	424	1121	––	––	––	––	.284	.374	––	––

ED FITZ GERALD   Edward Raymond Fitz Gerald. Born 5/21/1924, Santa Ynez, CA. Twelve year big league catcher with the Pirates, Indians, and Senators. Hit into a triple play on Opening Day in 1959. Travelled in the off—season with six brothers as part of barnstorming basketball team.

	G	AB	R	H	2B	3B	HR	RBI	BA	SA	TB	SB
1946 Sac	11	38	7	10	2	1	0	0	.263	.368	14	0
1947 Sac	144	411	62	149	22	9	5	49	.363	.496	204	26
	155	449	69	159	24	10	5	49	.354	.486	218	26

IRA FLAGSTEAD   Ira James Flagstead. Born 9/22/1893, Montague, MI. Died 3/13/1940, Olympia, WA. Thirteen years in big leagues; a five—time .300 hitter in majors. Excellent center fielder, started a big league record three double plays in one game on April 19, 1926.

	G	AB	R	H	2B	3B	HR	RBI	BA	SA	TB	SB
1931 Sea—P	68	229	38	53	15	2	1	28	.231	.328	75	3

DEE FONDY   Dee Virgil Fondy Jr. Born 10/31/1924, Slaton, TX. Sent to Los Angeles when Cubs recalled Chuck Connors in middle of the 1951 season, hit over .500 his first two weeks. Also had six hits in one game.

	G	AB	R	H	2B	3B	HR	RBI	BA	SA	TB	SB
1951 LA	70	274	46	103	16	6	11	45	.376	.599	164	7
1959 Sea—SD	140	498	51	128	18	2	2	46	.257	.313	156	4
	210	772	97	231	34	8	13	91	.299	.415	320	11

JACK FOURNIER   Jacques Frank Fournier. Born 9/28/1892, Au Sable, MI. Died 9/5/1973, Tacoma, WA. A good—hit, no—field first baseman, hit .313 during fifteen year big league career. Led the NL in homers in 1924.

	G	AB	R	H	2B	3B	HR	RBI	BA	SA	TB	SB
1909 Port	17	28	2	7	2	1	0	——	.250	.393	11	2
1910 Sac	14	27	4	7	4	0	0	——	.259	.407	11	2
1917 LA	144	512	76	156	29	6	7	——	.305	.426	218	38
1918 LA	104	400	52	130	26	13	4	——	.325	.485	194	37
1919 LA	169	638	108	209	36	19	11	——	.328	.495	316	44
	448	1605	242	509	97	39	22	——	.317	.467	750	123

JOHNNY FREDERICK   John Henry Frederick. Born 1/26/1901, Denver, CO. Died 6/18/1977, Tigard, OR. Set NL rookie record with a league best 52 doubles in 1929. Hit .308 lifetime in six seasons, all with Brooklyn. Set the major league record with six pinch—hit home runs in one season.

	G	AB	R	H	2B	3B	HR	RBI	BA	SA	TB	SB
1923 SLC	160	585	111	192	37	10	16	82	.328	.508	297	4
1924 SLC	186	790	171	279	67	7	28	132	.353	.562	444	8
1925 SLC	162	640	120	198	40	7	10	79	.309	.441	282	3
1926 Hol	186	667	87	185	33	4	8	63	.277	.375	250	3
1927 Hol	180	623	95	190	40	3	9	93	.305	.422	263	9
1935 Sac	170	628	116	228	34	11	3	93	.363	.467	293	6
1936 Port	170	644	132	227	44	9	9	103	.352	.491	316	4
1937 Port	177	667	110	201	46	8	12	107	.301	.448	299	0
1938 Port	176	617	92	197	37	5	5	102	.319	.420	259	3

JOHNNY FREDERICK (cont.)

	G	AB	R	H	2B	3B	HR	RBI	BA	SA	TB	SB
1939 Port	150	479	86	156	27	4	4	85	.326	.424	203	1
1940 Port	135	415	55	127	17	0	2	43	.306	.361	150	5
	1852	6755	1175	2180	422	68	106	982	.323	.452	3056	46

GENE FREESE

Eugene Lewis Freese. Born 1/8/1934, Wheeling, WV. Regular third baseman for 1961 Reds, battled his brother for job with 1955 Pittsburgh Pirates. Hit nine pinch–hit home runs in major league career.

	G	AB	R	H	2B	3B	HR	RBI	BA	SA	TB	SB
1956 Hol	68	223	36	61	10	2	11	36	.274	.484	108	6
1963 SD	54	196	32	55	9	0	12	34	.281	.510	100	3
1967 Haw	132	475	65	130	28	0	15	74	.274	.427	203	3
1968 Tac–Hw	83	271	30	73	10	2	6	42	.269	.387	105	4
	337	1165	163	319	57	4	44	186	.274	.443	516	16

RAY FRENCH

Raymond Edward French. Born 1/9/1897, Alameda, CA. Died 4/3/1978, Alameda, CA. Holds career mark in minors for at bats and games played at shortstop. Twice led Pacific Coast League in fielding and holds the PCL lifetime records in chances, put outs and assists.

	G	AB	R	H	2B	3B	HR	RBI	BA	SA	TB	SB
1915 Port	3	9	1	2	0	0	0	0	.222	.222	2	0
1919 Sea	88	299	27	66	10	7	0	––	.221	.301	90	6
1921 Ver	163	616	75	166	49	9	2	69	.269	.388	239	6
1922 Ver	200	741	112	207	29	8	4	83	.279	.356	264	27
1923 Ver	24	88	11	27	6	2	1	19	.307	.455	40	2
1925 Sac	167	680	97	184	31	6	0	47	.271	.334	227	32
1926 Sac	172	625	80	183	32	3	1	42	.293	.358	224	29
1927 Sac	190	636	89	165	30	4	5	87	.259	.343	218	14
1928 Sac	191	814	143	234	55	1	9	77	.287	.391	318	9
1929 Sac	161	619	102	183	36	6	1	53	.296	.378	234	8
1930 Sac	200	848	143	224	48	9	3	72	.264	.353	299	28
1931 Sac	176	644	76	157	25	7	1	67	.244	.309	199	15
1932 Sac	178	661	107	170	25	7	0	71	.257	.316	209	30
1933 Sac	172	624	80	168	24	5	4	75	.269	.343	214	23
1934 Sac–O	74	241	21	55	7	4	0	19	.228	.290	70	9
	2159	8145	1164	2191	407	78	31	––	.269	.350	2847	238

BARNEY FRIBERG

Augustaf Bernhardt Friberg. Born 8/18/1899, Manchester, NH. Died 12/8/1958, Swampscott, MA. Fourteen year major leaguer, played every position during his career. Five–time .300 hitter, he had a lifetime big league average of .281 with Cubs, Phils and Red Sox.

	G	AB	R	H	2B	3B	HR	RBI	BA	SA	TB	SB
1933 Miss	69	254	29	69	13	2	2	30	.272	.362	92	1

AUGIE GALAN

August John Galan. Born 5/25/1912, Berkeley, CA. Died 12/28/1993, Fairfield, CA. First big leaguer to go full season without grounding into a double play. Also first to hit homers from both sides of the plate in same game. Six–time .300 hitter despite deformed right arm.

AUGIE GALAN (cont.)

	G	AB	R	H	2B	3B	HR	RBI	BA	SA	TB	SB
1932 SF	183	712	122	207	37	12	6	75	.291	.402	286	14
1933 SF	189	745	164	265	51	22	9	102	.356	.519	387	41
1950 Oak	147	447	96	126	25	3	13	72	.282	.438	196	10
1951 Oak	118	323	69	99	15	1	13	64	.307	.480	155	4
	637	2227	451	697	128	38	41	313	.313	.460	1024	69

ART GARIBALDI
Arthur Edward Garibaldi. Born 8/21/1907, San Francisco, CA. Died 10/20/1967, Sacramento, CA. Returning to the PCL after a year with the St. Louis Cardinals, infielder was named league's MVP in 1937.

	G	AB	R	H	2B	3B	HR	RBI	BA	SA	TB	SB
1931 SF	130	478	75	150	41	11	4	77	.314	.471	225	12
1932 SF	183	740	115	227	57	6	5	81	.307	.420	311	49
1933 SF	183	729	110	225	39	9	7	102	.309	.416	303	26
1934 SF	186	725	91	207	56	6	1	86	.286	.383	278	28
1935 SF	171	731	135	218	53	12	7	89	.298	.432	316	26
1937 Sac	150	568	121	186	45	3	18	106	.327	.512	291	23
1939 Sac	171	637	99	186	41	9	16	85	.292	.460	290	25
1940 Sac–SD	165	582	83	146	31	4	5	70	.251	.344	200	6
1941 SD	107	329	46	94	14	2	5	49	.286	.386	127	5
1942 SD	100	298	27	67	14	0	0	25	.225	.272	81	3
	1546	5817	902	1706	391	62	68	770	.293	.417	2425	203

DEBS GARMS
Debs C. Garms. Born 6/26/1908, Bangs, TX. Died 12/16/1984, Glen Rose, TX. Won NL batting title in 1940. The batter who first hit safely off Johnny Vander Meer after his back–to–back no–hitters.

	G	AB	R	H	2B	3B	HR	RBI	BA	SA	TB	SB
1942 Sac	160	606	86	190	27	13	7	96	.314	.436	264	15
1946 SD	142	466	48	126	14	3	1	44	.270	.320	149	16
	302	1072	134	316	41	16	8	140	.295	.385	413	31

JOE GEDEON
Elmer Joseph Gedeon. Born 12/6/1894, San Francisco, CA. Died 5/19/1941, San Francisco, CA. Second baseman for the Yanks, Senators and Browns, was tipped off to 1919 Series fix by "friend" Swede Risberg. Won $600 betting on Reds; lifetime ban for "guilty knowledge".

	G	AB	R	H	2B	3B	HR	RBI	BA	SA	TB	SB
1912 SF	118	411	40	108	--	--	--	--	.263	--	--	26
1914 LA	39	106	12	29	5	2	1	8	.274	.387	41	5
1915 SLC	190	739	133	234	67	11	19	--	.317	.514	380	25
	347	1256	185	371	--	--	--	--	.295	--	--	56

JOHN WESLEY GILL
John Wesley Gill. Born 3/27/1905, Nashville, TN. Died 12/26/1984, Nashville, TN. An outfielder for parts of six major league seasons, had over 3,100 hits and 1,700 RBI in 24 minor league seasons.

	G	AB	R	H	2B	3B	HR	RBI	BA	SA	TB	SB
1937 SF	84	238	35	65	12	5	2	35	.273	.391	93	1
1940 Port	154	530	81	171	33	3	16	87	.323	.487	258	6
1941 Port	127	421	58	119	20	4	12	56	.283	.435	183	0

JOHN WESLEY GILL (cont.)

	G	AB	R	H	2B	3B	HR	RBI	BA	SA	TB	SB
1942 Port	124	387	48	117	28	1	11	57	.302	.465	180	7
1943 Port	121	393	62	127	38	7	2	60	.323	.471	185	2
1944 Port	127	425	48	122	27	2	3	49	.287	.381	162	6
1945 P–Sea	99	241	30	64	8	1	2	32	.266	.332	80	5
	836	2635	362	785	166	23	48	376	.298	.433	1141	27

JOE GINSBERG   Myron Nathan Ginsberg. Born 10/11/1926, New York, NY. Well–liked and a bit of a practical joker, spent 13 years in the majors, mostly as back–up catcher. Last start was first home game of '62 Mets.

	G	AB	R	H	2B	3B	HR	RBI	BA	SA	TB	SB
1955 Sea	147	475	48	139	27	3	7	66	.293	.406	193	6

JOE GORDON   Joseph Lowell Gordon. Born 2/18/1915, Los Angeles, CA. Died 4/14/1978, Sacramento, CA. An excellent gymnast who performed in halftime shows at basketball games, second baseman had more than 100 RBI four times in majors and was AL MVP in 1942. Led PCL in home runs and RBI in 1951 while serving as the player–manager for Sacramento.

	G	AB	R	H	2B	3B	HR	RBI	BA	SA	TB	SB
1936 Oak	143	533	73	160	33	4	6	56	.300	.411	219	9
1951 Sac	148	485	97	145	24	3	43	136	.299	.627	304	2
1952 Sac	122	370	39	91	18	0	16	46	.246	.424	157	5
1957 SF	1	3	0	2	0	0	0	0	.667	.667	2	0
	414	1391	209	398	75	7	65	238	.286	.490	682	16

CHARLIE GRAHAM   Charles Henry Graham. Born 4/24/1878, Santa Clara, CA. Died 8/29/1948, San Francisco, CA. A catcher in early days of PCL, played briefly with Boston in AL before the 1906 earthquake brought him back to help out family in San Francisco. Later long–time owner and president of SF Seals; force behind PCL attempt to become major league.

	G	AB	R	H	2B	3B	HR	RBI	BA	SA	TB	SB
1903 Sac	173	583	86	158	– –	– –	– –	– –	.271	– –	– –	25
1904 Tac	– –	488	52	119	18	1	3	– –	.244	.303	148	22
1905 Tac	156	484	– –	98	15	1	0	– –	.202	.238	115	17
1909 Sac	101	302	22	69	– –	– –	– –	– –	.228	– –	– –	– –
1910 Sac	7	16	0	1	0	0	0	– –	.063	.063	1	0
	– –	1873	– –	445	– –	– –	– –	– –	.238	– –	– –	– –

JACK GRAHAM   John Bernard Graham. Born 12/24/1916, Minneapolis, MN. Slugging first baseman was Pacific Coast League MVP in 1948. Was on a pace to break Tony Lazzeri's league home run record of 60 when he was injured in beaning by Red Adams fastball. Son of "Peaches" Graham.

	G	AB	R	H	2B	3B	HR	RBI	BA	SA	TB	SB
1948 SD	138	473	111	141	23	6	48	136	.298	.677	320	6
1950 SD	185	663	98	194	23	8	33	136	.293	.501	332	8
1951 SF–SD	152	536	91	145	27	1	30	105	.271	.493	264	0
1952 SD	167	552	87	151	31	7	22	88	.274	.475	262	8
	642	2224	387	631	104	22	133	465	.284	.530	1178	22

JACK GRANEY   John Gladstone Graney. Born 6/10/1886, St. Thomas, Ontario, Canada. Died 4/20/1978, Louisiana, MO. Exiled to Portland after beaning manager Nap Lajoie in batting practice. Cleveland later changed him from pitcher to outfielder. After fourteen years with the Indians, moved into the broadcast booth, the first ex—ballplayer to do so.

	G	AB	R	H	2B	3B	HR	RBI	BA	SA	TB	SB
1908 Port	46	105	7	24	1	1	0	--	.229	.257	27	1
1909 Port	137	385	48	97	--	--	--	--	.252	--	--	--
	183	490	55	121	--	--	--	--	.247	--	--	--

GEORGE GRANTHAM   George Farley Grantham. Born 5/20/1900, Galena, KS. Died 3/16/1954, Kingman, AZ. Played both first and second base in thirteen year big league career. Hit over .300 eight straight years.

	G	AB	R	H	2B	3B	HR	RBI	BA	SA	TB	SB
1921 Port	77	269	32	82	15	2	1	30	.305	.387	104	7
1935 Sea	47	168	30	48	9	1	1	13	.286	.369	62	1
	124	437	62	130	24	3	2	43	.297	.380	166	8

ART GRIGGS   Arthur Carle Griggs. Born 12/10/1883, Topeka, KS. Died 12/19/1938, Los Angeles, CA. Long—time manager in minors, began his athletic career as college football star. Played parts of seven years in the majors as a first baseman. Led the PCL in home runs and hitting in 1918.

	G	AB	R	H	2B	3B	HR	RBI	BA	SA	TB	SB
1916 Ver	127	386	48	106	26	5	7	--	.275	.422	163	9
1917 Ver-P	186	684	88	213	44	6	10	--	.311	.437	299	31
1918 Sac	89	344	49	130	16	4	12	--	.378	.552	190	22
1919 Sac	148	545	55	157	34	8	9	--	.288	.429	234	7
1920 LA	94	373	54	114	17	7	2	--	.306	.405	151	1
1921 LA	177	678	105	199	45	14	10	119	.294	.445	302	6
1922 LA	175	639	95	216	49	5	20	129	.338	.524	335	10
1923 LA	153	495	84	163	28	5	21	88	.329	.533	264	1
1926 Sea	89	234	27	81	16	3	5	36	.346	.504	118	0
	1238	4378	605	1379	275	57	96	--	.315	.470	2056	87

MARV GUDAT   Marvin John Gudat. Born 8/27/1904, Weser, TX. Died 3/1/1954, Los Angeles, CA. Began career as a pitcher, winning 56 games in the minors. Hit .306 lifetime in minors and played two seasons in major leagues, including the 1932 season with pennant—winning Chicago Cubs.

	G	AB	R	H	2B	3B	HR	RBI	BA	SA	TB	SB
1933 LA	183	741	154	247	41	8	10	113	.333	.451	334	25
1934 LA	188	758	150	242	36	13	4	125	.319	.417	316	43
1935 LA	176	735	125	227	28	4	2	65	.309	.366	269	52
1936 LA	102	346	52	112	15	3	1	46	.324	.393	136	13
1937 LA	164	621	100	206	45	6	6	73	.332	.452	281	7
1938 LA-O	73	216	37	64	13	1	2	32	.296	.394	85	6
1939 Oak	153	516	80	167	30	12	1	71	.324	.434	224	10
1940 Oak	173	626	81	196	26	7	1	67	.313	.382	239	13
1941 Oak	174	640	74	186	41	2	2	65	.291	.370	237	9
1942 Oak	112	369	32	100	18	3	0	41	.271	.336	124	4

MARV GUDAT (cont.)

	G	AB	R	H	2B	3B	HR	RBI	BA	SA	TB	SB
1943 H–SD	128	407	47	104	14	1	0	26	.256	.295	120	8
1944 SD	113	369	38	104	14	2	0	31	.282	.331	122	8
1945 SD	102	238	21	63	11	2	0	25	.265	.328	78	3
	1841	6582	991	2018	332	64	29	780	.307	.390	2565	201

DON GUTTERIDGE

Donald Joseph Gutteridge. Born 6/19/1912, Pittsburg, KS. Second baseman on St. Louis Browns championship team of 1944, led PCL in steals in 1941. Later managed the Chicago White Sox.

	G	AB	R	H	2B	3B	HR	RBI	BA	SA	TB	SB
1941 Sac	171	680	113	210	31	13	13	88	.309	.450	306	46

DICK GYSELMAN

Richard Renald Gyselman. Born 4/6/1908, San Francisco, CA. Died 9/20/1990, Seattle, WA. "The Thin Man" holds minor league record for games played at third base. Finished fourteen hits shy of 3,000 for minor league career. Led the PCL in doubles in 1938.

	G	AB	R	H	2B	3B	HR	RBI	BA	SA	TB	SB
1931 Miss	5	10	0	2	0	0	0	0	.200	.200	2	0
1932 Miss	58	226	26	72	7	6	1	34	.319	.416	94	0
1935 Sea	169	611	84	185	32	10	9	100	.303	.432	264	18
1936 Sea	172	655	93	185	33	9	10	77	.282	.406	266	15
1937 Sea	167	666	104	198	35	12	11	53	.297	.435	290	8
1938 Sea	175	701	110	214	53	6	12	86	.305	.449	315	12
1939 Sea	136	476	49	141	15	4	2	68	.296	.357	170	11
1940 Sea	175	608	80	176	27	7	2	73	.289	.367	223	12
1941 Sea	168	560	66	143	30	4	3	55	.255	.339	190	15
1942 Sea	178	647	71	181	25	5	2	64	.280	.343	222	6
1943 Sea	149	518	63	154	22	2	0	49	.297	.347	180	14
1944 Sea	160	607	78	185	28	4	0	49	.305	.364	221	23
1945 SD	154	576	102	185	31	4	2	74	.321	.399	230	27
1946 SD	171	619	77	174	22	8	0	58	.281	.342	212	16
1947 SD–Sea	133	446	54	113	16	3	1	36	.253	.309	138	11
	2170	7926	1057	2308	376	84	55	876	.291	.381	3017	188

STAN HACK

Stanley Camfield Hack. Born 12/6/1909, Sacramento, CA. Died 12/15/1979, Dixon, IL. "Smiling Stan" was favorite of Cub fans. Broke into baseball by taking leave of absence from Sacramento bank to try out with the local PCL team and never went back. Spent sixteen years as the Cubs third baseman, led NL in steals twice. Scored 100 runs seven times.

	G	AB	R	H	2B	3B	HR	RBI	BA	SA	TB	SB
1931 Sac	164	660	128	232	36	13	2	37	.352	.455	300	20

SAMMY HALE

Samuel Douglas Hale. Born 9/10/1896, Glen Rose, TX. Died 9/6/1974, Wheeler, TX. Bought from Portland by Mack's Athletics for $75,000 in 1923 after leading the AL in pinch–hits as a rookie in 1920.

	G	AB	R	H	2B	3B	HR	RBI	BA	SA	TB	SB
1921 Port	136	530	80	181	39	9	9	78	.342	.500	265	14
1922 Port	152	525	91	188	39	6	10	93	.358	.512	269	10

SAMMY HALE (cont.)

	G	AB	R	H	2B	3B	HR	RBI	BA	SA	TB	SB
1930 Port	36	140	19	41	10	3	1	18	.293	.429	60	4
1931 Port	133	555	95	179	35	5	2	80	.323	.414	230	7
	457	1750	285	589	123	23	22	269	.337	.471	824	35

FRED HANEY
Fred Girard Haney. Born 4/25/1898, Albuquerque, NM. Died 11/9/1977, Hollywood, CA. A four-time PCL stolen base champion. Already an experienced manager in minors and majors, was broadcaster for Hollywood Stars when brought out of the booth to run team. Later he managed Milwaukee to a World Series title. GM of expansion LA Angels.

	G	AB	R	H	2B	3B	HR	RBI	BA	SA	TB	SB
1919 LA	43	103	19	26	2	0	0	– –	.252	.272	28	7
1920 LA	31	90	8	13	0	1	0	– –	.144	.167	15	2
1929 LA	150	586	112	171	35	4	1	51	.292	.370	217	56
1930 LA	180	673	127	210	37	5	7	80	.312	.413	278	52
1931 LA	85	335	73	101	11	3	3	37	.301	.379	127	24
1932 LA	149	617	117	185	37	4	6	62	.300	.402	248	29
1933 Hol	176	710	134	228	05	7	2	85	.317	.394	283	63
1934 Hol	179	702	124	215	27	5	1	76	.306	.363	255	71
	993	3825	714	1149	184	29	20	– –	.300	.379	1451	304

TRUCK HANNAH
James Harrison Hannah. Born 6/5/1891, Larimore, ND. Died 4/27/1982, Fountain Valley, CA. A tough, sarcastic catcher for the New York Yankees from 1918–1920. Played behind the plate in PCL for twenty-one seasons. Manager for Los Angeles 1937–1939.

	G	AB	R	H	2B	3B	HR	RBI	BA	SA	TB	SB
1914 Sac	137	373	31	102	31	2	0	44	.273	.367	137	7
1915 SLC	138	436	59	118	28	1	3	– –	.271	.360	157	6
1916 SLC	152	469	68	122	23	1	9	– –	.260	.371	174	9
1917 SLC	187	569	85	166	39	2	3	– –	.292	.383	218	9
1921 Ver	140	452	67	138	29	0	5	49	.305	.403	182	4
1922 Ver	129	399	41	111	32	0	4	53	.278	.388	155	5
1923 Ver	119	370	49	128	23	0	6	55	.346	.457	169	1
1924 Ver	124	349	57	111	36	0	4	70	.318	.456	159	2
1925 Ver–P	132	350	36	99	25	2	3	45	.283	.391	137	5
1926 LA	131	389	38	92	12	1	4	55	.237	.303	118	3
1927 LA	114	317	36	84	13	0	7	37	.265	.372	118	2
1928 LA	97	262	18	71	8	0	3	27	.271	.336	88	0
1929 LA	67	136	11	29	5	0	1	15	.213	.272	37	1
1930 LA	125	329	40	88	13	0	4	48	.267	.343	113	1
1931 LA	71	204	19	54	3	0	0	28	.265	.279	57	0
1932 LA	5	5	0	0	0	0	0	0	.000	.000	0	0
1933 LA	11	13	1	5	1	0	0	3	.385	.462	6	0
1934 LA	20	50	5	11	1	0	0	9	.220	.240	12	0
1935 LA	16	33	0	4	0	0	0	1	.121	.121	4	0
1936 LA	1	0	0	0	0	0	0	0	– –	– –	0	0
1937 LA	1	1	0	1	0	0	0	0	1.000	1.000	1	0
	1917	5506	661	1534	322	9	56	– –	.279	.371	2042	55

GEORGE HARPER   George Washington Harper. Born 6/24/1892, Arlington, KY. Died 8/18/1978, Magnolia, AR. Outfielder in major leagues for eleven seasons, hit three home runs in one game September 20,1928. Played in the minor leagues well into his mid–40's.

	G	AB	R	H	2B	3B	HR	RBI	BA	SA	TB	SB
1914 LA	70	132	19	38	6	5	0	21	.288	.409	54	4
1915 LA	67	192	23	55	9	3	2	– –	.286	.396	76	7
1919 SF–Sea	70	264	33	71	7	1	2	– –	.269	.326	86	12
1930 LA	160	546	104	168	40	1	8	97	.308	.429	234	9
1931 LA–O	100	220	31	59	10	1	3	33	.268	.364	80	2
	467	1354	210	391	72	11	15	– –	.289	.391	530	34

JOE HARRIS   Joseph Harris. Born 5/20/1891, Coulters, PA. Died 12/10/1959, Plum Borough, PA. Eight–time .300 hitter in the majors, had a lifetime average of .318. Hit three home runs in the 1925 World Series.

	G	AB	R	H	2B	3B	HR	RBI	BA	SA	TB	SB
1929 Sac	54	190	37	65	16	1	6	42	.342	.532	101	0

SPENCER HARRIS   Anthony Spencer Harris. Born 8/12/1900, Duluth, MN. Died 7/3/1982, Minneapolis, MN. Career minor league leader in hits (3,617), doubles (743), and total bases (5,434).

	G	AB	R	H	2B	3B	HR	RBI	BA	SA	TB	SB
1938 SD	163	545	86	164	39	4	7	92	.301	.426	232	4
1939 Hol	138	383	61	130	32	7	6	58	.339	.507	194	1
1940 Sea	111	277	52	75	17	3	2	34	.271	.375	104	2
1941 Sea	133	414	74	125	29	1	4	53	.302	.406	168	6
1942 Sea	96	261	24	72	8	3	2	26	.276	.352	92	0
1943 Port	117	366	59	101	27	2	6	44	.276	.410	150	1
1944 Port	124	373	54	102	26	5	5	45	.273	.410	153	1
1945 P–H	114	316	43	79	17	2	3	46	.250	.345	109	4
	996	2935	453	848	195	27	35	398	.289	.410	1202	19

JEFF HEATH   John Geoffrey Heath. Born 4/1/1915, Ft. William, Ontario, Canada. Died 12/9/1975, Seattle, WA. A two–time AL All–Star outfielder, in majors for fourteen years, mostly for Cleveland. Twice led AL in triples. A broken leg in 1948 cost him his only chance to play in a World Series.

	G	AB	R	H	2B	3B	HR	RBI	BA	SA	TB	SB
1950 Sea	57	155	14	38	9	1	2	19	.245	.355	55	0

MICKEY HEATH   Minor Wilson Heath. Born 10/30/1903, Toledo, OH. Died 7/30/1986, Dallas, TX. Had a PCL record twelve straight hits in 1930. Illegally "hidden" by Tigers at Hollywood; after appealing to commissioner Landis he was traded to Cincinnati. Career hampered by rheumatic fever.

	G	AB	R	H	2B	3B	HR	RBI	BA	SA	TB	SB
1927 Hol	106	330	56	93	24	3	9	51	.282	.455	150	7
1928 Hol	191	662	118	203	38	12	19	109	.307	.486	322	10
1929 Hol	201	680	149	237	44	5	38	156	.349	.596	405	20
1930 Hol	174	546	146	177	16	3	37	136	.324	.568	310	19
	672	2218	469	710	122	23	103	452	.320	.535	1187	56

HARRY HEILMANN   Harry Edwin Heilmann. Born 8/3/1894, San Francisco, CA. Died 7/9/1951, Detroit, MI. A four—time AL batting champ. each time hitting over .390. Bought by Tigers from the Northwest League for $1,500 and was farmed out to San Francisco. Elected to Hall of Fame in 1952. Also served as Detroit Tigers broadcaster for seventeen years.

	G	AB	R	H	2B	3B	HR	RBI	BA	SA	TB	SB
1915 SF	98	371	57	135	23	4	12	— —	.364	.544	202	26

HEINE HEITMULLER   William Frederick Heitmuller. Born 1883, San Francisco, CA. Died 10/8/1912, Los Angeles, CA. A football and baseball star at the University of California. Won the PCL batting championship in in 1912, two weeks after succumbing to a fatal bout of typhoid fever.

	G	AB	R	H	2B	3B	HR	RBI	BA	SA	TB	SB
1906 Sea—O	153	542	56	166	25	14	2	— —	.306	.415	225	7
1907 Oak	199	763	94	200	44	1	4	— —	.262	.338	258	39
1908 Oak	205	791	104	225	39	1	12	— —	.284	.382	302	39
1911 LA	78	300	29	103	— — — —		— —	— —	.343	— —	— —	18
1912 LA	151	556	68	186	— — — —		15	— —	.335	— —	— —	27
	786	2952	351	880	— — — —		— —	— —	.298	— —	— —	130

ROLLIE HEMSLEY   Ralston Burdette Hemsley. Born 6/24/1907, Syracuse, OH. Died 7/31/1972, Washington, D.C. Caught in majors nineteen years, highlighted by Bob Feller's Opening Day no—hitter in 1940. After winning battle with the bottle was a two—time Minor League Manager of the Year.

	G	AB	R	H	2B	3B	HR	RBI	BA	SA	TB	SB
1947 Sea	88	240	27	63	11	2	3	31	.263	.363	87	1
1948 Sea	82	205	24	55	10	0	0	18	.268	.317	65	2
	170	445	51	118	21	2	3	49	.265	.342	152	3

BABE HERMAN   Floyd Caves Herman. Born 6/26/1903, Buffalo, NY. Died 11/27/1987, Glendale, CA. One of Brooklyn's "Daffiness Boys", holds Dodger season records for average, hits, total bases, and runs. Had .324 lifetime average in thirteen years. Hit for cycle three times in majors.

	G	AB	R	H	2B	3B	HR	RBI	BA	SA	TB	SB
1925 Sea	167	651	115	206	52	13	15	131	.316	.505	329	22
1939 Hol	90	350	69	111	36	5	13	71	.317	.560	196	2
1940 Hol	148	469	62	144	45	7	9	80	.307	.490	230	0
1941 Hol	110	272	41	94	16	1	11	63	.346	.533	145	2
1942 Hol	85	149	18	48	5	0	5	42	.322	.456	68	0
1943 Hol	81	147	15	52	8	1	4	22	.354	.503	74	1
1944 Hol	78	107	8	37	8	1	0	23	.346	.439	47	0
	759	2145	328	692	170	28	57	432	.323	.508	1089	27

BILLY HERMAN   William Jennings Herman. Born 7/7/1909, New Albany, IN. Died 9/5/1992, West Palm Beach, FL. Considered to be best hit and run man in history, was a ten—time All—Star. Hit .304 lifetime, with eight seasons over .300. Elected to the Hall of Fame in 1975.

	G	AB	R	H	2B	3B	HR	RBI	BA	SA	TB	SB
1950 Oak	71	202	32	62	8	0	4	29	.307	.406	82	2

GENE HERMANSKI   Eugene Victor Hermanski. Born 5/11/1920, Pittsfield, MA. Outfielder in major leagues for nine years with the Dodgers, Chicago Cubs and the Pirates. Hit three homers in a game for Brooklyn in 1948.

	G	AB	R	H	2B	3B	HR	RBI	BA	SA	TB	SB
1954 Oak	104	322	49	87	9	0	11	48	.270	.401	129	3

WILLARD HERSHBERGER   Willard Mc Kee Hershberger. Born 5/28/1910, Lemon Cove, CA. Died 8/3/1940, Boston, MA. Played at the same high school that graduated Walter Johnson and Arky Vaughan; was excellent catcher and contact hitter remembered today as major league baseball's only in−season suicide.

	G	AB	R	H	2B	3B	HR	RBI	BA	SA	TB	SB
1934 Hol	114	332	41	102	18	1	3	46	.307	.395	131	7
1936 Oak	89	259	25	68	6	4	1	40	.263	.328	85	5
	203	591	66	170	24	5	4	86	.288	.365	216	12

PINKY HIGGINS   Michael Franklin Higgins. Born 5/27/1909, Red Oak, TX. Died 3/21/1969, Dallas, TX. Three−time All−Star third baseman, set big league mark with twelve consecutive base hits in 1938. A four−time .300 hitter, later managed the Boston Red Sox for eight seasons.

	G	AB	R	H	2B	3B	HR	RBI	BA	SA	TB	SB
1932 Port	189	721	145	235	51	5	33	132	.326	.548	395	21

CHARLIE HIGH   Charles Edwin High. Born 12/1/1898, Ava, IL. Died 9/11/1960, Oak Grove, OR. One of three brothers to play in big leagues, the left−handed hitting outfielder briefly played for the Philadelphia A's.

	G	AB	R	H	2B	3B	HR	RBI	BA	SA	TB	SB
1922 Port	178	649	103	205	35	5	24	107	.316	.496	322	12
1923 Port	156	558	98	189	34	5	20	94	.339	.525	293	8
1924 Port	165	612	94	197	31	7	20	139	.322	.493	302	4
1925 Port	162	608	118	205	36	3	20	107	.337	.505	307	9
1932 Sea	25	88	8	21	1	1	0	8	.239	.273	24	0
	686	2515	421	817	137	21	84	455	.325	.496	1248	33

GEORGE HILDEBRAND   George Albert Hildebrand. Born 9/6/1878, San Francisco, CA. Died 5/30/1960, Woodland Hills, CA. Credited as inventor of the spitball, later spent twenty−three seasons as major league umpire. Involved in major controversy as home plate ump in calling Game Two of the 1922 World Series after ten innings because of "darkness".

	G	AB	R	H	2B	3B	HR	RBI	BA	SA	TB	SB
1903 Sac	185	702	129	208	−−	−−	−−	−−	.296	−−	−−	47
1904 SF	−−	835	134	237	42	7	4	−−	.284	.365	305	40
1905 SF	225	822	−−	217	39	11	2	−−	.264	.345	284	73
1906 SF	149	526	84	137	26	7	0	−−	.260	.337	177	18
1907 SF	186	648	73	155	27	3	1	−−	.239	.295	191	59
1908 SF	174	621	91	148	19	3	0	−−	.238	.279	173	37
1909 Sac	8	19	0	1	−−	−−	−−	−−	.053	−−	−−	0
	−−	4173	−−	1103	−−	−−	−−	−−	.264	.327	−−	274

MYRIL HOAG Myril Oliver Hoag. Born 3/9/1908, Davis, CA. Died 7/28/1971, High Springs, FL. Role as late inning defensive replacement for Bambino earned him the nickname "Babe Ruth's Caddie". As a pitcher—outfielder he won both the Florida State League batting and ERA titles in 1947.

	G	AB	R	H	2B	3B	HR	RBI	BA	SA	TB	SB
1926 Sac	2	3	0	1	0	0	0	2	.333	.333	1	0
1927 Sac	4	16	0	3	1	0	0	0	.188	.250	4	0
1929 Sac	116	414	47	116	25	2	6	54	.280	.394	163	5
1930 Sac	188	725	148	244	57	9	17	121	.337	.510	370	19
	310	1158	195	364	83	11	23	177	.314	.465	538	24

SHANTY HOGAN James Francis Hogan. Born 3/21/1906, Somerville, MA. Died 4/7/1967 Boston, MA. Once traded for Rogers Hornsby, had thirteen seasons in majors, six times hitting .300 or better. The catcher was a big target at 6—1 and 240 pounds and was also an excellent fielder.

	G	AB	R	H	2B	3B	HR	RBI	BA	SA	TB	SB
1938 SD	109	331	27	85	11	0	1	42	.257	.299	99	1

BROOKS HOLDER Richard Brooks Holder. Born 11/2/1915, Rising Star, TX. Outfielder played all but eighty—eight games of pro career in the PCL. Tied Truck Eagan's Pacific Coast League season mark for triples in 1939.

	G	AB	R	H	2B	3B	HR	RBI	BA	SA	TB	SB
1935 SF	18	48	9	12	0	0	0	4	.250	.250	12	4
1936 SF	152	581	110	100	27	11	1	50	.289	.379	220	17
1937 SF	135	486	87	155	27	8	2	65	.319	.420	204	10
1938 SF	172	585	122	193	26	8	2	95	.330	.412	241	11
1939 SF	173	636	115	200	34	24	5	87	.314	.467	297	14
1940 SF	152	521	63	143	19	7	1	60	.274	.344	179	6
1941 SF	170	624	119	175	30	10	2	53	.280	.370	231	11
1942 SF	179	652	113	194	36	9	6	51	.298	.408	266	4
1943 Hol	149	543	83	148	27	5	6	62	.273	.374	203	12
1944 Hol	161	583	119	163	28	8	6	54	.280	.386	225	21
1945 Hol	109	312	54	80	16	2	5	41	.256	.369	115	13
1946 Oak	155	477	88	135	15	3	13	59	.283	.409	195	14
1947 Oak	172	599	137	186	40	4	16	78	.311	.471	282	9
1948 Oak	148	482	99	143	15	3	10	57	.297	.402	194	11
1949 SF	76	237	45	74	17	0	5	36	.312	.447	106	0
1950 SF	158	511	113	151	26	1	11	77	.295	.415	212	2
1951 Port	125	377	65	115	20	1	6	54	.305	.411	155	0
	2404	8254	1541	2435	403	104	97	983	.295	.404	3337	159

DUTCH HOLLAND Robert Clyde Holland. Born 10/12/1903, Middlesex, NC. Died 6/16/1967, Lumberton, NC. Outfielder led the PCL in doubles and in total bases in 1930. Played briefly in majors with Braves and Indians.

	G	AB	R	H	2B	3B	HR	RBI	BA	SA	TB	SB
1930 Sea	200	792	130	263	72	11	20	141	.332	.527	417	16
1931 Sea	180	681	122	210	49	9	19	131	.308	.490	334	17
1932 Sea	130	519	101	174	36	2	15	76	.335	.499	259	15
	510	1992	353	647	157	22	54	348	.325	.507	1010	48

CHARLIE HOLLOCHER   Charles Jacob Hollocher. Born 6/11/1896, St. Louis, MO. Died 8/14/1940, St. Louis, MO. Led NL in hits and at–bats as a rookie shortstop for Cubs in 1918. Excellent fielder, batted .304 in major league career. Hampered by illness, committed suicide at age 44.

	G	AB	R	H	2B	3B	HR	RBI	BA	SA	TB	SB
1916 Port	14	21	1	4	1	0	0	– –	.190	.238	5	0
1917 Port	200	813	135	224	33	9	1	– –	.276	.342	278	33
	214	834	136	228	34	9	1	– –	.273	.339	283	33

WALLY HOOD   Wallace James Hood, Sr. Born 2/9/1895, Whittier, CA. Died 5/2/1965, Hollywood, CA. One of PCL's top sluggers, he and Cedric Durst hit HR on consecutive pitches vs SF in 1924. Later a PCL umpire.

	G	AB	R	H	2B	3B	HR	RBI	BA	SA	TB	SB
1920 SLC	111	398	49	122	24	8	1	– –	.307	.415	165	16
1922 Sea	134	507	86	160	26	11	11	71	.316	.475	241	25
1923 LA	193	745	108	253	59	10	21	128	.340	.530	395	19
1924 LA	195	757	135	256	48	17	22	184	.338	.534	404	0
1925 LA	195	758	149	248	63	13	27	157	.327	.551	418	31
1926 LA	170	502	81	151	41	2	13	82	.301	.468	235	9
1927 LA	174	600	85	179	35	3	17	116	.298	.452	271	7
1928 LA	167	599	98	174	43	2	20	106	.290	.469	281	9
1929 Sea	24	67	6	13	4	0	0	8	.194	.254	17	0
1930 Sac	22	63	9	15	2	0	0	7	.238	.270	17	1
	1385	4996	806	1571	345	66	132	– –	.314	.489	2444	117

HARRY HOOPER   Harry Bartholomew Hooper. Born 8/24/1887, Santa Clara County, CA. Died 12/18/1974, Santa Cruz, CA. Part of Boston Red Sox "Million Dollar Outfield", made barehanded catch to aid Boston's win in 1912 Series vs. Giants. Turned down career as a civil engineer to play baseball. Coached Princeton in 1930's. Elected to Hall of Fame in 1971.

	G	AB	R	H	2B	3B	HR	RBI	BA	SA	TB	SB
1927 Miss	78	218	35	62	9	0	1	19	.284	.339	74	4

DUMMY HOY   William Ellsworth Hoy. Born 5/23/1862, Houckstown, OH. Died 12/15/1961, Cincinnati, OH. According to baseball legend, this deaf mute outfielder was the reason umpires developed hand signals. Led NL in steals in 1888, AL in runs in 1901. Once tossed out three baserunners at home in one game. At age 99 threw out first ball at 1961 World Series.

	G	AB	R	H	2B	3B	HR	RBI	BA	SA	TB	SB
1903 LA	211	806	156	210	– –	– –	– –	– –	.261	– –	– –	46

FUZZY HUFFT   Irwin V. Hufft. Born 8/2/1903, Lebanon, MO. Slugging outfielder with gaudy numbers, yet amazingly never led the Pacific Coast League in any major offensive category.

	G	AB	R	H	2B	3B	HR	RBI	BA	SA	TB	SB
1926 Sea	165	550	86	171	23	8	16	94	.311	.469	258	8
1927 Sea	147	496	85	176	37	5	19	138	.355	.565	280	10
1928 Sea–M	160	561	108	208	46	8	30	143	.371	.642	360	7
1929 Miss	194	754	140	286	57	7	39	187	.379	.629	474	7

FUZZY HUFFT (cont.)

	G	AB	R	H	2B	3B	HR	RBI	BA	SA	TB	SB
1930 Miss	187	721	140	257	51	6	37	178	.356	.598	431	8
1931 M—O	176	645	119	221	49	9	14	92	.343	.512	330	10
1932 Oak	125	449	57	127	31	3	11	70	.283	.439	197	5
	1154	4176	735	1446	294	46	166	902	.346	.558	2330	55

MIKE HUNT   Arthur Leland Hunt. Born 10/12/1907, Santa Clara, CA. Led Pacific Coast League in home runs and RBI 1936 and 1937. Never played in the majors, although he did go to spring training with Braves in 1933.

	G	AB	R	H	2B	3B	HR	RBI	BA	SA	TB	SB
1930 SF	19	70	14	21	2	3	0	7	.300	.414	29	0
1931 SF	76	228	34	69	14	1	5	43	.303	.439	100	1
1932 SF	151	529	84	167	26	8	14	84	.316	.474	251	2
1933 M—SF	60	168	28	51	5	0	6	42	.304	.440	74	3
1934 Sea	175	644	125	223	42	5	30	128	.346	.567	365	8
1935 Sea	163	639	122	211	45	6	25	112	.330	.537	343	12
1936 Sea	169	670	116	212	50	6	30	135	.316	.543	364	6
1937 Sea	172	647	129	202	43	3	39	131	.312	.569	368	2
1938 Sea	157	539	98	157	26	6	13	77	.291	.434	234	1
1939 Sea	121	371	57	96	26	3	15	76	.259	.466	173	3
	1263	4505	807	1409	279	41	177	835	.313	.511	2301	38

DON HURST   Frank O'Donnell Hurst. Born 8/12/1905, Maysville, KY. Died 12/6/1952, Los Angeles, CA. Lefty—hitting first baseman, thrived in Baker Bowl for Phillies. Led NL with 143 RBI in 1932; in minors three years later.

	G	AB	R	H	2B	3B	HR	RBI	BA	SA	TB	SB
1936 LA	155	558	95	169	27	6	19	113	.303	.475	265	2
1937 LA	85	284	40	77	13	0	10	50	.271	.423	120	2
	240	842	135	246	40	6	29	163	.292	.457	385	4

MONTE IRVIN   Monford Merrill Irvin. Born 2/25/1919, Columbus, AL. A Negro League star, was first black player signed by the New York Giants. Great all—around athlete, if not for World War II, might have been chosen to break color line. Led NL in RBI 1951. Elected to Hall of Fame in 1973. A severe back injury ended his career four games into the 1957 season.

	G	AB	R	H	2B	3B	HR	RBI	BA	SA	TB	SB
1957 LA	4	10	1	3	0	0	1	2	.300	.600	6	0

CHARLIE IRWIN   Charles E. Irwin. Born 2/15/1869, Sheffield, IL. Died 9/21/1925, Chicago, IL. Ten—year major league third baseman with Cubs Reds and Dodgers. Was considered one of the best fielders of his time.

	G	AB	R	H	2B	3B	HR	RBI	BA	SA	TB	SB
1903 SF	209	773	135	235	——	——	——	——	.304	——	——	38
1904 SF	——	782	91	217	39	3	1	——	.277	.339	265	38
1905 SF	226	785	——	209	26	2	0	——	.266	.304	239	45
1906 SF	167	620	72	143	27	2	0	——	.231	.281	174	21
1907 SF	163	580	80	139	23	3	1	——	.240	.295	171	28
	——	3540	——	943	——	——	——	——	.266	.307	——	170

RANDY JACKSON   Ransom Joseph Jackson, Jr. Born 2/10/1926, Little Rock, AR. Ten year third baseman in majors, twice played in Cotton Bowl. Completed a 50–yard pass in the 1946 game on a Statue of Liberty play.

	G	AB	R	H	2B	3B	HR	RBI	BA	SA	TB	SB
1949 LA	14	44	6	14	3	0	2	6	.318	.523	23	0

RAY JACOBS   Raymond F. Jacobs. Born 1/2/1902, Salt Lake City, UT. Died 4/4/1952, Los Angeles, CA. A veteran Pacific Coast League infielder, played mostly first base. Played briefly for the Chicago Cubs in 1928.

	G	AB	R	H	2B	3B	HR	RBI	BA	SA	TB	SB
1923 LA	15	45	6	16	3	0	1	8	.356	.489	22	1
1924 LA	147	517	73	143	44	0	9	76	.277	.414	214	2
1925 LA	150	539	116	167	53	3	13	75	.310	.492	265	18
1926 LA	178	580	92	148	39	6	21	102	.255	.452	262	13
1927 LA	97	359	70	116	25	7	13	64	.323	.540	194	9
1928 LA	36	111	8	23	5	0	0	11	.207	.252	28	1
1929 LA	178	591	84	196	40	8	20	118	.332	.528	312	11
1930 LA	196	710	128	216	41	8	20	130	.304	.469	333	11
1931 LA	124	386	78	115	29	3	18	73	.298	.528	204	5
1932 Port	40	149	15	43	5	1	5	34	.289	.436	65	2
1933 Hol	159	564	107	160	35	0	36	125	.284	.537	303	9
1934 Hol	178	597	93	172	28	1	24	112	.288	.459	274	9
1935 Hol	115	402	62	119	17	3	13	69	.296	.450	181	11
1936 SD	106	332	42	93	23	1	5	46	.280	.401	133	8
	1719	5882	974	1727	387	41	198	1043	.294	.474	2790	110

TED JENNINGS   Theodore Michael Jennings. Born 11/23/1916, San Francisco, CA. Died 2/24/1994, Redwood City, CA. Steady third baseman for Seals and Solons. Set a Pacific Coast League record, scoring six runs in a game against Portland on September 14, 1939.

	G	AB	R	H	2B	3B	HR	RBI	BA	SA	TB	SB
1937 SF	109	367	73	106	20	8	2	39	.289	.403	148	9
1938 SF	130	488	70	138	26	12	5	65	.283	.416	203	7
1939 SF	115	378	69	99	16	9	4	44	.262	.384	145	4
1940 SF	175	680	108	217	37	18	13	89	.319	.484	329	12
1941 SF	66	273	50	89	13	8	5	43	.326	.487	133	5
1942 SF	122	376	45	110	23	3	3	60	.293	.394	148	1
1946 SF	136	495	83	150	21	5	3	53	.303	.384	190	11
1947 SF	87	151	24	46	8	2	0	21	.305	.384	58	6
1948 Sac	126	315	38	90	9	3	6	38	.286	.390	123	8
	1066	3523	560	1045	173	68	41	452	.297	.419	1477	63

JACKIE JENSEN   Jack Eugene Jensen. Born 3/9/1927, San Francisco, CA. Died 7/14/1982, Charlottesville, VA. An All–American football player; three–time American League All–Star and RBI champ. A great outfielder, lost out to Mickey Mantle in bid for Yankee centerfield job. The AL MVP in 1958, his career was cut short due to his fear of flying.

	G	AB	R	H	2B	3B	HR	RBI	BA	SA	TB	SB
1949 Oak	125	467	63	122	21	7	9	77	.261	.394	184	5

BOB JOHNSON   Robert Lee Johnson. Born 11/26/1906, Pryor, OK. Died 7/6/1982, Tacoma, WA. Half Cherokee, this outfielder had at least twenty home runs and ninety RBI in each of his first nine major league seasons. Always battling Connie Mack over salary, played ten years with Athletics as a regular and was an American League All–Star seven times.

	G	AB	R	H	2B	3B	HR	RBI	BA	SA	TB	SB
1929 Port	81	264	42	67	16	3	5	27	.254	.394	104	6
1930 Port	157	501	91	133	25	3	21	93	.265	.453	227	5
1931 Port	141	504	108	170	37	5	22	94	.337	.562	283	12
1932 Port	149	545	105	180	43	1	29	111	.330	.572	312	9
1947 Sea	130	342	44	101	28	1	7	50	.295	.444	152	6
1948 Sea	59	145	17	41	7	0	5	23	.283	.434	63	1
	717	2301	407	692	156	13	89	398	.301	.496	1141	39

ROY JOHNSON   Roy Cleveland Johnson. Born 2/23/1903, Pryor, OK. Died 9/11/1973, Tacoma, WA. The brother of Bob Johnson, set AL record of thirty–one errors in the outfield as a rookie with Detroit in 1929. A four-time .300 hitter in majors, led AL in doubles in 1929 and in triples in 1931.

	G	AB	R	H	2B	3B	HR	RBI	BA	SA	TB	SB
1926 SF	25	77	15	20	7	1	1	11	.260	.416	32	2
1927 SF	109	327	57	100	17	7	4	24	.306	.437	143	6
1928 SF	170	650	142	234	49	16	22	76	.360	.586	381	29
1944 Sea	115	369	38	96	14	5	2	35	.260	.341	126	12
1045 Sca	09	214	29	58	15	0	1	29	.271	.355	76	11
	488	1637	281	508	102	29	30	175	.310	.463	758	60

DOC JOHNSTON   Wheeler Roger Johnston. Born 9/9/1887, Cleveland, TN. Died 2/17/1961, Chattanooga, TN. Eleven year big league first baseman, in 1920 he and brother Jimmy became first siblings to play against each other in a World Series. A talkative, popular player, dubbed "The Human Telescope" for his ability to reach for throws from his fellow infielders.

	G	AB	R	H	2B	3B	HR	RBI	BA	SA	TB	SB
1923 Sea	156	584	82	180	30	7	3	73	.308	.399	233	21

JIMMY JOHNSTON   James Harle Johnston. Born 12/10/1889, Cleveland, TN. Died 2/14/1967, Chattanooga, TN. Shy and soft–spoken, not like his brother. Outfielder set PCL single–season record for steals in 1913. Was given a gold watch from the San Francisco fans in appreciation of his feat.

	G	AB	R	H	2B	3B	HR	RBI	BA	SA	TB	SB
1912 SF	16	30	2	8	––	––	––	––	.267	––	––	0
1913 SF	201	749	111	228	30	4	2	––	.304	.363	272	124
1915 Oak	206	788	140	274	52	8	11	––	.348	.476	375	82
	423	1567	253	510	82	12	13	––	.325	.418	655	206

SMEAD JOLLEY   Smead Powell Jolley. Born 1/14/1902, Wesson, AR. Died 11/17/1991, Alameda, CA. Won six minor league batting titles, with the final two coming in his last seasons. Won PCL Triple Crown in 1928. Began career as a pitcher, ended career with .366 batting average in the minors. Legendary lack of fielding prowess shortened big league career.

SMEAD JOLLEY (cont.)

	G	AB	R	H	2B	3B	HR	RBI	BA	SA	TB	SB
1925 SF	38	132	31	59	16	1	12	43	.447	.856	113	1
1926 SF	174	575	79	199	45	3	25	132	.346	.565	325	3
1927 SF	168	625	106	248	33	7	33	163	.397	.630	394	3
1928 SF	191	765	143	309	52	10	45	188	.404	.675	516	9
1929 SF	200	812	172	314	65	10	35	159	.387	.621	504	6
1934 Hol	171	631	117	227	49	7	23	133	.360	.569	359	7
1935 Hol	159	599	113	223	44	3	29	128	.372	.601	360	0
1938 H–O	119	414	48	145	25	9	6	54	.350	.498	206	2
1939 Oak	140	499	60	154	39	2	9	76	.309	.449	224	4
	1360	5052	869	1878	368	52	217	1076	.372	.594	3001	35

EDDIE JOOST   Edwin David Joost. Born 6/5/1916, San Francisco, CA. Two–time AL All–Star shortstop in 17 year major league career, helped set double play records and drew at least 100 walks six straight seasons.

	G	AB	R	H	2B	3B	HR	RBI	BA	SA	TB	SB
1933 Miss	25	64	8	16	0	1	0	1	.250	.281	18	0
1934 Miss	7	14	0	2	0	0	0	0	.143	.143	2	0
1935 Miss	147	533	72	153	32	6	1	83	.287	.375	200	8
1936 Miss	167	668	120	191	40	7	6	72	.286	.394	263	36
1956 SF	6	12	0	2	0	0	0	0	.167	.167	2	0
	352	1291	200	364	72	14	7	156	.282	.376	485	44

WALT JUDNICH   Walter Franklin Judnich. Born 1/24/1917, San Francisco, CA. Died 7/12/1971, Glendale, CA. Compared to Joe DiMaggio when in the Yankees farm system, twice hit .300 for the St. Louis Browns.

	G	AB	R	H	2B	3B	HR	RBI	BA	SA	TB	SB
1937 Oak	175	651	107	206	42	14	11	81	.316	.475	309	21
1949 SF	116	379	75	102	15	2	18	63	.269	.462	175	0
1950 Sea	166	505	91	144	22	1	19	84	.285	.446	225	3
1951 Sea	147	517	93	170	35	8	21	102	.329	.549	284	4
1952 Sea	177	668	93	192	41	5	15	105	.287	.431	288	4
1953 Sea	163	583	81	174	26	4	16	101	.298	.439	256	0
1954 Port	156	547	70	149	26	2	18	81	.272	.426	233	1
1955 P–SF	137	451	67	126	30	2	9	60	.279	.415	187	2
	1237	4301	677	1263	237	38	127	677	.294	.455	1957	35

WILLIE KAMM   William Edward Kamm. Born 2/2/1900, San Francisco, CA. Died 12/21/1988, Belmont, CA. Purchased from the San Francisco Seals by Chicago White Sox for $100,000, top fielder at third base for 13 years.

	G	AB	R	H	2B	3B	HR	RBI	BA	SA	TB	SB
1918 Sac	4	9	0	2	0	0	0	0	.222	.222	2	0
1919 SF	136	485	58	114	21	2	3	––	.235	.305	148	13
1920 SF	182	596	63	141	39	3	7	––	.237	.347	207	24
1921 SF	168	598	101	172	38	9	13	105	.288	.446	267	21
1922 SF	170	650	137	222	56	9	20	124	.342	.548	356	35
1936 Miss	9	19	2	6	––	––	––	––	.316	––	––	0
	669	2357	361	657	154	23	43	––	.279	.418	986	93

ALEX KAMPOURIS   Alex William Kampouris. Born 11/13/1912, Sacramento, CA. Died 5/29/1993, Sacramento, CA. Second baseman set the PCL record with seven RBI in one inning against Portland 7/9/1932.

	G	AB	R	H	2B	3B	HR	RBI	BA	SA	TB	SB
1932 Sac	148	549	80	154	33	3	11	88	.281	.412	226	10
1933 Sac	180	724	109	220	45	11	13	123	.304	.450	326	47
1934 Sac	112	422	68	117	17	3	19	64	.277	.467	197	21
1946 Sac	160	515	70	119	21	3	11	56	.231	.348	179	17
1947 Sac	132	368	60	106	20	2	10	49	.288	.435	160	5
1948 Sac	109	354	46	96	20	0	10	42	.271	.412	146	2
	841	2932	433	812	156	22	74	422	.277	.421	1234	102

JIM KEESEY   James Ward Keesey. Born 10/27/1902, Perryville, MD. Died 9/5/1951, Boise, ID. First baseman had two brief trials with Athletics. Had a lifetime batting average of .317 in minors with nearly 3,000 hits.

	G	AB	R	H	2B	3B	HR	RBI	BA	SA	TB	SB
1928 Port	186	678	107	228	52	7	9	104	.336	.473	321	18
1929 Port	185	705	107	246	54	8	12	124	.349	.499	352	17
1931 SF	163	665	103	238	40	10	10	113	.358	.403	020	14
1932 SF—P	175	674	105	208	35	8	5	122	.309	.407	274	6
1933 Port	83	334	33	100	19	2	4	56	.299	.404	135	1
1944 Sea	18	50	2	12	2	0	0	5	.240	.280	14	1
	810	3106	457	1032	202	35	40	524	.332	.458	1424	57

FRANK KELLEHER   Francis Eugene Kelleher. Born 8/22/1916, San Francisco, CA. Died 4/13/1979, Stockton, CA. Played outfield for Reds in 1942 and 1943. Probably the Hollywood Stars' most popular player ever, led the PCL in home runs and RBI in 1944 and in home runs in 1950.

	G	AB	R	H	2B	3B	HR	RBI	BA	SA	TB	SB
1938 Oak	18	60	3	8	1	1	1	6	.133	.233	14	0
1940 Sea	68	203	22	57	10	2	7	40	.281	.453	92	0
1944 Hol	130	487	90	160	34	2	29	121	.329	.585	285	0
1946 Hol	91	297	47	85	15	4	18	54	.286	.545	162	3
1947 Hol	121	427	80	134	30	7	21	93	.314	.564	241	5
1948 Hol	121	439	79	146	24	3	25	107	.333	.572	251	3
1949 Hol	176	609	122	154	26	1	29	90	.253	.442	269	4
1950 Hol	186	589	100	159	19	1	40	135	.270	.509	300	3
1951 Hol	146	470	82	119	16	3	28	94	.253	.479	225	2
1952 Hol	82	222	42	53	12	1	11	33	.239	.450	100	5
1953 Hol	109	249	36	82	22	3	15	65	.329	.622	155	1
1954 Hol	95	191	27	47	8	2	10	38	.246	.466	89	2
	1343	4243	730	1204	217	30	234	876	.284	.514	2183	28

GEORGE KELLY   George Lange Kelly. Born 9/10/1896, San Francisco, CA. Died 10/13/1984, Burlingame, CA. Nicknamed "High Pockets" because of six−foot−four frame, was one of John McGraw's favorite players. A .300 hitter six straight seasons. Elected to the Hall of Fame in 1973.

	G	AB	R	H	2B	3B	HR	RBI	BA	SA	TB	SB
1933 Oak	21	56	5	13	5	0	1	6	.232	.375	21	1

KEN KELTNER   Kenneth Frederick Keltner. Born 10/31/1916, Milwaukee, WI. Died 12/12/1991, New Berlin, WI. Third baseman for Cleveland all but thirteen games of his major league career; seven–time All–Star is chiefly remembered as bringing Joe DiMaggio's hitting streak to an end.

	G	AB	R	H	2B	3B	HR	RBI	BA	SA	TB	SB
1951 Sac	101	325	36	81	16	0	6	41	.249	.354	115	1

DUKE KENWORTHY   William Jennings Kenworthy. Born 7/4/1887, Cambridge, OH. Died 9/21/1950, Eureka, CA. Jumped from PCL to join Federal League with Kansas City. Led Feds in home runs in 1914.

	G	AB	R	H	2B	3B	HR	RBI	BA	SA	TB	SB
1913 Sac	177	622	104	185	32	16	8	– –	.297	.439	273	60
1916 Oak	200	735	99	231	54	5	1	– –	.314	.405	298	44
1917 LA	142	510	65	154	23	2	1	– –	.302	.361	184	29
1919 LA–Sea	146	520	57	118	10	3	3	– –	.227	.275	143	10
1920 Sea	180	616	74	193	45	14	5	– –	.313	.456	281	12
1921 Sea	172	654	105	224	56	7	5	101	.343	.472	309	21
1924 Port	31	77	8	17	5	0	1	14	.221	.325	25	1
	1048	3734	512	1122	225	47	24	– –	.300	.405	1513	177

BILL KNICKERBOCKER   William Hart Knickerbocker. Born 12/29/1911, Los Angeles, CA. Died 9/8/1963, Sebastapol, CA. Shortstop batted .303 from 1934–1936 as starter for Cleveland. Played ten seasons in majors.

	G	AB	R	H	2B	3B	HR	RBI	BA	SA	TB	SB
1943 Hol	68	236	19	67	13	1	0	26	.284	.347	82	1

ART KOEHLER   Arthur R. Koehler. Born 1894. Died 1/1960, Redding, CA. Catcher was Chicago native who failed a brief trial with the Detroit Tigers.

	G	AB	R	H	2B	3B	HR	RBI	BA	SA	TB	SB
1919 Port	96	299	26	74	15	1	1	– –	.247	.314	94	1
1920 Port	132	414	26	97	17	4	1	– –	.234	.302	125	7
1921 Oak	142	440	54	129	25	1	5	57	.293	.389	171	1
1922 Oak	153	478	38	116	22	2	3	40	.243	.316	151	2
1923 Sac	155	506	71	180	35	3	10	95	.356	.496	251	12
1924 Sac	130	396	48	135	27	0	9	78	.341	.477	189	2
1925 Sac	93	256	27	67	12	2	4	39	.262	.371	95	1
1926 Sac	170	578	69	174	25	2	10	98	.301	.403	233	7
1927 Sac	127	383	56	111	17	0	12	57	.290	.428	164	5
1928 Sac	111	370	56	113	18	1	8	60	.305	.424	157	1
1929 Sac	143	457	66	157	29	1	13	74	.344	.497	227	2
1930 Sac	126	369	36	103	15	0	3	47	.279	.344	127	4
1931 Sac	40	126	10	30	1	0	5	16	.238	.365	46	2
1932 Oak	7	14	2	3	– –	– –	– –	– –	.214	– –	– – – –	
	1625	5086	585	1489	258	17	84	– –	.293	.400	2033	47

MARK KOENIG   Mark Anthony Koenig. Born 7/19/1902, San Francisco, CA. Died 4/22/1993, Willows, CA. Considered himself the goat of the '26 World Series for key error, returned to hit .500 in '27 Series. Last surviving member of '27 Yankees, first PCL season led to famous role in '32 Series.

MARK KOENIG (cont.)

	G	AB	R	H	2B	3B	HR	RBI	BA	SA	TB	SB
1932 Miss	89	322	61	108	17	0	0	23	.335	.388	125	4
1937 Miss	39	90	10	26	2	1	0	19	.289	.333	30	1
	128	412	71	134	19	1	0	42	.325	.376	155	5

MERLIN KOPP   Merlin H. Kopp. Born 1/2/1892, Toledo, OH. Died 5/8/1960, Sacramento, CA. Outfielder won five minor league stolen base titles, with one of those coming in the Pacific Coast League in 1923.

	G	AB	R	H	2B	3B	HR	RBI	BA	SA	TB	SB
1920 Sac	198	740	119	193	19	11	9	– –	.261	.353	261	50
1921 Sac	168	663	114	186	29	7	12	59	.281	.400	265	45
1922 Sac	102	349	46	100	10	3	1	25	.287	.341	119	23
1923 Sac	201	829	178	279	40	17	5	62	.337	.444	368	80
1924 Sac	186	742	121	221	22	16	5	71	.298	.391	290	44
1925 Sac	202	805	133	227	25	9	8	76	.282	.365	294	27
1926 Sac	124	486	85	142	26	2	1	47	.292	.360	175	7
1927 Sac	158	608	110	166	34	5	5	64	.273	.370	225	14
1928 Sac	71	202	21	57	7	2	2	16	.282	.366	74	3
	1410	5424	927	1571	212	72	48	– –	.290	.382	2071	293

MIKE KREEVICH   Michael Andreas Kreevich. Born 6/10/1908, Mt. Olive, IL. Died 4/25/1994, Panama, IL. Sent to LA as property of Cubs, was traded to White Sox. Centerfielder hit .300 in three of first four seasons in majors.

	G	AB	R	H	2B	3B	HR	RBI	BA	SA	TB	SB
1932 LA	162	561	102	165	32	7	15	70	.294	.456	256	13

EDDIE LAKE   Edward Erving Lake. Born 3/18/1916, Antioch, CA. Had one of the strongest arms in baseball. Whenever a regular, this shortstop consistently drew 100 or more walks in both the majors and minors.

	G	AB	R	H	2B	3B	HR	RBI	BA	SA	TB	SB
1940 Sac	69	237	68	70	13	1	15	35	.295	.549	130	13
1942 Sac	176	633	118	176	38	3	19	69	.278	.438	277	23
1951 SF	158	579	106	151	17	1	27	58	.261	.434	251	7
1952 Oak	47	138	19	29	9	0	4	24	.210	.362	50	2
1953 Oak	105	262	41	59	13	0	2	15	.225	.298	78	0
	555	1849	352	485	90	5	67	201	.262	.425	786	45

BILL LANE   William Cleveland Lane. Born 1892, Macon, IL. Died 1/30/1954, San Pablo, CA. Outfielder stole 670 bases in the minors, never played in the majors. Led PCL in steals four times (1916, 1919, 1922, 1924).

	G	AB	R	H	2B	3B	HR	RBI	BA	SA	TB	SB
1916 Oak	197	691	93	191	37	3	4	– –	.276	.356	246	56
1917 Oak	173	564	90	130	20	4	4	– –	.230	.301	170	57
1919 Oak	173	647	122	165	22	4	3	– –	.255	.315	204	59
1920 Oak	155	589	100	160	29	10	3	– –	.272	.370	218	29
1921 Sea	168	639	130	189	51	8	7	54	.296	.433	277	47
1922 Sea	182	716	166	204	57	10	10	66	.285	.434	311	60
1923 Sea	180	695	131	216	46	11	4	62	.311	.426	296	44

BILL LANE (cont.)

	G	AB	R	H	2B	3B	HR	RBI	BA	SA	TB	SB
1924 Sea	149	598	125	201	49	6	1	45	.336	.443	265	45
1925 Sea	163	656	125	184	34	8	1	32	.280	.361	237	34
1926 Sea	160	600	111	163	34	6	3	61	.272	.363	218	37
	1700	6395	1193	1803	379	70	40	– –	.282	.382	2442	468

LYN LARY   Lynford Hobart Lary. Born 1/28/1906, Armona, CA. Died 1/9/1973, Downey, CA. A major league shortstop for twelve seasons, was purchased by Yankees from Oakland along with Jimmie Reese for a total of $125,000. Cost Lou Gehrig a home run title by running out of basepath thinking the fly ball had been caught. Scored 100 runs three times.

	G	AB	R	H	2B	3B	HR	RBI	BA	SA	TB	SB
1925 Oak	70	241	30	62	9	1	0	21	.257	.303	73	6
1926 Oak	170	566	55	143	19	5	7	44	.253	.341	193	6
1927 Oak	195	765	124	224	40	12	12	102	.293	.424	324	12
1928 Oak	167	614	79	193	34	10	7	94	.314	.436	268	19
	602	2186	288	622	102	28	26	261	.285	.392	858	43

COOKIE LAVAGETTO   Harry Arthur Lavagetto. Born 12/1/1912, Oakland, CA. Died 8/10/1990, Orinda, CA. Ten year major league infielder with the Dodgers and Pirates, was a four–time All–Star. His double with two out in ninth inning of Game 4 of 1947 World Series broke up Bill Bevens' no–hitter. One of Casey Stengel's "Nine Old Men" with Oakland in 1948.

	G	AB	R	H	2B	3B	HR	RBI	BA	SA	TB	SB
1933 Oak	152	509	83	159	29	8	7	100	.312	.442	225	18
1948 Oak	86	286	54	87	16	1	3	38	.304	.399	114	1
1949 Oak	142	459	76	133	23	1	6	58	.290	.383	176	2
1950 Oak	143	490	81	140	18	0	8	66	.286	.371	182	3
	523	1744	294	519	86	10	24	262	.298	.400	697	24

BILL LAWRENCE   William Henry Lawrence. Born 3/11/1906, San Mateo, CA. Briefly in majors with Detroit Tigers during 1932 season. Tied a PCL record for outfielders with eleven putouts in a game vs. LA, May 7, 1940.

	G	AB	R	H	2B	3B	HR	RBI	BA	SA	TB	SB
1929 Sea	41	106	12	26	0	1	1	7	.245	.292	31	4
1930 Sea	127	408	52	112	16	12	3	45	.275	.395	161	12
1931 Sea	162	618	100	200	28	12	2	99	.324	.417	258	14
1934 Sea	162	591	73	176	24	6	3	84	.298	.374	221	11
1935 Sea	166	608	97	194	27	11	7	86	.319	.434	264	23
1936 Sea	167	633	83	190	25	11	4	81	.300	.393	249	18
1937 Sea	136	439	55	110	20	7	0	54	.251	.328	144	5
1938 Sea	161	564	65	156	26	10	4	87	.277	.379	214	5
1939 Sea	158	566	71	167	19	15	3	92	.295	.398	225	8
1940 Sea	140	477	52	130	18	9	1	56	.273	.354	169	3
1941 Sea	73	241	33	67	8	5	1	29	.278	.365	88	4
1942 Sea	40	142	14	44	3	2	0	13	.310	.359	51	0
1943 Sea	80	256	17	62	6	3	0	17	.242	.289	74	1
	1613	5649	724	1634	220	104	29	750	.289	.380	2149	108

TONY LAZZERI   Anthony Michael Lazzeri. Born 12/6/1903, San Francisco, CA. Died 8/6/1946, San Francisco, CA. Created sensation in 1925 when he hit sixty home runs and set a still—standing single—season RBI record. Remembered for his epic battle with Grover Alexander in the 1926 World Series. Played fourteen years in majors; named to Hall of Fame in 1991.

	G	AB	R	H	2B	3B	HR	RBI	BA	SA	TB	SB
1922 SLC	45	78	9	15	4	2	1	8	.192	.333	26	0
1923 SLC	39	130	25	46	7	1	7	21	.354	.585	76	4
1924 SLC	85	293	51	83	15	3	16	61	.283	.519	152	8
1925 SLC	197	710	202	252	52	14	60	222	.355	.721	512	39
1941 SF	102	315	40	78	22	3	3	39	.248	.365	115	5
	468	1526	327	474	100	23	87	351	.311	.577	881	56

DUD LEE   Ernest Dudley Lee. Born 8/22/1899, Denver, CO. Died 1/7/1971, Denver, CO. Shortstop played in major leagues for Browns and Red Sox. Extremely popular among Hollywood fans; led the PCL in fielding in 1937.

	G	AB	R	H	2B	3B	HR	RBI	BA	SA	TB	SB
1926 Hol	165	558	56	127	19	5	0	42	.228	.280	156	8
1927 Hol	190	689	100	167	31	6	2	39	.242	.313	216	7
1928 Hol	191	802	119	219	35	4	5	77	.273	.345	277	7
1929 Hol	205	848	161	222	37	4	4	71	.262	.329	279	9
1930 Hol	187	717	122	197	24	4	3	57	.275	.332	238	27
1931 Hol	161	651	117	179	31	4	3	55	.275	.349	227	14
1932 Hol	163	611	85	162	26	2	1	44	.265	.319	195	10
1936 Port	162	613	77	153	23	3	0	49	.250	.297	182	9
1937 Port	174	631	85	148	22	3	0	49	.235	.279	176	2
1938 Port	69	227	16	56	8	1	0	14	.247	.291	66	2
	1667	6347	940	1630	256	36	18	497	.257	.317	2012	95

DUFFY LEWIS   George Edward Lewis. Born 4/18/1888, San Francisco, CA. Died 6/17/1979, Salem, NH. With Tris Speaker and Harry Hooper, he formed one of the game's all—time great outfields with the Red Sox. Won PCL batting title in 1924, edging Lefty O'Doul. At end of playing career, he spent three decades as the Traveling Secretary for the Boston Braves.

	G	AB	R	H	2B	3B	HR	RBI	BA	SA	TB	SB
1908 Oak	50	186	11	47	9	0	0	--	.253	.301	56	4
1909 Oak	200	748	72	209	--	--	--	--	.279	--	--	--
1922 SLC	164	566	111	205	52	2	20	108	.362	.567	321	5
1923 SLC	145	478	99	171	28	8	28	115	.358	.626	299	4
1924 SLC	154	528	128	207	55	5	28	154	.392	.674	356	7
1925 Port	130	442	65	130	17	2	15	71	.294	.443	196	5
	843	2948	486	969	--	--	--	--	.329	.558	--	--

GENE LILLARD   Robert Eugene Lillard. Born 11/12/1913, Santa Barbara, CA. Died 4/12/1991, Goleta, CA. Pitcher during the middle portion of his career, as a third baseman he twice led the Pacific Coast League in home runs (1933 and 1935). Ended his baseball career in minors as a catcher.

	G	AB	R	H	2B	3B	HR	RBI	BA	SA	TB	SB
1932 LA	40	141	21	44	7	3	5	28	.312	.511	72	2

GENE LILLARD (cont.)

	G	AB	R	H	2B	3B	HR	RBI	BA	SA	TB	SB
1933 LA	183	645	129	198	24	7	43	149	.307	.566	365	2
1934 LA	171	592	104	171	27	6	27	119	.289	.492	291	10
1935 LA	170	642	157	232	31	4	56	147	.361	.684	439	8
1937 SF	87	175	42	57	12	3	4	38	.326	.497	87	2
1938 LA	43	93	22	29	3	1	7	22	.312	.591	55	0
1940 LA	13	18	3	2	0	0	0	2	.111	.111	2	0
1942 Sac	29	97	9	33	5	0	3	20	.340	.485	47	2
1946 Sac	138	441	66	118	18	6	22	59	.268	.485	214	9
1947 Oak	110	291	45	75	16	0	7	46	.258	.385	112	1
1948 Oak	23	59	4	12	5	0	0	7	.203	.288	17	0
	1007	3194	602	971	148	30	174	637	.304	.533	1701	36

DARIO LODIGIANI

Dario Joseph Lodigiani. Born 6/6/1916, San Francisco, CA. Infielder was part of a junior high double play combo with Joe DiMaggio. Played six seasons in the majors with White Sox and A's.

	G	AB	R	H	2B	3B	HR	RBI	BA	SA	TB	SB
1935 Oak	10	38	8	15	— —	— —	— —	— —	.395	— —	— —	— —
1936 Oak	163	554	71	155	32	9	4	60	.280	.392	217	10
1937 Oak	162	538	83	176	35	14	18	84	.327	.545	293	12
1947 Oak	141	498	83	155	26	2	11	92	.311	.438	218	7
1948 Oak	162	581	77	176	29	2	7	72	.303	.396	230	7
1949 O–SF	181	662	92	178	30	0	10	65	.269	.360	238	11
1950 SF	150	536	88	161	25	2	6	68	.300	.388	208	1
1951 SF	120	387	36	117	19	0	5	45	.302	.390	151	6
	1089	3794	538	1133	196	29	61	486	.299	.414	1570	54

ERNIE LOMBARDI

Ernest Natali Lombardi. Born 4/6/1908, Oakland, CA. Died 9/26/1977, Santa Cruz, CA. A two–time NL batting champ and MVP in 1938, might have been the greatest hitter in baseball history if he had not also been the slowest. Elected to the Hall of Fame in 1985.

	G	AB	R	H	2B	3B	HR	RBI	BA	SA	TB	SB
1926 Oak	4	6	0	2	1	0	0	0	.333	.500	3	0
1927 Oak	16	20	2	3	0	0	1	6	.150	.300	6	0
1928 Oak	120	318	39	120	27	3	8	47	.377	.557	177	1
1929 Oak	164	516	70	189	36	3	24	109	.366	.587	303	3
1930 Oak	146	473	76	175	32	4	22	105	.370	.594	281	1
1948 Sac–O	102	284	25	75	13	0	11	55	.264	.426	121	1
	552	1617	212	564	109	10	66	322	.349	.551	891	6

DALE LONG

Richard Dale Long. Born 2/6/1926, Springfield, MO. Died 1/27/1991, Palm Coast, FL. Homered in eight straight games with Pirates in May, 1956. Also noted for playing in majors as a left–handed catcher.

	G	AB	R	H	2B	3B	HR	RBI	BA	SA	TB	SB
1951 SF	36	128	10	34	4	1	4	23	.266	.406	52	0
1953 Hol	172	599	106	163	34	7	35	116	.272	.528	316	5
1954 Hol	129	410	69	115	27	5	23	68	.280	.539	221	3
	337	1137	185	312	65	13	62	207	.274	.518	589	8

PEANUTS LOWREY   Harry Lee Lowrey. Born 8/27/1918, Los Angeles, CA. Died 7/2/1986, Inglewood, CA. A child actor in the "Our Gang" comedies; hit .310 for the 1945 Cubs as member of the team's last pennant—winner.

	G	AB	R	H	2B	3B	HR	RBI	BA	SA	TB	SB
1940 LA	70	216	36	54	7	1	1	12	.250	.306	66	12
1941 LA	164	653	110	203	39	4	6	69	.311	.410	268	26
1942 LA	96	393	64	101	17	0	5	39	.257	.338	133	10
1959 Sea	36	79	10	14	4	0	0	6	.177	.228	18	0
	366	1341	220	372	67	5	12	126	.277	.362	485	48

HUGH LUBY   Hugh Max Luby. Born 6/13/1913, Blackfoot, ID. Died 5/4/1986, Eugene, OR. Star second baseman on one of the best teams in PCL history, the 1946 San Francisco Seals. Appeared briefly in the majors with the A's and Giants. Played in 866 straight games from 1938 to 1942.

	G	AB	R	H	2B	3B	HR	RBI	BA	SA	TB	SB
1938 Oak	160	580	76	171	28	6	4	70	.295	.384	223	20
1939 Oak	176	681	94	193	35	6	3	56	.283	.366	249	20
1940 Oak	178	689	94	177	31	5	4	57	.257	.334	230	21
1941 Oak	178	677	82	204	39	5	5	73	.301	.396	268	17
1942 Oak	177	667	85	207	32	7	3	75	.310	.393	262	10
1943 Oak	157	587	75	184	31	0	3	69	.313	.382	224	16
1946 SF	176	678	110	199	30	6	2	60	.294	.364	247	22
1947 SF	187	711	122	189	30	10	9	70	.266	.374	266	12
1948 SF	175	646	113	185	26	5	12	77	.286	.398	257	19
	1564	5916	851	1709	282	50	45	607	.289	.376	2226	157

HARRY LUMLEY   Harry G. Lumley. Born 9/29/1880, Forest City, PA. Died 5/22/1938 Binghamton, NY. The PCL's first batting champion, left team to join the Brooklyn Dodgers and immediately led National League in triples and homers. A favorite of the Brooklyn faithful, led NL in slugging in 1906 and later served as the team's player—manager.

	G	AB	R	H	2B	3B	HR	RBI	BA	SA	TB	SB
1903 Sea	109	465	106	180	--	--	--	--	.387	--	--	28

CLARENCE MADDERN   Clarence James Maddern. Born 9/26/1921, Bisbee, AZ. Died 8/9/1986, Tucson, AZ. His grand—slam home run in a play—off game against San Francisco won the pennant for Los Angeles in 1947.

	G	AB	R	H	2B	3B	HR	RBI	BA	SA	TB	SB
1941 LA	5	15	--	3	--	--	--	--	.200	--	--	--
1942 LA	4	15	--	1	--	--	--	--	.067	--	--	--
1947 LA	129	458	78	152	22	4	15	83	.332	.496	227	1
1949 LA	129	495	69	152	25	3	14	83	.307	.455	225	1
1950 LA	162	573	81	162	29	7	14	102	.283	.431	247	0
1951 SD	99	373	57	116	22	4	14	76	.311	.504	188	1
1952 Sea	160	545	56	160	29	5	8	77	.294	.409	223	1
1953 Sea	133	411	62	121	27	1	14	65	.294	.467	192	1
1954 Sea	141	456	62	123	22	5	12	72	.270	.419	191	2
1955 SFPSD	88	223	22	60	15	1	4	39	.269	.399	89	0
	1050	3564	487	1050	191	30	95	597	.295	.448	1582	7

HARL MAGGERT   Harl Vess Maggert. Born 2/13/1883, Cromwell, IN. Died 1/7/1963, Fresno, CA. Led PCL in runs scored four times. Temperamental and difficult toward managers, hit stride as lead off hitter for LA. It was his acceptance of $300 from Babe Borton that led to the investigation into the allegation of games being thrown in PCL. Received lifetime ban in 1920.

	G	AB	R	H	2B	3B	HR	RBI	BA	SA	TB	SB
1909 Oak	59	211	26	56	13	1	1	– –	.265	.351	74	4
1910 Oak	221	745	91	189	34	1	9	– –	.254	.338	252	58
1911 Oak	114	437	74	137	16	13	8	– –	.314	.465	203	27
1913 LA	204	715	128	226	32	23	13	– –	.316	.480	343	89
1914 LA	203	754	127	217	25	20	3	82	.288	.386	291	51
1915 LA	201	736	147	226	38	14	12	– –	.307	.446	328	55
1916 LA	182	672	121	184	37	6	6	– –	.274	.374	251	42
1917 LA	165	597	96	153	29	5	0	– –	.256	.322	192	32
1918 SF	86	304	41	75	14	4	1	– –	.247	.329	100	19
1919 SLC	171	671	127	184	37	5	5	– –	.274	.367	246	36
1920 SLC	115	469	96	174	41	10	4	– –	.371	.527	247	29
	1721	6311	1074	1821	316	102	62	– –	.289	.400	2527	442

EMIL MAILHO   Emil Pierre Mailho. Born 12/16/1909, Berkeley, CA. Spent most of his career in the outfield of the Oakland Oaks or Atlanta Crackers. Played briefly with the 1936 A's. Retired with 2,511 career hits in minors.

	G	AB	R	H	2B	3B	HR	RBI	BA	SA	TB	SB
1931 Oak	10	15	3	5	0	1	0	1	.333	.467	7	0
1932 Oak	135	456	83	144	23	5	2	42	.316	.401	183	16
1933 Oak	180	690	142	209	34	12	4	58	.303	.404	279	52
1934 Oak	58	96	14	19	4	0	0	8	.198	.240	23	4
1935 Oak	172	652	117	230	42	17	2	88	.353	.479	312	36
1942 Oak	155	599	91	178	29	3	1	42	.297	.361	216	15
1943 Oak	155	598	100	188	37	8	2	46	.314	.413	247	13
1944 Oak	123	465	64	129	20	3	0	27	.277	.333	155	16
1945 SF	149	484	80	148	20	6	1	69	.306	.378	183	9
	1137	4055	694	1250	209	55	12	381	.308	.396	1605	161

FRANK MALZONE   Frank James Malzone. Born 2/28/1930, Bronx, NY. Long–time third baseman for the Boston Red Sox; five–time AL All–Star and three–time Gold Glove winner with a consistent and productive bat.

	G	AB	R	H	2B	3B	HR	RBI	BA	SA	TB	SB
1956 SF	87	324	34	96	14	3	6	42	.296	.414	134	1

LUIS MARQUEZ   Luis Angel Marquez. Born 10/28/1925, Aguadilla, PR. Died 3/1/1988 Aguadilla, PR. Outfielder had trials with Braves, Cubs and Pirates. Led the Pacific Coast League in stolen bases in 1950.

	G	AB	R	H	2B	3B	HR	RBI	BA	SA	TB	SB
1949 Port	132	511	87	150	26	7	4	46	.294	.395	202	32
1950 Port	194	775	136	241	41	19	9	86	.311	.448	347	38
1955 Port	112	381	60	119	24	1	8	57	.312	.444	169	5
1956 Port	155	602	122	207	27	10	25	110	.344	.547	329	18
1957 Port	167	610	92	169	31	6	31	85	.277	.500	305	13

LUIS MARQUEZ (cont.)

	G	AB	R	H	2B	3B	HR	RBI	BA	SA	TB	SB
1958 Port	109	335	43	89	13	6	8	42	.266	.412	138	2
	869	3214	540	975	162	49	85	426	.303	.464	1490	108

BILLY MARTIN   Alfred Manuel Martin. Born 5/16/1928, Berkeley, CA. Died 12/25/1989, Johnson City, NY. Came to PCL to play for Casey Stengel at end of 1947 season after batting .392 with 174 RBI in Ariz—Texas League. Hero of the 1952 and 1953 World Series. An AL All—Star in 1956. In spite of his fiery nature, he became one of baseball's greatest managers.

	G	AB	R	H	2B	3B	HR	RBI	BA	SA	TB	SB
1947 Oak	15	53	3	12	3	0	0	5	.226	.283	15	0
1948 Oak	132	401	60	111	28	2	3	42	.277	.379	152	7
1949 Oak	172	623	90	178	27	3	12	92	.286	.396	247	11
	319	1077	153	301	58	5	15	139	.279	.384	414	18

PEPPER MARTIN   Johnny Leonard Roosevelt Martin. Born 2/29/1904, Temple, OK. Died 3/5/1965, Mc Alester, OK. Four—time NL All—Star and sparkplug of the "Gashouse Gang"; known for his daring, aggressive play. Player—manager for Sacramento in 1942, led team to the pennant despite their being four games out of first place with only five games left to play.

	G	AB	R	H	2B	3B	HR	RBI	BA	SA	TB	SB
1941 Sac	92	245	40	79	17	6	2	35	.322	.465	114	10
1942 Sac	130	223	27	55	17	1	0	24	.247	.332	74	6
1945 SD	53	97	27	30	6	4	1	15	.309	.485	47	3
1946 SD	11	15	——	3	——	——	——	——	.200	——	—— ——	
	286	580	94	167	40	11	3	74	.288	.410	238	19

JOE MARTY   Joseph Anton Marty. Born 9/1/1913, Sacramento, CA. Died 10/4/1984, Sacramento, CA. The 1936 PCL batting champion, played in outfield for Chicago Cubs in 1938 World Series, hitting .500 with five RBI.

	G	AB	R	H	2B	3B	HR	RBI	BA	SA	TB	SB
1934 SF	142	513	73	141	28	4	2	55	.275	.357	183	19
1935 SF	159	609	124	175	29	16	6	98	.287	.417	254	25
1936 SF	164	599	110	215	49	14	17	92	.359	.573	343	33
1946 Sac	144	518	75	159	31	4	14	74	.307	.463	240	10
1947 Sac	168	568	86	186	37	9	13	100	.327	.493	280	8
1948 Sac	158	556	88	178	27	7	24	95	.320	.523	291	2
1949 Sac	148	477	72	156	35	1	16	112	.327	.505	241	3
1950 Sac	117	388	52	120	21	2	9	69	.309	.443	172	1
1951 Sac	111	370	46	106	24	1	12	81	.286	.454	168	2
1952 Sac	80	228	19	54	8	0	3	25	.237	.311	71	1
	1391	4826	745	1490	289	58	116	801	.309	.465	2243	104

GENE MAUCH   Gene William Mauch. Born 11/18/1925, Salina, KS. PCL All—Star in 1956, played parts of nine years in majors. An acknowledged expert on baseball's rules, later managed in majors for twenty—six years.

	G	AB	R	H	2B	3B	HR	RBI	BA	SA	TB	SB
1954 LA	153	565	81	162	26	2	11	58	.287	.398	225	12

GENE MAUCH (cont.)

	G	AB	R	H	2B	3B	HR	RBI	BA	SA	TB	SB
1955 LA	155	584	93	173	37	4	8	49	.296	.414	242	22
1956 LA	146	566	123	197	29	3	20	84	.348	.516	292	2
	454	1715	297	532	92	9	39	191	.310	.443	759	36

EDDIE MAYO

Edward Joseph Mayo. Born 4/15/1910, Holyoke, MA. Standout defensive player at both second and third, led the AL in fielding at both positions during career. Starred for world champ Tigers in 1945. Played major role in success of Angels in his seasons there. Suspended a year for allegedly spitting on an ump in '41, penalty reduced on appeal.

	G	AB	R	H	2B	3B	HR	RBI	BA	SA	TB	SB
1938 LA	118	416	69	138	25	5	9	59	.332	.481	200	9
1939 LA	127	464	65	122	24	1	6	61	.263	.358	166	3
1940 LA	162	643	119	206	34	8	11	85	.320	.449	289	17
1941 LA	109	412	71	118	30	3	13	72	.286	.468	193	8
1942 LA	171	635	71	195	31	3	12	110	.307	.422	268	10
	687	2570	395	779	144	20	51	387	.303	.434	1116	47

BILL MAZEROSKI

William Stanley Mazeroski. Born 9/5/1936, Wheeling, WV. The recognized master of turning the double play, set the single–season and career marks in that category. Seven–time All–Star and eight–time Gold Glove winner. His Series–winning home run off Ralph Terry in 1960 ranks as one of baseball's great moments.

	G	AB	R	H	2B	3B	HR	RBI	BA	SA	TB	SB
1955 Hol	21	47	4	8	0	0	1	3	.170	.234	11	0
1956 Hol	80	284	47	87	12	3	9	36	.306	.465	132	4
	101	331	51	95	12	3	10	39	.287	.432	143	4

MIKE MC CORMICK

Myron Winthrop McCormick. Born 5/6/1917, Angels Camp, CA. Died 4/14/1976, Los Angeles, CA. Outfielder for three different World Series teams, holds Series record for assists. Hit .300 as a rookie.

	G	AB	R	H	2B	3B	HR	RBI	BA	SA	TB	SB
1950 Oak	18	51	13	16	3	0	1	11	.314	.431	22	0
1952 Sac–P	94	315	40	79	11	2	2	26	.251	.317	100	1
1954 SF	1	4	0	1	0	0	0	0	.250	.250	1	0
	113	370	53	96	14	2	3	37	.259	.332	123	1

GEORGE MC DONALD

George Thomas McDonald. Born 4/12/1918, Seattle, WA. Long–time PCL first baseman, was childhood friend and an American Legion teammate of Hall of Famer Bobby Doerr.

	G	AB	R	H	2B	3B	HR	RBI	BA	SA	TB	SB
1934 Hol	19	46	6	9	0	0	0	8	.196	.196	9	0
1935 Hol	68	212	16	54	9	3	0	23	.255	.325	69	1
1936 SD	103	334	36	106	11	5	0	52	.317	.380	127	3
1937 SD	163	632	95	197	22	7	4	102	.312	.388	245	5
1938 SD	143	549	49	147	26	4	0	61	.268	.330	181	7
1939 SD	134	490	53	112	17	6	1	50	.229	.294	144	4
1940 SD	141	537	56	155	20	5	2	63	.289	.356	191	3

GEORGE MC DONALD (cont.)

	G	AB	R	H	2B	3B	HR	RBI	BA	SA	TB	SB
1941 SD	157	611	80	173	23	3	1	58	.283	.336	205	4
1942 SD	70	272	25	73	10	4	0	19	.268	.335	91	0
1943 SD	112	391	42	129	24	10	0	50	.330	.442	173	5
1944 SD	85	313	32	97	18	2	0	34	.310	.380	119	5
1945 Sea	151	552	81	183	26	5	1	69	.332	.402	222	26
1946 Sea–SD	142	506	55	140	21	5	1	56	.277	.344	174	7
1947 SD–Sac	10	26	5	5	1	0	0	1	.192	.231	6	0
1948 Sea	31	99	10	23	3	0	0	11	.232	.263	26	3
	1529	5570	641	1603	231	59	10	657	.288	.356	1982	73

LARRY MC LEAN   John Bannerman McLean. Born 7/18/1881, Cambridge, MA. Died 3/14/1921, Boston, MA. Big, lovable giant, except when under influence of alcohol. Involved in famous fight with John Mc Graw, which ended with his breaking a chair over a coach's head. Killed in a bar fight.

	G	AB	R	H	2B	3B	HR	RBI	BA	SA	TB	SB
1905 Port	180	667	––	187	41	3	1	––	.280	.355	237	8
1906 Port	82	248	21	88	15	7	2	––	.355	.490	123	10
	262	915	––	275	56	10	3	––	.301	.393	360	18

FRED MC MULLIN   Frederick William McMullin. Born 10/13/1891, Scammon, KS. Died 11/21/1952, Los Angeles, CA. Overheard a scheme to throw 1919 Series and insisted on being included. Banned for life.

	G	AB	R	H	2B	3B	HR	RBI	BA	SA	TB	SB
1915 LA	184	681	89	190	25	7	1	––	.279	.341	232	31

JOHN MC NAMARA   John Francis McNamara. Born 6/4/1932, Sacramento, CA. Good–field no–hit catcher, never played in the majors but managed six different big league teams over seventeen seasons.

	G	AB	R	H	2B	3B	HR	RBI	BA	SA	TB	SB
1956 Sac	76	181	22	31	5	1	1	18	.171	.227	41	1

EARL MC NEELY   George Earl McNeely. Born 5/12/1899, Sacramento, CA. Died 7/16/1971, Sacramento, CA. Eight year major league outfielder with Senators and Browns, hit bad–hop grounder that bounced over the head of Freddie Lindstrom to win the 1924 World Series for Washington.

	G	AB	R	H	2B	3B	HR	RBI	BA	SA	TB	SB
1922 Sac	106	315	29	67	8	1	0	15	.213	.244	77	10
1923 Sac	75	213	35	71	11	0	1	27	.333	.399	85	20
1924 Sac	112	460	93	153	33	4	8	41	.333	.474	218	14
1932 Sac	100	377	55	106	25	1	1	28	.281	.361	136	6
1933 Sac	94	279	79	86	18	2	5	20	.308	.441	123	15
1934 Sac	26	38	4	11	2	0	0	6	.289	.342	13	0
	513	1682	295	494	97	8	15	137	.294	.388	652	65

STEVE MESNER   Stephan Mathias Mesner. Born 1/13/1918, Los Angeles, CA. Died 4/6/1981, San Diego, CA. Broke in with Los Angeles at the age of sixteen and was only eighteen when he led the PCL in doubles in 1936.

STEVE MESNER (cont.)

	G	AB	R	H	2B	3B	HR	RBI	BA	SA	TB	SB
1934 LA	5	12	0	3	0	0	0	0	.250	.250	3	0
1935 LA	151	534	78	177	33	5	13	99	.331	.485	259	6
1936 LA	176	703	110	229	55	9	17	132	.326	.502	353	3
1937 LA	133	505	79	166	38	8	10	91	.329	.495	250	4
1940 SD	179	680	114	232	40	12	0	97	.341	.435	296	6
1942 Sac	178	680	83	205	24	6	1	74	.301	.359	244	3
1946 Sac	188	698	88	204	49	2	4	85	.292	.385	269	5
1947 Sac	176	636	84	162	30	5	2	71	.255	.327	208	0
1948 Sac–SD	172	586	75	174	35	1	8	76	.297	.401	235	3
1949 SD	114	343	49	102	17	1	0	40	.297	.353	121	1
1950 Port	69	194	24	44	7	1	0	16	.227	.273	53	0
	1541	5571	784	1698	328	50	55	781	.305	.411	2291	31

GEORGE METKOVICH

George Michael Metkovich. Born 10/8/1921, Angels Camp, CA. Ten year big league outfielder, had twenty–five game hitting streak with Red Sox in 1944. Won the PCL batting title in 1955.

	G	AB	R	H	2B	3B	HR	RBI	BA	SA	TB	SB
1943 SF	71	268	43	87	12	8	3	38	.325	.463	124	4
1948 Oak	134	500	116	168	23	7	23	88	.336	.548	274	9
1949 Oak	77	285	50	96	13	5	14	50	.337	.565	161	9
1950 Oak	184	739	152	233	34	8	24	141	.315	.480	355	23
1955 Oak	151	532	94	178	21	2	17	79	.335	.477	254	10
1956 Van	132	489	73	144	24	5	6	43	.294	.401	196	9
1957 SD	24	90	13	24	4	1	1	8	.267	.367	33	0
	773	2903	541	930	131	36	88	447	.320	.481	1397	64

BOB MEUSEL

Robert William Meusel. Born 7/19/1898, San Jose, CA. Died 11/28/1977, Downey, CA. Big strong–armed outfielder in the Yanks "Murderer's Row", led AL in home runs and RBI in 1925. Suspended with Babe Ruth in '22 for defiance of Judge Landis' rule against barnstorming.

	G	AB	R	H	2B	3B	HR	RBI	BA	SA	TB	SB
1917 Ver	45	164	16	51	11	3	0	––	.311	.415	68	3
1918 Ver	2	8	2	3	3	0	0	––	.375	.750	6	0
1919 Ver	163	655	113	221	39	14	14	––	.337	.504	330	31
1932 Hol	64	228	44	75	20	2	4	26	.329	.487	111	4
	274	1055	175	350	73	19	18	––	.332	.488	515	38

IRISH MEUSEL

Emil Frederick Meusel. Born 6/9/1893, Oakland, CA. Died 3/1/1963, Long Beach, CA. Brother of Bob, was a clean up hitter for McGraw's Giants of the early 1920's. Had four straight 100 RBI seasons.

	G	AB	R	H	2B	3B	HR	RBI	BA	SA	TB	SB
1913 LA	15	53	8	15	3	0	1	––	.283	.396	21	4
1915 LA	6	11	0	4	0	0	0	––	.364	.364	4	0
1917 LA	210	811	121	252	46	9	7	––	.311	.416	337	69
1928 Oak	108	374	52	100	25	5	11	65	.267	.449	168	4
1929 Sac	44	153	22	50	6	3	2	21	.327	.444	68	2
	383	1402	203	421	80	17	21	––	.300	.427	598	79

ROXY MIDDLETON   Robert Hugh Middleton. Born 8/15/1888, Servia, IN. Died 11/8/1966, Ft. Worth, TX. Outfielder in minors for eighteen years, he never played in majors. Retired after playing more than 2,500 games and collecting more than 2,900 career hits.

	G	AB	R	H	2B	3B	HR	RBI	BA	SA	TB	SB
1914 Oak	195	767	89	221	18	6	1	39	.288	.331	254	40
1915 Oak	199	750	81	216	22	6	3	— —	.288	.345	259	29
1916 Oak	185	713	83	195	19	2	2	— —	.273	.314	224	34
1917 Oak	187	696	89	183	33	6	0	— —	.263	.328	228	26
1918 Oak	94	377	47	114	12	3	3	— —	.302	.374	141	15
1919 Sac	166	644	88	188	14	5	5	— —	.292	.352	227	29
1920 Sac—Sea	179	718	96	206	25	4	2	— —	.287	.341	245	27
1921 Sea	116	384	61	106	13	3	2	26	.276	.341	131	7
	1321	5049	634	1429	156	35	18	— —	.283	.338	1709	207

HACK MILLER   Lawrence H. Miller. Born 1/1/1894, Chicago, IL. Died 9/17/1971, Oakland, CA. Son of a circus strong—man, able to bend iron bars and pound spikes into boards with his bare hands. Hit .323 lifetime in the majors, including a .352 average with the 1922 Cubs. Led the PCL in runs batted in and batting average in 1921.

	G	AB	R	H	2B	3B	HR	RBI	BA	SA	TB	SB
1917 Oak	193	696	76	206	40	12	3	— —	.296	.401	279	7
1918 Oak	102	414	45	131	22	3	6	— —	.316	.428	177	18
1919 Oak	54	217	36	75	10	5	5	— —	.346	.544	118	9
1920 Oak	199	806	107	280	45	10	17	— —	.347	.491	396	22
1921 Oak	184	726	130	252	54	10	11	137	.347	.494	359	14
1925 Oak	149	574	66	184	38	4	16	99	.321	.484	278	8
1926 Oak	33	42	3	11	2	0	0	4	.262	.310	13	1
	914	3475	463	1139	219	44	58	— —	.328	.466	1620	79

MINNIE MINOSO Saturnino Orestes Arrieta Armas Minoso. Born 11/29/1922, Matanza, Cuba. Six—time All—Star and winner of three Gold Gloves, was arguably the most popular player in Chicago White Sox history. Led AL in steals three straight years and triples twice. Oldest man to hit safely in the big leagues at age 53. Pinch—hit in the Northern League in 1993.

	G	AB	R	H	2B	3B	HR	RBI	BA	SA	TB	SB
1949 SD	137	532	99	158	19	7	22	75	.297	.483	257	13
1950 SD	169	599	130	203	40	10	20	115	.339	.539	323	30
1964 Ind	52	178	22	47	11	0	4	26	.264	.393	70	6
	358	1309	251	408	70	17	46	216	.312	.497	650	49

MIKE MITCHELL   Michael Francis Mitchell. Born 12/12/1879, Springfield, OH. Died 7/16/1961, Phoenix, AZ. Won 1906 PCL batting title. Led NL in triples twice while with the Cincinnati Reds. Was outfielder for eight years in majors; once traded to the Chicago Cubs by the Reds for Joe Tinker.

	G	AB	R	H	2B	3B	HR	RBI	BA	SA	TB	SB
1905 Port	146	530	— —	133	21	5	4	— —	.251	.332	176	26
1906 Port	164	578	96	203	31	12	6	— —	.351	.478	276	33
	310	1108	— —	336	52	17	10	— —	.303	.408	452	59

CARL MITZE   Carl A. Mitze. Born 11/7/1886, Marissa, IL. Died 5/29/1954, Marissa, IL. Nicknamed "Honus", led PCL catchers in fielding three times. Set league marks for assists in 1910 and for fielding percentage in 1914.

	G	AB	R	H	2B	3B	HR	RBI	BA	SA	TB	SB
1910 Oak	148	435	30	83	11	1	2	– –	.191	.234	102	12
1911 Oak	134	435	38	99	– –	– –	– –	– –	.228	– –	– –	11
1912 Oak	141	434	38	99	– –	– –	– –	– –	.228	– –	– –	8
1913 Oak	60	169	11	31	1	1	0	– –	.183	.201	34	3
1914 Oak	119	338	28	78	10	2	0	33	.231	.272	92	9
1915 Ver	114	346	32	80	11	2	2	– –	.231	.292	101	6
1916 Ver	58	166	28	40	6	1	1	– –	.241	.307	51	7
1917 Oak	123	387	35	86	11	2	0	– –	.222	.261	101	7
1918 Oak	66	199	21	39	9	1	0	– –	.196	.251	50	4
1919 Oak	111	330	34	82	20	1	0	– –	.248	.315	104	9
1920 Oak	131	406	42	100	11	1	0	– –	.246	.278	113	5
1921 Oak	58	174	15	36	4	1	0	11	.207	.241	42	2
1922 O–P	63	170	9	38	5	1	0	6	.224	.265	45	0
	1326	3989	361	891	– –	– –	– –	– –	.223	.268	– –	83

KID MOHLER   Ernest Follette Mohler. Born 12/13/1874, Oneida, IL. Died 11/4/1961, San Francisco, CA. A rarity as a left–handed throwing second baseman, was PCL's leading fielder in 1907. While playing for SF, he was often team's manager for road games. Later coach at Naval Academy.

	G	AB	R	H	2B	3B	HR	RBI	BA	SA	TB	SB
1903 Sea	115	427	85	134	– –	– –	– –	– –	.314	– –	– –	40
1904 Sea	209	790	159	252	40	6	5	– –	.319	.404	319	38
1905 SF	132	448	87	109	29	4	1	– –	.243	.333	149	39
1906 SF	163	555	76	172	24	4	2	– –	.310	.378	210	45
1907 SF	108	385	60	92	19	2	0	– –	.239	.299	115	25
1908 SF	201	723	118	184	28	6	1	– –	.254	.314	227	43
1909 SF	184	607	86	117	20	5	1	– –	.193	.247	150	58
1910 SF	198	670	71	128	25	0	1	– –	.191	.233	156	26
1911 SF	175	585	72	165	31	4	0	– –	.282	.349	204	25
1912 SF	110	381	37	97	10	0	0	– –	.255	.281	107	12
1914 Sac	49	167	18	34	4	1	0	15	.204	.240	40	5
	1644	5738	869	1484	– –	– –	– –	– –	.259	.316	– –	356

JOHN MONROE   John Allen Monroe. Born 8/24/1898, Farmersville, TX. Died 6/19/1956, Conroe, TX. Second baseman hit .321 over fifteen years in the minors. Played for Giants and Phillies in 1921. Tied PCL record for putouts by a second baseman in one game vs. Mission 9/13/1931.

	G	AB	R	H	2B	3B	HR	RBI	BA	SA	TB	SB
1926 Sac	200	779	122	230	52	10	13	97	.295	.438	341	26
1927 Sac	162	592	112	175	38	7	4	70	.296	.404	239	12
1928 Sac	171	731	124	235	45	4	10	84	.321	.435	318	14
1929 Sac	146	589	93	198	34	9	6	58	.336	.455	268	13
1930 Miss	188	689	158	241	39	2	28	106	.350	.534	368	7
1931 M–P	158	607	141	220	41	4	7	64	.362	.478	290	15
1932 Port	118	415	98	136	27	3	5	59	.328	.443	184	11

JOHN MONROE (cont.)

	G	AB	R	H	2B	3B	HR	RBI	BA	SA	TB	SB
1933 Port	152	576	126	186	33	6	7	62	.323	.438	252	20
	1295	4978	974	1621	309	45	80	600	.326	.454	2260	118

EDDIE MOORE   Graham Edward Moore. Born 1/8/1899, Barlow, KY. Died 2/10/1976, Ft. Myers, FL. Usually a utility infielder in majors, played a key role as a starter in pennant—winning season for Pittsburgh in 1925.

	G	AB	R	H	2B	3B	HR	RBI	BA	SA	TB	SB
1931 Oak	138	495	67	156	34	5	6	83	.315	.440	218	15

JOHNNY MOORE   John Francis Moore. Born 3/23/1902, Waterville, CT. Died 4/4/1991, Bradenton, FL. Outfielder hit .307 lifetime in major leagues over ten seasons. Won the Pacific Coast League batting title in 1941.

	G	AB	R	H	2B	3B	HR	RBI	BA	SA	TB	SB
1930 LA	142	546	120	187	45	2	26	101	.342	.575	314	15
1931 LA	80	317	66	116	34	4	6	69	.366	.555	176	8
1938 LA	140	492	81	150	33	7	21	86	.305	.528	260	2
1939 LA	131	491	83	148	24	5	17	99	.301	.475	233	2
1940 LA	120	380	41	118	20	2	9	69	.311	.445	169	2
1941 LA	134	474	77	157	31	10	18	100	.331	.553	262	2
1942 LA	134	487	59	169	28	6	7	85	.347	.472	230	3
1943 LA	81	217	22	63	11	1	1	31	.290	.364	79	1
1944 LA	85	120	11	39	9	0	3	30	.325	.475	57	2
1945 LA	71	65	5	23	4	0	4	26	.354	.600	39	0
	1118	3589	565	1170	239	37	112	696	.326	.507	1819	37

RAY MUELLER   Ray Coleman Mueller. Born 3/8/1912, Pittsburg, KS. Had fourteen year major league career as a catcher. First big league hit was a home run off Carl Hubbell. Named Pacific Coast League MVP in 1942.

	G	AB	R	H	2B	3B	HR	RBI	BA	SA	TB	SB
1942 Sac	166	565	64	168	24	6	16	102	.297	.446	252	3

FRED MULLER   Frederick William Muller. Born 12/21/1907, Newark, CA. Died 10/20/1976, Davis, CA. A product of the University of California, the slugging second baseman led the PCL in home runs in 1932 and 1936.

	G	AB	R	H	2B	3B	HR	RBI	BA	SA	TB	SB
1928 Sea	139	468	51	108	24	8	8	37	.231	.368	172	5
1929 Sea	125	436	43	111	12	4	10	37	.255	.369	161	1
1930 Sea	144	467	57	128	24	7	13	59	.274	.439	205	6
1931 Sea	182	687	82	193	43	6	15	105	.281	.426	293	8
1932 Sea	185	682	116	192	49	8	38	121	.282	.544	371	15
1933 Sea	83	294	63	96	15	6	20	66	.327	.622	183	5
1935 Oak	150	556	72	148	32	4	13	109	.266	.408	227	9
1936 Sea	157	561	94	171	32	7	30	105	.305	.547	307	11
1937 Sea	161	559	67	161	32	7	26	111	.288	.510	285	6
1938 Sea	170	627	101	186	33	7	20	110	.297	.467	293	4
1940 Port	68	244	17	57	10	0	3	31	.234	.311	76	0
	1564	5581	763	1551	306	64	196	891	.278	.461	2573	70

EDDIE MULLIGAN   Edward Joseph Mulligan. Born 8/27/1894, St. Louis, MO. Died 3/15/1982, San Rafael, CA. Acquired by Chicago White Sox in 1921 to replace Buck Weaver at third base. Also played pro soccer during his playing days. Later was president of California League for over twenty years. The Cal League's Rookie of the Year award is named in his honor.

	G	AB	R	H	2B	3B	HR	RBI	BA	SA	TB	SB
1919 SLC	137	465	68	125	22	6	5	– –	.269	.374	174	18
1920 SLC	179	662	116	198	35	11	6	– –	.299	.412	273	50
1923 SF	155	620	94	204	26	6	9	77	.329	.434	269	30
1924 SF	199	820	150	251	51	2	13	114	.306	.421	345	28
1925 SF	180	751	143	215	45	8	10	77	.286	.407	306	12
1926 SF	182	715	112	188	30	4	3	52	.263	.329	235	8
1927 SF	170	665	128	182	46	1	6	65	.274	.373	248	23
1929 Miss	181	734	144	205	34	5	3	56	.279	.351	258	42
1930 Miss	201	828	141	248	35	3	5	56	.300	.367	304	27
1931 Miss	94	390	57	109	17	6	0	27	.279	.354	138	12
1932 MSeaP	139	548	83	162	23	2	3	42	.296	.361	198	15
1933 Port	177	694	136	204	33	5	2	56	.294	.365	253	43
1934 Oak	184	722	118	194	32	5	0	44	.269	.327	236	45
1935 H–M	82	245	31	63	7	1	0	21	.257	.294	72	11
1936 SD	39	12	6	1	0	0	0	0	.083	.083	1	7
1937 SD	35	86	13	22	4	0	0	5	.256	.302	26	2
1938 SD	8	12	3	3	2	0	0	1	.250	.417	5	0
	2342	8969	1543	2574	442	65	65	– –	.287	.373	3341	373

SKEETER NEWSOME   Lamar Ashby Newsome. Born 10/18/1910, Phenix City, AL. Died 8/31/1989, Columbus, GA. Utility infielder in major leagues for twelve seasons with the Athletics, Red Sox and Phillies.

	G	AB	R	H	2B	3B	HR	RBI	BA	SA	TB	SB
1948 Sea	130	449	44	112	19	1	0	26	.249	.296	133	4

TED NORBERT   Theodore Joseph Norbert. Born 5/17/1908, Brooklyn, NY. Died 8/19/1991, San Juan, Puerto Rico. Was part of the deal that sent the young Joe DiMaggio from San Francisco Seals to the New York Yankees. The only man to win four Pacific Coast League home run titles, he led the PCL in RBI in 1938 and in batting average in 1942.

	G	AB	R	H	2B	3B	HR	RBI	BA	SA	TB	SB
1935 SF	149	524	86	158	46	5	11	103	.302	.471	247	30
1936 SF	165	597	103	187	41	9	21	126	.313	.518	309	16
1937 SF	144	497	93	151	32	2	16	91	.304	.473	235	7
1938 SF	178	677	101	192	46	5	30	163	.284	.499	338	7
1939 SF	162	564	96	172	46	4	25	104	.305	.534	301	9
1940 SF	173	594	109	190	32	2	20	94	.320	.481	286	5
1941 Port	149	503	72	140	21	1	20	73	.278	.443	223	1
1942 Port	149	481	88	182	25	4	28	99	.378	.622	299	4
1944 LA	111	363	58	105	21	5	10	57	.289	.457	166	1
1945 Sea	169	527	71	136	24	2	23	109	.258	.442	233	6
1946 Sea	20	43	5	13	2	0	1	4	.302	.419	18	0
	1569	5370	882	1626	336	39	205	1023	.303	.494	2655	86

IRV NOREN   Irving Arnold Noren. Born 11/29/1924, Jamestown, NY. Despite chronic knee problems, outfielder for eleven years in big leagues, making the 1954 AL All—Star team. Played in three WS for Yankees.

	G	AB	R	H	2B	3B	HR	RBI	BA	SA	TB	SB
1949 Hol	180	678	134	224	40	6	29	130	.330	.535	363	10
1962 Haw	76	135	13	32	3	0	4	25	.237	.348	47	0
1963 Haw	16	15	2	4	1	0	0	1	.267	.333	5	0
	272	828	149	260	44	6	33	156	.314	.501	415	10

RON NORTHEY   Ronald James Northey. Born 4/26/1920, Mahanoy City, PA. Died 4/16/1971, Pittsburgh, PA. Played twelve seasons in the majors with five teams, the last three seasons as a pinch—hitting specialist.

	G	AB	R	H	2B	3B	HR	RBI	BA	SA	TB	SB
1952 LA	92	235	22	60	4	0	11	38	.255	.413	97	1

LOU NOVIKOFF   Louie Alexander Novikoff. Born 10/12/1915, Glendale, AZ. Died 9/30/1970, South Gate, CA. A Hall of Fame softball player, "The Mad Russian" was one of baseball's most colorful players. Won the PCL Triple Crown in 1940. Poor outfielder reportedly afraid of Wrigley Field's ivy.

	G	AB	R	H	2B	3B	HR	RBI	BA	SA	TB	SB
1939 LA	36	135	36	61	11	4	8	37	.452	.770	104	2
1940 LA	174	714	147	259	44	6	41	171	.363	.613	438	3
1945 LA	101	390	60	121	27	6	9	52	.310	.479	187	5
1946 Sea	84	312	24	94	13	2	2	04	.301	.375	117	4
1947 Sea	171	647	90	210	44	7	21	114	.325	.512	331	1
1948 Sea	64	168	13	55	9	1	3	30	.327	.446	75	1
	630	2366	370	800	148	26	84	438	.338	.529	1252	16

REBEL OAKES   Ennis Talmadge Oakes. Born 12/17/1886, Homer, LA. Died 2/8/1948, Shreveport, LA. Led the PCL with 55 sacrifice hits in 1908. Seven year outfielder in majors, was player—manager in Federal League.

	G	AB	R	H	2B	3B	HR	RBI	BA	SA	TB	SB
1908 LA	192	736	98	212	25	8	0	––	.288	.344	253	36

PRINCE OANA   Henry Kauhane Oana. Born 1/22/1908, Waipahu, HI. Died 6/19/1976, Austin, TX. Not really a prince, ended career as a pitcher, with twenty—four victories in the Texas League in 1946.

	G	AB	R	H	2B	3B	HR	RBI	BA	SA	TB	SB
1930 SF	79	298	46	97	18	4	11	53	.326	.523	156	7
1931 SF	172	742	116	256	44	16	23	161	.345	.540	401	12
1932 SF	131	440	60	105	22	9	2	52	.239	.343	151	5
1933 Port	174	686	127	228	63	11	29	163	.332	.583	400	11
1934 Port	11	43	6	10	0	0	1	5	.233	.302	13	0
	567	2209	355	696	147	40	66	434	.315	.507	1121	35

JIMMY O'CONNELL   James Joseph O'Connell. Born 2/11/1901, San Francisco, CA. Died 11/11/1976, Bakersfield, CA. Contract purchased in 1922 from Seals by Giants for $75,000. Outfielder received a lifetime ban after confessing to offering the Phils' Heine Sand $500 to throw a game.

JIMMY O'CONNELL (cont.)

	G	AB	R	H	2B	3B	HR	RBI	BA	SA	TB	SB
1919 SF	8	32	3	10	1	0	0	– –	.313	.344	11	0
1920 SF	102	305	28	80	6	6	0	– –	.262	.321	98	5
1921 SF	170	600	113	202	32	9	17	101	.337	.505	303	23
1922 SF	187	671	133	225	39	10	13	92	.335	.481	323	39
	467	1608	277	517	78	25	30	– –	.322	.457	735	67

LEFTY O'DOUL

Francis Joseph O'Doul. Born 3/4/1897, San Francisco, CA. Died 12/7/1969, San Francisco, CA. Began career as a pitcher before arm trouble and a potent bat moved him to outfield. Won two NL batting titles and hit .349 over eleven big league seasons. Considered to be baseball's ambassador to Japan. Gifted hitting teacher, managed 23 years in PCL.

	G	AB	R	H	2B	3B	HR	RBI	BA	SA	TB	SB
1918 SF	49	120	9	24	3	0	1	– –	.200	.250	30	2
1921 SF	74	136	24	46	7	2	5	23	.338	.529	72	2
1924 SLC	140	416	84	163	31	4	11	101	.392	.565	235	11
1925 SLC	198	825	185	309	63	17	24	191	.375	.579	478	12
1926 Hol	180	659	88	223	29	3	20	116	.338	.483	318	10
1927 Hol	189	736	164	278	43	4	33	158	.378	.582	428	40
1935 SF	68	134	23	36	2	1	2	25	.269	.343	46	3
1936 SF	54	53	5	12	2	2	0	8	.226	.340	18	0
1937 SF	44	44	7	17	6	0	0	13	.386	.523	23	0
1938 SF	30	27	6	7	1	0	3	6	.259	.630	17	0
1939 SF	25	35	6	14	1	0	0	2	.400	.429	15	3
1940 SF	14	13	0	2	0	0	0	0	.154	.154	2	0
1944 SF	1	1	0	0	0	0	0	0	.000	.000	0	0
1945 SF	1	1	0	0	0	0	0	0	.000	.000	0	0
1956 Van	1	1	0	1	0	1	0	0	1.000	3.000	3	0
	1068	3201	601	1132	188	34	99	– –	.354	.526	1685	83

JIM OGLESBY

James Dorn Oglesby. Born 8/10/1905, Schofield, MO. Died 9/1/1955, Tulsa, OK. Consistent run producer, his forty–three game hitting streak in 1933 went virtually unnoticed, as it coincided with famous sixty–one game streak of Joe Di Maggio.

	G	AB	R	H	2B	3B	HR	RBI	BA	SA	TB	SB
1932 LA	64	263	46	85	16	0	5	61	.323	.441	116	5
1933 LA	186	723	122	226	49	6	20	137	.313	.480	347	14
1934 LA	188	725	102	226	44	4	15	139	.312	.446	323	11
1935 LA	173	678	133	237	56	5	24	132	.350	.553	375	18
	611	2389	403	774	165	15	64	469	.324	.486	1161	48

CHARLEY O'LEARY

Charles Timothy O'Leary. Born 10/15/1881, Chicago, IL. Died 1/6/1941, Chicago, IL. Infielder for eleven years in the majors, mostly with Tigers. Twenty–one years between big league hits, singled and scored a run as pinch–hitter for '34 Browns at age 51. As a Yankee coach, miraculously survived Babe Ruth's 1920 car accident.

	G	AB	R	H	2B	3B	HR	RBI	BA	SA	TB	SB
1914 SF	183	660	72	164	12	7	0	41	.248	.288	190	14

IVY OLSON   Ivan Massie Olson. Born 10/14/1885, Kansas City, MO. Died 9/1/1965, Inglewood, CA. Infielder in majors for fourteen years, mostly at shortstop. As Brooklyn's lead—off hitter, led the NL in base hits in 1919.

	G	AB	R	H	2B	3B	HR	RBI	BA	SA	TB	SB
1909 Port	206	797	96	171	—	—	—	—	.215	—	—	—
1910 Port	210	798	110	189	25	4	1	—	.237	.282	225	39
	416	1595	206	360	—	—	—	—	.226	—	—	—

BILLY ORR   William John Orr. Born 4/22/1891, San Francisco, CA. Died 3/10/1967, Santarium, CA. With the Philadelphia A's 1913–1914. After his return to the PCL, he led shortstops in fielding three times. Twice a victim of unassisted triple plays while in the Pacific Coast League.

	G	AB	R	H	2B	3B	HR	RBI	BA	SA	TB	SB
1912 Sac	87	324	29	83	—	—	—	—	.256	—	—	18
1914 Sac	131	498	46	152	16	8	1	38	.305	.376	187	13
1915 SLC	190	776	107	217	48	10	3	—	.280	.379	294	26
1916 SLC	179	683	94	170	32	4	5	—	.249	.329	225	16
1917 SLC	189	753	63	192	31	4	0	—	.255	.307	231	26
1918 SLC	97	359	42	94	15	1	0	—	.262	.309	111	17
1919 Sac	155	554	42	113	13	1	0	—	.204	.231	128	12
1920 Sac	178	673	76	178	21	2	5	—	.264	.324	218	9
1921 Sac	181	686	69	196	32	7	3	76	.286	.366	251	2
1922 Sac—Sea	125	421	46	126	24	3	2	57	.299	.385	162	10
1923 Sea	162	598	58	157	31	2	1	61	.203	.326	195	6
	1674	6325	672	1678	—	—	—	—	.265	.334	—	155

RAY ORTEIG   Raymond Joseph Orteig. Born 12/20/1921, Orchards, WA. Died 12/26/1993, Yakima, WA. Began his Pacific Coast League career as a third baseman, converted to catcher on his return to league in 1950.

	G	AB	R	H	2B	3B	HR	RBI	BA	SA	TB	SB
1947 SF	142	462	67	138	36	8	6	64	.299	.450	208	1
1948 SF	102	262	45	71	15	1	7	51	.271	.416	109	0
1950 SF	130	390	49	117	22	3	6	49	.300	.418	163	1
1951 SF	126	417	56	119	19	0	16	71	.285	.446	186	0
1952 SF	147	432	44	115	26	6	3	53	.266	.375	162	3
1953 Sea	158	489	76	135	15	1	28	99	.276	.483	236	2
1954 Sea	119	354	35	90	18	2	14	65	.254	.435	154	0
1955 Sea	39	98	15	29	5	0	4	20	.296	.469	46	2
1956 Sea	122	385	38	107	10	1	9	53	.278	.379	146	2
1957 Sea	122	343	30	90	21	3	3	47	.262	.367	126	2
1958 Sea	53	128	7	29	8	0	0	10	.227	.289	37	0
	1260	3760	462	1040	195	25	96	582	.277	.418	1573	13

MARV OWEN   Marvin James Owen. Born 3/22/1906, Agnew, CA. Died 6/22/1991, Mountain View, CA. Starting third baseman for the Tigers from 1933–1937, was involved in a celebrated fight with Ducky Medwick in the 1934 Series. Won pennant as a player/manager for Portland in 1945.

	G	AB	R	H	2B	3B	HR	RBI	BA	SA	TB	SB
1930 Sea	138	443	67	133	24	7	3	55	.300	.406	180	16

MARV OWEN (cont.)

	G	AB	R	H	2B	3B	HR	RBI	BA	SA	TB	SB
1941 Port	144	501	68	150	38	6	1	70	.299	.405	203	3
1942 Port	147	535	52	162	27	7	3	66	.303	.396	212	5
1943 Port	73	260	27	80	12	2	0	32	.308	.369	96	1
1944 Port	131	449	40	130	27	2	1	63	.290	.365	164	9
1945 Port	163	566	88	176	40	3	1	83	.311	.398	225	10
1946 Port	39	103	8	16	1	1	0	5	.155	.184	19	0
	835	2857	350	847	169	28	9	374	.296	.385	1099	44

ANDY PAFKO   Andrew Pafko. Born 2/25/1921, Boyceville, WI. Won PCL batting title and MVP Award in 1943. Strong–armed outfielder went on to become four–time NL All–Star with 213 home runs during his seventeen year career. Appeared in four World Series; very popular among fans.

	G	AB	R	H	2B	3B	HR	RBI	BA	SA	TB	SB
1943 LA	157	604	109	215	31	13	18	118	.356	.540	326	13

HAROLD PATCHETT   Harold Robert Patchett. Born 5/10/1912, Flint, MI. Died 4/7/1978, El Cajon, CA. Lettered in four sports at Adrian College; the outfielder had nearly 2,500 hits in minors. Led the PCL in triples in 1943.

	G	AB	R	H	2B	3B	HR	RBI	BA	SA	TB	SB
1937 SD	169	689	105	211	38	8	8	66	.306	.419	289	21
1938 SD	166	668	98	202	38	12	3	57	.302	.409	273	10
1939 SD	160	610	83	177	24	7	0	32	.290	.352	215	6
1940 SD	166	686	109	195	28	5	0	51	.284	.340	233	9
1941 SD	168	622	78	184	21	8	0	60	.296	.355	221	25
1942 SD	172	663	83	191	23	5	0	43	.288	.338	224	8
1943 SD	141	522	63	148	12	15	1	49	.284	.370	193	25
1944 SD	128	426	49	117	10	5	1	56	.275	.329	140	19
1945 O–Sea	157	580	85	178	21	6	0	47	.307	.364	211	19
1946 Sea	109	238	24	58	5	0	0	14	.244	.265	63	6
	1536	5704	777	1661	220	71	13	475	.291	.362	2062	148

ALBIE PEARSON   Albert Gregory Pearson. Born 9/12/1934, Alhambra, CA. The shortest player in the major leagues during his career, once struck for six extra base hits in a row, tying mark held by Babe Ruth and Lou Gehrig. 1958 AL Rookie of the Year and All–Star in 1963. Led AL in runs in 1962.

	G	AB	R	H	2B	3B	HR	RBI	BA	SA	TB	SB
1956 SF	31	101	18	30	5	2	0	6	.297	.386	39	2
1957 SF	158	592	89	176	22	11	5	50	.297	.397	235	9
	189	693	107	206	27	13	5	56	.297	.395	274	11

ROGER PECKINPAUGH   Roger Thorpe Peckinpaugh. Born 2/5/1891, Wooster, OH. Died 11/17/1977, Cleveland, OH. Considered to be the top shortstop of his era, was hero of the 1924 World Series and goat in 1925. At age of twenty–three, managed Yankees at the end of the 1914 season. Named the American League's Most Valuable Player in 1925.

	G	AB	R	H	2B	3B	HR	RBI	BA	SA	TB	SB
1911 Port	195	702	86	181	––	––	––	––	.258	––	––	35

PAUL PETTIT   George William Paul Pettit. Born 11/29/1931, Los Angeles,
CA. Signed by the Pittsburgh Pirates in 1950 as baseball's first $100,000
bonus baby, started out as a pitcher before a sore arm forced conversion
to outfield during the mid−1950's. Won 15 games for Hollywood in 1952;
only one in majors. Drove in ten runs in one game vs. Seattle 9/12/1957.

	G	AB	R	H	2B	3B	HR	RBI	BA	SA	TB	SB
1952 Hol	33	75	11	24	8	2	1	17	.320	.520	39	0
1954 Hol	9	6	0	2	0	0	0	0	.333	.333	2	0
1955 Hol	17	46	2	7	3	0	0	2	.152	.217	10	0
1956 Hol	114	284	39	67	11	0	10	45	.236	.380	108	1
1957 Hol	158	542	85	154	31	1	20	102	.284	.456	247	2
1958 SLC	32	86	13	23	5	0	3	15	.267	.430	37	0
1959 SLC−Se	130	431	65	109	24	5	16	68	.253	.443	191	3
1960 Sea	93	243	31	62	9	0	5	30	.255	.354	86	1
	586	1713	246	448	91	8	55	279	.262	.420	720	7

BABE PINELLI   Ralph Arthur Pinelli. Born 10/18/1895, San Francisco, CA.
Died 10/22/1984, Daly City, CA. Third baseman in major leagues for eight
seasons, twice hitting over .300. Hit two grand slams in one game in PCL
on 7/4/1929. NL umpire for twenty−two years, final appearance was as a
home plate umpire for Don Larsen's perfect game in 1956 World Series.

	G	AB	R	H	2B	3B	HR	RBI	BA	SA	TB	SB
1917 Port	79	211	21	42	5	2	0	−−	.199	.242	51	8
1918 Sac	94	348	40	93	9	6	0	−−	.267	.328	114	15
1919 Sac	150	548	76	138	20	3	1	−−	.252	.305	167	51
1921 Oak	181	720	127	244	38	5	2	57	.339	.414	298	47
1927 SF	49	142	20	46	5	2	0	14	.324	.387	55	2
1928 SF	114	422	62	131	26	0	2	31	.310	.386	163	3
1929 SF	167	679	109	211	34	4	5	65	.311	.395	268	12
1930 SF	140	579	95	181	22	1	3	55	.313	.370	214	16
1931 O−SF	155	553	71	148	29	6	0	63	.268	.342	189	11
1932 Oak	160	554	57	170	26	2	0	57	.307	.361	200	16
	1289	4756	678	1404	214	31	13	−−	.295	.361	1719	181

JIM POOLE   James Robert Poole. Born 5/12/1895, Taylorsville, NC. Died
1/2/1975, Hickory, NC. Led PCL in home runs in 1924. Spent three years
in majors, played in minors until age 51, collecting more than 3,000 hits.

	G	AB	R	H	2B	3B	HR	RBI	BA	SA	TB	SB
1921 Port	186	731	112	241	57	9	20	107	.330	.514	376	20
1922 Port	195	752	108	225	56	1	22	109	.299	.464	349	13
1923 Port	193	756	150	256	68	13	27	136	.339	.570	431	17
1924 Port	182	722	159	255	47	7	38	159	.353	.596	430	8
	756	2961	529	977	228	30	107	511	.330	.536	1586	58

JERRY PRIDDY   Gerald Edward Priddy. Born 11/9/1919, Los Angeles, CA.
Died 3/3/1980, North Hollywood, CA. Twelve years in majors as a second
baseman, was player−manager for Seattle in 1954. Briefly played on the
PGA tour after retirement. Was convicted of extortion against a steamship
company after claiming to have put a bomb aboard ship.

JERRY PRIDDY (cont.)

	G	AB	R	H	2B	3B	HR	RBI	BA	SA	TB	SB
1954 Sea	96	275	22	68	12	0	0	24	.247	.291	80	1
1955 Sea	16	36	3	12	2	0	1	7	.333	.472	17	0
1956 Sac–SF	75	175	15	52	8	0	2	20	.297	.377	66	0
	187	486	40	132	22	0	3	51	.272	.335	163	1

BILLY RAIMONDI   William Louis Raimondi. Born 12/1/1913, San Francisco, CA. One of the PCL's most popular, longest–serving, and least powerful players. A catcher who wore glasses, averaged one homer every 933 at bats. Played all nine positions in the final game of the 1943 season.

	G	AB	R	H	2B	3B	HR	RBI	BA	SA	TB	SB
1932 Oak	42	121	12	34	2	0	0	6	.281	.298	36	0
1933 Oak	101	270	35	78	23	2	0	34	.289	.389	105	3
1934 Oak	158	529	60	150	20	5	1	70	.284	.346	183	10
1935 Oak	112	355	46	91	15	2	0	38	.256	.310	110	3
1937 Oak	107	303	36	75	15	4	1	34	.248	.333	101	2
1938 Oak	140	441	44	119	15	2	0	47	.270	.313	138	4
1939 Oak	102	316	33	96	12	4	1	27	.304	.377	119	3
1940 Oak	108	358	34	85	13	5	0	43	.237	.302	108	4
1941 Oak	97	307	37	87	17	3	1	37	.283	.368	113	6
1942 Oak	128	415	47	102	16	1	0	33	.246	.289	120	6
1943 Oak	132	430	58	119	14	1	1	41	.277	.321	138	7
1944 Oak	143	452	53	131	19	3	0	45	.290	.345	156	10
1945 Oak	117	341	44	91	22	3	2	40	.267	.367	125	3
1946 Oak	112	347	34	104	19	4	0	32	.300	.378	131	6
1947 Oak	152	418	55	124	21	2	0	47	.297	.356	149	10
1948 Oak	126	302	40	86	17	1	0	31	.285	.348	105	14
1949 O–Sac	133	429	49	114	13	1	0	33	.266	.301	129	4
1950 Sac	110	277	41	67	15	1	0	16	.242	.303	84	4
1951 LA	52	107	18	31	4	0	0	9	.290	.327	35	0
1952 LA	11	12	1	3	1	0	0	2	.250	.333	4	0
1953 LA	3	2	0	0	0	0	0	0	.000	.000	0	0
	2186	6532	777	1787	293	44	7	665	.274	.335	2189	99

EARL RAPP   Earl Wellington Rapp. Born 5/20/1921, Corunna, MI. Died 2/13/1992, Swedesboro, NJ. Outfielder for five teams in three big league seasons, led the Pacific Coast League in 1955 in runs batted in.

	G	AB	R	H	2B	3B	HR	RBI	BA	SA	TB	SB
1948 Sea	168	564	88	168	36	6	17	96	.298	.473	267	10
1949 Oak	97	340	76	117	24	3	15	86	.344	.565	192	6
1950 Oak	181	639	133	222	49	8	24	145	.347	.562	359	7
1951 Oak	97	357	66	115	15	8	10	74	.322	.493	176	5
1953 SD	180	630	104	196	32	7	24	108	.311	.498	314	11
1954 SD	162	566	102	191	37	7	24	111	.337	.555	314	2
1955 SD	169	582	109	176	25	6	30	133	.302	.521	303	1
1956 SD	122	414	59	124	14	5	9	65	.300	.423	175	3
1957 SD–P	83	205	27	57	7	2	3	19	.278	.376	77	1
	1259	4297	764	1366	239	52	156	837	.318	.507	2177	46

JIMMIE REESE   James Harrison Reese. Born 10/1/1901, New York, NY. Died 7/13/1994, Santa Ana, CA. Spent over three quarters of a century in baseball, starting as a Los Angeles Angels batboy in 1917. Was paid with a silver dollar and a baseball each week from team owner Frank Chance. Arguably the greatest fielding second baseman in Coast League history.

	G	AB	R	H	2B	3B	HR	RBI	BA	SA	TB	SB
1920 LA	3	9	2	2	0	0	0	0	.222	.222	2	0
1924 Oak	8	32	8	6	2	0	0	——	.188	.250	8	——
1925 Oak	136	463	63	115	24	2	0	37	.248	.309	143	13
1926 Oak	183	709	113	189	32	11	4	48	.267	.360	255	11
1927 Oak	191	722	113	213	34	17	2	83	.295	.398	287	18
1928 Oak	132	478	60	118	10	5	1	35	.247	.295	141	5
1929 Oak	190	766	143	258	33	9	1	56	.337	.407	312	24
1933 LA	104	393	85	130	23	6	5	38	.331	.458	180	3
1934 LA	180	733	123	228	31	12	3	85	.311	.398	292	14
1935 LA	155	576	79	171	28	8	1	66	.297	.378	218	9
1936 LA	146	515	57	139	21	3	0	54	.270	.322	166	7
1937 SD	138	506	59	159	23	7	2	78	.314	.399	202	4
1938 SD	108	349	41	81	11	1	0	28	.232	.269	94	2
1940 LA	2	5	0	0	0	0	0	0	.000	.000	0	0
	1676	6256	946	1809	272	81	19	608	.289	.368	2300	110

HERMAN REICH   Herman Charles Reich. Born 11/23/1917, Bell, CA. First baseman played briefly in majors with the Washington Senators, the Cleveland Indians, and the Chicago Cubs——all in the 1949 season.

	G	AB	R	H	2B	3B	HR	RBI	BA	SA	TB	SB
1940 Port	164	592	62	136	21	2	11	54	.230	.328	194	7
1941 Port	151	556	82	170	21	3	11	66	.306	.414	230	8
1946 Port	170	629	64	190	27	3	9	75	.302	.397	250	5
1947 Port	153	533	76	150	23	2	18	98	.281	.433	231	13
1948 Port	187	677	94	219	38	1	19	100	.323	.467	316	7
1950 Sac	126	410	48	112	18	0	10	65	.273	.390	160	6
1951 Sac	134	388	58	96	9	1	9	49	.247	.345	134	3
1952 Sac—P	105	326	28	72	9	0	4	28	.221	.285	93	3
1953 Port	125	399	37	118	12	1	12	53	.296	.421	168	1
1954 P—Sea	62	131	15	34	9	0	2	19	.260	.374	49	0
	1377	4641	564	1297	187	13	105	607	.279	.393	1825	53

DINO RESTELLI   Dino Paul Restelli. Born 9/23/1924, St. Louis, MO. Hard hitting platoon outfielder, broke into majors with the Pittsburgh Pirates by slamming eight home runs in first ten games. Hit only five more in majors.

	G	AB	R	H	2B	3B	HR	RBI	BA	SA	TB	SB
1944 SF	38	137	23	47	10	5	1	19	.343	.511	70	6
1946 SF	26	39	0	4	0	0	0	2	.103	.103	4	0
1947 SF	119	356	61	104	20	4	10	55	.292	.455	162	6
1948 SF	145	505	86	146	43	8	10	80	.289	.465	235	6
1949 SF	72	268	47	94	21	2	10	65	.351	.556	149	7
1950 SF	99	290	65	99	17	0	17	62	.341	.576	167	1
1951 Hol	76	270	51	76	17	5	10	46	.281	.493	133	0

DINO RESTELLI (cont.)

	G	AB	R	H	2B	3B	HR	RBI	BA	SA	TB	SB
1952 Sac	69	249	39	89	14	4	7	31	.357	.530	132	4
1953 Port	73	256	47	87	21	1	12	41	.340	.570	146	7
1954 Port	117	357	53	93	12	0	12	44	.261	.395	141	9
1955 Port	21	57	7	18	1	0	2	6	.316	.439	25	0
	855	2784	479	857	176	29	91	451	.308	.490	1364	46

CARL REYNOLDS   Carl Nettles Reynolds. Born 2/1/1903, La Rue, TX. Died 5/29/1978, Houston, TX. Outfielder hit .302 lifetime in his twelve big league seasons. Batted over .300 six times, including .359 in 1930. Had home runs in three consecutive at bats against the Yankees 5/2/1930.

	G	AB	R	H	2B	3B	HR	RBI	BA	SA	TB	SB
1940 LA	41	80	10	20	3	1	0	13	.250	.313	25	1

HAL RHYNE   Harold J. Rhyne. Born 3/30/1899, Paso Robles, CA. Died 1/7/1971, Orangevale, CA. Considered a future star when sold to Pirates along with Paul Waner in 1925 for a reported $100,000; never lived up to early promise. Led PCL shortstops in fielding three times ('24, '25, '36).

	G	AB	R	H	2B	3B	HR	RBI	BA	SA	TB	SB
1922 SF	189	699	80	199	39	8	0	93	.285	.363	254	19
1923 SF	168	611	94	181	26	4	5	77	.296	.376	230	21
1924 SF	196	751	110	224	34	2	2	80	.298	.357	268	26
1925 SF	188	724	109	228	48	3	3	97	.315	.402	291	17
1928 SF	185	692	82	216	37	0	6	106	.312	.392	271	17
1934 SF	184	675	78	174	34	7	0	65	.258	.329	222	15
1935 SF	150	523	78	154	34	2	1	81	.294	.373	195	12
1936 SF	137	518	75	132	22	2	1	53	.255	.311	161	11
1937 SF	121	416	53	106	22	1	0	46	.255	.313	130	3
1938 SF	5	1	0	0	0	0	0	0	.000	.000	0	0
	1523	5610	759	1614	296	29	18	698	.288	.360	2022	141

HARRY RICE   Harry Francis Rice. Born 11/22/1901, Ware Station, IL. Died 1/1/1971, Portland, OR. Ten year major league outfielder, hit .300 or more five times and .299 lifetime. A good defensive player, hit .359 for St. Louis Browns in 1925. Struck out once every nineteen at bats in majors.

	G	AB	R	H	2B	3B	HR	RBI	BA	SA	TB	SB
1935 MSeaP	150	537	71	164	38	8	2	70	.305	.417	224	8

BILL RIGNEY   William Joseph Rigney. Born 1/29/1918, Alameda, CA. A big league infielder for Giants for eight years; manager in major leagues for eighteen seasons. Manager of the Giants at time of their move to San Francisco; he guided AL expansion Angels to third place finish in 1962.

	G	AB	R	H	2B	3B	HR	RBI	BA	SA	TB	SB
1938 Oak	24	83	11	22	7	0	0	4	.265	.349	29	0
1939 Oak	1	3	0	0	0	0	0	0	.000	.000	0	0
1941 Oak	173	605	76	126	26	7	3	61	.208	.289	175	8
1942 Oak	177	638	83	184	34	5	1	57	.288	.362	231	13
	375	1329	170	332	67	12	4	122	.250	.327	435	21

SWEDE RISBERG   Charles August Risberg. Born 10/13/1894, San Francisco, CA. Died 10/13/1975, Red Bluff, CA. A frequent brawler in the PCL, was co—ringleader and last surviving member of 1919 "Black Sox".

	G	AB	R	H	2B	3B	HR	RBI	BA	SA	TB	SB
1914 Ven	14	32	3	10	2	0	0	7	.313	.375	12	2
1915 Ver	175	602	94	165	31	6	10	— —	.274	.395	238	28
1916 Ver	185	691	101	182	51	5	6	— —	.263	.378	261	25
	374	1325	198	357	84	11	16	— —	.269	.386	511	55

JOHN RITCHEY   John Franklin Ritchey. Born 1/5/1923, San Diego, CA. Left—handed hitting catcher, broke the color line in PCL on signing Padre contract. Won the Negro American League in batting title in 1947.

	G	AB	R	H	2B	3B	HR	RBI	BA	SA	TB	SB
1948 SD	103	217	35	70	10	2	4	44	.323	.442	96	2
1949 SD	112	327	29	84	10	1	3	35	.257	.321	105	12
1950 Port	107	241	32	65	8	4	2	34	.270	.361	87	1
1951 Port	1	3	0	0	0	0	0	0	.000	.000	0	0
1953 Sac	147	454	62	132	18	8	5	55	.291	.399	181	10
1954 Sac	94	283	24	77	6	2	0	23	.272	.307	87	5
1955 SF	130	375	52	107	15	1	6	41	.285	.379	142	10
	694	1900	234	535	67	18	20	232	.282	.367	698	40

JUNGLE JIM RIVERA   Manuel Joseph Rivera. Born 7/22/1922, Brooklyn, NY. Batting champ and MVP in only PCL season, exciting player on base and in the field. Rogers Hornsby called him only player he'd pay to see.

	G	AB	R	H	2B	3B	HR	RBI	BA	SA	TB	SB
1951 Sea	166	657	135	231	40	16	20	112	.352	.553	363	33

FLOYD ROBINSON   Floyd Andrew Robinson. Born 5/9/1936, Prescott, AR. Three—time .300 hitter in majors, had 109 RBI for White Sox in 1962. Went six for six in a game against the Boston Red Sox July 22, 1962.

	G	AB	R	H	2B	3B	HR	RBI	BA	SA	TB	SB
1954 SD	3	6	0	0	0	0	0	0	.000	.000	0	0
1955 SD	4	2	1	0	0	0	0	0	.000	.000	0	0
1957 SD	140	498	93	139	11	5	11	41	.279	.388	193	27
1960 SD	101	374	60	119	20	6	13	48	.318	.508	190	13
1969 Haw	140	504	82	134	19	2	10	53	.266	.371	187	13
	388	1384	236	392	50	13	34	142	.283	.412	570	53

RAY ROHWER   Ray Rohwer. Born 6/5/1895, Dixon, CA. Died 1/24/1988, Davis, CA. Outfielder joined Pirates out of the University of California. In 1927 once had six trips to the plate in PCL game without an official at bat.

	G	AB	R	H	2B	3B	HR	RBI	BA	SA	TB	SB
1923 Sea	179	655	125	213	30	20	37	135	.325	.602	394	12
1924 Sea	176	644	120	209	42	15	33	155	.325	.590	380	11
1925 Port	177	677	139	226	44	3	40	153	.334	.585	396	12
1926 P—Sac	168	565	99	148	25	2	28	107	.262	.462	261	14
1927 Sac	133	422	70	141	32	4	14	95	.334	.528	223	11
1928 Sac	142	478	76	138	34	2	10	84	.289	.431	206	13

RAY ROHWER (cont.)

	G	AB	R	H	2B	3B	HR	RBI	BA	SA	TB	SB
1929 Sac	149	495	76	127	29	7	11	70	.257	.410	203	8
1930 Sac	124	392	56	117	27	6	13	83	.298	.497	195	6
1931 Sac	110	356	40	88	24	2	10	47	.247	.410	146	5
	1358	4684	801	1407	287	61	196	929	.300	.513	2404	92

JOHNNY ROMANO   John Anthony Romano. Born 8/23/1934, Hoboken, NJ. A two–time AL All–Star catcher during ten year major league career, twice topped twenty home runs in a season in the American League.

	G	AB	R	H	2B	3B	HR	RBI	BA	SA	TB	SB
1956 Van	81	241	35	58	9	3	8	41	.241	.402	97	2

AL ROSEN   Albert Leonard Rosen. Born 2/29/1924, Spartanburg, SC. Two time AL home run and RBI champ, the four–time All–Star third baseman missed out on the AL Triple Crown on last day of his 1953 MVP season.

	G	AB	R	H	2B	3B	HR	RBI	BA	SA	TB	SB
1949 SD	83	273	49	87	12	1	14	51	.319	.524	143	5

HARRY ROSENBERG   Harry Rosenberg. Born 6/22/1909, San Francisco, CA. Outfielder hit for a lifetime average of .326 in the minor leagues with over 2,000 hits, but had only five major league at bats.

	G	AB	R	H	2B	3B	HR	RBI	BA	SA	TB	SB
1930 Miss	70	239	60	88	19	2	11	53	.368	.603	144	3
1935 Sac	151	567	95	201	27	16	10	80	.354	.511	290	15
1936 Miss	172	668	103	223	33	15	3	99	.334	.442	295	11
1937 Miss	162	612	92	202	32	11	10	76	.330	.467	286	7
1938 Port	154	575	75	184	37	8	4	82	.320	.433	249	12
1939 Port	172	646	103	214	45	5	8	95	.331	.454	293	5
1940 Port	177	659	91	207	28	6	4	70	.314	.393	259	10
1941 Hol	120	420	58	120	31	2	1	55	.286	.376	158	9
1943 SF	26	94	11	34	4	1	0	18	.362	.426	40	0
	1204	4480	688	1473	256	66	51	628	.329	.450	2014	72

JACK ROTHROCK   John Houston Rothrock. Born 3/14/1905, Long Beach, CA. Died 2/2/1980, San Bernardino, CA. Played all nine positions during eleven year major league career. Led the "Gashouse Gang" with six runs batted in during the 1934 World Series against the Detroit Tigers.

	G	AB	R	H	2B	3B	HR	RBI	BA	SA	TB	SB
1938 LA	149	516	67	148	29	6	6	84	.287	.401	207	5
1939 LA	114	370	53	108	16	2	5	44	.292	.386	143	2
1940 LA–H	82	253	31	62	8	2	1	37	.245	.304	77	2
	345	1139	151	318	53	10	12	165	.279	.375	427	9

HARRY RUBY   Harry Ruby. Born 1/27/1895, New York, NY. Died 2/23/1974, Woodland Hills, CA. Song–writer for films, best remembered for "Hooray for Captain Spalding" & "Three Little Words". An ardent fan of baseball, he played in a couple of season ending games strictly as a lark. His love for the game was far bigger than his athletic talent.

HARRY RUBY (cont.)

	G	AB	R	H	2B	3B	HR	RBI	BA	SA	TB	SB
1935 Hol	1	2	0	0	0	0	0	0	.000	.000	0	0
1940 LA	1	0	0	0	0	0	0	0	——	——	0	0
	2	2	0	0	0	0	0	0	.000	.000	0	0

BILL RUMLER   William George Rumler. Born 3/27/1891, Milford, NE. Died 5/26/1966, Lincoln, NE. The 1919 PCL batting champion, was given a five year suspension for suspected involvement in PCL gambling scandal. He finally returned to baseball in 1929. Broken ankle in 1930 ended career.

	G	AB	R	H	2B	3B	HR	RBI	BA	SA	TB	SB
1919 SLC	151	591	98	214	42	17	17	——	.362	.577	341	15
1920 SLC	128	531	94	187	38	11	24	——	.352	.601	319	31
1929 Hol	140	503	110	194	39	3	26	120	.386	.630	317	6
1930 Hol	95	346	77	122	23	3	14	82	.353	.558	193	8
	514	1971	379	717	142	34	81	——	.364	.594	1170	60

BUD RYAN   John Budd Ryan. Born 10/6/1885, Denver, CO. Died 7/9/1956, Sacramento, CA. Led PCL in batting and home runs in 1911, played two years in Cleveland outfield. Later managed Sacramento for nine seasons.

	G	AB	R	H	2B	3B	HR	RBI	BA	SA	TB	SB
1908 Port	165	623	72	155	19	7	0	——	.249	.302	188	35
1909 Port	145	538	66	125	——	——	——	——	.232	——	——	——
1910 Port	206	784	86	100	28	0	13	——	.242	.348	273	25
1911 Port	190	741	120	247	——	——	23	——	.333	——	——	39
1914 Port	150	530	52	156	26	9	3	64	.294	.394	209	14
1915 SLC	193	754	129	256	59	9	12	——	.340	.489	369	21
1916 SLC	180	701	89	217	49	6	8	——	.310	.431	302	18
1917 SLC	194	730	102	233	47	2	9	——	.319	.426	311	28
1918 SLC	52	197	26	60	13	3	5	——	.305	.477	94	3
1920 Sac	105	393	42	117	26	6	7	——	.298	.448	176	7
1921 Sac	171	621	78	199	39	10	9	90	.320	.459	285	7
1922 Sac	172	623	94	190	48	10	4	83	.305	.433	270	16
1923 Sac	97	203	22	52	7	2	0	30	.256	.310	63	4
1925 Sac	14	——	——	——	——	——	——	——	.368	——	——	——
	2034	7438	978	2197	——	——	——	——	.295	.412	——	——

HEINE SAND   John Henry Sand. Born 7/3/1897, San Francisco, CA. Died 11/3/1958, San Francisco, CA. Infielder refused bribe by the Giants Jimmy O'Connell to throw a 1923 game so New York would win pennant. His testimony brought O'Connell and NY coach Cozy Dolan lifetime bans.

	G	AB	R	H	2B	3B	HR	RBI	BA	SA	TB	SB
1918 SLC	71	241	27	56	10	3	0	——	.232	.299	72	10
1919 SL–Sea	55	178	18	42	8	3	0	——	.236	.315	56	7
1920 SLC	112	352	47	76	14	3	1	——	.216	.281	99	11
1921 SLC	180	738	140	236	52	11	17	91	.320	.489	361	23
1922 SLC	191	748	121	200	46	14	21	95	.267	.451	337	13
1934 Miss	46	111	10	27	5	2	0	8	.243	.324	36	1
	655	2368	363	637	135	36	39	——	.269	.406	961	65

ED SAUER   Edward Sauer. Born 1/3/1920, Pittsburgh, PA. Died 7/1/1988, Thousand Oaks, CA. Younger brother of fifteen year major leaguer Hank Sauer, outfielder played in big leagues with the Cubs, Cardinals, and the and the Braves. Led the Pacific Coast League in stolen bases in 1946.

	G	AB	R	H	2B	3B	HR	RBI	BA	SA	TB	SB
1944 LA	108	392	61	115	25	4	5	52	.293	.416	163	19
1946 LA	184	685	102	187	36	3	20	82	.273	.422	289	45
1946 LA	150	568	87	159	45	5	17	66	.280	.467	265	17
1948 LA	150	571	90	174	41	3	16	121	.305	.471	269	20
1950 Hol	174	566	78	147	31	7	9	65	.260	.387	219	26
1951 HSDSF	136	459	70	121	22	1	16	61	.264	.420	193	10
	902	3241	488	903	200	23	83	447	.279	.431	1398	137

LES SCARSELLA   Leslie George Scarsella. Born 11/23/1913, Santa Cruz, CA. Died 12/17/1958, San Francisco, CA. Hit .313 for Reds as a rookie in 1936. Won the 1944 PCL batting title in closest race in league history.

	G	AB	R	H	2B	3B	HR	RBI	BA	SA	TB	SB
1941 Sea	170	637	86	205	25	10	10	110	.322	.440	280	14
1942 Sea–O	167	640	68	171	26	5	7	97	.267	.356	228	5
1943 Oak	157	589	67	192	32	6	3	85	.326	.416	245	12
1944 Oak	156	596	74	196	27	10	6	96	.329	.438	261	9
1945 Oak	139	508	95	165	37	10	10	77	.325	.496	252	11
1946 Oak	121	428	76	142	29	1	22	91	.332	.558	239	4
1947 Oak	89	341	47	87	19	5	13	56	.255	.455	155	1
1948 Oak	111	329	60	89	17	3	14	72	.271	.468	154	5
1949 Oak	64	226	31	59	10	1	12	44	.261	.473	107	1
	1174	4294	604	1306	222	51	97	728	.304	.447	1921	62

WALTER SCHMIDT   Walter Joseph Schmidt. Born 3/20/1887, Coal Hill, AR. Died 7/4/1973, Modesto, CA. Catcher bought his own contract from San Francisco Seals to join Pittsburgh. Brother of Tigers' "Boss" Schmidt.

	G	AB	R	H	2B	3B	HR	RBI	BA	SA	TB	SB
1911 SF	87	230	28	61	––	––	––	––	.265	––	––	21
1912 SF	134	370	30	97	––	––	––	––	.262	––	––	22
1913 SF	144	426	44	106	15	3	1	––	.249	.305	130	33
1914 SF	142	442	52	116	12	5	0	46	.262	.312	138	51
1915 SF	127	416	40	102	10	2	2	––	.245	.293	122	25
1916 Ver	30	88	9	18	6	0	1	––	.205	.307	27	3
1926 Miss	18	54	6	15	2	0	0	9	.278	.315	17	0
1927 Sea	108	314	33	85	18	0	0	34	.271	.328	103	3
1928 Sea	55	168	11	50	7	1	0	15	.298	.351	59	3
1929 SF	17	44	1	10	0	0	0	2	.227	.227	10	0
	862	2552	254	660	––	––	––	––	.259	.310	––	161

PETE SCHNEIDER   Peter Joseph Schneider. Born 8/20/1895, Los Angeles, CA. Died 6/1/1957, Los Angeles, CA. Began career as a pitcher, winning twenty for the Reds in 1917. Converted to outfield, with Vernon in 1923 hit five home runs in a game vs. Salt Lake on May 11th. Just missed a sixth when his double hit near the top of the outfield fence.

PETE SCHNEIDER (cont.)

	G	AB	R	H	2B	3B	HR	RBI	BA	SA	TB	SB
1919 Ver	10	9	0	3	1	0	0	– –	.333	.444	4	0
1920 Ver	16	40	6	10	0	0	2	– –	.250	.400	16	2
1921 Ver	138	458	72	149	29	8	14	69	.325	.515	236	5
1922 Ver	90	234	48	81	22	5	15	51	.346	.675	158	1
1923 Ver	163	598	104	215	43	23	19	110	.360	.604	361	3
1924 Ver	81	235	58	77	12	1	16	52	.328	.591	139	0
1925 Ver–Sac	15	53	8	7	1	2	0	5	.132	.226	12	3
	513	1627	296	542	108	39	66	– –	.333	.569	926	14

WES SCHULMERICH

Edward Wesley Schulmerich. Born 8/21/1901, Hillsboro, OR. Died 6/26/1985, Corvallis, OR. Star college football player at Oregon State; twice hit over .300 in majors. Liked to show off strength by running while carrying a teammate on each shoulder.

	G	AB	R	H	2B	3B	HR	RBI	BA	SA	TB	SB
1927 LA	31	115	14	37	7	1	0	14	.322	.400	46	0
1928 LA	192	717	100	227	33	5	19	96	.317	.456	327	9
1929 LA	134	360	70	118	22	0	19	77	.328	.547	197	6
1930 LA	180	692	102	203	51	7	28	130	.380	.595	412	12
1936 LA	142	462	68	139	30	6	14	85	.301	.483	223	2
1937 Port	19	54	6	13	1	0	1	8	.241	.315	17	1
	707	2400	420	797	144	19	81	410	.332	.509	1222	30

BILL SCHUSTER

William Charles Schuster. Born 8/14/1912, Buffalo, NY. Died 6/28/1987, El Monte, CA. Shortstop had major league trials with the Pirates, Braves, and Cubs. "Broadway Bill" is remembered as a legendary clown of the PCL, endearing him to fans but not to the umpires whom he often victimized with his antics.

	G	AB	R	H	2B	3B	HR	RBI	BA	SA	TB	SB
1940 Sea	176	645	99	188	31	4	2	74	.291	.361	233	26
1941 Sea–LA	136	492	71	136	21	2	2	53	.276	.339	167	25
1942 LA	179	640	80	191	41	4	6	78	.298	.403	258	26
1943 LA	157	618	117	170	42	6	5	67	.275	.387	239	16
1946 LA	176	626	89	179	34	4	4	69	.286	.372	233	26
1947 LA	174	687	84	180	27	5	6	70	.262	.342	235	17
1948 LA	151	617	85	163	23	5	11	60	.264	.371	229	8
1949 LA–Sac	163	616	86	158	23	1	8	68	.256	.336	207	19
1950 Sea	135	405	64	103	24	3	6	39	.254	.373	151	10
1952 Hol	3	6	1	2	0	0	0	1	.333	.333	2	0
	1450	5352	776	1470	266	34	50	579	.275	.365	1954	173

HANK SEVEREID

Henry Levai Severeid. Born 6/1/1891, Story City, IA. Died 12/17/1968, San Antonio, TX. The big Norwegian catcher took pride in his durability. The tough receiver played fifteen years in the majors. He caught 2,357 professional games overall. In the Texas League at the age of forty–six, he caught both ends of a doubleheader.

	G	AB	R	H	2B	3B	HR	RBI	BA	SA	TB	SB
1927 Sac	114	356	46	116	28	0	5	72	.326	.447	159	1

HANK SEVEREID (cont.)

	G	AB	R	H	2B	3B	HR	RBI	BA	SA	TB	SB
1928 Sac	118	385	51	116	21	3	10	59	.301	.449	173	0
1929 Sac–H	142	474	90	170	31	0	24	124	.359	.576	273	3
1930 Hol	129	376	62	138	24	1	13	93	.367	.540	203	6
1931 Hol	94	308	49	107	12	2	17	65	.347	.565	174	1
	597	1899	298	647	116	6	69	413	.341	.517	982	11

EARL SHEELY

Earl Homer Sheely. Born 2/12/1893, Bushnell, IL. Died 9/16/1952, Seattle, WA. A first baseman, hit .296 or better each of his first six seasons with the Chicago White Sox. Was the PCL batting champ in 1920 and 1930. Also won three consecutive PCL home run titles, 1918–1920. General manager of the Seattle Rainiers in the 1950's.

	G	AB	R	H	2B	3B	HR	RBI	BA	SA	TB	SB
1916 SLC	14	41	5	14	3	0	1	––	.341	.488	20	0
1917 SLC	193	749	97	227	46	7	19	––	.303	.459	344	14
1918 SLC	93	330	44	99	14	1	12	––	.300	.458	151	9
1919 SLC	168	646	107	197	35	1	28	––	.305	.492	318	15
1920 SLC	188	700	114	260	51	5	33	––	.371	.600	420	14
1928 Sac	165	630	102	240	46	3	21	128	.381	.563	355	3
1930 SF	183	718	120	289	35	1	29	180	.403	.575	413	6
1932 LA	117	417	65	133	26	0	11	102	.319	.460	192	6
1933 Port	137	454	77	163	30	1	13	100	.359	.515	234	0
1934 P–Sea	181	640	98	200	30	6	7	101	.313	.411	263	5
	1439	5325	829	1822	316	25	174	––	.342	.509	2710	72

NEILL SHERIDAN

Neill Rawlins Sheridan. Born 11/20/1921, Sacramento, CA. A gifted natural athlete, nicknamed "Wild Horse" for his unpredictable ways in the outfield. Played two games for the 1948 Boston Red Sox.

	G	AB	R	H	2B	3B	HR	RBI	BA	SA	TB	SB
1943 SF	1	1	0	0	0	0	0	0	.000	.000	0	0
1944 SF	42	150	30	44	5	2	4	21	.293	.433	65	6
1945 SF	148	527	78	153	35	7	3	68	.290	.400	211	30
1946 SF	116	357	58	96	18	4	5	55	.269	.384	137	9
1947 SF	153	618	94	177	27	9	16	95	.286	.437	270	9
1948 Sea	140	532	91	166	25	7	17	82	.312	.481	256	5
1949 Sea	147	486	81	126	19	3	14	67	.259	.397	193	10
1950 SF	104	319	51	92	18	2	12	54	.288	.470	150	3
1951 SF–SD	56	137	13	28	3	1	3	14	.204	.307	42	1
1953 O–Sac	170	591	77	173	43	5	13	83	.293	.448	265	12
1954 Sac–SF	22	59	5	9	2	2	0	3	.153	.254	15	0
	1099	3777	578	1064	195	42	87	542	.282	.425	1604	85

CHARLIE SILVERA

Charles Anthony Ryan Silvera. Born 10/13/1924, San Francisco, CA. New York Yankees' third–string catcher from 1948 to 1956, played more games in first two PCL seasons than in entire ten years in majors. Eligible to play in seven World Series, played in just one game.

	G	AB	R	H	2B	3B	HR	RBI	BA	SA	TB	SB
1947 Port	120	356	40	88	12	3	1	39	.247	.306	109	0

CHARLIE SILVERA (cont.)

	G	AB	R	H	2B	3B	HR	RBI	BA	SA	TB	SB
1948 Port	144	501	58	151	36	6	5	85	.301	.427	214	5
1960 SLC	44	110	8	24	5	0	0	9	.218	.264	29	1
	308	967	106	263	53	9	6	133	.272	.364	352	6

HARRY SIMPSON

Harry Leon Simpson. Born 12/3/1925, Atlanta, GA. Died 4/3/1979, Akron, OH. An excellent outfielder, nicknamed "Suitcase" due to the number of teams for which he played in his career. Led AL in triples twice. Topped the Pacific Coast League in 1950 in runs batted in.

	G	AB	R	H	2B	3B	HR	RBI	BA	SA	TB	SB
1950 SD	178	697	121	225	41	19	33	156	.323	.578	403	2
1960 SD	95	284	38	63	11	5	8	40	.222	.380	108	3
1961 SD	146	515	82	156	23	6	24	105	.303	.511	263	3
	419	1496	241	444	75	30	65	301	.297	.517	774	8

ROY SMALLEY

Roy Frederick Smalley, Jr. Born 6/9/1926, Springfield, MO. Shortstop for eleven years with the Chicago Cubs, Milwaukee Braves, and the Philadelphia Phillies; light hitter with a strong arm, but an erratic glove. Brother-in-law of teammate Gene Mauch; son Roy played in the majors.

	G	AB	R	H	2B	3B	HR	RBI	BA	SA	TB	SB
1944 LA	61	160	13	30	3	0	1	11	.188	.225	36	1
1946 LA	9	28	1	6	0	1	0	1	.214	.286	8	0
1960 Spo	67	172	20	45	5	1	8	10	.262	.442	76	1
	137	360	34	81	8	2	9	31	.225	.333	120	2

AL SMITH

Alphonse Eugene Smith. Born 2/7/1928, Kirkwood, MO. Spent twelve seasons in the majors, mostly in the outfield with the ChiSox and Cleveland Indians. A target of Comiskey Park boo-birds after being traded from Indians in exchange for the extremely popular Minnie Minoso.

	G	AB	R	H	2B	3B	HR	RBI	BA	SA	TB	SB
1950 SD	104	326	73	81	13	4	10	50	.248	.405	132	11
1951 SD	25	89	16	25	5	2	3	10	.281	.483	43	1
	129	415	89	106	18	6	13	60	.255	.422	175	12

ELMER SMITH

Elmer John Smith. Born 9/21/1892, Sandusky, OH. Died 8/3/1984, Columbia, KY. Outfielder in the major leagues for ten years; hit first grand slam in World Series history, off Burleigh Grimes in Game One of the 1920 World Series. Led the PCL in home runs in 1926 and 1927.

	G	AB	R	H	2B	3B	HR	RBI	BA	SA	TB	SB
1926 Port	185	669	150	225	28	7	46	133	.336	.605	405	20
1927 Port	182	653	158	240	52	7	40	141	.368	.652	426	11
1928 P-H	182	657	118	210	51	4	26	126	.320	.528	347	10
	549	1979	426	675	131	18	112	400	.341	.595	1178	41

RED SMITH

James Carlisle Smith. Born 4/6/1890, Greenville, SC. Died 10/11/1966, Atlanta, GA. Excellent defensive third baseman, played nine years with the Dodgers and the Braves. Missed chance to play in World Series for "Miracle Braves" when he broke his leg in last game of season.

RED SMITH (cont.)

	G	AB	R	H	2B	3B	HR	RBI	BA	SA	TB	SB
1920 Ver	186	616	71	180	25	4	1	––	.292	.351	216	10
1921 Ver	163	610	110	195	40	3	10	89	.320	.444	271	11
1922 Ver	190	719	120	251	51	6	8	101	.349	.470	338	7
1923 Ver–LA	160	548	102	179	31	3	7	60	.327	.432	237	7
	699	2493	403	805	147	16	26	––	.323	.426	1062	35

FRED SNODGRASS   Fred Charles Snodgrass. Born 10/19/1887, Ventura, CA. Died 4/5/1974, Ventura, CA. Often thought of as the goat of the 1912 World Series for his dropping a fly ball; was given a raise the next season by John McGraw. Played nine seasons in majors with Giants and Braves. Began career as a catcher, converted to the outfield in 1909.

	G	AB	R	H	2B	3B	HR	RBI	BA	SA	TB	SB
1905 LA	2	4	0	1	0	0	0	––	.250	.250	1	0
1906 LA	2	7	1	2	0	0	0	––	.286	.286	2	0
1917 Ver	170	642	97	178	34	3	0	––	.277	.340	218	34
	174	653	98	181	34	3	0	––	.277	.338	221	34

BILLY SOUTHWORTH   William Harrison Southworth. Born 3/9/1893, Harvard, NE. Died 11/15/1969, Columbus, OH. Outfielder spent thirteen years in the majors, hitting .300 six times and .297 lifetime. After retiring as a player, managed in big leagues for thirteen more seasons, winning four pennants and two World Series.

	G	AB	R	H	2B	3B	HR	RBI	BA	SA	TB	SB
1915 Port	25	100	19	32	6	0	5	––	.320	.530	53	3
1916 Port	171	627	97	188	31	8	12	––	.300	.432	271	32
	196	727	116	220	37	8	17	––	.303	.446	324	35

STAN SPENCE   Stanley Orville Spence. Born 3/20/1915, South Portsmith, KY. Died 1/9/1983, Kinston, NC. An excellent outfielder with a strong arm, was four–time All–Star with Washington Senators. Drove in one hundred runs with .316 batting average in 1944 before being drafted.

	G	AB	R	H	2B	3B	HR	RBI	BA	SA	TB	SB
1950 LA	146	438	65	100	16	1	22	66	.228	.420	184	1

JOE SPRINZ   Joseph Conrad Sprinz. Born 8/3/1902, St. Louis, MO. Died 1/12/1994, Fremont, CA. Catcher in majors for Cardinals. Gained broken jaw in attempt to catch ball dropped from blimp during 1939 World's Fair.

	G	AB	R	H	2B	3B	HR	RBI	BA	SA	TB	SB
1928 SF	158	505	59	119	20	1	4	49	.236	.303	153	10
1936 Miss	97	309	36	88	12	2	2	47	.285	.356	110	5
1937 Miss	103	307	34	79	6	3	0	36	.257	.296	91	5
1938 SF	132	402	57	120	21	2	0	42	.299	.361	145	6
1939 SF	90	276	35	86	9	4	0	26	.312	.373	103	2
1940 SF	118	378	26	94	12	2	0	51	.249	.291	110	2
1941 SF	47	131	13	22	2	0	0	15	.168	.183	24	1
1942 SF	106	302	23	73	6	6	0	33	.242	.301	91	1
1943 SF	92	298	21	63	7	1	0	22	.211	.242	72	3

JOE SPRINZ (cont.)

	G	AB	R	H	2B	3B	HR	RBI	BA	SA	TB	SB
1944 SF	92	272	38	75	6	2	0	28	.276	.313	85	3
1945 SF	106	307	37	93	3	2	0	33	.303	.326	100	5
1946 SF	35	93	6	26	1	0	0	14	.280	.290	27	0
	1176	3580	385	938	105	25	6	396	.262	.310	1111	43

OSCAR STANAGE

Oscar Harland Stanage. Born 3/17/1883, Tulare, CA. Died 11/11/1964, Detroit, MI. Ten year major league catcher with Detroit, was considered one of the best defensive receivers of his day.

	G	AB	R	H	2B	3B	HR	RBI	BA	SA	TB	SB
1921 LA	96	323	26	90	16	0	0	17	.279	.328	106	2
1922 Sac	96	307	25	82	15	0	1	31	.267	.326	100	4
	192	630	51	172	31	0	1	48	.273	.327	206	6

JIGGER STATZ

Arnold John Statz. Born 10/20/1897, Waukegan, IL. Died 3/16/1988, Corona Del Mar, CA. One of the best centerfielders in all of baseball, noted for his speed and range in the field. Spent eight years in majors and a record eighteen seasons with his only minor league team, the Los Angeles Angels. Led PCL in triples twice and steals three times.

	G	AB	R	H	2B	3B	HR	RBI	BA	SA	TB	SB
1920 LA	101	386	42	91	14	5	0	— —	.236	.298	115	11
1921 LA	153	584	126	181	21	7	2	34	.310	.380	222	52
1925 LA	130	545	90	144	27	7	2	45	.264	.350	191	17
1926 LA	199	823	150	291	68	18	4	59	.354	.495	407	19
1929 LA	195	799	173	246	41	7	3	75	.308	.388	310	37
1930 LA	161	558	95	201	43	12	5	84	.360	.507	283	37
1931 LA	184	748	141	248	42	13	6	107	.332	.447	334	45
1932 LA	188	737	153	256	43	12	6	93	.347	.463	341	21
1933 LA	182	767	144	249	29	8	10	73	.325	.422	324	17
1934 LA	183	760	168	246	39	13	6	66	.324	.433	329	61
1935 LA	171	716	132	236	40	7	2	65	.330	.413	296	53
1936 LA	158	631	134	203	37	7	3	62	.322	.417	263	43
1937 LA	154	558	90	162	32	5	2	57	.290	.376	210	18
1938 LA	167	630	131	200	41	4	2	44	.317	.405	255	12
1939 LA	145	557	89	173	38	5	4	62	.311	.418	233	9
1940 LA	144	453	97	131	30	3	1	48	.289	.375	170	11
1941 LA	75	142	8	38	3	1	0	21	.268	.303	43	1
1942 LA	100	263	33	60	9	2	2	22	.228	.300	79	2
	2790	10657	1996	3356	597	136	60	— —	.315	.413	4405	466

HANK STEINBACHER

Henry John Steinbacher. Born 3/22/1913, Sacramento, CA. Died 4/3/1977, Sacramento, CA. Outfielder played for for three years in majors with White Sox, batting .292 in part—time role.

	G	AB	R	H	2B	3B	HR	RBI	BA	SA	TB	SB
1930 Sac	59	153	27	48	6	0	0	26	.314	.353	54	5
1931 Sac	141	503	69	148	23	6	4	66	.294	.388	195	8
1932 Sac	159	578	79	186	35	11	5	82	.322	.446	258	9
1933 Sac	160	628	99	193	40	7	5	112	.307	.417	262	4

HANK STEINBACHER (cont.)

	G	AB	R	H	2B	3B	HR	RBI	BA	SA	TB	SB
1934 Sac	188	755	93	236	36	6	2	97	.313	.384	290	15
1935 Sac	170	661	95	204	35	7	4	85	.309	.401	265	10
1943 SF	156	569	75	181	32	15	2	105	.318	.438	249	6
1944 SF	137	492	54	122	27	8	1	86	.248	.341	168	10
1945 SF	19	46	5	14	2	2	0	10	.304	.435	20	0
	1189	4385	596	1332	236	62	23	669	.304	.402	1761	67

VERN STEPHENS
Vernon Decatur Stephens. Born 10/23/1920, McAlister, NM. Died 11/3/1968, Long Beach, CA. Slugging shortstop, was a seven time All–Star and three–time AL RBI champ. Led AL in homers in 1945.

	G	AB	R	H	2B	3B	HR	RBI	BA	SA	TB	SB
1955 Sea	52	160	22	54	9	0	7	36	.338	.525	84	0
1956 Sea	73	188	19	50	9	0	6	27	.266	.410	77	0
	125	348	41	104	18	0	13	63	.299	.463	161	0

HARVEY STOREY
Harvey Andrew Storey. Born 8/21/1916, Forest Grove, OR. A long–time Pacific Coast League third baseman, he began his career as a shortstop. Won a PCL batting title in 1946, joining Smead Jolley and Artie Wilson as the only men to win playing for two teams.

	G	AB	R	H	2B	3B	HR	RBI	BA	SA	TB	SB
1938 SF	39	83	19	24	2	1	0	15	.289	.337	28	2
1939 SF	127	459	67	161	23	8	9	85	.351	.495	227	5
1940 SF	63	232	31	75	8	2	1	36	.323	.388	90	5
1941 LA	137	465	45	130	22	0	2	50	.280	.340	158	5
1946 LA–P	157	556	75	181	44	9	17	89	.326	.529	294	3
1947 Port	182	681	96	208	51	5	14	119	.305	.457	311	9
1948 Port	181	627	97	191	35	4	18	91	.305	.459	288	3
1949 P–SD	146	491	61	148	22	4	17	97	.301	.466	229	3
1950 SD	123	297	39	79	23	2	6	54	.266	.418	124	0
1951 SD	104	352	34	89	20	0	14	54	.253	.429	151	0
1952 SD	15	12	1	0	0	0	0	1	.000	.000	0	0
	1274	4255	565	1286	250	35	98	691	.302	.447	1900	35

GEORGE STOVALL
George Thomas Stovall. Born 11/23/1878, Independence, MO. Died 11/5/1951, Burlington, IA. Carrying nickname "Human Torch", was first big league star to jump to the Federal League.

	G	AB	R	H	2B	3B	HR	RBI	BA	SA	TB	SB
1917 Ver	73	218	20	57	13	0	0	– –	.261	.321	70	5

PAUL STRAND
Paul Edward Strand. Born 12/19/1893, Carbonado, WA. Died 7/2/1974, Salt Lake City, UT. Pitcher turned outfielder, still holds the professional record for basehits in one season, which he set in 1923.

	G	AB	R	H	2B	3B	HR	RBI	BA	SA	TB	SB
1920 Sea	21	63	3	15	4	0	0	– –	.238	.302	19	2
1921 SLC	157	589	87	185	38	6	9	95	.314	.445	262	15
1922 SLC	178	752	138	289	52	13	28	138	.384	.600	451	10
1923 SLC	194	825	180	325	66	13	43	187	.394	.662	546	22

PAUL STRAND (cont.)

	G	AB	R	H	2B	3B	HR	RBI	BA	SA	TB	SB
1926 Port	105	386	56	126	21	4	11	52	.326	.487	188	3
1927 Port	176	622	86	221	39	4	18	105	.355	.518	322	11
	831	3237	550	1161	220	40	109	— —	.359	.552	1788	63

DICK STUART   Richard Lee Stuart. Born 11/7/1932, San Francisco, CA. Slugging first baseman loved hitting home runs and little else. Once, he hit sixty—six home runs in a minor league season. Led AL in RBI in 1963. Earned nickname "Dr. Strangeglove" for his lack of fielding acumen.

	G	AB	R	H	2B	3B	HR	RBI	BA	SA	TB	SB
1957 Hol	23	72	8	17	0	0	6	17	.236	.486	35	0
1958 SLC	80	315	61	98	14	1	31	76	.311	.657	207	0
1969 Phx	74	258	37	63	13	0	12	42	.244	.434	112	0
	177	645	106	178	27	1	49	135	.276	.549	354	0

GUS SUHR   August Richard Suhr. Born 1/3/1906, San Francisco, CA. Began career at shortstop but wild throws prompted move to first base. A left—handed hitter, found Recreation Park to his liking. Played more than a decade with Pirates, appearing in a then NL record 822 straight games.

	G	AB	R	H	2B	3B	HR	RBI	BA	SA	TB	SB
1925 SF	3	— —	— —	— —	— —	— —	— —	— —	.500	— —	— —	— —
1926 SF	173	611	86	172	33	4	14	71	.282	.417	255	6
1927 SF	195	679	143	199	42	9	27	110	.293	.501	340	6
1928 SF	191	741	156	233	64	9	22	133	.314	.514	381	5
1929 SF	202	785	196	299	62	6	51	177	.381	.670	526	19
1943 SF	149	527	60	130	25	7	1	65	.247	.326	172	1
1944 SF	164	588	81	164	36	5	0	75	.279	.357	210	6
1945 SF	138	399	64	124	26	5	0	56	.311	.401	160	3
	1215	4330	786	1321	288	45	115	695	.305	.472	2044	46

HOMER SUMMA   Homer Wayne Summa. Born 11/3/1898, Gentry, MO. Died 1/29/1966, Los Angeles, CA. Outfielder for ten years in majors, was a five—time .300 hitter and batted .302 lifetime. Spent most of big league career playing right field for the Cleveland Indians.

	G	AB	R	H	2B	3B	HR	RBI	BA	SA	TB	SB
1930 Port	97	376	52	119	20	1	4	47	.316	.407	153	10
1931 LA	187	754	141	257	40	6	4	89	.341	.426	321	25
1932 LA	134	543	88	161	29	7	0	64	.297	.376	204	7
1933 Sea	68	288	41	102	16	6	2	33	.354	.472	136	6
	486	1961	322	639	105	20	10	233	.326	.415	814	48

JIM THORPE   James Francis Thorpe. Born 5/28/1887, Prague, OK. Died 3/28/1953, Lomita, CA. Quite possibly the greatest athlete in the history of American sports. A member of the Football Hall of Fame and an Olympic gold medalist. Named the top American athlete of first half—century. Was in majors with New York Giants, Cincinnati Reds, and the Boston Braves.

	G	AB	R	H	2B	3B	HR	RBI	BA	SA	TB	SB
1922 Port	35	120	13	37	3	2	1	14	.308	.392	47	5

JACK TOBIN　　　John Thomas Tobin. Born 5/4/1892, St. Louis, MO. Died 12/10/1969, St. Louis, MO. Born, raised, and played almost entire career in St. Louis. Hit .309 lifetime in majors. Led PCL in hits and runs in 1917. Hit two grand slams off Walter Johnson during his career.

	G	AB	R	H	2B	3B	HR	RBI	BA	SA	TB	SB
1917 SLC	189	800	149	265	42	3	2	– –	.331	.399	319	41

AL TODD　　　Alfred Chester Todd. Born 1/7/1904, Troy, NY. Died 3/8/1985 Elmira, NY. Feisty catcher, holds the major league record for most games played behind the plate without a passed ball. Once slugged Dizzy Dean after a brushback pitch when both were in the Texas League.

	G	AB	R	H	2B	3B	HR	RBI	BA	SA	TB	SB
1942 LA	122	375	25	96	16	1	5	44	.256	.344	129	4

EARL TORGESON　　　Clifford Earl Torgeson. Born 1/1/1924, Snohomish, WA. Died 11/8/1990, Everett, WA. First baseman, inherited nickname of his idol, Earl Averill, who was also referred to as "The Earl of Snohomish". Was in major leagues for fifteen years; led the NL in runs scored in 1950.

	G	AB	R	H	2B	3B	HR	RBI	BA	SA	TB	SB
1941 Sea	4	10	1	5	1	0	0	0	.500	.600	6	0
1942 Sea	147	523	63	163	20	9	4	52	.312	.407	213	32
1946 Sea	103	354	46	101	18	5	5	53	.285	.407	144	20
	254	887	110	269	39	14	9	105	.303	.409	363	52

MIKE TRESH　　　Michael Tresh. Born 2/23/1914, Hazleton, PA. Died 10/4/1966, Detroit, MI. Light hitter, but an excellent defensive catcher; hit twice as many home runs in PCL as he did in twelve years in the majors.

	G	AB	R	H	2B	3B	HR	RBI	BA	SA	TB	SB
1937 Port	106	355	40	96	19	5	3	38	.270	.377	134	3
1950 SD	55	158	16	35	2	2	1	17	.222	.278	44	1
	161	513	56	131	21	7	4	55	.255	.347	178	4

FRENCHY UHALT　　　Bernard Bartholomew Uhalt. Born 4/27/1910, Bakersfield, CA. Speedy slap–hitting centerfielder, led the PCL in stolen bases in 1938. Had a brief trial with the Chicago White Sox in 1938. Had over 3,100 hits during his twenty–two year minor league career.

	G	AB	R	H	2B	3B	HR	RBI	BA	SA	TB	SB
1928 Oak	12	13	2	2	1	0	0	1	.154	.231	3	0
1929 Oak	27	102	17	36	5	1	0	17	.353	.422	43	4
1930 Oak	186	749	125	233	36	5	0	49	.311	.372	279	18
1931 Oak	174	691	90	201	31	8	1	62	.291	.363	251	21
1932 Oak	172	655	94	194	20	14	0	58	.296	.369	242	15
1933 Oak	171	632	129	221	41	8	4	89	.350	.459	290	62
1934 Oak	83	304	52	91	10	3	0	28	.299	.352	107	23
1935 Oak	158	581	102	188	28	8	4	52	.324	.420	244	33
1936 Oak	43	157	29	47	6	5	1	20	.299	.420	66	7
1938 Hol	166	635	113	211	39	11	5	65	.332	.452	287	32
1939 Hol	147	585	99	166	35	13	2	54	.284	.398	233	16
1940 Hol	170	651	117	175	24	4	1	52	.269	.323	210	23

FRENCHY UHALT (cont.)

	G	AB	R	H	2B	3B	HR	RBI	BA	SA	TB	SB
1941 Hol	148	534	95	154	15	12	2	44	.288	.373	199	18
1942 Hol	173	669	92	184	24	7	1	40	.275	.336	225	14
1943 SF	136	512	78	160	15	11	1	47	.313	.391	200	17
1944 SF	154	612	86	169	17	4	0	52	.276	.317	194	37
1945 SF	145	508	93	153	19	8	0	41	.301	.370	188	26
1946 SF	137	520	98	137	27	5	1	24	.263	.340	177	24
1947 SF	72	239	43	67	16	3	1	16	.280	.385	92	11
1948 Oak	25	44	7	9	1	0	0	3	.205	.227	10	0
	2499	9393	1561	2798	410	130	24	814	.298	.377	3540	401

GEORGE VAN HALTREN

George E. Van Haltren. Born 3/30/1866, St. Louis, MO. Died 9/29/1945, Oakland, CA. One of the overlooked stars of the 19th century, the pitcher turned centerfielder and lead—off man batted over .300 twelve times in majors and .316 lifetime while starring for Giants.

	G	AB	R	H	2B	3B	HR	RBI	BA	SA	TB	SB
1904 Sea	— —	941	159	253	35	10	4	— —	.269	.340	320	38
1905 Oak	220	860	— —	220	18	10	2	— —	.256	.307	264	47
1906 Oak	152	697	101	151	27	4	0	— —	.217	.267	186	36
1907 Oak	193	718	101	193	26	0	0	— —	.269	.305	219	47
1908 Oak	186	706	80	171	17	3	2	— —	.242	.283	200	30
1909 Oak	55	192	14	42	— —	— —	— —	— —	.219	— —	— —	— —
	— —	4114	— —	1030	— —	— —	— —	—	.250	.000	— —	— —

ARKY VAUGHAN

Joseph Floyd Vaughan. Born 3/9/1912, Clifty, AR. Died 8/30/1952, Eagleville, CA. Shortstop was nine—time All—Star who led NL in runs scored three times and won batting title in 1935. Also a perennial leader in doubles, triples, and on—base percentage. Excellent fielder; he quit for three years after dispute with Leo Durocher. Hall of Fame in 1985.

	G	AB	R	H	2B	3B	HR	RBI	BA	SA	TB	SB
1949 SF	97	281	50	81	10	6	2	26	.288	.388	109	6

JOHNNY VERGEZ

John Lewis Vergez. Born 7/9/1906, Oakland, CA. Died 7/15/1991, Davis, CA. Third baseman for the New York Giants from from 1931—34. Was player—manager for Oakland Oaks 1939—1943.

	G	AB	R	H	2B	3B	HR	RBI	BA	SA	TB	SB
1928 Oak	68	241	37	59	20	0	3	32	.245	.365	88	3
1929 Oak	199	711	142	230	39	5	46	165	.323	.586	417	11
1930 Oak	188	687	138	211	41	6	29	125	.307	.511	351	16
1936 Sac	93	354	40	97	20	7	7	42	.274	.429	152	8
1937 Sac	140	461	89	130	19	1	13	66	.282	.412	190	15
1938 Sac	167	583	90	145	30	1	16	80	.249	.386	225	19
1939 Oak	140	449	88	129	25	8	12	65	.287	.459	206	8
1940 Oak	79	259	46	70	14	2	4	31	.270	.386	100	5
1941 Oak	63	134	24	38	5	2	1	19	.284	.373	50	0
1942 Oak	107	335	40	88	10	5	3	31	.263	.349	117	5
1943 Oak	75	244	27	46	10	0	0	16	.189	.230	56	5
	1319	4458	761	1243	233	37	134	672	.279	.438	1952	95

OSCAR VITT   Oscar Joseph Vitt. Born 1/4/1890, San Francisco, CA. Died 1/31/1963, Oakland, CA. Cleveland manager in 1940, was target of player rebellion in middle of pennant race. Long–time manager in PCL.

	G	AB	R	H	2B	3B	HR	RBI	BA	SA	TB	SB
1910 SF	205	720	90	167	21	2	1	– –	.232	.271	195	41
1911 SF	124	401	51	108	– –	– –	– –	– –	.269	– –	– –	44
1922 SLC	163	642	104	202	39	6	4	52	.315	.413	265	8
1923 SLC	188	811	179	273	60	7	19	112	.337	.498	404	18
1924 SLC	112	435	106	145	33	5	15	90	.333	.536	233	4
1925 SLC	152	579	109	200	42	3	6	73	.345	.459	266	8
1926 Hol	110	341	35	86	12	5	1	25	.252	.326	111	11
1927 Hol	32	24	7	9	2	0	0	5	.375	.458	11	0
1928 Hol	1	1	0	0	0	0	0	0	.000	.000	0	0
	1087	3954	681	1190	– –	– –	– –	– –	.301	.418	– –	134

EDDIE WAITKUS   Edward Stephen Waitkus. Born 9/4/1919, Cambridge, MA. Died 9/15/1972, Boston, MA. Slick–fielding first baseman for "Whiz Kids", his 1949 shooting served as one basis for the novel, "The Natural". A National League All–Star in 1948, made a strong comeback in 1950.

	G	AB	R	H	2B	3B	HR	RBI	BA	SA	TB	SB
1942 LA	175	699	108	235	40	8	9	81	.336	.455	318	7

DICK WAKEFIELD   Richard Cummings Wakefield. Born 5/6/1921, Chicago, IL. Died 8/26/1985, Redford, MI. One of baseball's first bonus babies, he signed for $52,000 out of the University of Michigan in 1941.

	G	AB	R	H	2B	3B	HR	RBI	BA	SA	TB	SB
1950 Oak	87	246	41	72	22	0	7	38	.293	.467	115	2
1951 Oak	5	4	0	0	0	0	0	1	.000	.000	0	0
	92	250	41	72	22	0	7	39	.288	.460	115	2

LEE WALLS   Ray Lee Walls. Born 1/6/1933, San Diego, CA. Died 10/11/1993, Los Angeles, CA. One–time batboy for PCL Padres, played ten seasons in majors. Hit three homers in a game for the Cubs in 1958.

	G	AB	R	H	2B	3B	HR	RBI	BA	SA	TB	SB
1953 Hol	178	593	91	159	15	5	10	78	.268	.361	214	14
1954 Hol	162	601	88	174	23	5	16	93	.290	.424	255	18
1955 Hol	160	568	81	161	21	3	24	99	.283	.458	260	10
	500	1762	260	494	59	13	50	270	.280	.414	729	42

BUCKY WALTERS   William Henry Walters. Born 4/19/1909, Philadelphia, PA. Died 4/20/1991, Abington, PA. As a third baseman in the PCL, set record with five doubles in one game. Converted to pitching, won 198 games in majors, was six–time All–Star and MVP in the National League in 1939.

	G	AB	R	H	2B	3B	HR	RBI	BA	SA	TB	SB
1933 Miss	91	362	74	136	32	1	16	92	.376	.602	218	7

ROXY WALTERS   Alfred John Walters. Born 11/5/1892, San Francisco, CA. Died 6/3/1956, Alameda, CA. Spent eleven years in majors, mostly as a back–up catcher. In 1928, hit .382 and went 15–3 on mound in minors.

ROXY WALTERS (cont.)

	G	AB	R	H	2B	3B	HR	RBI	BA	SA	TB	SB
1926 Miss	86	253	19	46	7	0	0	15	.182	.209	53	0
1927 Miss	66	138	15	29	5	0	0	7	.210	.246	34	1
	152	391	34	75	12	0	0	22	.192	.223	87	1

LLOYD WANER   Lloyd James Waner. Born 3/16/1906, Harrah, OK. Died 7/22/1982, Oklahoma City, OK. Played eighteen years in majors, mostly in centerfield for Pirates. Had 200 or more hits in first four full big league seasons. "Little Poison" set NL rookie record with 223 hits in 1927, while scoring 133 runs. Lifetime .316 hitter, elected to Hall of Fame in 1967.

	G	AB	R	H	2B	3B	HR	RBI	BA	SA	TB	SB
1925 SF	31	44	7	11	2	0	0	1	.250	.295	13	1
1926 SF	6	20	0	4	1	0	0	0	.200	.250	5	0
	37	64	7	15	3	0	0	1	.234	.281	18	1

PAUL WANER   Paul Glee Waner. Born 4/16/1903, Harrah, OK. Died 8/29/1965, Sarasota, FL. Lloyd's older brother, "Big Poison" won three NL batting titles and led NL twice in triples, doubles and runs. The rightfielder was the National League Most Valuable Player in 1927, a year after being bought for $40,000 from San Francisco. Elected to Hall of Fame in 1952.

	G	AB	R	H	2B	3B	HR	RBI	BA	SA	TB	SB
1923 SF	112	325	54	120	30	4	3	39	.369	.514	167	4
1924 SF	160	587	113	209	46	5	8	07	.056	.492	289	12
1925 SF	174	699	167	280	75	7	11	130	.401	.575	402	8
	446	1611	334	609	151	16	22	266	.378	.533	858	24

AARON WARD   Aaron Lee Ward. Born 8/28/1896, Booneville, AR. Died 1/30/1961, New Orleans, LA. A productive infielder for the Yankees in the early 1920's despite propensity for strikeouts, eventually lost second base job when PCL slugging sensation Tony Lazzeri was acquired in 1926.

	G	AB	R	H	2B	3B	HR	RBI	BA	SA	TB	SB
1930 Sac	87	344	59	85	15	3	7	35	.247	.369	127	6

RABBIT WARSTLER   Harold Burton Warstler. Born 9/13/1903, North Canton, OH. Died 5/31/1964, North Canton, OH. Eleven year big league infielder with four teams. A weak hitter, was considered to be one of the best glove men of his era. Great arm allowed him to play extremely deep.

	G	AB	R	H	2B	3B	HR	RBI	BA	SA	TB	SB
1941 LA	89	276	33	70	8	4	0	25	.254	.312	86	0

ROY WEATHERLY   Cyril Roy Weatherly. Born 2/25/1915, Warren, TX. Died 1/19/1991, Woodville, TX. Nicknamed "Stormy", both as play on his name and his relationship with umpires, played ten years in majors, most of the time with Cleveland in a platoon role in the Indians outfield.

	G	AB	R	H	2B	3B	HR	RBI	BA	SA	TB	SB
1950 Oak	17	60	14	21	0	1	5	14	.350	.633	38	0
1951 Oak	58	230	37	78	14	1	8	60	.339	.513	118	0
	75	290	51	99	14	2	13	74	.341	.538	156	0

BUCK WEAVER   George Daniel Weaver. Born 8/18/1890, Pottstown, PA. Died 1/31/1956, Chicago, IL. Considered one of the best third basemen of his era, played several positions for the Seals in 1911. Though popular among fans, career ended with a lifetime ban for his "guilty knowledge" in the Black Sox scandal. Continually applied for reinstatement, to no avail.

	G	AB	R	H	2B	3B	HR	RBI	BA	SA	TB	SB
1911 SF	182	674	90	190	––	–– ––	––	.282	––	––	30

EARL WEBB   William Earl Webb. Born 9/17/1898, Bon Air, TN. Died 5/23/1965, Jamestown, TN. Slugging outfielder set the big league record for doubles in a season with sixty–seven for the Boston Red Sox in 1931.

	G	AB	R	H	2B	3B	HR	RBI	BA	SA	TB	SB
1929 LA	188	658	163	235	56	6	37	164	.357	.629	414	14

JIMMY WELSH   James Daniel Welsh. Born 10/9/1902, Denver, CO. Died Died 10/30/1970, Oakdale, CA. Two–time .300 hitter in majors, led NL in outfield assists during his first two big league seasons. Was part of trade made by Braves to acquire Rogers Hornsby from the Giants in 1928.

	G	AB	R	H	2B	3B	HR	RBI	BA	SA	TB	SB
1923 Sea	123	374	57	106	23	4	6	37	.283	.414	155	6
1924 Sea	164	599	125	205	38	12	16	90	.342	.526	315	17
1931 Miss	157	628	88	198	37	11	8	89	.315	.447	281	19
1932 M–Sea	158	627	98	194	47	4	7	75	.309	.431	270	11
1933 Sea	168	696	95	202	33	10	8	79	.290	.401	279	10
1934 Sea–O	55	206	18	40	4	2	1	12	.194	.248	51	2
	825	3130	481	945	182	43	46	382	.302	.432	1351	65

MAX WEST   Max Edward West. Born 11/28/1916, Dexter, MO. Starting outfielder for the National League in the 1940 All–Star game; hit a three–run home run. Drew PCL record 201 bases on balls in 1949 while leading league in home runs and runs batted in. Won three PCL home run titles. Later in sporting goods; designed the Angel uniforms used 1956–1957.

	G	AB	R	H	2B	3B	HR	RBI	BA	SA	TB	SB
1935 Sac	105	319	34	85	11	5	5	54	.266	.379	121	0
1936 Miss	158	579	79	178	22	11	1	91	.307	.389	225	5
1937 Miss	151	555	84	183	33	12	16	95	.330	.519	288	10
1947 SD	167	562	103	172	26	6	43	124	.306	.603	339	6
1949 SD	189	619	166	180	41	2	48	166	.291	.596	369	4
1950 SD	162	520	92	148	30	1	30	109	.285	.519	270	1
1951 LA	138	472	107	133	21	4	35	110	.282	.566	267	2
1952 LA	149	497	76	130	21	1	35	91	.262	.519	258	2
1953 LA	38	54	8	13	0	0	5	15	.241	.519	28	0
1954 LA	89	169	25	44	4	0	12	37	.260	.497	84	1
	1346	4346	774	1266	209	42	230	892	.291	.517	2249	31

WALLY WESTLAKE   Waldon Thomas Westlake. Born 11/8/1920, Gridley, CA. An NL All–Star outfielder in 1951, twice hit for the cycle in the major leagues. Spent ten seasons in majors, driving in 199 runs in 1949–1950 with the Pittsburgh Pirates. Traded to Cards in 1951 in seven player deal.

WALLY WESTLAKE (cont.)

	G	AB	R	H	2B	3B	HR	RBI	BA	SA	TB	SB
1942 Oak	169	593	57	159	26	6	7	74	.268	.368	218	10
1946 Oak	136	429	60	135	19	5	7	57	.315	.431	185	5
1955 O–P	73	236	32	61	7	2	5	32	.258	.369	87	2
1956 Sac	90	293	38	80	14	0	12	50	.273	.444	130	1
	468	1551	187	435	66	13	31	213	.280	.400	620	18

JO JO WHITE   Joyner Clifford White. Born 6/1/1909, Red Oak, GA. Died 10/9/1986, Tacoma, WA. Spent nine years in majors as outfielder for the Detroit Tigers and the war–time Athletics and Reds. Led PCL in steals in 1939 and won the league's batting championship in 1945.

	G	AB	R	H	2B	3B	HR	RBI	BA	SA	TB	SB
1939 Sea	165	648	126	186	27	8	1	54	.287	.358	232	47
1940 Sea	161	600	115	177	21	17	8	53	.295	.427	256	35
1941 Sea	147	547	80	159	26	16	2	49	.291	.408	223	28
1942 Sea	166	590	89	175	30	6	2	69	.297	.378	223	27
1945 Sac	177	688	162	244	46	10	1	87	.355	.455	313	40
1946 Sac–Sea	147	510	78	159	18	8	1	40	.312	.384	196	14
1947 Sea	125	382	64	119	23	3	3	47	.312	.411	157	8
1948 Sea	96	167	24	45	6	1	0	21	.269	.317	53	5
1949 Hol	31	56	4	13	1	0	0	4	.232	.250	14	0
	1215	4188	742	1277	198	69	18	424	.305	.398	1667	204

SAMMY WHITE   Samuel Charles White. Born 7/7/1928, Wenatchee, WA. Played in major leagues for eleven years, mostly catching for Boston Red Sox. All–Star in 1953, set a modern major league record by scoring three runs in an inning June 18, 1953 versus the Detroit Tigers. Owned bowling alley that was the scene of a mass murder in the 1970's.

	G	AB	R	H	2B	3B	HR	RBI	BA	SA	TB	SB
1949 Sea	60	173	23	52	2	2	2	20	.301	.370	64	2

JOE WILHOIT   Joseph William Wilhoit. Born 12/20/1891, Hiawatha, KS. Died 9/25/1930, Santa Barbara, CA. Set organized baseball record with a sixty–nine game hitting streak for Wichita in the Western League in 1919. That feat earned him a late season call–up by the Boston Red Sox. Had six hits in eighteen at bats in what proved to be his big league swan song.

	G	AB	R	H	2B	3B	HR	RBI	BA	SA	TB	SB
1913 Ven	10	20	7	5	0	1	0	— —	.250	.350	7	1
1914 Ven	55	192	38	67	7	0	2	15	.349	.417	80	8
1915 Ver	177	682	99	220	24	9	3	— —	.323	.397	271	27
1919 Sea	17	67	8	11	1	0	0	— —	.164	.179	12	3
1921 SLC	117	478	76	162	32	4	3	60	.339	.441	211	5
1922 SLC	169	624	99	198	36	4	6	81	.317	.417	260	10
1923 SLC	172	662	115	238	48	7	8	86	.360	.489	324	9
	717	2725	442	901	148	25	22	— —	.331	.428	1165	63

KEN WILLIAMS   Kenneth Roy Williams. Born 8/28/1890, Grants Pass, OR. Died 1/22/1959, Grants Pass, OR. Fourteen year major league outfielder, was the majors first "30–30" man in 1922 for St. Louis Browns. Led AL in home runs and RBI that year. Retired with a .319 career batting average and slugging percentage of .531, putting him in top twenty–five all–time.

	G	AB	R	H	2B	3B	HR	RBI	BA	SA	TB	SB
1916 Port	53	183	21	52	11	1	4	– –	.284	.421	77	14
1917 Port	192	737	117	231	43	8	24	– –	.313	.491	362	61
1930 Port	148	546	93	191	32	4	14	110	.350	.500	273	23
1931 Port	20	76	12	21	1	2	1	15	.276	.382	29	0
	413	1542	243	495	87	15	43	– –	.321	.481	741	98

TED WILLIAMS   Theodore Samuel Williams. Born 8/30/1918, San Diego, CA. Product of San Diego's Hoover High, broke into professional ball for the local PCL entry amid much fanfare. Later won six AL batting titles and would have won two more under today's rules. The last .400 hitter, retired with a slugging average second only to Babe Ruth. Hall of Fame in 1966.

	G	AB	R	H	2B	3B	HR	RBI	BA	SA	TB	SB
1936 SD	42	107	18	29	8	2	0	11	.271	.383	41	2
1937 SD	138	454	66	132	24	2	23	98	.291	.504	229	1
	180	561	84	161	32	4	23	109	.287	.481	270	3

MAURY WILLS   Maurice Morning Wills. Born 10/2/1932, Washington, D.C. A shortstop in the majors for fourteen years, was convinced by manager Bobby Bragan at Spokane to take up switch–hitting. Joined Dodgers in 1959; went on to lead the NL in steals six straight years, was an All–Star five times, won two Gold Gloves, and was National League MVP in 1962.

	G	AB	R	H	2B	3B	HR	RBI	BA	SA	TB	SB
1957 Sea	147	491	67	131	23	6	0	33	.267	.338	166	21
1958 Spo	144	534	69	135	20	7	2	37	.253	.328	175	25
1959 Spo	48	192	42	60	6	3	1	18	.313	.391	75	25
	339	1217	178	326	49	16	3	88	.268	.342	416	71

ARTIE WILSON   Arthur Lee Wilson. Born 10/28/1920, Springville, AL. A former Negro League star, drove pitchers crazy hitting soft line drives just beyond reach of the infielders. Won PCL batting title in 1949. Played for New York Giants in 1951. Sent to minors in May, replaced by Willie Mays.

	G	AB	R	H	2B	3B	HR	RBI	BA	SA	TB	SB
1949 SD–O	165	607	129	211	19	9	0	37	.348	.409	248	47
1950 Oak	196	848	168	264	27	17	1	48	.311	.387	328	31
1951 Oak	81	349	39	89	8	1	0	22	.255	.284	99	6
1952 Sea	160	683	95	216	15	8	1	59	.316	.366	250	25
1953 Sea	177	638	80	212	23	14	2	76	.332	.422	269	9
1954 Sea	163	660	92	222	24	16	0	50	.336	.421	278	20
1955 Port	155	616	88	189	20	2	2	23	.307	.356	219	12
1956 P–Sea	101	273	33	80	9	4	0	25	.293	.355	97	6
1957 Sac	75	315	34	83	10	6	0	17	.263	.333	105	3
1962 Port	25	55	3	9	0	1	0	2	.164	.200	11	0
	1298	5044	761	1575	155	78	6	359	.312	.377	1904	159

RED WILSON   Robert James Wilson. Born 3/7/1929, Milwaukee, WI. Ten year catcher in majors, was the Big Ten MVP while playing football for the Wisconsin Badgers in early '50's. Frank Lary's favorite catcher on Tigers.

	G	AB	R	H	2B	3B	HR	RBI	BA	SA	TB	SB
1952 Sea	155	562	76	167	32	9	7	75	.297	.423	238	3

HARRY WOLTER   Harry Meigs Wolter. Born 7/11/1884, Monterey, CA. Died 7/7/1970, Palo Alto, CA. Outfielder for seven major league seasons, won Pacific Coast League batting titles in 1914 and 1915. After retirement as an active player, he coached at Stanford for over a quarter—century.

	G	AB	R	H	2B	3B	HR	RBI	BA	SA	TB	SB
1905 SF–Sea	185	731	– –	176	15	2	0	– –	.241	.267	195	19
1906 Fre	137	549	71	157	16	10	1	– –	.286	.357	196	22
1914 LA	203	802	120	263	33	21	8	76	.328	.451	362	44
1915 LA	150	518	88	186	17	13	5	– –	.359	.471	244	29
1916 LA	173	615	85	182	28	12	6	– –	.296	.410	252	40
1918 Sac	73	294	30	65	8	1	2	– –	.221	.276	81	12
1919 Sac	158	578	83	190	26	4	10	– –	.329	.439	254	22
1920 SF	145	503	57	134	27	4	4	– –	.266	.360	181	14
	1224	4590	– –	1353	170	67	36	– –	.295	.385	1765	202

HARRY WOLVERTON   Harry Sterling Wolverton. Born 12/6/1873, Mt. Vernon, OH. Died 2/4/1937, Oakland, CA. Considered a top manager in minor leagues, was player—manager for New York Highlanders in 1912. Returned to PCL to manage, used himself as a pinch—hitting specialist.

	G	AB	R	H	2B	3B	HR	RBI	BA	SA	TB	SB
1910 Oak	179	618	51	156	16	1	2	– –	.256	.294	182	9
1911 Oak	153	491	47	145	– –	– –	– –	– –	.295	– –	– –	7
1913 Sac	23	24	0	3	1	0	0	– –	.125	.167	4	0
1914 Sac	24	23	0	6	0	0	0	3	.261	.261	6	0
1915 SF	17	17	1	8	1	0	0	– –	.471	.529	9	0
1916 SF	61	55	0	14	2	0	0	– –	.255	.291	16	1
1923 Sea	3	3	0	1	0	0	0	– –	.333	.333	1	0
	460	1231	99	335	– –	– –	– –	– –	.272	.295	– –	17

LARRY WOODALL   Charles Lawrence Woodall. Born 7/26/1894, Staunton, VA. Died 5/6/1963, Cambridge, MA. Ten year big league catcher, all with the Detroit Tigers. Later worked in the front office of the Boston Red Sox. Led Pacific Coast League catchers in fielding four straight years.

	G	AB	R	H	2B	3B	HR	RBI	BA	SA	TB	SB
1929 Port	110	347	38	98	11	3	1	34	.282	.340	118	0
1930 Port	106	336	51	116	23	1	1	44	.345	.429	144	4
1931 Port	104	376	44	100	16	0	0	35	.266	.309	116	0
1932 Sac	122	390	43	125	22	2	2	54	.321	.403	157	2
1933 Sac	104	346	38	108	13	0	2	31	.312	.367	127	3
1934 SF	129	402	33	101	12	0	0	39	.251	.281	113	1
1935 SF	79	257	25	91	11	2	0	43	.354	.412	106	1
1936 SF	55	163	15	45	6	0	0	18	.276	.313	51	1
1937 SF	95	305	23	89	7	1	0	44	.292	.321	98	1

LARRY WOODALL (cont.)

	G	AB	R	H	2B	3B	HR	RBI	BA	SA	TB	SB
1938 SF	66	194	15	57	7	1	1	17	.294	.356	69	0
1939 SF	83	213	13	51	5	0	0	26	.239	.263	56	0
	1053	3329	338	981	133	10	7	385	.295	.347	1155	13

GENE WOODLING   Eugene Richard Woodling. Born 8/16/1922, Akron, OH. Played seventeen years in majors for seven different teams. An All–Star with Orioles in 1959, won four minor league batting titles in his career.

	G	AB	R	H	2B	3B	HR	RBI	BA	SA	TB	SB
1948 SF	146	524	121	202	22	13	22	107	.385	.603	316	6

GLENN WRIGHT   Forrest Glenn Wright. Born 2/6/1901, Archie, MO. Died 4/6/1984, Olathe, KS. One of baseball's best shortstops during the 1920's and 1930's; four–time .300 hitter. Turned an unassisted triple play for the Pirates in 1925. Career shortened by arm injury incurred playing handball.

	G	AB	R	H	2B	3B	HR	RBI	BA	SA	TB	SB
1936 Sea	103	369	40	101	17	8	9	57	.274	.436	161	5

AL ZARILLA   Allen Lee Zarilla. Born 5/1/1919, Los Angeles, CA. Ten year big league outfielder, was an AL All–Star in 1948. Twice hit .325 or better and batted nearly .300 for the Browns' only pennant–winner in 1944.

	G	AB	R	H	2B	3B	HR	RBI	BA	SA	TB	SB
1954 Sea	113	347	40	75	11	4	3	32	.216	.297	103	2
1955 SD–H	42	90	6	18	4	0	2	14	.200	.311	28	0
	155	437	46	93	15	4	5	46	.213	.300	131	2

ROLLIE ZEIDER   Rollie Hubert Zeider. Born 11/16/1883, Auburn, IN. Died 9/12/1967, Garret, IN. Set an AL rookie stolen base record that stood for seventy–six years. Played in majors with all three Chicago big league teams. Led PCL in steals in 1908 with second most in league history.

	G	AB	R	H	2B	3B	HR	RBI	BA	SA	TB	SB
1907 SF	52	192	26	41	11	1	0	– –	.214	.281	54	10
1908 SF	201	742	93	182	26	7	1	– –	.245	.303	225	93
1909 SF	189	705	141	204	– –	– –	– –	– –	.289	– –	– –	– –
1920 LA	134	484	58	125	16	4	0	– –	.258	.308	149	14
1921 LA–Ver	118	402	39	87	11	0	0	35	.216	.244	98	9
1922 Ver	96	287	33	67	8	1	0	22	.233	.268	77	13
1923 Port	42	144	17	40	7	0	1	13	.278	.347	50	6
	832	2956	407	746	– –	– –	– –	– –	.252	.290	– –	– –

GUS ZERNIAL   Gus Edward Zernial. Born 6/27/1923, Beaumont, TX. Led PCL in RBI in 1948. Nicknamed "Ozark Ike" by Hollywood play–by–play man Fred Haney, led the American League in home runs and RBI in 1951. An AL All–Star in 1953, drove in 100 or more runs three straight years.

	G	AB	R	H	2B	3B	HR	RBI	BA	SA	TB	SB
1947 Hol	120	372	61	128	17	6	12	77	.344	.519	193	4
1948 Hol	186	737	130	237	47	7	40	156	.322	.567	418	3
	306	1109	191	365	64	13	52	233	.329	.551	611	7

SECTION III

Player Register — Pitchers

Included in this section are the year-by-year Pacific Coast League statistics for more than 220 of the most important, interesting, and talented pitchers to have appeared in the league during the years 1903 through 1957. While the selection of specific players in this section is subjective and at the discretion of the author, there were general criteria used in making selections.

Once again, players who appeared in 10 or more major league seasons and or 10 or more Pacific Coast League seasons were given priority. Allowances have been made for players not reaching those benchmarks but who still had significant major league or PCL careers. Other allowances have been made for careers shortened by injury, military service, racial barriers, untimely death, or other factors.

In addition, among those pitchers deemed noteworthy by the author are Jimmy Claxton, the only confirmed African-American to play in organized baseball between the time of Frank Grant and Jackie Robinson, comedian-actor Joe E. Brown, "Sleepy Bill" Burns, (a key figure in the "Black Sox" scandal), World Series near-hero Bill Bevens, and Ron Necciai, who once struck out 27 batters in a nine-inning minor league game. Those included because of long major league service as managers include Tommy Lasorda, Fred Hutchinson, and George Bamberger.

Each pitcher's listing in the register includes their year-by-year PCL playing record, biographical information showing full name, birth and death dates, and a few lines indicating PCL and or major league career highlights or other interesting information. For those pitchers whose Pacific Coast League careers began prior to 1957 and extends beyond the years covered in this book, their full PCL record is shown, including the seasons after 1957.

The statistical categories are self-explanatory. They include the year and team for which the player appeared (see the "Player Register — Hitters" section, page 160, for a list of abbreviations), wins and losses (W-L), win-loss percentage (PCT), games pitched (G), innings (IP), hits allowed (H), earned runs (ER), bases on balls (BB), strikeouts (SO), and earned run average (ERA). As explained in the "Sources and Methodology" section, fractions of an inning are calculated but not displayed because of space limitations. In addition to the above categories is one category not widely seen in statistical books. It is labeled as "EFF" and stands for efficiency. Rotisserie League players will know this category by the clunky appellation "hits plus walks divided by innings pitched." That is hard to abbreviate, and impossible when space is at a premium, so I have taken it upon myself to re-christen this statistic. I include it because I think it is easy to understand (it represents the number of baserunners allowed per inning through the pitcher's giving up a hit or a base on balls), and when combined with ERA seems a good indicator of a pitcher's effectiveness. It is especially valuable when looking at relief pitchers, whose earned run averages are often deceptive.

In the efficiency category, any ratio of 1.20 or under is excellent, anything below 1.00 is remarkable. Conversely, anything above 1.35 is outside the average realm.

Statistical information unavailable is indicated with "--." In calculating the Pacific Coast League career totals for each pitcher, the categories that include any unavailable information are not totaled unless the number of innings pitched involved is insignificant (one percent or less) in comparison with the pitcher's career total. The lifetime earned run averages and efficiency averages are computed only on seasons that have the necessary information, provided that information is available for at least 75 percent of the player's career, so for some pitchers, career totals will not foot to the averages displayed because of this approach.

HARRY ABLES   Harry Terrell Ables. Born 10/4/1884, Terrell, TX. Died 2/8/1951, San Antonio, TX. Set the single—season Texas League strikeout record in 1910. Averaged more than nine innings pitched per game in that season. Led the PCL in wins, innings pitched, and strikeouts in 1912.

	W	L	PCT	G	IP	H	ER	BB	SO	ERA	EFF
1911 Oak	22	11	.667	38	324	--	--	88	218	--	--
1912 Oak	25	18	.581	45	363	--	--	134	303	--	--
1913 Oak	9	15	.375	37	229	--	--	73	130	--	--
1914 Oak	13	17	.433	34	223	203	50	82	95	2.02	1.28
1915 Oak	8	16	.333	36	229	237	88	78	99	3.46	1.38
	77	77	.500	190	1368	--	--	455	845	--	--

RED ADAMS   Charles Dwight Adams. Born 10/7/1921, Parlier, CA. Pitched briefly for the Chicago Cubs in 1946. Led the Pacific Coast League in ERA in 1952 while with Portland. Later a long—time Dodger pitching coach.

	W	L	PCT	G	IP	H	ER	BB	SO	ERA	EFF
1942 LA	6	4	.600	11	67	69	31	31	21	4.16	1.49
1944 LA	10	7	.588	44	186	176	74	56	87	3.58	1.25
1945 LA	21	15	.583	41	298	269	90	90	160	2.72	1.20
1946 LA	9	4	.692	17	104	96	31	25	61	2.68	1.16
1947 LA	14	12	.538	34	236	230	92	57	134	3.51	1.22
1948 LA	14	11	.560	32	226	234	89	61	102	3.54	1.31
1949 LA–SD	8	7	.533	24	161	173	69	58	73	3.86	1.43
1950 Port	9	10	.474	41	181	172	93	76	92	4.62	1.37
1951 Port	11	9	.550	37	153	149	69	53	80	4.06	1.32
1952 Port	15	16	.484	37	269	211	65	67	162	2.17	1.03
1953 Port	9	10	.474	37	177	176	86	63	82	4.37	1.35
1954 Port	7	11	.389	34	129	152	73	48	62	5.11	1.55
1955 Port	12	12	.500	28	220	184	50	33	108	2.05	0.99
1956 P–LA	6	4	.600	18	100	125	50	21	36	4.49	1.46
1957 LA	2	5	.286	9	54	55	25	17	15	4.17	1.33
1958 Sac	0	1	.000	4	10	15	8	4	2	7.20	1.90
	153	138	.526	448	2571	2486	995	760	1277	3.48	1.26

HANK AGUIRRE   Henry John Aguirre. Born 1/31/1932, Azusa, CA. Died 9/5/1994, Detroit, MI. One of baseball's all—time worst hitting pitchers with a lifetime mark of .085. Pitched sixteen years in majors, leading AL in ERA in 1962. Also an American League All—Star for Detroit the same year.

	W	L	PCT	G	IP	H	ER	BB	SO	ERA	EFF
1957 SD	6	13	.316	24	132	116	55	69	100	3.75	1.40

VIC ALDRIDGE   Victor Eddington Aldridge. Born 10/25/1893, Indian Springs, IN. Died 4/17/1973, Terre Haute, IN. The number three man in the rotation for the Pirates in their pennant—winning seasons of 1925 and 1927; led the Pacific Coast League in earned run average in 1921.

	W	L	PCT	G	IP	H	ER	BB	SO	ERA	EFF
1919 LA	15	10	.600	31	221	221	71	56	87	2.89	1.25
1920 LA	18	15	.545	39	297	291	95	80	123	2.88	1.25
1921 LA	20	10	.667	33	283	231	68	62	116	2.16	1.04
	53	35	.602	103	801	743	234	198	326	2.63	1.17

BUZZ ARLETT   Russell Loris Arlett. Born 1/3/1899, Oakland, CA. Died 5/16/1964, Minneapolis, MN. Greatest switch–hitting slugger in the history of the minor leagues, was a pitcher before injuring his arm. Led the Pacific Coast League in victories in 1920 and innings pitched in 1920 and 1922.

	W	L	PCT	G	IP	H	ER	BB	SO	ERA	EFF
1918 Oak	4	9	.308	21	153	150	46	43	34	2.70	1.26
1919 Oak	22	17	.564	57	348	315	116	112	79	3.00	1.23
1920 Oak	29	17	.630	53	427	430	137	134	105	2.89	1.32
1921 Oak	19	18	.514	55	319	371	155	115	101	4.37	1.52
1922 Oak	25	19	.568	47	374	396	115	112	128	2.77	1.36
1923 Oak	4	9	.308	28	125	182	80	47	34	5.76	1.83
1924 Oak	0	0	– –	2	4	9	6	3	0	13.50	3.00
1925 Oak	0	0	– –	1	4	1	0	2	0	0.00	0.75
1926 Oak	2	0	1.000	5	14	13	2	3	4	1.29	1.14
1927 Oak	1	0	1.000	1	9	10	3	4	4	3.00	1.56
1928 Oak	1	0	1.000	7	27	19	2	8	7	0.67	1.00
1929 Oak	1	4	.200	17	61	84	39	17	17	5.75	1.66
1930 Oak	0	0	– –	3	3	3	3	1	0	9.00	1.33
	108	93	.537	297	1868	1983	704	601	513	3.39	1.38

LUIS ARROYO   Luis Enrique Arroyo. Born 2/18/1927, Penuelas, Puerto Rico. Two–time All–Star reliever, won fifteen games in 1961 and saved twenty–nine more for the world champion New York Yankees.

	W	L	PCT	G	IP	H	ER	BB	SO	ERA	EFF
1956 Hol	7	5	.583	22	115	110	36	45	76	2.81	1.34

JIM BAGBY   James Charles Jacob Bagby, Sr. Born 10/5/1889, Barnett, GA. Died 7/28/1954, Marietta, GA. Thirty–one wins for Cleveland in 1920. First pitcher to hit a homer in a World Series, in the same game that featured the first grand slam and only unassisted triple play in Series history. Reputedly considered by Ty Cobb to be the smartest pitcher he ever faced.

	W	L	PCT	G	IP	H	ER	BB	SO	ERA	EFF
1923 Sea	0	1	.000	1	2	– –	– –	– –	– –	– –	– –
1924 Sea	16	10	.615	32	202	274	107	41	40	4.76	1.56
1925 Sea	1	2	.333	5	18	– –	– –	– –	– –	– –	– –
	17	13	.567	38	222	– –	– –	– –	– –	– –	– –

WIN BALLOU   Noble Winfield Ballou. Born 11/30/1897, Mount Morgan, KY. Died 1/30/1963, San Francisco, CA. Called all of his teammates "Pard". In majors for four years and then pitched in the PCL until he was 46 years old.

	W	L	PCT	G	IP	H	ER	BB	SO	ERA	EFF
1930 LA	16	7	.696	44	238	243	100	95	129	3.78	1.42
1931 LA	24	13	.649	48	286	309	118	89	160	3.71	1.39
1932 LA	18	21	.462	55	305	357	148	87	157	4.36	1.45
1933 LA	12	19	.387	50	217	234	89	69	122	3.69	1.40
1934 SF	13	12	.520	50	210	216	79	64	117	3.39	1.33
1935 SF	18	8	.692	33	220	241	80	69	94	3.28	1.41
1936 SF	11	16	.407	40	220	278	117	63	132	4.79	1.55
1937 SF	13	12	.520	43	153	165	63	55	86	3.70	1.43
1938 SF	10	2	.833	45	86	82	23	36	43	2.41	1.37

WIN BALLOU (cont.)

	W	L	PCT	G	IP	H	ER	BB	SO	ERA	EFF
1939 SF	8	7	.533	44	99	92	31	48	37	2.82	1.41
1940 SF	6	7	.462	46	67	77	27	25	36	3.63	1.52
1941 SF	3	5	.375	24	38	--	--	--	--	--	--
1943 SF	1	1	.500	16	16	--	--	--	--	--	--
1944 SF	1	1	.500	13	14	20	--	7	5	--	1.93
	154	131	.540	551	2169	--	--	--	--	3.75	1.43

GEORGE BAMBERGER   George Irvin Bamberger. Born 8/1/1925, Staten Island, NY. Set PCL record in pitching sixty—eight straight innings without allowing a base on balls. Very successful pitching coach for the Baltimore Orioles; later named American League Manager of the Year for Milwaukee Brewers. Also managed NY Mets. Often accused of throwing a spitter.

	W	L	PCT	G	IP	H	ER	BB	SO	ERA	EFF
1950 Oak	17	13	.567	39	236	226	111	112	133	4.23	1.43
1952 Oak	14	6	.700	27	150	129	48	36	67	2.88	1.10
1953 Oak	15	18	.484	47	245	289	136	100	111	5.00	1.59
1954 Oak	11	8	.579	40	179	170	70	81	61	3.53	1.40
1955 Oak	12	14	.462	35	180	182	83	61	70	4.15	1.35
1956 Van	9	14	.391	30	186	215	84	45	69	4.07	1.40
1957 Van	14	12	.538	34	200	244	89	46	73	4.01	1.45
1958 Van	15	11	.577	31	184	183	50	26	71	2.45	1.14
1959 Van	11	7	.611	25	160	167	53	27	75	2.98	1.21
1960 Van	12	12	.500	35	206	238	87	34	89	3.80	1.32
1961 Van	12	6	.667	31	196	195	82	42	105	3.77	1.21
1962 Van	12	12	.500	34	228	227	80	37	135	3.16	1.16
1963 DFW	7	15	.318	35	169	205	85	29	86	4.53	1.38
	161	146	.524	443	2518	2670	1058	676	1145	3.78	1.33

CLYDE BARFOOT   Clyde Raymond Barfoot. Born 7/8/1891, Richmond, VA. Died 3/11/1971, Highland Park, CA. Won 314 minor league games; led the PCL in wins in 1925 and innings pitched in 1927. Won twenty—one games and led the Southern Association in earned run average at the age of 41.

	W	L	PCT	G	IP	H	ER	BB	SO	ERA	EFF
1925 Ver	26	15	.634	50	354	383	126	83	76	3.20	1.32
1926 Miss	13	14	.481	30	235	300	119	46	49	4.56	1.47
1927 Miss	15	18	.455	40	308	348	122	54	55	3.56	1.31
1928 LA	20	19	.513	44	311	343	133	59	57	3.84	1.29
1929 LA	18	12	.600	42	236	309	119	58	64	4.53	1.55
1930 LA	12	10	.545	36	186	247	104	42	32	5.03	1.55
	104	88	.542	242	1631	1930	723	342	333	3.99	1.39

DICK BARRETT   Tracey Souter Barrett. Born 9/28/1906, Montoursville, PA. Died 10/30/1966, Seattle, WA. A hard—living right—hander, won 325 minor laegue games, twice leading the Pacific Coast League in wins. War—time hurler for the Phillies and Chicago Cubs, led the NL with 20 losses in 1945.

	W	L	PCT	G	IP	H	ER	BB	SO	ERA	EFF
1935 Sea	22	13	.629	45	305	284	119	119	191	3.51	1.32
1936 Sea	22	13	.629	43	284	263	106	109	187	3.36	1.31

DICK BARRETT (cont.)

	W	L	PCT	G	IP	H	ER	BB	SO	ERA	EFF
1937 Sea	20	18	.526	43	275	274	119	118	186	3.89	1.43
1938 Sea	18	17	.514	46	328	297	118	132	188	3.24	1.31
1939 Sea	22	15	.595	40	308	300	110	113	144	3.22	1.34
1940 Sea	24	5	.828	37	258	197	71	121	164	2.48	1.23
1941 Sea	20	12	.625	40	291	270	89	108	163	2.75	1.30
1942 Sea	27	13	.675	40	330	229	63	101	178	1.72	1.00
1946 Port	9	21	.300	40	251	270	104	89	143	3.73	1.43
1947 Sea	14	17	.452	41	286	276	101	110	130	3.18	1.35
1948 Sea	15	13	.536	38	246	236	91	78	96	3.33	1.28
1949 Sea–SD	12	6	.667	26	135	126	56	68	62	3.73	1.44
1950 SD–H	9	5	.643	31	111	133	71	58	34	5.76	1.72
	234	168	.582	510	3408	3155	1218	1324	1866	3.22	1.31

SPIDER BAUM　　　Charles Adrian Baum. Born 5/28/1882, San Francisco, CA. Died 6/28/1955, Renton, WA. Won 325 games during career spent entirely in the minor leagues. His brother, Allan, served as President of the PCL for eight years, from 1912 through the 1919 season.

	W	L	PCT	G	IP	H	ER	BB	SO	ERA	EFF
1903 LA	1	2	.333	3	26	29	9	9	4	3.12	1.46
1904 LA	24	23	.511	47	––	––	––	––	––	––	––
1905 LA	24	28	.462	57	––	––	––	––	––	––	––
1909 Sac	21	20	.512	51	––	––	––	85	182	––	––
1910 Sac	17	20	.459	47	––	––	––	74	111	––	––
1911 Sac	17	15	.531	39	320	––	––	49	118	––	––
1912 Sac–Ver	14	13	.519	37	227	––	––	54	73	––	––
1913 Ven	23	19	.548	51	361	––	––	72	140	––	––
1914 SF	21	12	.636	40	303	295	68	74	120	2.02	1.22
1915 SF	30	15	.667	55	382	393	104	65	153	2.45	1.20
1916 SF	20	19	.513	56	330	331	103	90	110	2.81	1.28
1917 SF	24	17	.585	50	352	333	98	85	91	2.50	1.19
1918 SF	8	7	.533	22	156	131	35	42	30	2.02	1.11
1919 SF–SL	11	16	.407	36	219	236	84	41	69	3.45	1.26
1920 SLC	7	10	.412	30	149	204	84	32	48	5.07	1.58
	262	236	.526	621	––	––	––	––	––	––	––

GENE BEARDEN　　　Henry Eugene Bearden. Born 9/5/1920, Lexa, AR. Knuckleballer won twenty games in rookie season with Cleveland, leading American League in ERA. Won playoff game vs. Boston in 1948 and then worked 10 2/3 shutout innings in World Series. Not as effective after Oaks manager Casey Stengel came to AL and advised hitters to lay off knuckler.

	W	L	PCT	G	IP	H	ER	BB	SO	ERA	EFF
1946 Oak	15	4	.789	32	167	139	58	75	81	3.13	1.28
1947 Oak	16	7	.696	26	198	185	63	82	80	2.86	1.35
1954 Sea	11	13	.458	44	202	218	91	97	82	4.05	1.56
1955 SF	18	12	.600	43	248	268	97	66	84	3.52	1.35
1956 Sac	15	14	.517	34	207	215	80	56	54	3.48	1.31
1957 Sac	0	1	.000	4	23	13	5	8	10	1.99	0.93
	75	51	.595	183	1045	1038	394	384	391	3.39	1.36

BUD BEASLEY   Bud Louis Beasley. Born 12/8/1910, Melrose, NM. Had played only semi-pro ball in Reno plus short stint with the House of David when signed to Sacramento contract. Developed elaborate routines on the mound both to disrupt the batter and to entertain fans. Taught high school until June each season; 1995 marked his 61st year in the classroom.

	W	L	PCT	G	IP	H	ER	BB	SO	ERA	EFF
1944 Sac	5	6	.455	15	105	100	35	32	21	3.00	1.26
1945 Sac	12	4	.750	17	132	123	46	30	22	3.14	1.16
1946 Sac	6	3	.667	22	71	67	23	19	16	2.92	1.21
1947 Sac-Sea	3	2	.600	22	60	43	33	29	14	4.95	1.20
1948 Sea	0	0	--	21	--	--	--	--	--	--	--
	26	15	.634	97	--	--	--	--	--	3.35	1.20

BOOM BOOM BECK   Walter William Beck. Born 10/16/1904, Decatur, IL. Died 5/7/1987, Champaign, IL. Led the PCL in wins and strikeouts in 1935. Earned nickname from a famous story involving Hack Wilson.

	W	L	PCT	G	IP	H	ER	BB	SO	ERA	EFF
1935 Miss	23	18	.561	46	354	366	160	143	202	4.07	1.44
1936 Miss	18	21	.462	47	304	321	126	119	135	3.73	1.45
1937 Miss	11	22	.333	44	226	270	111	90	108	4.42	1.60
1938 H-Sea	7	10	.412	31	108	137	80	40	42	6.67	1.64
	59	71	.454	168	992	1094	477	392	487	4.33	1.50

GARY BELL   Gary Bell. Born 11/17/1936, San Antonio, TX. A three-time All-Star, both started and relieved in majors. After acquisition by Red Sox in mid-1967, he was a major factor in their "Impossible Dream" season.

	W	L	PCT	G	IP	H	ER	BB	SO	ERA	EFF
1957 SD	1	5	.167	10	56	53	31	33	54	4.98	1.54
1958 SD	6	2	.750	9	75	41	13	23	60	1.56	0.85
1970 Haw	0	2	.000	5	26	34	24	13	14	8.31	1.81
	7	9	.438	24	157	128	68	69	128	3.90	1.25

AL BENTON   John Alton Benton. Born 3/18/1911, Noble, OK. Died 4/14/1968, Lynwood, CA. In big leagues for fourteen years, had seventeen saves for pennant-winning Tigers in 1940. Is the only pitcher to surrender home runs to both Babe Ruth and Mickey Mantle.

	W	L	PCT	G	IP	H	ER	BB	SO	ERA	EFF
1949 Sac	2	1	.667	4	30	30	10	8	11	3.00	1.27
1951 Sac-SD	5	7	.417	43	130	142	58	43	48	4.02	1.42
1952 SD	6	1	.857	21	56	34	8	19	32	1.29	0.95
1953 SD	6	6	.500	50	82	77	26	28	24	2.85	1.28
	19	15	.559	118	298	283	102	98	115	3.08	1.28

BILL BEVENS   Floyd Clifford Bevens. Born 10/21/1916, Hubbard, OR. Died 10/26/1991, Salem, OR. Last appearance in big league uniform came in fourth game of the 1947 World Series. Pitching for the Yanks versus the Dodgers, lost on Lavagetto's two out double in ninth, only hit of the game.

	W	L	PCT	G	IP	H	ER	BB	SO	ERA	EFF
1942 Sea-H	4	11	.267	31	126	125	62	84	65	4.44	1.66

BILL BEVENS (cont.)

	W	L	PCT	G	IP	H	ER	BB	SO	ERA	EFF
1949 Sea	1	2	.333	4	23	30	12	8	3	4.70	1.65
1950 Sac-SD	3	8	.273	30	77	93	64	71	16	7.48	2.13
1952 SF	6	12	.333	33	155	159	77	79	64	4.47	1.54
	14	33	.298	98	381	407	215	242	148	5.08	1.70

JOE BLACK   Joseph Black. Born 2/8/1924, Plainfield, NJ. Began career in Negro Leagues, pitching seven years for the Baltimore Elite Giants. First black to win a World Series game. Named Rookie of the Year in 1952.

	W	L	PCT	G	IP	H	ER	BB	SO	ERA	EFF
1957 Sea	1	1	.500	10	24	34	13	6	14	4.94	1.69

EWELL BLACKWELL   Ewell Blackwell. Born 10/23/1922, Fresno, CA Nicknamed "The Whip" for distinctive underhand delivery, led NL in wins in 1947. Came within two outs of consecutive no-hitters for Cincinnati Reds that year, nearly matching Johnny Vander Meer's feat of nine years before.

	W	L	PCT	G	IP	H	ER	BB	SO	ERA	EFF
1955 SF-Sea	5	5	.500	23	112	120	51	47	31	4.09	1.49

SHERIFF BLAKE   John Frederick Blake. Born 9/17/1899, Ansted, WV. Died 10/31/1982, Beckley, WV. Pitched ten seasons in the majors, winning in double figures six straight times for the Chicago Cubs in the 1920's. The losing pitcher in famous 1929 World Series game when the Athletics rallied for ten runs in one inning to come back from 8-0 deficit against the Cubs.

	W	L	PCT	G	IP	H	ER	BB	SO	ERA	EFF
1923 Sea	13	20	.394	45	256	305	134	115	125	4.71	1.64

CY BLANTON   Darrell Elijah Blanton. Born 7/6/1908, Waurika, OK. Died 9/13/1945, Norman, OK. As a rookie in 1935, he led the NL in shutouts and ERA. Led NL in shutouts again the following year. Two-time All-Star, his career was cut short by mental illness. Died at age 37 in an insane asylum.

	W	L	PCT	G	IP	H	ER	BB	SO	ERA	EFF
1943 Hol	9	9	.500	24	150	150	45	43	70	2.70	1.29
1944 Hol	4	5	.444	14	68	72	24	23	44	3.18	1.40
1945 Hol	0	0	--	1	1	1	--	5	1	--	6.00
	13	14	.481	39	219	223	69	71	115	2.85	1.34

GEORGE BOEHLER   George Henry Boehler. Born 1/2/1892, Lawrenceburg, IN. Died 6/23/1958, Lawrenceburg, IN. Topped the PCL in strikeouts three times and led league in wins in 1927. Won thirty-eight games for Tulsa in the Texas League in 1922. The side-armer pitched in nine different major league seasons, but made only sixty appearances with a 7-12 record.

	W	L	PCT	G	IP	H	ER	BB	SO	ERA	EFF
1924 Oak	26	21	.553	53	396	380	176	172	216	4.00	1.39
1925 Oak	23	25	.479	58	417	387	190	209	278	4.10	1.43
1927 Oak	22	12	.647	39	296	269	102	75	160	3.10	1.16
1928 Oak	17	14	.548	41	257	276	117	124	140	4.09	1.55
1929 O-LA	2	6	.250	19	62	62	51	67	26	7.40	2.08
	90	78	.536	210	1428	1374	636	647	820	4.01	1.41

JULIO BONETTI   Julio Giacomo Bonetti. Born 7/14/1911, Genoa, Italy. Died 6/17/1952, Belmont, CA. Set a PCL record, later broken, pitching sixty—four innings in a row without giving up a base on balls. Seen passing money to known gamblers and banned from baseball in 1941.

	W	L	PCT	G	IP	H	ER	BB	SO	ERA	EFF
1939 LA	20	5	.800	34	238	252	86	24	69	3.25	1.16
1940 LA	14	10	.583	28	193	223	92	43	54	4.28	1.38
1941 LA	7	3	.700	18	111	126	40	20	37	3.24	1.32
	41	18	.695	80	542	601	218	87	160	3.62	1.27

ERNIE BONHAM   Ernest Edward Bonham. Born 8/16/1913, Ione, CA. Died 9/15/1949, Pittsburgh, PA. Two—time All—Star, led the AL in ERA as rookie in 1940. Won 103 games in big league career ended by a fatal illness. One of the first pitchers successful with the forkball, he was a twenty—one game winner for the Yankees in 1942. Led the AL in CG and shutouts that year.

	W	L	PCT	G	IP	H	ER	BB	SO	ERA	EFF
1937 Oak	17	16	.515	40	278	283	113	89	188	3.66	1.34

JOE BOWMAN   Joseph Emil Bowman. Born 6/17/1910, Argentine, KS. Died 11/22/1990, Kansas City, MO. Loser of twenty games for 1935 Phillies, his career was hampered by arm injuries. Batted a respectable .221 in majors, including twenty—four pinch—hits during his career.

	W	L	PCT	G	IP	H	ER	BB	SO	ERA	EFF
1931 Port	18	11	.621	39	246	265	104	62	126	3.80	1.33
1932 Port	10	7	.588	23	180	145	62	47	66	4.19	1.44
1933 Port	23	11	.676	38	283	330	131	65	155	4.17	1.40
1946 SD	1	2	.333	15	40	40	— —	22	16	— —	1.55
	52	31	.627	115	702	780	— —	196	363	4.04	1.39

ED BRANDT   Edward Arthur Brandt. Born 2/17/1905, Spokane, WA. Died 11/1/1944, Spokane, WA. A forkball specialist, his twenty—one defeats led NL as rookie for Boston in 1928. Won sixty—eight games in four year span for the Braves during the 1930's. An excellent hitter, batted .309 in 1933.

	W	L	PCT	G	IP	H	ER	BB	SO	ERA	EFF
1924 Sea	0	0	— —	4	19	— —	— —	— —	— —	— —	— —
1925 Sea	1	2	.333	5	21	— —	— —	— —	— —	— —	— —
1926 Sea	2	0	1.000	4	21	— —	— —	— —	— —	— —	— —
1927 Sea	19	11	.633	41	261	274	115	107	144	3.96	1.46
1939 Hol	2	3	.400	6	29	41	— —	10	9	— —	1.76
	24	16	.600	60	351	— —	— —	— —	— —	— —	— —

AL BRAZLE   Alpha Eugene Brazle. Born 10/19/1913, Loyal, OK. Died 10/24/1973, Grand Junction, CO. Led the PCL in ERA in 1943, earning the side—armer a chance in the majors after nearly a decade in the minors. He played ten years in the majors, twice leading the National League in saves.

	W	L	PCT	G	IP	H	ER	BB	SO	ERA	EFF
1943 Sac	11	8	.579	22	160	131	30	60	69	1.69	1.19
1955 Sac	0	1	.000	19	26	30	18	8	8	6.31	1.48
	11	9	.550	41	186	161	48	68	77	2.33	1.23

TOMMY BRIDGES   Thomas Jefferson Davis Bridges. Born 12/28/1906, Gordonsville, TN. Died 4/19/1968, Nashville, TN. Led AL in strikeouts and wins in 1936. Also led the AL in strikeouts in 1935. One of the game's top curveballers, was six–time All–Star and three–time twenty–game winner for the Detroit Tigers. Won clinching game of 1935 World Series.

	W	L	PCT	G	IP	H	ER	BB	SO	ERA	EFF
1947 Port	7	3	.700	13	104	84	19	31	73	1.64	1.11
1948 Port	15	11	.577	29	195	173	62	75	123	2.86	1.27
1949 Port	11	11	.500	28	184	179	78	75	110	3.82	1.38
1950 SF–Sea	0	0	– –	11	24	18	14	23	11	5.25	1.71
	33	25	.569	81	507	454	173	204	317	3.07	1.30

ERNIE BROGLIO   Ernest Gilbert Broglio. Born 8/27/1935, Berkeley, CA. Led NL in wins with twenty–one in 1960 for Cardinals; unfortunately he will be remembered as being part of infamous trade to the Cubs for Lou Brock.

	W	L	PCT	G	IP	H	ER	BB	SO	ERA	EFF
1953 Oak	2	4	.333	11	47	68	36	33	21	6.89	2.15
1954 Oak	5	8	.385	25	72	69	41	50	30	5.13	1.65
1955 Oak	0	0	– –	1	3	3	2	2	0	5.40	1.50
1958 Phx	8	1	.889	28	110	110	50	52	87	4.09	1.47
1966 Tac	5	4	.556	13	104	99	33	41	74	2.86	1.35
	20	17	.541	78	336	349	162	178	212	4.33	1.57

JIM BROSNAN   James Patrick Brosnan. Born 10/24/1929, Cincinnati, OH. Baseball's first in–season author with classic "The Long Season," he was a consistent and solid relief pitcher in the NL for nearly a decade.

	W	L	PCT	G	IP	H	ER	BB	SO	ERA	EFF
1955 LA	17	10	.630	31	223	188	59	66	133	2.38	1.14

HAL BROWN   Hector Harold Brown. Born 12/11/1924, Greensboro, NC. Nicknamed "Skinny". Rare knuckleball control pitcher, averaging just over two walks per nine innings during his fourteen seasons in the majors.

	W	L	PCT	G	IP	H	ER	BB	SO	ERA	EFF
1950 Sea	13	13	.500	46	222	242	115	78	87	4.66	1.44
1951 Sea	16	6	.727	27	168	151	57	36	70	3.05	1.11
1955 Oak	9	2	.818	12	92	71	30	12	37	2.95	0.91
	38	21	.644	85	482	464	202	126	194	3.77	1.22

JOE E. BROWN   Joseph Even Brown. Born 7/28/1892, Holgate, OH. Died 7/6/1973, Brentwood, CA. Famous comic in vaudeville and film, was great athlete as well. Starred in several popular baseball films in the '30's. Also played a classic role in Billy Wilder's film "Some Like It Hot." Played in the original Hollywood Stars' final game, striking out songwriter Harry Ruby.

	W	L	PCT	G	IP	H	ER	BB	SO	ERA	EFF
1935 Miss	0	0	– –	1	1	0	0	0	1	0.00	0.00

LLOYD BROWN   Lloyd Andrew Brown. Born 12/25/1904, Beeville, TX. Died 1/14/1974, Opa Locka, FL. Favorite victim of Lou Gehrig, won ninety–one games in twelve seasons in the majors. After playing for thirty years, hired as a scout for two of his old teams, the Senators and the Phillies.

LLOYD BROWN (cont.)

	W	L	PCT	G	IP	H	ER	BB	SO	ERA	EFF
1941 Sea	5	7	.417	33	105	112	49	31	46	4.20	1.36

ED BRYAN

Edwin C. Bryan. Born 3/26/1900, Belleville, IL. Won 217 games in minors, including a shutout in the PCL's first night game. Spent his entire career in Texas or the Pacific Coast League, never in the majors.

	W	L	PCT	G	IP	H	ER	BB	SO	ERA	EFF
1924 Ver	13	5	.722	24	173	168	63	42	34	3.27	1.21
1925 Ver	9	18	.333	45	251	310	137	59	72	4.91	1.47
1926 Miss	7	10	.412	49	194	223	73	46	41	3.39	1.39
1927 Miss	8	7	.533	43	164	219	94	49	45	5.15	1.63
1928 M–Sea	8	11	.421	34	191	243	100	51	48	4.71	1.54
1929 Sac	20	12	.625	48	328	401	161	80	79	4.41	1.46
1930 Sac	18	12	.600	38	250	304	117	67	84	4.21	1.48
1931 Sac	14	18	.438	44	280	348	134	60	71	4.31	1.46
1932 Sac	19	13	.594	40	271	295	114	55	59	3.79	1.29
1933 Sac	21	17	.553	43	318	441	182	54	78	5.15	1.56
1934 Port	11	24	.314	42	309	367	121	81	77	3.53	1.45
1935 P–Sea	15	19	.441	54	259	341	123	62	54	4.27	1.56
	163	166	.495	504	2989	3660	1419	706	742	4.27	1.46

LEW BURDETTE

Selva Lewis Burdette. Born 11/22/1926, Nitro, WV. The hero of the 1957 Series, with three complete game victories for the Braves, he was a two–time twenty game winner and a National League All–Star. Frequently accused of throwing a spitter. Threw a no–hitter against Phils on August 18, 1960. Winning pitcher in Harvey Haddix's "perfect game".

	W	L	PCT	G	IP	H	ER	BB	SO	ERA	EFF
1951 SF	14	12	.538	30	210	202	75	78	118	3.21	1.33
1967 Sea	0	1	.000	13	19	18	9	4	8	4.26	1.16
	14	13	.519	43	229	220	84	82	126	3.30	1.32

SLEEPY BILL BURNS

William Thomas Burns. Born 1/29/1880, San Seba, TX. Died 6/6/1953, Ramona, CA. Earned nickname for his noticeable lack of intensity on the mound. Later, was would–be "money man" behind the "Black Sox" scheme, turned star prosecution witness in the Chicago trial.

	W	L	PCT	G	IP	H	ER	BB	SO	ERA	EFF
1906 LA	16	16	.500	35	––	––	––	––	––	––	––
1907 LA	23	16	.590	45	––	––	––	82	144	––	––
1915 LA–O	14	15	.483	59	274	283	85	48	73	2.79	1.21
1916 Oak	10	14	.417	37	209	214	56	43	50	2.42	1.23
1917 Oak	4	5	.444	19	88	118	44	15	19	4.48	1.51
	67	66	.504	195	––	––	––	––	––	––	––

GUY BUSH

Guy Terrell Bush. Born 8/23/1901, Aberdeen, MS. Died 7/2/1985, Shannon, MS. Remembered as hurler who gave up Babe Ruth's last two home runs. Won 176 games in the majors, 152 with the Cubs. A twenty–game winner for Chicago in 1933.

	W	L	PCT	G	IP	H	ER	BB	SO	ERA	EFF
1938 LA	8	5	.615	26	108	121	47	16	44	3.92	1.27

RALPH BUXTON   Ralph Stanley Buxton. Born 6/7/1911, Wayburn, Sask., Canada. Died 1/6/1988, San Leandro, CA. Nicknamed "Pine Tar", the long time Oakland Oaks hurler was called up to pitch for the New York Yankees in 1949 by Casey Stengel after being out of the majors for eleven seasons.

	W	L	PCT	G	IP	H	ER	BB	SO	ERA	EFF
1934 LA	0	2	.000	2	13	––	––	––	––	––	––
1935 LA	7	7	.500	28	134	151	58	47	64	3.90	1.48
1936 LA	0	3	.000	11	39	––	––	––	––	––	––
1939 Oak	13	10	.565	37	200	188	64	72	95	2.88	1.30
1940 Oak	17	13	.567	38	252	229	86	90	149	3.07	1.27
1941 Oak	14	18	.438	39	243	255	95	103	97	3.52	1.47
1942 Oak	13	16	.448	33	204	207	77	65	74	3.39	1.33
1943 Oak	11	11	.500	29	183	169	56	51	92	2.75	1.20
1946 Oak	10	5	.667	31	119	109	34	32	68	2.57	1.18
1947 Oak	8	8	.500	29	125	128	54	42	52	3.89	1.36
1948 Oak	13	3	.813	34	96	78	34	29	52	3.19	1.11
1949 Oak	4	4	.500	25	77	67	29	32	58	3.39	1.29
1950 SF	6	3	.667	38	77	87	43	37	33	5.03	1.61
1952 Oak	0	0	––	2	1	4	4	4	1	36.00	8.00
	116	103	.530	376	1763	––	––	––	––	3.33	1.33

TOMMY BYRNE   Thomas Joseph Byrne. Born 12/31/1919, Baltimore, MD. Like Babe Ruth, he learned baseball in Baltimore orphanage. A wild, hard thrower who liked to tell batters what was coming, especially Ted Williams, who he loved to torment. Used the PCL as a comeback venue after being cut from majors in 1953. Excellent hitter, also played first base for Seattle.

	W	L	PCT	G	IP	H	ER	BB	SO	ERA	EFF
1954 Sea	20	10	.667	36	260	218	91	118	199	3.15	1.29

LEON CADORE   Leon Joseph Cadore. Born 11/20/1890, Chicago, IL. Died 3/16/1958, Spokane, WA. Won 68 games in ten big league seasons; best remembered for his twenty–six inning duel vs. Joe Oeschger May 1, 1920. Hit five home runs and batted .208 lifetime in the majors.

	W	L	PCT	G	IP	H	ER	BB	SO	ERA	EFF
1924 Ver	6	6	.500	15	92	117	63	29	32	6.16	1.59

MILO CANDINI   Mario Cain Candini. Born 8/3/1917, Manteca, CA. Pitched eight seasons in the majors with the Senators and Phillies, mostly out of the bullpen. One of the Pacific Coast League's best relievers, set a league record with sixty–nine appearances in 1952.

	W	L	PCT	G	IP	H	ER	BB	SO	ERA	EFF
1940 Oak	3	3	.500	10	42	––	––	––	––	––	––
1949 Oak	15	9	.625	34	176	167	79	67	88	4.04	1.33
1952 Oak	9	6	.600	69	133	121	38	49	69	2.57	1.28
1953 O–Sac	9	4	.692	57	74	87	40	42	39	4.86	1.74
1954 Sac	11	4	.733	44	72	55	18	30	42	2.25	1.18
1955 Sac	2	9	.182	42	71	74	27	24	34	3.41	1.37
1956 Sac	3	4	.429	49	66	53	15	25	39	2.04	1.18
1957 Sac	9	6	.600	57	100	88	22	30	47	1.98	1.18
	61	45	.575	362	735	––	––	––	––	3.11	1.32

BEN CANTWELL   Benjamin Caldwell Cantwell. Born 4/13/1902, Milan, TN. Died 12/4/1962, Salem, MO. Played eleven seasons in majors, mostly with Braves. Went from 20–10 record in 1933 to a 4–25 mark two years later.

	W	L	PCT	G	IP	H	ER	BB	SO	ERA	EFF
1939 Oak	13	15	.464	38	227	238	84	53	57	3.33	1.28
1940 Oak	13	5	.722	33	151	157	43	32	35	2.56	1.25
1941 Oak	0	1	.000	6	21	--	--	--	--	--	--
	26	21	.553	77	399	--	--	--	--	3.02	1.27

HUGH CASEY   Hugh Thomas Casey. Born 10/14/1913, Atlanta, GA. Died 7/3/1951, Atlanta, GA. Tough man and a tougher reliever for Brooklyn, he was the pitcher who threw a third strike past Mickey Owen in the '41 World Series. Befriended and once boxed Ernest Hemingway. Suicide at 37.

	W	L	PCT	G	IP	H	ER	BB	SO	ERA	EFF
1936 LA	5	8	.385	19	106	120	58	36	66	4.92	1.47

GEORGE CASTER   George Jasper Caster. Born 8/4/1907, Colton, CA. Died 12/18/1955, Lakewood, CA. Knuckleball pitcher for Browns, A's, and Tigers; three times lost nineteen or more games. Led the PCL in wins and strikeouts for the pennant—winning Portland Beavers in 1936.

	W	L	PCT	G	IP	H	ER	BB	SO	ERA	EFF
1929 Miss	5	4	.556	20	84	98	44	31	28	4.71	1.54
1930 Miss	8	10	.444	30	128	170	78	47	78	5.48	1.70
1931 Miss	13	17	.433	35	236	286	133	79	83	5.07	1.55
1932 M–LA	3	9	.250	28	87	115	59	37	16	6.08	1.74
1933 Sea	12	19	.387	47	264	325	170	126	114	5.80	1.71
1934 Sea–P	13	15	.464	34	233	245	88	95	104	3.40	1.46
1936 Port	25	13	.658	44	339	316	105	102	234	2.79	1.23
1947 H–SD	2	2	.500	23	31	38	15	22	13	4.35	1.94
	81	89	.476	261	1402	1593	692	539	670	4.44	1.52

SPUD CHANDLER   Spurgeon Ferdinand Chandler. Born 9/12/1907, Commerce, CA. Died 1/9/1990, St. Petersburg, FL. Nearly thirty at time of his major league debut, pitched entire career with Yankees, setting record for winning percentage among pitchers with 100 or more victories. The AL MVP in 1943, had two complete game wins in the World Series that year.

	W	L	PCT	G	IP	H	ER	BB	SO	ERA	EFF
1935 O–P	7	9	.438	34	179	203	85	51	82	4.27	1.42

CHARLIE CHECH   Charles William Chech. Born 4/27/1878, Madison, WI. Died 1/31/1938, Los Angeles, CA. Came out of the University of Wisconsin. Pitched four seasons in majors and won 239 games in the minors. Had an excellent curveball. Traded by Cleveland as part of a deal for Cy Young.

	W	L	PCT	G	IP	H	ER	BB	SO	ERA	EFF
1912 LA	25	14	.641	50	360	--	--	80	118	--	--
1913 LA	18	20	.474	42	305	295	--	86	84	--	--
1914 LA	20	16	.556	46	297	258	95	82	72	2.88	1.15
1915 LA–Ver	12	14	.462	34	228	240	83	46	60	3.28	1.26
1918 Ver	9	7	.563	20	141	128	33	18	24	2.11	1.04
	84	71	.542	192	1330	--	--	312	358	--	--

JIMMY CLAXTON   James E. Claxton. Born 1892, Wellington, B.C., Canada. Left–hander was on the Oakland roster for a week in 1916 under the name "Minnehaha" Claxton, an American Indian. In fact, he had played in the Bay Area Negro Leagues, and on that discovery, was cut from team after pitching in both games of a doubleheader. Retains distinction as only black to play organized baseball in this century prior to Jackie Robinson.

	W	L	PCT	G	IP	H	ER	BB	SO	ERA	EFF
1916 Oak	0	0	––	2	2	4	2	4	0	7.72	3.43

BERT COLE   Albert George Cole. Born 7/1/1896, San Francisco, CA. Died 5/30/1975, San Mateo, CA. A six year big league veteran; led PCL in wins in 1926. Later served the Pacific Coast League as an umpire.

	W	L	PCT	G	IP	H	ER	BB	SO	ERA	EFF
1920 SF	5	1	.833	16	63	46	13	21	26	1.87	1.07
1926 Miss	29	12	.707	41	325	306	95	93	102	2.63	1.23
1928 P–Sea	10	20	.333	41	246	317	141	58	73	5.16	1.52
1929 Miss	24	12	.667	42	279	301	107	90	103	3.45	1.40
1930 Miss	16	13	.552	37	267	320	137	70	100	4.61	1.46
1931 Miss	15	17	.469	39	273	294	116	70	110	3.82	1.33
1932 Miss	12	16	.429	30	236	253	92	51	79	3.51	1.29
1933 Miss	8	17	.320	30	203	293	136	59	44	6.02	1.73
1935 Miss	1	2	.333	7	36	––	––	––	––	––	––
	120	110	.522	283	1928	––	––	––	––	3.98	1.40

WILBUR COOPER   Arlie Wilbur Cooper. Born 2/24/1892, Bearsville, WV. Died 8/7/1973, Van Nuys, CA. A left–handed sinkerballer, one of the NL's most consistent pitchers. With Pittsburgh, was a four–time twenty–game winner and won at least seventeen for eight straight seasons.

	W	L	PCT	G	IP	H	ER	BB	SO	ERA	EFF
1927 Oak	15	12	.556	36	231	238	86	51	65	3.35	1.25
1928 Oak	10	16	.385	27	212	261	82	45	45	3.48	1.44
	25	28	.472	63	443	499	168	96	110	3.41	1.34

JOHNNY COUCH   John Daniel Couch. Born 3/31/1891, Vaughn, MT. Died 12/8/1975, San Mateo, CA. Replaced Rube Marquard in the rotation of the Cincinnati Reds in 1922, earning sixteen victories as a thirty–one year old rookie. Compiled a major league record of only 13–25 after that season.

	W	L	PCT	G	IP	H	ER	BB	SO	ERA	EFF
1915 SF	6	5	.545	21	98	95	27	46	34	2.47	1.43
1916 SF	18	15	.545	56	319	309	95	115	70	2.68	1.33
1919 SF	12	19	.387	48	267	261	97	117	62	3.27	1.42
1920 SF	22	17	.564	51	328	308	99	90	88	2.72	1.21
1921 SF	25	15	.625	54	345	353	118	68	90	3.08	1.22
1926 Port	0	1	.000	5	5	––	––	––	––	––	––
1927 Port	18	15	.545	47	232	277	104	62	41	4.03	1.46
1928 P–H	9	17	.346	44	236	304	128	46	51	4.88	1.48
1929 SF	9	8	.529	37	113	152	68	28	30	5.42	1.59
	119	112	.515	363	1943	2059	736	572	466	3.42	1.36

STAN COVELESKI   Stanley Anthony Coveleski. Born 7/13/1889, Shamokin, PA. Died 3/20/1984, South Bend, IN. Taught the spitball while in PCL, leading to Hall of Fame career. A control artist, once tossed seven innings in a game in which every pitch was either hit or a called strike. He won three games in the 1920 World Series. Won twenty or more five times.

	W	L	PCT	G	IP	H	ER	BB	SO	ERA	EFF
1915 Port	17	17	.500	64	293	279	87	82	171	2.67	1.23

HOWARD CRAGHEAD   Howard Oliver Craghead. Born 5/25/1908, Selma, CA. Died 7/15/1962, San Zielde, CA. Pitched briefly in the big leagues for Cleveland. Won 209 games in minors and led the Pacific Coast League in strikeouts in 1930. Also led the league in losses that same year.

	W	L	PCT	G	IP	H	ER	BB	SO	ERA	EFF
1926 Oak	2	3	.400	20	83	78	30	33	37	3.25	1.34
1927 Oak	4	4	.500	24	100	104	38	41	49	3.42	1.45
1928 Oak	18	13	.581	39	282	283	107	104	147	3.41	1.37
1929 Oak	21	12	.636	52	298	321	134	128	190	4.04	1.51
1930 Oak	21	22	.488	47	343	342	139	125	199	3.64	1.36
1931 Oak	13	15	.464	36	229	233	106	100	156	4.17	1.45
1934 Sea	16	21	.432	46	280	339	135	110	145	4.34	1.60
1935 Sea	18	16	.529	39	276	316	125	101	120	4.07	1.51
1936 Sea–SD	16	12	.571	40	235	233	94	83	109	3.60	1.34
1937 SD	16	13	.552	42	245	265	89	74	119	3.27	1.38
1938 SD	18	18	.500	47	271	279	88	79	138	2.86	1.32
1939 SD	11	16	.407	34	203	239	107	56	94	4.75	1.46
1940 SD	8	14	.364	38	175	205	95	74	66	4.88	1.59
	182	179	.504	504	3021	3237	1285	1108	1569	3.83	1.44

DOC CRANDALL   James Otis Crandall. Born 10/8/1887, Wadena, IN. Died 8/17/1951, Bell, CA. Very popular among New York Giant fans, was one of the first to specialize, and star, as reliever. Damon Runyan dubbed him as "The Physician of the Pitching Emergency". Lost a no–hitter in 1918 when he surrendered a base hit to his brother with two out in the ninth inning.

	W	L	PCT	G	IP	H	ER	BB	SO	ERA	EFF
1916 O–LA	11	17	.393	33	234	234	77	80	70	2.96	1.34
1917 LA	26	15	.634	49	364	343	112	83	91	2.77	1.17
1918 LA	16	9	.640	27	222	193	51	35	69	2.07	1.03
1919 LA	28	10	.737	47	355	328	95	43	99	2.41	1.05
1920 LA	15	13	.536	38	278	296	90	51	90	2.92	1.25
1921 LA	24	13	.649	40	328	311	114	53	106	3.13	1.11
1922 LA	17	19	.472	37	269	318	109	34	95	3.65	1.31
1923 LA	17	12	.586	30	258	265	89	28	84	3.10	1.14
1924 LA	19	11	.633	34	256	256	77	32	72	2.71	1.13
1925 LA	20	7	.741	39	239	250	92	40	89	3.46	1.21
1926 LA	20	8	.714	33	245	238	60	48	86	2.20	1.17
1928 Sac	6	4	.600	13	81	87	35	19	22	3.89	1.31
1929 Sac–LA	11	13	.458	34	202	252	94	58	50	4.18	1.53
	230	151	.604	454	3331	3371	1095	604	1023	2.96	1.19

BUDDY DALEY   Leavitt Leo Daley. Born 10/7/1932, Orange, CA. Taught himself to toss left–handed after polio shortened his right arm. Two–time All–Star, he won sixteen games in both 1959 and 1960 for the Athletics.

	W	L	PCT	G	IP	H	ER	BB	SO	ERA	EFF
1954 Sac	13	8	.619	30	180	175	56	55	117	2.80	1.28
1955 Sac	18	16	.529	40	259	268	99	87	118	3.44	1.37
1957 SD	3	0	1.000	5	33	24	3	6	35	0.83	0.92
	34	24	.586	75	472	467	158	148	270	3.01	1.30

FRANK DASSO   Francis Joseph Nicholas Dasso. Born 8/31/1917, Chicago, IL. Chicago high school star, plagued by wildness and lack of confidence throughout his career. Led PCL in strikeouts twice and in walks four times. Pitched in the major leagues for the Cincinnati Reds in 1945 and 1946.

	W	L	PCT	G	IP	H	ER	BB	SO	ERA	EFF
1940 SF	10	15	.400	37	212	205	78	121	126	3.31	1.54
1941 Hol	15	15	.500	43	230	232	100	116	147	3.91	1.51
1942 SD	15	18	.455	42	284	280	91	127	155	2.88	1.43
1943 SD	12	8	.600	27	177	170	54	93	154	2.75	1.49
1944 SD	20	19	.513	40	298	252	93	131	253	2.81	1.29
1946 Hol	12	5	.706	26	146	127	53	71	88	3.27	1.36
1947 H–Sac	9	18	.333	43	194	225	101	108	117	4.69	1.72
1948 Sac	0	1	.000	6	18	24	14	10	15	7.00	1.89
1949 Sac	17	10	.630	34	214	205	89	93	108	3.74	1.39
1950 Sac	4	9	.308	31	100	107	61	65	48	5.49	1.72
	114	118	.491	329	1873	1827	734	935	1211	3.53	1.47

CURT DAVIS   Curtis Benton Davis. Born 9/7/1903, Greenfield, MO. Died 10/13/1965, Covina, CA. One of three players traded by the Chicago Cubs to the Cardinals for Dizzy Dean, won 22 games for St. Louis in 1939. Two–time All–Star, was starting pitcher for Brooklyn in Game 1 of 1941 Series.

	W	L	PCT	G	IP	H	ER	BB	SO	ERA	EFF
1929 SF	17	13	.567	41	240	277	106	61	79	3.97	1.41
1930 SF	17	18	.486	44	305	389	165	80	103	4.87	1.54
1931 SF	14	14	.500	38	236	275	110	56	106	4.19	1.40
1932 SF	22	16	.579	44	326	290	81	57	122	2.24	1.06
1933 SF	20	16	.556	41	283	340	125	56	86	3.97	1.40
	90	77	.539	208	1391	1571	587	310	496	3.80	1.35

WHEEZER DELL   William George Dell. Born 6/11/1887, Tuscarora, NV. Died 8/24/1966, Independence, CA. Pitched four years in the majors; won 231 games in the minors. Led PCL in shutouts in 1920 and wins in 1921.

	W	L	PCT	G	IP	H	ER	BB	SO	ERA	EFF
1918 Ver	14	7	.667	27	208	170	39	74	78	1.69	1.17
1919 Ver	25	16	.610	50	352	303	93	99	162	2.38	1.14
1920 Ver	27	15	.643	54	370	368	123	126	123	2.99	1.34
1921 Ver	28	14	.667	49	336	311	110	112	134	2.95	1.26
1922 Ver	23	17	.575	49	369	328	130	104	143	3.17	1.17
1923 Ver–Sea	12	11	.522	39	236	276	106	72	88	4.04	1.47
1924 Sea	9	14	.391	38	183	215	113	86	74	5.56	1.64
	138	94	.595	306	2054	1971	714	673	802	3.13	1.29

AL DEMAREE　　　Albert Wentworth Demaree. Born 9/8/1884, Quincy, IL. Died 4/30/1962, Long Beach, CA. Later an artist specializing in sports cartoons, won eighty games over eight big league seasons; retired with a career ERA of 2.77. Once won both games of a doubleheader for the Phillies in 1915.

	W	L	PCT	G	IP	H	ER	BB	SO	ERA	EFF
1920 Sea	16	13	.552	32	251	229	73	64	63	2.61	1.17
1921 Sea	16	9	.640	39	247	284	115	59	69	4.19	1.39
1922 Port	2	2	.500	5	32	--	--	--	--	--	--
	34	24	.586	76	530	--	--	--	--	3.39	1.27

BILL DIETRICH　　　William John Dietrich. Born 3/29/1910, Philadelphia, PA. Died 6/20/1978, Philadelphia, PA. The bespectacled "Wild Bill" appeared in majors for sixteen seasons, achieving his best results during the war years. Pitched a no–hitter on June 1, 1937 for the White Sox versus the Browns.

	W	L	PCT	G	IP	H	ER	BB	SO	ERA	EFF
1932 Port	5	7	.417	18	112	117	48	51	58	3.85	1.50
1950 Oak	0	0	--	2	4	7	5	3	2	11.25	2.50
	5	7	.417	20	116	124	53	54	60	4.10	1.53

PETE DONOHUE　　　Peter Joseph Donohue. Born 11/5/1900, Athens, TX. Died 2/23/1988, Fort Worth, TX. A workhorse pitcher in the majors from 1922 to 1926, he won twenty games three times for the Cincinnati Reds.

	W	L	PCT	G	IP	H	ER	BB	SO	ERA	EFF
1933 Hol	1	2	.333	4	22	--	--	--	--	--	--

JEAN DUBUC　　　Jean Joseph Octave Dubuc. Born 9/15/1888, St. Johnsbury, VT. Died 8/28/1958, Ft. Myers, FL. An excellent batter, hit .200 or better for five straight seasons during the dead ball era. Won seventy–two games for Tigers in those years. Banned over knowledge of Chase–Zimmerman fix.

	W	L	PCT	G	IP	H	ER	BB	SO	ERA	EFF
1917 SLC	22	16	.579	42	351	323	122	146	98	3.13	1.33
1918 SLC	9	9	.500	19	158	171	63	78	44	3.60	1.58
	31	25	.554	61	509	494	185	224	142	3.27	1.41

RYNE DUREN　　　Rinold George Duren. Born 2/22/1929, Cazenovia, WI. Few threw as hard or struck as much fear in batter's hearts than this reliever. At beginning of each appearance, would peer through thick glasses and toss a 100 mph pitch to the screen. Once hit a player in the on–deck circle.

	W	L	PCT	G	IP	H	ER	BB	SO	ERA	EFF
1955 Sea	2	3	.400	7	34	28	14	22	38	3.74	1.49
1956 Van	11	11	.500	33	205	185	94	87	183	4.13	1.33
	13	14	.481	40	239	213	108	109	221	4.07	1.35

HOWARD EHMKE　　　Howard Jonathan Ehmke. Born 4/24/1894, Silver Creek, NY. Died 3/17/1959, Philadelphia, PA. Jumped PCL for Federal League in in 1915 to begin fifteen year big league career. A twenty–game winner for Red Sox in 1923. Sidearmer earned a place in baseball history by winning Game One of the 1929 World Series as surprise starter for the Athletics.

	W	L	PCT	G	IP	H	ER	BB	SO	ERA	EFF
1914 LA	12	11	.522	40	232	228	72	91	89	2.79	1.38

HOD ELLER   Horace Owen Eller. Born 7/5/1894, Muncie, IN. Died 7/18/1961, Indianapolis, IN. Winner of twenty games for pennant–winning Cincinnati Reds in 1919; not as effective after "shine ball" outlawed. Struck out six consecutive batters in Game Five of the 1919 World Series.

	W	L	PCT	G	IP	H	ER	BB	SO	ERA	EFF
1922 Oak	6	10	.375	22	108	135	56	44	33	4.67	1.66

JUMBO ELLIOTT   James Thomas Elliott. Born 10/22/1900, St. Louis, MO. Died 1/7/1970, Terre Haute, IN. Largest man in the big leagues during his career, (at times tipping the scales at over 250 pounds), tied for NL lead in victories with nineteen for the Philadelphia Phillies in 1931.

	W	L	PCT	G	IP	H	ER	BB	SO	ERA	EFF
1926 Sea	26	20	.565	48	367	329	104	121	203	2.55	1.23

ERIC ERICKSON   Eric George Adolph Erickson. Born 3/13/1892, Goteborg, Sweden. Died 5/19/1965, Jamestown, NY. Took pitcher's "triple crown" in the PCL in 1917, leading the league in victories, strikeouts, and ERA.

	W	L	PCT	G	IP	H	ER	BB	SO	ERA	EFF
1916 SF	12	9	.571	31	192	143	50	112	158	2.35	1.33
1917 SF	31	15	.674	62	444	322	95	153	307	1.93	1.07
	43	24	.642	93	636	465	145	265	465	2.05	1.15

CY FALKENBERG   Frederick Peter Falkenberg. Born 12/17/1880, Chicago, IL. Died 4/14/1961, San Francisco, CA. Pitching for Cleveland in 1913, he won twenty games and promptly became one of the biggest stars to make the jump to the Federal League. Won twenty–five games for Indianapolis the next year, leading league in strikeouts, shutouts, and innings pitched.

	W	L	PCT	G	IP	H	ER	BB	SO	ERA	EFF
1919 Oak	15	18	.455	44	314	295	101	75	115	2.89	1.18

SKEETER FANNING   Charles H. Fanning. Born 1884, Jacksonville, IL. Was consistently among PCL strikeout leaders; once drafted by A's and Browns. Pitched Seals' first game at Ewing Field. Led PCL in wins in 1913; tied for lead in shutouts in 1914. Pitched no–hitters against Portland and Vernon.

	W	L	PCT	G	IP	H	ER	BB	SO	ERA	EFF
1911 SF	5	6	.455	18	110	––	––	25	63	––	––
1912 SF	12	13	.480	35	245	––	––	52	150	––	––
1913 SF	28	15	.651	51	357	––	––	54	206	––	––
1914 SF	24	18	.571	54	369	329	93	76	168	2.27	1.10
1915 SF	25	15	.625	58	364	321	107	62	202	2.65	1.05
1916 SF	2	5	.286	20	80	74	32	32	36	3.60	1.33
	96	72	.571	236	1525	––	––	301	825	––	––

BOB FESLER   Robert Clellan Fesler. Born 8/21/1925, Nampa, ID. Died 8/28/1983, Seattle, WA. One of the very best fast–pitch softball pitchers of his time; Rainiers wanted to see if softball delivery would be as intimidating in baseball. The increase in distance proved too great, as his eleven walks and seven wild pitches in 7 2/3 innings attest.

	W	L	PCT	G	IP	H	ER	BB	SO	ERA	EFF
1955 Sea	0	2	.000	4	8	13	14	11	7	16.43	3.13

PAUL FITTERY   Paul Clarence Fittery. Born 10/10/1887, Lebanon, PA. Died 1/28/1974, Cartersville, GA. Topped the PCL in innings pitched, strikeouts, and walks in 1916. Led in innings pitched and strikeouts in 1921; also led in losses twice. A 48−8 record after age 40 in Georgia−Alabama League.

	W	L	PCT	G	IP	H	ER	BB	SO	ERA	EFF
1915 SLC	22	17	.564	58	312	312	105	111	177	3.03	1.35
1916 SLC	29	19	.604	65	448	407	148	158	203	2.97	1.26
1918 LA	11	13	.458	25	210	187	62	86	85	2.66	1.30
1919 LA	18	20	.474	47	301	286	101	121	102	3.02	1.35
1920 Sac	19	21	.475	46	331	326	113	110	153	3.07	1.32
1921 Sac	25	14	.641	49	361	370	116	82	164	2.89	1.25
1922 Sac	16	26	.381	49	334	346	123	107	152	3.31	1.36
1923 Sac	15	14	.517	40	225	265	96	71	83	3.84	1.49
	155	144	.518	379	2522	2499	864	846	1119	3.08	1.33

GUY FLETCHER   Guy Fletcher. Born 8/23/1913, East Bend, NC. Winner of 242 games over his twenty−one minor league seasons. Led the PCL in wins, complete games, and shutouts in 1949 after nearly retiring the winter before. In long professional career, he never pitched in the major leagues.

	W	L	PCT	G	IP	H	ER	BB	SO	ERA	EFF
1944 Sac	12	19	.387	38	268	249	84	94	126	2.82	1.28
1945 Sac	24	14	.632	45	335	292	87	92	144	2.33	1.15
1946 Sac	19	12	.613	36	225	230	84	74	92	3.36	1.35
1947 Sac−Sea	18	13	.581	43	284	279	114	87	121	3.61	1.29
1948 Sea	16	15	.516	37	249	269	102	82	114	3.69	1.41
1949 Sea	23	12	.657	42	318	317	116	113	162	3.28	1.35
1950 Sea	11	12	.478	35	217	249	105	83	88	4.35	1.53
1951 SF−SD	9	12	.429	28	170	181	65	62	91	3.44	1.43
1952 SD	14	16	.467	36	232	236	97	87	108	3.76	1.39
1954 Sac	1	1	.500	5	9	9	4	5	4	4.00	1.56
	147	126	.538	345	2307	2311	858	779	1050	3.35	1.34

JESSE FLORES   Jesse Sandoval Flores. Born 11/2/1914, Guadalajara, Mexico. Died 12/17/1991, Orange, CA. Long−time big league scout, won forty−four games in seven years with the Chicago Cubs, Philadelphia A's, and the Cleveland Indians. Tied for PCL lead in shutouts in 1952.

	W	L	PCT	G	IP	H	ER	BB	SO	ERA	EFF
1939 LA	9	9	.500	30	173	166	68	59	100	3.54	1.30
1940 LA	7	5	.583	32	132	131	65	67	99	4.43	1.50
1941 LA	12	15	.444	39	223	186	80	89	139	3.23	1.23
1942 LA	14	5	.737	37	185	151	54	63	100	2.63	1.16
1948 SD	11	19	.367	41	225	267	109	81	111	4.36	1.55
1949 SD	21	10	.677	36	279	283	94	74	139	3.03	1.28
1951 Sac	4	7	.364	34	65	63	29	27	32	4.02	1.38
1952 Sac	10	20	.333	32	240	223	74	60	123	2.78	1.18
1953 Sac−O	8	9	.471	29	153	180	67	34	47	3.94	1.40
1954 O−P	3	8	.273	37	91	101	37	27	34	3.65	1.40
	99	107	.481	347	1766	1751	677	581	924	3.45	1.32

TONY FREITAS   Antonio Freitas. Born 5/5/1908, Mill Valley, CA. Died 3/15/1994, Orangevale, CA. Chosen by SABR as minors' greatest pitcher, had 342 wins in the minors and twenty–five in the majors. Set PCL record with six straight twenty–win seasons. Also led league in CG four years in a row. Turned down chances to return to majors, preferred Sacramento.

	W	L	PCT	G	IP	H	ER	BB	SO	ERA	EFF
1929 Sac	2	4	.333	18	59	73	42	29	27	6.41	1.73
1930 Sac	19	6	.760	42	275	287	99	74	121	3.24	1.31
1931 Sac	19	13	.594	39	297	311	102	102	156	3.09	1.39
1932 Sac	6	4	.600	11	65	53	26	28	35	3.62	1.25
1933 Port	4	7	.364	11	75	102	33	15	48	3.98	1.57
1937 Sac	23	12	.657	37	290	262	92	36	108	2.86	1.03
1938 Sac	24	11	.686	38	290	298	86	46	159	2.67	1.19
1939 Sac	21	18	.538	43	332	350	106	37	172	2.87	1.17
1940 Sac	20	19	.513	41	332	350	100	48	146	2.71	1.20
1941 Sac	21	15	.583	41	300	297	90	38	112	2.70	1.12
1942 Sac	24	13	.649	44	295	322	96	36	98	2.93	1.21
1946 Sac	16	20	.444	40	296	307	77	50	126	2.34	1.21
1947 Sac	13	17	.433	41	215	242	92	46	104	3.85	1.34
1948 Sac	12	11	.522	31	192	221	66	32	59	3.09	1.32
1949 Sac	4	4	.500	31	78	88	35	26	31	4.04	1.46
1950 Sac	0	1	.000	9	11	14	11	12	4	9.00	2.36
	228	175	.566	517	3401	3577	1153	655	1506	3.05	1.24

LARRY FRENCH   Lawrence Herbert French. Born 11/1/1907, Visalia, CA. Died 2/9/1987, San Diego, CA. Winner of 197 games during major league career, contributed five wins to the Chicago Cubs' twenty–one game win streak during the 1935 pennant drive. Led the National League in winning percentage in 1942 before entering the Navy for World War II. Remained in the Navy for the next twenty–six years, retiring as a captain.

	W	L	PCT	G	IP	H	ER	BB	SO	ERA	EFF
1926 Port	1	0	1.000	7	17	––	––	––	––	––	––
1927 Port	11	12	.478	44	181	191	96	98	71	4.77	1.60
1928 Port	11	17	.393	43	251	274	113	128	105	4.05	1.60
	23	29	.442	94	449	––	––	––	––	4.35	1.60

ART FROMME   Arthur Henry Fromme. Born 9/3/1883, Quincy, IL. Died 8/24/1956, Los Angeles, CA. Had his best big league season in 1909 while with the Cincinnati Reds, winning nineteen games with a 1.90 ERA. Won a total of seventy–eight games in ten major league seasons with a 2.90 ERA. Led the Pacific Coast League in earned run average in 1916.

	W	L	PCT	G	IP	H	ER	BB	SO	ERA	EFF
1915 Ver	11	9	.550	25	154	141	39	42	45	2.28	1.19
1916 Ver	23	14	.622	44	319	268	68	89	91	1.92	1.12
1917 Ver	21	19	.525	42	350	428	100	84	89	2.57	1.46
1918 Ver	8	7	.533	20	169	150	44	30	55	2.34	1.07
1919 Ver	20	7	.741	45	250	254	62	56	83	2.23	1.24
1920 Ver	6	8	.429	21	108	106	32	22	19	2.67	1.19
1921 Ver	4	2	.667	13	47	54	20	15	10	3.83	1.47
	93	66	.585	210	1397	1401	365	338	392	2.35	1.24

DENNY GALEHOUSE   Dennis Ward Galehouse. Born 12/7/1911, Marshallville, OH. Clutch performer for the Browns on team's only pennant winner. Won first game of 1944 World Series. Surprise starter for Red Sox in a losing cause versus the Cleveland Indians in 1948 AL playoff game.

	W	L	PCT	G	IP	H	ER	BB	SO	ERA	EFF
1949 Sea	10	12	.455	25	143	158	65	31	74	4.09	1.32
1950 Sea	6	7	.462	36	109	127	53	40	49	4.38	1.53
	16	19	.457	61	252	285	118	71	123	4.21	1.41

HARRY GARDNER   Harry Ray Gardner. Born 9/20/1888, Portland, OR. Died 8/2/1961, Barlow, OR. Two-time twenty-game winner in the Pacific Coast League, pitched briefly in the big leagues with the Pittsburgh Pirates.

	W	L	PCT	G	IP	H	ER	BB	SO	ERA	EFF
1917 Port	7	6	.538	22	124	122	29	33	24	2.10	1.25
1918 Sac	12	8	.600	27	195	183	48	34	78	2.22	1.11
1919 Sac–Sea	10	12	.455	29	168	165	62	44	56	3.32	1.24
1920 Sea	20	15	.571	46	279	263	78	54	115	2.52	1.14
1921 Sea	18	12	.600	41	291	310	95	75	115	2.94	1.32
1922 Sea	17	15	.531	42	287	301	104	73	128	3.26	1.30
1923 Sea	22	12	.647	41	305	314	105	59	98	3.10	1.22
1924 Port	5	6	.455	16	99	139	59	22	33	5.36	1.63
	111	86	.563	264	1748	1797	580	394	647	2.99	1.25

AI GETTEL   Allen Jones Gettel. Born 9/17/1917, Norfolk, VA. Durable performer, led PCL in innings pitched for three straight seasons, from 1952 through 1954. Nicknamed "Cowboy", Lefty O'Doul used to pretend he was galloping on a horse to bring this right-hander into a game. Later acted in several movie westerns after his playing days ended.

	W	L	PCT	G	IP	H	ER	BB	SO	ERA	EFF
1949 Oak	4	0	1.000	12	55	44	22	27	29	3.60	1.29
1950 Oak	23	7	.767	53	241	234	97	89	128	3.62	1.34
1951 Oak	4	6	.400	14	72	74	42	26	42	5.25	1.39
1952 Oak	17	14	.548	46	284	261	104	91	132	3.30	1.24
1953 Oak	24	14	.632	42	309	293	110	75	141	3.20	1.19
1954 Oak	17	15	.531	46	284	257	97	79	140	3.07	1.18
1955 Oak	12	13	.480	40	218	226	99	85	101	4.09	1.43
1956 SD	2	4	.333	26	58	76	35	23	32	5.46	1.72
	103	73	.585	279	1521	1465	606	495	745	3.59	1.29

SAM GIBSON   Samuel Braxton Gibson. Born 8/5/1899, King, NC. Died 1/31/1983, High Point, NC. Good-natured right-hander, won 307 games in the minors and another thirty-two in the majors. Led the Pacific Coast League in innings, wins, strikeouts, and in ERA in 1931. One of the PCL's most consistent performers, he also led the league in ERA in 1939.

	W	L	PCT	G	IP	H	ER	BB	SO	ERA	EFF
1931 SF	28	12	.700	41	337	338	93	59	204	2.48	1.18
1933 Port	15	14	.517	33	234	248	104	60	132	4.00	1.32
1934 SF	21	17	.553	47	313	297	103	74	171	2.96	1.19
1935 SF	22	4	.846	38	252	269	97	48	121	3.46	1.26
1936 SF	18	15	.545	39	298	297	93	70	172	2.81	1.23

SAM GIBSON (cont.)

	W	L	PCT	G	IP	H	ER	BB	SO	ERA	EFF
1937 SF	19	8	.704	35	260	263	82	55	146	2.83	1.22
1938 SF	23	12	.657	38	284	243	84	59	151	2.66	1.06
1939 SF	22	9	.710	34	265	242	66	51	136	2.24	1.11
1940 SF	14	14	.500	35	263	245	83	57	126	2.84	1.15
1941 SF	13	7	.650	22	163	150	60	41	72	3.31	1.17
1942 SF	20	12	.625	34	249	277	77	41	87	2.78	1.28
1943 SF	6	5	.545	20	125	122	34	27	34	2.45	1.19
1944 SF	4	8	.333	18	114	124	50	26	27	3.95	1.32
1945 Oak	2	3	.400	18	65	76	23	14	17	3.18	1.38
	227	140	.619	452	3222	3191	1049	682	1596	2.93	1.20

LEFTY GOMEZ   Vernon Louis Gomez. Born 11/26/1908, Rodeo, CA. Died 2/17/1989, Greenbrae, CA. Winner of the AL pitcher's "Triple Crown" (wins, strikeouts, and ERA) in 1934 and 1937. Seven–time All–Star, was 6–0 in the World Series during his career. Elected to the Hall of Fame in 1972.

	W	L	PCT	G	IP	H	ER	BB	SO	ERA	EFF
1929 SF	18	11	.621	41	267	277	102	108	159	3.44	1.44

AL GOULD   Albert Frank Gould. Born 1/20/1893, Muscatine, IA. Died 8/8/1982, San Jose, CA. Pitched two seasons for Cleveland. Led the PCL in winning percentage in 1927. Twice led PCL pitchers in fielding. Tossed two complete game victories in a 1919 doubleheader against Seattle.

	W	L	PCT	G	IP	H	ER	BB	SO	ERA	EFF
1919 SLC	15	16	.484	44	325	337	127	125	96	3.52	1.42
1920 SLC	6	8	.429	21	140	166	67	46	44	4.30	1.51
1921 SLC	18	20	.474	53	248	296	136	88	83	4.94	1.55
1922 SLC	16	14	.533	52	278	370	163	98	91	5.28	1.68
1923 SLC	16	21	.432	60	268	388	178	92	94	5.98	1.79
1926 Oak	8	8	.500	42	143	134	47	55	29	2.96	1.32
1927 Oak	17	5	.773	34	167	157	67	53	76	3.61	1.26
1928 O–Sac	13	8	.619	55	209	203	70	61	58	3.01	1.26
1929 Sac	10	18	.357	55	223	290	127	82	71	5.12	1.67
1930 Sac–SF	5	9	.357	39	127	127	67	56	44	4.74	1.44
1931 H–P	3	4	.429	15	55	61	25	21	18	4.09	1.49
1932 Oak	0	0	––	5	5	––	––	––	––	––	––
1935 Port	0	2	.000	5	25	––	––	––	––	––	––
1936 Oak	0	1	.000	11	32	––	––	––	––	––	––
	127	134	.487	491	2246	––	––	––	––	4.43	1.51

MUDCAT GRANT   James Timothy Grant. Born 8/13/1935, Lacooche, FL. Helped lead Minnesota Twins to the 1965 AL pennant, topping the league in wins and shutouts. Led PCL in strikeouts and complete games in 1957.

	W	L	PCT	G	IP	H	ER	BB	SO	ERA	EFF
1957 SD	18	7	.720	34	218	169	56	102	178	2.31	1.24

DOLLY GRAY   William Denton Gray. Born 12/4/1878, Ishpeming, MI. Died 4/4/1956, Yuba City, CA. Nicknamed after a well–known song of the time; led PCL in wins in 1907. Major league record of 17–52 in three seasons.

DOLLY GRAY (cont.)

	W	L	PCT	G	IP	H	ER	BB	SO	ERA	EFF
1903 LA	25	20	.556	48	--	--	--	--	--	--	--
1904 LA	24	26	.480	--	--	--	--	--	--	--	--
1905 LA	30	16	.652	53	--	--	--	--	--	--	--
1906 LA	7	2	.778	9	--	--	--	--	--	--	--
1907 LA	32	14	.696	54	--	--	--	155	216	--	--
1908 LA	26	11	.703	47	--	--	--	--	--	--	--
1909 LA	1	0	1.000	1	--	--	--	--	--	--	--
1913 O-Ven	0	0	--	4	16	29	--	8	8	--	--
	145	89	.620	--	--	--	--	--	--	--	--

VEAN GREGG

Sylveanus Augustus Gregg. Born 4/13/1885, Chehalis, WA. Died 7/29/1964, Aberdeen, WA. Won twenty games in his first three years in the major leagues before hurting his arm. Set PCL record with fourteen shutouts in 1910 while also leading the circuit in victories and strikeouts.

	W	L	PCT	G	IP	H	ER	BB	SO	ERA	EFF
1910 Port	32	18	.640	53	--	--	--	141	376	--	--
1922 Sea	19	20	.487	46	327	338	122	74	150	3.36	1.26
1923 Sea	17	15	.531	47	281	259	86	71	173	2.75	1.17
1924 Sea	25	11	.695	49	326	341	105	75	175	2.90	1.28
	93	64	.592	195	--	--	--	361	874	--	--

PAUL GREGORY

Paul Edwin Gregory. Born 7/9/1908, Tomnolen, MS. Pitched for the Chicago White Sox in 1932 and 1933; was compared to his Hall of Fame teammate Ted Lyons early in his career. After retirement, was head of the Physical Education Department at Mississippi State University.

	W	L	PCT	G	IP	H	ER	BB	SO	ERA	EFF
1934 Sac	15	16	.484	34	221	251	101	72	70	4.11	1.46
1935 Sac	11	16	.407	37	236	285	112	51	83	4.27	1.42
1936 Sea	15	14	.517	41	241	278	104	79	96	3.88	1.48
1937 Sea	20	15	.571	41	276	315	119	88	80	3.88	1.46
1938 Sea	21	15	.583	40	260	243	106	74	128	3.67	1.22
1939 Sea	18	11	.621	39	245	256	111	79	86	4.08	1.37
1940 Sea	12	10	.545	38	199	213	81	71	92	3.66	1.43
1941 Sea	11	14	.440	31	197	204	80	50	56	3.65	1.29
1946 Sea-H	9	5	.643	38	79	87	34	21	35	3.87	1.37
1947 Hol	0	7	.000	26	51	67	35	21	19	6.18	1.73
	132	123	.518	365	2005	2199	883	606	745	3.96	1.40

BOB GROOM

Robert Groom. Born 9/12/1884, Belleville, IL. Died 2/19/1948, Belleville, IL. Played in majors for ten seasons; led AL in losses twice and the Federal League once. Wild right-hander, threw twenty-two wild pitches in 1907. Pitched no-hitters in both the PCL and the majors.

	W	L	PCT	G	IP	H	ER	BB	SO	ERA	EFF
1907 Sea	20	26	.435	52	--	--	--	158	191	--	--
1908 Sea	29	15	.659	55	--	--	--	--	--	--	--
	49	41	.544	107	--	--	--	--	--	--	--

HARRY GUMBERT   Harry Edward Gumbert. Born 11/5/1909, Elizabeth, PA. Began fifteen year major league career as a starter and ended it as a relief pitcher. Appeared in three World Series for Giants and Cardinals.

	W	L	PCT	G	IP	H	ER	BB	SO	ERA	EFF
1950 Sac	7	12	.368	40	138	160	82	34	38	5.35	1.41

RANDY GUMPERT   Randall Pennington Gumpert. Born 1/23/1918, Monocacy, PA. After winning a game for the A's as teenager in 1936; had to wait ten years for next big league victory. Selected to American League All–Star team in 1951.

	W	L	PCT	G	IP	H	ER	BB	SO	ERA	EFF
1953 LA	7	9	.438	36	100	101	34	28	52	3.07	1.29
1954 LA	4	4	.500	37	64	73	35	27	33	4.92	1.56
	11	13	.458	73	164	174	69	55	85	3.79	1.40

WARREN HACKER   Warren Louis Hacker. Born 11/21/1924, Marissa, IL. Led the NL in losses in 1953. Threw a no–hitter against Seattle 9/7/1951.

	W	L	PCT	G	IP	H	ER	BB	SO	ERA	EFF
1951 LA	8	15	.348	28	193	161	83	54	100	3.87	1.11
1964 Ind	4	9	.308	65	98	63	21	18	90	1.93	0.83
1965 Ind	3	6	.333	39	74	65	21	5	52	2.55	0.95
1966 Ind	3	7	.300	49	80	73	35	10	49	3.94	1.04
	18	37	.327	181	445	362	160	87	291	3.24	1.01

SEA LION HALL   Charles Louis Hall. Born 7/27/1885, Ventura, CA. Died 12/6/1943, Ventura, CA. One of the first relief specialists in majors. Threw two no–hitters in PCL and was five–time twenty–game winner in minors.

	W	L	PCT	G	IP	H	ER	BB	SO	ERA	EFF
1904 Sea	28	19	.596	51	––	––	––	––	––	––	––
1905 Sea	23	27	.460	57	––	––	––	––	––	––	––
1906 Sea	8	13	.381	24	––	––	––	––	––	––	––
1916 LA	6	6	.500	22	128	130	48	44	39	3.37	1.36
1917 LA	14	19	.424	49	313	306	106	104	73	3.04	1.31
1924 Sac	16	21	.432	45	305	359	143	96	51	4.22	1.49
	95	105	.475	248	––	––	––	––	––	––	––

EARL HAMILTON   Earl Andrew Hamilton. Born 7/19/1891, Gibson City, IL. Died 11/17/1968, Anaheim, CA. Spent fourteen years in the major leagues with the Browns, Tigers, Pirates, and Phils. Threw a no–hitter against the Detroit Tigers in 1912.

	W	L	PCT	G	IP	H	ER	BB	SO	ERA	EFF
1926 LA	24	8	.750	40	279	246	77	68	138	2.48	1.13
1927 LA	7	16	.304	30	145	194	88	50	49	5.46	1.68
	31	24	.564	70	424	440	165	118	187	3.50	1.32

WALLACE HEBERT   Wallace Andrew Hebert. Born 8/21/1907, Lake Charles, LA. Pitched three years with the St. Louis Browns, from 1931 thru 1933 with limited success; returned to majors in 1943 after nine seasons in the Pacific Coast League and pitched well for Pittsburgh. A side–arm lefty, nicknamed "Preacher". Shared the PCL lead in shutouts in 1936.

WALLACE HEBERT (cont.)

	W	L	PCT	G	IP	H	ER	BB	SO	ERA	EFF
1934 Hol	11	11	.500	37	170	200	80	49	53	4.23	1.46
1935 Hol	10	17	.370	39	219	276	120	50	79	4.94	1.49
1936 SD	18	12	.600	35	229	240	77	51	87	3.03	1.27
1937 SD	17	14	.549	39	244	257	82	42	90	3.02	1.23
1938 SD	12	16	.429	37	243	244	84	58	102	3.11	1.24
1939 SD	20	10	.667	39	299	295	104	64	104	3.13	1.20
1940 SD	15	18	.455	38	280	316	122	100	106	3.92	1.49
1941 SD	22	10	.688	39	279	294	93	58	102	3.00	1.26
1942 SD	22	15	.591	40	319	324	84	78	125	2.37	1.26
	147	123	.544	343	2282	2446	846	550	848	3.34	1.31

ROY HELSER

Royal H. Helser. Along with Don Pulford and Ad Liska, won twenty games to lead Portland Beavers to Pacific Coast League pennant in 1945. Led all Pacific Coast League pitchers with eight shutouts in 1944.

	W	L	PCT	G	IP	H	ER	BB	SO	ERA	EFF
1941 SF	1	1	.500	3	14	--	--	--	--	--	--
1942 Port	1	2	.333	5	32	--	--	--	--	--	--
1943 Port	2	1	.667	3	23	--	--	--	--	--	--
1944 Port	20	16	.556	37	280	260	75	120	156	2.41	1.36
1945 Port	20	14	.588	37	270	270	101	99	136	3.37	1.38
1946 Port	20	16	.556	38	293	276	99	118	175	3.04	1.34
1947 Port	10	11	.476	30	199	224	99	86	139	4.48	1.56
1948 Port	12	11	.522	29	195	196	104	78	132	4.80	1.41
1949 Port	16	10	.615	35	223	208	73	77	125	2.94	1.28
1950 Port	12	8	.600	22	144	145	51	47	71	3.19	1.33
1951 Port	8	16	.333	34	161	167	83	73	68	4.64	1.49
1952 Port	1	0	1.000	3	10	7	2	4	4	1.80	1.10
	123	106	.537	276	1844	--	--	--	--	3.48	1.38

CACK HENLEY

Clarence T. Henley. Born 1885, Sacramento, CA. Died 7/29/1929, Sacramento, CA. Pitched a twenty—four inning shutout against Oakland 6/8/1909, winning 1—0. Led PCL in victories and CG in 1910.

	W	L	PCT	G	IP	H	ER	BB	SO	ERA	EFF
1905 SF	24	19	.558	49	431	346	--	100	173	--	1.03
1906 SF	4	4	.500	8	--	--	--	--	--	--	--
1907 SF	24	15	.615	56	--	--	--	103	197	--	--
1908 SF	20	18	.526	54	--	--	--	84	151	--	--
1909 SF	31	10	.756	46	--	--	--	71	188	--	--
1910 SF	34	19	.642	57	--	--	--	76	224	--	--
1911 SF	17	14	.548	45	321	--	--	76	158	--	--
1912 SF	14	23	.378	45	324	--	--	54	161	--	--
1913 SF	15	15	.500	40	253	242	--	56	106	--	1.18
1914 Ven	17	13	.567	37	269	249	83	59	109	2.78	1.14
1915 Ver	15	21	.417	42	276	252	85	50	96	2.78	1.10
	215	171	.557	479	--	--	--	729	1563	--	--

BILL HENRY   William Rodman Henry. Born 10/15/1927, Alice, TX. Left–handed reliever, pitched in the majors for sixteen seasons, starred for Reds and Cubs in the late fifties and early sixties. An NL All–Star in 1960.

	W	L	PCT	G	IP	H	ER	BB	SO	ERA	EFF
1952 SD	7	9	.438	17	123	117	49	55	85	3.59	1.40
1956 SF	5	6	.455	29	105	115	55	34	50	4.73	1.42
	12	15	.444	46	228	232	104	89	135	4.11	1.41

OTTO HESS   Otto C. Hess. Born 11/13/1878, Berne, Switzerland. Died 2/24/1926, Tucson, AZ. Was in big leagues for ten seasons with Cleveland and Boston. Best season was 1906, with twenty–two wins and an ERA of 1.80. Also played in the outfield and at first base in the majors.

	W	L	PCT	G	IP	H	ER	BB	SO	ERA	EFF
1916 Ver	13	11	.542	37	191	179	57	86	63	2.69	1.39

KIRBY HIGBE   Walter Kirby Higbe. Born 4/8/1915, Columbia, SC. Died 5/6/1985, Columbia, SC. Pitched twelve years in big leagues. Acquired by Dodgers from Phillies for $100,000 and three players in 1941; led the NL in wins the next year. Authored an autobiography, "The High Hard One."

	W	L	PCT	G	IP	H	ER	BB	SO	ERA	EFF
1950 Sea	0	2	.000	4	20	22	11	14	13	4.95	1.80

ROY HITT   Roy Wesley Hitt. Born 6/22/1884, Carleton, NE. Died 2/8/1956, Pomona, CA. Won 209 games in the minor leagues, including five straight twenty–win seasons. Pitched one season for Cincinnati in 1907.

	W	L	PCT	G	IP	H	ER	BB	SO	ERA	EFF
1903 Oak	1	0	1.000	3	14	9	––	19	8	––	2.00
1904 LA–SF	0	2	.000	2	9	14	––	4	3	––	––
1905 SF	24	14	.632	42	346	245	––	122	218	––	––
1906 SF	32	12	.727	50	––	––	––	––	––	––	––
1909 Ver	15	29	.341	47	––	––	––	114	197	––	––
1910 Ver	26	18	.591	49	––	––	––	98	135	––	––
1911 Ver	21	15	.583	45	290	––	––	77	125	––	––
1912 Ver	21	12	.636	42	314	––	––	92	149	––	––
1913 Ven	22	15	.595	53	320	310	––	73	142	––	1.20
1914 Ven	25	18	.581	46	364	306	83	116	152	2.05	1.16
1915 Ver	15	11	.577	46	258	257	72	56	88	2.51	1.21
1916 Ver	0	1	.000	4	8	7	0	4	2	0.00	1.38
	202	147	.579	429	––	––	––	––	––	––	––

ART HOUTTEMAN   Arthur Joseph Houtteman. Born 8/7/1927, Detroit, MI. Dogged by injury and personal tragedies throughout career; played twelve seasons in majors. An AL All–Star in 1950. Led AL in losses in 1952.

	W	L	PCT	G	IP	H	ER	BB	SO	ERA	EFF
1957 Van	5	6	.455	17	91	92	40	27	50	3.97	1.31

TOM HUGHES   Thomas L. Hughes. Born 1/28/1884, Coal Creek, CO. Died 11/1/1961, Los Angeles, CA. Pitched in majors with the Yankees and the Braves. Won twenty games in 1915. Pitched no–hitters in the NL and the AL. Led NL in winning percentage in 1916. Had a career ERA of 2.56.

TOM HUGHES (cont.)

	W	L	PCT	G	IP	H	ER	BB	SO	ERA	EFF
1919 LA	1	0	1.000	1	5	4	1	4	1	1.80	1.60
1920 LA	7	4	.636	23	94	78	38	42	47	3.64	1.28
1921 LA	14	14	.500	36	241	203	76	89	130	2.84	1.21
1922 LA	17	9	.654	31	231	212	79	88	95	3.08	1.30
1923 LA	14	16	.467	36	235	265	112	93	88	4.29	1.52
1924 LA	12	14	.462	31	208	229	108	99	73	4.67	1.58
1925 LA	5	4	.556	23	89	88	39	38	36	3.94	1.42
	70	61	.534	181	1103	1079	453	453	470	3.70	1.39

FRED HUTCHINSON

Frederick Charles Hutchinson. Born 8/12/1919, Seattle, WA. Died 11/12/1964, Bradenton, FL. Led PCL in victories and in ERA in 1938, winning league's Most Valuable Player award. Spent eleven years in majors and later managed the Reds to the NL pennant in 1961. In his honor, award is given annually to baseball's Most Inspirational Player.

	W	L	PCT	G	IP	H	ER	BB	SO	ERA	EFF
1938 Sea	25	7	.781	35	290	241	80	99	145	2.48	1.17

ELMER JACOBS

William Elmer Jacobs. Born 8/10/1892, Salem, MO. Died 2/10/1958, Salem, MO. Right–hander went 49–81 during nine big league seasons. Led the Pacific Coast League in earned run average in 1926 and in strikeouts and ERA in 1928. Also led PCL in shutouts in 1928 and 1929.

	W	L	PCT	G	IP	H	ER	BB	SO	ERA	EFF
1921 Sea	19	14	.576	41	292	311	119	87	124	3.67	1.36
1922 Sea	23	17	.575	48	306	336	119	65	95	3.50	1.31
1923 Sea	24	10	.706	44	312	333	109	91	143	3.14	1.36
1925 LA	9	5	.643	15	121	112	37	24	50	2.75	1.12
1926 LA	20	12	.625	40	278	254	68	69	103	2.20	1.16
1928 SF	22	8	.733	37	277	277	79	64	159	2.56	1.23
1929 SF	21	11	.656	38	290	324	112	63	130	3.47	1.33
1930 SF	17	13	.567	38	275	335	119	81	120	3.89	1.51
1931 SF	12	11	.522	30	217	236	96	51	78	3.98	1.32
	167	101	.623	331	2369	2518	858	595	1002	3.26	1.31

LARRY JANSEN

Lawrence Joseph Jansen. Born 7/16/1920, Verboort, OR. The PCL's last thirty–game winner, led league in ERA, winning percentage, innings, and complete games in 1946. Went on to win twenty–one games in 1947 as a rookie with the New York Giants. Won twenty–three games in 1951. Later managed in the PCL and was a major league pitching coach.

	W	L	PCT	G	IP	H	ER	BB	SO	ERA	EFF
1941 SF	16	10	.615	32	238	220	74	75	70	2.80	1.24
1942 SF	11	14	.440	32	173	222	83	39	46	4.32	1.51
1945 SF	4	1	.800	7	55	63	25	12	34	4.09	1.36
1946 SF	30	6	.833	38	321	254	56	69	171	1.57	1.01
1955 Sea	7	7	.500	26	137	147	51	26	66	3.34	1.26
1956 Sea	11	2	.846	24	98	85	28	20	59	2.58	1.08
1957 Sea	10	12	.455	30	180	185	63	25	82	3.15	1.17
1958 Port	9	10	.474	22	158	142	55	24	85	3.13	1.05
1959 Port	1	0	1.000	11	24	26	7	4	11	2.63	1.25

LARRY JANSEN (cont.)

	W	L	PCT	G	IP	H	ER	BB	SO	ERA	EFF
1960 Port	3	0	1.000	9	18	11	3	6	13	1.50	0.94
	102	62	.622	231	1402	1355	445	300	637	2.86	1.18

CHET JOHNSON   Chester Lillis Johnson. Born 8/1/1917, Redmond, WA. Died 4/10/1983, Seattle, WA. Brother of Red Sox hurler Earl Johnson, was one of the great clowns of the PCL. Major league career lasted five games with the St. Louis Browns in 1946. The left−handed hurler struck out more than two thousand batters in the minor leagues while winning 204 games.

	W	L	PCT	G	IP	H	ER	BB	SO	ERA	EFF
1939 Hol	0	0	−−	4	10	22	−−	7	2	−−	2.90
1941 SF	0	0	−−	1	1	6	4	1	0	36.00	7.00
1943 SD	14	16	.467	35	242	256	88	97	106	3.27	1.46
1944 SD	12	11	.522	29	186	167	73	94	138	3.53	1.40
1945 Sea	14	12	.538	27	178	178	68	82	117	3.44	1.46
1950 SF	22	13	.629	45	310	316	121	132	164	3.51	1.45
1951 SF−O	7	18	.280	40	181	223	114	98	91	5.67	1.77
1952 Sac	10	17	.370	37	206	224	93	90	99	4.06	1.52
1953 Sac	12	14	.462	39	195	199	78	55	81	3.60	1.30
1954 Sac	8	15	.348	33	201	211	88	82	80	3.94	1.46
1955 Sac	10	9	.526	36	176	187	78	64	49	3.99	1.43
1956 Sac	2	1	.667	12	39	48	16	13	14	3.69	1.56
	111	126	.468	338	1925	2037	821	815	941	3.86	1.48

SYL JOHNSON   Sylvester W. Johnson. Born 12/31/1900, Portland, OR. Died 2/20/1985, Portland, OR. Right−handed control specialist in the big leagues for nineteen seasons, re−joined PCL at end of big league career.

	W	L	PCT	G	IP	H	ER	BB	SO	ERA	EFF
1920 Port	1	4	.200	10	45	53	19	16	13	3.83	1.54
1921 Port	12	26	.316	52	304	324	129	97	119	3.82	1.38
1925 Ver	3	17	.150	24	168	186	87	53	95	4.66	1.42
1941 Sea	13	7	.650	30	151	132	47	13	59	2.80	0.96
1942 Sea	1	3	.250	11	26	−−	−−	−−	−−	−−	−−
1943 Sea	8	7	.533	21	104	87	29	7	38	2.51	0.90
1944 Sea	2	1	.667	13	32	37	−−	2	13	−−	1.22
1945 Sea	6	3	.667	23	65	67	22	8	24	3.05	1.15
	46	68	.404	184	895	−−	−−	−−	−−	3.58	1.25

SAM JONES   Samuel Jones. Born 12/14/1925, Stewartsville, OH. Died 11/5/1971, Morgantown, WV. Former Negro League star with intimidating stuff, led NL in walks and strikeouts in the same season three times and in the PCL once. Two−time All−Star, led NL in wins and ERA in 1959. Held opposing PCL batters to a .188 batting average in 1951.

	W	L	PCT	G	IP	H	ER	BB	SO	ERA	EFF
1951 SD	16	13	.552	40	267	179	82	175	246	2.76	1.33

BOB JOYCE   Robert Emmett Joyce. Born 1/14/1915, Stockton, CA. Died 12/10/1981, San Francisco, CA. Development of slider transformed career. Led PCL in wins, ERA, shutouts, complete games, and innings in 1945.

BOB JOYCE (cont.)

	W	L	PCT	G	IP	H	ER	BB	SO	ERA	EFF
1936 LA	5	13	.278	33	149	195	79	64	37	4.77	1.74
1938 Oak	18	18	.500	51	287	270	96	100	66	3.01	1.29
1941 SF	6	12	.333	26	135	181	72	43	31	4.80	1.66
1942 SF	22	10	.688	38	234	255	83	41	59	3.19	1.26
1943 SF	20	12	.625	34	259	248	70	37	75	2.43	1.10
1944 SF	21	20	.512	41	324	338	101	73	105	2.80	1.27
1945 SF	31	11	.738	46	344	347	83	55	100	2.17	1.17
1947 SF	15	15	.500	35	261	309	105	52	55	3.62	1.38
1948 SF	4	6	.400	18	68	93	41	14	14	5.43	1.57
1949 Port	0	1	.000	4	8	13	9	5	1	10.13	2.25
	142	118	.546	326	2069	2249	739	484	543	3.21	1.32

RUDY KALLIO

Rudolph Kallio. Born 12/14/1892, Portland, OR. Died 4/6/1979, Newport, OR. Compiled a 9–18 record in his three major league seasons with Detroit Tigers and Boston Red Sox. Winner of 288 games in the minor leagues, most coming in the Pacific Coast League.

	W	L	PCT	G	IP	H	ER	BB	SO	ERA	EFF
1916 SF	3	1	.750	8	40	38	19	33	25	4.31	1.79
1917 SF	2	3	.400	7	48	36	15	30	19	2.81	1.38
1920 Port	9	10	.474	33	211	202	79	62	66	3.37	1.25
1921 P–SL	9	21	.300	49	277	351	138	82	107	4.48	1.56
1922 SLC	17	12	.586	46	264	275	102	92	118	3.48	1.39
1923 SLC	14	9	.609	41	234	305	123	96	106	4.73	1.71
1924 SLC	18	14	.563	37	244	269	105	93	102	3.87	1.48
1925 SLC	8	5	.615	16	109	119	44	34	46	3.63	1.40
1926 Sac	18	16	.529	44	326	323	117	85	123	3.23	1.25
1927 Sac	12	16	.429	40	239	273	111	85	69	4.18	1.50
1928 Sac	12	11	.522	33	179	187	86	58	65	4.32	1.37
1929 Sea	15	19	.441	44	278	349	125	91	85	4.04	1.58
1930 Sea	18	16	.529	38	267	281	109	92	140	3.67	1.40
1931 Sea–P	12	13	.480	31	194	238	123	81	78	5.71	1.64
1932 Sea	11	20	.355	39	285	338	120	105	121	3.79	1.55
1933 Port	17	7	.708	27	211	248	80	58	97	3.42	1.45
1934 P–Sea	13	18	.419	39	207	238	97	93	74	4.22	1.60
1940 Port	0	0	––	2	3	11	8	5	1	24.00	5.33
	208	211	.496	574	3616	4081	1601	1275	1442	3.98	1.48

VERN KENNEDY

Lloyd Vernon Kennedy. Born 3/20/1907, Kansas City, MO. Two–time American League All–Star; no–hit Cleveland in 1935. He won twenty–one games for the Chicago White Sox in 1936. Led the AL in losses in 1939 while pitching for St. Louis Browns and Detroit Tigers. The top senior pentatholon performer in the U.S. at age seventy.

	W	L	PCT	G	IP	H	ER	BB	SO	ERA	EFF
1946 SD	18	13	.581	34	225	185	73	103	95	2.92	1.28
1947 SD	9	15	.375	36	195	200	89	82	102	4.11	1.45
1948 Hol	9	12	.429	38	183	181	80	94	97	3.93	1.50
	36	40	.474	108	603	566	242	279	294	3.61	1.40

DICKIE KERR   Richard Henry Kerr. Born 7/3/1893, St. Louis, MO. Died
5/4/1963, Houston, TX. Honest member of "Black Sox", won two games in
1919 World Series. Won twenty—one games for Chicago in 1920. Rest of
his career was hampered by a combination of arm injuries and holdouts.

	W	L	PCT	G	IP	H	ER	BB	SO	ERA	EFF
1926 SF	3	8	.273	20	99	121	47	32	18	4.27	1.55

ELLIS KINDER   Ellis Raymond Kinder. Born 7/26/1914, Atkins, AR. Died
10/16/1968, Jackson, TN. Thirty—two years old on his major league debut
in 1946, earned nickname "Old Folks" during twelve year career. Led AL in
winning percentage and won twenty—three games for Red Sox in 1949.

	W	L	PCT	G	IP	H	ER	BB	SO	ERA	EFF
1957 SD	0	0	——	2	2	4	0	1	0	0.00	2.50

PHIL KNELL   Philip H. Knell. Born 1865, Mill Valley, CA. Nearly forty on
his arrival in PCL, was long time veteran of the California State League and
a two—time twenty game winner in the major leagues.

	W	L	PCT	G	IP	H	ER	BB	SO	ERA	EFF
1903 Sac	10	9	.526	29	——	——	——	——	——	——	——
1904 SF	9	23	.281	——	——	——	——	——	——	——	——
	19	32	.373	——	——	——	——	——	——	——	——

JACK KNOTT   John Henry Knott. Born 3/2/1907, Dallas, TX. Died 10/13/1981,
Brownwood, TX. Pitched eleven seasons in majors with the Browns, White
Sox, and A's. Played for only one first division team in the big leagues.

	W	L	PCT	G	IP	H	ER	BB	SO	ERA	EFF
1928 Miss	1	3	.250	6	32	——	——	——	——	——	——
1929 Miss	2	1	.667	9	23	——	——	——	——	——	——
1930 Miss	7	11	.389	32	183	243	111	67	57	5.45	1.69
	10	15	.400	47	238	——	——	——	——	——	——

JIM KONSTANTY   Casimir James Konstanty. Born 3/2/1917, Strykersville,
NY. Died 6/11/1976, Oneonta, NY. Ace reliever of the Phillies "Whiz Kids",
was selected National League Most Valuable Player. Was surprise starter
in Game One of the 1950 World Series, losing 1—0 to the Yankees.

	W	L	PCT	G	IP	H	ER	BB	SO	ERA	EFF
1957 SF	0	0	——	4	5	9	5	0	4	9.00	1.80

HARRY KRAUSE   Harry William Krause. Born 7/12/1887, San Francisco, CA.
Died 10/23/1940, San Francisco, CA. His 1.39 earned run average in 1909
set the American League record for a rookie. Sent to Pacific Coast League
because of a sore arm, became one of the league's best pitchers.

	W	L	PCT	G	IP	H	ER	BB	SO	ERA	EFF
1913 Port	17	11	.607	46	284	——	——	108	175	——	——
1914 Port	22	18	.550	46	356	302	88	114	155	2.22	1.17
1915 Port	11	15	.423	52	267	249	99	76	111	3.34	1.22
1917 Oak	28	26	.519	58	429	415	142	142	131	2.98	1.30
1918 Oak	10	11	.476	23	170	168	49	53	66	2.60	1.30
1919 Oak	3	3	.500	11	51	44	10	15	16	1.75	1.15
1920 Oak	11	16	.407	33	213	239	98	41	51	4.13	1.31

HARRY KRAUSE (cont.)

	W	L	PCT	G	IP	H	ER	BB	SO	ERA	EFF
1921 Oak	24	13	.649	47	294	292	95	59	111	2.91	1.19
1922 Oak	21	19	.525	46	344	367	122	65	134	3.19	1.26
1923 Oak	19	20	.487	43	328	345	113	60	113	3.10	1.23
1924 Oak	16	16	.500	37	242	265	110	51	122	4.09	1.31
1925 Oak	11	15	.423	31	223	280	121	52	96	4.88	1.49
1926 Oak	19	12	.613	34	263	257	93	46	114	3.18	1.15
1927 Oak	15	6	.714	29	172	186	68	28	51	3.56	1.24
1928 O–M	15	10	.600	27	180	202	87	36	56	4.35	1.32
1929 Miss	7	9	.438	31	167	234	99	35	55	5.34	1.61
	249	220	.531	594	3983	––	––	981	1557	3.39	1.28

RAY KREMER

Remy Peter Kremer. Born 3/23/1893, Oakland, CA. Died 2/8/1965, Pinole, CA. Tough on the mound and off, first reached the major leagues at the age of thirty–one. Spent ten years with the Pirates; led the National League in wins in 1926 and 1930. Led the NL twice in earned run average, winning titles in both 1926 and 1927. Won 143 games in majors.

	W	L	PCT	G	IP	H	ER	BB	SO	ERA	EFF
1914 Sac	2	8	.200	29	137	158	79	42	34	5.20	1.46
1917 Oak	9	15	.375	40	224	227	82	76	55	3.29	1.35
1918 Oak	5	14	.263	22	158	166	58	35	69	3.30	1.27
1919 Oak	15	23	.395	49	298	233	127	88	94	3.84	1.08
1920 Oak	13	22	.371	49	321	336	108	66	90	3.02	1.25
1921 Oak	16	14	.533	48	294	331	118	66	123	3.61	1.35
1922 Oak	20	18	.526	48	356	368	110	74	154	2.78	1.24
1923 Oak	25	16	.610	45	057	374	122	77	127	3.08	1.26
1933 Oak	1	5	.167	7	31	––	––	––	––	––	––
1934 Oak	0	1	.000	4	10	––	––	––	––	––	––
	106	136	.438	341	2186	––	––	––	––	3.37	1.27

EARL KUNZ

Earl Dewey Kunz. Born 12/25/1899, Sacramento, CA. Died 4/14/1963, Sacramento, CA. Pitched briefly in majors for Pittsburgh Pirates. Tied for Coast League lead in complete games with twenty–four in 1927.

	W	L	PCT	G	IP	H	ER	BB	SO	ERA	EFF
1920 Sac	3	11	.214	39	171	191	91	44	59	4.78	1.37
1921 Sac	14	12	.538	50	228	219	96	103	99	3.79	1.41
1922 Sac	15	18	.455	44	304	312	139	118	126	4.12	1.41
1924 Oak	23	18	.561	52	364	373	152	140	143	3.76	1.41
1925 Oak	13	18	.419	51	271	316	149	139	85	4.94	1.68
1926 O–SF	7	11	.389	47	166	160	66	65	45	3.58	1.36
1927 SF	18	19	.486	52	305	366	146	110	70	4.30	1.56
1928 Sac	4	8	.333	29	132	157	76	51	36	5.18	1.58
1929 Sac–Sea	4	5	.444	14	66	88	44	30	17	6.00	1.79
1930 Sea	8	8	.500	44	174	198	100	93	64	5.17	1.67
	109	128	.460	422	2182	2380	1059	893	744	4.37	1.50

TOMMY LASORDA

Thomas Charles Lasorda. Born 9/22/1927, Norristown, PA. Pitched briefly in majors for Brooklyn Dodgers; later succeeded Walter Alston as manager of the team in Los Angeles. Also pitched for KC A's.

TOMMY LASORDA (cont.)

	W	L	PCT	G	IP	H	ER	BB	SO	ERA	EFF
1957 LA	7	10	.412	29	132	134	57	59	72	3.90	1.47

BROOKS LAWRENCE   Ulysses Brooks Lawrence. Born 1/30/1925, Springfield, OH. Negro League veteran, had thirty–five wins for Reds over two seasons. Won fifteen games as a rookie for the Cardinals in 1954.

	W	L	PCT	G	IP	H	ER	BB	SO	ERA	EFF
1955 Oak	5	1	.833	7	38	29	10	10	24	2.37	1.03
1960 Sea	0	2	.000	8	11	15	5	7	4	4.09	2.00
	5	3	.625	15	49	44	15	17	28	2.76	1.24

LEFTY LEIFIELD   Albert Peter Leifield. Born 9/5/1883, Trenton, IL. Died 10/10/1970, Alexandria, VA. One of the aces of Pittsburgh's rotation during the first decade of the twentieth century, picked up 124 wins with 2.47 ERA in his major league career. Twenty–game winner for Pittsburgh in 1907.

	W	L	PCT	G	IP	H	ER	BB	SO	ERA	EFF
1913 SF	13	8	.619	22	160	––	––	29	55	––	––
1914 SF	21	19	.525	50	357	348	88	105	137	2.22	1.27
	34	27	.557	72	517	––	––	134	192	––	––

WALT LEVERENZ   Walter Fred Leverenz. Born 7/21/1888, Chicago, IL. Died 3/19/1973, Atascadero, CA. Went 8–31 in major league career; won 269 games in the minor leagues. Led the PCL in victories during the war–shortened 1918 season. Plagued by control problems throughout career.

	W	L	PCT	G	IP	H	ER	BB	SO	ERA	EFF
1911 LA	10	12	.455	30	194	––	––	58	61	––	––
1912 LA	23	13	.639	52	334	––	––	111	173	––	––
1915 Oak	0	6	.000	7	27	33	16	16	21	5.33	1.81
1917 SLC	22	18	.550	45	349	333	106	147	126	2.73	1.38
1918 SLC	16	5	.762	22	192	189	48	74	74	2.25	1.37
1919 SLC	13	11	.542	28	216	243	90	96	94	3.74	1.57
1920 SLC	18	13	.581	41	277	302	115	110	111	3.73	1.49
1921 SLC	11	19	.367	40	246	324	149	113	119	5.45	1.78
1922 Port	15	18	.455	37	266	297	94	86	103	3.18	1.44
1923 Port	17	11	.607	34	245	274	95	62	98	3.49	1.37
1924 Port	14	14	.500	29	218	268	106	75	84	4.38	1.57
1925 Port	11	11	.500	26	193	224	80	77	61	3.73	1.56
	170	151	.530	391	2758	––	––	1025	1125	3.63	1.50

DUTCH LIEBER   Charles Edwin Lieber. Born 2/1/1909, Alameda, CA. Died 12/31/1961, Sawtelle, CA. Righthander pitched one full season and part of another for the Philadelphia Athletics, winning one game. Best years came as a reliever for the Los Angeles Angels at the end of his PCL career.

	W	L	PCT	G	IP	H	ER	BB	SO	ERA	EFF
1929 Miss	1	0	1.000	5	11	––	––	––	––	––	––
1930 Miss	13	18	.419	38	240	303	138	85	85	5.17	1.61
1931 Miss	11	16	.407	42	213	260	115	51	63	4.86	1.46
1932 Miss	13	18	.419	41	241	309	108	46	60	4.03	1.47
1933 Miss	15	16	.484	43	253	345	142	61	80	5.05	1.60

DUTCH LIEBER (cont.)

	W	L	PCT	G	IP	H	ER	BB	SO	ERA	EFF
1934 Miss	19	13	.594	58	284	269	79	83	77	2.50	1.24
1936 LA	12	12	.500	34	183	223	97	56	55	4.77	1.52
1937 LA	8	10	.444	38	165	210	80	38	42	4.36	1.50
1938 LA	10	6	.625	39	167	174	59	32	57	3.18	1.23
1939 LA	4	2	.667	27	69	70	26	24	22	3.39	1.36
	106	111	.488	365	1826	2163	844	476	541	4.18	1.45

AL LIEN   Alfred Woodrow Lien. Born 2/2/1916, Canby, OR. Died 6/27/1967, Millbrae, CA. Left—hander tied for PCL lead in shutouts in 1951. Pitched a seventeen inning, 1—0 shutout against Hollywood on September 10, 1950.

	W	L	PCT	G	IP	H	ER	BB	SO	ERA	EFF
1942 SF	6	8	.429	19	120	116	37	25	49	2.77	1.17
1943 SF	13	12	.520	34	222	192	63	39	76	2.55	1.04
1946 SF	8	9	.471	32	143	145	46	52	67	2.90	1.38
1947 SF	11	12	.478	38	190	179	76	51	76	3.60	1.21
1948 SF	15	8	.652	34	184	192	69	31	81	3.38	1.21
1949 SF	17	18	.486	41	264	287	125	70	99	4.26	1.35
1950 SF	20	13	.606	46	276	292	126	86	106	4.11	1.37
1951 SF	13	10	.565	34	179	195	77	39	65	3.87	1.31
1952 SF	9	16	.360	37	207	232	99	57	60	4.30	1.40
1953 SF	12	8	.600	33	153	181	69	37	43	4.07	1.43
1954 SF	2	4	.333	24	74	87	39	24	30	4.76	1.51
	126	118	.516	372	2012	2098	826	511	752	3.70	1.30

JOHNNY LINDELL   John Harlan Lindell. Born 8/30/1916, Greeley, CA. Died 8/27/1985, Newport Beach, CA. PCL MVP in 1952, leading league in wins and strikeouts. Had an unusual career; began as a pitcher, moved to outfield after an arm injury, then went back to pitching with a knuckleball.

	W	L	PCT	G	IP	H	ER	BB	SO	ERA	EFF
1938 Oak	9	8	.529	33	166	177	63	77	68	3.42	1.53
1950 Hol	0	1	.000	2	7	4	0	4	2	0.00	1.14
1951 Hol	12	9	.571	26	190	163	64	112	89	3.03	1.45
1952 Hol	24	9	.727	37	282	223	79	108	190	2.52	1.17
	45	27	.625	98	645	567	206	301	349	2.87	1.35

AD LISKA   Adolph James Liska. Born 7/10/1906, Dwight, NE. Began career as pitcher with a conventional delivery and had limited success. Converted to submarine style at the suggestion of a Minneapolis coach who had once been a teammate of Carl Mays. Pitched in majors for Phillies and Senators. Legendary fast worker with pinpoint control, led the PCL in wins in 1937.

	W	L	PCT	G	IP	H	ER	BB	SO	ERA	EFF
1936 Port	15	12	.556	43	223	217	72	68	97	2.91	1.28
1937 Port	24	18	.571	45	319	319	109	74	135	3.07	1.23
1938 Port	16	18	.471	46	278	309	114	75	126	3.69	1.38
1939 Port	20	16	.556	42	285	314	106	54	137	3.35	1.29
1940 Port	9	12	.429	29	190	208	71	41	99	3.36	1.31
1941 Port	18	18	.500	42	301	335	124	87	154	3.71	1.40
1942 Port	15	21	.417	43	322	338	130	73	164	3.64	1.28

AD LISKA (cont.)

	W	L	PCT	G	IP	H	ER	BB	SO	ERA	EFF
1943 Port	17	11	.607	32	254	243	56	31	122	1.98	1.08
1944 Port	18	9	.667	32	236	236	65	40	124	2.48	1.17
1945 Port	20	12	.625	35	273	257	71	59	127	2.34	1.16
1946 Port	7	16	.304	35	195	208	67	43	87	3.09	1.29
1947 Port	10	10	.500	36	148	155	56	35	70	3.41	1.28
1948 Port	5	10	.333	22	107	134	64	33	47	5.38	1.56
1949 Port	4	11	.267	32	140	147	60	42	44	3.86	1.35
	198	194	.505	514	3271	3420	1165	755	1533	3.21	1.28

SLIM LOVE

Elmer Haughton Love. Born 8/1/1893, Love, MO. Died 11/30/1942, Memphis, TN. Set PCL full–season ERA record in 1914. Also led the PCL in ERA in 1915. Won thirteen games for the Yankees in 1918.

	W	L	PCT	G	IP	H	ER	BB	SO	ERA	EFF
1914 LA	10	9	.526	37	288	158	50	81	95	1.56	0.83
1915 LA	23	15	.605	59	359	259	78	138	173	1.95	1.10
1920 SF	12	19	.387	44	290	269	86	112	149	2.67	1.31
1921 Ver	5	14	.263	37	182	172	92	72	88	4.55	1.34
1922 Ver	2	2	.500	7	32	––	––	––	––	––	––
	52	59	.468	184	1151	––	––	––	––	2.46	1.13

TURK LOWN

Omar Joseph Lown. Born 5/30/1924, Brooklyn, NY. Starred in relief for Chicago White Sox in their pennant winning 1959 season. Also pitched for the Cubs and Reds during his eleven major league seasons.

	W	L	PCT	G	IP	H	ER	BB	SO	ERA	EFF
1954 LA	5	3	.625	30	73	54	20	46	52	2.48	1.38
1955 LA	12	5	.706	61	114	91	27	49	96	2.13	1.23
	17	8	.680	91	187	145	47	95	148	2.27	1.29

RED LUCAS

Charles Fred Lucas. Born 4/28/1902, Columbia, TN. Died 7/9/1986, Nashville, TN. Pitched fifteen seasons in majors with four teams. Won 157 games in big leagues; three times led the NL in complete games.

	W	L	PCT	G	IP	H	ER	BB	SO	ERA	EFF
1925 Sea	9	5	.643	26	121	119	38	33	47	2.82	1.25

WILLIE LUDOLPH

William Francis Ludolph. Born 1/21/1900, San Francisco, CA. Died 4/7/1952, Oakland, CA. Spent all but six innings of his career in the minors. Led PCL in ERA in 1933; no–hit Mission, 6/6/1931.

	W	L	PCT	G	IP	H	ER	BB	SO	ERA	EFF
1921 SF	1	0	1.000	4	18	15	6	9	6	3.00	1.33
1924 Ver	7	10	.412	26	138	148	71	36	45	4.63	1.33
1925 Ver	13	12	.520	42	266	287	108	89	60	3.65	1.41
1926 Miss	15	13	.536	43	253	259	107	88	85	3.81	1.37
1927 Miss	9	20	.310	41	238	287	133	72	74	5.03	1.51
1928 Miss	2	4	.333	8	49	57	18	17	12	3.31	1.51
1931 Oak	10	12	.455	39	184	229	101	50	72	4.94	1.52
1932 Oak	16	14	.533	38	271	269	83	62	99	2.76	1.22
1933 Oak	19	9	.679	38	262	277	90	59	74	3.09	1.28
1934 Oak	16	12	.571	37	231	262	102	53	58	3.97	1.36

WILLIE LUDOLPH (cont.)

	W	L	PCT	G	IP	H	ER	BB	SO	ERA	EFF
1935 Oak	20	13	.606	37	283	309	97	40	74	3.09	1.23
1936 Oak	21	6	.778	33	250	230	75	45	80	2.70	1.10
1937 Oak	7	4	.636	12	99	85	27	24	35	2.45	1.10
	156	129	.547	398	2542	2714	1018	644	774	3.60	1.32

RED LYNN

Japhet Monroe Lynn. Born 12/27/1913, Kenney, TX. Died 10/27/1977, Bellville, TX. Pitched three seasons in major leagues, winning a total of ten games. Led Pacific Coast League in wins in 1943 and 1948.

	W	L	PCT	G	IP	H	ER	BB	SO	ERA	EFF
1942 LA	12	13	.480	43	211	172	73	67	108	3.11	1.13
1943 LA	21	8	.724	36	248	218	68	64	110	2.47	1.14
1946 LA	17	16	.515	41	271	200	84	123	165	2.79	1.19
1947 LA	16	16	.500	42	273	251	102	110	145	3.36	1.32
1948 LA	19	10	.655	42	244	236	101	114	131	3.73	1.43
1949 LA–P	10	18	.357	37	194	203	100	95	85	4.64	1.54
1950 Port	14	10	.583	41	239	218	94	92	117	3.54	1.30
1951 Port	13	12	.520	41	192	190	00	87	68	3.75	1.44
1952 P–H	9	6	.600	39	121	130	57	56	30	4.24	1.54
1953 Hol	10	4	.714	53	143	158	59	63	42	3.72	1.55
	141	113	.555	415	2136	1976	818	871	1001	3.45	1.33

WALTER MAILS

John Walter Mails. Born 10/1/1895, San Quentin, CA. Died 7/5/1974, San Francisco, CA. Tossed 15 2/3 shutout innings in 1920 World Series after going undefeated in seven decisions to aid Cleveland pennant hopes after death of Ray Chapman. Preferred nickname "The Great Mails". Led PCL in strikeouts in 1923. Later worked in public relations for Seals.

	W	L	PCT	G	IP	H	ER	BB	SO	ERA	EFF
1917 Port	3	2	.600	7	49	28	12	37	18	2.20	1.33
1919 Sea–Sac	19	17	.528	47	301	265	105	99	134	3.14	1.21
1920 Sac	18	17	.514	43	292	238	104	187	105	3.21	1.46
1923 Oak	23	18	.561	49	356	338	117	125	206	2.96	1.30
1924 Oak	24	22	.522	56	382	388	158	140	190	3.73	1.38
1926 SF	9	13	.409	27	176	207	82	54	54	4.19	1.48
1927 SF	11	11	.500	40	217	240	106	75	102	4.39	1.45
1928 SF	20	12	.625	45	277	316	122	101	152	3.96	1.51
1929 SF	15	16	.484	38	250	306	135	103	119	4.86	1.64
1930 Port	11	16	.407	39	234	259	114	112	144	5.01	1.59
1931 Port	13	13	.500	37	212	234	118	140	124	5.01	1.76
1934 SF	4	13	.235	30	167	189	77	62	74	4.14	1.50
1935 SF	3	1	.750	16	41	52	22	19	16	4.83	1.73
1936 SF	0	0	––	8	10	21	––	10	5	––	3.10
	173	171	.503	482	2964	3081	1272	1264	1443	3.88	1.47

MORRIE MARTIN

Morris Webster Martin. Born 9/3/1922, Dixon, MO. Recipient of the Purple Heart in World War II, left–hander pitched in major leagues for ten seasons. Led the PCL in earned run average in 1957.

	W	L	PCT	G	IP	H	ER	BB	SO	ERA	EFF
1957 Van	14	4	.778	31	176	154	37	30	87	1.90	1.05

JAKIE MAY   Frank Spruiell May. Born 11/25/1895, Youngville, NC. Died 6/3/1970, Wendell, NC. Pitched fourteen seasons in majors with Cardinals, Reds, and Cubs. Led PCL in wins, ERA, and strikeouts in 1922.

	W	L	PCT	G	IP	H	ER	BB	SO	ERA	EFF
1922 Ver	35	9	.795	53	362	283	74	100	238	1.84	1.06
1923 Ver	19	22	.463	47	320	354	122	89	149	3.43	1.38
	54	31	.635	100	682	637	196	189	387	2.58	1.21

CARL MAYS   Carl William Mays. Born 11/12/1891, Liberty, KY. Died 4/4/1971, El Cajon, CA. Remembered for fatally beaning Ray Chapman. In 1921, led AL in wins with twenty–seven; one of five twenty–win seasons.

	W	L	PCT	G	IP	H	ER	BB	SO	ERA	EFF
1930 Port	5	9	.357	19	144	178	76	36	43	4.75	1.49

JOE MC GINNITY   Joseph Jerome McGinnity. Born 3/19/1871, Rock Island, IL. Died 11/14/1929, Brooklyn, NY. Led the NL in victories five times, setting the modern big league record of 434 innings pitched in 1903. Once won five games in six days while with the New York Giants. A minor league pitcher into his fifties, the "Iron Man" made the Hall of Fame in 1946.

	W	L	PCT	G	IP	H	ER	BB	SO	ERA	EFF
1914 Ven	1	4	.200	8	37	42	15	5	7	3.65	1.27

CAL MC LISH   Calvin Coolidge Julius Caesar Tuskahoma McLish. Born 12/1/1925, Anadarko, OK. Blasted twelve home runs in his PCL stint. Won thirty–five games for Cleveland in 1958 and 1959, a year after allowing four homers in one inning to Red Sox. Gene Mauch's favorite pitching coach.

	W	L	PCT	G	IP	H	ER	BB	SO	ERA	EFF
1949 LA	8	11	.421	29	150	164	96	107	68	5.76	1.81
1950 LA	20	11	.645	42	260	243	104	104	129	3.60	1.33
1952 LA	10	15	.400	34	212	215	89	60	84	3.78	1.30
1953 LA	16	11	.593	35	235	239	97	60	114	3.71	1.27
1954 LA	13	15	.464	37	245	261	96	74	120	3.53	1.37
1955 LA–SD	17	12	.586	35	233	230	80	69	116	3.09	1.28
	84	75	.528	212	1335	1352	562	474	631	3.79	1.37

HUGH MC QUILLAN   Hugh A. McQuillan. Born 9/15/1897, New York, NY. Died 8/26/1947, New York, NY. Spent ten years in the majors; won eighty–eight games. Purchased by the Giants from the Braves for $100,000 in '22, he helped New York to three straight National League pennants.

	W	L	PCT	G	IP	H	ER	BB	SO	ERA	EFF
1931 Sea–P	8	7	.533	28	152	187	84	64	58	4.97	1.65

CLIFF MELTON·   Clifford George Melton. Born 1/3/1912, Brevard, NC. Died 7/28/1986, Baltimore, MD. Had eighty–six victories in majors with the New York Giants, including twenty in his rookie season. Jug–eared pitcher was nicknamed "Mountain Music" for his guitar playing. His five shutouts in '47 led the Pacific Coast League.

	W	L	PCT	G	IP	H	ER	BB	SO	ERA	EFF
1946 SF	17	12	.586	33	248	228	78	72	99	2.83	1.21
1947 SF	17	11	.607	38	261	242	79	56	123	2.72	1.14

CLIFF MELTON (cont.)

	W	L	PCT	G	IP	H	ER	BB	SO	ERA	EFF
1948 SF	16	10	.615	31	215	204	75	48	98	3.14	1.17
1949 SF	5	6	.455	18	115	131	49	46	57	3.83	1.54
1950 SF	11	18	.379	45	240	271	136	96	120	5.10	1.53
	66	57	.537	165	1079	1076	417	318	497	3.48	1.29

CLARENCE MITCHELL

Clarence Elmer Mitchell. Born 2/22/1891, Franklin, NE. Died 11/6/1963, Grand Island, NE. Legal spitballer won 125 games in eighteen year major league career. Had best big league season at age 40 in 1931. Sometimes played first base, hitting .252 lifetime in the majors. In 1920 World Series, hit ball that started Bill Wambsganss' famous triple play.

	W	L	PCT	G	IP	H	ER	BB	SO	ERA	EFF
1934 Miss	19	12	.613	36	253	282	103	70	63	3.67	1.39
1935 Miss	6	11	.353	26	152	197	86	31	32	5.09	1.50
	25	23	.521	62	405	479	189	101	95	4.20	1.43

WILLIE MITCHELL

William Mitchell. Born 12/1/1888, Sardis, MS. Died 11/23/1973, Sardis, MS. Won eighty—four games over eleven seasons with the Indians and Tigers. Best season was in 1913, winning fourteen games with a 1.74 earned run average for Cleveland. Led Pacific Coast League in strikeouts in 1920 for the pennant—winning Vernon Tigers.

	W	L	PCT	G	IP	H	ER	BB	SO	ERA	EFF
1919 Ver	9	5	.643	26	155	166	45	45	73	2.61	1.36
1920 Ver	25	13	.658	52	348	283	92	86	161	2.38	1.06
1921 Ver	12	15	.444	39	249	277	112	66	122	4.05	1.38
	46	33	.582	117	752	726	249	197	356	2.98	1.23

WILCY MOORE

William Wilcy Moore. Born 5/20/1897, Bonita, TX. Died 3/29/1963, Hollis, OK. Became a reliever after suffering an arm injury in the minors. Sidearm sinker made him a star with the New York Yankees on the famous 1927 World Champions. Won nineteen games as a starter/reliever. Arm problems returned after that excellent rookie season.

	W	L	PCT	G	IP	H	ER	BB	SO	ERA	EFF
1938 Oak	2	1	.667	24	59	65	33	24	18	5.03	1.51

HUGH MULCAHY

Hugh Noyes Mulcahy. Born 9/9/1913, Brighton, MA. A National League All—Star in 1940, earned the nickname "Losing Pitcher" after leading National League in losses twice while pitching for Phillies.

	W	L	PCT	G	IP	H	ER	BB	SO	ERA	EFF
1947 Oak	1	6	.143	31	89	118	66	40	20	6.67	1.78

BOB MUNCRIEF

Robert Cleveland Muncrief. Born 1/28/1916, Madill, OK. Pitched in major leagues for twelve seasons with five teams. Thirteen wins for the pennant—winning St. Louis Browns in 1944. Also appeared in 1948 World Series with the Cleveland Indians against the Boston Braves.

	W	L	PCT	G	IP	H	ER	BB	SO	ERA	EFF
1939 Hol	11	11	.500	37	169	192	81	40	93	4.32	1.38
1950 LA	15	17	.469	43	244	263	104	61	138	3.84	1.33
1952 SF	6	13	.316	65	147	140	44	55	69	2.69	1.33

BOB MUNCRIEF (cont.)

	W	L	PCT	G	IP	H	ER	BB	SO	ERA	EFF
1953 SF	10	12	.455	61	169	156	50	39	83	2.67	1.16
1954 SF	3	7	.300	46	107	97	35	36	59	2.95	1.25
	45	60	.429	252	836	848	314	231	442	3.38	1.29

RED MUNGER   George David Munger. Born 10/4/1918, Houston, TX.
A two–time National League All–Star, pitched ten seasons in majors with
the Cardinals and Pirates. Led PCL in wins, ERA, and CG in 1955. Threw
a seven–inning, 1–0 no–hitter against the Sacramento Solons, 7/4/1953.

	W	L	PCT	G	IP	H	ER	BB	SO	ERA	EFF
1940 Sac	9	14	.391	41	190	163	67	99	96	3.17	1.38
1941 Sac	17	16	.515	46	261	223	89	87	159	3.07	1.19
1952 Hol	4	3	.571	14	64	51	19	20	33	2.67	1.11
1953 Hol	12	10	.545	37	166	177	62	58	61	3.36	1.42
1954 Hol	17	8	.680	38	218	178	56	63	96	2.31	1.11
1955 Hol	23	8	.742	36	272	223	56	57	133	1.85	1.03
1957 Sea	6	10	.375	22	138	155	56	48	55	3.65	1.47
	88	69	.561	234	1309	1170	405	432	633	2.78	1.22

RON NECCIAI   Ronald Andrew Necciai. Born 6/18/1932, Gallatin, PA.
Struck out twenty–seven batters against Welch of the Appalachian League
on May 13, 1952. Struck out twenty–four in his next start, including five in
one inning. Torn rotator cuff the next spring basically ended his career.

	W	L	PCT	G	IP	H	ER	BB	SO	ERA	EFF
1955 Hol	0	0	– –	3	10	5	3	13	1	2.61	1.74

ERNIE NEVERS   Ernest Alonzo Nevers. Born 6/11/1903, Willow River,
MN. Died 5/3/1976, San Rafael, CA. One of the all–time great college and
pro football stars, greatest moment came while playing for Stanford against
Notre Dame and legendary Four Horsemen in 1925 Rose Bowl. Pitched in
three seasons for the Browns and two in PCL before switching to the NFL.

	W	L	PCT	G	IP	H	ER	BB	SO	ERA	EFF
1928 Miss	14	11	.560	29	206	202	100	69	54	4.37	1.32
1929 Miss	7	8	.467	36	148	194	75	60	44	4.56	1.72
	21	19	.525	65	354	396	175	129	98	4.45	1.48

BOBO NEWSOM   Louis Norman Newsom. Born 8/11/1907, Hartsville, SC.
Died 12/7/1962, Orlando, FL. Colorful character remembered as oft traded
pitcher. Three–time twenty–game winner, joined PCL after missing entire
1932 season with a broken leg. Star of the 1940 World Series for Detroit in
a losing effort. Led Pacific Coast League in wins and strikeouts in 1933.

	W	L	PCT	G	IP	H	ER	BB	SO	ERA	EFF
1933 LA	30	11	.732	56	320	328	113	124	212	3.17	1.41

DOC NEWTON   Eustace James Newton. Born 10/26/1877, Indianapolis, IN.
Died 5/14/1931, Memphis, TN. Set NL single season record for errors by a
pitcher with seventeen in 1901. Carried that tradition into the PCL, making
a record twenty–eight errors for Los Angeles in 1904. Also set a record for
pitching victories that same year. Pitched PCL's first no–hitter, 11/8/1903.

DOC NEWTON (cont.)

	W	L	PCT	G	IP	H	ER	BB	SO	ERA	EFF
1903 LA–P	35	12	.745	51	––	––	––	––	––	––	––
1904 LA	39	17	.696	––	––	––	––	––	––	––	––
	74	29	.718	––	––	––	––	––	––	––	––

JOE OESCHGER Joseph Carl Oeschger. Born 5/24/1891, Chicago, IL. Died 7/28/1986, Rohnert Park, CA. Remembered for his twenty–six inning pitcher's duel with Brooklyn's Leon Cadore ending in 1–1 tie on 5/1/1920.

	W	L	PCT	G	IP	H	ER	BB	SO	ERA	EFF
1926 M–O	5	14	.263	32	146	156	68	46	44	4.19	1.38

AL OLSEN Albert William Olsen. Born 3/30/1921, San Diego, CA. Died 7/3/1994, San Marcos, CA. After baseball career, was athletic director at San Diego State. Grew up with Ted Williams in San Diego, throwing him an endless number of curveballs so he could learn to hit lefthanders.

	W	L	PCT	G	IP	H	ER	BB	SO	ERA	EFF
1939 SD	7	12	.368	34	164	161	86	94	76	4.72	1.55
1940 SD	7	7	.500	20	118	125	54	39	47	4.11	1.39
1941 SD	14	16	.467	38	247	237	102	90	107	3.72	1.32
1942 SD	18	16	.529	45	293	281	90	93	94	2.76	1.28
1943 SD	2	4	.333	9	50	61	23	8	7	4.14	1.38
1946 SD	17	15	.531	45	288	309	93	68	104	2.91	1.31
1947 SD	6	13	.316	46	162	196	85	41	48	4.72	1.46
1948 SD	10	14	.417	34	159	182	85	52	76	4.81	1.47
1949 SD	0	0	––	5	16	24	15	4	3	8.44	1.75
1950 SD	20	15	.571	39	272	284	112	56	96	3.71	1.25
1951 SD	7	10	.412	25	138	168	72	33	47	4.70	1.46
1952 SD	6	13	.316	30	147	172	60	26	67	3.67	1.35
	114	135	.458	370	2054	2200	877	604	772	3.84	1.36

WAYNE OSBORNE Wayne Harold Osborne. Born 10/11/1912, Watsonville, CA. Died 3/13/1987, Vancouver, WA. Tied for Pacific Coast League lead in shutouts in 1935 and led the league in wild pitches that same year. Pitched in two games for the Pirates in 1935 and five games for the Braves in 1936.

	W	L	PCT	G	IP	H	ER	BB	SO	ERA	EFF
1931 Port	1	0	1.000	8	24	––	––	––	––	––	––
1932 Miss	2	6	.250	20	100	132	59	35	29	5.31	1.67
1933 Miss	2	7	.222	43	146	192	85	57	55	5.25	1.71
1934 Miss	16	19	.457	45	266	278	108	87	107	3.65	1.37
1935 Miss	18	11	.621	41	253	260	100	75	101	3.56	1.32
1936 Miss	12	9	.571	28	172	195	76	75	88	3.98	1.57
1937 Miss	3	9	.250	31	120	143	70	74	33	5.25	1.81
1938 Hol	12	18	.400	37	246	280	137	116	77	5.01	1.61
1939 Hol	16	17	.485	42	277	316	142	77	77	4.61	1.42
1940 Hol	18	17	.514	43	262	285	118	86	67	4.06	1.42
1941 Hol	12	12	.500	33	207	233	97	65	67	4.22	1.44
1942 H–P	10	14	.417	34	175	225	105	64	46	5.40	1.65
1943 Port	9	5	.643	16	127	129	35	39	35	2.48	1.32
	131	144	.476	421	2374	2668	1132	850	782	4.33	1.50

ORVAL OVERALL   Orval Overall. Born 2/2/1881, Visalia, CA. Died 7/14/1947, Fresno, CA. Multi-sport athlete and University of California graduate, was star for Cubs in three World Series. Arm injury ended career at age 29. In 1913, he failed in a comeback attempt. Successful banker after retirement.

	W	L	PCT	G	IP	H	ER	BB	SO	ERA	EFF
1904 Tac	32	25	.561	--	--	--	--	--	--	--	--
1913 SF	8	9	.471	19	147	--	--	31	118	--	--
	40	34	.541	--	--	--	--	--	--	--	--

JOE PAGE   Joseph Francis Page. Born 10/28/1917, Cherry Valley, PA. Died 4/21/1980, Latrobe, PA. A three-time All-Star reliever, he starred for the Yankees in the late 1940's. Set a major league record for relief wins in 1947 with fourteen. Set unofficial record with twenty-seven saves in 1949.

	W	L	PCT	G	IP	H	ER	BB	SO	ERA	EFF
1951 SF	2	1	.667	6	21	21	8	13	7	3.43	1.62

MONTE PEARSON   Monte Pearson. Born 9/2/1909, Oakland, CA. Died 1/27/1978, Fresno, CA. A two-time AL All-Star, led the AL in ERA in 1936. Pitching for New York Yankees, he won all four of his World Series starts.

	W	L	PCT	G	IP	H	ER	BB	SO	ERA	EFF
1930 Oak	3	2	.600	24	53	57	34	30	25	5.77	1.64
1931 Oak	17	16	.515	40	234	260	116	123	158	4.46	1.64
1941 Hol	0	1	.000	1	5	--	--	--	--	--	--
	20	19	.513	65	292	317	150	153	183	4.70	1.64

KEN PENNER   Kenneth William Penner. Born 4/24/1896, Booneville, IN. Died 5/28/1959, Sacramento, CA. Pitched in portions of two major league seasons thirteen years apart. Won 330 games in the minor leagues.

	W	L	PCT	G	IP	H	ER	BB	SO	ERA	EFF
1917 Port	21	18	.538	59	375	418	139	120	100	3.33	1.43
1918 SLC	7	5	.583	16	118	135	46	50	40	3.52	1.57
1919 Port	15	20	.429	47	337	344	135	89	111	3.61	1.28
1920 Sac	19	23	.452	48	379	420	146	90	122	3.47	1.35
1921 Sac	17	14	.548	49	281	306	114	71	115	3.65	1.34
1922 Sac	11	17	.393	41	232	236	85	49	90	3.30	1.23
1923 Sac	12	17	.414	43	234	256	111	59	103	4.27	1.35
1924 Ver	24	13	.649	45	346	380	154	84	130	4.00	1.34
1925 Ver	2	6	.250	18	74	104	45	20	24	5.47	1.68
1942 Sac	0	1	.000	7	14	10	7	6	2	4.50	1.14
1943 Sac	0	0	--	3	3	2	2	2	2	6.00	1.33
	128	134	.489	376	2393	2611	984	640	839	3.70	1.36

JEFF PFEFFER   Edward Joseph Pfeffer. Born 3/4/1888, Seymour, IL. Died 8/15/1972, Chicago, IL. Pitched in majors for thirteen years, twice winning twenty games. Collected 158 victories in his career, mostly with Brooklyn.

	W	L	PCT	G	IP	H	ER	BB	SO	ERA	EFF
1925 SF	15	15	.500	36	193	240	113	57	62	5.27	1.54

BILL PIERCY   William Benton Piercy. Born 5/2/1896, El Monte, CA. Died 8/28/1951, Long Beach, CA. Nicknamed "Wild Bill", led PCL in strikeouts 1919 and in shutouts in 1916 and 1919. Also led once in walks, twice in hit batsmen, and three times in wild pitches. No-hitter vs. Oakland in 1915.

	W	L	PCT	G	IP	H	ER	BB	SO	ERA	EFF
1915 Ver	15	15	.500	47	292	250	71	90	104	2.19	1.17
1916 SLC	20	15	.556	50	292	287	106	132	108	3.26	1.43
1919 Sac	26	18	.591	54	369	304	93	148	163	2.27	1.22
1920 Ver	13	10	.565	38	232	209	63	112	94	2.44	1.38
1925 SLC	21	11	.656	41	255	268	126	118	102	4.44	1.51
1927 LA	12	20	.375	45	267	321	139	105	72	4.68	1.59
	107	89	.546	275	1708	1639	598	705	643	3.15	1.37

MARINO PIERETTI   Marino Paul Pieretti. Born 9/23/1920, Lucca, Italy. Died 1/30/1981, San Francisco, CA. Led the PCL in wins in 1944. In off-season, he would reportedly slaughter cattle with a baseball bat.

	W	L	PCT	G	IP	H	ER	BB	SO	ERA	EFF
1943 Port	8	11	.421	37	135	117	46	50	55	3.07	1.24
1944 Port	26	13	.667	48	322	280	88	125	139	2.46	1.26
1951 Port	18	13	.581	40	256	252	94	75	86	3.30	1.28
1952 Port	16	18	.471	44	276	262	105	82	77	3.42	1.25
1953 Sac	12	17	.414	46	249	252	115	87	91	4.16	1.36
1954 Sac	16	16	.500	36	277	275	107	84	122	3.48	1.30
1955 Sac	19	15	.559	40	293	271	98	73	110	3.01	1.17
1956 LA	7	9	.438	38	150	191	85	53	68	4.90	1.56
	122	112	.421	329	1964	1900	738	629	748	3.38	1.29

HERM PILLETTE   Herman Polycarp Pillette. Born 12/26/1895, St. Paul, OR. 4/30/1960, Sacramento, CA. Won 19 games as rookie with Detroit in 1922, led AL in losses the next season. Led PCL in losses three times. Pitched a no-hitter against Seattle, October 5, 1929. Son Duane also pitched in PCL.

	W	L	PCT	G	IP	H	ER	BB	SO	ERA	EFF
1920 Port	0	3	.000	5	17	24	14	8	6	7.41	1.88
1921 Port	13	30	.302	55	326	378	152	104	141	4.20	1.48
1925 Ver	11	26	.297	42	285	323	116	71	78	3.66	1.38
1926 Miss	21	16	.568	47	322	343	111	76	99	3.10	1.30
1927 Miss	13	20	.394	46	297	373	155	63	74	4.69	1.47
1928 Miss	16	18	.471	42	301	332	104	59	71	3.11	1.30
1929 Miss	23	13	.639	41	273	299	109	52	82	3.59	1.29
1930 Miss	18	14	.563	39	261	350	126	58	66	4.34	1.56
1931 Miss	16	11	.593	33	273	334	107	44	68	3.52	1.38
1932 Miss	11	12	.478	35	209	277	100	40	52	4.31	1.52
1933 M-Sea	13	14	.481	35	254	328	132	57	73	4.68	1.52
1934 Sea	17	11	.607	36	260	278	75	45	87	2.60	1.24
1935 Sea-H	14	15	.483	32	201	279	104	40	63	4.66	1.59
1936 SD	11	8	.579	31	191	180	67	37	63	3.16	1.14
1937 SD	4	5	.444	36	126	137	53	29	38	3.78	1.31
1938 SD	2	2	.500	26	78	92	23	18	29	2.65	1.41
1939 SD	8	6	.571	25	89	75	23	21	22	2.32	1.07
1940 SD	7	2	.778	22	89	95	28	18	31	2.82	1.26

HERM PILLETTE (cont.)

	W	L	PCT	G	IP	H	ER	BB	SO	ERA	EFF
1941 SD	1	2	.333	15	20	17	––	10	4	––	1.35
1942 SD	1	1	.500	11	24	34	––	9	7	––	1.79
1943 Sac	2	3	.400	28	41	47	––	13	7	––	1.46
1944 Sac	3	2	.600	15	37	34	––	9	7	––	1.16
1945 Sac	1	1	.500	7	12	12	––	1	3	––	1.08
	226	235	.490	704	3986	4641	––	882	1171	3.73	1.39

COTTON PIPPEN   Henry Harold Pippen. Born 4/2/1910, Cisco, TX. Died 2/15/1981, Williams, CA. Pitched in majors for the Cardinals, Athletics, and Tigers. Struck out Ted Williams on three pitches in the future Hall of Fame outfielder's pro debut with San Diego. Pitched seven–inning perfect game against Sacramento, May 31, 1943.

	W	L	PCT	G	IP	H	ER	BB	SO	ERA	EFF
1936 Sac	16	9	.640	33	215	246	85	51	65	3.56	1.38
1937 Sac	15	14	.517	35	238	270	111	59	75	4.20	1.38
1938 Sac	17	8	.680	32	223	228	78	40	68	3.15	1.20
1940 Oak	10	13	.435	26	172	175	68	48	63	3.56	1.30
1941 Oak	17	16	.515	40	263	282	104	69	104	3.56	1.33
1942 Oak	11	17	.393	38	211	249	98	66	51	4.18	1.49
1943 Oak	20	15	.571	36	270	273	91	69	56	3.03	1.27
1944 Oak	8	11	.421	23	176	170	62	31	77	3.17	1.14
1946 Oak	14	11	.560	30	184	189	58	56	58	2.84	1.33
1947 Oak	1	5	.167	9	52	66	23	15	11	3.98	1.56
1948 P–Sac	––	––	––	4	––	––	––	––	––	––	––
	129	119	.520	306	2004	2148	778	504	628	3.49	1.32

BILL POSEDEL   William John Posedel. Born 8/2/1906, San Francisco, CA. Died 11/28/1989, Livermore, CA. Later a major league pitching coach, was in the big leagues five seasons, winning fifteen games for the 1939 Braves.

	W	L	PCT	G	IP	H	ER	BB	SO	ERA	EFF
1929 Port	0	0	––	7	17	––	––	––	––	––	––
1930 Port	1	2	.333	12	34	––	13	––	––	3.44	––
1931 Port	7	6	.538	27	131	172	76	59	39	5.22	1.76
1935 Port	12	7	.632	21	161	191	66	31	93	3.69	1.38
1936 Port	20	10	.667	39	265	270	83	87	175	2.82	1.35
1937 Port	21	12	.636	44	300	294	103	87	172	3.09	1.27
1947 Sea	12	8	.600	27	131	144	62	40	34	4.26	1.40
1957 Port	0	1	.000	1	1	1	1	1	1	9.00	2.00
	73	46	.613	178	1040	––	––	––	––	3.55	1.39

RAY PRIM   Raymond Lee Prim. Born 12/30/1906, Salitpa, AL. Pitched six seasons in the majors with Senators, Phils and Cubs. Won thirteen games with a 2.40 ERA for last Cub pennant–winners. Control artist; left–hander held PCL opponents to a league low .226 batting average in 1944.

	W	L	PCT	G	IP	H	ER	BB	SO	ERA	EFF
1936 LA	13	8	.619	29	161	186	80	48	69	4.47	1.45
1937 LA	21	13	.618	39	293	317	121	59	176	3.72	1.28
1938 LA	17	10	.630	31	230	243	84	42	126	3.29	1.24

RAY PRIM (cont.)

	W	L	PCT	G	IP	H	ER	BB	SO	ERA	EFF
1939 LA	20	17	.541	39	280	302	111	43	107	3.57	1.23
1940 LA	18	11	.621	38	240	227	69	47	110	2.59	1.14
1941 LA	16	15	.516	36	255	261	81	38	119	2.86	1.17
1942 LA	21	10	.677	39	277	265	76	39	121	2.47	1.10
1944 LA	22	10	.688	41	286	238	54	40	139	1.70	0.97
1947 LA	2	3	.400	9	39	42	11	8	14	2.54	1.28
	150	97	.607	301	2061	2081	687	364	981	3.00	1.19

BILL PROUGH   Herschel Clinton Prough. Born 11/25/1888, Martle, IN. Died 11/29/1936, Richmond, IN. Pitched only one game in the majors; led PCL in losses in 1915 and 1916, in shutouts in 1917 and in CG in 1918.

	W	L	PCT	G	IP	H	ER	BB	SO	ERA	EFF
1914 Oak	14	23	.378	45	328	342	104	75	175	2.86	1.27
1915 Oak	15	25	.375	52	357	371	122	72	194	3.08	1.24
1916 Oak	18	23	.439	48	389	373	116	57	142	2.69	1.11
1917 Oak	22	22	.500	50	374	391	98	54	108	2.36	1.19
1918 Oak	13	12	.520	25	226	218	49	33	68	1.95	1.11
1919 Sac	12	13	.480	32	185	182	52	22	69	2.53	1.10
1920 Sac	20	20	.500	48	348	361	124	40	105	3.21	1.15
1921 Sac	20	12	.625	44	320	326	107	61	118	3.01	1.21
1922 Sac	11	14	.440	29	243	268	93	42	77	3.44	1.28
1923 Sac	20	11	.645	39	285	326	114	38	81	3.60	1.28
1924 Sac	10	17	.070	35	242	294	133	50	75	4.95	1.42
	175	192	.477	447	3296	3452	1112	544	1212	3.04	1.21

BOB PURKEY   Robert Thomas Purkey. Born 7/14/1929, Pittsburgh, PA. Knuckleball pitcher with excellent control, won twenty—three games for the the Reds in 1962. Won 129 games over thirteen—year big league career.

	W	L	PCT	G	IP	H	ER	BB	SO	ERA	EFF
1956 Hol	6	8	.429	20	118	125	44	23	60	3.36	1.25

JACK QUINN   John Picus Quinn. Born 7/5/1883, Mahanoy City, PA. Died 4/17/1946, Pottsville, PA. Spitballer in majors until age 50. Oldest player to hit a homer in big leagues (age 47). Led PCL in ERA and strikeouts in 1918.

	W	L	PCT	G	IP	H	ER	BB	SO	ERA	EFF
1916 Ver	16	13	.552	51	289	292	94	85	149	2.93	1.30
1917 Ver	24	20	.545	52	409	415	107	84	160	2.35	1.22
1918 Ver	13	9	.591	26	213	167	35	20	99	1.48	0.88
1934 Hol	1	1	.500	6	18	29	12	4	3	6.00	1.83
	54	43	.557	135	929	903	248	193	411	2.40	1.18

KEN RAFFENSBERGER   Kenneth David Raffensberger. Born 8/8/1917, York, PA. Twice led the National League in losses, earning a victory in the All—Star game in the first of those seasons. Fifteen years in big leagues.

	W	L	PCT	G	IP	H	ER	BB	SO	ERA	EFF
1942 LA	17	18	.486	51	242	258	93	51	138	3.46	1.28
1943 LA	19	11	.633	35	244	228	58	53	134	2.14	1.15
	36	29	.554	86	486	486	151	104	272	2.80	1.21

VIC RASCHI   Victor John Angelo Raschi. Born 3/28/1919, West Springfield, MA. Died 10/14/1988, Groveland, NJ. Nicknamed "The Springfield Rifle"; a four–time All–Star, won 82 games in first four full seasons with Yankees.

	W	L	PCT	G	IP	H	ER	BB	SO	ERA	EFF
1947 Port	8	2	.800	12	85	74	26	42	68	2.75	1.36

CHARLIE ROOT   Charles Henry Root. Born 3/17/1899, Middletown, OH. Died 11/5/1970, Hollister, CA. Remembered as pitcher who gave up Babe Ruth's "Called Shot". Pitched sixteen seasons and won 201 games for the Chicago Cubs, leading NL in wins in 1927. Player–manager at Hollywood.

	W	L	PCT	G	IP	H	ER	BB	SO	ERA	EFF
1924 LA	21	16	.568	55	322	316	132	102	199	3.69	1.30
1925 LA	25	13	.658	52	324	268	103	91	211	2.86	1.11
1942 Hol	11	14	.440	30	215	205	76	39	103	3.18	1.13
1943 Hol	15	5	.750	25	166	170	57	28	70	3.09	1.19
1944 Hol	3	5	.375	21	87	91	31	28	58	3.22	1.37
	75	53	.586	183	1114	1050	399	288	641	3.22	1.20

SCHOOLBOY ROWE   Lynwood Thomas Rowe. Born 1/11/1910, Waco, TX. Died 1/8/1961, El Dorado, AR. Won forty–three games over the 1934 and 1935 seasons to lead Detroit Tigers to back–to–back AL titles. Winner of sixteen in a row in 1934. After winning nineteen in 1936, shoulder injuries hampered his effectiveness and he was never the same.

	W	L	PCT	G	IP	H	ER	BB	SO	ERA	EFF
1950 SD	0	4	.000	16	40	44	29	24	12	6.53	1.70

DUTCH RUETHER   Walter Henry Ruether. Born 9/13/1893, Alameda, CA. Died 6/16/1970, Phoenix, AZ. A member of the 1927 Yankees; he led the NL in percentage in 1919. Led the PCL in wins and percentage in 1928. Managed Seattle 1934–36; scouted for Giants from 1947 until his death.

	W	L	PCT	G	IP	H	ER	BB	SO	ERA	EFF
1911 Port	0	1	.000	1	6	––	––	2	6	––	––
1913 LA–Sac	0	0	––	4	12	7	––	10	5	––	1.46
1915 SLC	0	3	.000	9	34	43	26	21	25	6.95	1.90
1916 SLC	4	5	.444	12	80	62	22	41	43	2.49	1.29
1928 SF	29	7	.806	36	303	330	102	57	110	3.03	1.28
1929 Miss	14	9	.609	30	208	247	109	64	76	4.71	1.49
1930 Sea	17	15	.531	35	254	318	97	78	61	3.43	1.56
1931 Sea–P	9	13	.409	24	160	208	89	40	43	5.00	1.55
1932 Miss	3	9	.250	28	103	124	48	30	29	4.21	1.50
1933 Oak	0	1	.000	3	14	––	––	––	––	––	––
1934 Sea	0	0	––	7	9	––	––	––	––	––	––
1935 Sea	0	0	––	4	7	––	––	––	––	––	––
1936 Sea	0	0	––	10	––	––	––	––	––	––	––
	76	63	.547	203	1189	––	––	––	––	3.88	1.46

JACK SALVESON   John Theodore Salveson. Born 1/5/1914, Fullerton, CA. Died 12/28/1974, Norwalk, CA. A bespectacled right–hander; was the last player ever signed personally by John McGraw. Had a small role in "Pride of the Yankees", beaning Lou Gehrig. Led PCL in ERA in 1940 and 1950.

JACK SALVESON (cont.)

	W	L	PCT	G	IP	H	ER	BB	SO	ERA	EFF
1936 LA	21	7	.750	35	251	249	77	70	127	2.76	1.27
1937 LA	5	5	.500	16	73	76	25	10	24	3.08	1.18
1938 LA	11	10	.524	32	205	237	94	44	91	4.13	1.37
1939 Oak	12	15	.444	46	233	290	99	42	75	3.82	1.42
1940 Oak	19	13	.594	38	286	278	73	43	71	2.30	1.12
1941 Oak	15	20	.429	42	288	321	120	63	100	3.75	1.33
1942 Oak	24	12	.667	39	310	297	89	60	93	2.58	1.15
1946 Port	15	14	.517	35	261	248	72	41	119	2.48	1.11
1947 Port	17	14	.548	37	287	334	116	52	96	3.64	1.34
1948 Sac–O	13	18	.419	41	245	300	129	55	95	4.74	1.45
1949 Hol	11	7	.611	42	148	150	49	35	59	2.98	1.25
1950 Hol	15	4	.789	30	165	155	52	37	62	2.84	1.16
1951 Hol	15	10	.600	36	219	224	77	55	74	3.16	1.27
1952 SD	10	10	.500	26	168	196	71	34	57	3.80	1.37
1953 SD–O	1	7	.125	12	60	75	39	22	16	5.85	1.62
	204	166	.551	507	3199	3430	1182	663	1159	3.33	1.28

MANNY SALVO   Manuel Salvo. Born 6/30/1913, Sacramento, CA. Five of his ten wins for the Boston Braves in 1940 were shutouts. Winner of thirty–three major league games over five seasons. Led the Pacific Coast League in strikeouts in 1937 and 1938. Led in shutouts in 1935 and 1937.

	W	L	PCT	G	IP	H	ER	BB	SO	ERA	EFF
1932 Sac	7	4	.636	28	127	147	64	38	28	4.54	1.46
1933 Sac	5	11	.313	19	114	139	49	18	49	3.86	1.37
1934 Sac	15	18	.455	45	271	283	100	82	112	3.32	1.35
1935 Sac	11	17	.393	44	248	244	92	83	121	3.33	1.32
1936 SD	15	12	.556	45	239	244	88	74	145	3.31	1.33
1937 SD	19	13	.594	46	278	275	95	107	196	3.08	1.37
1938 SD	22	9	.710	40	239	205	69	82	191	2.60	1.20
1944 Oak	18	7	.720	27	210	192	50	38	58	2.14	1.10
1946 SD	3	6	.333	13	92	96	34	20	20	3.33	1.26
1947 SD	14	13	.519	34	200	215	85	44	77	3.83	1.30
1948 SD–Sac	5	7	.417	36	121	122	59	46	59	4.39	1.39
1949 Sac	5	5	.500	30	75	70	31	26	47	3.72	1.28
	139	122	.533	407	2215	2232	816	658	1103	3.32	1.30

CARL SCHEIB   Carl Alvin Scheib. Born 1/1/1927, Gratz, PA. Pitched eleven seasons in the major leagues, all but three games with the Athletics. Was the youngest player ever to appear in AL game at his debut in 1943.

	W	L	PCT	G	IP	H	ER	BB	SO	ERA	EFF
1954 Port	3	3	.500	19	59	65	35	16	35	5.34	1.37
1955 Port	7	4	.636	31	73	67	28	20	40	3.45	1.19
	10	7	.588	50	132	132	63	36	75	4.30	1.27

HENRY SCHMIDT   Henry M. Schmidt. Born 6/26/1873, Brownsville, TX. Died 4/23/1926, Nashville, TN. Winner of twenty–one games in only major league season with Brooklyn in 1903; he returned to the West Coast where he had originally been discovered because he did not like living in the East.

HENRY SCHMIDT (cont.)

	W	L	PCT	G	IP	H	ER	BB	SO	ERA	EFF
1904 Oak	26	28	.481	--	--	--	--	--	--	--	--
1905 Oak	18	17	.514	41	--	--	--	--	--	--	--
1906 F–LA	0	6	.000	8	--	--	--	--	--	--	--
	44	51	.463	--	--	--	--	--	--	--	--

JIM SCOTT   James Scott. Born 4/23/1888, Deadwood, SD. Died 4/7/1957, Palm Springs, CA. Nicknamed "Death Valley", the 235–pound hurler twice won twenty games for the Chicago White Sox. Stationed in San Francisco during World War One, enjoyed area so much he bought out contract from Chicago and joined Seals. Led the Pacific Coast League in ERA in 1920.

	W	L	PCT	G	IP	H	ER	BB	SO	ERA	EFF
1919 SF	13	11	.542	30	237	204	64	71	76	2.43	1.16
1920 SF	23	14	.622	44	354	329	90	82	122	2.29	1.16
1921 SF	18	15	.545	42	296	335	120	68	64	3.65	1.36
1922 SF	25	9	.735	35	276	262	68	52	75	2.22	1.14
1923 SF	11	9	.550	28	173	211	78	51	58	4.06	1.51
1924 SF	4	7	.364	12	77	103	40	23	12	4.68	1.64
	94	65	.591	191	1413	1444	460	347	407	2.93	1.27

TOM SEATON   Thomas Gordon Seaton. Born 8/30/1889, Blair, NE. Died 4/10/1940, El Paso, TX. A knuckleballer, led NL with twenty–seven wins in 1913 and quickly jumped to Federal League. Accused in scheme to throw games with teammate Casey Smith in 1920. Both were blacklisted.

	W	L	PCT	G	IP	H	ER	BB	SO	ERA	EFF
1909 Port	4	3	.571	12	--	--	--	--	--	--	--
1910 Port	17	17	.500	52	--	--	--	102	128	--	--
1911 Port	24	16	.600	51	382	--	--	114	218	--	--
1917 LA	8	8	.500	22	129	104	42	71	62	2.93	1.36
1918 SF	11	8	.579	24	167	139	47	48	75	2.53	1.12
1919 SF	25	16	.610	42	354	335	112	115	107	2.84	1.27
1920 SF	3	2	.600	10	--	--	--	--	--	--	--
	92	70	.568	213	--	--	--	--	--	--	--

TOM SEATS   Thomas Edward Seats. Born 9/24/1911, Farmington, NC. Died 5/10/1992, San Ramon, CA. Shut out the Sacramento Solons in both games of a doubleheader, August 6, 1944. Reportedly victimized by stage fright in majors. At Brooklyn in 1945, Leo Durocher supposedly suggested a whiskey "cure"; Branch Rickey quickly ended the experiment.

	W	L	PCT	G	IP	H	ER	BB	SO	ERA	EFF
1937 Sac	11	10	.524	38	186	225	80	53	76	3.87	1.49
1938 Sac	1	4	.200	9	38	--	--	--	--	--	--
1939 Sac	21	14	.600	40	292	293	98	63	130	3.02	1.22
1941 SF	14	18	.438	38	261	278	88	58	114	3.03	1.29
1942 SF	10	18	.357	38	250	282	102	56	89	3.67	1.35
1943 SF	14	11	.560	32	229	243	63	41	75	2.48	1.24
1944 SF	25	13	.658	39	320	295	84	51	129	2.36	1.08
1946 SD	11	18	.379	36	236	226	82	52	96	3.13	1.18
1947 SD	17	17	.500	45	306	337	124	39	130	3.65	1.23

TOM SEATS (cont.)

	W	L	PCT	G	IP	H	ER	BB	SO	ERA	EFF
1948 SD	12	14	.462	43	258	296	119	39	114	4.15	1.30
1949 SDOH	2	2	.500	29	66	72	34	29	25	4.64	1.53
	138	139	.498	387	2442	--	--	--	--	3.27	1.26

SPEC SHEA

Frank Joseph Shea. Born 10/2/1920, Naugatuck, CT. Was second to Larry Jansen in earned run average in the PCL in 1946. All—Star in his rookie season with the 1947 Yankees, won fourteen games, plus two more in World Series. Pitched four years each for Yankees and Senators.

	W	L	PCT	G	IP	H	ER	BB	SO	ERA	EFF
1946 Oak	15	5	.750	24	174	125	32	60	124	1.66	1.06

TOM SHEEHAN

Thomas Clancy Sheehan. Born 3/31/1894, Grand Ridge, IL. Died 10/29/1982, Chillicothe, OH. Lifetime record in the major leagues of 17—39, including 1—16 mark for the infamous 1916 Philadelphia A's. A top scout for the New York Giants in the late 1940's and 1950's. Made the manager of the Giants in 1960 at the age of 66 after team's move to SF.

	W	L	PCT	G	IP	H	ER	BB	SO	ERA	EFF
1932 Hol	18	6	.684	31	181	182	61	50	87	3.03	1.28
1933 Hol	21	13	.618	38	271	318	128	88	95	4.25	1.50
1934 Hol	16	14	.533	37	237	252	97	77	102	3.68	1.39
	50	33	.602	106	689	752	286	215	284	3.74	1.40

FRANK SHELLENBACK

Frank Victor Shellenback. Born 12/16/1898, Joplin, MO. Died 8/17/1969, Newton, MA. Spitballer left off the list of those allowed to throw the pitch in majors after it was outlawed, threw it legally in PCL and set league record for career victories. From the middle of 1930 to August of 1931, he won thirty—four out of thirty—five, including the playoffs.

	W	L	PCT	G	IP	H	ER	BB	SO	ERA	EFF
1920 Ver	18	12	.600	47	299	262	90	79	104	2.71	1.14
1921 Ver	18	10	.643	39	268	286	95	64	84	3.19	1.31
1922 Ver	1	1	.500	5	9	15	--	12	1	--	3.00
1923 Ver	19	19	.500	43	286	362	139	53	98	4.37	1.45
1924 Ver	14	7	.667	29	212	273	86	38	55	3.65	1.47
1925 Sac	14	17	.452	38	264	297	96	61	91	3.27	1.36
1926 Hol	16	12	.571	34	230	220	76	49	93	2.97	1.17
1927 Hol	19	12	.613	34	265	271	90	68	106	3.05	1.28
1928 Hol	23	11	.676	38	272	274	101	66	125	3.34	1.25
1929 Hol	26	12	.684	46	335	365	148	68	163	3.97	1.29
1930 Hol	19	7	.731	36	252	304	130	59	111	4.64	1.44
1931 Hol	27	7	.794	36	306	305	97	61	127	2.85	1.20
1932 Hol	26	10	.722	36	322	343	112	48	119	3.13	1.21
1933 Hol	21	12	.636	38	314	373	158	74	124	4.53	1.42
1934 Hol	14	12	.538	34	229	259	106	50	80	4.17	1.35
1935 Hol	14	9	.609	26	200	236	76	33	82	3.42	1.35
1936 SD	6	7	.462	15	102	104	40	13	38	3.53	1.15
1937 SD	0	1	.000	6	16	23	10	7	7	5.63	1.88
1938 SD	0	0	--	3	2	4	3	1	1	13.50	2.50
	295	178	.624	583	4184	4576	1653	904	1609	3.56	1.31

LARRY SHERRY   Lawrence Sherry. Born 7/25/1935, Los Angeles, CA. Born with club feet, went on play in the majors for eleven years. Starred as a rookie for Dodgers in both the 1959 pennant race and World Series. Had thirteen relief wins in 1960. Brother Norm also played for Dodgers.

	W	L	PCT	G	IP	H	ER	BB	SO	ERA	EFF
1957 LA	0	1	.000	5	21	22	12	10	17	5.23	1.55
1958 Spo	6	14	.300	29	154	160	84	88	84	4.91	1.61
1959 Spo	0	0	– –	1	1	2	1	1	0	9.00	3.00
1968 Sea–Hw	6	6	.500	34	88	77	28	25	62	2.86	1.16
1969 Tuc	6	5	.545	25	61	83	34	16	45	5.02	1.62
	18	26	.409	94	325	344	159	140	208	4.41	1.49

ERNIE SHORE   Ernest Grady Shore. Born 3/24/1891, East Bend, NC. Died 9/24/1980, Winston–Salem, NC. Remembered for the greatest relief effort in major league history. Took over after Babe Ruth walked first batter and was ejected. Proceeded to pick off the baserunner and retired the next 26 hitters for an unusual and unprecedented "perfect game".

	W	L	PCT	G	IP	H	ER	BB	SO	ERA	EFF
1921 Ver–SF	2	5	.286	19	66	90	49	18	10	6.68	1.64

CLYDE SHOUN   Clyde Mitchell Shoun. Born 3/20/1912, Mountain City, TN. Died 3/20/1968, Mountain Home, TN. Traded by Cubs to the Cardinals for Dizzy Dean in 1938, pitched fourteen years in majors for five teams. Threw a no–hitter against the Boston Braves on May 15, 1944.

	W	L	PCT	G	IP	H	ER	BB	SO	ERA	EFF
1950 Oak	16	10	.615	41	233	242	118	74	84	4.56	1.36
1951 Oak	2	4	.333	7	41	44	25	12	16	5.49	1.37
	18	14	.563	48	274	286	143	86	100	4.70	1.36

ELMER SINGLETON   Bert Elmer Singleton. Born 6/26/1918, Ogden, UT. Pitched a no–hitter for 12 2/3 innings against Sacramento, April 24, 1952, before giving up three hits and losing 1–0. Led the Pacific Coast League in earned run average in 1956. Also led the league in shutouts twice. Was in majors for eight seasons with the Braves, Pirates, Senators, and Cubs.

	W	L	PCT	G	IP	H	ER	BB	SO	ERA	EFF
1942 Port	1	2	.333	6	14	– –	– –	– –	– –	– –	– –
1949 SF	8	14	.364	41	188	198	84	76	123	4.02	1.46
1950 SF	5	10	.333	29	119	108	56	61	79	4.24	1.42
1951 SF	5	3	.625	20	77	83	26	15	44	3.04	1.27
1952 SF	17	15	.531	37	276	235	82	76	170	2.67	1.13
1953 SF	15	17	.469	37	253	239	91	74	126	3.23	1.24
1954 SF	13	13	.500	30	213	201	71	65	102	3.00	1.25
1955 Sea	19	12	.613	35	249	210	61	45	150	2.20	1.02
1956 Sea	18	8	.692	29	226	212	64	58	110	2.55	1.19
1958 Port	13	12	.520	28	197	199	73	32	73	3.34	1.17
1960 Sac–Sp	14	5	.737	31	210	208	79	43	117	3.39	1.20
1961 Van–Sea	10	11	.455	28	191	168	71	49	98	3.35	1.14
1962 Sea	7	9	.438	20	119	140	54	20	53	4.08	1.34
1963 Sea	1	0	1.000	6	10	12	1	1	4	0.90	1.30
	146	131	.527	377	2342	2213	813	615	1249	3.14	1.21

EDDIE SMITH   Edgar Smith. Born 12/14/1913, Columbus, NJ. The losing pitcher in Bob Feller's 1940 Opening Day no—hitter, led the AL in losses in 1942 with the White Sox. Pitched ten seasons in the major leagues.

	W	L	PCT	G	IP	H	ER	BB	SO	ERA	EFF
1948 H–Sac	13	14	.481	35	194	218	84	72	101	3.90	1.49

ALLEN SOTHORON   Allen Sutton Sothoron. Born 4/29/1893, Laura, OH. Died 6/17/1939, St. Louis, MO. Legal spitballer, in 1916 he led PCL in wins. Won 92 games in ten big league seasons, including twenty for the St. Louis Browns in 1919, two years after leading AL in losses. Managed the Browns in 1933 for four games between terms of Bill Killefer and Rogers Hornsby.

	W	L	PCT	G	IP	H	ER	BB	SO	ERA	EFF
1916 Port	30	17	.638	57	397	341	117	158	202	2.65	1.26

GERRY STALEY   Gerald Lee Staley. Born 8/21/1920, Brush Prairie, WA. Three—time All—Star, had 54 wins from 1952 through 1954 with Cardinals. Switched to bullpen in 1956, starred five seasons with Chicago White Sox. Played a major role in Chicago's American League pennant in 1959.

	W	L	PCT	G	IP	H	ER	BB	SO	ERA	EFF
1946 Sac	13	12	.520	31	236	222	77	79	89	2.94	1.28
1962 Port	2	4	.333	48	73	88	35	15	42	4.32	1.41
	15	16	.484	79	309	310	112	94	131	3.26	1.31

JOE STANKA   Joe Donald Stanka. Born 7/23/1931, Hammon, OK. Won 100 games in Japan, more than any other American ex—big leaguer. Hero of 1964 Japan Series, starting and winning last two games on consecutive days to clinch the championship. Also named league MVP that season.

	W	L	PCT	G	IP	H	ER	BB	SO	ERA	EFF
1953 LA	0	0	––	1	2	1	1	2	1	4.50	1.50
1954 LA	0	0	––	2	4	1	0	2	1	0.00	0.75
1955 LA	0	0	––	2	4	8	4	2	2	9.00	2.50
1956 Sac	5	14	.263	31	173	156	83	84	108	4.31	1.38
1957 Sac	10	14	.417	33	203	192	79	88	133	3.51	1.38
1958 Sac	10	14	.417	30	195	173	79	91	113	3.65	1.35
1959 Sac	12	12	.500	29	204	206	74	67	104	3.26	1.34
	37	54	.407	128	785	737	320	336	462	3.67	1.37

LEFTY STEWART   Walter Cleveland Stewart. Born 9/23/1900, Sparta, TN. Died 9/26/1974, Knoxville, TN. Won one hundred games in ten big league seasons, including twenty of the St. Louis Browns' sixty—four wins in 1930.

	W	L	PCT	G	IP	H	ER	BB	SO	ERA	EFF
1936 Miss	11	13	.458	32	166	223	86	45	54	4.66	1.61

SAILOR STROUD   Ralph Vivian Stroud. Born 5/15/1885, Ironia, NJ. Died 4/11/1970, Stockton, CA. Lacked consistency and a fastball at big league level. Pitched three years in majors with Tigers and Giants. Posted some impressive stats at Salt Lake City, especially for a pitcher relying on curve balls in the high altitude. Led the PCL with eight shutouts in 1914.

SAILOR STROUD (cont.)

	W	L	PCT	G	IP	H	ER	BB	SO	ERA	EFF
1913 Sac	25	15	.625	51	315	— —	— —	68	202	— —	— —
1914 Sac	20	18	.526	43	331	288	74	62	130	2.01	1.06
1919 SLC	14	11	.560	28	215	204	92	37	75	3.85	1.12
1920 SLC	26	13	.667	42	323	292	115	112	149	3.20	1.25
1924 SL–Sac	0	4	.000	10	19	— —	— —	— —	— —	— —	— —
1925 SLC	5	5	.500	30	81	90	42	26	34	4.67	1.43
1926 H–LA	4	6	.400	24	93	106	40	31	34	3.87	1.47
1927 Sac	0	0	— —	3	7	— —	— —	— —	— —	— —	— —
1928 Port	0	1	.000	7	24	— —	— —	— —	— —	— —	— —
	94	73	.563	238	1408	— —	— —	— —	— —	— —	— —

ED STUTZ

Edward Francis Stutz. Born 10/26/1913, San Francisco, CA. Died 2/12/1959, Corte Madera, CA. Had a career–high nineteen complete games in 1940. Curveball specialist led the PCL in hits allowed in 1937.

	W	L	PCT	G	IP	H	ER	BB	SO	ERA	EFF
1932 SF	0	1	.000	13	50	65	23	25	20	4.11	1.79
1933 SF	6	9	.400	41	157	222	97	71	51	5.57	1.87
1934 SF	8	10	.444	32	138	135	45	53	35	2.94	1.37
1935 SF	11	13	.458	41	163	209	87	50	62	4.81	1.59
1936 SF	17	18	.486	42	243	309	120	74	90	4.44	1.58
1937 SF	15	9	.625	41	241	331	125	75	89	4.66	1.68
1938 SF	10	11	.476	35	196	241	98	50	51	4.50	1.48
1939 SF	13	16	.448	37	237	263	88	56	65	3.34	1.35
1940 SF	19	14	.576	39	252	297	99	78	65	3.54	1.49
1941 SF	14	16	.467	36	233	255	83	70	50	3.21	1.39
1942 SF	8	10	.444	40	179	254	83	40	42	4.17	1.64
1946 SF	3	2	.600	21	48	51	23	18	22	4.31	1.44
	124	129	.490	418	2137	2632	971	660	642	4.09	1.54

YANK TERRY

Lancelot Yank Terry. Born 2/11/1911, Bedford, IN. Pitched five seasons in majors with Red Sox, most of the time during the war years. 1941 PCL MVP after leading league in wins, strikeouts, ERA, and innings.

	W	L	PCT	G	IP	H	ER	BB	SO	ERA	EFF
1941 SD	26	8	.765	40	315	264	81	74	172	2.31	1.07
1946 LA	12	15	.444	33	192	186	61	47	84	2.86	1.21
	38	23	.623	73	507	450	142	121	256	2.52	1.13

BILL THOMAS

William C. Thomas. Born 1/9/1905, St. Louis, MO. The all–time winningest pitcher in minor league history with 383 victories; never played in major leagues. A thirty–five game winner at age forty–one in the Evangeline League. Pitched over 1,000 minor league games and holds the minor league career records for wins, losses, games, and innings pitched.

	W	L	PCT	G	IP	H	ER	BB	SO	ERA	EFF
1937 Sea–P	11	17	.393	44	242	261	103	40	85	3.83	1.24
1938 Port	18	19	.486	44	292	345	114	48	117	3.51	1.35
1939 Port	20	17	.541	49	303	386	162	64	151	4.81	1.49
1940 P–SD	16	20	.444	44	294	323	128	70	96	3.91	1.34
1941 SD	15	17	.469	44	272	298	100	61	78	3.31	1.32

BILL THOMAS (cont.)

	W	L	PCT	G	IP	H	ER	BB	SO	ERA	EFF
1942 SD–H	9	13	.409	44	163	176	48	35	57	2.65	1.29
1943 Hol	11	21	.344	52	249	294	108	66	78	3.90	1.45
	100	124	.446	321	1815	2083	763	384	662	3.78	1.36

FAY THOMAS   Fay Wesley Thomas. Born 10/10/1904, Holyrood, KS. Died 8/16/1990, Chatsworth, CA. Used forkball to dominate PCL hitters, though he could not duplicate success in the majors. Won twenty–two straight in 1933–1934 to set the PCL record. Led Pacific Coast League in strikeouts three times and set single–season record for winning percentage in 1934. Played tackle on the University of Southern California football team.

	W	L	PCT	G	IP	H	ER	BB	SO	ERA	EFF
1930 Sac	18	20	.474	52	298	292	131	131	228	3.95	1.42
1931 Oak	12	10	.545	25	163	159	70	59	123	3.86	1.33
1932 Oak	12	19	.387	34	255	216	92	93	196	3.25	1.21
1933 LA	20	14	.588	42	300	364	125	104	159	3.75	1.56
1934 LA	28	4	.875	41	295	246	85	118	204	2.59	1.23
1936 LA	15	10	.600	28	206	219	71	75	134	3.10	1.43
1937 LA	23	11	.676	40	294	275	105	112	181	3.21	1.32
1938 LA	18	8	.692	31	200	196	73	68	123	3.29	1.32
1939 LA	17	13	.567	35	246	216	75	91	139	2.75	1.25
1940 LA	6	11	.353	30	161	185	89	64	77	4.98	1.55
1941 LA	10	13	.435	28	154	168	70	65	72	4.09	1.51
1943 P–H	0	3	.000	5	20	23	12	7	3	5.40	1.50
	179	136	.568	391	2592	2559	998	987	1639	3.46	1.37

SLOPPY THURSTON   Hollis John Thurston. Born 6/2/1899, Fremont, NE. Died 9/14/1973, Los Angeles, CA. Once struck out side on nine pitches in the majors. Also once allowed six home runs in a game to tie a big league record. An excellent hitter, he often played first base or outfield for Seals.

	W	L	PCT	G	IP	H	ER	BB	SO	ERA	EFF
1920 SLC	9	13	.409	39	220	260	107	50	76	4.38	1.41
1921 SLC	7	13	.350	35	158	224	98	40	64	5.58	1.67
1922 SLC	15	16	.484	49	255	301	111	44	69	3.92	1.35
1928 SF	9	7	.563	26	137	184	70	22	37	4.59	1.50
1929 SF	22	11	.667	37	282	338	138	45	78	4.40	1.36
1934 Miss	15	10	.600	31	233	260	83	65	66	3.20	1.39
1935 Miss	15	10	.600	29	201	244	107	49	46	4.80	1.46
1936 Miss	13	10	.565	34	197	247	99	55	68	4.52	1.53
1937 Sea	1	5	.167	10	41	––	––	––	––	––	––
1938 Oak	0	1	.000	1	2	––	––	––	––	––	––
	106	96	.525	291	1726	––	––	––	––	4.35	1.44

LOU TOST   Louis Eugene Tost. Born 6/1/1911, Cumberland, WA. Died 2/22/1967, Santa Clara, CA. Had 10–10 record in rookie season in majors with Braves and appeared in only four more big league games after that.

	W	L	PCT	G	IP	H	ER	BB	SO	ERA	EFF
1935 Miss	0	0	––	9	16	––	––	––	––	––	––
1937 Miss	9	8	.529	39	204	220	80	82	102	3.52	1.48

LOU TOST (cont.)

	W	L	PCT	G	IP	H	ER	BB	SO	ERA	EFF
1938 Hol	11	16	.407	39	220	214	85	91	103	3.48	1.39
1939 Hol	5	10	.333	33	121	141	67	41	54	4.98	1.50
1940 Hol	4	6	.400	46	135	140	61	50	72	4.07	1.41
1941 Hol	13	10	.565	47	243	273	104	71	112	3.85	1.42
1946 Sea	16	13	.552	33	240	204	72	68	158	2.70	1.13
1948 Sac–O	12	15	.444	42	226	236	93	68	107	3.70	1.35
1949 Oak	14	7	.667	43	157	158	70	48	78	4.01	1.31
1950 Oak	6	5	.545	30	94	101	52	40	47	4.98	1.50
	90	90	.500	361	1656	1687	684	559	833	3.75	1.37

DIZZY TROUT   Paul Howard Trout. Born 6/29/1915, Sandcut, IN. Died 2/28/1972, Chicago, IL. Two–time All–Star, he led AL in wins in 1943 and in ERA in 1944 while winning twenty–seven for Tigers. Free spirit; pitched fifteen years in the majors, all but a half–season with Detroit. Attempted to make comeback in 1957 after impressive showing in an Old Timers game.

	W	L	PCT	G	IP	H	ER	BB	SO	ERA	EFF
1957 Van	0	2	.000	3	11	10	1	5	6	0.84	1.41

JIM TURNER   James Riley Turner. Born 8/6/1903, Antioch, TN. Won twenty games as thirty–three year old rookie with Boston Braves in 1937. Led NL in ERA, complete games, and shutouts as well. Also pitched for Cincinnati on 1940 World Championship team. Later a big league pitching coach for twenty–four years with Yanks and Reds. Control pitcher with good curve.

	W	L	PCT	G	IP	H	ER	BB	SO	ERA	EFF
1930 Hol	21	9	.700	36	258	303	109	58	92	3.80	1.40
1931 Hol	17	14	.548	45	292	340	139	80	106	4.28	1.44
1932 Hol	11	10	.524	40	194	238	99	55	52	4.59	1.51
1947 Port	0	0	––	2	3	5	2	3	1	6.00	2.67
	49	33	.598	123	747	886	349	196	251	4.20	1.45

HAL TURPIN   Harold Turpin. Born 9/28/1905, Yoncalla, OR. Joined with Dick Barrett in leading the Seattle pitching staff in late thirties and early forties. Led PCL in wins in 1939 and winning percentage in 1941 and 1942.

	W	L	PCT	G	IP	H	ER	BB	SO	ERA	EFF
1927 SF	6	4	.600	29	97	119	48	21	26	4.45	1.44
1929 SF	0	0	––	2	4	––	––	2	0	––	––
1930 SF	10	11	.476	45	205	247	88	41	65	3.86	1.40
1931 SF–Sea	9	14	.391	39	197	267	111	50	64	5.07	1.61
1932 Sea	1	1	.500	3	17	15	6	3	2	3.18	1.06
1933 Port	6	9	.400	16	104	130	34	23	35	2.93	1.47
1934 Port	15	22	.405	42	320	376	144	58	89	4.05	1.36
1935 Port	3	4	.429	12	47	73	44	21	17	8.43	2.00
1937 Sea	9	11	.450	24	157	175	80	50	64	4.59	1.43
1938 Sea	17	14	.548	37	217	220	70	53	81	2.90	1.26
1939 Sea	23	10	.697	37	270	273	75	46	100	2.50	1.18
1940 Sea	23	11	.676	37	297	289	90	65	96	2.73	1.19
1941 Sea	20	6	.769	37	269	274	75	35	68	2.51	1.15
1942 Sea	23	9	.719	36	321	309	74	44	67	2.07	1.10

HAL TURPIN (cont.)

	W	L	PCT	G	IP	H	ER	BB	SO	ERA	EFF
1943 Sea	7	6	.538	14	106	111	34	17	25	2.89	1.21
1944 Sea	13	15	.464	31	229	238	79	33	52	3.10	1.18
1945 Sea	18	8	.692	31	229	244	61	26	29	2.40	1.18
1946 Sac	0	3	.000	5	16	24	--	7	2	--	1.94
	203	158	.562	477	3102	3384	1113	595	882	3.25	1.28

DAZZY VANCE

Clarence Arthur Vance. Born 3/4/1891, Adair County, IA. Died 2/16/1961, Homosassa Springs FL. Already thirty−one by the time he won first big league game, rode fastball to Hall of Fame career. Led the NL in strikeouts seven straight years. Also led the National League in shutouts four times, earned run average three times, and in victories twice.

	W	L	PCT	G	IP	H	ER	BB	SO	ERA	EFF
1919 Sac	10	18	.357	48	294	264	92	81	86	2.82	1.17

JOHNNY VANDER MEER

John Samuel Vander Meer. Born 11/2/1914, Prospect Park, NJ. Led NL in strikeouts three times in−between streaks of wildness. Was named minor league Player of the Year in 1936. Only major league pitcher to throw consecutive no−hitters.

	W	L	PCT	G	IP	H	ER	BB	SO	ERA	EFF
1951 Oak	2	6	.250	13	63	78	36	35	37	5.14	1.79

RUBE VICKERS

Harry Porter Vickers. Born 5/17/1878, Pittsford, MI. Died 12/9/1958, Belleville, MI. Won twenty−two games in the major leagues, all but four of them coming in 1908 for the Philadelphia A's. He holds the PCL single−season record for wins, (shared with Doc Newton), innings pitched, and strikeouts, all coming in the 1906 season.

	W	L	PCT	G	IP	H	ER	BB	SO	ERA	EFF
1905 Sea	12	6	.667	19	162	121	--	31	103	--	0.94
1906 Sea	39	20	.661	64	517	395	--	139	409	--	1.03
	51	26	.662	83	679	516	--	170	512	--	1.01

LAURIE VINCI

Laurie Vinci. Born 1902. Died 1/6/1970, Redwood City, CA. Left−hander often plagued by wildness; he led the Pacific Coast League in wild pitches and hit batsmen in 1926. Also led PCL in walks in 1927 and in 1928. Released in mid−season by Seattle in 1935 to become team trainer.

	W	L	PCT	G	IP	H	ER	BB	SO	ERA	EFF
1924 Sac	6	8	.429	25	124	125	62	61	39	4.50	1.50
1925 Sac	10	19	.345	40	219	247	118	117	86	4.85	1.66
1926 Sac	15	21	.417	51	298	286	115	128	137	3.47	1.39
1927 Sac	11	19	.367	44	232	255	123	119	105	4.78	1.61
1928 Sac	23	11	.676	51	330	327	131	129	141	3.57	1.38
1929 Sac	13	20	.394	42	242	317	144	96	99	5.35	1.70
1930 Sac	7	18	.280	42	219	259	120	76	79	4.93	1.53
1931 Sac	3	11	.214	36	172	218	99	62	62	5.18	1.63
1932 Sac	13	13	.500	36	214	223	98	80	71	4.12	1.42
1933 Sac	18	12	.600	39	262	372	106	103	80	3.64	1.81
1934 Sac−Sea	6	10	.375	41	194	171	68	81	58	3.15	1.30
1935 Sea	1	5	.167	32	95	146	83	54	44	7.86	2.11

LAURIE VINCI (cont.)

	W	L	PCT	G	IP	H	ER	BB	SO	ERA	EFF
1938 Oak	0	1	.000	2	3	––	––	––	––	––	––
	126	168	.429	481	2604	2946	1267	1106	1001	4.38	1.56

RUBE WALBERG   George Elvin Walberg. Born 7/27/1899, Seattle, WA. Died 10/27/1978, Tempe, AZ. Enjoyed a long major league career, playing all but two games with A's and Red Sox. Won 155 games in major leagues including twenty in 1931, when he led American League in innings pitched.

	W	L	PCT	G	IP	H	ER	BB	SO	ERA	EFF
1922 Port	9	13	.409	33	209	233	104	79	84	4.48	1.49

BILL WALKER   William Henry Walker. Born 10/7/1903, East St. Louis, IL. Died 6/14/1966, East St. Louis, IL. Pitched ten seasons in the big leagues with the New York Giants and St. Louis Cardinals. Led NL in ERA in 1929 and in ERA and shutouts in 1931.

	W	L	PCT	G	IP	H	ER	BB	SO	ERA	EFF
1938 Sac	17	12	.586	31	226	222	74	59	99	2.95	1.24
1939 Sea	16	18	.471	42	241	239	89	76	82	3.32	1.31
1940 Sea	12	14	.462	36	202	220	94	72	51	4.19	1.45
	45	44	.506	109	669	681	257	207	232	3.46	1.33

BOB WEILAND   Robert George Weiland. Born 12/14/1905, Chicago, IL. Died 11/9/1988, Chicago, IL. Threw a shutout in major league debut. Was not until ninth season in majors that he won in double figures; then won a total of thirty–one games over the 1937 and 1938 seasons for Cardinals.

	W	L	PCT	G	IP	H	ER	BB	SO	ERA	EFF
1940 LA	12	7	.632	25	164	130	69	77	87	3.78	1.26
1941 LA	1	4	.200	17	57	61	24	38	23	3.79	1.74
	13	11	.542	42	221	191	93	115	110	3.78	1.38

BILL WERLE   William George Werle. Born 12/21/1920, Oakland, CA. Star at University of California, had a 12–13 record for last place Pirates in 1949. Led the PCL in winning percentage and complete games in 1948. A long–time major league scout after his playing days.

	W	L	PCT	G	IP	H	ER	BB	SO	ERA	EFF
1943 SF	1	2	.333	9	26	––	––	––	––	––	––
1944 SF	14	19	.424	36	289	331	130	84	129	4.05	1.44
1946 SF	12	8	.600	33	175	173	44	59	72	2.26	1.33
1947 SF	12	12	.500	36	205	231	75	42	80	3.29	1.33
1948 SF	17	7	.708	34	250	256	76	61	136	2.74	1.27
1955 Port	17	8	.680	33	221	248	87	30	76	3.54	1.26
1956 Port	16	15	.516	35	247	330	121	40	82	4.41	1.50
1957 P–SD	9	8	.529	26	174	219	75	17	58	3.88	1.36
1958 SD	10	8	.556	28	171	191	59	34	65	3.11	1.32
1959 SD	5	8	.385	32	128	153	62	29	47	4.36	1.42
1960 SD–Tac	·7	8	.467	26	134	149	61	17	66	4.10	1.24
1961 Tac–Hw	7	8	.467	22	143	159	56	27	66	3.52	1.30
	127	111	.534	350	2163	2440	846	440	877	3.56	1.35

JIMMY WHALEN   William L. Whalen. Born 1880, San Francisco, CA. Died 1/12/1915, Sacramento, CA. Led the Pacific Coast League in wins in 1905. Career shortened by a broken leg suffered in 1911.

	W	L	PCT	G	IP	H	ER	BB	SO	ERA	EFF
1903 SF	28	21	.571	51	443	404	— —	145	106	— —	1.24
1904 SF	32	23	.582	59	492	436	— —	137	143	— —	1.16
1905 SF	32	25	.561	65	512	383	— —	108	214	— —	0.96
1909 Sac	23	18	.561	51	— —	— —	— —	82	127	— —	— —
1910 Sac	14	22	.389	44	— —	— —	— —	85	80	— —	— —
1912 Ver	2	4	.333	11	52	— —	— —	20	12	— —	— —
	131	113	.537	281	— —	— —	— —	577	682	— —	— —

DOC WHITE   Guy Harris White. Born 4/9/1879, Washington D.C. Died 2/17/1969, Silver Spring, MD. Won 189 games over his thirteen big league seasons, mostly for Chicago White Sox "Hitless Wonders". Set AL records with five shutouts in a row and sixty—five straight innings without a walk.

	W	L	PCT	G	IP	H	ER	BB	SO	ERA	EFF
1914 Ven	17	13	.567	39	259	268	70	56	99	2.43	1.25
1915 Ver	2	3	.400	11	44	53	17	10	10	3.45	1.42
	19	16	.543	50	303	321	87	66	109	2.58	1.28

BILL WIGHT   William Robert Wight. Born 4/12/1922, Rio Vista, CA. Pitched twelve seasons in the big leagues with eight teams. Lost twenty games for the White Sox in 1948. Led PCL in winning percentage and ERA in 1954.

	W	L	PCT	G	IP	H	ER	BB	SO	ERA	EFF
1954 SD	17	5	.773	28	210	175	45	72	87	1.93	1.18
1959 Sea	1	3	.250	4	16	24	13	9	7	7.31	2.06
	18	8	.692	32	226	199	58	81	94	2.31	1.24

ED WILLETT   Robert Edgar Willett. Born 3/7/1884, Norfolk, VA. Died 5/10/1934, Wellington, KS. Won 95 games for Detroit Tigers over six—year period, 1908—1913. Hit two home runs in one game for the Tigers in 1912.

	W	L	PCT	G	IP	H	ER	BB	SO	ERA	EFF
1918 SLC	2	4	.333	9	47	59	25	11	14	4.79	1.49

LEFTY WILLIAMS   Claud Preston Williams. Born 3/9/1893, Aurora, MO. Died 11/4/1959, Laguna Beach, CA. His three losses in 1919 World Series raised suspicion that was unfortunately well—founded. Banned forever in 1920. Won forty—five games in the two seasons before career was halted. Led the PCL in wins, strikeouts, winning percentage, and innings in 1915.

	W	L	PCT	G	IP	H	ER	BB	SO	ERA	EFF
1914 Sac	13	20	.394	37	276	256	63	64	167	2.05	1.16
1915 SLC	33	12	.733	64	419	364	132	115	294	2.84	1.14
	46	32	.590	101	695	620	195	179	461	2.53	1.15

TED WILLIAMS   Theodore Samuel Williams. Born 8/30/1918, San Diego, CA. Pitched once in relief for the San Diego Padres in a one—sided game. His performance solidified his future as an outfielder.

	W	L	PCT	G	IP	H	ER	BB	SO	ERA	EFF
1936 SD	0	0	— —	1	1	2	2	1	0	13.50	2.25

JIM WILSON   James Alger Wilson. Born 2/20/1922, San Diego, CA. Three times an All–Star, career almost ended by Hank Greenberg line drive that fractured his skull. Led PCL in wins, strikeouts, shutouts and CG in 1950.

	W	L	PCT	G	IP	H	ER	BB	SO	ERA	EFF
1950 Sea	24	11	.686	41	293	254	96	76	228	2.95	1.13

PINKY WOODS   George Rowland Woods. Born 5/22/1915, Waterbury, CT. Died 10/30/1982, Los Angeles, CA. Sidearmer for Red Sox for three years, career hampered by a spiking that cost him his big toe. Led PCL in losses in 1948; tied for league lead in wins in 1949.

	W	L	PCT	G	IP	H	ER	BB	SO	ERA	EFF
1947 Hol	13	10	.565	28	179	204	89	82	79	4.47	1.60
1948 Hol	15	20	.429	44	279	303	140	167	161	4.52	1.68
1949 Hol	23	12	.657	49	275	287	126	100	128	4.12	1.41
1950 Hol	10	11	.476	32	184	188	76	81	91	3.72	1.46
1951 Hol	12	9	.571	28	162	178	73	54	97	4.06	1.43
1952 Hol	11	9	.550	29	160	149	69	75	79	3.88	1.40
1953 Hol	0	1	.000	2	––	––	––	––	––	––	––
	84	72	.538	212	1239	1309	573	559	635	4.16	1.51

JIMMY ZINN   James Edward Zinn. Born 1/31/1895, Benton, AR. Died 2/26/1991, Memphis, TN. Once released for striking out Babe Ruth during an exhibition game against orders. Tied for PCL lead in wins in 1930; held out in 1931. Also played outfield and first base in minors; hit .303 lifetime.

	W	L	PCT	G	IP	H	ER	BB	SO	ERA	EFF
1930 SF	26	12	.684	39	316	336	143	80	132	4.07	1.32
1931 SF	9	7	.563	20	146	167	54	31	49	3.32	1.35
1932 SF	18	15	.545	37	258	301	128	53	95	4.47	1.37
1933 SF	20	19	.513	42	317	337	145	69	99	4.12	1.28
1934 SF	14	17	.452	36	320	328	124	64	71	3.48	1.22
1935 SF–Sac	7	7	.500	26	134	187	66	29	42	4.43	1.61
	94	77	.550	200	1492	1656	660	326	488	3.98	1.33

SECTION IV

Franchise Register

This section deals with the Pacific Coast League through its various franchises during the years 1903 through 1957. The league began with six teams: Portland and Seattle in the north and Sacramento, Oakland, San Francisco and Los Angeles in the south. From that point until the major league's invasion of its territory, the circuit ranged in size from four to eight teams, the latter representing the number of franchises from 1919 forward. These teams represented 14 different cities at various times through 11 different franchises. Only three organizations (San Francisco, Los Angeles, and Oakland/Vancouver) were in operation continuously from 1903 through 1957.

Franchises and cities overlapped during the league's history. There were two separate Mission teams as well as two teams representing Hollywood, Seattle, Portland, and three for Sacramento. Two franchises folded following the 1906 season; the original Seattle team and Fresno, the latter having begun its existence in Sacramento and winning the 1904 pennant in Tacoma before returning to Sacramento late in 1905 and then finding its way to the Raisin Capitol the next season. All eight franchises operating in the Pacific Coast League in 1957 had been in continuous operation since 1919.

The tables on the following pages are arranged by franchise, both alphabetically and chronologically, sorted by the city originally represented. Each city in which the team was based is listed in the heading. For each year of operation, there is a listing of each team's home stadium (or the location of the stadium if the name is unknown), manager(s), and season record. Lines in bold typeface with the manager's name in capital letters indicate pennant-winning seasons. In case of the pennant-winning team having had more than one manager during the season, only the manager of the team at the end of the season is in bold typeface.

At the end of each franchise listing is a tabulation of the team's record, broken down by city where applicable, and a franchise cumulative record including overall winning percentage.

303

FRANCHISE – LOS ANGELES (1903–1957)

YR	HOME PARK	MANAGER	FINISH	RECORD		
1903	Chutes Park	JAMES MORLEY	FIRST	133	–	78
1904	Chutes Park	Tim Flood	Second	119	–	97
1905	Chutes Park	POP DILLON	FIRST	120	–	94
1906	Chutes Park	Pop Dillon	Third	95	–	87
1907	Chutes Park	POP DILLON	FIRST	115	–	74
1908	Chutes Park	POP DILLON	FIRST	110	–	78
1909	Chutes Park	Pop Dillon	Third	118	–	97
1910	Chutes Park	Pop Dillon	Fifth	101	–	121
1911	Chutes Park	Pop Dillon	Sixth	82	–	127
1912	Washington Park	Pop Dillon	Third	110	–	93
1913	Washington Park	Pop Dillon	Fifth	100	–	108
1914	Washington Park	Pop Dillon	Second	116	–	94
1915	Washington Park	Pop Dillon	Third	110	–	98
1916	Washington Park	FRANK CHANCE	FIRST	119	–	79
1917	Washington Park	Frank Chance	Second	116	–	94
1918	Washington Park	Red Killefer	Second	57	–	47
1919	Washington Park	Red Killefer	Second	108	–	72
1920	Washington Park	Red Killefer	Third	102	–	95
1921	Washington Park	RED KILLEFER	FIRST	108	–	80
1922	Washington Park	Red Killefer	Third	111	–	88
1923	Washington Park	Marty Krug	Sixth	93	–	109
1924	Washington Park	Marty Krug	Second	107	–	92
1925	Washington/Wrigley	Marty Krug	Fourth	105	–	93
1926	Wrigley Field	MARTY KRUG	FIRST	121	–	81
1927	Wrigley Field	Marty Krug	Eighth	80	–	116
1928	Wrigley Field	Marty Krug	Sixth	87	–	104
1929	Wrigley Field	Marty Krug	Fifth	104	–	98
		Jack Lelivelt				
1930	Wrigley Field	Jack Lelivelt	Second	113	–	84
1931	Wrigley Field	Jack Lelivelt	Fourth	98	–	89
1932	Wrigley Field	Jack Lelivelt	Fifth	96	–	93
1933	Wrigley Field	JACK LELIVELT	FIRST	114	–	73
1934	Wrigley Field	JACK LELIVELT	FIRST	137	–	50
1935	Wrigley Field	Jack Lelivelt	Second	98	–	76
1936	Wrigley Field	Jack Lelivelt	Fifth	88	–	88
1937	Wrigley Field	Truck Hannah	Fifth	90	–	88
1938	Wrigley Field	TRUCK HANNAH	FIRST	105	–	73
1939	Wrigley Field	Truck Hannah	Third	97	–	79
1940	Wrigley Field	Jigger Statz	Second	102	–	75
1941	Wrigley Field	Jigger Statz	Seventh	72	–	98
1942	Wrigley Field	Jigger Statz	Second	104	–	74
1943	Wrigley Field	BILL SWEENEY	FIRST	110	–	45
1944	Wrigley Field	BILL SWEENEY	FIRST	99	–	70
1945	Wrigley Field	Bill Sweeney	Seventh	76	–	107
1946	Wrigley Field	Bill Sweeney	Fourth	94	–	89

FRANCHISE — LOS ANGELES (cont.)

YR	HOME PARK	MANAGER	FINISH	RECORD	
1947	**Wrigley Field**	**BILL KELLY**	**FIRST**	**106**	**– 81**
1948	Wrigley Field	Bill Kelly	Third	102	– 86
1949	Wrigley Field	Bill Kelly	Eighth	74	– 113
1950	Wrigley Field	Bill Kelly	Seventh	86	– 114
1951	Wrigley Field	Stan Hack	Third	86	– 81
1952	Wrigley Field	Stan Hack	Sixth	87	– 93
1953	Wrigley Field	Stan Hack	Third	93	– 87
1954	Wrigley Field	Bill Sweeney	Sixth	73	– 92
1955	Wrigley Field	Bob Scheffing	Third	91	– 81
1956	**Wrigley Field**	**BOB SCHEFFING**	**FIRST**	**107**	**– 61**
1957	Wrigley Field	Clay Bryant	Sixth	80	– 88

FRANCHISE RECORD   5525 – 4822
                                                    .534

FRANCHISE — OAKLAND/VANCOUVER (1903—1957)

YR	HOME PARK	MANAGER	FINISH	RECORD	
1903	Freeman's Park	Peter Lohman	Sixth	89	– 126
1904	Freeman's Park	Peter Lohman	Fourth	116	– 109
1905	Freeman's Park	Peter Lohman	Fourth	103	– 119
		George Van Haltren			
1906	Freeman's Park	George Van Haltren	Fifth	77	– 110
1907	Freeman's Park	George Van Haltren	Third	97	– 101
1908	Freeman's Park	George Van Haltren	Fourth	83	– 116
1909	Freeman's Park	George Van Haltren	Fifth	88	– 125
		Bill Reidy			
1910	Freeman's Park	Harry Wolverton	Second	122	– 98
1911	Freeman's Park	Harry Wolverton	Third	111	– 99
1912	**Freeman's Park**	**BUD SHARPE**	**FIRST**	**120**	**– 83**
1913	Oaks Park	Carl Mitze	Sixth	90	– 120
		Art Devlin			
1914	Oaks Park	Art Devlin	Sixth	79	– 133
		Tyler Christian			
1915	Oaks Park	Tyler Christian	Fifth	93	– 113
		Rowdy Elliott			
1916	Oaks Park	Rowdy Elliott	Sixth	72	– 136
		Del Howard			
1917	Oaks Park	Del Howard	Fifth	103	– 108
1918	Oaks Park	Del Howard	Sixth	40	– 63
1919	Oaks Park	Del Howard	Fifth	86	– 96
1920	Oaks Park	Del Howard	Sixth	95	– 103
1921	Oaks Park	Del Howard	Fifth	101	– 85
1922	Oaks Park	Del Howard	Sixth	88	– 112

FRANCHISE — OAKLAND/VANCOUVER (cont.)

YR	HOME PARK	MANAGER	FINISH	RECORD
1923	Oaks Park	Ivan Howard	Seventh	91 — 111
1924	Oaks Park	Ivan Howard	Fourth	103 — 99
1925	Oaks Park	Ivan Howard	Sixth	88 — 112
1926	Oaks Park	Ivan Howard	Second	111 — 92
1927	**Oaks Park**	**IVAN HOWARD**	**FIRST**	**120 — 75**
1928	Oaks Park	Ivan Howard	Fifth	91 — 100
1929	Oaks Park	Ivan Howard	Fourth	111 — 91
1930	Oaks Park	Carl Zamloch	Fifth	97 — 103
1931	Oaks Park	Carl Zamloch	Fifth	86 — 101
1932	Oaks Park	Carl Zamloch	Seventh	80 — 107
1933	Oaks Park	Ray Brubaker	Fifth	93 — 92
1934	Oaks Park	Ray Brubaker	Fifth	90 — 98
1935	Oaks Park	Oscar Vitt	Third	91 — 83
1936	Oaks Park	Billy Meyer	Second	95 — 81
1937	Oaks Park	Billy Meyer	Seventh	79 — 98
1938	Oaks Park	Dutch Zwilling	Eighth	65 — 113
1939	Oaks Park	John Vergez	Seventh	78 — 98
1940	Oaks Park	John Vergez	Third	94 — 84
1941	Oaks Park	John Vergez	Fifth	81 — 95
1942	Oaks Park	John Vergez	Sixth	85 — 92
1943	Oaks Park	John Vergez	Fifth	73 — 82
1944	Oaks Park	Dolf Camilli	Third	86 — 83
1945	Oaks Park	Dolf Camilli	Fifth	90 — 93
1946	Oaks Park	Casey Stengel	Second	111 — 72
1947	Oaks Park	Casey Stengel	Fourth	96 — 90
1948	**Oaks Park**	**CASEY STENGEL**	**FIRST**	**114 — 74**
1949	Oaks Park	Charlie Dressen	Second	104 — 83
1950	**Oaks Park**	**CHARLIE DRESSEN**	**FIRST**	**118 — 82**
1951	Oaks Park	Mel Ott	Fifth	80 — 88
1952	Oaks Park	Mel Ott	Second	104 — 76
1953	Oaks Park	Augie Galan	Seventh	77 — 103
1954	Oaks Park	Charlie Dressen	Third	85 — 82
1955	Oaks Park	Lefty O'Doul	Seventh	77 — 95

FRANCHISE MOVED TO VANCOUVER

1956	Capilano Stadium	Lefty O'Doul	Eighth	67 — 98
1957	Capilano Stadium	Charlie Metro	Second	97 — 70

OAKLAND RECORD	4897 — 5183
VANCOUVER RECORD	164 — 168
FRANCHISE RECORD	5061 — 5351
	.486

FRANCHISE – PORTLAND (1903–1917)

YR	HOME PARK	MANAGER	FINISH	RECORD
1903	Vaughn Street Park	Sammy Vigneaux Fred Eley	Fifth	95 – 108
1904	Vaughn Street Park	Fred Eley Dan Dugdale Ike Butler	Sixth	79 – 136
1905	Vaughn Street Park	Walter Mc Creedie	Fifth	94 – 110
1906	**Vaughn Street Park**	**WALTER MCCREEDIE**	**FIRST**	**115 – 60**
1907	Vaughn Street Park	Walter Mc Creedie	Fourth	72 – 114
1908	Vaughn Street Park	Walter Mc Creedie	Second	95 – 90
1909	Vaughn Street Park	Walter Mc Creedie	Second	112 – 87
1910	**Vaughn Street Park**	**WALTER MCCREEDIE**	**FIRST**	**114 – 87**
1911	**Vaughn Street Park**	**WALTER MCCREEDIE**	**FIRST**	**113 – 79**
1912	Vaughn Street Park	Walter Mc Creedie	Fourth	85 – 100
1913	**Vaughn Street Park**	**WALTER MCCREEDIE**	**FIRST**	**109 – 86**
1914	**Vaughn Street Park**	**WALTER MCCREEDIE**	**FIRST**	**113 – 84**
1915	Vaughn Street Park	Walter Mc Creedie	Sixth	78 – 116
1916	Vaughn Street Park	Walter Mc Creedie	Fifth	93 – 98
1917	Vaughn Street Park	Walter Mc Creedie	Fourth	98 – 102

FRANCHISE RECORD   1465 – 1457
    .501

FRANCHISE – PORTLAND (1919–1957)

YR	HOME PARK	MANAGER	FINISH	RECORD
1919	Vaughn Street Park	Walter Mc Creedie	Seventh	78 – 96
1920	Vaughn Street Park	Walter Mc Creedie	Eighth	81 – 103
1921	Vaughn Street Park	Walter Mc Creedie	Eighth	51 – 134
1922	Vaughn Street Park	Duke Kenworthy Terry Turner Al Demaree J. B. Middleton	Seventh	87 – 112
1923	Vaughn Street Park	J. B. Middleton	Third	107 – 89
1924	Vaughn Street Park	Duke Kenworthy Frank Brazill	Seventh	88 – 110
1925	Vaughn Street Park	Duffy Lewis Truck Hannah	Fifth	92 – 104
1926	Vaughn Street Park	Ernie Johnson	Fourth	100 – 101
1927	Vaughn Street Park	Ernie Johnson	Fifth	95 – 95
1928	Vaughn Street Park	Ernie Johnson Bill Rodgers	Seventh	79 – 112
1929	Vaughn Street Park	Bill Rodgers	Sixth	90 – 112
1930	Vaughn Street Park	Larry Woodall	Eighth	81 – 117
1931	Vaughn Street Park	Spencer Abbott	Third	100 – 87

FRANCHISE — PORTLAND (cont.)

YR	HOME PARK	MANAGER	FINISH	RECORD	
1932	**Vaughn Street Park**	**SPENCER ABBOTT**	**FIRST**	**111 —**	**78**
1933	Vaughn Street Park	Spencer Abbott	Second	105 —	77
1934	Vaughn Street Park	Walter Mc Creedie	Eighth	66 —	117
		Terry Turner			
		George Burns			
		George Blackerby			
1935	Vaughn Street Park	Bud Ryan	Fourth	87 —	86
		Billy Cissell			
1936	**Vaughn Street Park**	Max Bishop	**FIRST**	**96 —**	**79**
		BILL SWEENEY			
1937	Vaughn Street Park	Bill Sweeney	Fourth	90 —	86
1938	Vaughn Street Park	Bill Sweeney	Sixth	79 —	96
1939	Vaughn Street Park	Bill Sweeney	Eighth	75 —	98
1940	Vaughn Street Park	Johnny Frederick	Eighth	56 —	122
1941	Vaughn Street Park	Oscar Vitt	Eighth	71 —	97
1942	Vaughn Street Park	Frank Brazill	Eighth	67 —	110
1943	Vaughn Street Park	Merv Shea	Fifth	79 —	76
1944	Vaughn Street Park	Marv Owen	Second	87 —	82
1945	**Vaughn Street Park**	**MARV OWEN**	**FIRST**	**112 —**	**68**
1946	Vaughn Street Park	Marv Owen	Seventh	74 —	109
1947	Vaughn Street Park	Jim Turner	Third	97 —	89
1948	Vaughn Street Park	Jim Turner	Fifth	89 —	99
1949	Vaughn Street Park	Bill Sweeney	Sixth	85 —	102
1950	Vaughn Street Park	Bill Sweeney	Fourth	101 —	99
1951	Vaughn Street Park	Bill Sweeney	Fourth	83 —	85
1952	Vaughn Street Park	Clay Hopper	Fourth	92 —	88
1953	Vaughn Street Park	Clay Hopper	Fourth	92 —	88
1954	Vaughn Street Park	Clay Hopper	Eighth	71 —	94
1955	Vaughn Street Park	Clay Hopper	Fifth	86 —	86
1956	Civic Stadium	Tommy Holmes	Third	86 —	82
		Bill Sweeney			
1957	Civic Stadium	Bill Sweeney	Eighth	60 —	108
		Frank Carswell			
		Bill Posedel			

	FRANCHISE RECORD	3326 — 3773
		.468

FRANCHISE — SACRAMENTO/TACOMA/FRESNO (1903–1906)

YR	HOME PARK	MANAGER	FINISH	RECORD	
1903	Oak Park	Mique Fisher	Second	105 —	105

FRANCHISE MOVED TO TACOMA

FRANCHISE - SACRAMENTO/TACOMA/FRESNO (cont.)

YR	HOME PARK	MANAGER	FINISH	RECORD	
1904	**Athletic Park**	**MIQUE FISHER**	**FIRST**	**130** -	**94**
1905	Athletic Park	Mique Fisher	Third	106 -	107

(Due to poor attendance, became road team in last part of 1905.)

FRANCHISE MOVED TO FRESNO

1906	Recreation Park	Mique Fisher	Sixth	64 -	117
		FRANCHISE RECORD		405 -	423
				.489	

FRANCHISE - SACRAMENTO/MISSION/SALT LAKE CITY/ HOLLYWOOD/SAN DIEGO (1909-1957)

YR	HOME PARK	MANAGER	FINISH	RECORD	
1909	Oak Park	Charlie Graham	Fourth	97 -	107
1910	Buffalo Park	Charlie Graham	Sixth	83 -	128
1911	Buffalo Park	Patsy O'Rourke	Fourth	95 -	109
1912	Buffalo Park	Patsy O'Rourke	Sixth	73 -	121
		Deacon Van Buren			
1913	Buffalo Park	Harry Wolverton	Second	103 -	94
1914	Buffalo Park	Harry Wolverton	Fifth	90 -	121

Recreation Park (team moved to San Francisco late in the 1914 season.

FRANCHISE MOVED TO SALT LAKE CITY

1915	Bonneville Park	Cliff Blankenship	Second	108 -	89
1916	Bonneville Park	Cliff Blankenship	Third	99 -	96
		Bill Bernhard			
		Bill O'Connor			
1917	Bonneville Park	Bill Bernhard	Third	102 -	97
1918	Bonneville Park	Walter Mc Creedie	Fifth	48 -	49
1919	Bonneville Park	Eddie Herr	Third	88 -	83
1920	Bonneville Park	Ernie Johnson	Fifth	95 -	92
1921	Bonneville Park	Gavvy Cravath	Seventh	73 -	110
1922	Bonneville Park	Duffy Lewis	Fourth	95 -	106
1923	Bonneville Park	Duffy Lewis	Fifth	94 -	105
1924	Bonneville Park	Duffy Lewis	Fifth	101 -	100
1925	Bonneville Park	Oscar Vitt	Second	116 -	84

FRANCHISE MOVED TO HOLLYWOOD

1926	Wrigley Field	Oscar Vitt	Sixth	94 -	107
1927	Wrigley Field	Oscar Vitt	Sixth	92 -	104

FRANCHISE — SAC/MISSION/SLC/HOLLY/SAN DIEGO (cont)

YR	HOME PARK	MANAGER	FINISH	RECORD
1928	Wrigley Field	Oscar Vitt	Second	112 — 79
1929	Wrigley Field	Oscar Vitt	Third	113 — 89
1930	**Wrigley Field**	**OSCAR VITT**	**FIRST**	**119 — 81**
1931	Wrigley Field	Oscar Vitt	Second	104 — 83
1932	Wrigley Field	Oscar Vitt	Second	106 — 83
1933	Wrigley Field	Oscar Vitt	Third	107 — 80
1934	Wrigley Field	Oscar Vitt	Third	97 — 88
1935	Wrigley Field	Frank Shellenback	Eighth	73 — 99

FRANCHISE MOVED TO SAN DIEGO

YR	HOME PARK	MANAGER	FINISH	RECORD
1936	Lane Field	Frank Shellenback	Second	95 — 81
1937	Lane Field	Frank Shellenback	Third	97 — 81
1938	Lane Field	Frank Shellenback	Fifth	92 — 85
1939	Lane Field	Cedric Durst	Fifth	83 — 93
1940	Lane Field	Cedric Durst	Fourth	92 — 85
1941	Lane Field	Cedric Durst	Third	101 — 76
1942	Lane Field	Cedric Durst	Fourth	91 — 87
1943	Lane Field	Cedric Durst / George Detore	Seventh	70 — 85
1944	Lane Field	George Detore	Eighth	75 — 94
1945	Lane Field	Pepper Martin	Sixth	82 — 101
1946	Lane Field	Pepper Martin / Jim Brillheart	Sixth	78 — 108
1947	Lane Field	Rip Collins	Eighth	79 — 107
1948	Lane Field	Rip Collins / Jim Brillheart	Seventh	83 — 105
1949	Lane Field	Bucky Harris	Fourth	96 — 92
1950	Lane Field	Del Baker	Second	114 — 86
1951	Lane Field	Del Baker	Sixth	79 — 88
1952	Lane Field	Lefty O'Doul	Fifth	88 — 92
1953	Lane Field	Lefty O'Doul	Sixth	88 — 92
1954	**Lane Field**	**LEFTY O'DOUL**	**FIRST**	**102 — 67**
1955	Lane Field	Bob Elliott	Second	92 — 80
1956	Lane Field	Bob Elliott	Seventh	72 — 96
1957	Lane Field	Bob Elliott / George Metkovich	Fourth	89 — 79

SACRAMENTO RECORD	541 —	680
SALT LAKE CITY RECORD	1019 —	1011
HOLLYWOOD RECORD	1017 —	893
SAN DIEGO RECORD	1938 —	1960
FRANCHISE RECORD	4515 —	4544
		.498

FRANCHISE - SACRAMENTO (1918-1957)

YR	HOME PARK	MANAGER	FINISH	RECORD	
1918	Buffalo Park	Bill Rodgers	Fourth	48 -	48
1919	Buffalo Park	Bill Rodgers	Fourth	85 -	83
1920	Buffalo Park	Bill Rodgers	Seventh	89 -	109
1921	Buffalo Park	Bill Rodgers	Second	105 -	80
1922	Moreing Field	Charlie Pick	Eighth	76 -	124
1923	Moreing Field	Charlie Pick	Second	112 -	87
1924	Moreing Field	Charlie Pick	Eighth	88 -	112
		Bud Ryan			
1925	Moreing Field	Bud Ryan	Seventh	82 -	119
1926	Moreing Field	Bud Ryan	Fifth	99 -	102
1927	Moreing Field	Bud Ryan	Fourth	100 -	95
1928	Moreing Field	Bud Ryan	Second	112 -	79
1929	Moreing Field	Bud Ryan	Seventh	85 -	117
1930	Moreing Field	Bud Ryan	Third	102 -	96
1931	Moreing Field	Bud Ryan	Fifth	86 -	101
1932	Moreing Field	Bud Ryan	Third	101 -	88
		Earl Mc Neely			
1933	Moreing Field	Earl Mc Neely	Fourth	96 -	85
1934	Moreing Field	Earl Mc Neely	Seventh	79 -	109
1935	Moreing Field	Earl Mc Neely	Seventh	75 -	100
		Kettle Wirtz			
1936	Cardinal Field	Bill Killefer	Eighth	65 -	111
1937	**Cardinal Field**	**BILL KILLEFER**	**FIRST**	**102 -**	**76**
1938	Cardinal Field	Bill Killefer	Third	95 -	82
1939	Cardinal Field	Bernard Borgmann	Fourth	88 -	88
1940	Cardinal Field	Bernard Borgmann	Fifth	90 -	88
1941	Cardinal Field	Pepper Martin	Second	102 -	75
1942	**Cardinal Field**	**PEPPER MARTIN**	**FIRST**	**105 -**	**73**
1943	Cardinal Field	Ken Penner	Eighth	41 -	114
1944	Doubleday Field	Earl Sheely	Seventh	76 -	93
1945	Doubleday Field	Earl Sheely	Third	95 -	85
1946	Edmonds Field	Earl Sheely	Fifth	94 -	92
1947	Edmonds Field	Dick Bartell	Seventh	83 -	103
1948	Edmonds Field	Joe Orengo	Eighth	75 -	113
1949	Edmonds Field	Del Baker	Third	102 -	85
1950	Edmonds Field	Red Kress	Eighth	81 -	119
		Joe Marty			
1951	Edmonds Field	Joe Gordon	Seventh	75 -	92
1952	Edmonds Field	Joe Gordon	Eighth	66 -	114
1953	Edmonds Field	Gene Desautels	Eighth	75 -	105
1954	Edmonds Field	Gene Desautels	Seventh	73 -	94
		Tony Freitas			
1955	Edmonds Field	Tony Freitas	Eighth	76 -	96
1956	Edmonds Field	Tommy Heath	Fifth	84 -	84
1957	Edmonds Field	Tommy Heath	Seventh	63 -	105

FRANCHISE - SACRAMENTO (cont.)

YR	HOME PARK	MANAGER	FINISH	RECORD
		FRANCHISE RECORD		3426 - 3821
				.473

FRANCHISE - SAN FRANCISCO (1903-1957)

YR	HOME PARK	MANAGER	FINISH	RECORD
1903	Eighth & Harrison	Charles Irwin	Fourth	107 - 110
1904	Eighth & Harrison	Charles Irwin	Fifth	101 - 117
1905	Eighth & Harrison	A. Parke Wilson	Second	125 - 100
1906	Eighth & Harrison	A. Parke Wilson	Fourth	91 - 84
	Freeman's Park			
1907	Recreation Park	Danny Long	Second	104 - 99
1908	Recreation Park	Danny Long	Third	100 - 104
1909	Recreation Park	DANNY LONG	FIRST	132 - 80
1910	Recreation Park	Danny Long	Third	114 - 106
1911	Recreation Park	Danny Long	Fifth	95 - 112
1912	Recreation Park	Danny Long	Fifth	89 - 115
1913	Recreation Park	Danny Long	Fourth	104 - 103
1914	Rec Park/Ewing Field	Danny Long	Third	115 - 96
1915	Recreation Park	HARRY WOLVERTON	FIRST	118 - 89
1916	Recreation Park	Harry Wolverton	Fourth	104 - 102
1917	Recreation Park	Harry Wolverton	FIRST	119 - 93
		RED DOWNS		
1918	Recreation Park	Charlie Graham	Third	51 - 51
1919	Recreation Park	Charlie Graham	Sixth	84 - 94
1920	Recreation Park	Charlie Graham	Fourth	103 - 96
1921	Recreation Park	Charlie Graham	Third	106 - 82
1922	Recreation Park	DOTS MILLER	FIRST	127 - 72
1923	Recreation Park	Dots Miller	FIRST	124 - 77
		BABE ELLISON		
1924	Recreation Park	Babe Ellison	Third	108 - 93
1925	Recreation Park	BABE ELLISON	FIRST	128 - 71
1926	Recreation Park	Nick Williams	Eighth	84 - 116
1927	Recreation Park	Nick Williams	Second	106 - 90
1928	Recreation Park	NICK WILLIAMS	FIRST	120 - 71
1929	Recreation Park	Nick Williams	Second	114 - 87
1930	Recreation Park	Nick Williams	Fourth	101 - 98
1931	Seals Stadium	NICK WILLIAMS	FIRST	107 - 80
1932	Seals Stadium	Jake Caveney	Fourth	96 - 90
1933	Seals Stadium	Jake Caveney	Sixth	81 - 106
1934	Seals Stadium	Jake Caveney	Fourth	93 - 95
1935	Seals Stadium	LEFTY O'DOUL	FIRST	103 - 70
1936	Seals Stadium	Lefty O'Doul	Seventh	83 - 93
1937	Seals Stadium	Lefty O'Doul	Second	98 - 80

FRANCHISE — SAN FRANCISCO (cont.)

YR	HOME PARK	MANAGER	FINISH	RECORD
1938	Seals Stadium	Lefty O'Doul	Fourth	93 — 85
1939	Seals Stadium	Lefty O'Doul	Second	97 — 78
1940	Seals Stadium	Lefty O'Doul	Seventh	81 — 97
1941	Seals Stadium	Lefty O'Doul	Fifth	81 — 95
1942	Seals Stadium	Lefty O'Doul	Fifth	88 — 90
1943	Seals Stadium	Lefty O'Doul	Second	89 — 66
1944	Seals Stadium	Lefty O'Doul	Third	86 — 83
1945	Seals Stadium	Lefty O'Doul	Fourth	96 — 87
1946	**Seals Stadium**	**LEFTY O'DOUL**	**FIRST**	**115 — 68**
1947	Seals Stadium	Lefty O'Doul	Second	105 — 82
1948	Seals Stadium	Lefty O'Doul	Second	112 — 76
1949	Seals Stadium	Lefty O'Doul	Seventh	84 — 103
1950	Seals Stadium	Lefty O'Doul	Fifth	100 — 100
1951	Seals Stadium	Lefty O'Doul	Eighth	74 — 93
1952	Seals Stadium	Tommy Heath	Seventh	78 — 102
1953	Seals Stadium	Tommy Heath	Fifth	91 — 89
1954	Seals Stadium	Tommy Heath	Fourth	84 — 84
1955	Seals Stadium	Tommy Heath	Sixth	80 — 92
1956	Seals Stadium	Eddie Joost Joe Gordon	Sixth	77 — 88
1957	**Seals Stadium**	**JOE GORDON**	**FIRST**	**101 — 67**
		FRANCHISE RECORD		5447 — 4947 .524

FRANCHISE — SEATTLE (1903—1906)

YR	HOME PARK	MANAGER	FINISH	RECORD
1903	Fifth & Republican	A. Parke Wilson	Third	98 — 100
1904	Fifth & Republican	A. Parke Wilson Russ Hall	Third	114 — 106
1905	Fifth & Republican	Russ Hall	Sixth	93 — 111
1906	Fifth & Republican	Russ Hall	Second	99 — 83
		FRANCHISE RECORD		404 — 400 .502

FRANCHISE — SEATTLE (1919—1957)

YR	HOME PARK	MANAGER	FINISH	RECORD
1919	Dugdale Field	Wil Clymer Charles Mullen	Eighth	62 — 108

FRANCHISE — SEATTLE (1919—1957)

YR	HOME PARK	MANAGER	FINISH	RECORD	
1920	Dugdale Field	Buzzy Wares	Second	102 —	91
1921	Dugdale Field	Buzzy Wares	Fourth	103 —	82
		Duke Kenworthy			
1922	Dugdale Field	Walter Mc Creedie	Fifth	90 —	107
		John Adams			
1923	Dugdale Field	Harry Wolverton	Fourth	99 —	97
		Red Killefer			
1924	**Dugdale Field**	**RED KILLEFER**	**FIRST**	**109 —**	**91**
1925	Dugdale Field	Red Killefer	Third	103 —	91
1926	Dugdale Field	Red Killefer	Seventh	89 —	111
1927	Dugdale Field	Red Killefer	Third	98 —	92
1928	Dugdale Field	J.B. Middleton	Eighth	64 —	127
1929	Dugdale Field	Ernie Johnson	Eighth	67 —	135
1930	Dugdale Field	Ernie Johnson	Sixth	92 —	107
1931	Dugdale Field	Ernie Johnson	Eighth	83 —	104
1932	Dugdale Field	Ernie Johnson	Sixth	90 —	95
	Civic Stadium	George Burns			
1933	Civic Stadium	George Burns	Eighth	65 —	119
1934	Civic Stadium	George Burns	Sixth	81 —	102
		Dutch Ruether			
1935	Civic Stadium	Dutch Ruether	Sixth	80 —	93
1936	Civic Stadium	Dutch Ruether	Fourth	93 —	82
1937	Civic Stadium	Johnny Bassler	Sixth	81 —	96
1938	Sick's Stadium	Jack Lelivelt	Second	100 —	75
1939	**Sick's Stadium**	**JACK LELIVELT**	**FIRST**	**101 —**	**73**
1940	**Sick's Stadium**	**JACK LELIVELT**	**FIRST**	**112 —**	**66**
1941	**Sick's Stadium**	**BILL SKIFF**	**FIRST**	**104 —**	**70**
1942	Sick's Stadium	Bill Skiff	Third	96 —	82
1943	Sick's Stadium	Bill Skiff	Third	85 —	70
1944	Sick's Stadium	Bill Skiff	Fifth	84 —	85
1945	Sick's Stadium	Bill Skiff	Second	105 —	78
1946	Sick's Stadium	Bill Skiff	Seventh	74 —	109
		Jo Jo White			
1947	Sick's Stadium	Jo Jo White	Fifth	91 —	95
1948	Sick's Stadium	Jo Jo White	Fourth	93 —	95
1949	Sick's Stadium	Jo Jo White	Fifth	95 —	93
		Bill Lawrence			
1950	Sick's Stadium	Paul Richards	Sixth	96 —	104
1951	**Sick's Stadium**	**ROGERS HORNSBY**	**FIRST**	**99 —**	**68**
1952	Sick's Stadium	Bill Sweeney	Third	96 —	84
1953	Sick's Stadium	Bill Sweeney	Second	98 —	82
1954	Sick's Stadium	Jerry Priddy	Fifth	77 —	85
1955	**Sick's Stadium**	**FRED HUTCHINSON**	**FIRST**	**95 —**	**77**
1956	Sick's Stadium	Luke Sewell	Second	91 —	77
1957	Sick's Stadium	Lefty O'Doul	Fifth	87 —	80

FRANCHISE – SEATTLE (cont.)

YR	HOME PARK	MANAGER	FINISH	RECORD
		FRANCHISE RECORD		3530 – 3578
				.497

FRANCHISE – VERNON/VENICE/VERNON/ MISSION/HOLLYWOOD (1909–1957)

YR	HOME PARK	MANAGER	FINISH	RECORD
1909	Maier Park	Happy Hogan	Sixth	80 – 131
1910	Maier Park	Happy Hogan	Fourth	113 – 107
1911	Maier Park	Happy Hogan	Second	118 – 88
1912	Maier Park	Happy Hogan	Second	118 – 83

FRANCHISE MOVED TO VENICE

YR	HOME PARK	MANAGER	FINISH	RECORD
1913	Washington & Venice	Happy Hogan	Third	107 – 102
1914	Washington & Venice	Happy Hogan	Fourth	113 – 98

FRANCHISE MOVED BACK TO VERNON

YR	HOME PARK	MANAGER	FINISH	RECORD
1915	Maier/Wash Park	Happy Hogan	Fourth	102 – 104
		Dick Bayless		
		Doc White		
1916	Maier/Wash Park	Ham Patterson	Second	115 – 91
1917	Maier/Wash Park	George Stovall	Sixth	84 – 128
1918	**Maier/Wash Park**	**BILL ESSICK**	**FIRST**	**58 – 44**
1919	**Maier/Wash Park**	**BILL ESSICK**	**FIRST**	**111 – 70**
1920	**Maier/Wash Park**	**BILL ESSICK**	**FIRST**	**110 – 88**
1921	Maier/Wash Park	Bill Essick	Sixth	96 – 90
1922	Maier/Wash Park	Bill Essick	Second	123 – 76
1923	Maier/Wash Park	Bill Essick	Eighth	77 – 122
1924	Maier/Wash Park	Bill Essick	Sixth	97 – 104
1925	Maier/Wash Park	Bill Essick	Eighth	80 – 120
		Rube Ellis		

FRANCHISE MOVED TO SAN FRANCISCO–BECAME MISSION

YR	HOME PARK	MANAGER	FINISH	RECORD
1926	Recreation Park	Walter Mc Creedie	Third	106 – 94
		Walter Schmidt		
		Bill Leard		
1927	Recreation Park	Bill Leard	Seventh	86 – 110
		Harry Hooper		
1928	Recreation Park	Red Killefer	Fourth	99 – 92
1929	**Recreation Park**	**RED KILLEFER**	**FIRST**	**123 – 78**
1930	Recreation Park	Red Killefer	Seventh	91 – 110

FRANCHISE – VERNON/VENICE/VERNON/ MISSION/HOLLYWOOD (cont.)

YR	HOME PARK	MANAGER	FINISH	RECORD
1931	Seals Stadium	George Burns	Seventh	84 – 103
		Joe Devine		
1932	Seals Stadium	Joe Devine	Eighth	71 – 117
		Fred Hofmann		
1933	Seals Stadium	Fred Hofmann	Seventh	79 – 108
1934	Seals Stadium	Gabby Street	Second	101 – 85
1935	Seals Stadium	Gabby Street	Fifth	87 – 87
1936	Seals Stadium	Willie Kamm	Fifth	88 – 88
1937	Seals Stadium	Willie Kamm	Eighth	73 – 105

FRANCHISE MOVED TO HOLLYWOOD

YR	HOME PARK	MANAGER	FINISH	RECORD
1938	Wrigley Field	Red Killefer	Seventh	79 – 99
1939	Gilmore Stadium/	Red Killefer	Sixth	82 – 94
	Gilmore Field			
1940	Gilmore Field	Bill Sweeney	Sixth	84 – 94
1941	Gilmore Field	Bill Sweeney	Fourth	85 – 91
1942	Gilmore Field	Oscar Vitt	Seventh	75 – 103
1943	Gilmore Field	Charlie Root	Fifth	73 – 82
1944	Gilmore Field	Charlie Root	Sixth	83 – 86
1945	Gilmore Field	Buck Fausett	Eighth	73 – 110
1946	Gilmore Field	Buck Fausett	Third	95 – 88
		Jimmy Dykes		
1947	Gilmore Field	Jimmy Dykes	Sixth	88 – 98
1948	Gilmore Field	Jimmy Dykes	Sixth	84 – 104
		Lou Stringer		
		Mule Haas		
1949	**Gilmore Field**	**FRED HANEY**	**FIRST**	**109 – 78**
1950	Gilmore Field	Fred Haney	Third	104 – 96
1951	Gilmore Field	Fred Haney	Second	93 – 74
1952	**Gilmore Field**	**FRED HANEY**	**FIRST**	**109 – 71**
1953	**Gilmore Field**	**BOBBY BRAGAN**	**FIRST**	**106 – 74**
1954	Gilmore Field	Bobby Bragan	Second	101 – 68
1955	Gilmore Field	Bobby Bragan	Third	91 – 81
1956	Gilmore Field	Clay Hopper	Fourth	85 – 83
1957	Gilmore Field	Clyde King	Third	94 – 74

VERNON RECORD		1482 – 1446
VENICE RECORD		220 – 200
MISSION RECORD		1088 – 1177
HOLLYWOOD RECORD		1793 – 1748

FRANCHISE RECORD		4583 – 4571
		.501

SECTION V

Yearly Standings

This section shows the annual standings of the Pacific Coast League during the years 1903 through 1957. Split-season standings are not shown. In years that featured a split-season schedule, the first-half winner is noted with a (1) next to the team name. The second-half winner is noted with a (2).

For seasons in which playoffs were held, the playoff winner is shown in boldface type.

1903

	W	–	L	PCT
Los Angeles	133	–	78	.630
Sacramento	105	–	105	.500
Seattle	98	–	100	.495
San Francisco	107	–	110	.493
Portland	95	–	108	.468
Oakland	89	–	126	.414

1904

	W	–	L	PCT
Tacoma (1)(2)	130	–	94	.580
Los Angeles	119	–	97	.551
Seattle	114	–	106	.518
Oakland	116	–	109	.516
San Francisco	101	–	117	463
Portland	79	–	136	.367

1905

	W	–	L	PCT
Los Angeles (2)	120	–	94	.561
San Francisco	125	–	100	.556
Tacoma (1)	106	–	107	.498
Oakland	103	–	119	.464
Portland	94	–	110	.461
Seattle	93	–	111	.456

1906

	W	–	L	PCT
Portland	115	–	60	.657
Seattle	99	–	83	.544
Los Angeles	95	–	87	.522
San Francisco	91	–	84	.520
Oakland	77	–	110	.412
Fresno	64	–	117	.354

1907

	W	–	L	PCT
Los Angeles	115	–	74	.608
San Francisco	104	–	99	.512
Oakland	97	–	101	.490
Portland	72	–	114	.387

1908

	W	–	L	PCT
Los Angeles	110	–	78	.585
Portland	95	–	90	.514
San Francisco	100	–	104	.490
Oakland	83	–	116	.417

1909

	W	–	L	PCT
San Francisco	132	–	80	.623
Portland	112	–	87	.563
Los Angeles	118	–	97	.549
Sacramento	97	–	107	.475
Oakland	88	–	125	.413
Vernon	80	–	131	.379

1910

	W	–	L	PCT
Portland	114	–	87	.567
Oakland	122	–	98	.555
San Francisco	114	–	106	.518
Vernon	113	–	107	.514
Los Angeles	101	–	121	.455
Sacramento	83	–	128	.393

1911

	W	–	L	PCT
Portland	113	–	79	.589
Vernon	118	–	88	.573
Oakland	111	–	99	.529
Sacramento	95	–	109	.466
San Francisco	95	–	112	.459
Los Angeles	82	–	127	.392

1912

	W	–	L	PCT
Oakland	120	–	83	.591
Vernon	118	–	83	.587
Los Angeles	110	–	93	.542
Portland	85	–	100	.459
San Francisco	89	–	115	.436
Sacramento	73	–	121	.376

1913

	W – L	PCT
Portland	109 – 86	.559
Sacramento	103 – 94	.523
Venice	107 – 102	.512
San Francisco	104 – 103	.502
Los Angeles	100 – 108	.481
Oakland	90 – 120	.429

1914

	W – L	PCT
Portland	113 – 84	.574
Los Angeles	116 – 94	.552
San Francisco	115 – 96	.545
Venice	113 – 98	.536
Sac–Mission	90 – 121	.427
Oakland	79 – 133	.373

1915

	W – L	PCT
San Francisco	118 – 89	.570
Salt Lake City	108 – 89	.548
Los Angeles	110 – 98	.529
Vernon	102 – 104	.495
Oakland	93 – 113	.451
Portland	78 – 116	.402

1916

	W – L	PCT
Los Angeles	119 – 79	.601
Vernon	115 – 91	.558
Salt Lake City	99 – 96	.508
San Francisco	104 – 102	.505
Portland	93 – 98	.487
Oakland	72 – 136	.346

1917

	W – L	PCT
San Francisco	119 – 93	.561
Los Angeles	116 – 94	.552
Salt Lake City	102 – 97	.513
Portland	98 – 102	.490
Oakland	103 – 108	.488
Vernon	84 – 128	.396

1918

	W – L	PCT
Vernon	58 – 44	.569
Los Angeles	57 – 47	.548
San Francisco	51 – 51	.500
Sacramento	48 – 48	.500
Salt Lake City	48 – 49	.495
Oakland	40 – 63	.388

1919

	W – L	PCT
Vernon	111 – 70	.613
Los Angeles	108 – 72	.600
Salt Lake City	88 – 83	.515
Sacramento	85 – 83	.506
Oakland	86 – 96	.473
San Francisco	84 – 94	.472
Portland	78 – 96	.448
Seattle	62 – 108	.365

1920

	W – L	PCT
Vernon	110 – 88	.556
Seattle	102 – 91	.528
Los Angeles	102 – 95	.518
San Francisco	103 – 96	.518
Salt Lake City	95 – 92	.508
Oakland	95 – 103	.480
Sacramento	89 – 109	.449
Portland	81 – 103	.440

1921

	W – L	PCT
Los Angeles	108 – 80	.574
Sacramento	105 – 80	.568
San Francisco	106 – 82	.564
Seattle	103 – 82	.557
Oakland	101 – 85	.543
Vernon	96 – 90	.516
Salt Lake City	73 – 110	.399
Portland	51 – 134	.276

1922

	W	–	L	PCT
San Francisco	127	–	72	.638
Vernon	123	–	76	.618
Los Angeles	111	–	88	.558
Salt Lake City	95	–	106	.473
Seattle	90	–	107	.457
Oakland	88	–	112	.440
Portland	87	–	112	.437
Sacramento	76	–	124	.380

1926

	W	–	L	PCT
Los Angeles	121	–	81	.599
Oakland	111	–	92	.547
Mission	106	–	94	.530
Portland	100	–	101	.498
Sacramento	99	–	102	.493
Hollywood	94	–	107	.468
Seattle	89	–	111	.445
San Francisco	84	–	116	.420

1923

	W	–	L	PCT
San Francisco	124	–	77	.617
Sacramento	112	–	87	.563
Portland	107	–	89	.546
Seattle	99	–	97	.505
Salt Lake City	94	–	105	.472
Los Angeles	93	–	109	.460
Oakland	91	–	111	.450
Vernon	77	–	122	.387

1927

	W	–	L	PCT
Oakland	120	–	75	.615
San Francisco	106	–	90	.541
Seattle	98	–	92	.516
Sacramento	100	–	95	.513
Portland	95	–	95	.500
Hollywood	92	–	104	.469
Mission	85	–	110	.430
Los Angeles	80	–	116	.408

1924

	W	–	L	PCT
Seattle	109	–	91	.545
Los Angeles	107	–	92	.538
San Francisco	108	–	93	.537
Oakland	103	–	99	.510
Salt Lake City	101	–	100	.502
Vernon	97	–	104	.483
Portland	88	–	110	.444
Sacramento	88	–	112	.440

1928

	W	–	L	PCT
San Francisco(1)	120	–	71	.628
Hollywood	112	–	79	.586
Sacramento (2)	112	–	79	.586
Mission	99	–	92	.518
Oakland	91	–	100	.476
Los Angeles	87	–	104	.433
Portland	79	–	112	.414
Seattle	64	–	127	.335

1925

	W	–	L	PCT
San Francisco	128	–	71	.643
Salt Lake City	116	–	84	.580
Seattle	103	–	91	.531
Los Angeles	105	–	93	.530
Portland	92	–	104	.469
Oakland	88	–	112	.440
Sacramento	82	–	119	.408
Vernon	80	–	120	.400

1929

	W	–	L	PCT
Mission (1)	123	–	78	.612
San Francisco	114	–	87	.567
Hollywood (2)	113	–	89	.559
Oakland	111	–	91	.550
Los Angeles	104	–	98	.515
Portland	90	–	112	.446
Sacramento	85	–	117	.421
Seattle	67	–	135	.332

1930

	W – L	PCT
Hollywood (2)	119 – 81	.595
Los Angeles (1)	113 – 84	.574
Sacramento	102 – 96	.515
San Francisco	101 – 98	.508
Oakland	97 – 103	.485
Seattle	92 – 107	.462
Mission	91 – 110	.453
Portland	81 – 117	.409

1931

	W – L	PCT
San Francisco(2)	107 – 80	.572
Hollywood (1)	104 – 83	.556
Portland	100 – 87	.535
Los Angeles	98 – 89	.524
Oakland	86 – 101	.460
Sacramento	86 – 101	.460
Mission	84 – 103	.449
Seattle	83 – 104	.444

1932

	W – L	PCT
Portland	111 – 78	.587
Hollywood	106 – 83	.561
Sacramento	101 – 88	.534
San Francisco	96 – 90	.516
Los Angeles	96 – 93	.508
Seattle	90 – 95	.486
Oakland	80 – 107	.428
Mission	71 – 117	.378

1933

	W – L	PCT
Los Angeles	114 – 73	.610
Portland	105 – 77	.577
Hollywood	107 – 80	.572
Sacramento	96 – 85	.530
Oakland	93 – 92	.503
San Francisco	81 – 106	.433
Mission	79 – 108	.422
Seattle	65 – 119	.353

1934

	W – L	PCT
Los Angeles (1)(2)	137 – 50	.733
Mission	101 – 85	.543
Hollywood	97 – 88	.524
San Francisco	93 – 95	.495
Oakland	90 – 98	.479
Seattle	81 – 102	.443
Sacramento	79 – 109	.420
Portland	66 – 117	.361

1935

	W – L	PCT
San Francisco(2)	103 – 70	.595
Los Angeles (1)	98 – 76	.563
Oakland	91 – 83	.523
Portland	87 – 86	.503
Mission	87 – 87	.500
Seattle	80 – 93	.462
Sacramento	75 – 100	.429
Hollywood	73 – 99	.424

1936

	W – L	PCT
Portland	96 – 79	.549
Oakland	95 – 81	.540
San Diego	95 – 81	.540
Seattle	93 – 82	.531
Los Angeles	88 – 88	.500
Mission	88 – 88	.500
San Francisco	83 – 93	.472
Sacramento	65 – 111	.369

1937

	W – L	PCT
Sacramento	102 – 76	.573
San Francisco	98 – 80	.551
San Diego	97 – 81	.545
Portland	90 – 86	.511
Los Angeles	90 – 88	.506
Seattle	81 – 96	.458
Oakland	79 – 98	.446
Mission	73 – 105	.388

1938

	W – L	PCT
Los Angeles	105 – 73	.590
Seattle	100 – 75	.571
Sacramento	95 – 82	.537
San Francisco	93 – 85	.522
San Diego	92 – 85	.520
Portland	79 – 96	.451
Hollywood	79 – 99	.444
Oakland	65 – 113	.365

1942

	W – L	PCT
Sacramento	105 – 73	.590
Los Angeles	104 – 74	.584
Seattle	96 – 82	.539
San Diego	91 – 87	.511
San Francisco	88 – 90	.494
Oakland	85 – 92	.480
Hollywood	75 – 103	.421
Portland	67 – 110	.379

1939

	W – L	PCT
Seattle	101 – 73	.580
San Francisco	97 – 78	.554
Los Angeles	97 – 79	.551
Sacramento	88 – 88	.500
San Diego	83 – 93	.472
Hollywood	82 – 94	.466
Oakland	78 – 98	.443
Portland	75 – 98	.434

1943

	W – L	PCT
Los Angeles	110 – 45	.710
San Francisco	89 – 66	.574
Seattle	85 – 70	.548
Portland	79 – 76	.510
Hollywood	73 – 82	.471
Oakland	73 – 82	.471
San Diego	70 – 85	.452
Sacramento	41 – 114	.265

1940

	W – L	PCT
Seattle	112 – 66	.629
Los Angeles	102 – 75	.576
Oakland	94 – 84	.528
San Diego	92 – 85	.520
Sacramento	90 – 88	.506
Hollywood	84 – 94	.472
San Francisco	81 – 97	.455
Portland	56 – 122	.315

1944

	W – L	PCT
Los Angeles	99 – 70	.586
Portland	87 – 82	.515
San Francisco	86 – 83	.509
Oakland	86 – 83	.509
Seattle	84 – 85	.497
Hollywood	83 – 86	.491
Sacramento	76 – 93	.450
San Diego	75 – 94	.444

1941

	W – L	PCT
Seattle	104 – 70	.598
Sacramento	102 – 75	.576
San Diego	101 – 76	.571
Hollywood	85 – 91	.483
San Francisco	81 – 95	.460
Oakland	81 – 95	.460
Los Angeles	72 – 98	.424
Portland	71 – 97	.424

1945

	W – L	PCT
Portland	112 – 68	.622
Seattle	105 – 78	.574
Sacramento	95 – 85	.528
San Francisco	96 – 87	.525
Oakland	90 – 93	.492
San Diego	82 – 101	.448
Los Angeles	76 – 107	.415
Hollywood	73 – 110	.399

1946

	W – L	PCT
San Francisco	115 – 68	.628
Oakland	111 – 72	.607
Hollywood	95 – 88	.519
Los Angeles	94 – 89	.514
Sacramento	94 – 92	.505
San Diego	78 – 108	.419
Portland	74 – 109	.404
Seattle	74 – 109	.404

1947

	W – L	PCT
Los Angeles	106 – 81	.567
San Francisco	105 – 82	.561
Portland	97 – 89	.522
Oakland	96 – 90	.516
Seattle	91 – 95	.489
Hollywood	88 – 98	.473
Sacramento	83 – 103	.446
San Diego	79 – 107	.425

1948

	W – L	PCT
Oakland	114 – 74	.606
San Francisco	112 – 76	.596
Los Angeles	102 – 86	.543
Seattle	93 – 95	.495
Portland	89 – 99	.473
Hollywood	84 – 104	.447
San Diego	83 – 105	.441
Sacramento	75 – 113	.399

1949

	W – L	PCT
Hollywood	109 – 78	.583
Oakland	104 – 83	.556
Sacramento	102 – 85	.545
San Diego	96 – 92	.511
Seattle	95 – 93	.505
Portland	85 – 102	.455
San Francisco	84 – 103	.449
Los Angeles	74 – 113	.396

1950

	W – L	PCT
Oakland	118 – 82	.590
San Diego	114 – 86	.570
Hollywood	104 – 96	.520
Portland	101 – 99	.505
San Francisco	100 – 100	.500
Seattle	96 – 104	.480
Los Angeles	86 – 114	.430
Sacramento	81 – 119	.405

1951

	W – L	PCT
Seattle	99 – 68	.593
Hollywood	93 – 74	.557
Los Angeles	86 – 81	.515
Portland	83 – 85	.494
Oakland	80 – 88	.476
San Diego	79 – 88	.473
Sacramento	75 – 92	.449
San Francisco	74 – 93	.443

1952

	W – L	PCT
Hollywood	109 – 71	.606
Oakland	104 – 76	.578
Seattle	96 – 84	.533
Portland	92 – 88	.511
San Diego	88 – 92	.489
Los Angeles	87 – 93	.483
San Francisco	78 – 102	.433
Sacramento	66 – 114	.367

1953

	W – L	PCT
Hollywood	106 – 74	.589
Seattle	98 – 82	.544
Los Angeles	93 – 87	.517
Portland	92 – 88	.511
San Francisco	91 – 89	.506
San Diego	88 – 92	.489
Oakland	77 – 103	.428
Sacramento	75 – 105	.417

1954

	W	–	L	PCT
San Diego	102	–	67	.604
Hollywood	101	–	68	.598
Oakland	85	–	82	.509
San Francisco	84	–	84	.500
Seattle	77	–	85	.475
Los Angeles	73	–	92	.442
Sacramento	73	–	94	.437
Portland	71	–	94	.430

1956

	W	–	L	PCT
Los Angeles	107	–	61	.637
Seattle	91	–	77	.542
Hollywood	86	–	82	.512
Portland	85	–	83	.506
Sacramento	84	–	84	.500
San Francisco	77	–	88	.467
San Diego	72	–	96	.429
Vancouver	67	–	98	.406

1955

	W	–	L	PCT
Seattle	95	–	77	.552
San Diego	92	–	80	.535
Hollywood	91	–	81	.529
Los Angeles	91	–	81	.529
Portland	86	–	86	.500
San Francisco	80	–	92	.465
Oakland	77	–	95	.448
Sacramento	76	–	96	.442

1957

	W	–	L	PCT
San Francisco	101	–	67	.601
Vancouver	97	–	70	.581
Hollywood	94	–	74	.560
San Diego	89	–	79	.530
Seattle	87	–	80	.521
Los Angeles	80	–	88	.476
Sacramento	63	–	105	.375
Portland	60	–	108	.357

SECTION VI

Individual Leaders — Offense

On the following seven pages are listed the leaders, by year, in the Pacific Coast League for 12 different offensive categories during the years 1903 through 1957. Information for some categories is not available for all seasons; for those years in which records are unavailable, that notation is made within the category along with the years affected.

Below are the single-season records for each of the categories listed in this section:

Batting Average:	Ox Eckhardt, Mission .414 (1933)
Hits:	Paul Strand, Salt Lake City 325 (1923)
Doubles:	Paul Waner, San Francisco 75 (1925)
Triples:	Truck Eagan, Sacramento 24 (1903)
	Brooks Holder, San Francisco 24 (1939)
Home Runs:	Tony Lazzeri, Salt Lake City 60 (1925)
Runs Batted In:	Tony Lazzeri, Salt Lake City 222 (1925)
Stolen Bases:	Jimmy Johnston, San Francisco 124 (1913)
Runs Scored:	Tony Lazzeri, Salt Lake City 202 (1925)
Total Bases:	Ike Boone, Mission 553 (1929)
Bases on Balls:	Max West, San Diego 201 (1949)
Strikeouts:	Steve Bilko, Los Angeles 150 (1957)
Sacrifice Hits:	Buzzy Wares, Oakland 74 (1910)

BATTING AVERAGE

1903	Harry Lumley, Sea	.387
1904	Emil Frisk, Sea	.337
1905	Kitty Brashear, LA	.303
1906	Mike Mitchell, Port	.351
1907	Truck Eagan, Oak	.335
1908	Babe Danzig, Port	.298
1909	Henry Melchoir, SF	.298
1910	Hunky Shaw, SF	.281
1911	Bud Ryan, Port	.333
1912	Heine Heitmuller, LA	.335
1913	Dick Bayless, Ver	.324
1914	Harry Wolter, LA	.328
1915	Harry Wolter, LA	.359
1916	Duke Kenworthy, Oak	.314
1917	Morrie Rath, SLC	.341
1918	Art Griggs, Sac	.378
1919	Bill Rumler, SLC	.002
1920	Earl Sheely, SLC	.371
1921	Hack Miller, Oak	.347
1922	Paul Strand, SLC	.384
1923	Paul Strand, SLC	.394
1924	Duffy Lewis, SLC	.392
1925	Paul Waner, SF	.401
1926	Bill Bagwell, Port	.391
1927	Smead Jolley, SF	.397
1928	Smead Jolley, SF	.404
1929	Ike Boone, Miss	.407
1930	Earl Sheely, SF	.403
1931	Ox Eckhardt, Miss	.369
1932	Ox Eckhardt, Miss	.371
1933	Ox Eckhardt, Miss	.414
1934	Frank Demaree, LA	.383
1935	Ox Eckhardt, Miss	.399
1936	Joe Marty, SF	.359
1937	Harlin Pool, Sea	.334
1938	Smead Jolley, Hol–Oak	.350
1939	Dom Dallessandro, SD	.368
1940	Lou Novikoff, LA	.363
1941	Johnny Moore, LA	.331
1942	Ted Norbert, Port	.378
1943	Andy Pafko, LA	.356
1944	Les Scarsella, Oak	.329
1945	Jo Jo White, Sac	.355
1946	Harvey Storey, LA–Port	.326
1947	Hilly Layne, Sea	.367
1948	Gene Woodling, SF	.385
1949	Artie Wilson, SD–Oak	.348

BATTING AVERAGE (cont.)

1950	Frankie Baumholtz, LA	.379
1951	Jim Rivera, Sea	.352
1952	Bob Boyd, Sac	.320
1953	Bob Dillinger, Sac	.366
1954	Harry Elliott, SD	.350
1955	George Metkovich, Oak	.335
1956	Steve Bilko, LA	.360
1957	Ken Aspromonte, SF	.334

HITS

1903	Deacon Van Buren, Sea	281
1904	Emil Frisk, Sea	272
1905	Lou Nordyke, Tac	227
1906	Art Kruger, Oak	211
1907	Truck Eagan, Oak	237
1908	Heine Heitmuller, Oak	225
1909	Chick Gandil, Sac	214
1910	Tom Tennant, SF	231
1911	Bud Ryan, Port	247
1912	Dick Bayless, Ver	228
1913	Bill Rodgers, Port	239
1914	Harry Wolter, LA	263
1915	Jimmy Johnston, Oak	274
1916	Finners Quinlan, SLC	241
1917	Johnny Tobin, SLC	265
1918	Hack Miller, Oak	131
1919	Sam Crawford, LA	239
1920	Hack Miller, Oak	280
1921	Paddy Siglin, SLC	270
1922	Paul Strand, SLC	289
1923	Paul Strand, SLC	325
1924	Babe Ellison, SF	307
1925	Lefty O'Doul, SLC	309
1926	Jigger Statz, LA	291
1927	Lefty O'Doul, SF	278
1928	Smead Jolley, SF	309
1929	Ike Boone, Miss	323
1930	Earl Sheely, SF	289
1931	Ed Coleman, Port	275
	Ox Eckhardt, Miss	275
1932	Lou Finney, Port	268
1933	Ox Eckhardt, Miss	315
1934	Frank Demaree, LA	269
1935	Ox Eckhardt, Miss	283
1936	Bobby Doerr, SD	238
1937	Nino Bongiovanni, Port	236

HITS (cont.)

1938	Rip Russell, LA	216
1939	Dom Di Maggio, SF	239
1940	Lou Novikoff, LA	259
1941	Nanny Fernandez, SF	231
1942	Eddie Waitkus, LA	235
1943	Andy Pafko, LA	215
1944	Les Scarsella, Oak	196
1945	Jo Jo White, Sac	244
1946	Bill Ramsey, Sea–Sac	219
1947	Tony Lupien, Hol	237
1948	Gus Zernial, Hol	237
1949	Al White, Sac	244
1950	Artie Wilson, Oak	264
1951	Jim Rivera, Sea	231
1952	Artie Wilson, Sea	216
1953	Bob Dillinger, Sac	236
1954	Harry Elliott, SD	224
1955	Nippy Jones, Sac	206
1956	Steve Bilko, LA	215
1957	Jim Marshall, Van	188

DOUBLES

1903	Charles Schwartz, O–Sea	58
1904	Truck Eagan, Tac	52
	Carlos Smith, Sea	52
1905	Lou Nordyke, Tac	57
1906	Gavvy Cravath, LA	33
1907	Gavvy Cravath, LA	45
	Truck Eagan, Oak	45
1908	Babe Danzig, Port	39
	Heine Heitmuller, Oak	39
1909	William Hogan, Oak	50
1910	Walter Carlisle, Ver	49
1911	Art Kruger, Port	57
1912	Louis Litschi, Ver	52
1913	Tom Tennant, Sac	47
1914	Art Kores, Port	54
1915	Joe Gedeon, SLC	67
1916	Duke Kenworthy, Oak	54
1917	Lloyd Farmer, Port	50
	Biff Schaller, SF	50
1918	Brick Eldred, SLC	26
	Jack Fournier, LA	26
1919	Bill Rumler, SLC	42
1920	Brick Eldred, Sea	59
1921	Paddy Siglin, SLC	67

DOUBLES (cont.)

1922	Paddy Siglin, SLC	60
1923	Les Sheehan, SLC	72
1924	Roy Leslie, SLC	73
1925	Paul Waner, SF	75
1926	Jigger Statz, LA	68
1927	Buzz Arlett, Oak	54
	Edward Rose, Miss	54
1928	Gus Suhr, SF	64
1929	Buzz Arlett, Oak	70
1930	Dutch Holland, Sea	72
1931	Ed Coleman, Port	53
	Billy Rhiel, Port	53
1932	Art Garibaldi, SF	57
1933	Prince Oana, SF	63
1934	Art Garibaldi, SF	56
1935	Moose Clabaugh, Port	56
	Jim Oglesby, LA	56
1936	Steve Mesner, LA	55
1937	Buster Adams, Sac	49
1938	Dick Gyselman, Sea	53
1939	Allan Strange, Sea	55
1940	George Archie, Sea	46
1941	Nanny Fernandez, SF	46
	Jack Sturdy, Sac	46
1942	Buster Adams, Sac	43
	Kermit Lewis, SF	43
1943	Bill Schuster, LA	42
1944	Bill Matheson, Sea	36
	Gus Suhr, SF	36
	Ed Wheeler, SD	36
1945	Cyril Moran, Hol	56
1946	Steve Mesner, Sac	49
1947	Harvey Storey, Port	51
1948	Lou Stringer, Hol	50
1949	Leo Thomas, Port	43
1950	Frankie Baumholtz, LA	53
1951	Jim Rivera, Sea	40
1952	Walt Judnich, Sea	41
1953	Bob Usher, LA	51
1954	Harry Elliott, SD	42
1955	Gene Mauch, LA	37
1956	Bobby Balcena, Sea	38
1957	Bobby Balcena, Sea	40

TRIPLES

1903	Truck Eagan, Sac	24

TRIPLES (cont.)

1904	Emil Frisk, Sea	14
1905	George Hildebrand, SF	11
	Joe Nealon, SF	11
1906	Heine Heitmuller, Sea–Oak	14
1907	Walter Mc Creedie, Port	12
1908	Otis Johnson, Port	17
1909	Chick Gandil, Sac	16
1910	Walter Carlisle, Ver	10
	Henry Perry, Sac	10
1911	Walter Carlisle, Ver	17
1912	Johnny Kane, Ver	16
1913	Ivan Howard, LA	23
	Harl Maggert, LA	23
1914	Art Kores, Port	21
	Harry Wolter, LA	21
1915	Walter Carlisle, Port–Ver	14
	Harl Maggert, LA	14
1916	Ray Bates, Ver	12
	Phil Koerner, LA	12
	Harry Wolter, LA	12
1917	Floyd Farmer, Port	12
	Hack Miller, Oak	12
	Rod Murphy, Oak	12
	Denis Wilie, Port	12
1918	Jack Fournier, LA	13
1919	Jack Fournier, LA	19
1920	Sam Crawford, LA	21
1921	Dixie Carroll, LA	22
1922	Nelson Hawks, Ver	15
1923	Pete Schneider, Ver	23
1924	Buzz Arlett, Oak	19
1925	Lefty O'Doul, SLC	17
1926	Jigger Statz, LA	18
1927	Jimmie Reese, Oak	17
1928	Roy Johnson, SF	16
1929	Ox Eckhardt, Miss	17
1930	Jess Hill, Hol	13
1931	Prince Oana, SF	16
	Ernie Sulik, SF	16
1932	Lou Almada, Miss	16
1933	Augie Galan, SF	22
1934	Marv Gudat, LA	13
	Jigger Statz, LA	13
1935	Joe Di Maggio, SF	18
1936	John Glynn, Oak	16
1937	Ernie Koy, Oak	16
1938	Max Marshall, Sac	14

TRIPLES (cont.)

1939	Brooks Holder, SF	24
1940	John Barrett, SF	22
1941	Nanny Fernandez, SF	16
	Jo Jo White, Sea	16
1942	Debs Garms, Sac	13
	Ralph Hodgin, SF	13
	Roy Hughes, Oak	13
	Mel Mazzera, SD	13
1943	Andy Pafko, LA	13
	Harold Patchett, SD	13
1944	Bill Ramsey, Sac	12
1945	John O'Neil, Port	13
1946	Danny Escobar, Port	11
1947	Johnny Rucker, Sea–Sac	19
1948	Gene Woodling, SF	13
1949	Al White, Sac	10
1950	Luis Marquez, Port	19
	Harry Simpson, SD	19
1951	George Schmees, Hol	17
1952	Bob Boyd, Sea	18
1953	Artie Wilson, Sea	14
1954	Artie Wilson, Sea	16
1955	Billy Hall, Hol	9
	Milt Smith, SD	9
	Jerry Streeter, Sac	9
1956	Carlos Bernier, Hol	15
1957	Albie Pearson, SF	11

HOME RUNS

1903	Truck Eagan, Sac	13
1904	Truck Eagan, Tac	25
1905	Truck Eagan, Tac	21
1906	Mike Mitchell, Port	6
1907	Walter Carlisle, LA	14
1908	Heine Heitmuller, Oak	12
1909	Otis Johnson, Port	13
1910	Ping Bodie, SF	30
1911	Bud Ryan, Port	23
1912	Bert Coy, Oak	19
1913	Bert Coy, Oak	18
1914	Ty Lober, Port	9
1915	Biff Schaller, SF	20
1916	Bunny Brief, SLC	33
1917	Ken Williams, Port	24
1918	Art Griggs, Sac	12
	Earl Sheely, SLC	12

HOME RUNS (cont.)

1919	Earl Sheely, SLC	28
1920	Earl Sheely, SLC	33
1921	Paddy Siglin, SLC	22
1922	Paul Strand, SLC	28
1923	Paul Strand, SLC	43
1924	Jim Poole, Port	38
1925	Tony Lazzeri, SLC	60
1926	Elmer Smith, Port	46
1927	Elmer Smith, Port	40
1928	Smead Jolley, SF	45
1929	Ike Boone, Miss	55
1930	Dave Barbee, Sea–Hol	41
1931	Dave Barbee, Hol	47
1932	Fred Muller, Sea	38
1933	Gene Lillard, LA	43
1934	Frank Demaree, LA	45
1935	Gene Lillard, LA	56
1936	Mike Hunt, Sea	30
	Fred Muller, Sea	30
1937	Mike Hunt, Sea	39
1938	Ted Norbert, SF	30
1939	Rip Collins, LA	26
1940	Lou Novikoff, LA	41
1941	Ted Norbert, Port	20
1942	Ted Norbert, Port	28
1943	John Ostrowski, LA	21
1944	Frank Kelleher, Hol	29
1945	Ted Norbert, Sea	23
1946	Loyd Christopher, LA	26
1947	Max West, SD	43
1948	Jack Graham, SD	48
1949	Max West, SD	48
1950	Frank Kelleher, Hol	40
1951	Joe Gordon, Sac	43
1952	Max West, LA	35
1953	Dale Long, Hol	35
1954	Jim Marshall, Oak	31
1955	Steve Bilko, LA	37
1956	Steve Bilko, LA	55
1957	Steve Bilko, LA	56

RUNS BATTED IN

1903–1913	Records Unavailable	
1914	Rube Ellis, LA	120
1915–1920	Records Unavailable	
1921	Hack Miller, Oak	137

RUNS BATTED IN (cont.)

1922	Paul Strand, SLC	138
1923	Paul Strand, SLC	187
1924	Babe Ellison, SF	188
1925	Tony Lazzeri, SLC	222
1926	Buzz Arlett, Oak	140
1927	Smead Jolley, SF	163
1928	Smead Jolley, SF	188
1929	Ike Boone, Miss	218
1930	Earl Sheely, SF	180
1931	Ed Coleman, Port	183
1932	George Burns, Port	140
1933	Joe Di Maggio, SF	169
1934	Frank Demaree, LA	173
1935	Joe Di Maggio, SF	154
1936	Mike Hunt, Sea	135
1937	Mike Hunt, Sea	131
1938	Ted Norbert, SF	163
1939	Rip Collins, LA	128
1940	Lou Novikoff, LA	171
1941	Nanny Fernandez, SF	129
1942	Kermit Lewis, SF	115
1943	Andy Pafko, LA	118
1944	Frank Kelleher, Hol	121
1945	Harold Patchett, Oak–Sea	110
1946	Ferris Fain, SF	112
1947	Max West, SD	124
1948	Gus Zernial, Hol	156
1949	Max West, SD	166
1950	Harry Simpson, SD	156
1951	Joe Gordon, Sac	136
1952	Tookie Gilbert, Oak	118
1953	Dale Long, Hol	116
1954	Jim Marshall, Oak	123
1955	Earl Rapp, SD	133
1956	Steve Bilko, LA	164
1957	Steve Bilko, LA	140

STOLEN BASES

1903	Danny Shay, SF	83
1904	Bob Ganley, Oak	72
1905	Larry Schlafly, Port–LA	77
1906	Johnny Kane, Sea	65
1907	George Hildebrand, SF	59
1908	Rollie Zeider, SF	93
1910	Ivan Howard, LA	77
1911	George Cutshaw, Oak	90

STOLEN BASES (cont.)   RUNS SCORED

1912	Bill Leard, Oak	80		1903	Dummy Hoy, LA	156
1913	Jimmy Johnston, SF	124		1904	Emil Frisk, Sea	179
1914	Bill Rodgers, Port	71		1905	Records Unavailable	
1915	Jimmy Johnston, Oak	82		1906	Henry Spencer, SF	133
1916	Bill Lane, Oak	56		1907	Walter Carlisle, LA	113
1917	Irish Meusel, LA	69		1908	Kid Mohler, SF	118
1918	Charlie Pick, SF	55		1909	Rollie Zeider, SF	141
1919	Bill Lane, Oak	59		1910	Walter Carlisle, Ver	134
1920	Rod Murphy, Sea	63		1911	Walter Carlisle, Ver	181
1921	Patsy Mc Gaffigan, Sac	55		1912	Walter Carlisle, Ver	177
1922	Bill Lane, Sea	60		1913	Harl Maggert, LA	128
1923	Merlin Kopp, Sac	80		1914	Harl Maggert, LA	127
1924	Bill Lane, Sea	45		1915	Harl Maggert, LA	147
1925	Bill Hunnefield, Port	42		1916	Bunny Brief, SLC	149
1926	Evar Swanson, Miss	43		1917	Jack Tobin, SLC	149
1927	Lefty O'Doul, SF	40		1918	Charlie Pick, SF	65
1928	Evar Swanson, Miss	49		1919	Harl Maggert, SLC	127
1929	Fred Haney, LA	56		1920	Denis Wilie, Oak	135
1930	Fred Haney, LA	52		1921	Paddy Siglin, SLC	156
1931	Jigger Statz, LA	45		1922	Bill Lane, Sea	166
1932	Art Garibaldi, SF	49		1923	Paul Strand, SLC	180
1933	Fred Haney, Hol	63		1924	Howard Lindemore, SLC	180
1934	Fred Haney, Hol	71		1925	Tony Lazzeri, SLC	202
1935	Jigger Statz, LA	53		1926	Evar Swanson, Miss	157
1936	Jigger Statz, LA	43		1927	Lefty O'Doul, SF	164
1937	George Myatt, SD	33		1928	Earl Averill, SF	178
1938	Frenchy Uhalt, Hol	32		1929	Gus Suhr, SF	196
1939	Jo Jo White, Sea	47		1930	Frank Crosetti, SF	171
1940	John Barrett, Sea	40		1931	Frank Crosetti, SF	141
1941	Don Gutteridge, Sac	46			John Monroe, Port	141
1942	Barney Olsen, LA	33			Jigger Statz, LA	141
1943	Oral Burnett, Sac	32			Homer Summa, LA	141
1944	Bill Ramsey, Sea	45		1932	Jigger Statz, LA	153
1945	Gene Handley, Sac	56		1933	Augie Galan, SF	164
1946	Ed Sauer, LA	45		1934	Frank Demaree, LA	190
1947	Dain Clay, SD	40		1935	Joe Di Maggio, SF	173
	Tony Lupien Hol	40		1936	Jigger Statz, LA	134
1948	Jackie Tobin, SF	37		1937	Nino Bongiovanni, Port	136
1949	Artie Wilson, SD—Oak	47		1938	Jigger Statz, LA	131
1950	Luis Marquez, Port	38		1939	Dom Di Maggio, SF	165
1951	Bob Boyd, Sac	41		1940	Lou Novikoff, LA	147
1952	Carlos Bernier, Hol	65		1941	Ferris Fain, SF	122
1953	Tom Saffell, Hol	29		1942	Eddie Lake, Sac	118
1954	Tom Saffell, Hol	48		1943	Bill Schuster, LA	117
1955	Carlos Bernier, Hol	29		1944	Cecil Garriott, LA	148
1956	Carlos Bernier, Hol	48		1945	Jo Jo White, Sac	162
1957	Solly Drake, Port	36		1946	Ferris Fain, SF	117

RUNS SCORED (cont.)

1947	Tony Lupien, Hol	147
1948	Dain Clay, SD	133
1949	Max West, SD	166
1950	Artie Wilson, Oak	168
1951	Jim Rivera, Sea	135
1952	Carlos Bernier, Hol	105
1953	Jackie Tobin, Sea	116
1954	Al Federoff, SD	110
1955	Earl Rapp, SD	109
1956	Steve Bilko, LA	163
1957	Steve Bilko, LA	111

TOTAL BASES

1903	Truck Eagan, Sac	405
1904	Emil Frisk, Sea	379
1905	Truck Eagan, Tac	333
1906	Mike Mitchell, Port	276
1907	Truck Eagan, Oak	316
1908	Heine Heitmuller, Oak	302
1909	Chick Gandil, Sac	347
1910	Ping Bodie, SF	336
1911	Bud Ryan, Port	391
1912	Walter Carlisle, Ver	314
1913	Harl Maggert, LA	343
1914	Harry Wolter, LA	362
1915	Joe Gedeon, SLC	380
1916	Bunny Brief, SLC	374
1917	Ken Williams, Port	362
1918	Jack Fournier, LA	194
1919	Sam Crawford, LA	358
1920	Earl Sheely, SLC	420
1921	Paddy Siglin, SLC	409
1922	Paul Strand, SLC	451
1923	Paul Strand, SLC	546
1924	Babe Ellison, SF	496
1925	Tony Lazzeri, SLC	512
1926	Buzz Arlett, Oak	444
1927	Lefty O'Doul, SF	428
1928	Smead Jolley, SF	516
1929	Ike Boone, Miss	553
1930	Dutch Holland, Sea	427
1931	Ed Coleman, Port	467
1932	Pinky Higgins, Port	395
1933	Joe Di Maggio, SF	414
1934	Frank Demaree, LA	384

TOTAL BASES (cont.)

1935	Joe Di Maggio, SF	456
1936	Mike Hunt, Sea	364
1937	Mike Hunt, Sea	368
1938	Ted Norbert, SF	338
	Rip Russell, LA	338
1939	Dom Di Maggio, SF	365
1940	Lou Novikoff, LA	438
1941	Nanny Fernandez, SF	366
1942	Buster Adams, Sac	340
1943	Andy Pafko, LA	326
1944	Frank Kelleher, Hol	285
1945	Jo Jo White, Sac	313
1946	Loyd Christopher, LA	296
1947	Tony Lupien, Hol	362
1948	Gus Zernial, Hol	418
1949	Max West, SD	369
1950	Harry Simpson, SD	403
1951	Jim Rivera, Sea	363
1952	Tookie Gilbert, Oak	298
1953	Fred Richards, LA	335
1954	Harry Elliott, SD	319
1955	Steve Bilko, LA	356
1956	Steve Bilko, LA	410
1957	Steve Bilko, LA	353

BASES ON BALLS

1903 – 1938	Records Unavailable	
1939	Dom Dallessandro, SD	92
1940	Frenchy Uhalt, Hol	101
1941	Ferris Fain, SF	96
1942	Eddie Lake, Sac	107
1943	Rupert Thompson, Port	102
1944	Cecil Garriott, LA	124
1945	Gene Handley, Sac	103
1946	Brooks Holder, Oak	131
1947	Brooks Holder, Oak	136
1948	Cecil Garriott, LA	116
1949	Max West, SD	201
1950	Les Fleming, SF	126
1951	Eddie Lake, SF	112
1952	Joe Brovia, Port	109
1953	Joe Brovia, Sac	105
1954	Al Federoff, SD	108
1955	Earl Rapp, SD	103
1956	Steve Bilko, LA	104
1957	Steve Bilko, LA	108

STRIKEOUTS

1903–1940	Records Unavailable	
1941	Buster Adams, Sac	103
1942	Wally Westlake, Oak	108
1943	John Ostrowski, LA	109
1944	James Hill, Hol	84
1945	Neill Sheridan, SF	89
1946	Alex Kampouris, Sac	116
1947	Lou Stringer, LA	98
1948	Gus Zernial, Hol	130
1949	Jim Baxes, Hol	123
1950	Al Lyons, Sea	108
1951	Ed Barr, Port	101
1952	Lou Stringer, Hol–SD	91
1953	Richard Faber, SD	97
1954	Ted Beard, Hol–SF	97
1955	Steve Bilko, LA	104
1956	Jim Pisoni, Van	138
1957	Steve Bilko, LA	150

SACRIFICE HITS

1903	Deacon Van Buren, Sea	71
1904	Tim Flood, LA	48
1905	Tommy Sheehan, Tac	54
1906	John Gochnaur, SF	46
1907	George Van Haltren, Oak	48
1908	Rebel Oakes, LA	55
1909	Kid Mohler, SF	59
1910	Buzzy Wares, Oak	74
1911	Buzzy Wares, Oak	51
1912	Joe Berger, LA	52
1913	Harold Mc Ardle, SF	50
1914	Charley O'Leary, SF	67
1915	Fred Mc Mullin, LA	48
1916	Gus Gleischmann, Ver	56
1917	Morrie Rath, SLC	58
1918	Zeb Terry, LA	32
1919	Bunny Fabrique, LA–Sea	49
1920	Karl Crandall, SLC	45
1921	Ike Mc Auley, LA	59
1922	Denis Wilie, Oak	54
1923	Walter Mearkle, Sea	43
1924	Cliff Brady, Sea	62
1925	Ray Brubaker, Oak	44
1926	John Monroe, Sac	48
1927	John Kerr, Hol	64
1928	John Kerr, Hol	57

SACRIFICE HITS (cont.)

1929	W. H. Rollings, LA	60
1930	Carl Dittmar, LA	47
1931	Billy Rhiel, Port	32
1932	Floyd Ellsworth, Sea	30
	Augie Galan, SF	30
1933	Eddie Mulligan, Port	41
1934	Hal Rhyne, SF	37
1935	Leroy Anton, Oak	28
1936	Leroy Anton, Oak	26
1937	Dud Lee, Port	34
1938	Bill Lawrence, Sea	23
1939	Charles English, LA	33
1940	Bud Stewart, SD	31
1941	Don Gutteridge, Sac	26
1942	Hugh Luby, Oak	25
	Ned Stickle, Sea	25
1943	Frenchy Uhalt, SF	19
1944	Joe Futernick, SF	38
1945	Bob Gorbould, Sea	30
1946	Lindsay Brown, Port	22
1947	Roy Nicely, SF	22
1948	Gene Handley, SD	29
1949	John O'Neil, Hol	22
1950	Len Ratto, Sac	35
1951	Frank Austin, Port	35
1952	Monty Basgall, Hol	27
1953	Jim Moran, SF	21
1954	Buddy Peterson, SD	39
1955	Dick Smith, Hol	27
1956	Bob Usher, SD	17
1957	Eddie Basinski, Port–Sea	22

SECTION VII

Individual
Leaders — Pitching

On the following pages are listed the leaders, by year, in the Pacific Coast League for 14 different pitching categories, plus a listing of all no-hitters, during the years 1903 through 1957. Information for some categories is not available for all seasons; pitching records are especially sketchy for the years 1903 through 1913. For those years in which records are unavailable, that notation is made within the category along with the years affected.

For the categories of earned run average, opponent batting average, and efficiency, a minimum of 150 innings pitched is necessary to be considered league leader.

Below are the single-season records for each of the categories listed in this section (Jack Quinn's earned run average in 1918 is considered unofficial since the statistics were compiled from box scores, not from league records):

Wins:	Doc Newton, LA 39 (1904)
	Rube Vickers, Sea 39 (1906)
ERA:	Jack Quinn, Ver 1.48 (1918) unofficial
	Slim Love, LA 1.56 (1914) official
Strikeouts:	Rube Vickers, Sea 409 (1906)
Winning Pct:	Fay Thomas, LA .875 (1934)
Shutouts:	Vean Gregg, Port 14 (1910)
Comp Games:	Frank Browning, SF 54 (1909)
Innings:	Rube Vickers, Sea 526 (1906)
Hits Allowed:	Al Klawitter, Oak 415 (1914)
Hit Batsmen:	George Boice, Oak 31 (1909)
Wild Pitches:	Bob Groom, Port 22 (1907)
	Bill Piercy, Sac 22 (1919)
Bases on Balls:	Elmer Ponder, SLC 215 (1925)
Opponent Batting:	Sam Jones, SD .188 (1951)
Losses:	Ike Butler, Port 31 (1903 & 1904)
Efficiency:	Slim Love, LA 0.88 (1914)

WINS

1903	Doc Newton, LA—Port	35
1904	Doc Newton, LA	39
1905	Jimmy Whalen, SF	32
1906	Rube Vickers, Sea	39
1907	Dolly Gray, LA	32
1908	Bob Groom, Port	29
1909	Frank Browning, SF	32
1910	Cack Henley, SF	34
1911	Bill Steen, Port	30
1912	Harry Ables, Oak	25
	Charlie Chech, LA	25
1913	Skeeter Fanning, SF	28
1914	Irv Higginbotham, Port	31
1915	Lefty Williams, SLC	33
1916	Allen Sothoron, Port	30
1917	Eric Erickson, SF	31
1918	Doc Crandall, LA	16
	Walt Leverenz, SLC	16
1919	Doc Crandall, LA	28
1920	Buzz Arlett, Oak	29
1921	Wheezer Dell, Ver	28
1922	Jakie May, Ver	35
1923	Ray Kremer, Oak	25
1924	Oliver Mitchell, SF	28
1925	Clyde Barfoot, Ver	26
1926	Bert Cole, Miss	29
1927	George Boehler, Oak	22
1928	Dutch Ruether, SF	29
1929	Frank Shellenback, Hol	26
1930	Ed Baecht, LA	26
	Jimmy Zinn, SF	26
1931	Sam Gibson, SF	28
1932	Frank Shellenback, Hol	26
1933	Bobo Newsom, LA	30
1934	Fay Thomas, LA	28
1935	Boom Boom Beck, Miss	23
1936	George Caster, Port	25
1937	Ad Liska, Port	24
1938	Fred Hutchinson, Sea	25
1939	Hal Turpin, Sea	23
1940	Dick Barrett, Sea	24
1941	Yank Terry, SD	26
1942	Dick Barrett, Sea	27
1943	Red Lynn, LA	21
1944	Marino Pieretti, Port	26
1945	Bob Joyce, SF	31
1946	Larry Jansen, SF	30

WINS (cont.)

1947	Cliff Chambers, LA	24
1948	Red Lynn, LA	19
1949	Guy Fletcher, Sea	23
	Harold Saltzman, Port	23
	Pinky Woods, Hol	23
1950	Jim Wilson, Sea	24
1951	Bill Ayers, Oak	20
	Marv Grissom, Sea	20
1952	Johnny Lindell, Hol	24
1953	Al Gettel, Oak	24
1954	Roger Bowman, Hol	22
1955	Red Munger, Hol	23
1956	Rene Valdes, Port	22
1957	Leo Kiely, SF	21

EARNED RUN AVERAGE

1914	Slim Love, LA	1.56
1915	Slim Love, LA	1.95
1916	Art Fromme, Ver	1.92
1917	Eric Erickson, SF	1.90
1918	Jack Quinn, Ver	1.48
1919	Curly Brown, LA	2.03
1920	Jim Scott, SF	2.29
1921	Vic Aldridge, LA	2.16
1922	Jakie May, Ver	1.84
1923	Vean Gregg, Sea	2.75
1924	Doc Crandall, LA	2.71
1925	Doug Mc Weeney, SF	2.70
1926	Elmer Jacobs, LA	2.20
1927	Johnny Miljus, Sea	2.36
1928	Elmer Jacobs, SF	2.56
1929	Lefty Gomez, SF	3.43
1930	Ed Baecht, LA	3.23
1931	Sam Gibson, SF	2.48
1932	Curt Davis, SF	2.24
1933	Willie Ludolph, Oak	3.09
1934	Dutch Lieber, Miss	2.50
1935	Mike Meola, LA	3.00
1936	Lou Koupal, Sea	2.42
1937	Bill Shores, SF	2.47
1938	Fred Hutchinson, Sea	2.48
1939	Sam Gibson, SF	2.24
1940	Jack Salveson, Oak	2.30
1941	Yank Terry, SD	2.31
1942	Dick Barrett, Sea	1.72
1943	Al Brazle, Sac	1.69

EARNED RUN AVERAGE (cont.)

1944	Clem Dreisewerd, Sac	1.61
1945	Bob Joyce, SF	2.17
1946	Larry Jansen, SF	1.57
1947	Bob Chesnes, SF	2.32
1948	Con Dempsey, SF	2.10
1949	Willard Ramsdell, Hol	2.60
1950	Jack Salveson, Hol	2.84
1951	Jim Davis, Sea	2.44
1952	Red Adams, Port	2.17
1953	Memo Luna, SD	2.67
1954	Bill Wight, SD	1.93
1955	Red Munger, Hol	1.85
1956	Elmer Singleton, Sea	2.55
1957	Morrie Martin, Van	1.90

STRIKEOUTS

1903	Joe Corbett, LA	198
1904–1905 Records Unavailable		
1906	Rube Vickers, Sea	409
1907	Eli Cates, Oak	226
1908	Rube Suter, SF	256
1909	Jimmy Wiggs, Oak	268
1910	Vean Gregg, Port	377
1911	Rube Suter, SF	339
1912	Harry Ables, Oak	303
1913	Bill James, Port	215
1914	Ed Klepfer, Ven	212
1915	Lefty Williams, SLC	294
1916	Paul Fittery, SLC	203
1917	Eric Erickson, SF	307
1918	Jack Quinn, Ver	99
1919	Bill Piercy, Sac	163
1920	Willie Mitchell, Ver	161
1921	Paul Fittery, Sac	164
1922	Jakie May, Ver	238
1923	Walter Mails, Oak	206
1924	George Boehler, Oak	216
1925	George Boehler, Oak	278
1926	Jumbo Elliott, Sea	203
1927	George Boehler, Oak	160
1928	Elmer Jacobs, SF	159
1929	Howard Craghead, Oak	190
1930	Fay Thomas, Sac	228
1931	Sam Gibson, SF	204
1932	Fay Thomas, Oak	196
1933	Bobo Newsom, LA	212

STRIKEOUTS (cont.)

1934	Fay Thomas, LA	204
1935	Boom Boom Beck, Miss	202
1936	George Caster, Port	234
1937	Manny Salvo, SD	196
1938	Manny Salvo, SD	191
1939	Tony Freitas, Sac	172
1940	Dick Barrett, Sea	164
1941	Yank Terry, SD	172
1942	Dick Barrett, Sea	178
1943	Frank Dasso, SD	154
1944	Frank Dasso, SD	253
1945	Vallie Eaves, SD	187
1946	Eddie Erautt, Hol	234
1947	Cliff Chambers, LA	175
1948	Con Dempsey, SF	171
1949	Con Dempsey, SF	164
1950	Jim Wilson, Sea	228
1951	Sam Jones, SD	246
1952	Johnny Lindell, Hol	190
1953	Joe Hatten, LA	152
1954	Tommy Bryne, Sea	199
1955	Bob Garber, Hol	199
1956	Dick Drott, LA	184
1957	Jim Grant, SD	178

WINNING PERCENTAGE

1903	Doc Newton, LA–Port	.745
1904	Doc Newton, LA	.696
1905	Dolly Gray, LA	.652
1906	Rube Vickers, Sea	.722
1907	Dolly Gray, LA	.696
1908	Walter Nagle, LA	.706
1909	Cack Henley, SF	.756
1910	John Lively, Oak	.674
1911	Bill Steen, Port	.667
1912	John Killilay, Oak	.789
1913	John Williams, Sac	.708
1914	John Ryan, LA	.686
1915	Lefty Williams, SLC	.733
1916	John Ryan, LA	.744
1917	Brad Hogg, LA	.675
1918	Walt Leverenz, SLC	.762
1919	Curly Brown, LA	.758
1920	Sailor Stroud, SLC	.667
1921	Art Reinhart, LA	.750
1922	Jakie May, Ver	.795

WINNING PERCENTAGE (cont.)

1923	Henry Courtney, SF	.760
1924	Ed Bryan, Ver	.722
1925	Marty Griffin, SF	.800
	Doug Mc Weeney, SF	.800
1926	Earl Hamilton, LA	.750
1927	Al Gould, Oak	.773
1928	Dutch Ruether, SF	.806
1929	Frank Shellenback, Hol	.684
1930	Tony Freitas, Sac	.760
1931	Frank Shellenback, Hol	.794
1932	Jimmy De Shong, Sac	.760
1933	Dick Ward, LA	.735
1934	Fay Thomas, LA	.875
1935	Sam Gibson, SF	.846
1936	Willie Ludolph, Oak	.778
1937	Sam Gibson, SF	.704
1938	Fred Hutchinson, Sea	.781
1939	Julio Bonetti, LA	.800
1940	Dick Barrett, Sea	.828
1941	Hal Turpin, Sea	.769
1942	Hal Turpin, Sea	.719
1943	Jodie Phipps, LA	.773
1944	Manny Salvo, Oak	.720
1945	Bob Joyce, SF	.738
1946	Larry Jansen, SF	.833
1947	Bob Chesnes, SF	.733
1948	Bill Werle, SF	.708
1949	Herb Karpel, Sea	.700
1950	Jim Wilson, Sea	.686
1951	Hal Brown, Sea	.727
	Ben Wade, Hol	.727
1952	Johnny Lindell, Hol	.727
1953	Royce Lint, Port	.688
1954	Bill Wight, SD	.773
1955	Lou Kretlow, Sea	.824
1956	Dave Hillman, LA	.750
1957	Bill Abernathie, SF	.867

SHUTOUTS

1903–1905	Records Unavailable	
1906	Rube Vickers, Sea	11
1907–1909	Records Unavailable	
1910	Vean Gregg, Port	14
1911–1913	Records Unavailable	
1914	Skeeter Fanning, SF	8
	Hub Pernoll, SF	8

SHUTOUTS (cont.)

1914	Sailor Stroud, Sac	8
1915	Chief Johnson, Ver	5
	John Ryan, LA	5
1916	Bill Piercy, SLC	8
1917	Bill Prough, Oak	8
1918	Curly Brown, LA	5
	Lefty O'Doul, SF	5
1919	Bill Piercy, Sac	7
1920	Wheezer Dell, Ver	7
1921	Lefty O'Doul, SF	7
1922	Jakie May, Ver	7
1923	Vean Gregg, Sea	5
	Walter Mails, Oak	5
1924–1927	Records Unavailable	
1928	Elmer Jacobs, SF	6
1929	Elmer Jacobs, SF	4
	Roy Mahaffey, Port	4
1930	Ray Keating, Sac–Port	6
1931	Sam Gibson, SF	5
	Frank Shellenback, Hol	5
1932	Curt Davis, SF	9
1933	Bobo Newsom, LA	7
1934	Herm Pillette, Sea	5
1935	Dick Barrett, Sea	4
	K. A. Douglass, Oak	4
	Wayne Osborne, Miss	4
	Manny Salvo, Sac	4
	Jake Wade, Port	4
1936	Dick Barrett, Sea	5
	Wallace Hebert, SD	5
1937	Manny Salvo, SD	8
1938	Bob Joyce, Oak	7
1939	Tony Freitas, Sac	9
1940	Dick Newsome, SD	7
1941	Jess Flores, LA	6
	Tony Freitas, Sac	6
	Jack Salveson, Oak	6
1942	Sam Gibson, SF	9
1943	Ad Liska, Port	7
1944	Roy Helser, Port	8
1945	Guy Fletcher, Sac	7
	Bob Joyce, SF	7
1946	Eddie Erautt, Hol	8
1947	Cliff Melton, SF	5
1948	Tommy Bridges, Port	7
1949	Con Dempsey, SF	5
	Guy Fletcher, Sea	5

SHUT OUTS (cont.)

1949	Charley Schanz, Sea	5
1950	Jim Wilson, Sea	8
1951	Warren Hacker, LA	5
	Sam Jones, SD	5
	Al Lien, SF	5
1952	Jess Flores, Sac	5
	Joe Hatten, LA	5
	Memo Luna, SD	5
	Elmer Singleton, SF	5
1953	Vernon Kindsfather, Sea	7
1954	Eddie Erautt, SD	7
1955	Elmer Singleton, Sea	9
1956	Rene Valdes, Port	8
1957	Bob Smith, SF	6
	George Witt, Hol	6

COMPLETE GAMES

1903–1908	Records Unavailable	
1909	Frank Browning, SF	54
1910	Cack Henley, SF	47
1911	Flame Delhi, LA	43
1912	Al Klawitter, Port	44
1913–1917	Records Unavailable	
1918	Bill Prough, Oak	22
	Jack Quinn, Ver	22
1919–1922	Records Unavailable	
1923	Ray Kremer, Oak	35
1924	George Boehler, Oak	30
	Ken Penner, Ver	30
1925	George Boehler, Oak	34
1926	Jumbo Elliott, Sea	37
1927	George Boehler, Oak	24
	Jim Joe Edwards, Sea	24
	Ray Keating, Sac	24
	Earl Kunz, Sac	24
	Frank Shellenback, Hol	24
1928	Elmer Knight, Sea–Port	28
	Dutch Ruether, SF	28
1929	Roy Mahaffey, Port	32
1930	Ed Baecht, LA	32
1931	Frank Shellenback, Hol	34
1932	Frank Shellenback, Hol	35
1933	Ed Bryan, Sac	31
1934	Hal Turpin, Port	32
1935	Boom Boom Beck, Miss	32
1936	George Caster, Port	33

COMPLETE GAMES (cont.)

1937	Tony Freitas, Sac	31
1938	Tony Freitas, Sac	32
1939	Tony Freitas, Sac	30
1940	Tony Freitas, Sac	28
	Dick Newsome, SD	28
	Hal Turpin, Sea	28
1941	Ad Liska, Port	30
1942	Jack Salveson, Oak	34
1943	Charley Schanz, SD	28
1944	Tom Seats, SF	34
1945	Bob Joyce, SF	35
1946	Larry Jansen, SF	31
1947	Tom Seats, SD	24
1948	Bill Werle, SF	23
1949	Guy Fletcher, Sea	26
	Charley Schanz, Sea	26
1950	Jim Wilson, Sea	26
1951	Sam Jones, SD	21
1952	Johnny Lindell, Hol	26
1953	Al Gettel, Oak	30
1954	Tommy Byrne, Sea	24
1955	Red Munger, Hol	25
	Marino Pieretti, Sac	25
1956	Rene Valdes, Port	18
1957	Jim Grant, SD	18

INNINGS PITCHED

1903–1905	Records Unavailable	
1906	Rube Vickers, Sea	526
1907–1910	Records Unavailable	
1911	Flame Delhi, LA	446
1912	Harry Ables, Oak	363
1913	Bob Koestner, Ven	411
1914	Irv Higginbotham, Port	418
1915	Lefty Williams, SLC	418
1916	Paul Fittery, SLC	448
1917	Eric Erickson, SF	444
1918	Bill Prough, Oak	226
1919	Red Oldham, Port	370
1920	Buzz Arlett, Oak	427
1921	Paul Fittery, Sac	361
1922	Buzz Arlett, Oak	374
1923	Ray Kremer, Oak	357
1924	George Boehler, Oak	396
1925	George Boehler, Oak	417
1926	Jumbo Elliott, Sea	367

INNINGS PITCHED (cont.)

1927	Clyde Barfoot, Miss	308
1928	Elmer Knight, Sea—Port	331
1929	Roy Mahaffey, Port	370
1930	Ed Baecht, LA	364
1931	Sam Gibson, SF	337
1932	Curt Davis, SF	326
1933	Bobo Newsom, LA	320
1934	Leroy Herrmann, SF	325
1935	Boom Boom Beck, Miss	345
1936	George Caster, Port	339
1937	Ad Liska, Port	319
1938	Dick Barrett, Sea	328
1939	Tony Freitas, Sac	332
1940	Tony Freitas, Sac	332
1941	Yank Terry, SD	315
1942	Dick Barrett, Sea	330
1943	Charley Schanz, Sea	276
1944	Bob Joyce, SF	324
1945	Bob Joyce, SF	344
1946	Larry Jansen, SF	321
1947	Tom Seats, SD	306
1948	Pinky Woods, Hol	279
1949	Charley Schanz, Sea	321
1950	Bill Evans, Sac	317
1951	Sam Jones, SD	267
1952	Al Gettel Oak	284
1953	Al Gettel Oak	309
1954	Al Gettel Oak	284
1955	Marino Pieretti, Sac	293
1956	Rene Valdes, Port	254
1957	Charlie Rabe, Sea	238

HITS ALLOWED

1903—1913	Records Unavailable	
1914	Al Klawitter, Oak	415
1915	Spider Baum, SF	393
1916	Paul Fittery, SLC	407
1917	Art Fromme, Ver	428
1918	Bill Prough, Oak	218
1919	Red Oldham, Port	355
1920	Buzz Arlett, Oak	430
1921	Herm Pillette, Port	378
1922	Buzz Arlett, Oak	396
1923	Al Gould, SLC	388
1924	Bill Hughes, Sac	405
1925	George Boehler, Oak	387

HITS ALLOWED (cont.)

1926	George Payne, Port	381
1927	Herm Pillette, Miss	373
1928	Jack Knight, Sea—Port	356
1929	Jack Knight, Port—SF	414
1930	Curt Davis, SF	389
1931	Ed Bryan, Sac	348
1932	Phil Page, Sea	375
1933	Ed Bryan, Sac	441
1934	Hal Turpin, Port	376
1935	Boom Boom Beck, Miss	366
1936	John Chambers, Sac	342
1937	Ed Stutz, SF	331
1938	Bill Thomas, Port	345
1939	Bill Thomas, Port	386
1940	Tony Freitas, Sac	350
1941	Ad Liska, Port	335
1942	Ad Liska, Port	338
1943	Bill Thomas, Hol	294
1944	Bob Joyce, SF	338
1945	Bob Joyce, SF	347
1946	Al Olsen, SD	309
1947	Tom Seats, SD	337
1948	Vince Di Biasi, Port	306
1949	Charley Schanz, Sea	324
1950	Chet Johnson, SF	316
1951	Bob Spicer, LA	262
1952	Marino Pieretti, Port	262
1953	Al Gettel, Oak	293
1954	Marino Pieretti, Sac	275
1955	Marino Pieretti, Sac	271
1956	Bill Werle, Port	330
1957	George Bamberger, Van	244

HIT BATSMEN

1903—1906	Records Unavailable	
1907	Bob Groom, Port	28
1908	Records Unavailable	
1909	George Boice, Oak	31
1910	Ed Willett, Ver	28
1911	Harry Stewart, Ver	21
1912	Frank Miller, SF	20
1913	Jack Killilay, Oak	20
1914	Hub Pernoll, SF	20
1915	Tex Pruiett, Oak	26
1916	Paul Fittery, SLC	23
1917	Casey Smith, SF	20

HIT BATSMEN (cont.)		WILD PITCHES	
1918 Records Unavailable		1903–1906 Records Unavailable	
1919 Bill Piercy, Sac	23	1907 Bob Groom, Port	22
1920 Paul Fittery, Sac	22	1908–1909 Records Unavailable	
1921 Paul Fittery, Sac	22	1910 Jack Lively, Oak	10
1922 Bill James, Ver	22	1911 Frank Miller, SF	20
1923 Fritz Coumbe, SLC	15	1912 Harry Ables, Oak	16
Jakie May, Ver	15	Frank Miller, SF	16
1924 George Boehler, Oak	27	1913 Judge Munsell, Sac	16
1925 George Boehler, Oak	25	1914 Ed Klepfer, Ven	16
1926 Laurie Vinci, Sac	17	1915 Bill Hughes, LA	17
1927 Bill Piercy, LA	26	1916 Ray Boyd, Oak	16
1928 Walt Kinney, Hol	14	1917–1918 Records Unavailable	
1929 Pete Daglia, Oak	19	1919 Bill Piercy, Sac	22
1930 Pete Daglia, Oak	17	1920 Walter Mails, Sac	20
1931 George Caster, Port	15	1921 Herm Pillette, Port	16
1932 John Walters, Sea	23	1922 Harry Biemiller, Port	15
1933 Buzz Wetzel, Hol	10	1923 Sheriff Blake, Sea	14
1934 Le Roy Herrmann, SF	12	1924 Guy Williams, SF	14
1935 Tom Conlan, Oak	10	1925 Bill Piercy, SLC	15
1936 Boom Boom Beck, Miss	12	1926 Laurie Vinci, Sac	17
1937 Clarence Pickrel, Sea	10	1927 Bill Piercy, LA	13
1938 Ad Liska, Port	10	1928 Curt Fullerton, Hol–Port	13
1939 Les Fleming, Hol	6	1929 Bert Cole, Miss	13
Al Olsen, SD	6	1930 Fay Thomas, Sac	11
1940 Dick Newsome, SD	10	1931 Tom Flynn, Sac	11
1941 Woody Rich, SD	12	Mal Moss, LA	11
1942 Joe Orrell, Port	13	1932 Ed Baecht, LA	13
1943 Chet Johnson, SD	8	1933 Clarence Fieber, Oak	9
1944 Frank Dasso, SD	12	1934 Fay Thomas, LA	10
1945 Roy Helser, Port	12	Jack Wilson, Port	10
1946 Roy Helser, Port	9	1935 Wayne Osborne, Miss	11
Red Lynn, LA	9	1936 Fay Thomas, LA	7
1947 Hugh Orphan, Sac–Hol	12	1937 Dick Barrett, Sea	11
1948 Pinky Woods, Hol	12	1938 Bill Shores, SF	15
1949 Charlie Gassaway, Oak	11	1939 Dick Barrett, Sea	11
1950 Pinky Woods, Hol	13	1940 Ralph Buxton, Oak	15
1951 Lew Burdette, SF	14	1941 Dick Barrett, Sea	12
1952 George Boemler, SF	8	Bill Caplinger, Sac	12
1953 Bob Kerrigan ,SD	8	1942 Ralph Buxton, Oak	13
Charley Schanz, Sac	8	1943 Vince Di Biasi, Oak	8
1954 Buddy Daley, Sac	13	1944 Marino Pieretti, Port	12
1955 Karl Drews, Oak	12	Bill Werle, SF	12
1956 John Carmichael, SD	11	1945 Glenn Elliott, Sea	11
Riverboat Smith, SF	11	1946 Dick Barrett, Port	13
1957 Bob Alexander, Port	9	1947 Bob Chesnes, SF	11
Ed Gasque, SD	9	1948 Pinky Woods, Hol	13
Dolan Nichols, SD–Port	9	1949 Willard Ramsdell, Hol	13

WILD PITCHES (cont.)

1950	George Bamberger, Oak	13
1951	Bill Ayers, Oak	15
1952	Vern Kindsfather, Sea	13
1953	Royce Lint, Port	11
1954	Jim Atkins, Oak	11
	Eddie Erautt, SD	11
1955	Johnny Briggs, Sac	15
1956	Riverboat Smith, SF	13
1957	Roger Osenbaugh, Sac	14

BASES ON BALLS

1903–1906	Records Unavailable	
1907	Bob Groom, Port	158
1908–1909	Records Unavailable	
1910	Slim Nelson, Oak	196
1911	Elmer Koestner, Port	127
1912	Harry Ables, Oak	134
1913	Gene Krapp, Port	134
1914	Roy Hitt, Ven	116
1915	Slim Love, LA	138
1916	Paul Fittery, SLC	158
	Allen Sothoron, Port	158
1917	Eric Erickson, SF	153
1918	Paul Fittery, LA	86
1919	Lyle Bigbee, Sea	148
	Bill Piercy, Sac	148
1920	Walter Mails, Sac	187
1921	Sam Ross, Port	138
1922	Bill James, Ver	137
1923	Walter Mails, Oak	125
	John Singleton, SLC	125
1924	George Boehler, Oak	172
1925	Elmer Ponder, SLC	215
1926	Dick Moudy, SF	146
1927	Laurie Vinci, Sac	119
1928	Laurie Vinci, Sac	129
1929	Lou Mc Evoy, Oak	134
1930	Pete Daglia, Oak	149
1931	Walter Mails, Port	140
1932	John Walters, Sea	130
1933	George Caster, Sea	126
1934	Joe Sullivan, Hol	132
1935	Jake Wade, Port	166
1936	Boom Boom Beck, Miss	119
1937	Dick Barrett, Sea	118
1938	Dick Barrett, Sea	132

BASES ON BALLS (cont.)

1939	Pat Tobin ,SD	119
1940	Dick Barrett, Sea	121
	Frank Dasso, SF	121
1941	Frank Dasso, Hol	116
1942	Blix Donnelly, Sac	128
1943	Charley Schanz, Sea	130
1944	Frank Dasso, SD	131
1945	Vallie Eaves, SD	127
1946	Red Lynn, LA	123
1947	Albert Treichel, SD	151
1948	Pinky Woods, Hol	167
1949	Bob Kelly, LA	127
1950	Hank Behrman, Oak	138
1951	Sam Jones, SD	175
1952	Johnny Lindell, Hol	108
1953	Al Widmar, Sea	108
1954	Don Ferrarese, Oak	174
1955	Johnny Briggs, Sac	118
1956	Pete Mesa, SD	137
1957	Bennie Daniels, Hol	121

OPPONENT BATTING AVERAGE

1903–1914	Records Unavailable	
1915	Slim Love, LA	.207
1916	Eric Erickson, SF	.218
1917	Eric Erickson, SF	.211
1918	Records Unavailable	
1919	Ray Kremer, Oak	.207
1920	Walter Mails, Sac	.212
1921	Vic Aldridge, LA	.227
1922	Jakie May, Ver	.215
1923	Vean Gregg, Sea	.245
1924	Carroll Canfield, Sac	.252
1925	Charlie Root, LA	.227
1926	Earl Hamilton, LA	.238
1927	George Boehler, Oak	.250
1928	Gordon Rhodes, Hol	.254
1929	Ed Baecht, LA	.243
1930	Ed Baecht, LA	.258
1931	Frank Shellenback, Hol	.258
1932	Fay Thomas, Oak	.234
1933	Dick Ward, LA	.232
1934	Roy Henshaw, LA	.208
1935	Dick Barrett, Sea	.243
1936	Joe La Rocca, Oak	.238
1937	Tony Freitas, Sac	.239

OPP. BATTING AVERAGE (cont.)

1938	Sam Gibson, SF	.227
1939	Lawrence Powell, SF	.218
1940	Dick Barrett, Sea	.209
1941	Hi Bithorn, Hol	.225
1942	Dick Barrett, Sea	.196
1943	Al Brazle, Sac	.207
1944	Ray Prim, LA	.226
1945	Wandel Mossor, Port	.207
1946	Spec Shea, Oak	.203
1947	Bob Chesnes, SF	.214
1948	Dewey Adkins, LA	.232
1949	Orval Grove, Sac	.215
1950	Earl Harrist, Oak	.229
1951	Sam Jones, SD	.188
1952	Mel Queen, Hol	.208
1953–1957	Records Unavailable	

LOSSES

1903	Ike Butler, Port	31
1904	Ike Butler, Port	31
1905	Bill Essick, Port	30
1906	Bill Reidy, Oak	28
1907	Bob Groom, Port	26
1908	Oscar Jones, SF	24
1909	Roy Hitt, Ver	29
1910	Jack Fitzgerald, Sac	25
1911	Flame Delhi, LA	23
1912	Bob Koestner, Port	24
1913	Bob Koestner, Ven	26
1914	Al Klawitter, Oak	26
1915	Bill Prough, Oak	25
1916	Sammy Beer, Oak	23
	Ray Boyd, Oak	23
	Bill Prough, Oak	23
1917	Harry Krause, Oak	26
	Roy Mitchell, Ver	26
1918	Speed Martin, Oak	16
1919	Ray Kremer, Oak	23
	Red Oldham, Port	23
1920	Ken Penner, Sac	23
1921	Herm Pillette, Port	30
1922	Paul Fittery, Sac	26
1923	Jakie May, Ver	22
1924	Jim Christian, Ver	22
	Walter Mails, Oak	22
1925	Herm Pillette, Ver	25

LOSSES (cont.)

1926	Dick Moudy, SF	22
1927	Willie Ludolph, Miss	20
	Bill Piercy, LA	20
	Herm Pillette, Miss	20
1928	Hap Collard, Sea	23
1929	Roy Mahaffey, Port	25
1930	Howard Craghead, Oak	22
1931	Pete Daglia, Oak	20
1932	Win Ballou, LA	21
1933	Phil Page, Sea	24
1934	Ed Bryan, Port	24
1935	Ed Wells, Hol	20
1936	Boom Boom Beck, Miss	21
1937	K. A. Douglass, Oak	23
1938	Ken Sheehan, Oak	27
1939	Tony Freitas, Sac	18
	Bill Walker, Sea	18
1940	Ray Harrell, Port	23
1941	Jack Salveson, Oak	20
1942	Joe Orrell, Port	22
1943	John Pintar, Sac	27
1944	Bob Joyce, SF	20
1945	Bob Ferguson, SD	21
	Newt Kimball, Hol	21
1946	Dick Barrett, Port	21
1947	Frank Dasso, Hol–Sac	18
1948	Pinky Woods, Hol	20
1949	Omer Anthony, LA	19
	Herman Besse, Sea	19
1950	Bill Evans, Sac	22
1951	Chet Johnson, SF–Oak	18
1952	Jess Flores, Sac	20
1953	Bill Boemler, SF	17
	Ken Gables, Sac	17
	Marino Pieretti, Sac	17
	Elmer Singleton, SF	17
1954	Bob Hall, Hol–Sea	17
	Joe Hatten, LA	17
1955	Buddy Daley, Sac	16
1956	Eddie Erautt, SD	19
1957	John Carmichael, SD–Port	18

EFFICIENCY

1903–1913	Records Unavailable	
1914	Slim Love, LA	0.83
1915	Skeeter Fanning, SF	1.05

EFFICIENCY (cont.)

1916	Bill Prough, Oak	1.11
1917	Eric Erickson, SF	1.07
1918	Jack Quinn, Ver	0.88
1919	Doc Crandall, LA	1.05
1920	Willie Mitchell, Ver	1.06
1921	Vic Aldridge, LA	1.04
1922	Jakie May, Ver	1.06
1923	Doc Crandall, LA	1.14
1924	Doc Crandall, LA	1.13
1925	Charlie Root, LA	1.11
1926	Earl Hamilton, LA	1.13
1927	George Boehler, Oak	1.16
1928	Ray Keating, Sac	1.22
1929	Ed Baecht, Port—LA	1.24
1930	Ed Baecht, LA	1.30
1931	Sam Gibson, SF	1.18
1932	Curt Davis, SF	1.06
1933	Jimmy Zinn, SF	1.28
1934	Sam Gibson, SF	1.19
1935	Willie Ludolph, Oak	1.23
1936	Willie Ludolph, Oak	1.10

EFFICIENCY (cont.)

1937	Joe Berry, LA	1.02
1938	Sam Gibson, SF	1.06
1939	Sam Gibson, SF	1.11
1940	Jack Salveson, Oak	1.12
1941	Syl Johnson, Sea	0.96
1942	Dick Barrett, Sea	1.00
1943	Al Lien, SF	1.04
1944	Ray Prim, LA	0.97
1945	Guy Fletcher, Sac	1.15
1946	Larry Jansen, SF	1.01
1947	Cliff Melton, SF	1.14
1948	Con Dempsey, SF	1.14
1949	Gordon Maltzberger, Hol	1.16
1950	Jim Wilson, Sea	1.13
1951	Hal Brown, Sea	1.11
1952	Red Adams, Port	1 03
1953	Glenn Elliott, Port	1.15
1954	Lino Donoso, Hol	1.10
1955	Red Adams, Port	0.99
1956	Elmer Singleton, Sea	1.20
1957	Morrie Martin, Van	1.05

NO–HITTERS

Pitcher, Team	Date	Opponent	Score	Inn
Doc Newton, LA	Nov. 8, 1903	Oakland	2–0	9
Frank Barber, SF	Jul. 13, 1904	Oakland	1–0	9
Sea Lion Hall, Sea	Apr. 5, 1905	Oakland	6–0	9
Jimmy Whalen, SF	Jul. 26, 1905	Seattle	2–0	7
Bobby Keefe, Tac	Nov. 18, 1905	Oakland	3–0	9
Sea Lion Hall, Sea	May 12, 1906	Oakland	2–0	9
Eli Cates, Oak	Sep. 2, 1906	Fresno	7–0	9
Fred Brown, SF	Oct. 12, 1906	Oakland	3–0	9
Bob Groom, Port	Jun. 16, 1907	Los Angeles	1–0	9
Eli Cates, Oak	Jun. 25, 1907	Portland	2–1	9
Bob Koestner, LA	Apr. 16, 1909	San Francisco	4–0	9
Jimmy Wiggs, Oak	May 12, 1909	San Francisco	3–0	9
Frank Browning, SF	Jul. 5, 1909	Sacramento	3–0	9
Alex Carson, Port	Jul. 22, 1909	Los Angeles	1–0	10
Frank Miller, SF	Aug. 20, 1910	Vernon	3–1	9
Vean Gregg, Port	Sep. 2, 1910	Los Angeles	2–0	9
Frank Arellanes, Sac	Oct. 17, 1910	Vernon	0–2	8
Rube Suter, SF	Apr. 25, 1911	Oakland	1–0	9
Harry Ables, Oak	Jun. 13, 1911	Los Angeles	2–1	9
Ferdinand Henkle, Port	Jul. 5, 1911	Sacramento	1–0	9
Red Toner, SF	May 21, 1912	Portland	2–0	9
Bill Malarkey, Oak	Jun. 30, 1912	San Francisco	0–0 (1)	9
John Ryan, LA	May 18, 1913	Portland	6–0	9
Roy Hitt, Ven	Jul. 19, 1914	San Francisco	2–0	9
Johnny Lush, Port	Sep. 20, 1914	Venice	0–1	9
Bill Evans, Port	Oct. 16, 1914	Oakland	3–0	9
Skeeter Fanning, SF	Oct. 25, 1914	Portland	7–0	9
Bill Piercy, Ver	Jul. 25, 1915	Oakland	3–0	9
Skeeter Fanning, SF	Jun. 23, 1916	Vernon	4–1	9
Chief Johnson, Ver	Apr. 15, 1917	Portland	6–0	9
Suds Sutherland, Port	Jun. 25, 1919	San Francisco	11–0	9
Cy Falkenberg, Oak	Aug. 19, 1919	Seattle	6–0	9
Wheezer Dell, Ver	Sep. 21, 1922	Oakland	1–0	9
Jim Scott, SF	Apr. 14, 1923	Oakland	5–0	9
Herm Pillette, Miss	Oct. 5, 1929	Seattle	4–0	9
Jimmy Zinn, SF	May 14, 1930	Sacramento	8–0	9
Willie Ludolph, Oak	Jun. 6, 1931	Mission	4–0	9
Mal Moss, LA	Jun. 12, 1931	Sacramento	5–1	9
Tony Freitas, Sac	Nov. 5, 1932	Oakland	2–0 (2)	9
Ed Walsh Jr, Oak	Aug. 17, 1933	San Francisco	5–0	9
Ernie Bonham, Oak	Jul. 4, 1937	Seattle	2–0	7
Joe Berry, LA	Jul. 19, 1938	Oakland	4–0	7
Dick Ward, SD	Aug. 30, 1938	Los Angeles	1–0 (3)	12
Hal Turpin, Sea	Apr. 12, 1942	San Diego	2–0	9
Cotton Pippen, Oak	May 31, 1943	Sacramento	10–0 (4)	7

NO—HITTERS

Pitcher, Team	Date	Opponent	Score		Inn
George Comellas, LA	May 7, 1944	San Francisco	2—0		9
Manny Salvo, Oak	Jul. 19, 1944	Sacramento	2—0		9
Joe Demoran, Sea	Apr. 4, 1946	Los Angeles	3—0		9
Ad Liska, Port	Apr. 21, 1946	Hollywood	1—0		7
Red Mann, Sac	May 31, 1946	Seattle	6—0		9
Tommy Bridges, Port	Apr. 20, 1947	San Francisco	2—0		9
Dick Barrett, Sea	May 15, 1948	Sacramento	2—0	(5)	7
Paul Calvert, Sea	May 27, 1951	Sacramento	4—0		9
Warren Hacker, LA	Sep. 7, 1951	Seattle	4—0		9
Elmer Singleton, SF	Apr. 24, 1952	Sacramento	0—1	(6)	12
Hal Gregg, Oak	May 1, 1952	Portland	3—0		7
Roger Bowman, Oak	Jul. 3, 1952	Hollywood	5—0		9
Joe Hatten, LA	Jun. 7, 1953	San Diego	6—0		7
Red Munger, Hol	Jul. 4, 1953	Sacramento	1—0		7
Jim Atkins, Oak	Aug. 25, 1953	San Francisco	2—0		7
Bubba Church, LA	Aug. 3, 1954	Portland	3—0		9
Bob Alexander, Port	Aug. 17, 1954	Oakland	3—0		7
Roger Bowman, Hol	Sep. 12, 1954	Portland	10—0	(7)	7
George Piktuzas, LA	Jul. 21, 1955	San Francisco	2—1		9
Elmer Singleton, Sea	Jul. 24, 1955	San Diego	2—0		7
Chris Van Cuyk, Oak	Jul. 26, 1955	Los Angeles	2—0		7

(1) Gave up one hit in the tenth inning, game ended in scoreless tie because of a time limit.
(2) Night game.
(3) Gave up hit with one out in the thirteenth, won the game in sixteen innings.
(4) Perfect game.
(5) Perfect game.
(6) Gave up three hits with two out in the thirteenth inning and lost game.
(7) Perfect game to force one game playoff with San Diego for PCL pennant.

SECTION VIII

Individual
Leaders — Fielding

On the following pages are listed the fielding leaders, by year and by position, in the Pacific Coast League for the years 1903 through 1957. At each position is listed the leader in fielding percentage and errors. In addition, the yearly leaders in assists among catchers and outfielders is listed.

To be considered eligible for leading the league in fielding percentage, a player must have appeared in at least one-half of his team's games at the position. Leaders are not carried to the ten-thousandths of a point; all players with the same fielding percentage carried to three places are listed as leader, provided the player appeared in at least half of his team's games at the position.

Pitchers must be an exception to this rule. In years where no pitcher achieved a 1.000 fielding average, the leader is as listed in the *1947 Old's Coast League Annual*. In those years where several pitchers ended the season at the 1.000 mark, the pitcher with the most chances accepted is listed as the leader.

Below are the single-season records for the years 1903 through 1957 in each of the categories listed in this section (Babe Borton's fielding percentage is considered unofficial since his fielding statistics were taken from the *Los Angeles Times*, not from league records):

Fielding—1st Base:	Babe Borton, Ver .997 (1920) unofficial
	Bill Sweeney, Port .997 (1938 & 1939)
Fielding—2nd Base:	Jim Moran, SF .992 (1955)
Fielding—3rd Base:	Marv Owen, Port .986 (1945)
Fielding—Shortstop:	Bud Hardin, LA .981 (1954)
Fielding—Outfield:	Frank Osborn, Sac-Port 1.000 (1932)
	Pete Scott, Sea 1.000 (1932)
Fielding—Catcher	Larry Woodall, Sac .996 (1932)
	John Ritchey, SD .996 (1949)
Fielding—Pitcher	Numerous tied with 1.000
Errors—1st Base:	Babe Danzig, Port 86 (1908)
Errors—2nd Base:	George Wheeler, LA 78 (1903)
	George Cutshaw, Oak 78 (1910)

Errors—3rd Base:	Heine Jansing, Sea 99 (1903)
Errors—Shortstop:	Russ Hall, Sea 119 (1904)
Errors—Outfield:	Bill O'Hara, Oak-Sea 45 (1903)
Errors—Catcher:	Ly Gorton, Oak 45 (1903)
Errors—Pitcher:	Doc Newton, LA 28 (1904)
Assists—Outfield:	Wilbur Murdock, Oak 63 (1903)
Assists—Catcher:	Mickey La Longe, Oak-Sac 281 (1910)

FIRST BASE

1903	Pop Dillon, LA	.984
1904	Jay Streib, Oak	.981
1905	Pop Dillon, LA	.985
1906	Records Unavailable	
1907	Pop Dillon, LA	.988
1908	Pop Dillon, LA	.987
1909	Pop Dillon, LA	.993
1910	Pop Dillon, LA	.989
1911	Pop Dillon, LA	.987
1912	Bud Sharpe, Oak	.989
1913	Ham Patterson, Ver	.980
1914	Babe Borton, Ver	.992
1915	Jack Ness, Oak	.991
1916	Jack Barry, Oak	.991
1917	Gus Gleischman, Ver	.990
	Earl Sheely, SLC	.990
1918	Jack Fournier, LA	.992
1919	Jack Fournier, LA	.992
1920	Babe Borton, Ver	.997
1921	Fred Mollwitz, Sac	.995
1922	Fred Mollwitz, Sac	.993
1923	Fred Mollwitz, Sac	.994
1924	Roy Leslie, SLC	.900
1925	George Lafayette, O–P	.993
1926	Roy Leslie, Hol	.092
1927	Jack Fenton, Oak	.992
1928	Jim Keesey, Port	.994
1929	Jim Keesey, Port	.995
1930	Ray Jacobs, LA	.994
1931	George Burns, Miss–LA	.991
1932	Le Roy Anton, Oak	.991
	Dolf Camilli, Sac	.991
	Jim Keesey, Port	.991
1933	Dolf Camilli, Sac	.992
1934	Le Roy Anton, Oak	.994
1935	Jim Oglesby, LA	.994
1936	Roy Mort, Miss	.993
1937	Bob Gibson, Oak	.994
1938	Bill Sweeney, Port	.997
1939	Bill Sweeney, Port	.997
1940	George Archie, Sea	.994
1941	George Mc Donald, SD	.993
	Les Scarsella, Sea	.993
1942	Maurice Sturdy, Sac	.995
1943	George Mc Donald, SD	.996
1944	Reggie Otero, LA	.992
1945	Ed Zipay, Sac	.992

FIRST BASE (cont.)

1946	Reggie Otero, LA	.995
1947	Vince Shupe, SD	.992
	Tony Lupien, Hol	.992
1948	Nick Etten, Oak	.995
1949	Chuck Stevens, Hol	.993
	Vince Shupe, SD–Port	.993
1950	Elbie Fletcher, LA	.994
1951	Chuck Stevens, Hol	.994
1952	Tookie Gilbert, Oak	.992
1953	Gordon Goldsberry, Sea	.994
	Dale Long, Hol	.994
	Hank Arft, Port	.994
1954	Jim Westlake, SF	.992
	Hank Arft, Port	.992
1955	Ed Mickelson, Port	.996
1956	Dick Sisler, SD	.993
	Ed Mickelson, Port	.993
1957	Jim Marshall, Van	.996

SECOND BASE

1903	Perle Casey, Sac	.961
1904	Perle Casey, Tac	953
1905	Perle Casey, Tac	.966
1906	Records Unavailable	
1907	Kid Mohler, SF	.964
1908	Perle Casey, Port	.953
1909	Fred Raymer, Sac	.975
1910	Roy Brashear, Ver	.962
1911	Roy Brashear, Ver	.956
1912	Roy Brashear, Ver	.951
1913	Bill Leard, Oak	.966
1914	Ralph Young, Sac	.957
1915	Joe Gedeon, SLC	.962
1916	Bill Rodgers, Port	.965
1917	Bill Rodgers, Port	.958
1918	Franz Hosp, Ver	.975
1919	Bob Fisher, Ver	.970
1920	Patsy Mc Gaffigan, Sac	.975
1921	Patsy Mc Gaffigan, Sac	.975
1922	Paddy Siglin, SLC	.972
1923	Pete Kilduff, SF	.975
1924	Pete Kilduff, SF	.977
1925	Cliff Brady, Sea	.972
	Emmett Mc Cann, Port	.972
1926	Pete Kilduff, SF	.978
1927	Jimmie Reese, Oak	.984

SECOND BASE (cont.)

1928	Johnny Kerr, Hol	.977
1929	Jimmie Reese, Oak	.979
1930	Jake Caveney, SF	.980
1931	Loris Baker, LA	.975
1932	Ray Brubaker, Oak	.977
1933	Jimmie Reese, Oak	.969
1934	Jimmie Reese, Oak	.972
1935	Andy Harrington, Sea	.986
1936	Al Wright, Miss	.979
1937	Pete Coscarart, Port	.970
1938	Dib Williams, Sac	.980
1939	Lou Stringer, LA	.976
1940	Al Niemiec, Sea	.988
1941	Al Niemiec, Sea	.981
1942	Al Niemiec, Sea	.974
	Ham Schulte, Hol–Oak	.974
1943	Roy Hughes, Oak	.988
1944	Gene Handley, Sac	.970
1945	Glen Stewart, Oak	.978
1946	Hugh Luby, SF	.980
1947	Hugh Luby, SF	.981
1948	Tony York, Sea	.978
1949	Dario Lodigiani, Oak–SF	.976
1950	Johnny Lucadello, LA–Sac	.987
1951	Eddie Basinski, Port	.974
1952	Jim Moran, SF	.981
1953	Jim Moran, SF	.988
1954	Jim Moran, SF	.982
1955	Jim Moran, SF	.992
1956	Spider Jorgensen, Van	.984
1957	Sparky Anderson, LA	.985

THIRD BASE

1903	Jud Smith, LA	.923
1904	Charlie Irwin, SF	.937
1905	Tommy Sheehan, Tac	.954
1906	Records Unavailable	
1907	Charlie Irwin, SF	.958
1908	Tom Mc Ardle, SF	.946
1909	Jud Smith, LA	.943
1910	Tommy Sheehan, Port	.964
1911	Oscar Vitt, SF	.948
1912	George Metzger, LA	.956
1913	George Metzger, LA	.948
1914	George Metzger, LA	.950

THIRD BASE (cont.)

1915	Louis Litschi, Ver	.951
	George Metzger, LA	.951
1916	J. C. Galloway, LA	.957
1917	Bob Davis, LA	.953
1918	Tex Westerzil, Ver	.974
1919	Tex Westerzil, Ver–Port	.972
1920	Tex Westerzil, Port	.961
1921	Willie Kamm, SF	.963
1922	Charlie Deal, Port	.960
1923	Oscar Vitt, SLC	.964
1924	Charlie Deal, Port	.981
1925	Oscar Vitt, SLC	.974
1926	Oscar Vitt, Hol	.982
1927	Eddie Mulligan, SF	.969
1928	William Rodda, Miss	.974
1929	Eddie Mulligan, SF	.957
1930	Leonard Backer, Sac	.965
1931	Babe Pinelli, Oak–SF	.959
1932	Leonard Backer, Sac	.975
1933	Leonard Backer, Sac	.966
1934	Joe Coscarart, Sea	.963
1935	Gil English, Port	.964
1936	Ernie Holman, Oak	.954
1937	Pinky May, Oak	.958
1938	John Warner, Oak	.961
1939	Charles English, LA	.952
1940	Eddie Mayo, LA	.983
1941	Marv Owen, Port	.954
1942	Eddie Mayo, LA	.961
1943	Harry Clements, Hol	.965
1944	Marv Owen, Port	.964
1945	Marv Owen, Port	.986
1946	Steve Mesner, Sac	.955
1947	Hilly Layne, Sea	.965
1948	Lee Handley, SD	.958
1949	Strick Shofner, SF	.960
	Hilly Layne, Sea	.960
1950	Dario Lodigiani, SF	.957
1951	Leo Thomas, Port	.968
1952	Spider Jorgensen, Oak	.972
1953	Leo Thomas, Sea	.972
1954	Leo Thomas, Sea	.973
1955	Milt Smith, SD	.971
1956	George Risley, Sac	.959
1957	Rudy Regalado, SD	.971

SHORTSTOP

1903	James Toman, LA	.924
1904	James Toman, LA	.920
1905	Jake Atz, Port—LA	.928
1906	Records Unavailable	
1907	Bert Delmas, LA	.938
1908	Rollie Zeider, SF	.965
1909	Terry Mc Kune, Oak	.949
1910	Bill Lindsay, Ver	.954
1911	Bert Delmas, LA	.955
1912	Joe Berger, LA	.958
1913	Roy Corhan, SF	.951
1914	Ernie Johnson, LA	.949
1915	Zeb Terry, LA	.949
1916	Kid Butler, Oak—LA	.955
1917	Zeb Terry, LA	.958
1918	Zeb Terry, LA	.971
1919	Billy Orr, Sac	.954
1920	Johnny Mitchell, LA	.962
1921	Billy Orr, Sac	.957
1922	Ike Mc Auley, LA	.940
1923	Billy Orr, Sea	.955
1924	Hal Rhyne, SF	.956
1925	Hal Rhyne, SF	.901
1926	Johnny Mitchell, LA	.952
1027	Lyn Lary, Oak	.961
	Gordon Slade, Miss	.961
1028	Gordon Slade, Miss	.970
1929	Gordon Slade, Miss	.974
1930	Carl Dittmar, LA	.970
1931	Carl Dittmar, LA	.962
1932	Ray French, Sac	.958
1933	Ray French, Sac	.958
1934	Clyde Beck, Miss	.970
1935	Clyde Beck, Miss	.957
1936	Hal Rhyne, SF	.964
1937	Dud Lee, Port	.959
1938	Tom Carey, Hol	.966
1939	Ed Cihocki, LA	.966
1940	Lindsay Brown, Port	.951
1941	Lindsay Brown, Port	.960
1942	Lindsay Brown, Port	.957
1943	Billy Schuster, LA	.955
1944	Tod Davis, Hol	.948
1945	Jack Calvey, Sac	.943
1946	Lindsay Brown, Port	.950
1947	John O'Neil, Sea	.961
1948	Frankie Zak, Port	.966

SHORTSTOP (cont.)

1949	Len Ratto, Sac	.962
1950	Frankie Austin, Port	.972
1951	Len Ratto, Sac	.959
1952	Frankie Austin, Port	.958
1953	Frankie Austin, Port	.970
1954	Bud Hardin, LA	.981
1955	Richie Myers, Sac	.973
1956	Joe Koppe, Sac	.955
1957	Harry Malmberg, SF	.970

OUTFIELD

1903	George Mc Laughlin, Sac	.981
1904	George Hildebrand, SF	.962
1905	Deacon Van Buren, Port	.979
1906	Records Unavailable	
1907	Gavvy Cravath, LA	.973
1908	Harry Melchoir, SF	.976
1909	Harry Melchoir, SF	.981
1910	Curt Bernard, LA	.978
1911	Bud Ryan, Port	.985
1912	Deacon Van Buren, Sac	.986
1913	Art Kruger, LA	.986
1914	Dick Bayless, Ver	.984
1915	Johnny Kane, Ver	.984
1916	Jimmy Shinn, SLC	.981
1917	Rube Ellis, LA	.985
1918	Sam Crawford, LA	.993
1919	Dick Cox, Port	.994
1920	George Maisel, Port	.993
1921	Jigger Statz, LA	.990
1922	Fred Shulte, Sea—Oak	.988
1923	Hugh High, Ver	.988
1924	Mike Menosky, Ver	.993
1925	Ray Rohwer, Port	.984
1926	Jigger Statz, LA	.997
1927	Harry Callaghan, Sea	.993
1928	Evar Swanson, Miss	.991
1929	Bill Rumler, Hol	.990
1930	Frank Osborn, Sac	.982
1931	Ernest Kelly, Miss	.995
1932	Frank Osborn, Sac—P	1.000
	Pete Scott, Sea	1.000
1933	Al Moore, Port—Miss	.985
1934	Hank Steinbacher, Sac	.987
1935	Jerry Donovan, SF	.995
1936	Jigger Statz, LA	.993

OUTFIELD (cont.)

1937	Harold Patchett, SD	.993
1938	Dom Dallessandro, SD	.996
1939	Ted Norbert, SF	.988
1940	Bill Lawrence, Sea	.992
1941	Ted Norbert, Port	.990
1942	Kermit Lewis, SF	.987
	Tommy Thompson, Port	.987
1943	Bill Matheson, Sea	.991
1944	Harold Patchett, SD	.986
	Frenchy Uhalt, Oak	.986
1945	Tony Criscola, SD	.990
1946	Culley Rikard, Hol	.994
1947	Andrew Skurski, Hol	.996
1948	Jim Delsing, Hol	.997
1949	Irv Noren, Hol	.989
	Frank Kelleher, Hol	.989
1950	Cecil Garriott, LA	.994
1951	Walt Judnich, Sea	.996
	Loyd Christopher, Oak	.996
1952	Joe Brovia, Port	.996
1953	Bill Mc Cawley, SF	.996
1954	Bill Humphrey, Sac-Hol	.993
1955	Bob Coats, LA	.994
1956	Bobby Balcena, Sea	.997
1957	Floyd Robinson, SD	.997

CATCHER

1903	Harry Spies, LA	.974
1904	Harry Spies, LA	.978
1905	Harry Spies, LA	.975
1906	Records Unavailable	
1907	Gabby Street, SF	.969
1908	Claude Berry, SF	.959
1909	Charlie Lewis, Oak	.981
1910	Carl Mitze, Oak	.979
1911	Walt Kuhn, Port	.978
1912	Carl Mitze, Oak	.984
1913	Walter Schmidt, SF	.983
1914	Carl Mitze, Oak	.987
1915	Tubby Spencer, Ver	.985
1916	Clarence Brooks, LA	.982
1917	Walter Boles, LA	.978
1918	Walter Boles, LA	.984
1919	Al De Vormer, Ver	.976
1920	Hick Cady, Sac	.983
1921	Truck Hannah, LA	.972

CATCHER (cont.)

1922	Archie Yelle, SF	.980
1923	Danny Murphy, Ver	.987
1924	Del Baker, Oak	.989
1925	Frank Tobin, Port	.987
1926	Truck Hannah, LA	.987
1927	Hank Severeid, Sac	.982
1928	Johnny Bassler, Hol	.994
1929	Johnny Bassler, Hol	.988
1930	Truck Hannah, LA	.983
1931	Larry Woodall, Port	.995
1932	Larry Woodall, Sac	.996
1933	Larry Woodall, Sac	.986
1934	Larry Woodall, SF	.992
1935	Gene Desautels, Hol	.981
1936	Johnny Bassler, Sea	.986
1937	Bill Cronin, Port	.988
1938	Shanty Hogan, SD	.990
1939	George Detore, SD	.987
1940	Gilly Campbell, Sea	.988
1941	Gilly Campbell, Sea-LA	.989
1942	Billy Raimondi, Oak	.990
1943	Hal Sueme, Port	.987
1944	Bill Salkeld, SD	.992
1945	Norm Schleuter, Sac	.988
1946	Hal Sueme, Sea	.991
1947	Charlie Silvera, Port	.983
1948	Charlie Silvera, Port	.987
1949	John Ritchey, SD	.996
1950	Ray Noble, Oak	.993
1951	Les Peden, LA	.992
1952	Lonnie Summers, SD	.992
1953	Leonard Neal, Oak	.990
	Ray Orteig, Sea	.990
	Eddie Malone, Hol	.990
1954	Anthony Tornay, SF	.989
1955	Joe Ginsberg, Sea	.990
1956	Sammy Calderone, Port	.988
	Bill Hall, Hol	.988
1957	Dick Aylward, Sea	.995

PITCHER

1903	Jake Thielman, Port	.981
1904	Bobby Keefe, Tac	.962
1905	Spider Baum, LA	.976
1906	Records Unavailable	
1907	Oscar Jones, SF	.980

PITCHER (cont.)

1908	Deacon Wright, Oak	.973
1909	Alex Carson, Port	.988
1910	Jimmy Whalen, Sac	.986
1911	Frank Arellanes, Sac	1.000
1912	Judge Munsell, Sac	1.000
1913	Harry Krause, Oak	1.000
1914	Spider Baum, SF	1.000
1915	Harry Gregory, SLC	1.000
1916	Herb Kelly, Port	1.000
1917	Pete Standridge, LA	1.000
1918	Roy Mitchell, Ver	1.000
1919	Wally Schultz, LA	1.000
1920	Bill Prough, Sac	1.000
1921	Elmer Jacobs, Sea	.990
1922	Roy Gilder, Ver	1.000
1923	Ira Colwell, Oak	1.000
1924	Hugh Bedient, Port	1.000
1925	Oliver Mitchell, SF	1.000
1926	Earl Hamilton, LA	.985
1927	Al Gould, Oak	1.000
1928	Al Gould, Oak—Sac	1.000
1929	Elmer Jacobs, SF	1.000
1930	Elmer Hansen, Sea	1.000
1931	Claude Willoughby, SF	1.000
1932	Jimmy Zinn, SF	1.000
1933	Joe Bowman, Port	1.000
1934	Tom Sheehan, Hol	1.000
1935	Henry Ulrich, Port	1.000
1936	Berlyn Horne, SD	1.000
1937	Jim Chaplin, SD	1.000
1938	Wayne Osborne, Port	1.000
1939	Bob Muncrief, Hol	1.000
1940	Byron Humprheys, SD	1.000
1941	Al Olsen, SD	1.000
1942	Italo Chelini, Oak	1.000
1943	Pat Mc Laughlin, Hol	1.000
1944	Hal Turpin, Sea	1.000
1945	Hal Turpin, Sea	1.000
1946	Jack Salveson, Port	1.000
1947	Rugger Ardizoia, Hol	1.000
	Sig Jakucki, Sea—Sac	1.000
1948	Ken Holcombe, Sac	1.000
1949	Red Lynn, LA—Port	1.000
1950	Harry Feldman, SF	1.000
1951	Vic Lombardi, Hol	1.000
1952	Al Widmar, Sea	1.000
1953	Bill Moisan, LA	1.000

PITCHER (cont.)

1954	Eddie Erautt, SD	1.000
1955	Red Adams, Port	1.000
1956	Bill Werle, Port	1.000
1957	Marshall Bridges, Sac	1.000

ERRORS—FIRST BASE

1903	Charlie Townsend, Sac	58
1904	Kitty Brashear, Sea	55
1905	Joe Nealon, SF	48
1906	Records Unavailable	
1907	G. S. Bigbee, Oak	45
1908	Babe Danzig, Port	86
1909	Kitty Brashear, Ver	63
1910	Tom Tennant, SF	44
1911	Babe Danzig, Sac	43
1912	William Rapps, Port	22
1913	Charley Moore, LA	35
1914	Bill Abstein, LA	37
1915	Harry Heilmann, SF	25
1916	Gus Gleischman, Ver	40
1917	Phil Koerner, SF	28
1918	Records Unavailable	
1919	Lu Blue, Port	42
1920	Lu Blue, Port	33
1921	Jimmy O'Connell, SF	40
1922	Jim Poole, Port	35
1923	Jim Poole, Port	33
1924	Jim Poole, Port	32
1925	J. W. Davis, Sac	42
1926	J. W. Davis, Sac	36
1927	O.C. Mc Daniel, Miss	29
1928	O.C. Mc Daniel, Miss	19
1929	Jack Sherlock, Miss	28
1930	Mickey Heath, Hol	32
1931	Jack Fenton, Port	59
1932	Babe Dahlgren, Miss	30
1933	Babe Dahlgren, Miss	24
1934	Jim Oglesby, LA	24
1935	Roy Mort, Miss	15
	Les Powers, SF	15
1936	Harley Boss, SF	19
1937	Harley Boss, SF	24
1938	Larry Barton, Sac	19
1939	Larry Barton, Sac	20
1940	Ferris Fain, SF	24
1941	Ferris Fain, SF	22

ERRORS–FIRST BASE (cont.)

1942	Ferris Fain, SF	26
1943	Cyril Moran, Hol	20
1944	Gus Suhr, SF	18
1945	Cyril Moran, Hol	23
1946	Ferris Fain, SF	29
1947	Willard Matheson, SF	20
1948	Fenton Mole, Port	15
1949	Heinz Becker, Sea	19
1950	Chuck Stevens, Hol	19
1951	Bob Boyd, Sac	18
	Joe Lafata, Oak–Port	18
1952	Jack Graham, SD	19
1953	Tom Alston, SD	21
1954	Nippy Jones, Sac	23
1955	Nippy Jones, Sac	19
1956	Nippy Jones, Sac	20
1957	Steve Bilko, LA	12
	Bill Glynn, Sea–SD	12

ERRORS–SECOND BASE

1903	George Wheeler, LA	78
1904	Larry Schlafly, Oak	77
1905	Larry Schlafly, Port–LA	73
1906	Records Unavailable	
1907	George Haley, Oak	66
1908	Kid Mohler, SF	69
1909	Ivan Howard, LA	59
1910	George Cutshaw, Oak	78
1911	Patsy O'Rourke, Sac	64
1912	Patsy O'Rourke, Sac	66
1913	Duke Kenworthy, Sac	59
1914	Red Downs, SF	72
1915	Fred Mc Mullin, LA	53
1916	Red Downs, SF	73
1917	Bobby Vaughn, LA–Ver	50
1918	Records Unavailable	
1919	Marty Krug, SLC	51
1920	Marty Krug, SLC	47
1921	Paddy Siglin, SLC	50
1922	Howard Lindemore, LA	43
1923	Les Sheehan, SLC	40
	Paddy Siglin, Sac	40
1924	Spencer Adams, Oak	56
1925	Clyde Beck, LA	42
1926	John Monroe, Sac	53
1927	Gus Suhr, SF	44

ERRORS–SECOND BASE (cont.)

1928	Gus Suhr, SF	39
1929	Mickey Finn, Miss	32
	Charles Falk, Hol	32
1930	John Monroe, Miss	45
1931	John Monroe, Miss–Port	35
1932	Art Garibaldi, SF	56
1933	Alex Kampouris, Sac	47
1934	Al Wright, Miss	38
1935	Billy Cissell, Port	39
1936	Pete Coscarart, Port	41
1937	Al Wright, SF	36
1938	Al Wright, SF	26
1939	Billy Cissell, Hol	40
1940	Billy Cissell, Hol	45
1941	Buddy Blattner, Sac	32
	Al Wright, Port	32
1942	Mel Skelley, SD	33
1943	Nippy Jones, Sac	44
1944	Del Young, SF	33
1945	Gene Handley, Sac	31
1946	Alex Kampouris, Sac	27
1947	Lou Stringer, LA	21
1948	Lou Stringer, Hol	27
1949	Billy Martin, Oak	29
1950	Bob Wilson, SD	28
1951	Gene Handley, Hol	28
1952	Eddie Basinski, Port	29
1953	Monty Basgall, Hol	31
1954	Al Federoff, SD	34
1955	Billy Consolo, Oak	28
1956	Ken Aspromonte, SF	26
1957	Sparky Anderson, LA	15
	Ken Aspromonte, SF	15
	Owen Friend, Van	15

ERRORS–THIRD BASE

1903	Heine Jansing, Sea	99
1904	Brick Deveraux, Oak	94
1905	Brick Deveraux, Oak	54
	Charlie Irwin, SF	54
1906	Records Unavailable	
1907	Anson Mott, Port	60
1908	Jud Smith, LA	42
1909	Otis Johnson, Port	57
	Anson Mott, Ver	57
1910	Louis Boardman, Sac	53

ERRORS—THIRD BASE (cont.)

1911	Jimmy Shinn, Sac	68
1912	Gus Hetling, Oak	55
1913	Joseph Cartwright, SF	44
1914	Ed Hallinan, Sac	40
1915	Bob Jones, SF	48
1916	Bob Jones, SF	44
1917	Charlie Pick, SF	53
1918	Records Unavailable	
1919	Willie Kamm, SF	42
1920	Willie Kamm, SF	53
1921	Don Brown, SLC	39
1922	Red Smith, Ver	33
1923	Red Smith, Ver—LA	39
1924	Frank Brazill, Port	42
1925	George Makin, Oak	49
1926	Frank Brazill, LA	32
1927	Jim Mc Laughlin, Sac	25
1928	Jim Mc Laughlin, Sac	22
	Babe Pinelli, SF	22
1929	Johnny Vergez, Oak	44
1930	Fritz Knothe, Sea	42
1931	Fritz Knothe, Sea	46
1932	Julie Wera, SF	52
1933	Gene Lillard, LA	43
1934	Leo Ostenberg, Sac	48
1935	Gene Lillard, LA	34
1936	Steve Barath, SF	46
1937	Dick Gyselman, Sea	40
1938	Johnny Vergez, Sac	40
1939	Art Garibaldi, Sac	49
1940	Ted Jennings, SF	48
1941	Mel Duezabou, Oak	63
1942	Dick Gyselman, Sea	39
1943	Charles English, LA	27
1944	Ed Wheeler, SD	36
1945	Dick Gyselman, SD	40
1946	Ted Jennings, SF	43
1947	Steve Mesner, Sac	35
1948	Hilly Layne, Sea	28
1949	Jim Baxes, Hol	43
1950	Minnie Minoso, SD	27
1951	Rocky Krsnich, Sea	26
1952	Donald Eggert, Port	35
1953	Eddie Bockman, Sac	31
1954	Bruce Edwards, LA	22
1955	Donald Eggert, Port	30
1956	Milt Smith, Sea	29

ERRORS—THIRD BASE (cont.)

1957	Kal Segrist, Van	30

ERRORS—SHORTSTOP

1903	Danny Shay, SF	108
1904	Russ Hall, Sea	119
1905	John Gochnaur, SF	98
1906	Records Unavailable	
1907	Truck Eagan , Oak	67
1908	Phil Cooney, Port	79
1909	Jimmy Shinn, Sac	98
1910	Buzzy Wares, Oak	107
1911	Buzzy Wares, Oak	92
1912	Al Cook, Oak	87
1913	Al Cook, Oak	84
1914	Roy Corhan, SF	82
1915	Roy Corhan, SF	83
1916	Chuck Ward, Port	65
1917	Charlie Hollocher, Port	62
1918	Records Unavailable	
1919	Sammy Bohne, Oak	58
1920	Ike Mc Auley, LA	58
1921	Jake Caveney, SF	70
1922	Heine Sand, SLC	68
1923	Ike Mc Auley, LA	62
	Hal Rhyne, SF	62
1924	Jack Warner, Ver	70
1925	Tony Lazzeri, SLC	85
1926	Lyn Lary, Oak	59
1927	Billy Cissell, Port	76
1928	Carl Dittmar, LA	69
1929	Frank Crosetti, SF	72
1930	Dud Lee, Hol	62
1931	Frank Crosetti, SF	60
1932	F. W. Ellsworth, Sea	72
1933	Carl Sever, Miss—SF	77
1934	Jim Levey, Hol	67
1935	Chet Smith, Sea	69
1936	George Myatt, SD	79
1937	George Myatt, SD	58
1938	Joe Orengo, Sac	46
1939	Joe Hoover, Hol	53
1940	Steve Mesner, SD	62
1941	Nanny Fernandez, SF	83
1942	Joe Hoover, Hol	68
1943	John Caulfield, Oak	76
1944	John Caulfield, Oak	65

ERRORS–SHORTSTOP (cont.)

1945	John Caulfield, Oak	77
1946	Jack Calvey, Sac	57
1947	Roy Nicely, SF	59
1948	Roy Nicely, SF	51
1949	Roy Nicely, SF	43
1950	Len Ratto, Sac	45
1951	Gene Baker, LA	52
1952	Gene Baker, LA	55
1953	Buddy Peterson, SD	44
1954	Buddy Peterson, SD	39
1955	Buddy Peterson, SD	41
	Dick Smith, Hol	41
1956	Clarence Moore, SD	50
1957	Maury Wills, Sea	48

ERRORS–OUTFIELD

1903	Bill O'Hara, Oak–Sea	45
1904	Bob Ganley, Oak	33
1905	George Mc Laughlin, Tac	33
1906	Records Unavailable	
1907	Jimmy Smith, Oak	30
1908	John Bassey, Port	28
1909	Felix Martinke, Ver	35
1910	Henry Perry, Sac	29
1911	Walter Carlisle, Ver	26
1912	Tom Daley, LA	21
1913	Jimmy Johnston, SF	20
1914	Walter Carlisle, Ven	25
1915	Harl Maggert, LA	24
1916	Finners Quinlan, SLC	22
1917	Ken Williams, Port	18
1918	Records Unavailable	
1919	E. J. Mulvey, SLC	16
1920	Hack Miller, Oak	20
1921	Hack Miller, Oak	20
1922	Dixie Carroll, LA	27
1923	Wally Hood, LA	24
1924	Buzz Arlett, Oak	19
1925	M. J. Wolfer, Ver	19
1926	Tony Governor, Oak	18
1927	Edward Rose, Miss	22
1928	Wes Shulmerich, LA	24
1929	Charlie Bates, Port	26
1930	Walter French, Port	22
1931	Frenchy Uhalt, Oak	23
1932	Lou Almada, Sea	21

ERRORS–OUTFIELD (cont.)

1933	Lou Almada, Sea	19
1934	Ernest Kelly, Oak	20
1935	Mike Hunt, Sea	24
	Smead Jolley, Hol	24
1936	Moose Clabaugh, Port	16
1937	Ernie Koy, Oak	20
1938	Dom Di Maggio, SF	14
	Jess Hill, Oak	14
	Mike Hunt, Sea	14
1939	Jo Jo White, Sea	16
1940	John Barrett, SF	17
1941	Wallace Carroll, LA–SF	19
1942	Buster Adams, Sac	13
1943	Johnny Dickshot, Hol	16
1944	Frank Shone, Port	19
1945	Frank Shone, Port	20
1946	Don White, SF	17
1947	Neill Sheridan, SF	19
1948	Neill Sheridan, Sea	16
1949	Jackie Jensen, Oak	16
1950	Luis Marquez, Port	12
1951	Jim Rivera, Sea	16
1952	Len Attyd, Oak–Sac	10
1953	Pete Milne, Oak	12
1954	Len Attyd, Sac	12
	Granville Gladstone, Port	12
1955	George Metkovich, Oak	12
1956	George Metkovich, Van	12
1957	Bill Causion, Hol	11

ASSISTS–OUTFIELD

1903	Wilbur Murdock, Oak	63
1904	George Van Haltren, Sea	58
1905	George Hildebrand, SF	40
	Mike Lynch, Tac	40
1906	Records Unavailable	
1907	Walter Mc Creedie, Port	43
1908	George Van Haltren, Oak	48
1909	Charley Doyle, Sac	44
1910	Pinky Swander, Oak	43
1911	Ivan Howard, LA	44
1912	Tom Daley, LA	39
1913	Bert Coy, Oak	40
1914	Dick Bayless, Ven	37
	Mike Fitzgerald, SF	37
1915	William Speas, Port	47

ASSISTS—OUTFIELD (cont.)

1916	Finners Quinlan, SLC	43
1917	Irish Meusel, LA	44
1918	Records Unavailable	
1919	Bill Lane, Oak	36
1920	Denney Wilie, Oak	40
1921	Denney Wilie, Oak	38
1922	Denney Wilie, Oak	39
1923	Wally Hood, LA	45
1924	Johnny Frederick, SLC	31
1925	M. J. Wolfer, Ver	30
1926	Ike Boone, Miss	43
1927	Earl Averill, SF	45
1928	Smead Jolley, SF	35
1929	Ike Boone, Miss	44
1930	Myril Hoag, Sac	31
1931	Louis Almada, Sea	31
1932	Lou Finney, Port	27
	Jim Welsh, Miss—Sea	27
1933	Joe Di Maggio, SF	32
1934	Hank Steinbacher, Sac	27
1935	Joe Di Maggio, SF	32
1936	Vince Di Maggio, SD	31
1937	Rupert Thompson, SD	27
1938	Dom Di Maggio, SF	29
1939	Dom Di Maggio, SF	27
1940	Bud Stewart, SD	27
1941	Brooks Holder, SF	19
1942	Kermit Lewis, SF	29
1943	Rupert Thompson, Port	22
1944	Frank Kelleher, Hol	24
1945	Tony Criscola, SD	27
1946	Don White, SF	19
1947	Neill Sheridan, SF	22
1948	Dain Clay, SD	25
1949	Irv Noren, Hol	30
1950	Joe Brovia, Port	20
1951	Ed Sauer, Hol—SD—SF	17
1952	Bob Usher, LA	17
1953	Sam Chapman, Oak	25
1954	Harry Elliott, SD	23
1955	Art Schult, Sea	19
1956	Roman Mejias, Hol	24
1957	Albie Pearson, SF	28

ERRORS—CATCHER

1903	Ly Gorton, Oak	45

ERRORS—CATCHER (cont.)

1904	Farmer Steelman, Port	32
1905	Jim Byrnes, Oak	35
1906	Records Unavailable	
1907	John Bliss, Oak	30
1908	Claude Berry, SF	39
1909	Gus Fisher, Port	34
1910	Drummond Brown, Ver	38
1911	Pinch Thomas, Sac	33
1912	Harry Cheek, Sac	14
1913	Rowdy Elliott, Ven	34
1914	Rowdy Elliott, Ven	29
1915	Truck Hannah, SLC	30
1916	Jack Roche, Port	25
1917	Truck Hannah, SLC	42
1918	Records Unavailable	
1919	Rowdy Elliott, Oak	31
1920	Ed Baldwin, Sea	21
1921	Ed Baldwin, LA	22
1922	Oscar Stanage, Sac	20
1923	John Peters, SLC	25
1924	John Peters, SLC	18
1925	Merv Shea, Sac	35
1926	Art Koehler, Sac	21
1927	Gus Sanberg, LA	13
1928	Joe Sprinz, SF	21
1929	Charles Borreani, Sea	18
	Robert Reed, SF	18
1930	Joe Palmisano, Port	18
1931	Bill Brenzel, Miss	17
1932	Frank Cox, Sea	16
	Fred Hofmann, Miss	16
1933	John Bottarini, SF	18
1934	John Bottarini, Sea	22
1935	Chink Outen, Miss	18
1936	John Bottarini, LA	25
1937	Bob Collins, LA	24
1938	George Dickey, Port	15
1939	Bob Collins, LA	13
1940	Joe Annunzio, Port	12
1941	Billy Raimondi, Oak	18
1942	John Leovich, Port	19
1943	Billy Raimondi, Oak	14
1944	Jim Hill, Hol	23
1945	Jim Hill, Hol	19
1946	Al Unser, Hol	19
1947	Ed Fitz Gerald, Sac	20
1948	Mickey Grasso, Sea	24

ERRORS–CATCHER (cont.)

1949	Mickey Grasso, Sea	18
1950	Jim Gladd, Port	13
1951	Frank Kerr, SD	11
1952	Bob Wilson, Sea	16
1953	John Ritchey, Sac	20
1954	Alfred Evans, LA	13
	Leonard Neal, Oak	13
1955	Bill Hall, Hol	14
	Jim Robertson, Port	14
1956	John Romano, Van	15
1957	Cuno Barragan, Sac	15

ASSISTS–CATCHER

1903	Charlie Graham, Sac	226
1904	Charlie Graham, Tac	205
1905	Parke Wilson, SF	208
1906	Records Unavailable	
1907	Gabby Street, SF	220
1908	Claude Berry, SF	201
1909	Claude Berry, SF	227
1910	Mick La Longe, O–Sac	281
1911	Pinch Thomas, Sac	247
1912	Charles Mitze, Oak	205
1913	Rowdy Elliott, Ven	244
1914	Rowdy Elliott, Ven	217
1915	Walter Boles, LA	183
	Gus Fisher, Port	183
1916	Truck Hannah, SLC	201
1917	Truck Hannah, SLC	253
1918	Records Unavailable	
1919	Pete Lapan, LA–Sea	133
1920	Johnny Bassler, LA	190
1921	Truck Hannah, Ver	133
1922	Art Koehler, Oak	122
1923	Art Koehler, Sac	128
1924	Ed Baldwin, Sea	111
1925	Merv Shea, Sac	109
1926	Art Koehler, Sac	133
1927	Rodney Whitney, Miss	99
1928	Johnny Bassler, Hol	125
1929	Ernie Lombardi, Oak	95
1930	Ernie Lombardi, Oak	105
1931	Bill Brenzel, Miss	89
1932	Johnny Bassler, Hol	120
1933	John Fitzpatrick, Mis	113
1934	Billy Raimondi, Oak	112

ASSISTS–CATCHER (cont.)

1935	Gene Desautels, Hol	97
1936	Gene Desautels, SD	109
1937	Bob Collins, LA	121
1938	Bob Collins, LA	97
1939	Bob Collins, LA	93
1940	Joe Sprinz, SF	71
1941	Cliff Dapper, Hol	91
1942	Ray Mueller, Sac	115
1943	Billy Raimondi, Oak	90
1944	Billy Raimondi, Oak	91
1945	Del Ballinger, SD	102
1946	Al Unser, Hol	97
1947	Ed Fitz Gerald, Sac	80
	Eddie Malone, LA	80
1948	Mickey Grasso, Sea	81
1949	Mickey Grasso, Sea	74
1950	Dee Moore, SD	70
1951	Les Peden, LA	70
1952	Les Peden, LA	111
1953	Anthony Tornay, SF	82
1954	Anthony Tornay, SF	58
1955	Joe Ginsberg, Sea	86
1956	Sammy Calderone, Port	69
1957	Bill Hall, Hol	59

ERRORS–PITCHER

1903	Doc Newton, LA–Port	21
1904	Doc Newton, LA	28
1905	Sea Lion Hall, Sea	24
1906	Records Unavailable	
1907	Bob Groom, Port	12
	Barney Joy, SF	12
1908	D. A. Hardy, Oak	15
1909	George Boice, Oak	14
	Curly Brown, Sac	14
	Jack Graney, Port	14
1910	Alex Carson, Ver	15
	Roy Hitt, Ver	15
	Ed Willett, Ver	15
1911	Bill Steen, Port	12
1912	Harry Gregory, Oak	10
1913	Harry Gregory, Oak–LA	14
	Bob Koestner, Ven	14
1914	Harry Gregory, Sac	10
1915	Tom Hughes, LA	10
	Johnny Lush, Port	10

ERRORS—PITCHER (cont.)   ERRORS—PITCHER (cont.)

	Tex Pruiett, Oak	10		Art Herring, Sac	7
1916	Paul Fittery, SLC	11		Jake Wade, Port	7
1917	Casey Smith, SF	12	1936	Sam Gibson, SF	8
1918	Records Unavailable		1937	Ray Prim, LA	8
1919	Bill Pertica, LA	9	1938	William Schmidt, Sac	7
	Casey Smith, SF	9	1939	Bill Walker, Sea	7
1920	Buzz Arlett, Oak	10	1940	Joe Orrell, Port	9
	Bob Geary, Sea	10	1941	Joe Berry, LA	9
	Sam Ross, Port	10	1942	Dick Barrett, Sea	8
	Jim Scott, SF	10	1943	Bill Thomas, Hol	9
1921	Ray Crumpler, SF	10	1944	Ray Harrell, SF	10
1922	Bill James, Ver	13	1945	Don Pulford, Port	7
1923	Elmer Ponder, LA	10	1946	Lou Tost, Sea	9
1924	Earl Kunz, Oak	10	1947	Dick Barrett, Sea	6
1925	George Boehler, Oak	10		Al Treichel, SD	6
1926	Herm Pillette, Miss	9	1948	Charlie Gassaway, Oak	7
1927	Jim Joe Edwards, Sea	10	1949	Steve Nagy, SF	7
1928	Walter Mails, SF	8	1950	Bob Gillespie, Sac	6
	Herbert May, SF	6	1951	Jim Davis, Sea	5
1929	Joe Cascarella, Port	7		Earl Harrist, Oak	5
	Pete Daglia, Oak	7		Sam Jones, SD	5
1930	Herm Pillette, Miss	6		Marino Pieretti, Port	5
	Fay Thomas, Sac	6		Jack Salveson, Hol	5
1931	Tony Freitas, Oak	7	1952	Paul Pettit, Hol	6
	Monte Pearson, Oak	7	1953	Chet Johnson, Sac	5
1932	Rudy Kallio, Sea	7	1954	Gene Bearden, Sea	8
1933	John Babich, Miss	10	1955	Gene Bearden, SF	9
1934	Herm Pillette, Sea	7	1956	Marino Pieretti, LA	5
1935	Paul Gregory, Sac	7	1957	Hank Aguirre, SD	7

SECTION IX

League Leaders — Teams

On the following pages are listed the year-by-year league leaders, by team, in five offensive and two defensive categories in Pacific Coast League for the years 1903 through 1957. (Information in other categories is too sketchy to be included here.)

These records are presented to provide a profile of the changes in the league over the years 1903 through 1957; fluctuations in scoring and power, better defense, less reliance on moving runners along via sacrifice, etc.

Below are the single-season records for the years 1903 through 1957 in each of the categories listed in this section:

Batting Average:	Salt Lake City .327 (1923 & 1924)
Runs Per Game:	Salt Lake City 7.0 (1924)
Home Runs:	Salt Lake City 204 (1923)
Stolen Bases:	San Francisco 413 (1913)
Sacrifice Hits:	Oakland 324 (1927)
Fielding Percentage:	Hollywood .979 (1950)
Double Plays:	San Francisco 210 (1948)

BATTING AVERAGE

1903	Portland	.278
1904	Seattle	.280
1905	Seattle	.238
1906–1909	Records Unavailable	
1910	San Francisco	.226
1911	Vernon	.266
1912	Oakland	.272
1913	Portland	.276
1914	Portland	.276
1915	Salt Lake City	.284
1916	Salt Lake City	.273
1917	Salt Lake City	.285
1918	Los Angeles	.267
1919	Salt Lake City	.284
1920	Salt Lake City	.295
1921	Oakland	.305
1922	San Francisco	.298
1923	Salt Lake City	.327
1924	Salt Lake City	.327
1925	Salt Lake City	.321
1926	Mission	.290
1927	Portland	.307
1928	San Francisco	.308
1929	Mission	.319
1930	San Francisco	.318
1931	San Francisco	.314
1932	Portland	.293
1933	Mission	.308
1934	Los Angeles	.299
1935	San Francisco	.305
1936	Los Angeles	.292
1937	San Francisco	.286
1938	San Francisco	.292
1939	Portland	.296
1940	San Diego	.291
1941	Sacramento	.283
1942	Sacramento	.283
1943	Los Angeles	.281
1944	Los Angeles	.270
1945	Sacramento	.289
1946	Hollywood	.261
1947	Hollywood	.285
1948	Oakland	.286
1949	Oakland	.284
1950	Oakland	.289
1951	Oakland	.275
1952	Hollywood	.270

BATTING AVERAGE (cont.)

1953	Los Angeles	.276
1954	San Diego	.276
1955	San Francisco	.268
1956	Los Angeles	.297
1957	San Francisco	.278

RUNS PER GAME

1903	Records Unavailable	
1904	Seattle	5.4
1905	San Francisco	3.6
1906–1909	Records Unavailable	
1910	San Francisco	3.1
1911	Vernon	4.7
1912	Vernon	4.6
1913	Sacramento	3.9
1914	Los Angeles	4.3
1915	Salt Lake City	5.1
1916	Salt Lake City	4.9
1917	Salt Lake City	4.4
1918	Sacramento	4.2
1919	Salt Lake City	5.0
1920	Salt Lake City	5.2
1921	Salt Lake City	5.7
1922	San Francisco	5.4
1923	Salt Lake City	6.5
1924	Salt Lake City	7.0
1925	Salt Lake City	6.8
1926	Los Angeles	4.8
1927	San Francisco	5.7
1928	San Francisco	5.9
1929	Mission	6.0
1930	Hollywood	6.5
1931	Los Angeles	6.0
1932	Los Angeles	5.4
1933	Los Angeles	5.8
1934	Los Angeles	5.9
1935	San Francisco	5.8
1936	Los Angeles	5.0
1937	Sacramento	5.1
1938	San Francisco	5.1
1939	Los Angeles	5.2
1940	Los Angeles	4.9
1941	Hollywood	4.6
1942	Sacramento	4.4
1943	Los Angeles	4.9
1944	Los Angeles	4.5

RUNS PER GAME (cont.)

1945	Sacramento	5.4
1946	San Francisco	4.3
1947	Oakland	5.0
1948	Oakland	5.4
1949	Oakland	5.3
1950	Oakland	5.8
1951	Los Angeles	5.1
1952	Hollywood	4.6
1953	Seattle	4.5
1954	San Diego	4.5
1955	San Francisco	4.3
1956	Los Angeles	6.0
1957	San Francisco	4.7

HOME RUNS

1903	Records Unavailable	
1904	Tacoma	46
1905–1912	Records Unavailable	
1913	Sacramento	47
1914	Venice	38
1915	San Francisco	99
1916	Salt Lake City	65
1917	Portland	52
1918	Salt Lake City	30
1919	Salt Lake City	80
1920	Salt Lake City	91
1921	Salt Lake City	122
1922	Salt Lake City	138
1923	Salt Lake City	204
1924	Salt Lake City	194
1925	Salt Lake City	197
1926	Portland	156
1927	San Francisco	155
1928	San Francisco	182
1929	San Francisco	193
1930	Hollywood	182
1931	Hollywood	136
1932	Seattle	118
1933	Los Angeles	147
1934	Los Angeles	127
1935	Los Angeles	117
1936	Seattle	121
1937	Seattle	128
1938	Sacramento	121
1939	Los Angeles	117
1940	Los Angeles	115

HOME RUNS (cont.)

1941	Sacramento	87
1942	Sacramento	78
1943	Los Angeles	97
1944	Los Angeles	73
1945	Los Angeles	63
1946	Hollywood	92
1947	Los Angeles	151
1948	Los Angeles	178
1949	San Diego	187
1950	San Diego	173
1951	Los Angeles	167
1952	Los Angeles	145
1953	Los Angeles	153
1954	Los Angeles	140
1955	Los Angeles	143
1956	Los Angeles	202
1957	Los Angeles	167

STOLEN BASES

1903	Records Unavailable	
1904	Los Angeles	364
1905–1910	Records Unavailable	
1911	Los Angeles	370
1912	Los Angeles	337
1913	San Francisco	413
1914	Los Angeles	356
1915	San Francisco	349
1916	Vernon	252
1917	San Francisco	385
1918	San Francisco	174
1919	Oakland	276
1920	Seattle	242
1921	Sacramento	247
1922	Sacramento	226
1923	Sacramento	298
1924	Seattle	167
1925	Seattle	173
1926	Los Angeles	137
1927	Hollywood	130
1928	Portland	128
1929	Los Angeles	193
1930	Los Angeles	184
1931	Seattle	179
1932	Seattle	150
1933	Oakland	227
1934	Los Angeles	195

STOLEN BASES (cont.)

1935	San Francisco	178
1936	San Diego	151
1937	Sacramento	131
1938	Sacramento	107
1939	Seattle	148
1940	Seattle	137
1941	Sacramento	162
1942	Seattle	132
1943	Seattle	134
1944	Seattle	161
1945	Seattle	182
1946	Seattle	134
1947	San Diego	130
1948	Oakland	101
1949	Oakland	127
1950	Seattle	116
1951	Sacramento	80
1952	Hollywood	142
1953	Hollywood	93
1954	Hollywood	160
1955	Hollywood	120
1956	Hollywood	123
1957	Portland	74

SACRIFICE HITS

1903	Records Unavailable	
1904	Tacoma	279
1905—1910 Records Unavailable		
1911	San Francisco	313
1912	Los Angeles	317
1913	Sacramento	274
1914	Los Angeles	308
1915	Los Angeles	314
1916	Vernon	262
1917	Los Angeles	285
1918	Records Unavailable	
1919	Oakland	294
1920	Vernon	311
1921	Los Angeles	295
1922	Vernon	318
1923	Los Angeles	271
1924	Oakland	288
1925	Los Angeles	240
1926	Oakland	287
1927	Oakland	324
1928	Oakland	298

SACRIFICE HITS (cont.)

1929	Hollywood	314
1930	Los Angeles	292
1931	Sacramento	187
1932	Portland	180
1933	Portland	148
1934	San Francisco	208
1935	Los Angeles	156
1936	Los Angeles	155
1937	Oakland	138
1938	Seattle	153
1939	San Diego	203
1940	Seattle	194
1941	Seattle	180
1942	Sacramento	194
1943	San Diego	158
1944	Los Angeles	170
1945	Seattle	206
1946	Oakland	163
1947	San Diego	144
1948	San Diego	139
1949	Hollywood	185
1950	Hollywood	195
1951	Hollywood	173
1952	Hollywood	199
1953	Los Angeles	141
1954	San Francisco	157
1955	Hollywood	155
1956	Hollywood	109
1957	Seattle	136

FIELDING PERCENTAGE

1903	Records Unavailable	
1904	San Francisco	.949
1905	Tacoma	.958
1906—1910 Records Unavailable		
1911	San Francisco	.962
1912	Oakland	.962
1913	Portland	.963
1914	Venice	.965
1915	Vernon	.964
1916	Oakland	.963
1917	Los Angeles	.965
1918	Records Unavailable	
1919	Los Angeles	.969
1920	Vernon	.972
1921	Sacramento	.972

FIELDING PCT. (cont.) FIELDING PCT. (cont.)

1922	San Francisco	.964	1940	Seattle	.972
1923	Sacramento	.968	1941	San Diego	.972
1924	San Francisco	.967	1942	Los Angeles	.973
1925	San Francisco	.968	1943	Los Angeles	.978
1926	Los Angeles	.971	1944	Portland	.966
1927	Oakland	.973	1945	Sacramento	.968
1928	Sacramento	.973	1946	Los Angeles	.969
1929	Mission	.975	1947	Los Angeles	.974
1930	Los Angeles	.974	1948	San Diego	.975
1931	Portland	.970	1949	Hollywood	.974
1932	Sacramento	.974	1950	Hollywood	.979
1933	Sacramento	.972	1951	Los Angeles	.976
1934	Los Angeles	.970	1952	Portland	.976
1935	Portland	.970	1953	Seattle	.978
1936	Mission	.973	1954	Hollywood	.977
1937	Oakland	.971	1955	San Diego	.976
1938	Seattle	.975	1956	Seattle	.973
1939	Los Angeles	.975	1957	San Diego	.977

DOUBLE PLAYS DOUBLE PLAYS (cont.)

1903–1939	Records Unavailable		1948	San Francisco	210
1940	San Diego	201	1949	Oakland	196
1941	San Francisco	167	1950	Sacramento	206
1942	San Diego	170	1951	Hollywood	170
1943	Seattle	148	1952	Portland	187
1944	Hollywood	159	1953	Portland	204
	Oakland	159	1954	San Francisco	185
1945	Sacramento	186	1955	Sacramento	197
1946	San Diego	186	1956	Portland	207
1947	Seattle	206	1957	Vancouver	191

SECTION X

Statistical Corrections

This section lists corrections made to the official records carried in the various guides published throughout the years. The columns show the player and team, followed by the original number carried in the official records (listed under the heading "Old"), and the corrected figure shown in this book (under the heading "New").

BATTING AVERAGES

Year	Player, Team	Old	New
1903	Andrews, Port-Sea	.279	.281
	Freeman, Port	.303	.304
	Hoy, LA	.260	.261
	Hurlburt, LA	.260	.261
	Messerly, Oak-Port	.249	.248
	Vigneaux, Port	.190	.194
1904	Castro, Port	.265	.263
	Murphy, Port-Sea	.243	.244
	Shea, Port-SF	.195	.196
	J. Smith, LA	.280	.279
	H. Spencer, Port	.240	.238
1905	Frary, Sea	.237	.238
	W. Hogan, Oak	.238	.228
	Streib, Oak-Sea	.204	.203
	Van Haltren, Oak	.255	.256
1906	Arellanes, Fre	.164	.165
	Blankenship, Sea	.259	.253
	Brashear, LA	.388	.369
	Cartwright, Fre	.216	.217
	Cates, Oak	.159	.199
	Cravath, LA	.284	.283
	Croll, Sea	.259	.248
	Dashwood, Fre	.185	.186
	Delmas, LA-Fre	.242	.245
1906	Dillon, LA	.330	.329
	Eagan, Fre	.260	.261

BATTING AVERAGES (cont.)

Year	Player, Team	Old	New
1906	Dillon, LA	.330	.329
	Eager, LA	.156	.157
	Francks, Oak	.209	.227
	Graham, Oak	.212	.217
	Hackett, Oak	.196	.192
	Haley, Oak	.221	.222
	Henderson, Port	.270	.268
	Hitt, SF	.293	.301
	Hogan, Fre	.175	.178
	Householder, Sea-SF	.303	.305
	Irwin, SF	.230	.231
	McCreedie, Port	.301	.309
	McHale, Port	.310	.311
	McLean, Port	.315	.355
	Mohler, SF	.310	.309
	Moore, Port-LA	.200	.198
	Mott, Sea	.183	.184
	Nagle, LA	.247	.248
	Randolph, Oak-SF-LA	.168	.169
	Sears, SF	.216	.211
	Smith, Oak	.236	.235
	Sweeney, Port	.285	.283
	Toman, LA	.188	.190
	Van Buren, Sea	.270	.269
	Van Haltren, Oak	.216	.217
	Wilson, SF	.234	.235
	Wolter, Fre	.285	.286
1908	Bassey, Port	.250	.246
	Dillon, LA	.270	.271
	Ellis, LA	.270	.269
1909	Daringer, Sac	.198	.197
	Mott, Ver	.178	.179
	Mundorff, SF	.265	.266
	Myers, Sac	.291	.292
1910	Dillon, LA	.239	.238
	Heister, Sac	.217	.216
	Lindsay, Ver	.181	.196
	Wolverton, Oak	.255	.256
1911	Powell, SF	.290	.289
1912	Agnew, Ver	.282	.283
	Bancroft, Port	.213	.212
	Hartley, SF	.305	.306
	Van Buren, Sac	.314	.313
1913	Chadbourne, Port	.284	.283
	Mundorff, SF	.269	.270
1914	Carlisle, Ven	.263	.262
1916	Doane, Ver	.272	.271
	Fisher, Port	.289	.288

BATTING AVERAGES (cont.)

Year	Player, Team	Old	New
1916	Gleischmann, SLC	.244	.245
	Mitze, Oak	.240	.241
	Shinn, SLC	.279	.280
	Vann, SLC-Oak	.309	.308
	Williams, Port	.285	.284
1917	Callahan, Ver	.232	.233
	Daley, Ver	.277	.276
	Mitchell, Ver	.273	.272
1919	Mitze, Oak	.243	.248
1920	Koerner, SF	.262	.263
1922	King, Port	.257	.258
1925	Agnew, SF	.325	.326
	Brazill, Sea	.394	.395
	Daly, Sea	.227	.228
	Hunnefield, Port	.282	.291
	Makin, Oak	.256	.257
	McCann, Port	.310	.309
	Warner, Ver	.295	.296
	Watson, Sac	.291	.296
	Whaley, LA	.258	.257
	Yarrison, Port	.226	.227
1926	Agnew, SF	.252	.251
	Camilli, SF	.311	.312
	Hemingway, LA	.279	.278
	Krug, LA	.390	.389
	Rohwer, Port-Sac	.254	.262
1927	Yelle, SF	.259	.260
1928	Backer, Sac	.266	.267
	Borreani, Sea	.241	.240
	Burkett, LA	.260	.261
	Johnson, Port	.309	.310
	Rehg, Hol	.306	.307
	Sigafoos, Port	.299	.296
	Thurston, SF	.347	.348
1930	Summa, Port	.317	.316
1931	Campbell, LA	.306	.307
	Dahlgren, Miss	.243	.244
	Powers, Oak	.299	.300
1932	De Viveiros, Sac-Oak-LA	.224	.225
	Dittmar, LA	.299	.298
	Moore, Port	.335	.336
1933	Reese, LA	.330	.331
1935	Beck, Miss	.192	.191
	Steinbacher, Sac	.308	.309
1945	Scarsella, Oak	.327	.325
1949	Fallon, Hol	.218	.217
	Marsh, Sac	.212	.211
	Ostrowski, LA	.318	.314

BATTING AVERAGES (cont.)

Year	Player, Team	Old	New
1949	Shupe, SD-Port	.275	.276
	Terwilliger, LA	.278	.275
1950	Wilson, Oak	.312	.311

EARNED RUN AVERAGES

Year	Player, Team	Old	New
1914	Chech, LA	2.89	2.88
	Ehmke, LA	2.80	2.79
	Harkness, Ven	4.91	4.90
	Koestner, Ven	4.00	3.99
	Kremer, Sac	5.23	5.20
	Lush, Port	1.44	1.43
	McGinnity, Ven	3.66	3.65
	Pruiett, Oak	3.26	3.25
	White, Ven	2.44	2.43
	L. Williams, Sac	2.06	2.05
1915	Beer, Oak	2.80	2.73
	Boyd, Oak	2.64	2.62
	Brown, SF	2.76	2.75
	Burns, LA-Oak	2.80	2.79
	Cavet, SF	4.30	4.29
	Chech, LA-Ver	3.29	3.28
	Couch, SF	2.45	2.47
	Coveleski, Port	2.68	2.67
	Evans, Port	3.19	3.20
	Fittery, SLC	3.12	3.03
	Fromme, Ver	2.29	2.28
	Killilay, SF-SLC	3.30	3.31
	Klawitter, Oak	2.98	2.97
	La Roy, SLC	3.99	3.97
	Piercy, Ver	2.20	2.19
	Pruiett, Oak	2.96	2.95
	Ryan, LA	2.73	2.72
	West, Ver-SLC-LA	4.30	4.31
	J. Williams, SLC-LA	4.06	4.05
1916	Arellanes, Ver	2.47	2.46
	Beer, Oak	3.94	3.09
	Brown, SF	3.17	3.16
	Decanniere, Ver	2.18	2.20
	Erickson, SF	2.37	2.35
	Fanning, SF	3.71	3.60
	Fittery, SLC	3.30	2.97
	Hagerman, Port	4.33	4.30
	B. Hall, SLC	4.05	4.04
	S. Hall, LA	3.38	3.37
1916	Hess, Ver	2.70	2.69

EARNED RUN AVERAGES (cont.)

Year	Player, Team	Old	New
1916	Higginbotham, Port-Oak	4.48	4.29
	Hoff, SLC	3.76	3.75
	Hogg, LA	2.65	2.64
	Horstmann, LA	2.57	2.56
	Hughes, SLC	3.88	3.87
	E. Johnson, Ver	3.04	3.03
	Kelly, Port	2.80	2.78
	Klawitter, Oak-SLC	4.09	4.08
	Martin, Oak	2.82	2.81
	Mitchell, Ver	2.34	2.33
	Noyes, Port	3.15	3.14
	Perritt, SF	4.12	4.10
	Piercy, SLC	3.27	3.26
	Prough, Oak	2.69	2.68
	Scoggins, LA	3.77	3.70
1917	Burns, Oak	4.49	4.48
	Decanniere, Ver-SF	3.20	3.19
	Dubuc, SLC	3.18	3.13
	Fromme, Ver	2.58	2.57
	S. Hall, LA	3.05	3.04
	Hoff, SLC	4.93	4.91
	Houck, Port	2.22	2.21
	James, Port	3.95	3.94
	Kirmeyer, SLC	5.16	5.17
	Marion, Ver	4.41	4.42
	Quinn, Ver	2.36	2.35
	Seaton, LA	2.94	2.93
	Smith, SF	2.34	2.33
1919	Baum, SLC-SF	3.44	3.45
	Brenton, Sea	3.36	3.81
	Bromley, SF-Sac	4.43	4.45
	Couch, SF	3.30	3.27
	Dawson, Ver	2.56	2.96
	Falkenberg, Oak	2.92	2.89
	Gearin, Oak	3.44	3.46
	Gould, SLC	3.53	3.52
	Harstad, Port	4.04	3.99
	Main, SLC	3.84	3.87
	Prough, Sac	2.52	2.53
	Regan, Sea	4.10	5.20
	Rieger, Sea	2.63	2.67
	Schultz, LA	4.38	4.37
	Smith, SF	3.56	3.57
	Stroud, SLC	3.84	3.85
	Sutherland, Port	3.46	3.45
	Vance, Sac	3.32	2.82
1921	Faeth, Sac-Ver	2.93	4.25
	Thurston, SLC	3.91	4.31

EARNED RUN AVERAGES (cont.)

Year	Player, Team	Old	New
1922	Walberg, Port	4.39	4.48
1923	Geary, SF	3.64	3.61
	Myers, SLC	6.00	6.04
	Singleton, SLC	6.25	6.28
1924	Christian, Ver	3.96	3.94
	Mitchell, SF	4.20	4.06
	Mulcahy, SLC	6.40	6.50
	Root, LA	3.96	3.69
1925	Keating, Sac	4.99	5.02
	Pruett, Oak	2.92	3.49
	Root, LA	2.87	2.86
1926	Kallio, Sac	3.24	3.23
	Krause, Oak	3.18	2.87
	Leverette, Port	3.76	6.52
	Meeker, Port	3.91	3.77
	Moudy, SF	3.21	4.05
	Shea, Sac	3.75	3.79
1927	French, Port	4.55	4.77
	Hamilton, LA	5.46	5.09
	Shea, Sac	4.05	4.09
	Sparks, Oak	4.03	4.04
1928	Crandall, LA	3.88	3.89
	Fullerton, Hol-Port	3.12	3.45
	Martin, Sea-Miss	5.57	5.58
	McEvoy, Oak	3.34	3.35
	Peters, LA	3.62	3.99
	Shellenback, Hol	3.13	3.34
	Wright, LA	4.32	4.33
1929	Chesterfield, Port-Hol	4.11	4.25
	Couch, SF	5.41	5.42
	Krause, Miss	5.33	5.34
1930	Baecht, LA	3.23	3.24
	Ballou, LA	3.77	3.78
	Cascarella, Port	6.60	6.61
	House, Sea	5.35	4.82
	Kunz, Sea	5.05	5.17
	Nelson, Miss	6.84	6.85
	Pearson, Oak	5.78	5.77
	Zahniser, Sea	3.99	4.06
1931	Bryan, Sac	4.35	4.31
	Craghead, Oak	4.12	4.17
	Johns, Hol	5.17	5.16
	Kallio, Sea-Port	5.77	5.71
	McDougall, SF	3.22	3.27
	Moss, LA	4.55	4.59
	Shealy, LA	6.60	6.61
	Vinci, Sac	5.21	5.18
1932	Briggs, Sac	4.76	4.74

EARNED RUN AVERAGES (cont.)

Year	Player, Team	Old	New
1932	Cole, Miss	3.52	3.51
	Dietrich, Port	3.47	3.86
	Douglass, SF	4.72	4.70
	Fieber, Oak	5.76	5.77
	Flynn, Sac	4.23	4.22
	Freitas, Sac	3.61	3.60
	Kallio, Sea	3.80	3.79
	Moss, LA	4.70	4.68
	Ortman, Hol	4.07	4.06
	Osborne, Miss	5.32	5.31
	Phebus, Oak	5.18	5.17
	Shellenback, Hol	3.14	3.13
	Stine, SF	5.19	5.17
	Sweetland, LA	6.28	6.26
	Turner, Hol	4.61	4.59
	Walsh, Miss-Oak-LA	6.11	6.10
	Zinn, SF	4.48	4.47
1933	Bryan, Sac	5.26	5.15
	Stitzel, LA	4.79	4.80
1935	Buxton, LA	3.86	3.90
	Darrow, Oak	5.19	5.21
	Harris, LA	4.96	4.95
	Johnson, Miss	6.26	6.28
	Nitcholas, Miss	5.09	5.07
	Osborne, Miss	3.53	3.56
	Pickrel, Sea	5.15	5.26
	Turpin, Port	8.46	8.43
	Vinci, Sea	7.83	7.86
1940	Ballou, SF	3.62	3.63
	Fallin, Port	5.80	5.79
	Gibson, SF	2.83	2.84
	Hebert, SD	3.91	3.92
	Jensen, SF	5.12	5.13
	Newsome, SD	2.62	2.63
1941	Coffman, LA	5.73	5.74
	Prim, LA	2.85	2.86
1952	Flores, Sac	2.77	2.78
	Linde, Port	3.10	3.11

OTHER CORRECTIONS

1903   Casey, Sac; hits listed as 137, should be 237.
Cravath, LA; hits listed as 319, should be 219.
Eagan, Sac; hits listed as 202; should be 262.
Hoy, LA; at bats listed as 896, should be 806.
Newton, LA-Port; wins listed as 25 in *Reach Guide*, should be 35.

OTHER CORRECTIONS (cont.)

1905	Ike Walters, SF-Sea; actually is Harry Wolter.
1908	House, Sac; hits listed as 100, should be 109.
	Olson, Port; hits listed as 71, should be 171.
1915	Middleton, Oak; hits listed as 260, should be 216.
1918	Downey, Easterly, Eldred, Griggs, Pinelli, Wilie with Sacramento, not San Francisco.
1919	Brown, LA; listed as allowing 81 earned runs, should be 71.
	Crandall, LA; at bats listed as 257, should be 140.
	Seaton was with San Francisco, not Portland.
1923	Guisto, Oak; at bats listed as 166, should be 116.
	Murphy, Ver; hits listed as 235, should be 225.
1926	Wendell, Port; hits listed as 40, should be 49.
1927	Piercy, LA; wins listed as 17, should be 12.
1944	Prim, LA; games pitched listed as 31, should be 41.